Introduction to
Literature

Fifth Edition

Introduction to
Literature

Isobel M. Findlay University of Saskatchewan

Wendy R. Katz St. Mary's University

Kenneth A. MacKinnon St. Mary's University

Richard J.H. Perkyns St. Mary's University

Gillian Thomas St. Mary's University

THOMSON
—✳—™
NELSON

Australia   Canada   Mexico   Singapore   Spain   United Kingdom   United States

Introduction to Literature
Fifth Edition

by Isobel M. Findlay, Wendy R. Katz, Kenneth A. MacKinnon,
Richard J.H. Perkyns, and Gillian Thomas

Editorial Director and Publisher:
Evelyn Veitch

Executive Editor:
Anne Williams

Acquisitions Editor:
Pamela Armstrong-Duprey

Marketing Manager:
Lisa Rahn

Senior Developmental Editor:
Mike Thompson

Permissions Coordinator:
Patricia Buckley

Production Editor:
Julie van Veen

Copy Editor/Proofreader:
Wayne Herrington

Production Coordinator:
Ferial Suleman

Creative Director:
Angela Cluer

Interior Design:
The Brookview Group Inc.

Interior Design Modifications:
Gabriel Sierra

Cover Design:
Angela Cluer

Cover Image:
Susan Cunningham
"Daylight Containment"
screenprint

Compositor:
Rachel Sloat

Printer:
Transcontinental

National Library of Canada Cataloguing in Publication

Introduction to literature / [edited by] Isobel Findlay ... [et al.]. – 5th ed.

Includes index.
ISBN 0-17-641546-7

1. English literature.
2. American literature.
3. Canadian literature (English). I. Findlay, Isobel

PN6014.I68 2003   820.8
C2003-904754-7

PREFACE

In this edition, as in the fourth, we have retained works that consistently interest and stimulate class discussion and have discarded those that, for various reasons, no longer prove as engaging as they did. We remain committed to Canadian literatures and the larger historical and cultural contexts within which they operate. Over the last few decades, literature has been changed by an increasingly inclusive society that respects the rights and responsibilities of people of different genders, classes, cultures, and ethnic and religious backgrounds. In order to preserve the compact size of the anthology while reflecting diverse audiences and authors and an ever-expanding canon of literature in English, we have maintained the focus on three genres: essays, poetry, and short fiction.

We have retained chronological order within each genre according to authors' dates of birth, have included dates of publication of all works (printed on the right at the end of each selection), and have revised introductions to amplify the history of the different genres. We feel that the benefits of historical order outweigh those of structural alternatives that highlight formal features or follow alphabetical order of authors' names or thematic arrangement. An emphasis on the historical conditions of production and reproduction of the genres helps students understand the writer as social actor operating within and responding to specific historical and cultural contexts.

We have resisted thematic ordering to encourage a broad range of approaches and readings of the work. We do, however, offer a few suggestions toward a thematic approach in the introductions to each of the genres and indicate some connections between certain works in the brief author profiles and footnotes. We have also attempted to suggest multi-genre comparisons; for example, there are works by Margaret Atwood in all three genres, and by authors such as D.H. Lawrence, Langston Hughes, Margaret Laurence, and Rhea Tregebov in two genres.

Selections from the three genres have been considerably revised to reflect changing needs, to provide updated material, and to represent a wider range of women's and postcolonial writing in English. The essay section, for example, includes much highly topical material and registers the essay's role in reshaping self and society, its capacity to conserve as much as to contest the way things are. Several essays explore the subject of language's ability to include and exclude, to limit and liberate, while others contribute to discussions on the environment, the consumer society, colonial legacies, war and terrorism, women's issues and human justice, and the challenges of social inclusion and cohesion in multicultural Canada. The poetry section has been revised to include a better balance of periods and sub-genres and to represent more of the formal, cultural, social, and other diversity of poetry written by men and women in English. In particular, we have added excerpts from long poems, expanded representation of the medieval period and the seventeenth and eighteenth centuries, increased the range of eighteenth-century women's poetry, and strengthened Aboriginal representation. At times these considerations and the desire to extend thematic range and encourage comparisons among writers, themes, and genres have meant that we cannot always represent poets by more than one poem. The short fiction has been similarly revised to include new material, extending thematic, technical, and cultural range, while amplifying the history of the form and elaborating its powers and utility within the literary and sociocultural domains.

Footnotes, though kept to a minimum, are included for quick reference and to aid ready understanding without resources and reference books. In poetry, particularly, the footnote often suggests only one of the many potential layers of meaning of a word or phrase. Notes are provided for dialect or foreign phrases, some place names, mythological allusions, and folkloric references, for example. We have tried to resist the temptation to steer the reader toward particular interpretations by means of footnote material. Basic vocabulary found in most desk dictionaries is not included in footnotes, with the exception of a few words that we have found may give some difficulty or are being used in a non-standard sense. Like the glossary entries, which have been revised and augmented for this edition, the brief biographical profiles that precede each author's work are intended to be suggestive rather than comprehensive.

New to this edition is the Writing about Literature section, offering students instruction on essay writing. Stressing process as much as product, the advice is designed to help students build confidence and develop the tact and tactics to represent effectively their arguments and appreciation of literature. Instructors are also advised of the availability of an Instructor's Manual, which contains a wealth of advice on pedagogy, diverse approaches to the texts, and different options for organizing course delivery.

ACKNOWLEDGMENTS

If all writing is collaborative, it is especially so in the case of revising an anthology. This new edition builds on the success of previous editions and the impressive work of the editorial team of Wendy R. Katz, Kenneth A. MacKinnon, Richard J.H. Perkyns, and Gillian Thomas. In addition, I thank those instructors who provided valuable suggestions for this edition: Shafi Ahmad, University of Ottawa; Richard Arnold, University of Lethbridge; Stuart Blott, Vanier College; Paul Denham, University of Saskatchewan; Alice den Otter, Lakehead University; Jannie Edwards, Grant MacEwan College; Robert Fleming, Kwantlen University College; Karen Hofmann, University College of the Cariboo; Susan Holbrook, University of Windsor; Gerry Manning, University of Guelph; Greg McSweeney, Dawson College; Kim Michasiw, York University; Deanna Roozendaal, Camosun College; Ray Shankman, Vanier College; Mary Silcox, McMaster University; Peter Slade, Red Deer College; Veronica Thompson, Mount Royal College; Jerry Wasserman, University of British Columbia.

This edition is also the richer for the thoughtful feedback and suggestions of students and colleagues at the University of Saskatchewan, and, in particular, Len Findlay, John Lavery, Anthony Murphy, Doug Thorpe, and Carrie Ronstadler. I would also like to thank my editors at Nelson—Mike Thompson, Pamela Duprey, Julie van Veen, Anne Williams—and copy editor Wayne Herrington for their encouragement and valuable advice.

Isobel M. Findlay

A NOTE FROM THE PUBLISHER

Thank you for selecting *Introduction to Literature*, Fifth Edition, by Isobel M. Findlay, Wendy R. Katz, Kenneth A. MacKinnon, Richard J.H. Perkyns, and Gillian Thomas. The authors and publisher have devoted considerable time to the careful development of this book. We appreciate your recognition of this effort and accomplishment.

CONTENTS▬▬▬▬■

ESSAYS

POETRY

SHORT FICTION

Essays

INTRODUCTION _____

Virginia Woolf warns that we should not be overly preoccupied with pursuing the essay's origins ("whether it derives from Socrates or Sianney the Persian").[1] In order to understand its present, however, it is helpful to know something of the essay's past, particularly in English. It is a form intimately connected to change, to writing as learning and exploring, to the making and remaking of the self and society promoted by the Reformation and Renaissance. A feature of an emergent native culture, increasing literacy, new publishing practices, and new possibilities for mobility in an increasingly urban society, the essay is closely associated with the establishment of English national identity as much as with new notions of individual identity explored in Reformation theology and Humanist education and realized in a new mercantilist economy and expanding professional class. Ever since, the essay has remained linked to efforts to rethink public and private issues and connections between them. The essays reproduced here attest to the richness of such rethinking.

From its beginnings in English, the essay was a contested form, one of the sites of the so-called Battle of the Styles, a struggle expressed in ongoing efforts to isolate from the broad range of "literary" options a style appropriate to the "impersonal" stance of scientific and other rationalist discourses. If the essay was in part defined by its difference from earlier prose forms marked by elaborate footnoting and citation of authorities, there was no unanimity about appropriate length, themes (ranging from the private and domestic to the public and political), or style (whether direct or digressive, formal or informal, courtly or colloquial, aphoristic or alliterative). The Renaissance essay is represented by the Latinate prose of Roger Ascham (1515–1568), the exaggerated, alliterative aphorisms of John Lyly (1554–1606), the proverbial and pointed style of Francis Bacon (1561–1626), represented here by his "Of Studies," and the epigrammatic wit of John Donne (1572–1631). Each option had its fierce adherents. There was not then, nor is there now, one true way to write an essay.

_____

1. "The Modern Essay," *The Common Reader*, First Series (New York: Harcourt, Brace & World, 1925), 216.

While definitions of the essay form have often been structured around oppositions (personal/impersonal, literary/non-literary), such oppositions are neither natural nor universal. Rather, they are instruments of authority concerned to control the unruly and unpredictable consequences of literacies and language, and especially of what Samuel Johnson termed the "fatal Cleopatra" of figurative language. In twentieth-century anthologies and rhetorics, essays are frequently defined negatively: they are not treatises or fiction and are hence "nonfiction," and, as such, often carefully labelled expository, descriptive, narrative, persuasive, or argumentative types. However, categories and hierarchies of types and styles do little justice to the range, diversity, and complexity of a form that has proven powerfully assimilative of other forms (autobiography, narrative, epigram, anecdote, for example) while resisting confinement within rigid classification systems. Throughout its history, the essay has entertained as it educated, described and narrated as it explained and persuaded. From this combinative power derive the pleasures and provocations found in this particular literary form.

In short, the essay has resisted prescription and conscription, remaining amenable to those who would protest as much as to those who would preserve the status quo. If it has served certain interests claiming impersonality and objectivity, the essay has also accommodated such historically marginalized groups as women, the lower classes, people of colour, Aboriginal peoples, and religious and political dissenters in their resolve to challenge the status quo and especially the stereotypes and oversimplified oppositions dear to dominant forms of rationality.

For most university courses, students are required to write some form of essay, be it a piece of literary criticism, history term paper, scientific discussion of research findings, business proposal, or study of a judicial decision. It is therefore useful for students to have the opportunity to examine various approaches to the essay form and to appreciate its intellectual and artistic power as well as its cultural, social, political, or more narrowly utilitarian potential. The readings in this section show the scope of the form both thematically and expressively, and they demonstrate the skill and rhetorical strategies required to organize material, arrange paragraphs, and communicate accurately and vividly. When Lewis Mumford examines the role of mechanization in cultural development, he presents his argument so precisely and rationally that students might well consider his writing a model of the formal essay. The format of works included here ranges from Mumford's formality, to such lighter, journalistic articles as Margaret Atwood's "Through the One-Way Mirror," to John Ralston Saul's probing of the dictionary or encyclopedia style of inquiry, to George Orwell's narrative power, to Peter Robertson's scholarly use of endnotes that might serve as a model for research essays.

Although the majority of the essays included here were written in the twentieth century, the selections begin with Francis Bacon's seventeenth-century essay "Of Studies," reflecting on the differences between the expert and the learned, on the opportunities and challenges of learning, and on scientific method. In the eighteenth century the essay became a crucial genre in an emergent public sphere of clubs and coffeehouses, periodicals, journals, polite conversation, and rational judgment. In the face of privilege and political absolutism, thinkers and writers developed critical commentary and new discourses of rights. Even as rationality became the instrument of men's and women's aspirations, however, it became itself an object of critique, as in the 1729 satire "A Modest Proposal," by Jonathan Swift. A parody of the new rationalist discourse of political economy, the essay demonstrates the inevitable limits of any supposedly pure and universal rationality, while coming passionately to the defence of the oppressed in Ireland. It is a powerful comment on the capacity of professional knowledge to reduce and distort human experience, to rationalize the most inhumane behaviour. This "proposal" is widely considered to be one of the most brilliant pieces of ironic prose in the English language and all the more remarkable in that, while apparently advocating savagery, it so effectively expresses indignation and compassion. Its impact is as forcible today, when millions face famine and starvation, as when it was written, nearly three hundred years ago.

Although not the first of its kind, Mary Wollstonecraft's introductory essay to her 1792 *A Vindication of the Rights of Woman* represents the best of Romantic feminism. A powerful indictment of women's education as the source of women's subjection, Wollstonecraft's work exposes the injustices of women's situation, while claiming women's rights as human rights. And Heather Mallick, writing about Carol Shields, paints a picture of the pain of exclusion literary and other women still face. The tradition of women producing a literature and style of their own to counter misconstruction in mainstream media and to revalue women's work and artistic practice has been continued by such recent writers as Joyce Nelson. Nelson's "The Temple of Fashion" satirizes the new religion of consumerism and a fashion business fuelled by sweatshops and piecework in the Third World and elsewhere. In her "Buying a Gladiatorial Myth," Naomi Klein comments on the gender of power and terror, on the persistence of myth and history, and on the connections between consumption and cold warriors in the wake of September 11.

In "Phrases and Philosophies for the Use of the Young," Oscar Wilde reworks the aphoristic models of Francis Bacon to "disagree with three-fourths of all England on all points of view," which Wilde claimed in a lecture to be "one of the first elements of sanity." The tradition of satirical writing is further illustrated in "The War Prayer" by Samuel Langhorne Clemens, better known as "Mark Twain." His parable on war, individual and national pride, idiocy and idealism, and religious appeals to support righteous action contains a still-devastating irony. Equally penetrating in its satirical intent is Atwood's "Through the One-Way Mirror," with its irreverent study and revisioning of a familiar preoccupation, Canadian–American relations.

Several of the essays in this volume are concerned with the use and abuse of language in human thought and interaction, the ways language serves to include while excluding outsiders, to define while limiting the ways available for thinking about a subject. In "The Grail of Balance," Saul links the possibilities for human action to the sayable and thinkable and hence to the power of dictionaries and encyclopedias. As capable of questioning as of condoning the powers that be, of freeing or subjecting citizens, the dictionary operates by liberating or limiting debate. In the current fragmentation of discourses and knowledges, Saul detects the loss of public language that could lead to meaningful action—and connects this loss to a renewed need for dictionaries as instruments of change. David Suzuki's essay "A Planet for the Taking" promotes a paradigm shift by unsettling blind faith in scientific and technological progress. Suzuki shows how choice of words skews our vision, so that we can delude ourselves that our practices and procedures are natural and we can "manage" while we "harvest" and "cull" resources.

Illustrating from another medium of communication, Robertson challenges the reader's basic assumption that what we see in a photograph must be the truth. He suggests that a photograph can be used to manipulate the viewer, just as Suzuki asserts that language and narrowly focused scientific methodology can manipulate understanding and action. Readers may also be interested to compare on issues of representation the essays with Lynda Barry's short story, "Automatic Timer," or the poems of Derek Walcott, Wole Soyinka, George Elliott Clarke, or Daphne Marlatt, among others. Like clarity and plainness, transparency bears watching.

The word *essay*, derived from the French verb *essayer*, suggests that writers are sometimes trying out or testing their ideas on discerning and critical readers. Indeed, during the eighteenth century, an essayist might be one who wrote essays, but might also be one who made experiments. Hence, all essays are partial and provisional, initiating a discussion and offering the first or current, not the last, word on the subject at hand. In so doing, essayists may draw on personal experience to advance more general claims. Margaret Laurence begins her essay by estranging the reader from habitual forms of perception: "A strange place it was, the place where the world began." As we read on, we realize that she is not only familiarizing readers with her own origins in order to have them revalue the Canadian prairies but also connecting that microcosm to the larger experience of Canada and the consequences of a history of colonization.

In her chapter of autobiography, Isabelle Knockwood also offers a distinctive personal experience. She explains how the establishment of the Indian Residential School in Shubenacadie, Nova Scotia, threatened the traditional language and culture of the Mi'kmaw people. Yet the rich Mi'kmaw lore, with its stories and ceremonies, many at least seven centuries old, proves a resilient fund of wisdom. While registering the violence of colonial ignorance and ethnocentrism, Knockwood keeps the focus on familiarizing readers with the too-little-known world of values and conventions whereby the Mi'kmaq live in harmony with all their relations.

Both Knockwood and Drew Hayden Taylor take a personal approach to issues that are concerned with identity and values as well as with wider issues of public policy and cultural diversity. However, in his "Pretty Like a White Boy," Taylor relies on humour to describe his own, often deeply wounding, experiences of racism. And Neil Bissoondath explores in "I'm Not Racist But ..." the consequences of ethnic and other stereotypes and the challenges of Canada's policy of multiculturalism. Rhea Tregebov also investigates questions of personal and cultural identity in "Some Notes on the Story of Esther," in which she makes comparisons between her position as a woman in male culture and that as a Jew in Christian culture. Tregebov traces her first authentic writing to her own developing consciousness of both identities.

The paradoxes of British colonial rule in Burma—its attempts to manage fear, hatred, power, powerlessness, privilege, and racism—are explored in George Orwell's "Shooting an Elephant." The effect of the particular experience described in the essay is a profound insight into, and indictment of, the imperial system Orwell had supported as a police officer. Whereas Orwell writes from the self-critical colonizer's perspective, South African writer Njabulo S. Ndebele represents the perspective of the colonized, although both reflect on the masks each wears and the writer's imperative to unmask, to expose the arbitrariness and injustice of the official line. Despite an era of public reconciliation and a "rhetoric of hope" in the "new South Africa," Ndebele ponders the "wall of ignorance" that still in 1991 divides him from his project of writing a novel about a young Afrikaner. In reconstructing the past, Ndebele reflects on the barely concealed horrors and the difficulties of contending with "the logic of apartheid," the heinous instrument of unequal power. Even in the present, the "liberated" are confined by the cultural, social, and economic structures of the supposedly ousted oppressor, and hence those "liberated" from apartheid ironically succeed by enjoying that which had been constructed "at [their own] expense." These neocolonial and postcolonial ironies (and the oppressors' appropriation of the discourse of struggle and liberation) explain why Ndebele insists on remembering the past and resisting the corrosive effects of guilt and shame if the structures of oppression are to be dislodged and justice secured.

An early derivation of the word *essay* is from the Latin word *exagium*, which refers to the act of weighing something on scales. In another sense, then, writing an essay can be seen as a matter of judgment, the art of assessment. When, in the eighteenth century, the essay became firmly established as a literary form in English, the reader expected discussion of the subject at hand to be not only rational, but clear, discerning, and accessible. The essay was no longer purely academic; its ideas became available to a popular audience. Many of the readings in this section suggest an awareness of this tradition of essay writing, inasmuch as they provoke their readers to thought, while demonstrating intensely felt experience and passionately held beliefs and inviting readers to reflect and act on their own values, identity, knowledge, and experience.

Francis Bacon (1561–1626)

Educated at Cambridge and Gray's Inn, Francis Bacon was a politician, civil servant, and philosopher. He became Lord Chancellor of England under James I before conviction for bribery ended his career in 1621. Thereafter, he devoted himself to philosophical writing on learning, on idols and other obstacles to knowledge, and on the experience and experiment of scientific method.

Of Studies

1   Studies serve for delight, for ornament, and for ability. Their chief use for delight is in privateness and retiring; for ornament, is in discourse; and for ability, is in the judgement and disposition of business. For expert men can execute and perhaps judge of particulars, one by one; but the general counsels and the plots and marshalling of affairs come best from those that are learned. To spend too much time in studies is sloth; to use them too much for ornament is affectation; to make judgement wholly by their rules is the humour of a scholar. They perfect Nature and are perfected by experience. For natural abilities are like natural plants, that need pruning by study; and studies themselves do give forth directions too much at large, except they be bounded in by experience. Crafty men condemn studies; simple men admire them; and wise men use them; for they teach not their own use, but that is a wisdom without them and above them, won by observation. Read not to contradict and confute, nor to believe and take for granted, nor to find talk and discourse, but to weigh and consider. Some books are to be tasted, others to be swallowed, and some few to be chewed and digested: that is, some books are to be read only in parts; others to be read but not curiously; and some few to be read wholly and with diligence and attention. Some books also may be read by deputy, and extracts made of them by others, but that would be only in the less important arguments and the meaner sort of books; else distilled books are like common distilled waters, flashy things. Reading maketh a full man; conference a ready man, and writing an exact man. And therefore if a man write little, he had need have a great memory; if he confer little, he had need have a present wit; and if he read little, he had need have much cunning to seem to know that he doth not. Histories make men wise; poets, witty; the mathematics, subtle; natural philosophy, deep; moral, grave; logic and rhetoric, able to contend. *Abuent studia in*

mores.[1] Nay, there is no stond[2] or impediment in the wit but may be wrought out by fit studies, like as diseases of the body may have appropriate exercises. Bowling is good for the stone and reins[3]; shooting for the lungs and breast; gentle walking for the stomach; riding for the head; and the like. So if a man's wit be wandering, let him study the mathematics, for in demonstrations, if his wit be called away never so little, he must begin again. If his wit be not apt to distinguish or find differences, let him study the schoolmen; for they are *Cymini sectores.*[4] If he be not apt to beat over matters and to call up one thing to prove and illustrate another, let him study the lawyers' cases. So every defect of the mind may have a special receipt.

(*1625*)

---

1. Studies transform people's behaviour (Ovid, *Heroides*).
2. Obstacle.
3. Bladder and kidneys.
4. Hair-splitters, such as medieval scholars Thomas Aquinas and John Duns Scotus.

Jonathan Swift (1667–1745)

Born in Ireland of English parents, Swift was an Anglican clergyman as well as a controversial political satirist. A thoroughgoing irony governs "A Modest Proposal" (1729) as well as the earlier Gulliver's Travels *(1726), both of which display Swift's superb prose style.*

A Modest Proposal

For preventing the Children of Poor People in Ireland, from Being a Burden to Their Parents or Country; and for Making Them Beneficial to the Public[1]

1   It is a melancholy object to those who walk through this great town, or travel in the country, when they see the streets, the roads, and cabin doors crowded with beggars of the female sex, followed by three, four or six children, *all in rags*, and importuning every passenger for an alms. These mothers, instead of being able to work for their honest livelihood, are forced to employ all their time in strolling, to beg sustenance for their helpless infants, who, as they grow up, either turn thieves for want of work, or leave their dear native country to fight for the Pretender[2] in Spain, or sell themselves to the Barbados.[3]

2   I think it is agreed by all parties that this prodigious number of children in the arms, or on the backs, or at the heels of their mothers, and frequently of their fathers, is in the present deplorable state of the kingdom a very great additional grievance; and therefore whoever could find out a fair, cheap, and easy method of making these children sound and useful members of the commonwealth would deserve so well of the public as to have his statue set up for a preserver of the nation.

3   But my intention is very far from being confined to provide only for the children of professed beggars; it is of a much greater extent, and

1. This essay was provoked by the impoverished conditions, resulting from exorbitant rents and successive crop failures, that were endured by the Irish peasantry.

2. James, the Old Pretender (1688–1766), son of the deposed James II of England, claimant to the English and Scottish thrones. Irish Catholics were recruited to fight against England in the French and Spanish armies. Irish troops were involved in an unsuccessful expedition planned in 1719 by Cardinal Alberoni of Spain to restore the Pretender to the English throne.

3. As slaves.

shall take in the whole number of infants at a certain age who are born of parents in effect as little able to support them as those who demand our charity in the streets.

4   As to my own part, having turned my thoughts, for many years, upon this important subject, and maturely weighed the several schemes of other projectors, I have always found them grossly mistaken in their computation. It is true a child, just dropped from its dam, may be supported by her milk for a solar year with little other nourishment, at most not above the value of two shillings, which the mother may certainly get, or the value in scraps, by her lawful occupation of begging; and it is exactly at one year old that I propose to provide for them, in such a manner as, instead of being a charge upon their parents, or the parish, or wanting food and raiment for the rest of their lives, they shall, on the contrary, contribute to the feeding and partly to the clothing of many thousands.

5   There is likewise another great advantage in my scheme, that it will prevent those voluntary abortions, and that horrid practice of women murdering their bastard children, alas, too frequent among us; sacrificing the poor innocent babes, I doubt, more to avoid the expense than the shame; which would move tears and pity in the most savage and inhuman breast.

6   The number of souls in Ireland being usually reckoned one million and a half, of these I calculate there may be about two hundred thousand couples whose wives are breeders; from which number I subtract thirty thousand couples who are able to maintain their own children, although I apprehend[4] there cannot be so many under the present distresses of the kingdom; but this being granted, there will remain an hundred and seventy thousand breeders. I again subtract fifty thousand for those women who miscarry, or whose children die by accident or disease within the year. There only remain an hundred and twenty thousand children of poor parents, annually born: The question therefore is, how this number shall be reared, and provided for; which, as I have already said, under the present situation of affairs, is utterly impossible by all the methods hitherto proposed: for we can neither employ them in handicraft, or agriculture; we neither build houses (I mean in the country), nor cultivate land:[5] they can very seldom pick up a livelihood by stealing until they arrive at six years old, except where they are of towardly parts,[6] although, I confess they learn the rudiments much earlier, during which time they can however be properly looked upon only as *probationers*; as I have been informed by a principal gentleman in the County of Cavan,[7] who protested to me

---

4. Am apprehensive that, anticipate with fear.
5. English legislation restricted cultivation of land, which prevented the Irish from growing sufficient food crops.
6. Fitting ability.
7. One of three counties of the old province of Ulster, now part of the Irish Republic.

that he never knew above one or two instances under the age of six, even in a part of the kingdom so renowned for the quickest proficiency in that art.

7   I am assured by our merchants that a boy or a girl, before twelve years old, is no saleable commodity, and even when they come to this age, they will not yield above three pounds, or three pounds and half a crown at most on the Exchange; which cannot turn to account either to the parents or kingdom, the charge of nutriment and rags having been at least four times that value.

8   I shall now therefore humbly propose my own thoughts, which I hope will not be liable to the least objection.

9   I have been assured by a very knowing American of my acquaintance in London, that a young healthy child well nursed is at a year old most delicious, nourishing, and wholesome food, whether stewed, roasted, baked, or boiled; and I make no doubt that it will equally serve in a fricassee or a ragout.

10   I do therefore humbly offer it to public consideration, that of the hundred and twenty thousand children already computed, twenty thousand may be reserved for breed, whereof only one-fourth part to be males; which is more than we allow to sheep, black cattle, or swine; and my reason is that these children are seldom the fruits of marriage, a circumstance not much regarded by our savages, therefore one male will be sufficient to serve four females. That the remaining hundred thousand may at a year old be offered in sale to the persons of quality, and fortune, through the kingdom; always advising the mother to let them suck plentifully in the last month, so as to render them plump, and fat for a good table. A child will make two dishes at an entertainment for friends; and when the family dines alone, the fore- or hindquarter will make a reasonable dish, and seasoned with a little pepper or salt will be very good boiled on the fourth day, especially in winter.

11   I have reckoned upon a medium, that a child just born will weigh twelve pounds, and in a solar year if tolerably nursed increases to twenty-eight pounds.

12   I grant this food will be somewhat dear, and therefore very *proper for landlords*, who, as they have already devoured most of the parents, seem to have the best title to the children.

13   Infants' flesh will be in season throughout the year, but more plentiful in March, and a little before and after: for we are told by a grave author,[8] an eminent French physician, that fish being a prolific diet, there are more children born in Roman Catholic countries about nine months after Lent than at any other season; therefore reckoning a year after Lent, the markets will be more glutted than usual, because the number of Popish infants is at least three to one in this kingdom; and

---

8. Rabelais (1494?–1553), famous French satirist.

therefore it will have one other collateral advantage by lessening the number of Papists among us.

14   I have already computed the charge of nursing a beggar's child (in which list I reckon all cottagers,[9] labourers, and four-fifths of the farmers) to be about two shillings *per annum*, rags included; and I believe no gentleman would repine to give ten shillings for the carcass of a good fat child, which, as I have said, will make four dishes of excellent nutritive meat, when he hath only some particular friend or his own family to dine with him. Thus the squire will learn to be a good landlord, and grow popular among his tenants, the mother will have eight shillings net profit, and be fit for work until she produces another child.

15   Those who are more thrifty (*as I must confess the times require*) may flay the carcass; the skin of which, artificially dressed, will make admirable gloves for ladies, and summer boots for fine gentlemen.

16   As to our City of Dublin, shambles[10] may be appointed for this purpose, in the most convenient parts of it; and butchers we may be assured will not be wanting, although I rather recommend buying the children alive, and dressing them hot from the knife, as we do roasting pigs.

17   A very worthy person, a true lover of his country, and whose virtues I highly esteem, was lately pleased, in discoursing on this matter, to offer a refinement upon my scheme. He said that many gentlemen of this kingdom, having of late destroyed their deer, he conceived that the want of venison might be well supplied by the bodies of young lads and maidens, not exceeding fourteen years of age, nor under twelve; so great a number of both sexes in every country being now ready to starve, for want of work and service: and these to be disposed of by their parents if alive, or otherwise by their nearest relations. But with due deference to so excellent a friend, and so deserving a patriot, I cannot be altogether in his sentiments. For as to the males, my American acquaintance assured me from frequent experience that their flesh was generally tough and lean, like that of our schoolboys, by continual exercise, and their taste disagreeable, and to fatten them would not answer the charge. Then as to the females, it would, I think with humble submission, be a loss to the public, because they would soon become breeders themselves: And besides, it is not improbable that some scrupulous people might be apt to censure such a practice (although indeed very unjustly) as a little bordering upon cruelty; which, I confess, hath always been with me the strongest objection against any project, how well soever intended.

18   But in order to justify my friend, he confessed that this expedient was put into his head by the famous Psalmanazar,[11] a native of the

9. Agricultural labourers.

10. Slaughterhouses.

11. (1679?–1763), literary imposter born in southern France, who posed as a Formosan and wrote a description of the island. Later, he reformed and became a Hebraic scholar.

island Formosa, who came from thence to London, above twenty years ago, and in conversation told my friend that in his country when any young person happened to be put to death, the executioner sold the carcass to persons of quality, as a prime dainty; and that, in his time, the body of a plump girl of fifteen, who was crucified for an attempt to poison the emperor, was sold to his Imperial Majesty's Prime Minister of State, and other great mandarins of the court, in joints from the gibbet, at four hundred crowns. Neither indeed can I deny that if the same use were made of several plump young girls in this town, who, without one single groat[12] to their fortunes, cannot stir abroad without a chair,[13] and appear at a playhouse, and assemblies in foreign fineries, which they never will pay for, the kingdom would not be the worse.

19   Some persons of a desponding spirit are in great concern about that vast number of poor people, who are aged, diseased, or maimed; and I have been desired to employ my thoughts what course may be taken to ease the nation of so grievous an encumbrance. But I am not in the least pain upon that matter, because it is very well known that they are every day dying, and rotting, by cold, and famine, and filth, and vermin, as fast as can be reasonably expected. And as to the younger labourers they are now in almost as hopeful a condition. They cannot get work, and consequently pine away for want of nourishment, to a degree, that if at any time they are accidentally hired to common labour, they have not strength to perform it; and thus the country and themselves are in a fair way of being soon delivered from the evils to come.

20   I have too long digressed, and therefore shall return to my subject. I think the advantages by the proposal which I have made are obvious and many, as well as of the highest importance.

21   For first, as I have already observed, it would greatly lessen the number of Papists, with whom we are yearly overrun, being the principal breeders of the nation, as well as our most dangerous enemies; and who stay at home on purpose with a design to deliver the kingdom to the Pretender; hoping to take their advantage by the absence of so many good Protestants, who have chosen rather to leave the country than stay at home, and pay tithes against their conscience to an idolatrous Episcopal curate.[14]

22   Secondly, The poorer tenants will have something valuable of their own, which by law may be made liable to distress, and help to pay their landlord's rent, their corn and cattle being already seized, and *money a thing unknown*.

23   Thirdly, Whereas the maintenance of an hundred thousand children, from two years old, and upwards, cannot be computed at less

---

12. Small coin, obsolete by Swift's day. Figuratively, very little money.

13. Sedan chair: a covered chair suspended on two poles used to transport a person.

14. Nonconformist Protestants, claiming freedom of conscience, often resisted payment of tithes to the Established Anglican church.

than ten shillings apiece *per annum*, the nation's stock will be thereby increased fifty thousand pounds *per annum*; besides the profit of a new dish, introduced to the tables of all gentlemen of fortune in the kingdom, who have any refinement in taste; and the money will circulate among ourselves, the goods being entirely of our own growth and manufacture.

24   Fourthly, The constant breeders, besides the gain of eight shillings sterling *per annum*, by the sale of their children, will be rid of the charge of maintaining them after the first year.

25   Fifthly, This food would likewise bring great custom to taverns, where the vintners will certainly be so prudent as to procure the best receipts for dressing it to perfection, and consequently have their houses frequented by all the fine gentlemen, who justly value themselves upon their knowledge in good eating; and a skillful cook, who understands how to oblige his guests, will contrive to make it as expensive as they please.

26   Sixthly, This would be a great inducement to marriage, which all wise nations have either encouraged by rewards or enforced by laws and penalties. It would increase the care and tenderness of mothers toward their children, when they are sure of a settlement for life, to the poor babes, provided in some sort by the public to their annual profit instead of expense. We should see an honest emulation[15] among the married women, *which of them could bring the fattest child to market*. Men would become as fond of their wives, during the time of pregnancy, as they are now of their mares in foal, their cows in calf, or sows when they are ready to farrow; nor offer to beat or kick them (as it is too frequent a practice) for fear of a miscarriage.

27   Many other advantages might be enumerated. For instance, the addition of some thousand carcasses in our exportation of barrelled beef; the propagation of swine's flesh, and improvement in the art of making good bacon, so much wanted among us by the great destruction of pigs, too frequent at our tables, and are no way comparable in taste or magnificence to a well-grown, fat yearling child, which roasted whole will make a considerable figure at a Lord Mayor's feast, or any other public entertainment. But this and many others I omit, being studious of brevity.

28   Supposing that one thousand families in this city would be constant customers for infants' flesh, besides others who might have it at merrymeetings, particularly at weddings and christenings, I compute that Dublin would take off annually about twenty thousand carcasses, and the rest of the kingdom (where probably they will be sold somewhat cheaper) the remaining eighty thousand.

29   I can think of no one objection that will possibly be raised against this proposal, unless it should be urged that the number of people will be thereby much lessened in the kingdom. This I freely own, and it was

---

15. Rivalry.

indeed one principal design in offering it to the world, I desire the reader will observe, that I calculate my remedy *for this one individual Kingdom of Ireland, and for no other that ever was, is, or, I think, ever can be upon earth.* Therefore let no man talk to me of other expedients.[16] *Of taxing our absentees*[17] *at five shillings a pound: Of using neither clothes, nor household furniture, except what is of our own growth and manufacture: Of utterly rejecting the materials and instruments that promote foreign luxury: Of curing the expensiveness of pride, vanity, idleness, and gaming in our women: Of introducing a vein of parsimony, prudence, and temperance: Of learning to love our Country, wherein we differ even from* LAPLANDERS, *and the inhabitants of* TOPINAMBOO:[18] *Of quitting our animosities and factions, nor act any longer like the Jews, who were murdering one another at the very moment their city was taken: Of being a little cautious not to sell our country and consciences for nothing: Of teaching landlords to have a least one degree of mercy toward their tenants. Lastly, of putting a spirit of honesty, industry, and skill into our shopkeepers, who, if a resolution could now be taken to buy our native goods, would immediately unite to cheat and exact upon us in the price, the measure, and the goodness; nor could ever yet be brought to make one fair proposal of just dealing, though often and earnestly invited to it.*

30   Therefore I repeat, let no man talk to me of these and the like expedients; until he hath at least a glimpse of hope that there will ever be some hearty and sincere attempt to put them into practice.

31   But as to myself, having been wearied out for many years with offering vain, idle, visionary thoughts, and at length utterly despairing of success, I fortunately fell upon this proposal, which as it is wholly new, so it hath something *solid* and *real*, of no expense and little trouble, full in our own power, and whereby we can incur no danger in *disobliging* ENGLAND. For this kind of commodity will not bear exportation, the flesh being too tender a consistence to admit a long continuance in salt; *although perhaps I could name a country*[19] *which would be glad to eat up our whole nation without it.*

32   After all I am not so violently bent upon my own opinion as to reject any offer, proposed by wise men, which shall be found equally innocent, cheap, easy, and effectual. But before something of that kind shall be advanced in contradiction to my scheme, and offering a better, I desire the author, or authors, will be pleased maturely to consider two points. First, as things now stand, how they will be able to find food and raiment for an hundred thousand useless mouths and backs. And secondly, there being a round million of creatures in human figure,

---

16. These "other expedients" would include those suggested by Swift himself in his anonymously published pamphlet *Proposal for the Universal Use of Irish Manufacture* (1720). This work was the subject of a legal prosecution.

17. Absentee landlords.

18. An area in Brazil.

19. England.

throughout this kingdom, whose whole subsistence put into a common stock would leave them in debt two millions of pounds sterling; adding those, who are beggars by profession, to the bulk of farmers, cottagers, and labourers with their wives and children, who are beggars in effect; I desire those politicians, who dislike my overture, and may perhaps be so bold to attempt an answer, that they will first ask the parents of these mortals whether they would not at this day think it a great happiness to have been sold for food at a year old, in the manner I prescribe, and thereby have avoided such a perpetual scene of misfortunes as they have since gone through; by the oppression of landlords; the impossibility of paying rent without money or trade; the want of common sustenance, with neither house nor clothes to cover them from the inclemencies of the weather; and the most inevitable prospect of entailing the like, or greater miseries upon their breed forever.

33   I profess in the sincerity of my heart that I have not the least personal interest in endeavouring to promote this necessary work, having no other motive than the *public good of my country, by advancing our trade, providing for infants, relieving the poor, and giving some pleasure to the rich*. I have no children by which I can propose to get a single penny; the youngest being nine years old, and my wife past childbearing.

(1729)

Mary Wollstonecraft (1759–1797)

A powerful radical who died in childbirth, Mary Wollstonecraft penned cri-
tiques of private property, political oppression, and the subjection of women.
Her A Vindication of the Rights of Woman, *from which we reproduce the*
introduction, is a crucial document in the history of Western feminism. As
well as denouncing misogynist representations of women in literature,
Wollstonecraft argued forcefully for political, economic, and legal equality
for women.

Introduction to *A Vindication of the Rights of Woman*

1   After considering the historic page, and viewing the living world with
anxious solicitude, the most melancholy emotions of sorrowful indignation have depressed my spirits, and I have sighed when obliged to
confess, that either nature has made a great difference between man
and man, or that the civilization which has hitherto taken place in the
world has been very partial. I have turned over various books written
on the subject of education, and patiently observed the conduct of parents and the management of schools; but what has been the result?—
a profound conviction that the neglected education of my
fellow-creatures is the grand source of the misery I deplore; and that
women, in particular, are rendered weak and wretched by a variety of
concurring causes, originating from one hasty conclusion. The conduct and manners of women, in fact, evidently prove that their minds
are not in a healthy state; for, like the flowers which are planted in too
rich a soil, strength and usefulness are sacrificed to beauty; and the
flaunting leaves, after having pleased a fastidious eye, fade, disregarded
on the stalk, long before the season when they ought to have arrived
at maturity.—One cause of this barren blooming I attribute to a false
system of education, gathered from the books written on this subject
by men who, considering females rather as women than human creatures, have been more anxious to make them alluring mistresses than
affectionate wives and rational mothers; and the understanding of the
sex has been so bubbled by this specious homage, that the civilized
women of the present century, with a few exceptions, are only anxious
to inspire love, when they ought to cherish a nobler ambition, and by
their abilities and virtues exact respect.

2   In a treatise, therefore, on female rights and manners, the works which have been particularly written for their improvement must not be overlooked; especially when it is asserted, in direct terms, that the minds of women are enfeebled by false refinement; that the books of instruction, written by men of genius, have had the same tendency as more frivolous productions; and that, in the true style of Mahometanism,[1] they are treated as a kind of subordinate beings, and not as a part of the human species, when improveable reason is allowed to be the dignified distinction which raises men above the brute creation, and puts a natural sceptre in a feeble hand.

3   Yet, because I am a woman, I would not lead my readers to suppose that I mean violently to agitate the contested question respecting the equality or inferiority of the sex; but as the subject lies in my way, and I cannot pass over it without subjecting the main tendency of my reasoning to misconstruction, I shall stop a moment to deliver, in a few words, my opinion.—In the government of the physical world it is observable that the female in point of strength is, in general, inferior to the male. This is the law of nature; and it does not appear to be suspended or abrogated in favour of woman. A degree of physical superiority cannot, therefore, be denied—and it is a noble prerogative! But not content with this natural pre-eminence, men endeavour to sink us still lower, merely to render us alluring objects for a moment; and women, intoxicated by the adoration which men, under the influence of their senses, pay them, do not seek to obtain a durable interest in their hearts, or to become the friends of the fellow creatures who find amusement in their society.

4   I am aware of an obvious inference:—from every quarter have I heard exclamations against masculine women; but where are they to be found? If by this appellation men mean to inveigh against their ardour in hunting, shooting, and gaming, I shall most cordially join in the cry; but if it be against the imitation of manly virtues, or, more properly speaking, the attainment of those talents and virtues, the exercise of which ennobles the human character, and which raise females in the scale of animal being, when they are comprehensively termed mankind;—all those who view them with a philosophic eye must, I should think, wish with me, that they may every day grow more and more masculine.

5   This discussion naturally divides the subject. I shall first consider women in the grand light of human creatures, who, in common with men, are placed on this earth to unfold their faculties; and afterwards I shall more particularly point out their peculiar designation.

6   I wish also to steer clear of an error which many respectable writers have fallen into; for the instruction which has hitherto been addressed to women, has rather been applicable to *ladies*, if the little indirect

---

1. Variant of "Mahomedanism," i.e., Islam.

advice, that is scattered through Sandford and Merton,[2] be excepted; but, addressing my sex in a firmer tone, I pay particular attention to those in the middle class, because they appear to be in the most natural state. Perhaps the seeds of false-refinement, immorality, and vanity have ever been shed by the great. Weak, artificial beings, raised above the common wants and affections of their race, in a premature unnatural manner, undermine the very foundation of virtue, and spread corruption through the whole mass of society! As a class of mankind they have the strongest claim to pity; the education of the rich tends to render them vain and helpless, and the unfolding mind is not strengthened by the practice of those duties which dignify the human character.—They live only to amuse themselves, and by the same law which in nature invariably produces certain effects, they soon only afford barren amusement.

7   But as I purpose taking a separate view of the different ranks of society, and the moral character of women, in each, this hint is, for the present, sufficient; and I have only alluded to the subject, because it appears to me to be the very essence of an introduction to give a cursory account of the contents of the work it introduces.

8   My own sex, I hope, will excuse me, if I treat them like rational creatures, instead of flattering their *fascinating* graces, and viewing them as if they were in a state of perpetual childhood, unable to stand alone. I earnestly wish to point out in what true dignity and human happiness consists—I wish to persuade women to endeavour to acquire strength, both of mind and body, and to convince them that the soft phrases, susceptibility of heart, delicacy of sentiment, and refinement of taste are almost synonymous with epithets of weakness, and that those beings who are only the objects of pity and that kind of love, which has been termed its sister, will soon become objects of contempt.

9   Dismissing then those pretty feminine phrases, which the men condescendingly use to soften our slavish dependence, and despising that weak elegancy of mind, exquisite sensibility, and sweet docility of manners, supposed to be the sexual characteristics of the weaker vessel, I wish to show that elegance is inferior to virtue, that the first object of laudable ambition is to obtain a character as a human being, regardless of the distinction of sex; and that secondary views should be brought to this simple touchstone.

10   This is a rough sketch of my plan; and should I express my conviction with the energetic emotions that I feel whenever I think of the subject, the dictates of experience and reflection will be felt by some of my readers. Animated by this important object, I shall disdain to cull my phrases or polish my style;—I aim at being useful, and sincerity will render me unaffected; for, wishing rather to persuade by the force of my arguments, than dazzle by the elegance of my language, I shall

---

2. Thomas Day (1748–1789), *The History of Sandford and Merton*, 3 vols. (1783–89). Wollstonecraft reviewed the third volume for the *Analytical Review*.

not waste my time in rounding periods, or in fabricating the turgid bombast of artificial feelings, which, coming from the head, never reach the heart.—I shall be employed about things, not words!—and anxious to render my sex more respectable members of society, I shall try to avoid that flowery diction which has slided from essays into novels, and from novels into familiar letters and conversation.

11   These pretty superlatives, dropping glibly from the tongue, vitiate the taste, and create a kind of sickly delicacy that turns away from simple unadorned truth; and a deluge of false sentiments and over-stretched feelings, stifling the natural emotions of the heart, render the domestic pleasures insipid, that ought to sweeten the exercise of those severe duties, which educate a rational and immortal being for a nobler field of action.

12   The education of women has, of late, been more attended to than formerly; yet they are still reckoned a frivolous sex, and ridiculed or pitied by the writers who endeavour by satire or instruction to improve them. It is acknowledged that they spend many of the first years of their lives in acquiring a smattering of accomplishments; meanwhile strength of body and mind are sacrificed to libertine notions of beauty, to the desire of establishing themselves,—the only way women can rise in the world,—by marriage. And this desire making mere animals of them, when they marry they act as such children may be expected to act:—they dress; they paint, and nickname God's creatures.—Surely these weak beings are only fit for a seraglio!³—Can they be expected to govern a family with judgment, or take care of the poor babes whom they bring into the world?

13   If then it can be fairly deduced from the present conduct of the sex, from the prevalent fondness for pleasure which takes place of ambition and those nobler passions that open and enlarge the soul; that the instruction which women have hitherto received has only tended, with the constitution of civil society, to render them insignificant objects of desire—mere propagators of fools!—if it can be proved that in aiming to accomplish them, without cultivating their understandings, they are taken out of their sphere of duties, and made ridiculous and useless when the short-lived bloom of beauty is over,⁴ I presume that *rational* men will excuse me for endeavouring to persuade them to become more masculine and respectable.

14   Indeed the word masculine is only a bugbear: there is little reason to fear that women will acquire too much courage or fortitude; for their apparent inferiority with respect to bodily strength must render them, in some degree, dependent on men in the various relations of

---

3. Shakespeare, *Hamlet*, III, i, 142–46. Seraglio: harem.

4. A lively writer, I cannot recollect his name, asks what business women turned of forty have to do in the world? [Wollstonecraft's note.] Wollstonecraft may be thinking of a character in Frances Burney (1752–1840), *Evelina; or, The History of a Young Lady's Entrance into the World* (1778).

life; but why should it be increased by prejudices that give a sex to virtue, and confound simple truths with sensual reveries?

15   Women are, in fact, so much degraded by mistaken notions of female excellence, that I do not mean to add a paradox when I assert, that this artificial weakness produces a propensity to tyrannize, and gives birth to cunning, the natural opponent of strength, which leads them to play off those contemptible infantine airs that undermine esteem even whilst they excite desire. Let men become more chaste and modest, and if women do not grow wiser in the same ratio, it will be clear that they have weaker understandings. It seems scarcely necessary to say, that I now speak of the sex in general. Many individuals have more sense than their male relatives; and, as nothing preponderates where there is a constant struggle for an equilibrium, without it has naturally more gravity, some women govern their husbands without degrading themselves, because intellect will always govern.

(*1792*)

Samuel Langhorne Clemens (Mark Twain) (1835–1910)

A popular American stylist and satirist, Clemens wrote (under the pen name "Mark Twain") humorous sketches and tales, along with travel narratives, novels—The Adventures of Huckleberry Finn *(1884) being the most famous of these—and literary criticism. The tone of this essay is typical of Twain's work.*

The War Prayer [1]

1   It was a time of great and exalting excitement. The country was up in arms, the war was on, in every breast burned the holy fire of patriotism; the drums were beating, the bands playing, the toy pistols popping, the bunched firecrackers hissing and spluttering; on every hand and far down the receding and fading spread of roofs and balconies a fluttering wilderness of flags flashed in the sun; daily the young volunteers marched down the wide avenue gay and fine in their new uniforms, the proud fathers and mothers and sisters and sweethearts cheering them with voices choked with happy emotion as they swung by; nightly the packed mass meetings listened, panting, to patriot oratory which stirred the deepest deeps of their hearts, and which they interrupted at briefest intervals with cyclones of applause, the tears running down their cheeks the while; in the churches the pastors preached devotion to flag and country, and invoked the God of Battles, beseeching His aid in our good cause in outpouring of fervid eloquence which moved every listener. It was indeed a glad and gracious time, and the half dozen rash spirits that ventured to disapprove of the war and cast a doubt upon its righteousness straightway got such a stern and angry warning that for their personal safety's sake they quickly shrank out of sight and offended no more in that way.

2   Sunday morning came—next day the battalions would leave for the front; the church was filled; the volunteers were there, their young faces alight with martial dreams—visions of the stern advance, the gathering momentum, the rushing charge, the flashing sabers, the flight of the foe, the tumult, the enveloping smoke, the fierce pursuit,

---

1. According to Charles Neider, editor of *Complete Essays*, this was dictated in 1904–05 but was not published until after Clemens's death.

the surrender!—then home from the war, bronzed heroes, welcomed, adored, submerged in golden seas of glory! With the volunteers sat their dear ones, proud, happy, and envied by the neighbors and friends who had no sons and brothers to send forth to the field of honor, there to win for the flag, or, failing, die the noblest of noble deaths. The service proceeded; a war chapter from the Old Testament was read; the first prayer was said; it was followed by an organ burst that shook the building, and with one impulse the house rose, with glowing eyes and beating hearts, and poured out that tremendous invocation—

"God the all-terrible! Thou who ordainest,
Thunder thy clarion and lightning thy sword!"

Then came the "long" prayer. None could remember the like of it for passionate pleading and moving and beautiful language. The burden of its supplication was, that an ever-merciful and benignant Father of us all would watch over our noble young soldiers, and aid, comfort, and encourage them in their patriotic work; bless them, shield them in the day of battle and the hour of peril, bear them in His mighty hand, make them strong and confident, invincible in the bloody onset; help them to crush the foe, grant to them and to their flag and country imperishable honor and glory—

3   An aged stranger entered and moved with slow and noiseless step up the main aisle, his eyes fixed upon the minister, his long body clothed in a robe that reached to his feet, his head bare, his white hair descending in a frothy cataract to his shoulders, his seamy face unnaturally pale, pale even to ghastliness. With all eyes following him and wondering, he made his silent way; without pausing, he ascended to the preacher's side and stood there, waiting. With shut lids the preacher, unconscious of his presence, continued his moving prayer, and at last finished it with the words, uttered in fervent appeal, "Bless our arms, grant us the victory, O Lord our God, Father and Protector of our land and flag!"

4   The stranger touched his arm, motioned him to step aside—which the startled minister did—and took his place. During some moments he surveyed the spellbound audience with solemn eyes, in which burned an uncanny light; then in a deep voice he said:

5   "I come from the Throne—bearing a message from Almighty God!" The words smote the house with a shock; if the stranger perceived it he gave no attention. "He has heard the prayer of His servant your shepherd, and will grant it if such shall be your desire after I, His messenger, shall have explained to you its import—that is to say, its full import. For it is like unto many of the prayers of men, in that it asks for more than he who utters it is aware of—except he pause and think.

6   "God's servant and yours has prayed his prayer. Has he paused and taken thought? Is it one prayer? No, it is two—one uttered, the other not. Both have reached the ear of Him Who heareth all supplications,

the spoken and the unspoken. Ponder this—keep it in mind. If you would beseech a blessing upon yourself, beware! lest without intent you invoke a curse upon a neighbor at the same time. If you pray for the blessing of rain upon your crop which needs it, by that act you are possibly praying for a curse upon some neighbor's crop which may not need rain and can be injured by it.

7   "You have heard your servant's prayer—the uttered part of it. I am commissioned of God to put into words the other part of it—that part which the pastor—and also you in your hearts—fervently prayed silently. And ignorantly and unthinkingly? God grant that it was so! You heard these words: 'Grant us the victory, O Lord our God!' That is sufficient. The *whole* of the uttered prayer is compact into those pregnant words. Elaborations were not necessary. When you have prayed for victory you have prayed for many unmentioned results which follow victory—*must* follow it, cannot help but follow it. Upon the listening spirit of God the Father fell also the unspoken part of the prayer. He commandeth me to put it into words. Listen!

8   "O Lord our Father, our young patriots, idols of our hearts, go forth to battle—be Thou near them! With them—in spirit—we also go forth from the sweet peace of our beloved firesides to smite the foe. O Lord our God, help us to tear their soldiers to bloody shreds with our shells; help us to cover their smiling fields with the pale forms of their patriot dead; help us to drown the thunder of the guns with the shrieks of their wounded, writhing in pain; help us to lay waste their humble homes with a hurricane of fire; help us to wring the hearts of their unoffending widows with unavailing grief; help us to turn them out roofless with their little children to wander unfriended the wastes of their desolated land in rags and hunger and thirst, sports of the sun flames of summer and the icy winds of winter, broken in spirit, worn with travail, imploring Thee for the refuge of the grave and denied it— for our sakes who adore Thee, Lord, blast their hopes, blight their lives, protract their bitter pilgrimage, make heavy their steps, water their way with their tears, stain the white snow with the blood of their wounded feet! We ask it, in the spirit of love, of Him Who is the Source of Love, and Who is the ever-faithful refuge and friend of all that are sore beset and seek His aid with humble and contrite hearts. Amen."

9   (*After a pause.*) "Ye have prayed it; if ye still desire it, speak! The messenger of the Most High waits."

10   It was believed afterward that the man was a lunatic, because there was no sense in what he said.

(*1923*)

Oscar Wilde (1854–1900)

Educated at Trinity College, Dublin, and Magdalen College, Oxford, and winner of the Newdigate Prize for poetry, Oscar Wilde seemed destined for a glittering career. His plays, reviews, essays, and poetry, marked by epigram and irony, were as popular as they were provocative, and his life proved as notorious as his literary career. The aphorisms here, first published in the undergraduate magazine The Chameleon, *were used as evidence of Wilde's immorality during the trial for libel that he brought against the Marquess of Queensbury.*

Phrases and Philosophies for the Use of the Young

1   The first duty in life is to be as artificial as possible. What the second duty is no one has as yet discovered.

2   Wickedness is a myth invented by good people to account for the curious attractiveness of others.

3   If the poor only had profiles there would be no difficulty in solving the problem of poverty.

4   Those who see any difference between soul and body have neither.

5   A really well-made buttonhole is the only link between Art and Nature.

6   Religions die when they are proved to be true. Science is the record of dead religions.

7   The well-bred contradict other people. The wise contradict themselves.

8   Nothing that actually occurs is of the smallest importance.

9   Dulness is the coming of age of seriousness.

10   In all unimportant matters, style, not sincerity, is the essential. In all important matters, style, not sincerity, is the essential.

11   If one tells the truth one is sure, sooner or later, to be found out.

12   Pleasure is the only thing one should live for. Nothing ages like happiness.

13   It is only by not paying one's bills that one can hope to live in the memory of the commercial classes.

14   No crime is vulgar, but all vulgarity is crime. Vulgarity is the conduct of others.

15   Only the shallow know themselves.

16   Time is waste of money.

17   One should always be a little improbable.

18   There is a fatality about all good resolutions. They are invariably made too soon.

19   The only way to atone for being occasionally a little overdressed is by being always absolutely over-educated.

20   To be premature is to be perfect.

21   Any preoccupation with ideas of what is right or wrong in conduct shows an arrested intellectual development.

22   Ambition is the last refuge of the failure.

23   A truth ceases to be true when more than one person believes in it.

24   In examinations the foolish ask questions that the wise cannot answer.

25   Greek dress was in its essence inartistic. Nothing should reveal the body but the body.

26   One should either be a work of art, or wear a work of art.

27   It is only the superficial qualities that last. Man's deeper nature is soon found out.

28   Industry is the root of all ugliness.

29   The ages live in history through their anachronisms.

30   It is only the gods who taste of death. Apollo has passed away, but Hyacinth, whom men say he slew, lives on. Nero and Narcissus are always with us.

31   The old believe everything: the middle-aged suspect everything: the young know everything.

32   The condition of perfection is idleness: the aim of perfection is youth.

33   Only the great masters of style ever succeed in being obscure.

34   There is something tragic about the enormous number of young men there are in England at the present moment who start life with perfect profiles, and end by adopting some useful profession.

35   To love oneself is the beginning of a life-long romance.

(1894)

Lewis Mumford (1895–1990)

A native New Yorker, Lewis Mumford was an American social philosopher
and university professor who wrote on city planning, architecture, and the
dehumanizing effects of technology. Mumford's works include Technics and
Civilization *(1933) and* The Culture of Cities *(1938).*

Mechanization of Modern Culture

1   Where did the machine first take form in modern civilization? There
was plainly more than one point of origin. Our mechanical civilization
represents the convergence of numerous habits, ideas, and modes of
living, as well as technical instruments; and some of these were, in the
beginning, directly opposed to the civilization they helped to create.
But the first manifestation of the new order took place in the general
picture of the world: during the first seven centuries of the machine's
existence the categories of time and space underwent an extraordinary
change, and no aspect of life was left untouched by this transformation. The application of quantitative methods of thought to the study
of nature had its first manifestation in the regular measurement of
time; and the new mechanical conception of time arose in part out of
the routine of the monastery. Alfred Whitehead[1] has emphasized the
importance of the scholastic belief in a universe ordered by God as one
of the foundations of modern physics: but behind that belief was the
presence of order in the institutions of the Church itself.

2   The technics of the ancient world were still carried on from
Constantinople and Baghdad to Sicily and Cordova: hence the early
lead taken by Salerno[2] in the scientific and medical advances of the
Middle Ages. It was, however, in the monasteries of the West that the
desire for order and power, other than that expressed in the military
domination of weaker men, first manifested itself after the long uncertainty and bloody confusion that attended the breakdown of the
Roman Empire. Within the walls of the monastery was sanctuary:
under the rule of the order surprise and doubt and caprice and irregularity were put at bay. Opposed to the erratic fluctuations and pulsa-
tions of the worldly life was the iron discipline of the rule. Benedict[3]

---

1. Alfred North Whitehead (1861–1947), British mathematician and philosopher.
2. Seaport on the western coast of southern Italy. Salerno University was founded in
   1150 and was one of the leading Italian places of learning.
3. Saint Benedict of Nursia (c. 480–c. 544) devised the first orderly regimen for
   monastic life, which became known as "The Rule of Saint Benedict."

added a seventh period to the devotions of the day, and in the seventh century, by a bull of Pope Sabinianus,[4] it was decreed that the bells of the monastery be rung seven times in the twenty-four hours. These punctuation marks in the day were known as the canonical hours, and some means of keeping count of them and ensuring their regular repetition became necessary.

3 According to a now discredited legend, the first modern mechanical clock, worked by falling weights, was invented by the monk named Gerbert who afterwards became Pope Sylvester II, near the close of the tenth century. This clock was probably only a water clock,[5] one of those bequests of the ancient world either left over directly from the days of the Romans, like the water-wheel itself, or coming back again into the West through the Arabs. But the legend, as so often happens, is accurate in its implications if not in its facts. The monastery was the seat of a regular life, and an instrument for striking the hours at intervals or for reminding the bell-ringer that it was time to strike the bells, was an almost inevitable product of this life. If the mechanical clock did not appear until the cities of the thirteenth century demanded an orderly routine, the habit of order itself and the earnest regulation of time-sequences had become almost second nature in the monastery. Coulton agrees with Sombart[6] in looking upon the Benedictines, the great working order, as perhaps the original founders of modern capitalism: their rule certainly took the curse off work and their vigorous engineering enterprises may even have robbed warfare of some of its glamor. So one is not straining the facts when one suggests that the monasteries—at one time there were 40,000 under the Benedictine rule—helped to give human enterprise the regular collective beat and rhythm of the machine; for the clock is not merely a means of keeping track of the hours, but of synchronizing the actions of men.

4 Was it by reason of the collective Christian desire to provide for the welfare of souls in eternity by regular prayers and devotions that time-keeping and the habits of temporal order took hold of men's minds: habits that capitalist civilization presently turned to good account? One must perhaps accept the irony of this paradox. At all events, by the thirteenth century there are definite records of mechanical clocks, and by 1370 a well-designed "modern" clock had been built by Heinrich von Wyck at Paris. Meanwhile, bell towers had come into existence, and the new clocks, if they did not have, till the fourteenth century, a dial and

---

4. Pope from 604 to 606 who succeeded Gregory the Great.

5. In ancient Greece and Rome, time was measured by *clepsydrae*, or water clocks, globes of earthenware or glass filled with water that then escaped at a steady rate through a tiny hole. These devices were used to set time limits for speeches in the court of justice.

6. George Gordon Coulton (1858–1947), English historian who also wrote on monasticism, notably *Five Centuries of Religion* (1923–50). Werner Sombart (1863–1941), German economic historian, author of *The Quintessence of Capitalism: A Study of the History and Psychology of the Modern Businessman* (1915).

a hand that translated the movement of time into a movement through space, at all events struck the hours. The clouds that could paralyze the sundial, the freezing that could stop the water clock on a winter night, were no longer obstacles to time-keeping; summer or winter, day or night, one was aware of the measured clank of the clock. The instrument presently spread outside the monastery; and the regular striking of the bells brought a new regularity into the life of the workman and the merchant. The bells of the clock tower almost defined urban existence. Time-keeping passed into time-serving and time-accounting and time-rationing. As this took place, Eternity ceased gradually to serve as the measure and focus of human actions.

5   The clock, not the steam-engine, is the key-machine of the modern industrial age. For every phase of its development the clock is both the outstanding fact and the typical symbol of the machine: even today no other machine is so ubiquitous. Here, at the very beginning of modern technics, appeared prophetically the accurate automatic machine which, only after centuries of further effort, was also to prove the final consummation of this technics in every department of industrial activity. There had been power-machines, such as the water-mill, before the clock; and there had also been various kinds of automata, to awaken the wonder of the populace in the temple, or to please the idle fancy of some Moslem caliph: machines one finds illustrated in Hero and Al-Jazari.[7] But here was a new kind of power-machine, in which the source of power and the transmission were of such a nature as to ensure the even flow of energy throughout the works and to make possible regular production and a standardized product. In its relationship to determinable quantities of energy, to standardization, to automatic action, and finally to its own special product, accurate timing, the clock has been the foremost machine in modern technics: and at each period it has remained in the lead: it marks a perfection toward which other machines aspire. The clock, moreover, served as a model for many other kinds of mechanical works, and the analysis of motion that accompanied the perfection of the clock, with the various types of gearing and transmission that were elaborated, contributed to the success of quite different kinds of machine. Smiths could have hammered thousands of suits of armor or thousands of iron cannon, wheelwrights could have shaped thousands of great water-wheels or crude gears, without inventing any of the special types of movement developed in clockwork, and without any of the accuracy of measurement and fineness of articulation that finally produced the accurate eighteenth-century chronometer.

---

7. Hero of Alexandria, Greek geometer, and writer on mechanical subjects of the second half of the first century. His works include a description of a coin-operated slot machine and a type of steam engine. Al-Jazari, twelfth-century engineer in the service of Nasir al-Din, king of Diyar Bakr in Mesopotamia. Al-Jazari's *Book of Knowledge of Mechanical Devices* contains sketches and descriptions of reservoirs, fountains, and several varieties of water clocks.

6   The clock, moreover, is a piece of power-machinery whose "product" is seconds and minutes: by its essential nature it dissociated time from human events and helped to create the belief in an independent world of mathematically measurable sequences: the special world of science. There is relatively little foundation for this belief in common human experience; throughout the year the days are of uneven duration, and not merely does the relation between day and night steadily change, but a slight journey from East to West alters astronomical time by a certain number of minutes. In terms of the human organism itself, mechanical time is even more foreign: while human life has regularities of its own, the beat of the pulse, the breathing of the lungs, these change from hour to hour with mood and action, and in the longer span of days, time is measured not by the calendar but by the events that occupy it. The shepherd measures from the time the ewes lambed; the farmer measures back to the day of sowing or forward to the harvest; if growth has its own duration and regularities, behind it are not simply matter and motion but the facts of development: in short, history. And while mechanical time is strung out in a succession of mathematically isolated instants, organic time—what Bergson[8] calls duration—is cumulative in its effects. Though mechanical time can, in a sense, be speeded up or run backward, like the hands of a clock or the images of a moving picture, organic time moves in only one direction—through the cycle of birth, growth, development, decay, and death—and the past that is already dead remains present in the future that has still to be born.

7   Around 1345, according to Thorndike,[9] the division of hours into sixty minutes and of minutes into sixty seconds became common: it was this abstract framework of divided time that became more and more the point of reference for both action and thought, and in the effort to arrive at accuracy in this department, the astronomical exploration of the sky focused attention further upon the regular, implacable movements of the heavenly bodies through space. Early in the sixteenth century a young Nuremberg mechanic, Peter Henlein, is supposed to have created "many-wheeled watches out of small bits of iron" and by the end of the century the small domestic clock had been introduced in England and Holland. As with the motor car and the airplane, the richer classes first took over the new mechanism and popularized it: partly because they alone could afford it, partly because the new bourgeoisie were the first to discover that, as Franklin[10] later put it, "time is money." To become "as regular as clockwork" was the bourgeois ideal, and to own a watch was for long a definite symbol of success. The increasing tempo of civilization led to a demand for greater power: and in turn power quickened the tempo.

---

8. Henri Bergson (1859–1941), French philosopher.

9. Lynn Thorndike (1882–1965), author of *The History of Medieval Europe* (1917).

10. Benjamin Franklin (1706–1790), American statesman and scientist who coined the famous dictum "time is money" in his *Advice to Young Tradesmen* (1748).

8   Now, the orderly punctual life that first took shape in the monasteries is not native to mankind, although by now Western peoples are so thoroughly regimented by the clock that it is "second nature" and they look upon its observance as a fact of nature. Many Eastern civilizations have flourished on a loose basis in time: the Hindus have in fact been so indifferent to time that they lack even an authentic chronology of the years. Only yesterday, in the midst of the industrializations of Soviet Russia, did a society come into existence to further the carrying of watches there and to propagandize the benefits of punctuality. The popularization of time-keeping, which followed the production of the cheap standardized watch, first in Geneva, then in America around the middle of the last century, was essential to a well-articulated system of transportation and production.

9   To keep time was once a peculiar attribute of music: it gave industrial value to the workshop song or the tattoo or the chantey of the sailors tugging at a rope. But the effect of the mechanical clock is more pervasive and strict: it presides over the day from the hour of rising to the hour of rest. When one thinks of the day as an abstract span of time, one does not go to bed with the chickens on a winter's night: one invents wick, chimneys, lamps, gaslights, electric lamps, so as to use all the hours belonging to the day. When one thinks of time, not as a sequence of experiences, but as a collection of hours, minutes, and seconds, the habits of adding time and saving time come into existence. Time took on the character of an enclosed space: it could be divided, it could be filled up, it could even be expanded by the invention of labor-saving instruments.

10   Abstract time became the medium of existence. Organic functions themselves were regulated by it: one ate, not upon feeling hungry, but when prompted by the clock: one slept, not when one was tired, but when the clock sanctioned it. A generalized time-consciousness accompanied the wider use of clocks: dissociating time from organic sequences, it became easier for the men of the Renaissance to indulge the fantasy of reviving the classic past or of reliving the splendors of antique Roman civilization: the cult of history, appearing first in daily ritual, finally abstracted itself as a special discipline. In the seventeenth century journalism and periodic literature made their appearance: even in dress, following the lead of Venice as fashion-center, people altered styles every year rather than every generation.

11   The gain in mechanical efficiency through co-ordination and through the closer articulation of the day's events cannot be overestimated: while this increase cannot be measured in mere horsepower, one has only to imagine its absence today to foresee the speedy disruption and eventual collapse of our entire society. The modern industrial régime could do without coal and iron and steam more easily than it could do without the clock.

(1934)

George Orwell (1903–1950)

Novelist, essayist, and political journalist, Orwell was born Eric Arthur
Blair in Motihari, Bengal, and educated at Eton. He worked with the Indian
Imperial Police in Burma, an experience recalled in the title essay of
Shooting an Elephant (1950), and fought on the Republican side in the
Spanish Civil War. He is best remembered for his powerful satires
Animal Farm (1945) and Nineteen Eighty-Four (1948) and for his
essays on politics, language, poverty, and colonialism.

Shooting an Elephant

1   In Moulmein, in Lower Burma, I was hated by large numbers of people—the only time in my life that I have been important enough for this to happen to me. I was sub-divisional police officer of the town, and in an aimless, petty kind of way anti-European feeling was very bitter. No one had the guts to raise a riot, but if a European woman went through the bazaars alone somebody would probably spit betel juice[1] over her dress. As a police officer I was an obvious target and was baited whenever it seemed safe to do so. When a nimble Burman tripped me up on the football field and the referee (another Burman) looked the other way, the crowd yelled with hideous laughter. This happened more than once. In the end the sneering yellow faces of young men that met me everywhere, the insults hooted after me when I was at a safe distance, got badly on my nerves. The young Buddhist priests were the worst of all. There were several thousands of them in the town and none of them seemed to have anything to do except stand on street corners and jeer at Europeans.

2   All this was perplexing and upsetting. For at that time I had already made up my mind that imperialism was an evil thing and the sooner I chucked up my job and got out of it the better. Theoretically—and secretly, of course—I was all for the Burmese and all against their oppressors, the British. As for the job I was doing, I hated it more bitterly than I can perhaps make clear. In a job like that you see the dirty work of Empire at close quarters. The wretched prisoners huddling in the stinking cages of the lock-ups, the grey, cowed faces of the long-term convicts, the scarred buttocks of the men who had been flogged

---

1. The seed of the betel palm, chewed with its leaves and lime to provide a mild stimulant.

with bamboos—all these oppressed me with an intolerable sense of guilt. But I could get nothing into perspective. I was young and ill-educated and I had had to think out my problems in the utter silence that is imposed on every Englishman in the East. I did not even know that the British Empire is dying, still less did I know that it is a great deal better than the younger empires that are going to supplant it. All I knew was that I was stuck between my hatred of the empire I served and my rage against the evil-spirited little beasts who tried to make my job impossible. With one part of my mind I thought of the British Raj[2] as an unbreakable tyranny, as something clamped down, *in saecula saeculorum*,[3] upon the will of prostrate peoples; with another part I thought that the greatest joy in the world would be to drive a bayonet into a Buddhist priest's guts. Feelings like these are the normal by-products of imperialism; ask any Anglo-Indian official, if you can catch him off duty.

3   One day something happened which in a roundabout way was enlightening. It was a tiny incident in itself, but it gave me a better glimpse than I had had before of the real nature of imperialism—the real motives for which despotic governments act. Early one morning the sub-inspector at a police station the other end of the town rang me up on the phone and said that an elephant was ravaging the bazaar. Would I please come and do something about it? I did not know what I could do, but I wanted to see what was happening and I got on to a pony and started out. I took my rifle, an old .44 Winchester and much too small to kill an elephant, but I thought the noise might be useful *in terrorem*. Various Burmans stopped me on the way and told me about the elephant's doings. It was not, of course, a wild elephant, but a tame one which had gone "must."[4] It had been chained up as tame elephants always are when their attack of "must" is due, but on the previous night it had broken its chain and escaped. Its mahout,[5] the only person who could manage it when it was in that state, had set out in pursuit, but he had taken the wrong direction and was now twelve hours' journey away, and in the morning the elephant had suddenly reappeared in the town. The Burmese population had no weapons and were quite helpless against it. It had already destroyed somebody's bamboo hut, killed a cow and raided some fruit-stalls and devoured the stock; also it had met the municipal rubbish van, and when the driver jumped out and took to his heels, had turned the van over and inflicted violence upon it.

4   The Burmese sub-inspector and some Indian constables were waiting for me in the quarter where the elephant had been seen. It was a very poor quarter, a labyrinth of squalid bamboo huts, thatched with

---

2. The British Raj: British sovereignty in India and Burma.

3. For ages and ages.

4. A state of frenzy to which elephants are subject at irregular intervals.

5. Elephant trainer and driver.

palm-leaf, winding all over a steep hillside. I remember that it was a cloudy stuffy morning at the beginning of the rains. We began questioning the people as to where the elephant had gone, and, as usual, failed to get any definite information. That is invariably the case in the East; a story always sounds clear enough at a distance, but the nearer you get to the scene of events the vaguer it becomes. Some of the people said that the elephant had gone in one direction, some said that he had gone in another, some professed not even to have heard of any elephant. I had almost made up my mind that the whole story was a pack of lies, when we heard yells a little distance away. There was a loud, scandalized cry of "Go away, child! Go away this instant!" and an old woman with a switch in her hand came round the corner of a hut, violently shooing away a crowd of naked children. Some more women followed, clicking their tongues and exclaiming; evidently there was something there that the children ought not to have seen. I rounded the hut and saw a man's dead body sprawling in the mud. He was an Indian, a black Dravidian coolie,[6] almost naked, and he could not have been dead many minutes. The people said that the elephant had come suddenly upon him round the corner of the hut, caught him with its trunk, put its foot on his back and ground him into the earth. This was the rainy season and the ground was soft, and his face had scored a trench a foot deep and a couple of yards long. He was lying on his belly with arms crucified and head sharply twisted to one side. His face was coated with mud, the eyes wide open, the teeth bared and grinning with an expression of unendurable agony. (Never tell me, by the way, that the dead look peaceful. Most of the corpses I have seen looked devilish.) The friction of the great beast's foot had stripped the skin from his back as neatly as one skins a rabbit. As soon as I saw the dead man I sent an orderly to a friend's house nearby to borrow an elephant rifle. I had already sent back the pony, not wanting it to go mad with fright and throw me if it smelled the elephant.

5   The orderly came back in a few minutes with a rifle and five cartridges, and meanwhile some Burmans had arrived and told us that the elephant was in the paddy fields below, only a few hundred yards away. As I started forward practically the whole population of the quarter flocked out of their houses and followed me. They had seen the rifle and were all shouting excitedly that I was going to shoot the elephant. They had not shown much interest in the elephant when he was merely ravaging their homes, but it was different now that he was going to be shot. It was a bit of fun to them, as it would be to an English crowd; besides, they wanted the meat. It made me vaguely uneasy. I had no intention of shooting the elephant—I had merely sent for the rifle to defend myself if necessary—and it is always unnerving to have a crowd following you. I marched down the hill, looking and feeling a fool, with the rifle over my shoulder and an ever-growing

---

6. A labourer belonging to one of the Dravidian-speaking groups of southern India.

army of people jostling at my heels. At the bottom when you got away from the huts there was a metalled road and beyond that a miry waste of paddy fields a thousand yards across, not yet ploughed but soggy from the first rains and dotted with coarse grass. The elephant was standing eighty yards from the road, his left side towards us. He took not the slightest notice of the crowd's approach. He was tearing up bunches of grass, beating them against his knees to clean them and stuffing them into his mouth.

6   I had halted on the road. As soon as I saw the elephant I knew with perfect certainty that I ought not to shoot him. It is a serious matter to shoot a working elephant—it is comparable to destroying a huge and costly piece of machinery—and obviously one ought not to do it if it can possibly be avoided. And at that distance, peacefully eating, the elephant looked no more dangerous than a cow. I thought then and I think now that his attack of "must" was already passing off; in which case he would merely wander harmlessly about until the mahout came back and caught him. Moreover, I did not in the least want to shoot him. I decided that I would watch him for a little while to make sure that he did not turn savage again, and then go home.

7   But at that moment I glanced round at the crowd that had followed me. It was an immense crowd, two thousand at the least and growing every minute. It blocked the road for a long distance on either side. I looked at the sea of yellow faces above the garish clothes—faces all happy and excited over this bit of fun, all certain that the elephant was going to be shot. They were watching me as they would watch a conjurer about to perform a trick. They did not like me, but with the magical rifle in my hands I was momentarily worth watching. And suddenly I realized that I should have to shoot the elephant after all. The people expected it of me and I had got to do it; I could feel their two thousand wills pressing me forward, irresistibly. And it was at this moment, as I stood there with the rifle in my hands, that I first grasped the hollowness, the futility of the white man's dominion in the East. Here was I, the white man with his gun, standing in front of the unarmed native crowd—seemingly the leading actor of the piece; but in reality I was only an absurd puppet pushed to and fro by the will of those yellow faces behind. I perceived in this moment that when the white man turns tyrant it is his own freedom that he destroys. He becomes a sort of hollow, posing dummy, the conventionalized figure of a sahib.[7] For it is the condition of his rule that he shall spend his life in trying to impress the "natives" and so in every crisis he has got to do what the "natives" expect of him. He wears a mask, and his face grows to fit it. I had got to shoot the elephant. I had committed myself to doing it when I sent for the rifle. A sahib has got to act like a sahib; he has got to appear resolute, to know his own mind and do definite things. To come all that way, rifle in hand, with two thousand people

7. Once a form of respectful address for a European man in India.

marching at my heels, and then to trail feebly away, having done nothing—no, that was impossible. The crowd would laugh at me. And my whole life, every white man's life in the East, was one long struggle not to be laughed at.

8   But I did not want to shoot the elephant. I watched him beating his bunch of grass against his knees, with that preoccupied grandmotherly air that elephants have. It seemed to me that it would be murder to shoot him. At that age I was not squeamish about killing animals, but I had never shot an elephant and never wanted to. (Somehow it always seems worse to kill a *large* animal.) Besides, there was the beast's owner to be considered. Alive, the elephant was worth at least a hundred pounds; dead, he would only be worth the value of his tusks—five pounds, possibly. But I had got to act quickly. I turned to some experienced-looking Burmans who had been there when we arrived, and asked them how the elephant had been behaving. They all said the same thing: he took no notice of you if you left him alone, but he might charge if you went too close to him.

9   It was perfectly clear to me what I ought to do. I ought to walk up to within, say, twenty-five yards of the elephant and test his behaviour. If he charged I could shoot, if he took no notice of me it would be safe to leave him until the mahout came back. But also I knew that I was going to do no such thing. I was a poor shot with a rifle and the ground was soft mud into which one would sink at every step. If the elephant charged and I missed him, I should have about as much chance as a toad under a steam-roller. But even then I was not thinking particularly of my own skin, only the watchful yellow faces behind. For at that moment, with the crowd watching me, I was not afraid in the ordinary sense, as I would have been if I had been alone. A white man mustn't be frightened in front of "natives"; and so, in general, he isn't frightened. The sole thought in my mind was that if anything went wrong those two thousand Burmans would see me pursued, caught, trampled on and reduced to a grinning corpse like that Indian up the hill. And if that happened it was quite probable that some of them would laugh. That would never do. There was only one alternative. I shoved the cartridges into the magazine and lay down on the road to get a better aim.

10   The crowd grew very still, and a deep, low, happy sigh, as of people who see the theatre curtain go up at last, breathed from innumerable throats. They were going to have their bit of fun after all. The rifle was a beautiful German thing with crosshair sights. I did not know that in shooting an elephant one should shoot to cut an imaginary bar running from ear-hole to ear-hole. I ought, therefore, as the elephant was sideways on, to have aimed straight at his ear-hole; actually I aimed several inches in front of this, thinking the brain would be further forward.

11   When I pulled the trigger I did not hear the bang or feel the kick— one never does when a shot goes home—but I heard the devilish roar of glee that went up from the crowd. In that instant, in too short a

time, one would have thought, even for the bullet to get there, a mysterious, terrible change had come over the elephant. He neither stirred nor fell, but every line of his body altered. He looked suddenly stricken, shrunken, immensely old, as though the frightful impact of the bullet had paralysed him without knocking him down. At last, after what seemed a long time—it might have been five seconds, I dare say—he sagged flabbily to his knees. His mouth slobbered. An enormous senility seemed to have settled upon him. One could have imagined him thousands of years old. I fired again into the same spot. At the second shot he did not collapse but climbed with desperate slowness to his feet and stood weakly upright, with legs sagging and head drooping. I fired a third time. That was the shot that did for him. You could see the agony of it jolt his whole body and knock the last remnant of strength from his legs. But in falling he seemed for a moment to rise, for as his hind legs collapsed beneath him he seemed to tower upwards like a huge rock toppling, his trunk reaching skyward like a tree. He trumpeted, for the first and only time. And then down he came, his belly towards me, with a crash that seemed to shake the ground even where I lay.

12   I got up. The Burmans were already racing past me across the mud. It was obvious that the elephant would never rise again, but he was not dead. He was breathing very rhythmically with long rattling gasps, his great mound of a side painfully rising and falling. His mouth was wide open—I could see far down into caverns of pale pink throat. I waited a long time for him to die, but his breathing did not weaken. Finally I fired my two remaining shots into the spot where I thought his heart must be. The thick blood welled out of him like red velvet, but still he did not die. His body did not even jerk when the shots hit him, the tortured breathing continued without a pause. He was dying, very slowly and in great agony, but in some world remote from me where not even a bullet could damage him further. I felt that I had got to put an end to that dreadful noise. It seemed dreadful to see the great beast lying there, powerless to move and yet powerless to die, and not even to be able to finish him. I sent back for my small fire and poured shot after shot into his heart and down his throat. They seemed to make no impression. The tortured gasps continued as steadily as the ticking of a clock.

13   In the end I could not stand it any longer and went away. I heard later that it took him half an hour to die. The Burmans were arriving with dahs[8] and baskets even before I left, and I was told they had stripped his body almost to the bones by the afternoon.

14   Afterwards, of course, there were endless discussions about the shooting of the elephant. The owner was furious, but he was only an Indian and could do nothing. Besides, legally I had done the right thing, for a mad elephant has to be killed, like a mad dog, if its owner

---

8. Dah: a heavy knife used in Burma.

fails to control it. Among the Europeans opinion was divided. The older men said I was right, the younger men said it was a damn shame to shoot an elephant for killing a coolie, because an elephant was worth more than any damn Coringhee coolie. And afterwards I was very glad that the coolie had been killed; it put me legally in the right and it gave me sufficient pretext for shooting the elephant. I often wondered whether any of the others grasped that I had done it solely to avoid looking a fool.

(1936)

Margaret Laurence (1926–1987)

Known for her novels about prairie life, Margaret Laurence was

a major Canadian novelist whose A Jest of God *(1966) and* The Diviners

(1974) both received the Governor General's Award. "Where the World

Began" explores the shaping influence of the prairie town of her childhood.

See "The Loons," p. 465.

Where the World Began

1   A strange place it was, that place where the world began. A place of incredible happenings, splendours and revelations, despairs like multitudinous pits of isolated hells. A place of shadow-spookiness, inhabited by the unknowable dead. A place of jubilation and of mourning, horrible and beautiful.

2   It was, in fact, a small prairie town.

3   Because that settlement and that land were my first and for many years only real knowledge of this planet, in some profound way they remain my world, my way of viewing. My eyes were formed there. Towns like ours, set in a sea of land, have been described thousands of times as dull, bleak, flat, uninteresting. I have had it said to me that the railway trip across Canada is spectacular, except for the prairies, when it would be desirable to go to sleep for several days, until the ordeal is over. I am always unable to argue this point effectively. All I can say is—well, you really have to live there to know that country. The town of my childhood could be called bizarre, agonizingly repressive or cruel at times, and the land in which it grew could be called harsh in the violence of its seasonal changes. But never merely flat or uninteresting. Never dull.

4   In winter, we used to hitch rides on the back of the milk sleigh, our moccasins squeaking and slithering on the hard rutted snow of the roads, our hands in ice-bubbled mitts hanging onto the box edge of the sleigh for dear life, while Bert grinned at us through his great frosted moustache and shouted the horses into speed, daring us to stay put. Those mornings, rising, there would be the perpetual fascination of the frost feathers on windows, the ferns and flowers and eerie faces traced there during the night by unseen artists of the wind. Evenings, coming back from skating, the sky would be black but not dark, for you could see a cold glitter of stars from one side of the earth's rim to the other. And then the sometime astonishment when you saw the Northern Lights flaring across the sky, like the scrawled signature of God. After a blizzard, when the snowploughs hadn't yet got through, school

would be closed for the day, the assumption being that the town's young could not possibly flounder through five feet of snow in the pursuit of education. We would then gaily don snowshoes and flounder for miles out into the white dazzling deserts, in pursuit of a different kind of knowing. If you came back too close to night, through the woods at the foot of the town hill, the thin black branches of poplar and chokecherry now meringued with frost, sometimes you heard coyotes. Or maybe the banshee wolf-voices were really only inside your head.

5   Summers were scorching, and when no rain came and the wheat became bleached and dried before it headed, the faces of farmers and townsfolk would not smile much, and you took for granted, because it never seemed to have been any different, the frequent knocking at the back door and the young men standing there, mumbling or thrusting defiantly their request for a drink of water and a sandwich if you could spare it. They were riding the freights, and you never knew where they had come from, or where they might end up, if anywhere. The Drought and Depression were like evil deities which had been there always. You understood and did not understand.

6   Yet the outside had its continuing marvels. The poplar bluffs and the small river were filled and surrounded with a zillion different grasses, stones, and weed flowers. The meadowlarks sang undaunted from the twanging telephone wires along the gravel highway. Once we found an old flat-bottomed scow, and launched her, poling along the shallow brown waters, mending her with wodges[1] of hastily chewed Spearmint, grounding her among the tangles of soft yellow marsh marigolds that grew succulently along the banks of the shrunken river, while the sun made our skins smell dusty-warm.

7   My best friend lived in an apartment above some stores on Main Street (its real name was Mountain Avenue, goodness knows why), an elegant apartment with royal-blue velvet curtains. The back roof, scarcely sloping at all, was corrugated tin, of a furnace-like warmth on a July afternoon, and we would sit there drinking lemonade and looking across the back lane at the Fire Hall. Sometimes our vigil would be rewarded. Oh joy! Somebody's house burning down! We had an almost-perfect callousness in some ways. Then the wooden tower's bronze bell would clonk and toll like a thousand speeded funerals in a time of plague, and in a few minutes the team of giant black horses would cannon forth, pulling the fire wagon like some scarlet chariot of the Goths, while the firemen clung with one hand, adjusting their helmets as they went.

8   The oddities of the place were endless. An elderly lady used to serve, as her afternoon tea offering to other ladies, soda biscuits spread with peanut butter and topped with a whole marshmallow. Some considered this slightly eccentric, when compared with chopped egg sand-

---

1. Chunks or lumps.

wiches, and admittedly talked about her behind her back, but no one ever refused these delicacies or indicated to her that they thought she had slipped a cog. Another lady dyed her hair a bright and cheery orange, by strangers often mistaken at twenty paces for a feather hat. My own beloved stepmother wore a silver fox neckpiece, a whole pelt, *with the embalmed (?) head still on.* My Ontario Irish grandfather said, "sparrow grass," a more interesting term than asparagus. The town dump was known as "the nuisance grounds," a phrase fraught with weird connotations, as though the effluvia of our lives was beneath contempt but at the same time was subtly threatening to the determined and sometimes hysterical propriety of our ways.

9   Some oddities were, as idiom had it, "funny ha ha"; others were "funny peculiar." Some were not so funny at all. An old man lived, deranged, in a shack in the valley. Perhaps he wasn't even all that old, but to us he seemed a wild Methuselah[2] figure, shambling among the underbrush and the tall couchgrass, muttering indecipherable curses or blessings, a prophet who had forgotten his prophesies. Everyone in town knew him, but no one knew him. He lived among us as though only occasionally and momentarily visible. The kids called him Andy Gump,[3] and feared him. Some sought to prove their bravery by tormenting him. They were the medieval bear baiters, and he the lumbering bewildered bear, half blind, only rarely turning to snarl. Everything is to be found in a town like mine. Belsen,[4] writ small but with the same ink.

10   All of us cast stones in one shape or another. In grade school, among the vulnerable and violet girls we were, the feared and despised were those few older girls from what was charmingly termed "the wrong side of the tracks." Tough in talk and tougher in muscle, they were said to be whores already. And may have been, that being about the only profession readily available to them.

11   The dead lived in that place, too. Not only the grandparents who had, in local parlance, "passed on" and who gloomed, bearded or bonneted, from the sepia photographs in old albums, but also the uncles, forever eighteen or nineteen, whose names were carved on the granite family stones in the cemetery, but whose bones lay in France. My own young mother lay in that graveyard, beside other dead of our kin, and when I was ten, my father too, only forty, left the living town for the dead dwelling on the hill.

12   When I was eighteen, I couldn't wait to get out of that town, away from the prairies. I did not know then that I would carry the land and town all my life within my skull, that they would form the mainspring and source of the writing I was to do, wherever and however far away I might live.

---

2. Biblical patriarch said to have lived 969 years.

3. A character in the 1920s comic strip *The Gumps*, who often spoke in soliloquies.

4. Notorious Nazi concentration camp during World War II.

13   This was my territory in the time of my youth, and in a sense my life since then has been an attempt to look at it, to come to terms with it. Stultifying to the mind it certainly would be, and sometimes was, but not to the imagination. It was many things, but it was never dull.

14   The same, I now see, could be said for Canada in general. Why on earth did generations of Canadians pretend to believe this country dull? We knew perfectly well it wasn't. Yet for so long we did not proclaim what we knew. If our upsurge of so-called nationalism seems odd or irrelevant to outsiders, and even to some of our own people (*what's all the fuss about?*), they might try to understand that for many years we valued ourselves insufficiently, living as we did under the huge shadows of those two dominating figures, Uncle Sam and Britannia. We have only just begun to value ourselves, our land, our abilities. We have only just begun to recognize our legends and to give shape to our myths.

15   There are, God knows, enough aspects to deplore about this country. When I see the killing of our lakes and rivers with industrial wastes, I feel rage and despair. When I see our industries and natural resources increasingly taken over by America, I feel an overwhelming discouragement, especially as I cannot simply say "damn Yankees." It should never be forgotten that it is we ourselves who have sold such a large amount of our birthright for a mess of plastic Progress. When I saw the War Measures Act being invoked in 1970,[5] I lost forever the vestigial remains of the naïve wish–belief that repression could not happen here, or would not. And yet, of course, I had known all along in the deepest and often hidden caves of the heart that anything can happen anywhere, for the seed of both man's freedom and his captivity are found everywhere, even in the microcosm of a prairie town. But in raging against our injustices, our stupidities, I do so as *family*, as I did, and still do in writing about those aspects of my town which I hated and which are always in some ways aspects of myself.

16   The land still draws me more than other lands. I have lived in Africa and in England, but splendid as both can be, they do not have the power to move me in the same way as, for example, that part of southern Ontario where I spent four months last summer in a cedar cabin beside a river. "Scratch a Canadian, and you find a phony pioneer," I used to say to myself in warning. But all the same it is true, I think, that we are not yet totally alienated from physical earth, and let us only pray we do not become so. I once thought that my lifelong fear and mistrust of cities made me a kind of old-fashioned freak; now I see it differently.

---

5. In 1970, the Liberal government of Pierre Trudeau proclaimed the War Measures Act in response to the kidnapping of British trade commissioner James Cross and Quebec labour minister Pierre Laporte by a small group of Quebec separatists. More than four hundred Quebec residents, among them musicians, writers, teachers, and students, were jailed. No charges were laid.

17 The cabin has a long window across its front western wall, and sitting at the oak table there in the mornings, I used to look out at the river and at all the tall trees beyond, green-gold in the early light. The river was bronze; the sun caught it strangely, reflecting upon its surface the near-shore sand ripples underneath. Suddenly, the crescenting of a fish, gone before the eye could clearly give image to it. The old man next door said these leaping fish were carp. Himself, he preferred muskie, for he was a real fisherman and the muskie gave him a fight. The wind most often blew from the south, and the river flowed toward the south, so when the water was wind-riffled, and the current was strong, the river seemed to be flowing both ways. I liked this, and interpreted it as an omen, a natural symbol.

18 A few years ago, when I was back in Winnipeg, I gave a talk at my old college. It was open to the public, and afterward a very old man came up to me and asked me if my maiden name had been Wemyss. I said yes, thinking he might have known my father or my grandfather. But no. "When I was a young lad," he said, "I once worked for your great-grandfather, Robert Wemyss, when he had the sheep ranch at Raeburn." I think that was a moment when I realized all over again something of great importance to me. My long-ago families came from Scotland and Ireland, but in a sense that no longer mattered so much. My true roots were here.

19 I am not very patriotic, in the usual meaning of that word. I cannot say "My country right or wrong" in any political, social or literary context. But one thing is inalterable, for better or worse, for life.

20 This is where my world began. A world which includes ancestors— both my own and other people's ancestors who become mine. A world which formed me, and continues to do so, even while I fought it in some of its aspects, and continue to do so. A world which gave me my own lifework to do, because it was here that I learned the sight of my own particular eyes.

(1971)

Isabelle Knockwood (b. 1931)

Isabelle Knockwood is a Mi'kmaw elder who attended the Indian Residential School at Shubenacadie, Nova Scotia, from 1936 to 1947. During the 1960s, she lived in Boston and was active in the American Indian Movement. Shortly after graduating with a B.A. in anthropology from Saint Mary's University in 1992, she published Out of the Depths, *an account of the experiences of children at the Residential School, from which this essay is taken.*

Origins

1   When the government established the Indian Residential School in Shubenacadie in 1929, the Mi'kmaw population had been decreasing for some time. The official census shows a Mi'kmaw population of just over 2000 in 1934. Despite the threat to our survival as a people, we still had a language and a culture of our own. The world of Mi'kmaw language and culture from which the children were taken when they went to the Residential School had its roots in the knowledge of many generations.

2   When I was a little girl, one of my chores was to help the old people get settled when they came to our house to visit. They were between seventy and one hundred years old. The younger ones walked two miles through the woods from one end of the reserve to our place across the meadow. My father would be working in his *nipign* [an arbour made with leafy branches]. He would take a dipper of cold spring water with him and go to meet them. First, they would greet each other with a kiss on both cheeks, then they would stop and take a nice cold drink, chat a bit, then follow my father home. Sometimes one of my brothers would go with him to carry the water and other times he carried it himself. My mother and the rest of the children would watch from our yard. When the old people came, the children were instructed to help them to sit down, and to serve them a warm drink, usually tea, which was followed by a meal. Then they took out their clay pipes and Daddy passed around tobacco. When they had something important to say, they would tap their canes on the ground or floor, and the others would stop talking and listen. Some elders would not let us touch their pipes or their canes, which they kept always close by. After they had eaten, we gathered up their dishes and they would thank us. The best part came when the old people would place their feeble hands on our heads and give us their blessing.

3   Then came story time.

4   The elders would sit in a circle and smoke their pipes. Some of them would be leaning on their canes listening to the stories. Once in a while, they'd say, A'a! There was much laughter, merriment, joking and reminiscing about the past. But when the sun started to set, the mood changed. The elders would be drowsy and some would be leaning on their canes with their eyes closed. Once in a while, one of them would get up and lie on the ground and take a nap. The Council Fire would be lit, a fresh cup of tea or *pitewey* [any type of warm drink] was made and pipes were refilled.

5   Sometimes they talked all night and throughout several days. Children were never allowed to interrupt or walk in front of the people or in between them when they were talking. *Muk-bed-des-kow* we were told. This means, "Don't walk in front of people who are talking." This custom stems back to the old belief that everyone is a spirit and a conversation between people is a spiritual experience because they are also exchanging their most valuable possession, their word. I usually sat by my mother's knee and kept very quiet because I did not want to be told to leave. I wanted to hear all the interesting stories about my ancestors. I was listening and learning. Now, I realize that I was witnessing the Talking Stick ceremony.

6   Some of the elders who met at my parents' place for the Talking Stick ceremony knew the area where we lived, not as Shubenacadie, but as *Sipekne'katik* [the land of the wild turnips]. In their youth they had travelled long distances in big birch-bark canoes, the whole family travelling with all their belongings, taking the family dog along for protection. They paddled to Dartmouth by way of the Shubenacadie Canal to the *Mi'kmawi-gospeml* [Micmac Lakes] and then down to the salt water. They often crossed over the Bay of Fundy, paddling while on their knees in the bottom of the canoes which made them less likely to tip over. There had been a Mi'kmaw settlement at Shubenacadie since ancient times, and the area was considered especially good for its salmon fishing, for the abundance of sweetgrass and for the ash tree used in basket-making. The stories we heard the elders tell referred not just to their own experiences but to those who had lived generations earlier. The elders started their stories by saying, "*Sa'gewey na*," which means, "This originates in antiquity." This indicated to the listeners that what they were about to say was passed down to them through their great grandparents. So some of the legends that I and my brothers and sister heard were at least seven generations old.

7   The stories were ancient, and the language in which they were told was even older. According to my mother, Deodis, the Mi'kmaw language evolved from the sounds of the land, the winds and the waterfalls. As far as we know, there is no other language like it spoken anywhere else in the world.

8   One of the principal ways of teaching young children was through the telling of legends that embodied thousands of years of experience

in living off the land. The storytellers emphasized living harmoniously with the two-legged, the four-legged, the winged ones and those that swim in the waters—all our relations. Even the plants are said to have a spirit and are our relations. When we have our sacred ceremonies, like the sweat lodge, we end it by saying, *No'kamaq*, which means, "All my relations."

9   Our elders were the most respected members of the Mi'kmaw community. They were the mental storehouse for the genealogy of every member of the tribe. Young people who wanted to marry always consulted them to find out whether they were related or not. The custom of consulting elders is called *"Wji-kluluey."* Elders also had a vast knowledge of survival skills. They knew the seasonal cycles of edible and medicinal plants, and the migrations of animals, birds and fish, and they knew which hunting and trapping methods worked best with certain weather conditions. Mi'kmaw lore is rich with stories about how the people communicated with all these elements. The young people were educated through these stories. Children who were acting inappropriately were told a legend. Some of these were moral tales concerning appropriate action and others were lessons in survival techniques illustrated by animal behaviour.

10 Although the early Mi'kmaq[1] were free of such contagious diseases as tuberculosis and syphilis, they were vulnerable to natural ills such as bone fractures, sprains, and even arthritis, so everyone knew some herbal medicine. The older ones taught the younger ones, and many times medicine and food were the same thing. People suffering from depression or grief talked to an elder who took them for a walk in the woods to find a medicine tree, a pine tree. The sufferers were instructed to lean their backs up against the tree and to stay in that position until they felt its strength running up their spines. After the healing, an offering was made to the tree in acknowledgement and appreciation. Recently I found an old photograph in the Nova Scotia Museum of one such tree—a huge pine tree which used to stand on the Indian Brook Reserve. When I showed the photograph to my brother he said, "Yes, that's the tree the people used to gather under, but the priest came and cut it down."

11 Traditionally we were all taught to take responsibility for the protection and nourishment of others, especially the very old, who had the wisdom and knowledge of the past, and the very young, who held the future. Older brothers and sisters were absolutely required to look after their younger siblings. When they went to the Residential School, being unable to protect their young brothers and sisters became a source of life-long pain. Survival among the Mi'kmaq was always based

---

1. The spelling "Mi'kmaq" indicates its use as a noun, the earliest form of the word. After European settlers arrived, the adjectival form "Mi'kmaw" was needed. Both forms are commonly rendered as "Micmac" by speakers and writers unfamiliar with the language.

on sharing. For example, people chewed food for the elders who had lost their teeth and for infants who had no teeth. Growing children were never denied food and were fed whenever they were hungry.

12 Women breast-fed their own babies, but when a woman had twins sometimes she didn't produce enough milk to feed both, so she gave one to another woman to nurse. This did not mean the second mother kept the child as her own, but rather a strong bonding occurred between the child, the natural mother and the wet nurse. There were no restrictions on visitation rights or the natural mother's right to take back the responsibility of raising her own child. Lorraine Sack told me, "When my father was a week old, his mother gave him up. Aunt Jane took him and breast-fed him, and he always said that although we are not really related to the Sacks he wanted us to accept them as our relatives because it was she who saved his life."

13 Direct eye contact was definitely not allowed between the younger and older generations. Partly this was because it can be interpreted in so many ways, including challenging authority, arrogance, hostility, belligerence, and invasion of privacy, but mostly it was because of the sexual connotations associated with eye contact. When people come to your home, you are allowed to look at their faces to see what kind of message they are bringing, whether it is sad or glad, so that you will know how to act appropriately. After that, it is considered rude to look at their eyes. At the school however, when we followed our training and avoided looking directly into the faces of the priest or the nuns, we were punished for being insolent.

14 Our whole family used to go into the bush together to gather basket wood, birch-bark, medicine and berries for the winter. Sometimes, we also accompanied Daddy when he went moose hunting. He would walk ahead to read the signs of animal tracks so that the family would not accidentally stumble across the trail of a mother bear with cubs or walk in the path of a moose during the rutting season. He also had to clear the trail of overhanging branches that could injure the eyes and to watch out for hornets' nests. It was he who decided where to camp at night, taking care to be close to a spring-water supply. If Daddy was hunting, we'd stay until he got a deer, which could be just overnight. But during the blueberry-picking season, we'd stay until we had our winter's supply, which could take days. Some excursions combined different types of work, such as hunting and cutting trees for winter firewood or making baskets and axe handles. Medicines and herbs were gathered anytime between spring and fall. When my brothers were very young they usually walked behind with my mother, but as they grew older, they went ahead with my father and learned the art of clearing the trail. My mother always was the last one in line and acted as a guard. We always felt safe and protected everywhere we went. After carefully selecting the campsite, my father made a frame for the lean-to out of logs which he covered with branches of trees with the leaves left on. My mother made the beds out of spruce boughs, while

we kids carried the drinking water from the spring and gathered fire-wood. At night, we slept in front of the campfire with the night sky overhead. Daddy would sit at one side of the lean-to and tend the fire while Mom sat on the other side with us five kids in between. Usually the youngest boy slept near Daddy and one of the girls next to Mom, whoever got there first. My parents would talk late into the night until we fell asleep and when we woke up in the morning, they were still there. It seemed to me they were guarding their children all through the night.

15 Deodis, my mother, had gathered much of her traditional knowl-edge from the people who brought her up. She was an orphan who was adopted by a couple living on the Cambridge Reserve.[2] This was in the early part of the twentieth century and in those days, everyone had chores to do. When Deodis was about seven years old, her duty was to collect kindling for the elderly couple who lived on the hill. One night she forgot, so Aunt Sabet put a lantern on one of the branches of the old pine tree so Deodis would have light to work by. When she had an apron full of dry wood, she took it up to the old people's house. N'sukwes was sitting on a rocking chair looking out the window and waiting for her firewood. It was already dark inside when Deodis arrived. Deodis made a fire and some *pitewey*. Uncle Charlie was lying on top of the bed with his coat over his head and with his shoes still on. Deodis asked if he was sleeping and N'sukwes said that he was sick. "You better go and get Aunt Sabet and tell her to bring some *ki'kwesu'skw* [flag-root] for fever." So Deodis ran down the hill and returned with Aunt Sabet and her medicine. Aunt Sabet opened the door and stopped short. She had smelled the fever. She told Deodis to stand by the door while she uncovered Uncle Charlie's face. When she removed the coat, she saw that his face was swollen and had ugly red blotches all over it. She quickly covered up his face again and stepped back in fright. "*Lapigotewit*" [smallpox] she gasped. "It's going to kill us all." She gently but firmly pushed Deodis out the door and closed it. "I'll come back later," she called out. Once outside, Aunt Sabet explained to Deodis that there was no cure for smallpox and that it had already killed many Mi'kmaq and everyone was afraid of it because tra-ditional aboriginal herbs did not work on this white man's disease. "But I will show you how to protect yourself with the winds.

16 "Always start by facing in the direction where the sun comes up. Bow to the winds that blow from that direction. Greet the Great Spirit of the wind by touching your forehead with your index finger and middle finger to clear your mind. Then touch your lips to make your words true and then touch your breast to give you a kind heart. Ask the wind to blow away the evil spirits that brought the smallpox and to protect you from getting it. Do that four times, each time facing each of the directions."

2. In the Annapolis Valley of Nova Scotia.

17   As it turned out Uncle Charlie did recover and the only visible sign that he had had smallpox was that his face was covered with large scars about as round as a dime.

18   My mother passed on some of her traditional knowledge to me. Like other Mi'kmaw mothers, she took care to teach us things which would keep us safe. For example, when she was walking with me in the forest, she told me to listen to my footsteps as I went along so when I retraced my steps back home I would recognize the different sounds and realize if I was going the wrong way before going too far.

19   When we were taken into the bush as tiny children we began learning about the environment from the cradle-board strapped to our mother's back or from sleeping and waking up in a hammock between two trees. As our mother walked along, we saw the changing land-scapes. Day after day, from sunrise to sunset, in all kinds of weather, the sky, the trees, the ground, and the waters are what we saw. Upon wakening in the morning, our first sight was usually the branches and leaves silhouetted against the ever-changing sky and the last thing before the dream world took over, we saw the moon and stars and the milky way of the night world.

20   Many parents recognized that their children would need other kinds of knowledge to get along in the white world. My father, John Knockwood, who was also known as John Subbadis (John the Baptist), had never attended school, but had taught himself to read and write by reading the *Halifax Herald* from cover to cover every week. He'd buy the paper at the City Market every Friday after selling baskets, axe handles and herbal medicines—he had to keep the herbal medicines under the table because their sale was illegal and he was risking arrest by selling them. When he came across words he didn't understand in his newspaper he would ask the non-Native customers to explain, and so gradually he learned to read and write English. Deodis was also self-taught, although she used to tell me that she had a grade four educa-tion. When she was seven years old, she had been sent to a Kentville public school where she was called a "squaw," stoned and chased home to the reserve every day. One day, instead of running, she turned on her tormentors and beat them up. She scratched, kicked and bit, and gave them the "dead man's grip," by which she meant she refused to let go of the handful of hair she had grabbed. Consequently, she was expelled. Aunt Sabet told her, "You may stay home now, because you went to school for four days." To Deodis, this meant that she was in grade four. She was very proud that she had taught herself to sign her name and to make out a grocery list.

21   In any Mi'kmaw family the worst act a child could commit was to endanger the lives of the younger children. Once, for example, all five of us jumped on the bumper of a moving car. Some white people had come to our house to buy baskets and when they drove away, we went joyriding on their bumper. As a punishment, we were switched. It was believed that the bushes have a spirit and were good medicine. Now

you're going to get your "medicine," we were told. The sting was remembered for a long time. Doug Knockwood remembers one occasion when he received his "medicine" from a birch switch:

> My mother and grandfather and uncle were very traditional people and had a different way of correcting and teaching me which was by talking to me and by using switches on the ankles. That switch on the ankles taught me more than getting a belt across the ass because when my mother had to resort to the switch, I knew that I had done something very serious, like the time I ran away when Mom was home alone. She came three miles after me with a little birch switch. Every couple hundred feet she would ask, "Are you going to run away again?" And I'd say, "No." Then I'd get a whip across the ankles and I'd step dance for a little while.

22   The highest reward was to be praised by *Sagmawinu* at a public gathering. That is when an elder stands up before the whole community and tells what you have done to benefit everyone. Earning an eagle feather is a great honour because it proves that you have received public recognition for something done for the community and not for yourself. The eagle feather symbolizes high ideals because it comes from a bird that flies higher than any other bird and comes closest to the source of life's energy which is the sun.

23   Those who established the Indian Residential schools across Canada regarded all we had learned from our parents and grandparents with contempt and hatred. As Bernie Knockwood sees it: "They were making a value judgement based on white middle class values. Looking at it from the Native perspective—even though you were hungry and dirty, you knew that you were being loved because when there was food, you were the first one to be fed." Although his grandparents reared him in poverty Bernie still remembers their pride and their dignity:

> One of the things I remember is when I used to go picking sweetgrass with my grandmother. She used it in her fancy baskets. I always have a braid in my room which I use for smudging [using the smoke for cleansing] and which reminds me of my grandmother. Whenever I went to my grandparents' house, the first thing that I noticed was the aroma of sweetgrass. I can remember in Parrsborough, my grandmother would take one side of the street and I'd take the other and we'd go door-to-door trying to sell baskets. On good days, if we sold our baskets, we'd buy a bus ticket and food and we'd go visit my grandmother's friend. She lived on the end of this fairly long driveway. Off on the left, there was a small marsh with a freshwater stream which would flood when the tide came in. Before the bus came in, we'd spend a good part of the afternoon picking sweetgrass. Back on the bus home, people would make rude comments about the stink from the sweetgrass. My grandmother, who was just a tiny woman, would just sit there with her head held high and look at me and say, "Don't listen to them *Nkwis* [son]." To this day, I can still hear her. Other times, we'd be walking on that road after dark

because we never sold a basket. We'd walk all the way and get back around twelve o'clock. Gramp would be waiting for us near the spring with a lantern.

Bernie's grandfather made axe handles to sell in the neighbouring towns:

> From the time he gathered the wood and made the handles, it took three weeks of hard work. That's working day-in and day-out, sometimes all night. And those axe handles were just as smooth with no knots and just as straight. I remember sitting there and him showing me how to "glass" them and sand them with sand paper. I felt proud for what I could do. It wasn't much but I felt that anything I could do was a help.... In the morning, he'd hitchhike into Parrsborough. And I would sit up on the hill and watch for the Acadian Lines bus. If it stopped, it meant that Gramp sold his axe handles but if it didn't stop, I would go down to that spring with the lantern and I'd see him coming through the dark. I'd run down and take the handles and we'd go home. And we'd be talking all the way up. He'd tell me, "It was a rough day today. Nobody wants handles. Tomorrow morning, I'll catch the Advocate bus and go to Amherst and I won't come home until I sell them all."

Part of his grandparents' devotion to him was shown in their refusal to teach him the Mi'kmaw language:

> After work, I'd take the shavings from their work and pile them up against a tree for a pillow and I'd lay there in the sun and listen to them talk. They would always speak in Mi'kmaw and I couldn't understand what they were saying. I asked my grandmother, "Why don't you teach me how to speak Mi'kmaw?" And she told me, "You don't need to know how to speak Mi'kmaw. We know how to speak Mi'kmaw and all we did was starve. When you speak Mi'kmaw, you starve. We don't want you to starve."

Like many other Mi'kmaq who went through the residential school system, Bernie is now beginning to reclaim part of the cultural legacy that the school tried so hard to exterminate:

> Going to the Residential School didn't kill what was in us. And now we're trying to get back some semblance of what we were. But there's no way we can go back to do what our grandparents used to do because we don't want to give up what we have now, but what I would like to see is at least a large proportion of our philosophy and our way of doing things restored so that we will be able to incorporate it into our lives as a part of our core value for ourselves and our children and our children's children.

(1992)

David Suzuki (b. 1936)

Geneticist David Suzuki was born in Vancouver and is arguably Canada's best-known science educator and environmentalist. His international reputation as a commentator on science and society has been enhanced by his accessible journalism and regular appearances on television and radio.

A Planet for the Taking

1   Canadians live under the remarkable illusion that we are technologically advanced people. Everything around us denies that assumption. We are, in many ways, a Third World country, selling our natural resources in exchange for the high technology of the industrialized world. Try going through your home and looking at the country of origin of your clothes, electrical appliances, books, car. The rare technological product that does have Canada stamped on it is usually from a branch plant of a multinational company centred in another country. But we differ from traditional Third World countries. We have a majority population of Caucasians and a very high level of literacy and affluence. And we have been able to maintain our seemingly advanced social state by virtue of an incredible bounty of natural resources.

2   Within the Canadian mystique there is also a sense of the vastness of this land. The prairies, the Arctic, the oceans, the mountains are ever present in our art and literature. This nation is built on our sense of the seeming endlessness of the expanse of wilderness and the output of nature and we have behaved as if this endlessness were real. Today we speak of renewable resources but our "harvest" procedures are more like a mining operation. We extract raw resources in the crudest of ways, gouging the land to get at its inner core, spewing our raw wastes into the air, water and soil in massive amounts while taking fish, birds, animals and trees in vast quantities without regard to the future. So we operate under a strange duality of mind: we have both a sense of the importance of the wilderness and space in our culture and an attitude that it is limitless and therefore we needn't worry.

3   Native cultures of the past may have been no more conservation-minded than we are but they lacked the technology to make the kind of impact that we do today. Canadians and Americans share one of the great natural wonders, the Great Lakes, which contain 20 percent of the world's fresh water, yet today even this massive body of water is terribly polluted and the populations of fish completely mixed-up by human activity. We speak of "managing" our resources but do it in

a way that resembles the sledgehammer-on-the-head cure for a headache. On the west coast of Canada, Natives lived for millennia on the incredible abundance of five species of salmon. Today, the massive runs are gone and many biologists fear that the fish may be in mortal jeopardy because of both our fishing and management policies. Having improved fishing techniques this century to the point of endangering runs yet still knowing very little of the biology of the fish, we have assumed that we could build up the yield by simply dumping more back. But it wasn't known that sockeye salmon fry, for example, spend a year in a freshwater lake before going to sea. Millions of sockeye fry were dumped directly into the Fraser River where they died soon after. In Oregon, over-fishing and hydroelectric dams decimated coho populations in the Columbia River. In one year, over 8 million fry were released of which only seven were ever caught. No one knows what's happening to the rest.

4   We act as if a fish were a fish, a duck a duck or a tree a tree. If we "harvest" one, we renew it by simply adding one or two back. But what we have learned is that all animals and plants are not equivalent. Each organism reflects the evolutionary history of its progenitors; in the case of salmon, each race and subrace of fish has been exquisitely honed by nature to return to a very specific part of the Pacific watershed. Similarly, in the enormous area of prairie pothole country in the centre of the continent, migratory birds do not just space themselves out according to the potholes that are empty. Scientists have discovered that the birds have been selected to return to a very restricted part of that area. And of course, our entire forestry policy is predicated on the ridiculous idea that a virgin stand of fir or cedar which has taken millennia to form and clings to a thin layer of topsoil can be replaced after clear-cut logging simply by sticking seedlings into the ground. How can anyone with even the most rudimentary understanding of biology and evolution ignore the realities of the complex interaction between organisms and the environment and attempt to manipulate wild populations as if they were tomato plants or chickens?

5   I believe that in large part our problems rest on our faith in the power of science and technology. At the beginning of this century, science, when applied by industry and medicine, promised a life immeasurably better and there is no doubt that society, indeed the planet, has been transformed by the impact of new ideas and inventions of science. Within my lifetime, I've seen the beginning of television, oral contraception, organ transplants, space travel, computers, jets, nuclear weapons, satellite communication, and polio vaccine. Each has changed society forever and made the world of my youth recede into the pages of history. But we have not achieved a technological utopia. The problems facing us today are immense and many are a direct consequence of science and technology. What has gone wrong?

6   I believe that the core of our 20th century dilemma lies in a fundamental limitation of science that most scientists, especially those in the

life sciences, fail to recognize. Most of my colleagues take it for granted that our studies will ultimately be applicable to the "big picture," that our research will have beneficial payoffs to society eventually. That is because the thrust of modern science has been predicated on the Newtonian idea that the universe is like an enormous machine whose entire system will be reconstructed on the basis of our understanding of the parts. This is the fundamental reductionist faith in science: the whole is equal to the sum of its parts. It does make a lot of sense—what distinguishes science from other activities that purport to provide a comprehensive "world view" is its requirement that we focus on a part of nature isolated to as great an extent as possible from the rest of the system of which it is a part. This has provided enormous insights into that fragment of nature, often accompanied by power to manipulate it. But when we attempt to tinker with what lies in the field of our view, the effects ripple far beyond the barrel of the microscope. And so we are constantly surprised at the unexpected consequences of our inter- ference. Scientists only know nature in "bits and pieces" and assume that higher levels of organization are simply the expression of the component parts. This is what impels neurobiologists to study the chemical and electrical behaviour of single neurons in the faith that it will ultimately lead to an understanding of what creativity and imagi- nation are, a faith that I don't for a moment think will ever be fulfilled (although a lot of useful information will accrue).

7   Physicists, who originally set this view in motion, have this century, with the arrival of relativity and quantum theory, put to rest the notion that we will ever be able to reconstruct the entire universe from fun- damental principles. Chemists know that a complete physical descrip- tion of atoms of oxygen and hydrogen is of little value in predicting the behaviour of a water molecule. But biologists scream that any sense that there are properties of organization that don't exist at lower levels is "vitalism," a belief that there is some mystical life force in living organisms. And so biochemists and molecular biologists are intent on understanding the workings of organisms by learning all they can about sub-cellular organization.

8   Ironically, ecology, long scorned by molecular biologists as an inexact science, is now corroborating physics. In studying ecosystems, we are learning that a simple breakdown into components and their behaviour does not provide insight into how an entire collection of organisms in a natural setting will work. While many ecologists do continue to "model" ecosystems in computers in the hope that they will eventually derive a predictive model, their science warns of the hazards of treating it too simply in management programs.

9   At present, our very terminology suggests that we think we can manage wild plants and animals as though they were domesticated organisms. We speak of "herds" of seals, of "culling," "harvesting," "stocks." The ultimate expression of our narrow view (and self-inter- ested rationalizations) is seen in how we overlook the enormous envi-

ronmental impact of our pollution, habitat destruction and extraction, and blame seals and whales for the decline in fish populations or wolves for the decrease in moose—and then propose bounties as a solution!

10   But Canadians do value the spiritual importance of nature and want to see it survive for future generations. We also believe in the power of science to sustain a high quality of life. And while the current understanding of science's power is, I believe, misplaced, in fact the leading edges of physics and ecology may provide the insights that can get us off the current track. We need a very profound perceptual shift and soon.

(1985)

Margaret Atwood (b. 1939)

One of Canada's foremost literary figures, Atwood has established an inter-
national reputation for her fiction and poetry. She is also known for her
essays, literary criticism, and editorial work. "Through the One-Way
Mirror" reveals her abiding concern with the question of national identity.
See "Happy Endings," p. 511, and Atwood's poems, p. 317.

Through the One-Way Mirror

1   The noses of a great many Canadians resemble Porky Pig's. This comes
from spending so much time pressing them against the longest unde-
fended one-way mirror in the world. The Canadians looking through
this mirror behave the way people on the hidden side of such mirrors
usually do: they observe, analyze, ponder, snoop and wonder what all
the activity on the other side means in decipherable human terms.

2   The Americans, bless their innocent little hearts, are rarely aware
that they are even being watched, much less by the Canadians. They
just go on doing body language, playing in the sandbox of the world,
bashing one another on the head and planning how to blow things up,
same as always. If they think about Canada at all, it's only when things
get a bit snowy or the water goes off or the Canadians start fussing over
some piddly detail, such as fish. Then they regard them as unpatriotic;
for Americans don't really see Canadians as foreigners, not like the
Mexicans, unless they do something weird like speak French or beat
the New York Yankees at baseball. Really, think the Americans, the
Canadians are just like us, or would be if they could.

3   Or we could switch metaphors and call the border the longest unde-
fended backyard fence in the world. The Canadians are the folks in the
neat little bungalow, with the tidy little garden and the duck pond. The
Americans are the other folks, the ones in the sprawly mansion with
the bad-taste statues on the lawn. There's a perpetual party, or something, going on there—loud music, raucous laughter, smoke billowing
from the barbecue. Beer bottles and Coke cans land among the
peonies. The Canadians have their own beer bottles and barbecue
smoke, but they tend to overlook it. Your own mess is always more
forgivable than the mess someone else makes on your patio.

4   The Canadians can't exactly call the police—they suspect that the
Americans are the police—and part of their distress, which seems permanent, comes from their uncertainty as to whether or not they've
been invited. Sometimes they do drop by next door, and find it exciting

but scary. Sometimes the Americans drop by their house and find it clean. This worries the Canadians. They worry a lot. Maybe those Americans want to buy up their duck pond, with all the money they seem to have, and turn it into a cesspool or a water-skiing emporium.

5   It also worries them that the Americans don't seem to know who the Canadians are, or even where, exactly, they are. Sometimes the Americans call Canada their backyard, sometimes their front yard, both of which imply ownership. Sometimes they say they are the Mounties and the Canadians are Rose Marie. (All these things have, in fact, been said by American politicians.) Then they accuse the Canadians of being paranoid and having an identity crisis. Heck, there is no call for the Canadians to fret about their identity, because everyone knows they're Americans, really. If the Canadians disagree with that, they're told not to be so insecure.

6   One of the problems is that Canadians and Americans are educated backward from one another. The Canadians—except for the Québécois, one keeps saying—are taught about the rest of the world first and Canada second. The Americans are taught about the United States first, and maybe later about other places, if they're of strategic importance. The Vietnam War draft dodgers got more culture shock in Canada than they did in Sweden. It's not the clothing that is different, it's those mental noises.

7   Of course, none of this holds true when you get close enough, where concepts like "Americans" and "Canadians" dissolve and people are just people, or anyway some of them are, the ones you happen to approve of. I, for instance, have never met any Americans I didn't like, but I only get to meet the nice ones. That's what the businessmen think too, though they have other individuals in mind. But big-scale national mythologies have a way of showing up in things like foreign policy, and at events like international writers' congresses, where the Canadians often find they have more to talk about with the Australians, the West Indians, the New Zealanders and even the once-loathed snooty Brits, now declining into humanity with the dissolution of the empire, than they do with the impenetrable and mysterious Yanks.

8   But only sometimes. Because surely the Canadians understand the Yanks. Shoot, don't they see Yank movies, read Yank mags, bobble around to Yank music and watch Yank telly, as well as their own, when there is any?

9   Sometimes the Canadians think it's their job to interpret the Yanks to the rest of the world; explain them, sort of. This is an illusion: they don't understand the Yanks as much as they think they do, and it isn't their job.

10   But, as we say up here among God's frozen people, when Washington catches a cold, Ottawa sneezes. Some Canadians even refer to their capital city as Washington North and wonder why we're paying those guys in Ottawa when a telephone order service would be

cheaper. Canadians make jokes about the relationship with Washington which the Americans in their thin-skinned, bunion-toed way, construe as anti-American (they tend to see any nonworshipful comment coming from that grey, protoplasmic fuzz outside their borders as anti-American). They are no more anti-American than the jokes Canadians make about the weather: it's there, it's big, it's hard to influence, and it affects your life.

11   Of course, in any conflict with the Dreaded Menace, whatever it might be, the Canadians would line up with the Yanks, probably, if they thought it was a real menace, or if the Yanks twisted their arms or other bodily parts enough or threatened a "scorched-earth policy" (another real quote). Note the qualifiers. The Canadian idea of a menace is not the same as the U.S. one. Canada, for instance, never broke off diplomatic relations with Cuba, and it was quick to recognize China. Contemplating the U.S.–Soviet growling match, Canadians are apt to recall a line from Blake: "They became what they beheld." Certainly both superpowers suffer from the imperial diseases once so noteworthy among the Romans, the British and the French: arrogance and myopia. But the bodily-parts threat is real enough, and accounts for the observable wimpiness and flunkiness of some Ottawa politicians. Nobody, except at welcoming-committee time, pretends this is an equal relationship.

12   Americans don't have Porky Pig noses. Instead they have Mr. Magoo eyes, with which they see the rest of the world. That would not be a problem if the United States were not so powerful. But it is, so it is.

(1984)

Joyce Nelson (b. 1943)

Canadian cultural historian Joyce Nelson turns a sharply critical eye on the "religion of acquisition" practised in our shopping malls in "The Temple of Fashion," an essay from her Sign Crimes/Road Kill: From Mediascape to Landscape *(1992).*

The Temple of Fashion

1   "The act of acquiring has taken the place of all other actions, the sense of having has obliterated all other senses," the British art critic and cultural historian John Berger observed in his 1972 book *Ways of Seeing.* By the mid-1970s, acquisition had achieved the status of a new religion in the West. The appearance of a new advertising buzz-word, *spirit,* was a clear signal of this development.

2   Once Coca-Cola had merely claimed to add "life" to our lives. Now everything from a cola through a department store and a hotel chain to a fashion designer began to make even bolder assertions. In slogans such as "the Pepsi Spirit," "Simpson's Spirit," "the Spirit of Hyatt," and Yves Saint-Laurent's "New Spirit of Masculinity," advertisers proclaimed the new religion of buying. More recently, the word *soul* has entered the advertising lexicon as another religious additive to enhance acquisition.

3   In such a context, shopping malls have become the cathedrals of our time: vast horizontal-Gothic places of worship that draw the faithful together in communal rites central to the new religion. While the Prime Movers in this religion are the TV God and its consort, the advertising industry, the shopping cathedrals are themselves temples of technomagic where steps move effortlessly beneath one's feet, doors open automatically, celestial Muzak hymns permeate the atmosphere, and the wave of a credit card completes the sacred transaction. Isolated from the mundane reality of urban existence, the shopping mall is sacred space, climate-controlled and patrolled, devoted to the ease of acquisition: the meaning of life in the postwar West.

4   This religion has evolved its own holy days (such as Boxing Day solstice) and holy seasons (Back-to-School octave). It also has its important sites of pilgrimage (in Canada, the West Edmonton Mall and Toronto's Eaton Centre), although every North American city has its lesser malls where the same litany of brand names holds out the promise of salvation. Nevertheless, this is a religion in which both faith and good works are necessary. This facet of the religion is nowhere

more apparent than in the domain of Fashion, whose side chapels in each shopping cathedral remind us that last season's profession of faith is up for renewal.

5   According to the arcane hermeneutics of the Fashion Bible, one risks damnation by last year's colour or the slightest oversight of tie, lapel, or faux nail. Thus, the Gospels according to Armani and Alfred Sung, Ralph Lauren and Christian Dior are continually being reinterpreted for our edification and enlightenment. While slogans such as Calvin Klein's "Eternity for Men" and Alfred Sung's "Timeless" collection evoke an eschatological promise signifying the end-time of shopping, it is a central tenet within the religion (and certainly dogma in Fashion) that our indulgences are never plenary. "Shop Till You Drop" is the vulgar—but correct—grasp of this aspect of consumer theology.

6   Fortunately, the high priests of Fashion (particularly the college of ecclesiastics gathered at *Women's Wear Daily*) continually disseminate guidance on each chapter and verse of the Fashion Bible. Their perennial lists of "Best Dressed" and "Worst Dressed" remind us that even those not banished to the purgatory of obscurity risk hellfire by sinning against Fashion commandments that are perpetually under revision.

7   For this reason, there exists a wealth of inspirational literature and illustrated texts to assist us in our salvific efforts. *Vogue*, *Esquire*, *Gentleman's Quarterly*, and *Flare* provide not only the necessary iconography for the consumer aspirant's meditation but also details on those Fashion sins (venial and mortal) that can impede our progress. The pages of such inspirational texts also offer devotional readings on the lives of the Fashion saints: popular saints of the past like St. Marilyn and St. James Dean; current beatified exemplars like Madonna and Billy Idol; and our living martyr to Fashion, Elizabeth Taylor. But such devotional reading and contemplation are only preparations for the greater liturgies of the mall.

8   Window shopping brings the congregation into closer proximity to the Fashion priesthood and the means of redemption, but before we enter any of the mall's side chapels there is usually an impressive form of statuary to mediate our passage. Modern mannequins have evolved with the mall itself, becoming increasingly elaborate, detailed, and even startling in their effect.

9   The old form of mannequin (like the old form of storefront) was, for the most part, simply uninspiring; its wig askew, its coiffure outmoded, its facial expression vague and nondescript, its limbs akimbo or missing, its stand ridiculous or pathetic. Only by the greatest leap of faith could the consumer attain the proper buying spirit through a glance at such a guardian of the portals.

10   The new mannequins, on the other hand, are appropriate statuary for the impressive cathedrals that surround them. Figures of anatomical perfection, these statues with their erect nipples, painted fingernails, detailed eye makeup, stunning hairdos, high cheekbones,

and long sinewy legs remind us at a glance just what it is that we, as mundane Fashion consumers, aspire to. While the male statuary is somewhat less intimidating, it too bespeaks the contemporary codes of the Fashion cult: chiselled jaws, muscled but sleek torsos, long-legged figures of power.

11   But it is the faces of the new statuary that are most significant in their religious function: aloof, haughty, disdaining, beyond appeal. Inspiring neither solace nor prayer, these figures at the portals are part of the shrines of envy and are meant to inspire a certain measure of fear.

12   To gaze at one of these detailed figures is an oddly unsettling experience (though in truth they are meant to be only glimpsed in passing). Typically, the statue is posed so that its haughty gaze is directed above or away from us, as though we were quite obviously beneath contempt. At the same time, the statue's fetish of forever-perfect and hyperrealistic detail cruelly reminds us of our own imperfections. Whether we are fully conscious of the effect or not, we enter the chapels of Fashion subtly diminished and suitably envious.

13   Such feelings enhance the redemptive power of the array of apparel within. Each article of clothing promises to increase our status and transform us in turn into objects of envy, in our own eyes and the imagined eyes of others. Here, the numinous brand name confers its accretion of socially envious connotations, religiosity, and sacred trust. This veneer laid upon mere cloth by the high priests of Fashion is necessary for passing through the challenging ritual of the changing room.

14   Within this confessional enclosure, one is confronted by the attendant mirror revealing all the sins of the flesh that mar one's progress: the cellulite thighs, the body hair, the paunch, the girth, the less-than-perfect contours reminding us that the spirit is willing but the flesh is weak. Making promises to join the modern-day *flagellantes* in daily workout routine, we proceed to put on the desired article of clothing that promises to miraculously transform our lives.

15   The moment of beholding ourselves dressed in the desired brand name has also been prefigured and prepared by the statue at the chapel's portal. Like it, we must harden our gaze, overlook that small inner voice of protest about price, and focus on a future vision of ourselves as the envied possessor of this article of apparel that most of the faithful will have already seen (and desired) in the inspirational Fashion texts. We know that the envious others will recognize at a glance that we have joined the elect.

16   Where once it was possible for the faithful to identify, from a momentary glimpse, the habit of a Franciscan friar or Benedictine nun, so now the congregation is steeped in the familiar cut and style of various designer looks. Indeed, one can dress oneself entirely from head to foot in Ralph Lauren or YSL, Lee or Esprit. As the most dedicated of the Fashion faithful realize, it is the brand, not the cloth, that clothes us. So the slogan says, "Life's Necessities: Food, Shelter and Lee Jeans."

17   As we become the objects of our own devotion, the high point in the shopping mall liturgy approaches: the transforming ritual of the credit card. Through its instantaneous magic, we momentarily redeem ourselves and enter the ecstasy of acquisition, consuming and consumed by the bliss of possession.

18   It is precisely this ease of acquisition that is fundamental to the new religion. The technomagic of the credit card is in keeping with the whole aura of effortlessness that pervades the mall. Indeed, the many objects on display seem magically conjured out of nothing to fulfil the promise of advertising images' sleight-of-hand. For all intents and purposes, these millions of objects seem to have no origin, no history of labour and creation. Only the shopping agnostic would think to consider such questions as: who made these things, and under what conditions?

19   For example, most of our brand-name clothing is made by Third World garment workers, primarily women, who are grossly underpaid and exploited by North American contractors paying as little as ten cents an hour for the labour. In the export-processing zones of the Philippines, Thailand, Hong Kong, Mexico, Indonesia, and dozens of other countries, non-unionized workers typically work sixteen-hour days for the most meagre of wages, assembling the host of products that fill our malls. Even Canada's high priest of Fashion, Alfred Sung, employs Hong Kong labour to work at a fraction of Canadian wages in sewing the apparel of the elect.

20   But the religion of acquisition excludes any knowledge of the actual work that goes into the making of our products. For most of the consumer faithful, these millions of objects simply appear "as seen on TV" or in the photo magazines: as though untouched by human hands, as though the image itself (like an idea in the mind of God) had somehow spawned its progeny, as it were, "in the flesh." Like Doubting Thomases, we touch and buy their tangibility to reaffirm our faith. Thus, while some have dubbed this new religion the Church of Perpetual Indulgence, it may more accurately be described as the Church of the Wholly Innocent: wilfully apolitical, purposely unknowing, steeped in the mystification and technomagic of our time.

(1992)

Peter Robertson (b. 1944)

Peter Robertson is employed by the National Archives of Canada, where he works as an archivist with the National Photography Collection. He is the author of Relentless Verity—Canadian Military Photographers since 1885 *(1973) and a contributing author to* Private Realms of Light: Amateur Photography in Canada, 1839–1939 *(1984).*

More Than Meets the Eye

1   Somebody once said that the camera never lies. Those who support that generalisation include the many Canadians who, during the past decade, have used increasingly larger numbers of photographs as historical documents. Sacrificing quality for quantity, they have overlooked the fact that photographs, for a number of reasons, can present a somewhat less than truthful image of the past. Surely it is time for archivists to understand these limitations and to moderate the undiscriminating attitude with which many of their patrons are approaching photographs.

2   Following Louis Daguerre's invention of photography in 1839, people seeing a photograph for the first time often remarked on the quality of verity. In the words of one observer, "Every object is retraced with mathematical preciseness, ... a degree of perfection that could be attained by no other means."[1] Truthfulness was a useful weapon in photography's protracted struggle for equality with, if not superiority over, traditional visual arts such as painting. What photographers were claiming was that photographs were able to depict the same subjects as paintings, and with greater truthfulness. In his definitive book *Art and Photography*, Dr. Aaron Scharf comments on the assertiveness of photographers, who "saw little reason why photography should not be considered as a Fine Art" and "conscious of the mechanical limitations of their medium ... developed new, often elaborate means for augmenting the artistic content of their work."[2] One of the most significant "mechanical limitations" was of course the inability of nineteenth-century photographic equipment to record adequately people and objects that were in motion. Partly because of this problem and partly because of their collective desire to surpass painting, photographers tended to concentrate on subjects that were both motionless *and* artistic, such as portraits, buildings, and landscapes.

3   What effect did the process of building a relationship with his clients have on the outlook of a photographer reaching for success in his pro-

fession? The client, in simplest terms, was the person who engaged the photographer to take his portrait, and who expected satisfactory results for the money thus spent. Published in 1864, the widely-used manual *The Camera and the Pencil* exhorted: "Let us never lose sight of the fact that we must, if practicable, *please all* who seek our services ... to secure the patronage of *every visitant* ... to promise compliance with their wishes."[3] Recognizing that an unflattering portrait might offend a client, photographers routinely employed people who specialized in retouching negatives. According to a textbook entitled *The Art of Retouching*, published in 1880, the duty of the retoucher was "to make with facility any alteration taste may suggest, such as a fixed, staring and unnatural look, assumed by so many persons while sitting for a portrait, into an easy, natural smile; or to change the forced, sinister smirk into a calm and pleasing expression."[4] Retouching paid dividends, because satisfied clients were apt to return for additional portraits, and for exterior and interior views of their homes and businesses. This "portrait-home-business" sequence is present, for example, in William Topley's photographs of the prominent Ottawa lumber barons H.F. Bronson, J.R. Booth and W.C. Edwards taken between 1880 and 1920. Judging from the examples published in the book *Portrait of a Period*, similar patterns would emerge from an analysis of the photographs taken by William Notman, the shining example of the successful nineteenth-century Canadian photographer.[5]

4   Nineteenth-century photography was not only a process struggling to rise above its technical limitations and to achieve the status of art, but also a profession striving for social and economic respectability. For example, photographers in the United States and Canada often used the purely honorary title of "Professor" to impress the public with their knowledge. Furthermore, they generally displayed an acute understanding of modern advertising techniques. Consider the following typical notice, which appeared in 1888:

> There is perhaps no establishment in Port Arthur that shows more conspicuously the rapid developments and improvements in the photographic art, than that of J.F. Cooke. This studio is spacious and well arranged. The light and all other requisites for a first-class establishment are perfect. Photography, in all its branches, is here executed in the highest style of art. Mr. Cooke is an artist of rare talent and ability, and that this fact is appreciated by the public, is evinced by the large and influential patronage he now enjoys.[6]

Fortunate indeed was a photographer like William Topley who was able to use the title "Photographer by Appointment to His Excellency the Marquis of Lorne and Her Royal Highness the Princess Louise." The more influential the patron, the better for business.

5   Having acquired a reputation with, and made money from, clients who were influential people in their community, photographers sometimes became part of the movement known as "boosterism," a phe-

nomenon in part manifested by the flood of illustrated brochures, pamphlets and books extolling the virtues of Canadian cities and industries during the period from 1880 to 1914. For example, Frank Micklethwaite's photographs of Toronto, widely published in periodicals and books, document a prosperous, progressive city: bustling city streets, office buildings, banks, industries, colleges and schools, churches, spacious parks, quiet residential streets. Micklethwaite's photographs, however, present an image of the city which is accurate but incomplete—incomplete because nobody commissioned him to photograph its slum housing, neglected children, and sweated labour.

6   Twentieth-century Canadian boosterism hides behind a variety of euphemistic titles: publicity, public relations, advertising, propaganda, information services, media relations. Whatever name it assumes, the concept implies the use of certain techniques by newspapers, businesses, and by organizations such as governments, to influence people's thoughts and actions. These organizations are able to employ and train photographers, to enforce guidelines or regulations stating how the photographers are to perform their assignments and, through a number of editorial processes, to determine just which photographs the public will see.

7   One organization which has always recruited and trained its own photographers is the Department of National Defence. The reason for this policy, according to one report, is "that the fullest and most complete control over activities and personnel may be exercised by the military authorities" and thus "not only to provide an historical record but

Boosterism: Frank Micklethwaite's photograph of Upper Canada College during the 1890s helped spread Toronto's self-image of a prosperous, progressive city.

Source: Frank W. Micklethwaite/National Archives of Canada/RD353.

to provide informational and inspirational material for ... the maintenance of public morale and the stimulation of recruiting."[7] Drawing an
example from the world of business, one notes that the vice-president
of Pringle and Booth, one of the largest commercial studios in Toronto,
recently criticized the tendency of photography students to use "old
barns and fences" as subjects, and referred approvingly to a plaque in
his firm's office reading: "We do not make pictures to hang on walls.
We create photographs to be reproduced in major media to sell mer-
chandise."[8]

8   The manipulation of photographs may take the form of an order
like the one which prohibited R.C.A.F. photographers in wartime from
including in their photographs subjects like the complete aircrew of an
aircraft, lest that information benefit the enemy.[9] Manipulation is
present too in the widespread use of photographs taken with wide-
angle lenses in advertisements which convey a false and misleading
impression of, say, the interior of a new car.

9   Distortion can result from the cropping or retouching of negatives
and prints to delete unwanted details, such as the pennant number and
radar aerials visible in a wartime negative of the destroyer H.M.C.S.
Ottawa. Captions are another means of manipulating photographs, as
these two examples will attest:

> The Canadian Corps who cracked the Hitler Line in Italy were
> given a well-earned rest by the shores of the blue Mediterranean.

*The other side of the coin: Taken by Arthur S. Goss, official photographer
for the City of Toronto, this photograph shows the rear of 512 Front
Street, Toronto, on 27 August 1914.*

Source: Arthur S. Goss/City of Toronto Archives/RG 8-32-315.

Academically, Indian students are considered to be as bright as any other group of youngsters. Here, a grade 8 class at Mount Elgin Indian day school at the Caradoc Agency ... are at work learning geography.

Whoever wrote the first caption must have been a frustrated travel agent; the colour of the Mediterranean is immaterial, but researchers will certainly want to know the names and units of the soldiers in the photograph, the exact location and date, plus the name of the photographer. Some member of the Information Division of the Department of Citizenship and Immigration wrote the second caption; perhaps that person should remove his foot from his mouth and stop perpetuating racial stereotypes.

10   The editor who makes the decision to release or not to release a photograph practises manipulation. For example, a colleague who is organizing the Montreal *Gazette* collection of some 130 000 negatives taken between 1938 and 1968 reports that an average of only one in ten of these photographs was published in that newspaper. There is also the example of the photograph showing the blanket-wrapped body of a Canadian soldier killed in Korea in 1951; branded with the rubber stamp "Banned," this photograph vanished into the files for the next twenty-five years. Even when released to the public, a photograph can present a distorted image. Many people have seen the well-known Canadian Press photograph of Robert Stanfield fumbling a football during the 1974 federal election campaign. Yet how many people have

Controlling a photograph: Censors removed both the pennant numbers and radar aerials from this photo of H.M.C.S. Ottawa *taken in 1940, making the picture less suitable in some ways as an historical document.*

Source: National Archives of Canada/C85886.

Distortion: Surely the phrase "academically, Indian students are considered to be as bright as any other group of youngsters" influences the information conveyed by this photograph!

Source: National Archives of Canada/C85885.

noticed the photographer's subsequent statement that, of the many photographs he took on that occasion, the one selected for national exposure was the one showing the only time that the leader of the Progressive Conservative Party fumbled the ball? Other photographs inflicted upon the public may be described politely as re-enactments and impolitely as fakes. The most notorious examples are Captain Ivor Castle's photographs which purport to show Canadian troops in action during the Battle of the Somme in 1916. Bearing captions like "A Canadian Battalion go over the top," these photographs appeared in both official and popular histories for over fifty years, symbolizing Canadian participation in the First World War. It was one of Castle's colleagues, William Rider-Rider, who supplied the evidence which finally destroyed their credibility:

> These alleged battle pictures were "made," or rather pieced together, from [photographs of] shell bursts taken at a British trench mortar school outside St. Pol, and those taken at rehearsal attacks of men going over the top with canvas breech covers on their rifles ... [consequently] I had a lot to live down when I visited some units ... [such comments as] "Want to take us going over the top? Another faker?"[10]

11   We are now observing the proliferation of re-enacted photographs as a byproduct of the current nostalgia boom throughout North America. A number of individuals and groups in the United States are

What the public did not see: The blanket-wrapped body of a soldier of the 2nd Battalion, Royal Canadian Regiment, killed in Korea on 3 November 1951.

Source: Department of National Defence/National Archives of Canada/C70696.

producing early photographs like daguerreotypes and tintypes showing, for example, people dressed in Civil War uniforms. There is a group in Toronto which specializes in recreating and photographing scenes characteristic of the 1940s prompting one observer to comment, "This is the possible future direction of photography ... perhaps the staged, created photograph will be the wave of the future."[11] Certainly the potential exists: so realistic were publicity photographs taken during the filming of the television documentary *The National Dream* that some have already appeared in textbooks passing as actual illustrations of the construction of the Canadian Pacific Railway.[12] Because of their careful attention to period detail, re-enacted photographs may well pose problems of authentication for archivists in the near future.

12   Those researchers who lack discrimination perpetuate the careless use of historical photographs. Far too many researchers are content to compile a sheaf of photostatic copies of photographs already used in other publications, and then mail these to the National Photography Collection as a request for more copies of the same. The result is further exposure of those tired old visual clichés. If only researchers would make the effort to choose from the full range of photographs available on their particular subjects, either through visits or through detailed letters asking for assistance! Other researchers, representing publishing companies or television networks, appear armed with a long list of every person, place and event mentioned in their assigned

Re-enactment or fake?: Officially captioned "A Canadian Battalion go over the top, October 1916," Captain Ivor Castle's photograph actually shows Canadian troops in training at school far behind the front line.

Source: W.I. Castle/Department of National Defence/National Archives of Canada/PA648.

manuscript or program script. As long as they obtain one photograph matching every item on this list, regardless of its suitability, these people are satisfied. Frequently, researchers do not realize that cameras have not been on the spot recording every single event in Canadian history for the past one hundred and forty years. A classic example of this misconception was the representative of a well-known publishing company who persisted in asking for photographs of the sinking of the H.M.C.S. *Fraser* in 1940, apparently unaware that the ship sank a few minutes after a collision which occurred in the middle of the night— hardly the time for a photographer to stand around recording the scene. Whenever photographs of a subject do not exist, researchers often resort to the questionable practice of using photographs taken out of context, using the rationalization that nobody will know the difference. The author of a recent British book faced the necessity of using out-of-context photographs by writing captions clearly stating that "although a photograph of such-and-such an event does not exist, this photograph taken on a different occasion shows the same conditions."[13] Canadian picture researchers should treat their audience with the same honesty.

13   Archivists are the people who enjoy direct contact with collections of original negatives and prints. What can we do to understand the limitations of the photographs in our custody, and to promote their intelligent use as historical documents? We can approach photographs with an ever-skeptical attitude, aware that something which is both old

and a photograph is not necessarily an objective document. We can study photographs for evidence of the various types of distortion and manipulation mentioned in this article, and can check captions for accuracy and objectivity. We can learn as much as possible about the photographer who took the photographs, either through research into textual sources or through personal interviews: his qualifications, his attitudes, his economic status. We can communicate all this information to the public by stripping away the layers of misinformation from photographs, by bringing complete collections of photographs, bearing accurate and complete captions, into public view, by giving impartial advice to researchers, by making speeches to organizations and by publishing articles about our research, and by critically reviewing the use of historical photographs in all media.[14] Archivists can and should read the message that there is more than meets the eye in a photograph.

(1976)

NOTES

1. Report of Joseph-Louis Gay-Lussac, in *An Historical and Descriptive Account of the Various Processes of the Daguerreotype* (London: McLean, 1839), 35.

2. Aaron Scharf, *Art and Photography* (London: The Penguin Press, 1968), xiii.

3. M.A. Root, *The Camera and the Pencil, or the Heliographic Art* (Philadelphia: D. Appleton & Co., 1864), 90–91.

4. J.P. Ourdan, *The Art of Retouching* (New York: E. & H.T. Anthony, 1880), 12–13.

5. J. Russell Harper and Stanley Triggs, eds., *Portrait of a Period: A Collection of Notman Photographs 1856 to 1915* (Montreal: McGill University Press, 1967).

6. *The New West* (Winnipeg: Canadian Historical Publishing Co., 1888), 30. However, a contemporary mercantile directory stated that Cooke's estimated capital was less than $500 and that his credit rating was limited.

7. F.C. Badgley to W.S. Thompson, 3 January 1940, Public Archives of Canada (hereinafter PAC), Records of the Wartime Information Board, RG36, 31, vol. 16, file 9-A-6.

8. *Canadian Photography* 5 (June 1974): 23.

9. Interview of Harry Price by Peter Robertson, 23 August 1972, PAC, Sound Recordings Accession 1972-47, Henry E. Price Collection.

10. Interview of William Rider-Rider by Peter Robertson, 18–19 May 1971, PAC, Sound Recordings Accession 1972-27, William Rider-Rider Collection.

11. Robert Fulford, "A Journey in Time," *Saturday Night* 91 (March 1976): 58.

12. Statement by M. Omer Lavallée of CP Rail, Montreal, Que., March 1976.

13. Martin Middlebrook, *The Nuremberg Raid* (London: Allen Lane, 1973).

14. See for example Richard Huyda's review of the books *Macdonald: His Life and Times* and *The John A. Macdonald Album* in *Archivaria* 2 (1976).

John Ralston Saul (b. 1947)

Educated at McGill and King's College, London (where he earned a Ph.D.),
John Ralston Saul is a prize-winning, internationally acclaimed novelist
and essayist who has also run a Paris-based investment firm and worked
as an oil executive. Saul is one of Canada's most distinguished writers,
thinkers, and public intellectuals, and his philosophical trilogy, Voltaire's
Bastards: The Dictatorship of Reason in the West, The Doubter's
Companion, *and* The Unconscious Civilization, *offers a provocative*
analysis of dominant Western structures.

The Grail of Balance

1   Our civilization is unable to do what individuals cannot say. And individuals are unable to say what they cannot think. Even thought can only advance as fast as the unknown can be stated through conscious organized language, an apparently self-defeating limitation.

2   The power of dictionaries and encyclopaedias is thus enormous. But what kind of power? The very possibility of it invites positive or negative use. A dictionary can as easily be a liberating force as one of control.

3   In the humanist view, the alphabet can be a tool for examining society; the dictionary a series of questions, an enquiry into meaning, a weapon against received wisdom and therefore against the assumptions of established power. In other words, the dictionary offers an organized Socratic approach.

4   The rational method is quite different. The dictionary is abruptly transformed into a dispensary of truth; that is, into an instrument which limits meaning by defining language. This bible becomes a tool for controlling communications because it directs what people can think. In other words, it becomes the voice of Platonic élitism.

5   Humanism versus definition. Balance versus structure. Doubt versus ideology. Language as a means of communication versus language as a tool for advancing the interests of groups.

6   The power of mere words and sentences may be particular to the West. Other civilizations are driven more by the image or by metaphysics. These lead them to treat the relationship between the oral and the written as secondary. But in the West, almost everything we need to know about the state of our society can be extracted from the relative power of oral versus written language.

7   The heavier the hand of the written, the more likely it is that language will have a deadened, predictable quality about it, justified by an obscure scholasticism. The whole thing then falls easily into the service of ideology and superstition. In societies such as these—such as ours—definition becomes an attempt to close doors by answering questions.

8   As for oral language, it is periodically unleashed as the only force capable of freeing society from the strangling effects of the written and the ideological. Like a burst of wind it opens the shuttered windows of scholasticism, blows out the dust of received wisdom and, in the phrase of Stéphane Mallarmé, purifies the language of a tribe. In those periods, dictionaries and encyclopaedias come into their own as aggressive, questioning tools which embrace doubt and consideration.

9   The dichotomy between the humanist and the rational is simple. How are citizens to enter into public debate if the concepts which define our society and decide the manner in which we are governed are open neither to understanding nor to questioning? If this is impossible or even difficult, then society comes to a standstill. If this immobility is prolonged, the results are catastrophic.

10   The way out for the citizenry is always the same. The language— our language—must be reclaimed from the structures of conventional wisdom and expertise. Populations know from experience that that change can only come through what will seem at first to be outrageous statements, provocation and a stubborn refusal to accept the smooth, calm, controlling formulae of conventional wisdom.

11   The ideologies of this century have prospered through the exploitation of what amounts to modern superstitions, each of which is justified by closely argued definitions divorced from reality. Even the most horrifying of superstitious acts—the Holocaust—was the product of decades of written, intellectual justification, which the rest of society failed to destroy as an expressible option by passively allowing the arguments to stand.

12   Our current ideologies revolve around economic determinism. They use expert argument to turn almost any form of injustice into an inevitability. This infection of the citizenry with passivity is, in fact, what we used to call superstition. Whatever is defined as true we feel obliged to accept as inevitable. Knowledge, which we believed would free us, has somehow become the instrument of our imprisonment. How can a dictionary do other than attack such mystification?

13   Erasmus was perhaps the first to try to kill the modern scholastic system by questioning the power of written truths. With *Adagio* (1508—a collection of three thousand proverbs from classical writers) and *In Praise of Folly* (1509—a satire on scholasticism), he attacked with both enumeration and comedy. His apparent aim was to redis-

cover the simplicity of early Christianity. But beyond that he was searching for the humanist equilibrium.

14   The religious wars—with their roar of deftly argued hatred and violence—seemed to overwhelm his message. But Erasmus had sent out a long-term signal. He had declared himself in favour of the oral approach to language, communication and understanding. Thus Europe's leading intellectual rejected the ideologies, both old and new.

15   The next major step nevertheless contradicted Erasmus. It continued in the unfortunate direction of the new rational and national powers unleashed more or less during the wars of religion. Cardinal Richelieu hired Claude Favre de Vangelas to organize the first dictionary of the *Académie Française* (1694—*Dictionnaire de la langue française*). Favre saw "elevated usage as the proper legislator of language."[1] He wanted to establish a "new High Mode" to replace Latin. The aim was to create a dictionary of absolute authority and so to fix French in place, like an exotic butterfly pinned in a display case, at a high level of politically correct rhetoric.

16   He was apparently unaware of Chancelier François Olivier's maxim "The higher the monkey climbs, the more he shows his ass."[2] Indeed, each time French has attained its natural greatness over the last three centuries, it has done so by rejecting "elevated usage" in favour of clear, flexible language inspired by a burst of oral genius.

17   In any case, the great humanist purification was about to begin. Ephrin Chambers's two-volume *Cyclopaedia or an Universal Dictionary of Arts and Sciences* appeared in 1728. The claims he made for his work were modest—to provide "an explication of the terms and an account of the things signified therein." Explanation and account. He did not pretend to define truth.

18   Samuel Johnson began with the intent of imitating Favre de Vangelas. By nature he believed that "all change is of itself evil." But by 1755, when his own dictionary was published, he had realized that language was either alive and uncontrollable or controlled and therefore dead.

> ... Academies have been instituted to guard the avenues of ... language, to retain fugitives, and to repulse intruders; but their vigilance and activity have hitherto been vain; sounds are too volatile and subtle for legal restraints; to enchain syllables, and to lash the wind, are equally the undertakings of pride, unwilling to measure its desires by its strengths.[3]

Then came the great innovation. Denis Diderot's *Encyclopédie* appeared in seventeen volumes between 1751 and 1766.[4] For the first time, an alphabetical analysis of civilization looked, not backwards but forward through innovative social ideas.[5] It was a tool for change and its publication was therefore dogged by arrests and censorship. Voltaire's *Dictionnaire Philosophique*, which appeared in varying forms over the same period, was even more consciously designed as a weapon of portable and flexible linguistic guerilla warfare.[6] By the early twentieth century, the multi-volumed Larousse encyclopaedia was describing Diderot's as an instrument of war.

19   But why war? And against what? Against a language which did not serve its civilization. A language which did not communicate. What the attack led by Voltaire and Diderot demonstrated was that the large and elegant beast of eighteenth-century society was an over-dressed and overly made-up sick animal.

20   The last steps in this opening up of communications and thought came with the *Encyclopaedia Britannica* (1718–71) and Noah Webster's two-volume dictionary in 1828.[7] Then the settling-in stage began. This was quickly succeeded by a mania for massive tomes filled with dry and sectarian definitions turned towards the past. These were in the image of a successful, self-satisfied civilization.

21   Flaubert poked fun at it with his little *Dictionnaire des Idées Reçues* (1880),[8] as did Ambrose Bierce in *The Devil's Dictionary* (1911).[9] But they were prodding an unmovable and increasingly unconscious animal, slumbering in comfortable self-confidence. In the twentieth century, the tools of debate and change of the eighteenth century have become scholastic monuments to truth. Since dictionaries now define not only meaning, but decide whether words really exist, people argue over which should be included. And they turn to their Oxford or their Webster's not to challenge themselves but to be reassured.

22   Today our civilization is not slumbering in unconscious self-confidence. Rather it resembles the wounded and confused animal of the eighteenth century. We are again the prisoners of scholastic rhetoric, which has blocked useful public communications by dividing our language up into thousands of closed specialist dialects. The result is the disappearance of almost any public language which could have a real impact on structures and actions. Instead we have an illusion of unlimited oral communications which are, in practical terms, a vast and murmuring silence.

23   Our élites interpret this situation as a confirmation of their indispensability. The citizenry, on the other hand, seem to have taken their distances from the existing structure and its languages. They react to the waves of expert truth which continue to wash over them with a sort of mute indifference.

24   An uninvolved outsider might interpret this as the first stages of a purification rite. Indifference is often the manner behind which humans consider change.

25   Given our history, it should be possible to decipher our intent. We are trying to think our way out of a linguistic prison. This means we need to create new language and new interpretations, which can only be accomplished by re-establishing the equilibrium between the oral and the written.

26   This is a situation in which dictionaries should again be filled with doubt, questioning and considerations. They can then be used as practical weapons of change.

(1994)

NOTES

1. Tom McArthur, *Worlds of Reference* (Cambridge: Cambridge University Press, 1986), 94.

2. Quoted in Michel de Montaigne, *Essais*, Volume II, 1588, Chapter 17, "De la praesumption": "Plus haut monte le singe, plus il montre son cul."

3. Samuel Johnson, *A Dictionary of the English Language* (1755; facsimile, London: Times Books Ltd., 1983). Quoted from the introduction. Johnson's original had no page numbers.

4. Denis Diderot, *L'Encyclopédie, un dictionnaire raisonné des sciences, des arts et des métiers*, edited by Alain Pons (Paris: Flammarion, 1986).

5. McArthur, *Worlds of Reference*, 105.

6. The edition in eight volumes quoted throughout is: Voltaire, *Dictionnaire Philosophique* (Paris: Librairie de Fortic, 1826).

7. Noah Webster, *An American Dictionary of the English Language* (New York: Johnson Reprint Corporation, 1970). This is a reprint of the original Webster's Dictionary, published in 1828.

8. Actually published posthumously in 1911.

9. Originally published as *The Cynic's Word Book* in 1906.

Njabulo S. Ndebele (b. 1948)

Born in Johannesburg, South Africa, and educated at the universities of
Cambridge and Denver, Ndebele is the author of Fools and Other Stories
(1983) and South African Literature and Culture *(1994), from which the*
essay reprinted here is taken. He first presented the essay at the New Nation
Writers Conference, December 1991, Witwatersrand University.

Guilt and Atonement:
Unmasking History for the Future

1   A few years ago I began to write a novel which I called "The Mask of the Fatherland." It was meant to be about a young Afrikaner boy in the South African Defence Force who during the war in Angola discovers the many masks that he and his tribe have had to wear over the centuries as they tried to justify their mission on earth. After much planning and research, I found I could not write the novel. At the root of the problem was that I simply did not know my main character. I did not know the simplest things about him. What was his mother fond of saying to him? Did he dream of his childhood sweetheart? Did he have problems revealing his feelings? Who were his neighbourhood friends, and what kind of mischief as boys did they get into? Does he have any strong thoughts about TV, about the Space Shuttle? What kind of home conditions his thinking? All I had was a treasure house of stereotypes for which I had no use.

2   I look at the times in which we live right now and I ask the question: am I in a position to write this novel? I know that I still cannot write it. At bottom is the fact that I do not know the people that my hero belongs to as a real, living community. At this time when Berlin walls of various kinds are falling, I am aware of a wall that is as formidable as ever. It is the wall of ignorance. At this time when the spirit of reconciliation is supposed to bring South Africans together, South Africans don't know one another as a people. Can we as a nation write the novel of the future under these conditions? If so, what are the preconditions for such novels to be written? What does it take for us to know one another? What *will* it take?

3   The African struggle for liberation was coming along. Somewhere it appeared to flounder and then it stopped to take another form. What characterises the nature of the transformation is that those who opened the prison doors were not victorious crowds pursuing a

defeated enemy in flight. They were opened by an enemy who had declared that he was now a friend. To date, he still holds the keys. When it suits him, he haggles over conditions, trying to prescribe the manner in which the new friendship is to be carried out, prompting the following questions. Are those who did not forcibly bring down the doors victorious? Have those who still hold the keys been defeated? There is a stand-off that offers no certitude. We are aware of those who are driven by hope, the supposed victors, and those who are driven by fear, the supposed losers. The danger is that a situation such as this can breed the most debilitating ambiguity in which we oscillate between hope and despair with a frequency that induces undefined bitterness and cynicism.

4   This situation of ambiguity may very well suggest that what we see is a chaotic play of masks: the masks of conciliation or reconciliation whose colourfulness may suggest a fragile essence, the absence of an underlying form. One such mask is the expression "the new South Africa." It is a sonorous expression fraught with much meaning and meaninglessness all at once. It spawns various masks that suggest many possible forms that this "new South Africa" may take. Who, anyway, invented the phrase? Was it the anxious "defeated" or the hopeful "victors"? Whatever the case might be, at the end of the day we still ask: what exactly is behind each mask? What is the reality so steadfastly hidden by the rhetoric of hope and anxiety?

5   It is part of the writer's task to strive to unmask. We are confronted by so many surfaces in our day-to-day lives. So many masks. Writing enables us to crack the surface and break through to the often deliberately hidden essence. What we find may either bring joy or sadness, hope or despair, but almost always yields insight. It is this masking and unmasking that often constitutes the terrain of conflict between the writer and official culture. Writers strive to remove the blanket which officialdom insists on spreading and laying over things. When officialdom is under attack and lacks confidence, it is the new one that constructs masks.

6   Let us step back and reconstruct the situation briefly. It is interesting to note that we have just come from a situation in which the South African government (*this very present government*) did not even attempt to mask anything. On the contrary, it seems to have even enjoyed what most of us saw as obscene exhibitionism. It was characterised by brazen acts of public cruelty and terrible laws. It was a public dance of indecency choreographed from parliament. Some masking, of course, took place at the level of ideology. Attempts were made to justify the manifest and most observable horror through the propounding of apartheid philosophy.

7   Of course the oppressed had no option but to live with and to subsist in the terrible reality created. From that perspective, denied a say in matters pertaining to their health, housing, education, employment, recreation, they focused their attention on the justificatory arguments,

since we cannot but respond to speech. They grappled with the logic of apartheid.

8 February 2, 1990 represented the strategic withdrawal of the argument. "Strategic" because, indeed, it was known all along that the argument was a lie, that it had been constructed for a purpose: to systematically entrench white power through a range of instruments of domination. Now all is in place, the red herring can be done away with and it will seem like defeat. In fact, this is victory at the very moment that defeat is being proclaimed.

9 Of course, it will take generations in a normal time sequence for blacks to produce enough academics, engineers, industrialists, doctors, corporate managers, archivists, pilots, etc. to make a real competitive difference in the actual play of power in the governance of the country. Their land of milk and honey, according to the current flow of events, still seems a remote possibility.

10 In fact, just as they had no option but to accept the conditions of life imposed on them, if they want to experience some semblance of freedom, in the short term, they have no option but to fit into the available business and civil service culture and rise through the ranks. Suddenly, where the various structures of such a culture represented exclusion and repulsive, exploitative white power, now they may represent opportunity. The glitter of apartheid: buildings, banks, etc., previously an index of the oppressed's powerlessness, now represent, disturbingly, the possibility of fulfilment.

11 But such fulfilment comes at a price. Everything has been thought out for us: our inventive capacity is harnessed according to the demands of a structured business and industrial culture. The brazen oppression of the past can now become the seductive oppression of having to build and consolidate and enjoy what was achieved at our expense. There will be the attractive tendency to accept all this as the spoils of struggle. But who are likely to take advantage of this situation?

12 This situation is likely to split the black community into those who, worn out by the struggle, seek immediate relief, and those who, seeing the dangers of a short-term accommodation, wish to press ahead. Indeed, the ambiguities and contradictions of the times throw up painful choices to grapple with intellectually.

13 Terrible choices! We can choose between absorption and accommodation on the one hand, and, on the other hand, the quest for a self-created reality. The former promises short-term relief for the few who can make it, and discontent for the vast masses who see no relief in sight. The latter choice may even prompt the question: was the armed struggle perhaps abandoned too soon? Could a year or two not have driven home more dramatically to the whites of our country the real nature of the demand of the oppressed for liberation? Did all the painful struggles of the past terminate so abruptly so that an all-white cricket team can go to India triumphantly without the baggage of

guilt? Who did it represent? Certainly not me. Do people who still ask for old national emblems really know what is going on? Where is the future we have wanted to build with our hands and our imaginations from the ashes of the past?

14   Terrible choices! We can choose between freedom through the agony of destructive strife and struggle, on the one hand, and on the other, the anxiety born of the need for security, the choice to hang on to a known reality, no matter how problematic (after all there can be legitimate burn-out after long years of struggle and hope for deliverance); between reconstruction and accommodative consolidation; between war and negotiation.

15   One of the prices we can pay for choosing the illusion of freedom is to forget about the past and enjoy the present as much as we can. After all, apartheid laws are gone, what do we want now?

16   In fact, there is a concerted attempt by those responsible for apartheid to forget about the past and to convince everyone else to do so. Not too long ago, Roelof ("Pik") Botha, addressing the Australian press club, declared that he has also fought against apartheid. So the ANC, PAC and other liberation groups really have no special claim to the attention of the world. Of course, Pik Botha has his heroic, invisible scars to show for it: he has been banned, tortured, detained without trial, forced into exile, maimed in SADF raids in Lesotho and Botswana and then recalled to be rewarded with a cabinet post by the government of his nightmares. This tactic represents not only a brazen distortion of historical fact, but can also be regarded as an obscene attempt to appropriate the struggles of those who have been victims of his government in order to belittle the significance of the liberation struggle. What gives him the right to do this? I registered in myself the flickers of rage as I listened to our Minister of Foreign Affairs perform.

17   Certainly it now seems to me that the negotiation atmosphere has created a false moral equation between the Nationalist Party (the authors of our horror novel) and its government on the one hand, and the liberation movement on the other. It is an equation that has given our white compatriots a right they previously and still do not have: the right to judge our struggle. It is an equation in which the liberation movement perhaps saw the possibility of some strategic gains for the struggle. But clearly, the government saw the possibility of consolidating white power without the baggage of the past. In effect, there is no equation but conflicting interests in a balance in which one thing that is certain is the uncertainty of the future.

18   One should not be seen to be harping on the evils of the past. But we have to cry out when the past is being deliberately forgotten in order to ensure that what was gained by it can now be enjoyed without compunction. It is crucial at this point that the past be seen as a legitimate point of departure for talking about the challenges of the present and the future. The past, no matter how horrible it has been, can redeem us. It can be the moral foundation on which to build the pil-

lars of the future. If so, what are the implications of keeping the past alive?

19   Should the oppressor now feel guilty about it? Guilt, in this situation, may be healthy. It may represent a healthy recognition of the moral flaws of the past and the extent of one's responsibility for them.

20   But guilt is like pain: not many of us would like or wish to inflict it on others. We cannot call forth the guilt of others. Guilty people are not pleasant people to live with. They are tense, unpredictable, and unhappy. Guilt on a massive social scale is not healthy.

21   And the oppressed? Should they feel shame? Yes, to the extent that they should recognise their humiliation and vow never to go through it again. Beyond that, a prolonged feeling of shame on a massive social scale may perpetuate inferiority.

22   Yes. It is at this point that we move away from shame and guilt to call for the atonement of justice. It is justice we must demand, not guilt. We must demand justice.

23   But the balance of forces at this juncture is such that we may not even be able to get justice. Is justice possible in a situation in which the following questions are still being asked? Given the current balance of forces and the need for democracy and equality in the short term:

How do we dispossess those who took the land by unfair means?
How do we remove from power those who won it by conquest?
How do we take away privileges and resources from those who accumulated them by unfair means?

Because of the balance of forces, I am unable to answer these questions. This inability I find debilitating. It spawns frustration and may even lead to something I have steadfastly fought in the past: bitterness. For indeed, to borrow from Jay Reddy's quotation in her address, "the end of apartheid seems to represent for the white minority a defeat in which they have lost nothing." It leads me to the uncomfortable perception that at a time when justice has to prevail (because the advent of freedom represents historical redress), there seems no objective basis on which to promote it. There is no manifest objective base to support the moral law. Entrenched privilege, entrenched and pervasive institutional and social power, entrenched poverty, ill health, joblessness, lack of opportunity, lack of housing: all these persist *with a vengeance*! All these still constitute the universal reality of our times.

24   Guilt? it is not something we need to spend too much time on. Guilt is irrelevant. But why is it likely to crop up in discussions of the need for redress? Essentially because the struggle is unresolved. Its end has not been decisive. Paradoxically, it may benefit the whites to keep us demanding their guilt. For guilt is a red herring that gives us the illusion that in dealing with it we are engaged in combat. It enables us to deal with the illusion while leaving the reality intact. It may even represent the reinvention of protest. The demand for justice, on the other

hand, is more immediately and concretely threatening: *it keeps our attention firmly on the search for the actual process of redress.*

25   Those who have lost should properly experience loss, not guilt. Those who feel guilty may feel this way precisely because they have not lost, and yet see the legitimacy of the demands on them, and the possibility and even the need to lose something. The bold and the arrogant among them may even say: why should I feel guilty anyway? I deserve everything I have. Of course, yes. They deserve every bit of it, because at the individual level, people may very well have worked hard for what they possess. Of course, no. The entire social context in which those personal struggles took place was seriously flawed. Ultimately, individuals who have benefited from that flawed environment cannot deny responsibility. To deny responsibility is to affirm indirectly the perception that there has indeed been no change.

26   There is one area of negotiation that produces many heated words: Affirmative Action. It is designed not to make people lose jobs, but to ensure that those who have been left out previously through parliamentary injustice can find jobs. And there lie the problems.

27   Whenever I hear this expression, affirmative action, I boil inside. Affirmative action represents concessions that the powerful make for the oppressed. In the land of its origins, the United States of America, affirmative action is a strategy to manage the demand for redress for those who can never hope ever to seize the instruments of government as a group. The context of their struggle has been civil rights, not national liberation. In South Africa, to adopt this strategy is to distort our perceptions of the objective goal; it enables us to assume the mentality of being a dominated minority, rather than experience ourselves as a struggling, free majority, free even to make mistakes. Free, to quote Babel, to write our bad novels.

28   Affirmative action is a programme for the oppressed. Free people talk about the need for education and skills in a reconstructive national environment. Free people appreciate the need to learn from experience. They are not chained to keeping going something they had no part in establishing; they are not chained to the need to maintain efficiency that does not contain the content of their lives. They learn through the sweat and frustrations of reconstruction. They know that the future will not be easy; that there are new things to be learned; that during the struggle they accumulated so much experience that as a result there is so much that they are good at, and that it is that experience that must form the new society.

29   The maintenance of corporate efficiency will not be sufficient justification to keep people oppressed, to deny people freedom. Reference is always being made to the "chaos" in the north. One will not deny many of the allegations. But in reality, the "chaos" up north is the chaos of historically free people making their own and understandable mistakes, which they learn from. It is a much better lesson for it calls

for the kind of creative involvement in the search for solutions which makes people experience themselves as true participants in history.

30   Paulo Freire[1] has said that only the oppressed can free both themselves and their oppressors from the shackles of the past. But for the oppressed to feel that the moral high ground belongs to them, they have to experience themselves as having the power to be magnanimous, generous, and forgiving. Do the oppressed feel that power in our country at this point in our history?

31   No. I cannot and can never demand other people's guilt; but I do want justice. I cannot ask people to confess their sins, or to indulge in any kind of self-flagellation (unless they do so voluntarily—even though I would never enjoy the sight of them doing so). Guilt is too personal a feeling. To demand it of someone is to invade a personal domain that can result in humiliation. It results in no solace for both sides. Justice, on the other hand, yields not humiliation but knowledge and responsibility.

32   And the search for justice is the path by which the struggle for redress is dramatised, and the means by which the struggle between fairness and unfairness is made visible through a legitimate institutional instrument. It leads to decisive corrective action.

33   The past is knocking constantly on the doors of our perceptions, refusing to be forgotten, because it is deeply embedded in the present. To neglect it at this most crucial of moments in our history is to postpone the future.

(1991)

---

1. (b. 1921), author of *Pedagogy of the Oppressed* (1970) among other highly influential works.

Rhea Tregebov (b. 1953)

Born in Saskatoon, Saskatchewan, Rhea Tregebov was raised in Winnipeg and now lives in Toronto. Her publications include Remembering History *(1982)—a Pat Lowther Prize–winner—and* No One We Know *(1986). See "What Makes You Sure," p. 351.*

Some Notes on the Story of Esther[1]

1 To look at the parallels between the position of women in male culture and Jews in Christian culture, replace for the moment the word "Jew" with "woman."

2 "So you're a woman! My mother was a woman but my sisters and I were all raised as men."

3 "I didn't find out my mother was a woman until I was fourteen. It just wasn't important to her, so she didn't mention it."

4 "My parents gave me a female education, but I'm not any gender now."

5 "Are you a woman? That's funny, you don't look female!"

6 I could go on. What becomes apparent is the shared ambiguity to our role: not until we explicitly identify ourselves as different are we perceived as such.

7 Women are visibly women; Jews may or may not be visibly Jews. We are, however, mutually expected to be one of the guys or, more specifically, one with the guys. Not until we declare ourselves as outside the norm are we perceived as standing in opposition to things-as-they-are.

8 It is a vexed question, this question of our visibility or invisibility as Jews. We can, in many cases, "pass" in a way Blacks or Natives or Asians cannot. At a recent Passover dinner, in reply to my remark that "This is the one day I get to be Jewish" (I am very sporadically observant), a Black friend said, "And lucky me—I get to be Black every day."

9 The parallel, however, may well extend to people whose background is mixed, or whose "racial" identity, because it does not match the stereotype (be it because of appearance or of class), may be uncertain. This uncertainty does carry its own pain, and I would suggest that, precisely because of the possibility of "passing," the risk of inter-

---

1. Biblical Jewish queen of Persia who, during a period when anti-Semitic feelings ran high, saved her people from massacre.

nalization is perhaps greater for those of us who are ambiguously what we are.

10   Our invisibility requires that we declare ourselves as standing in opposition. Women are generally expected to be sympathetic with, if not proponents of, male culture. Jews in turn are expected to be sympathetic towards and supportive of Christian culture. This includes the expectation of sympathy with the anti-woman and anti-Semitic aspects of the culture: the woman/Jew who is the target of the sexist/anti-Semitic joke is expected to laugh along.

11   The assumption demands a basic denial of one's identity. The conversations begin, "Oh, you're not like other women/Jews!" (you aren't who you are) and then inevitably continue with a litany of the ills and evils women/Jews embody—a litany with which the listener is expected to agree.

12   We have learned to respond by refusing any ground of agreement; by openly expressing our anger, our refusal of complicity. By insisting on having our differences, our difference defined; and thus, even in this minimal way, insisting on being acknowledged.

13   I (along with many others) use the two terms, "other" and "different," in very specific ways. Women are genuinely *different* from men in terms of our biology, our historical position and many of the facts of our lives. Jews are genuinely *different* from Christians in our religious beliefs, our historical position and many of our cultural values.

14   Both groups, however, have suffered from the *otherness* imposed upon us by the dominant culture. Our difference is not, however, regarded as a positive attribute. We are instead viewed as other, as "un-men" or "not-men"; as "un-Christians" or "not-Christians"; shadowy beings whose otherness defines and describes the dominant group, not ourselves. Since we are continually battling external definitions—definitions which are more than merely negative; they are an annihilation of our selves—our lives come to take on an artificiality which never really leaves us. The word which kept coming to mind again and again, with a peculiar resonance, was "imposter." As false men, false Christians,[2] until the point at which we declare our difference, at which we explicitly eliminate the ambiguity of our role, we act as imposters, deceivers.

15   Within the patriarchy, femaleness is perceived in so distorted a fashion that we cannot act simply as women, but are compelled to act as female impersonators. We so contort ourselves, either in acquiescing to the distortions or in constantly reacting in opposition to them, that a "naturalness," an ease, a sense of sitting *bien dans sa peau*,[3] is rare if not impossible.

---

2. The scope of this essay does not permit a consideration of those "false Americans," the Canadians, much as I wish it did. [Author's note.]

3. Comfortable with oneself.

16   The same may be said of the Jew. Say "Jew." I flinch. It is painful for me to admit it, but so deeply, so ineradicably have I internalized the anti-Semitism I grew up with, that I cannot hear, cannot say the word "Jew" without experiencing it as an epithet, without sensing the negative resonance it has acquired over millennia of attack.

17   There does exist for writers the possibility of "passing" and all the dangers inherent in such a move. Writers can, up to a point, remain anonymous. (This is of course a possibility for Black and other "visible" writers as well.) In the past we adopted male pen names. It was also not uncommon to adopt British pseudonyms, or to change one's name. I still see young women writers hiding their identifying first names under initials, at least until they get that first book accepted for publication. But there is also the more subtle and more destructive attempt to "pass" in terms of content, in terms of not acknowledging or not fully acknowledging who we are, or whom we're writing for.

18   So how do we, as writers, women, Jews, integrate into our work what we really are, as opposed to these refutations or denials, these shadows of otherness, these acquiescences? What it all means to me as a writer is, first of all, that if I spent the first five years of my writing career writing as a man, I certainly spent the first ten years writing as a Christian. And then, of course, there are the fifteen years I spent reading as a man. As a young woman raised and educated without access to an articulated feminism, I identified with men, I identified with the male authors I read. A kind of literary tomboyism. I would certainly feel some sort of discomfort when I came across sexism in my reading, but I had no word for it, I had no way of placing it. My primary response was "I am not a woman like that," not "Women are not like that." And as a young writer, while I began to experience a sense of exclusion, while the strain of identifying with male authors and teachers and any accompanying sexual bias increased, the wish, unexpressed, to be one of the boys continued. I had my "us" and "them" confused.

19   And so I did not begin writing authentically until that point at which an articulated feminism made it possible for me to identify myself—not so much merely as a *feminist*, but at the primary level as *female*. This many all sound incredible to younger women, but I don't think at the same time it was an uncommon experience. Much of it was the struggle, still ongoing, against the prevalent notion that the male (and the Christian) are universal. If you speak as a man and Christian, you address everyone. The words "male" and "Christian" are not necessary as qualifiers: it's not the Oxford (Norton, Penguin, etc.) anthology of male, Christian literature, it's the Oxford anthology of literature. Whereas, when we speak as women, as Jews, the assumption is that this is a specialty literature, that we are speaking only to a select (read insignificant) group.

20   The eruption of feminist consciousness in my writing was followed years later by a less well-defined consciousness of my Jewishness.

Although I had been writing for a decade, only in 1982 did I first begin work on a piece which dealt specifically and at length with Jewish content. "I'm talking from my time" was a performance piece/slide show which juxtaposed images and words of my husband's ninety-six-year-old Russian Jewish grandmother with my own poetry.

21   Any writer's reasons for writing a given piece are, necessarily, multiple. But I do feel I was impelled to work on it, from a reactive position, in response to the feeling of being invisible. I remember the shock when a Québécoise writer talked to me about "you Anglos." (In North End Winnipeg, anyone whose first language was English was called English, even if they were of Scottish, Irish, Welsh, or Brazilian origin. No Jew was an Anglo.) There was some kind of pervasive filter in the Toronto milieu in which I wrote that could not see or wished to eradicate the differences that began, increasingly, to define me for myself: my Western roots, my un-bourgeois, left-wing background, my Jewishness. I felt myself becoming vague, bleached. Ambiguous.

22   I was, in addition, responding to the mainstream (mostly American) writing about Jewish experience; its sexism (the castrating Jewish mother); its painful pandering to stereotypes (the grasping, materialistic, bourgeois Jew); its eye on the Christian audience. In summary, its assertion of our otherness.

23   As women and Jews we share a common posture; a tenuous, ambiguous position in a social structure which is emphatically not our own and yet which we know and understand intimately, profoundly. The parallels are not, of course, exact, but they can act in powerfully similar ways in our lives, and in our lives as writers in particular. Our writing, once it is conscious, can grow to be an assertion of our difference, and a refutation of the otherness imposed upon us.

(1990)

Neil Bissoondath (b. 1955)

Born in Trinidad, Neil Bissoondath immigrated to Canada and became a teacher after completing a B.A. at York University. A scholarship from the Banff School of Fine Arts allowed him to finish his first book, Digging Up the Mountains *(1986), and begin his exploration in fiction and in essays of the consequences of ethnic and other stereotypes and of Canada's policy of multiculturalism. His other books include* A Casual Brutality *(1988),* Selling Illusions: The Cult of Multiculturalism in Canada *(1994), and* Doing the Heart Good *(2002).*

"I'm Not Racist But ... "

1   Someone recently said that racism is as Canadian as maple syrup. I have no argument with that. History provides us with ample proof. But, for proper perspective, let us remember that it is also as American as apple pie, as French as croissants, as Jamaican as ackee, as Indian as aloo,[1] as Chinese as chow mein, as ... Well, there's an entire menu to be written. This is not by way of excusing it. Murder and rape, too, are international, multicultural, as innate to the darker side of the human experience. But we must be careful that the inevitable rage evoked does not blind us to the larger context.

2   The word "racism" is a discomforting one: It is so vulnerable to manipulation. We can, if we so wish, apply it to any incident involving people of different colour. And therein lies the danger. During the heat of altercation, we seize, as terms of abuse, on whatever is most obvious about the person. It is, often, a question of unfortunate convenience. A woman, because of her sex, easily becomes a female dog or an intimate part of her anatomy. A large person might be dubbed "a stupid ox," a small person "a little" whatever. And so a black might become "a nigger," a white "a honky," an Asian "a paki," a Chinese "a chink," an Italian "a wop," a French-Canadian "a frog."

3   There is nothing pleasant about these terms; they assault every decent sensibility. Even so, I once met someone who, in a stunning surge of naiveté, used them as simple descriptives and not as terms of racial abuse. She was horrified to learn the truth. While this may have

---

1. Ackee: tropical tree, *Blighia sapida*, the fruit of which is edible when cooked; aloo: potato.

been an extreme case, the point is that the use of such patently abusive words may not always indicate racial or cultural distaste. They may indicate ignorance or stupidity or insensitivity, but pure racial hatred—such as the Nazis held for Jews, or the Ku Klux Klan for blacks—is a thankfully rare commodity.

4   Ignorance, not the willful kind but that which comes from lack of experience, is often indicated by that wonderful phrase, "I'm not racist but ..." I think of the mover, a friendly man, who said, "I'm not racist, but the Chinese are the worst drivers on the road." He was convinced this was so because the shape of their eyes, as far as he could surmise, denied them peripheral vision.

5   Or the oil company executive, an equally warm and friendly man, who, looking for an apartment in Toronto, rejected buildings with East Indian tenants not because of their race—he was telling me this, after all—but because he was given to understand that cockroaches were symbols of good luck in their culture and that, when they moved into a new home, friends came by with gift-wrapped cockroaches.

6   Neither of these men thought of himself as racist, and I believe they were not, deep down. (The oil company executive made it clear he would not hesitate to have me as a neighbour; my East Indian descent was of no consequence to him, my horror of cockroaches was.) Yet their comments, so innocently delivered, would open them to the accusation, justifiably so if this were all one knew about them. But it is a charge which would undoubtedly be wounding to them. It is difficult to recognize one's own misconceptions.

7   True racism is based, more often than not, on willful ignorance, and an acceptance of—and comfort with—stereotype. We like to think, in this country, that our multicultural mosaic will help nudge us into a greater openness. But multiculturalism as we know it indulges in stereotype, depends on it for a dash of colour and the flash of dance. It fails to address the most basic questions people have about each other. Do those men doing the Dragon Dance really all belong to secret criminal societies? Do those women dressed in saris really coddle cockroaches for luck? Do those people in dreadlocks all smoke marijuana and live on welfare? Such questions do not seem to be the concern of the government's multicultural programs, superficial and exhibitionistic as they have become.

8   So the struggle against stereotype, the basis of all racism, becomes a purely personal one. We must beware of the impressions we create. A friend of mine once commented that, from talking to West Indians, she has the impression that their one great cultural contribution to the world is in the oft-repeated boast that "We (unlike everyone else) know how to party."

9   There are dangers, too, in community response. We must be wary of the self-appointed activists who seem to pop up in the media at every given opportunity spouting the rhetoric of retribution, mining distress for personal, political and professional gain. We must be skeptical

about those who depend on conflict for their sense of self, the non-whites who need to feel themselves victims of racism, the whites who need to feel themselves purveyors of it. And we must be sure that, in addressing the problem, we do not end up creating it. Does the *Miss Black Canada Beauty Contest* still exist? I hope not. Not only do I find beauty contests offensive, but a racially segregated one even more so. What would the public reaction be, I wonder, if every year CTV broadcast the *Miss White Canada Beauty Pageant*? We give community-service awards only to blacks: Would we be comfortable with such awards only for whites? In Quebec, there are The Association of Black Nurses, The Association of Black Artists, The Congress of Black Jurists. Play tit for tat: The Association of White Nurses, White Artists, White Jurists: visions of apartheid. Let us be frank, racism for one is racism for others.

10   Finally, and perhaps most important, let us beware of abusing the word itself.

(1989)

Heather Mallick (b. 1959)

Heather Mallick grew up in various towns and cities across Canada but remembers most fondly her high school years in Kapuskasing, Ontario. She earned a journalism degree from Ryerson and a B.A. and M.A. in English literature from the University of Toronto and maintains an interest in Virginia Woolf. Nominated four times for National Newspaper Awards, winning in 1994 for Critical Writing and in 1996 for Feature Writing, Mallick has worked as a reporter at The Toronto Star *and* The Globe and Mail, *as chief copy editor at* The Financial Post, *and as review editor at* The Sunday Sun *in Toronto. She now writes the As If column for* The Globe's *Focus section.*

Women Clamouring at the Gates, but the Boys Still Won't Open Up

1   Wanting and not getting. That's the big female secret, the story of what women are in for when they leave their hopeful years behind. "What we see is an alignment of locked doors." Carol Shields has painted the pain of this exclusion beautifully in her new (and possibly her last, as she is dying)[1] novel.

2   Any woman, and any smart man, will know what she means. "And what made you think for a moment we'd let you in, little lady?" sneers the ground-floor bouncer.

3   *Unless* is a great novel, the best she has written since I borrowed her *A Fairly Conventional Woman* from a small-town library at a dreary fake-woodgrain, pressed-chipboard time in my life 20 years ago, and found her highly unconventional. Odd how these writers dismissed as "women writers" or "feminine voices" are the most subversive.

4   In *Unless*, Reta Winters, a mother of three teenaged daughters, ponders the quasi-suicidal path of her 19-year-old. She writes to various literary snoots, wondering if the girl was damaged by the way men send women over "to the side pocket of the snooker table" where they are made to disappear. Did young Norah learn that she could have "goodness but not greatness" and did it break her heart?

---

1. Carol Shields died in July 2003.

5   In the book, Winters writes to a male editor about his *Great Minds of the Western Intellectual World: Galileo, Kant, Hegel, Bacon, Newton, Plato, Locke and Descartes*. Their sepia heads form a band across the page, "a ceaseless conveyor belt of noble thought," and not a woman among them. "You'll respond with a long list of rights women have won and you will insist that the playing field is level, but you must see that it is not." She wonders if her daughter saw the page and understood "how casually and completely she is shut out of the universe."

6   Post *Unless*, Shields recalled to an interviewer how the critic George Steiner once told an audience that there were no important 20th-century women writers. Shields challenged him. He could think of a couple from the 19th, he allowed. She was there when Martin Amis said much the same thing to another audience. This time, Shields didn't speak up. She now defines feminism as "simply an acknowledgment that women are human."

7   But they don't make humanity's lists. The world's "leading writers" (few women included) recently compiled a list of the top 100 books of all time. Only 11 were written by women. The supposedly liberal Guardian subsequently asked 12 distinguished bookish types—11 of them male—to comment. They mentioned nearly 30 books that should have been on the list but were not. Not a single one was written by a woman. No one found this unusual.

8   The long list of a newish, British prize for humorous fiction is released. There are 25 books, only one by a woman. No one points out that this is ludicrous and, indeed, profoundly unfunny. There's no Arabella Weir on it, by the way. She's the novelist and comedian who invented "The Girl Men Can't Hear." A woman and her boyfriend get into a cab. She gives the driver elaborate instructions on their destination. Pause. "Where to guv?" the driver says.

9   I read the index page of the New Yorker and wonder why no one ever notices that it is, to all intents and purposes, a men's magazine, written almost exclusively by men. Clogged with epics about the American ice-machine industry and whether seat-belt usage ever reached the rates predicted when it was mandated, it is a hymn to Asperger's Syndrome, obsessed with numbers and uncomprehending of emotional life and social cues. That's because it ignores half the human race. It reeks of exclusion, like an airless men's club, in the same way that all-female magazines stink of air freshener.

10   There shouldn't be female quotas, smart men and women will say. True. But there are quotas for men and they average 90 per cent, a big black anvil landing on the heads of women who want their voices heard without trying to imitate male voices.

11   I was pleased when the Americans (land of Susan B. Anthony!) set a quota for women in the new Afghan assembly. It may only have been 10 per cent, but a marvellous improvement on the Taliban quota of zero. And then, that day, I began counting, how many women in this field, how many women in that, and the smile was wiped off my face—

what a Swiffer-like feminine analogy, if that does not detract from my point—when I realized that most organizations don't even reach Afghan levels.

12   "Imagine someone writing a play called *Death of a Saleswoman*," Shields's protagonist says. "What a joke." For who could be bothered?

13   "I am trying to put forward my objection gently," she writes. "I'm not screaming as you may think. I'm not even whining, and certainly not stamping my little lady-size foot. Whispering is more like it."

14   And there you have it, a whisper from one of Canada's greatest writers, so typical of her because even though it is a howl of anger, it is reasoned in its delivery.

15   It is like crying pale pink tears, and much more effective than a scream.

(2002)

Drew Hayden Taylor (b. 1962)

Drew Hayden Taylor, born on the Curve Lake Reserve in Ontario, has worked in radio, television, and theatre as a journalist, author, and director. Two one-act plays, Toronto at Dreamer's Rock *and* Education Is Our Right, *in addition to the full-length play* The Bootlegger's Blues, *were published in 1990.*

Pretty Like a White Boy: The Adventures of a Blue Eyed Ojibway

1   In this big, huge world, with all its billions and billions of people, it's safe to say that everybody will eventually come across personalities and individuals that will touch them in some peculiar yet poignant way. Individuals that in some way represent and help define who you are. I'm no different, mine was Kermit the Frog. Not just because Natives have a long tradition of savouring Frogs' legs, but because of his music. If you all may remember, Kermit was quite famous for his rendition of "It's Not Easy Being Green." I can relate. If I could sing, my song would be "It's Not Easy Having Blue Eyes in a Brown Eyed Village."

2   Yes, I'm afraid it's true. The author happens to be a card-carrying Indian. Once you get past the aforementioned eyes, the fair skin, light brown hair, and noticeable lack of cheekbones, there lies the heart and spirit of an Ojibway storyteller. Honest Injun, or as the more politically correct term may be, honest aboriginal.

3   You see, I'm the product of a white father I never knew, and an Ojibway woman who evidently couldn't run fast enough. As a kid I knew I looked a bit different. But, then again, all kids are paranoid when it comes to their peers. I had a fairly happy childhood, frolicking through the bullrushes. But there were certain things that, even then, made me notice my unusual appearance. Whenever we played cowboys and Indians, guess who had to be the bad guy, the cowboy.

4   It wasn't until I left the Reserve for the big bad city, that I became more aware of the role people expected me to play, and the fact that physically I didn't fit in. Everybody seemed to have this preconceived idea of how every Indian looked and acted. One guy, on my first day of college, asked me what kind of horse I preferred. I didn't have the heart to tell him "hobby."

5   I've often tried to be philosophical about the whole thing. I have both white and red blood in me, I guess that makes me pink. I am a "Pink" man. Try to imagine this, I'm walking around on any typical Reserve in Canada, my head held high, proudly announcing to everyone, "I am a Pink Man." It's a good thing I ran track in school.

6   My pinkness is constantly being pointed out to me over and over and over again. "You don't look Indian?" "You're not Indian, are you?" "Really?!?" I got questions like that from both white and Native people, for a while I debated having my Status card tattooed on my forehead.

7   And like most insecure people and specially a blue eyed Native writer, I went through a particularly severe identity crisis at one point. In fact, I admit it, one depressing spring evening, I dyed my hair black. Pitch black.

8   The reason for such a dramatic act, you may ask? Show Business. You see, for the last eight years or so, I've worked in various capacities in the performing arts, and as a result I'd always get calls to be an extra or even try out for an important role in some Native oriented movie. This anonymous voice would phone, having been given my number, and ask if I would be interested in trying out for a movie. Being a naturally ambitious, curious, and greedy young man, I would always readily agree, stardom flashing in my eyes and hunger pains from my wallet.

9   A few days later I would show up for the audition, and that was always an experience. What kind of experience you may ask? Picture this, the picture calls for the casting of seventeenth-century Mohawk warriors living in a traditional longhouse. The casting director calls the name "Drew Hayden Taylor" and I enter.

10   The casting director, the producer, and the film's director look up from the table and see my face, blue eyes flashing in anticipation. I once was described as a slightly chubby beachboy. But even beachboys have tans. Anyway, there would be a quick flush of confusion, a recheck of the papers, and a hesitant "Mr. Taylor?" Then they would ask if I was at the right audition. It was always the same. By the way, I never got any of the parts I tried for, except for a few anonymous crowd shots. Politics tells me it's because of the way I look, reality tells me it's probably because I can't act. I'm not sure which is better.

11   It's not just film people either. Recently I've become quite involved in Theatre, Native theatre to be exact. And one cold October day I was happily attending the Toronto leg of a province-wide tour of my first play, *Toronto at Dreamer's Rock*. The place was sold out, the audience very receptive and the performance was wonderful. Ironically one of the actors was also half white.

12   The director later told me he had been talking with the actor's father, an older Non-Native type chap. Evidently he had asked a few questions about me, and how I did my research. This made the director

curious and he asked about his interest. He replied "He's got an amazing grasp of the Native situation for a white person."

13   Not all these incidents are work related either. One time a friend and I were coming out of a rather upscale bar (we were out YUPPIE watching) and managed to catch a cab. We thanked the cab driver for being so comfortably close on such a cold night, he shrugged and nonchalantly talked about knowing what bars to drive around. "If you're not careful, all you'll get is drunk Indians." I hiccuped.

14   Another time this cab driver droned on and on about the government. He started out by criticizing Mulroney, and eventually to his handling of the Oka crisis. This perked up my ears, until he said "If it were me, I'd have tear-gassed the place by the second day. No more problem." He got a dime tip. A few incidents like this and I'm convinced I'd make a great undercover agent for one of the Native political organizations.

15   But then again, even Native people have been known to look at me with a fair amount of suspicion. Many years ago when I was a young man, I was working on a documentary on Native culture up in the wilds of Northern Ontario. We were at an isolated cabin filming a trapper woman and her kids. This one particular nine-year-old girl seemed to take a shine to me. She followed me around for two days both annoying me and endearing herself to me. But she absolutely refused to believe that I was Indian. The whole film crew tried to tell her but to no avail. She was certain I was white.

16   Then one day as I was loading up the car with film equipment, she asked me if I wanted some tea. Being in a hurry I declined the tea. She immediately smiled with victory crying out "See, you're not Indian, all Indians drink tea!"

17   Frustrated and a little hurt I whipped out my Status card and thrust it at her. Now there I was, standing in a Northern Ontario winter, showing my Status card to a nine-year-old non-status Indian girl who had no idea what one was. Looking back, this may not have been one of my brighter moves.

18   But I must admit, it was a Native woman that boiled everything down in one simple sentence. You may know that woman, Marianne Jones from "The Beachcombers" television series. We were working on a film together out west and we got to gossiping. Eventually we got around to talking about our respective villages. Hers on the Queen Charlotte Islands, or Haida Gwaii as the Haida call them, and mine in central Ontario.

19   Eventually childhood on the Reserve was being discussed and I made a comment about the way I look. She studied me for a moment, smiled, and said "Do you know what the old women in my village would call you?" Hesitant but curious, I shook my head. "They'd say you were pretty like a white boy." To this day I'm still not sure if I like that.

20   Now some may argue that I am simply a Métis with a Status card. I disagree, I failed French in grade 11. And the Métis as everyone knows have their own separate and honourable culture, particularly in western Canada. And of course I am well aware that I am not the only person with my physical characteristics.

21   I remember once looking at a video tape of a drum group, shot on a Reserve up near Manitoulin Island. I noticed once of the drummers seemed quite fairheaded, almost blond. I mentioned this to my girl-friend of the time and she shrugged saying "Well, that's to be expected. The highway runs right through the Reserve."

22   Perhaps I'm being too critical. There's a lot to be said for both cul-tures. For example, on the left hand, you have the Native respect for Elders. They understand the concept of wisdom and insight coming with age.

23   On the white hand, there's Italian food. I mean I really love my mother and family but seriously, does anything really beat good Veal Scallopini? Most of my aboriginal friends share my fondness for this particular brand of food. Wasn't there a warrior at Oka named Lasagna? I found it ironic, though curiously logical, that Columbus was Italian. A connection I wonder?

24   Also Native people have this wonderful respect and love for the land. They believe they are part of it, a mere chain in the cycle of exis-tence. Now, as many of you know, this conflicts with the accepted Judeo-Christian i.e. western view of land management. I even believe somewhere in the first chapters of the Bible it says something about God giving man dominion over Nature. Check it out, Genesis 4:?, "Thou shalt clear cut." So I grew up understanding that everything around me is important and alive. My Native heritage gave me that.

25   And again, on the white hand, there's breast implants. Darn clever them white people. That's something Indians would never have invented, seriously. We're not ambitious enough. We just take what the Creator decides to give us, but no, not the white man. Just imagine it, some serious looking white man, and let's face it people, we know it was a man who invented them, don't we? So just imagine some serious looking white doctor sitting around in his laboratory muttering to himself, "Big tits, big tits, hmm, how do I make big tits?" If it was an Indian, it would be "Big tits, big tits, white women sure got big tits" and leave it at that.

26   So where does that leave me on the big philosophical scoreboard, what exactly are my choices again; Indians—respect for elders, love of the land. White people—food and big tits. In order to live in both cul-tures I guess I'd have to find an Indian woman with big tits who lives with her grandmother in a cabin out in the woods and can make Fettuccini Alfredo on a wood stove.

27   No let me make this clear. I'm not writing this for sympathy, or out of anger, or even some need for self-glorification. I am just setting the

facts straight. For as you read this, a new Nation is born. This is a declaration of independence, my declaration of independence.

28   I've spent too many years explaining who and what I am repeatedly, so as of this moment, I officially secede from both races. I plan to start my own separate nation. Because I am half Ojibway, and half Caucasian, we will be called the Occasions. And I of course, since I'm founding the new nation, will be a Special Occasion.

(1991)

Naomi Klein (b. 1970)

Montreal-born Naomi Klein is an award-winning journalist and author of such international successes as No Logo: Taking Aim at the Brand Bullies *(2000) and* Fences and Windows: Dispatches from the Front Lines of the Globalization Debate *(2002). Her articles and columns have appeared in such publications as* The Globe and Mail, The Guardian, The Nation, The New Statesman, *and* The New York Times, *and she has been a guest lecturer at Harvard, Yale, and New York universities.*

Buying a Gladiatorial Myth

1   Since the Pentagon released its own Osama Bin Laden video last month, the Al-Qaeda leader's every gesture, chuckle and word has been dissected. But his co-star, identified in the transcript only as "Shaykh," has received little scrutiny. Too bad, since he offers a rare window into the psychology of men who think of mass murder as a great game.

2   A theme that comes up repeatedly in Bin Laden's guests' monologues is the idea that they are living in times as grand as those described in the Koran. This war, he observes, is like "in the days of the prophet Mohammed. Exactly like what's happening right now." He goes on to say: "It is the same, like the old days, such as Abu Bakr and Othman and Ali and others.[1] In these days, in our times."

3   It's easy to chalk up this nostalgia to the usual theory about Bin Laden's followers being stuck in the Middle Ages. But the comments seem to reflect something more. It's not some ascetic medieval lifestyle that he longs for, but the idea of living in mythic times, when men were god-like, battles were epic and history was spelled with a capital H.

4   "Screw you, Francis Fukuyama,"[2] he seems to be saying, "history hasn't ended yet. We are making it, right here, right now!"

5   It's an idea we've heard from many quarters since September 11, a return of the great narrative: chosen men, evil empires, master plans, and great battles. All are ferociously back in style. The Bible, the

---

1. Abu Bakr (573–634), regarded by some as the first caliph of Islam (632–34); Ali (600?–661), fourth caliph and son-in-law of Mohammed, prophet and founder of Islam; and Othman (also Osman, 1259–1326), founder of the Ottoman Dynasty and Empire.
2. Francis Fukuyama (b. 1952), author of *The End of History and the Last Man* (1992).

Koran, "the clash of civilisations," *The Lord of the Rings*—all of them suddenly playing out "in these days, in our times." This grand redemption narrative is our most persistent myth, and it has a dangerous flip side. When a few men decide to live their myths, to be larger than life, it can't help but have an impact on all the lives that unfold in regular sizes. People suddenly look insignificant by comparison, easy to sacrifice in the name of some greater purpose.

6   When the Berlin Wall fell, it was supposed to have buried this epic narrative in its rubble. This was capitalism's decisive victory. Ideology is dead, let's go shopping. The end-of-history theory was understandably infuriating to those whose sweeping ideas lost the gladiatorial battles, whether it was global communism or, in Bin Laden's case, an imperial version of Islam.

7   What is becoming clear since September 11, however, is that history's end also turned out to be a hollow victory for the United States' cold warriors. It seems that since 1989, many of them have missed their epic narrative as if it were a lost limb. Without ideology, shopping was … just shopping. During the Cold War, consumption in the US wasn't only about personal gratification; it was the economic front of the great battle. When Americans went shopping, they were participating in the lifestyle that the Commies supposedly wanted to crush. When kaleidoscopic outlet malls were contrasted with Moscow's grey and barren shops, the point wasn't just that we in the West had easy access to Levi's 501s. In this narrative, our malls stood for freedom and democracy, while their empty shelves were metaphors for control and repression.

8   But when the Cold War ended and this ideological backdrop was yanked away, the grander meaning behind the shopping evaporated. The response from the corporate world was "lifestyle branding": an attempt to restore consumerism as a philosophical or political pursuit by selling powerful ideas instead of mere products. Ad campaigns began equating Benetton sweaters with fighting racism, Ikea furniture with democracy, computers with revolution.

9   Lifestyle branding filled shopping's "meaning" vacuum for a time, but it wasn't enough to satisfy the ambitions of the old-school cold warriors. Cultural exiles in a world they had created, disgruntled hawks spent their most triumphant decade not basking in their new uncontested power but grouching about how America had gone "soft," become feminised. It was an orgy of indulgence personified by Oprah Winfrey and Bill Clinton.

10   But since September 11, history is back with a capital H. Shoppers are once again foot-soldiers in a battle between good and evil, wearing new stars-and-stripes bras by Elita and popping special-edition red, white and blue M&Ms.

11   When US politicians urge their citizens to fight terrorism by shopping, it is about more than feeding an ailing economy. It's about once again wrapping the day-to-day in the mythic.

(2002)

Poetry

INTRODUCTION_____

" I , too, dislike it." So says American poet Marianne Moore (p. 236) of poetry, acknowledging the strong feelings prompted by the genre, while urging readers to ponder definitions and reconsider stereotyped notions of its proper medium and message, its supposed irrelevance to the real world of use, experience, and action. Such depleted notions of poetry persist despite the ubiquity of poetry in people's lives, whether in books or magazines, nursery rhymes, song lyrics, hymns and psalms, advertising jingles, greeting card verses, or political slogans. Whether in the study, on the bleachers, or in the shower, there is no escaping poetry.

Whereas poetry is a matter of universality and expressive abilities ("What oft was thought but ne'er so well expressed," according to Alexander Pope), it is "almost a remembrance" for John Keats and "the spontaneous overflow of powerful feelings" for William Wordsworth. Poetry is a matter not so much of emotions as of social and political engagement for Mary Leapor or Mary Alcock, Lord Byron or Percy Bysshe Shelley, or of national pride and identity for W.B. Yeats, A.J.M. Smith, John Betjeman, Derek Walcott, and others. For yet others, such as George Herbert, John Milton, or Gerard Manley Hopkins, poetry is a valuable form of religious expression, while for Adrienne Rich it is a powerful source of "self-exploration" and means of rewriting a culture's dominant myths. For D.G. Rossetti, poetry is "fundamental brainwork," and American poet Wallace Stevens insists that poetry's intellectual challenge should "resist the intelligence almost successfully." If poetry has no single or stable meaning across time and cultures, it remains difficult even to make absolute distinctions between prose and poetry. Consider, for example, the poetic prose of Margaret Laurence's essay, "Where the World Began," or the prosaic features of such poems as Robert Bly's "Visiting Emily Dickinson's Grave with Robert Francis" and Marlene Nourbese Philip's "Discourse on the Logic of Language."

Poetry, in the most widely used descriptive sense of the term, refers simply to composition in verse form, although some purists would reserve the term for only the "very best" of verse. Often popularly associated with preciousness in the pejorative sense or with concealment and complexity, even incomprehensibility—the hidden meanings of mysterious inspiration—like prose, poetry frequently follows all the normal patterns of grammar, syntax, and punctuation. As a mode of composition, poetry undoubtedly differs from prose not only in its compression and concentration, but also in its capacity to clarify meaning through additional conventions such as delimited line lengths, rhythmic patterns, and sometimes rhyme.

Poetry is the oldest literary form. Wherever we look in the history of literature we find that poetry, in its various forms, existed long before any form of prose. In its beginnings, too, poetry was public and popular and not elitist, self-expressive, or private; that is, it was composed by the people for the people and figured prominently in the formation of group identity and collective memory. Consider the powerfully evocative words of the *Beowulf* epic poet recording the history of a people, acts of heroism, and effects of earthly things in this oldest of the long poems in English.

Much of the earliest poetry in English was also set to music. For example, the anonymous popular ballads and short lyric (pp. 122–126) would originally have been sung rather than spoken in oral transmission. Ballads were stories in verse that aimed not only to entertain and educate by narrating events, which were often tragic, but also to evoke the mood, atmosphere, or feeling commonly associated with the event. Through dialogue and vivid, but sketchy, description (and often repetition and refrains), they tell only the important details, inviting the listener to reconstruct the rest of the story and recognize its implications. Prominent in the Scots "Sir Patrick Spens" are the two lines of standard English spoken by the "eldern knicht" who advises the king. That the knight's advice to the ignorant and decadent king leads to the death of Sir Patrick Spens and his men suggests where the Scots locate responsibility for their tragic social and political conditions. We are likewise able to guess who has slain the knight in the Scots version of "The Twa Corbies," and when we do so, we feel its grisly atmosphere all the more. We have included two versions of this particular ballad to show how different ballad communities, or cultural contexts of composition and circulation, produce very different renditions. Whereas the English version, complete with moral tag, confidently invokes a deity overlooking a scene of loyalty and love in the face of valiant death, the Scots version vividly captures the distress of a people who feel almost literally cannibalized. Most of the body of folk literature in English was not written down until the eighteenth century, and since Scotland retained this traditional poetry in greater abundance than did England at that time, many versions of the poems familiar to us are preserved in Scots. W.H. Auden's "One Evening" is a literary ballad imitative of the popular tradition.

Although most of the later poetry in this section was not written for musical accompaniment (with the exception of Robert Burns's "Auld Lang Syne," a tribute to memory and friendship sung by millions of English speakers at least once a year), almost all of it can be readily seen to embody a musical element in the use of rhythm and in the choice of words for the sound of sense (Keats's "Ode to Autumn," or Lewis Carroll's "Jabberwocky," for example). Interestingly, children take great pleasure in words used rhythmically long before they enjoy being told a story. The rhythm of poetry, like that of music, with which poetry has long been associated, seems to appeal to something quite basic in our physical and emotional beings, something that affects us prior to, while anticipating, our understanding of the actual language. In the real world of advertising, poetry's capacity to move and memorialize has made it a prominent means of arresting audiences, activating appetites, and shaping actions. This sound of poetry is a most important characteristic: a poem has to be heard as well as seen. Indeed, American poet Ezra Pound has said that "poetry begins to atrophy when it gets too far from music"; Elizabeth Barrett Browning's "A Musical Instrument," Dionne Brand's "Blues Spiritual for Mammy Prater," and George Elliott Clarke's poetry all celebrate the relationship between music and poetry.

Traditionally, English versification has been based on metrical principles (Anglo-Saxon verse, represented by the *Beowulf* excerpt and imitated in Earle Birney's "Anglosaxon Street," had been structured around accentual balance and alliteration in half lines). Metre (from the Greek *metron* or measure) is the pattern of stressed and unstressed syllables that structures the rhythm of formal verse in English. To Geoffrey Chaucer we owe the introduction into English of new metrical forms, including the heroic couplet (rhymed pairs of ten-syllable lines). Metre was developed out of the tendency in English to accent certain syllables in relation to others and was regularized to aid memory and underline meaning. This inclination imparts what we call a "rising rhythm" to English speech. We often begin with an unstressed syllable and proceed immediately to a stressed syllable. Andrew Marvell's "Had we but world enough, and time" illustrates the point. This metrical rhythm is called iambic, and the iambic foot is the most commonly employed metrical unit in the language (for additional information on metre, see the Glossary). A single line is a sort of verse sentence, and the poetic device whereby grammatical pauses and sentences are played off against line length is used frequently. The relationship in a verse line between stressed and relatively unstressed syllables is another important determinant of how poetry expresses emotion and reinforces meaning.

Good poetry varies a great deal from the strict metrical rhythm, and iambic and other stress patterns are guides rather than prescriptions for versification. In fact, whatever metre or combination of metres is used as the basis for the rhythm of a poem, some sort of controlled, purposeful variation from the metrical norm is likely. A stanza in which there is no variation ignores the expressive capacities of speech and shows, in its monotony, the dangers of excessive rhythmic regularity. Such regularity can, however, be used to advantage in a poem such as William Blake's "London" to intensify the monotonous regularity of oppressed lives—or, as at the end of George Herbert's "The Collar," to signal accommodation to faith after a period of rebellion (marked by equally disruptive rhythms). Other measuring devices besides metre have been used (and been found to work) in much modern poetry as a basis for versification.

What we call "free verse" (which emerged in the later nineteenth century) is "free" only in the sense that it has liberated itself from the traditional preference for keeping strict count of stresses and syllables—just as it redefines other notions of appropriate order, whether logical, social, linguistic, and so on. It is not without its own unit of measurement, however. The poetry in this anthology encompasses a variety of traditional and free-versification methods. While a basic knowledge of types of versification is very helpful in the understanding of poetry, it can never substitute for the reader's developing an attentive and intelligent "ear" for the pattern of sounds created in a poem. Generally, the sense of a poem becomes more readily comprehensible and memorable when the poem has been heard, either literally or through the reader's auditory imagination.

Rhythm is heard in the poetic voice that becomes more prominent with new understandings of individual identity in the Reformation and Renaissance, though Chaucer's "General Prologue" to *The Canterbury Tales* already does some justice to the individuality and diversity of the pilgrims—religious and secular, old and young, and men and women of different professions, ranks, and reputations. The speaker of a poem—that is, its voice—is the poetic equivalent of the narrator in a short story. The poet usually creates, in more or less detail, an individual speaker who has a separate creative existence. Drawing on but diverging from the conventional Italian or Petrarchan form of the sonnet and its typical topic of unrequited love, Shakespeare and his precursors (from Thomas Wyatt to Sir Philip Sidney) dramatize new, highly individualized and even argumentative voices, while elaborating new emphases and ironies in love relationships. Their treatment of earlier love traditions ranges from the subtle to the satiric anti-Petrarchan voice of Shakespeare's "My mistress' eyes are nothing like the sun." A similar pattern of conventional and anti-conventional voices and views is evident in the pastoral tradition of such poems as Christopher Marlowe's "The Passionate Shepherd to His Love" and Sir Walter Ralegh's "The Nymph's Reply to the Shepherd" and later anti-pastorals such as C. Day Lewis's "Song," or even Wordsworth's "Composed upon Westminster Bridge, 3 September 1802" or Matthew Arnold's "Dover Beach" (and Anthony Hecht's "The Dover Bitch").

With an equally strong sense of voice and dramatic presence, John Donne, Herbert, Milton, and Marvell probe the power of human reason (and its limits). In poems that are as dense as they are technically sophisticated, they explore secular and sacred themes, illuminating the abstract and philosophical through ingenious conceits. In the dramatic monologue, a kind of poem in which the speaker converses in revealing ways with a silent listener (see, for example, Robert Browning's "My Last Duchess" or T.S. Eliot's "The Love Song of J. Alfred Prufrock" or even Marvell's "To His Coy Mistress"), we find a clearly identifiable character. Others are not so obviously fictional characters, and some even seem almost indistinguishable from the poets themselves. Some speakers use a formal tone; others, informal. Some voices are prophetic, political, philosophical, or otherwise public; others are altogether private. In all cases, however, the speaker views, experiences, and interprets life to varying degrees. Our understanding of a particular poem is contingent upon our understanding of the speaker's role.

Love, death, nature, war, and religion are among the most traditional subjects chosen for poetic expression, although it is interesting to trace the ways that poetry contributes to even as it reflects changes in attitudes and emphases over time. It is equally interesting to compare poems of the same period focused on the same topic. Consider, for example, Blake and Wordsworth on London, or Marvell and Lady Mary Chudleigh on gender relations. Poets may give voice to subjects that intimately characterize their native lands and issues of identity. Canadian poets such as Sir Charles G.D. Roberts, Bliss Carman, A.J.M. Smith, and Al Purdy give the reader a sense of the vastness of the nation and its geography, often suggesting a sense of isolation. Powerful, too, are the anti-colonial sentiments of Phillis Wheatley, Derek Walcott, Wole Soyinka, Jeannette Armstrong, Louise Halfe, Marilyn Dumont, and others. As in the case of the popular ballads at the beginning of this section, such poems challenge versions of official history to change our views of Aboriginal and other oppressed peoples.

Poems may be inspired by a variety of experiences and scenes, but no subject, scene, or experience is naturally poetic. While some poems spring from an immediate experience, others owe something to the poet's reading. Some poets acknowledge the achievement of others: Bly writes about Dickinson, and Leonard Cohen addresses E.J. Pratt. In "Thoughts about the Person from Porlock," Stevie Smith makes fun of Samuel Taylor Coleridge's own account of the origins of "Kubla Khan." The "Cinderella" theme has inspired Anne Sexton and other women writers (Rich, Audre Lorde, Sylvia Plath, Marge Piercy, Margaret Atwood, Daphne Marlatt, Lorna Crozier, Halfe, among others) to rewrite the conventional myths women have had to learn about relationships and sexuality—and are supposed to retell. Pope draws on the epistolary tradition, as does Halfe later in her address to the pope or Dumont addressing Sir John A. Macdonald or Chief Lindsay Marshall addressing "Dear successive fathers." Other poems, like ballads or narrative poems (Chaucer's "General Prologue," the anonymous "Sir Patrick Spens," or "Out, Out—" by Robert Frost), tell a complete story. Frost's "Home Burial," like some of the short fiction, uses the playwright's craft of revealing character and situation through dialogue. Some poetry has a theatrical connection: Wilfred Owen's "Disabled" suggested the main plot of Irish playwright Sean O'Casey's *The Silver Tassie* (the title of which comes from a Robert Burns poem).

Some of the earlier poems, like Samuel Johnson's "On the Death of Dr. Robert Levet," were written for specific occasions. Modern poets characteristically focus on events or perceptions to which their inner-most feelings add a special significance but that are not necessarily a matter of public record. Indeed, many modern poems explore changing relations between public and private lives. Atwood's "This Is a Photograph of Me," for example, contrasts the public nature of a pho-tograph with the private sensibility that responds to it. In fact, the lyric poem, which is an intensely personal poetic expression, is now the most frequently used poetic form. The ode, the sonnet, the dramatic monologue, and the elegy are all different kinds of lyrical expression.

Poetry often makes considerable demands on the reader because it tends to concentrate and compress expression rather than offer lengthy explanations. Consequently, the reader must provide some of the con-nections and explanations that have been distilled out of the poem. For this reason, poetry is frequently both more involving and more memo-rable than prose. Readers of the poem thus become more active partic-ipants in the creative process. Poet and critic T.S. Eliot has said that poetry should communicate before it is understood. Poetry does not have to be obscure to be profound. Herbert's "The Collar" and Alden Nowlan's "Warren Pryor"—works written three centuries apart—are but two examples of poetry containing deceptively simple language that has deeper meaning than at first appears. A poem may be difficult to comprehend at first, but with several readings (and attention to the formal features as well as literary, historical, and biographical contexts), possible interpretations begin to emerge. Understanding poetry is not like solving a mathematical problem; there is not necessarily a right or a wrong way to interpret the poem. One of the fascinations of poetry is that it can stimulate discussion and controversy when readers bring dif-ferent experiences, knowledge, and preconceptions to the ideas the poet is expressing.

The meaning of a poem cannot finally be separated from the poet's diction and verse form, which are essential components in the creative process. And many of the most recent poets here ponder the language or discourses they inhabit and that inhabit them (Soyinka, Marlatt, Nourbese Philip, Halfe, Clarke). Poets best achieve concentration and compression by careful use of language, both literal and figurative. Figurative language extends the literal meaning of the work or phrase or construction in order to achieve a particular effect. When in "The Fish" Moore describes how "submerged shafts of the / sun, / split like spun / glass, move themselves with spotlight swiftness," she is using a simile to enact the optical effects of a highly specific situation in terms that connect the natural and the artificial. Nature can be the source of forced or stilted comparisons no less than culture—a point made most trenchantly in Shakespeare's famous negation, "My mistress' eyes are nothing like the sun." When Shakespeare says, in Sonnet 116, that love is "an ever-fixed mark / That looks on tempests and is never shaken," he is using a metaphor, a device with even greater potential for enriched but concise expression, one he draws from even as he subverts

Petrarchan traditions. These two figures of speech, and others, such as personification, metonymy, and synecdoche, indicate comparison or shared identity; some, such as antithesis, paradox, or oxymoron, suggest contrast or irreducible difference. Others still, such as alliteration and onomatopoeia, which are also illustrated by the quotation above from "The Fish," are based on the sound and sequencing of language. Figurative language demands that we see pictures or images of the thing being described. Imagery comprehends all aspects of poetic diction, including figurative language, connotative meanings, symbolism, and auditory impact. Consider, for example, Halfe's voice or voices connecting past and present as if, as it were, they are a performative metaphor or fable of identity. We must remember, however, that figures of speech are not an end in themselves; the mere listing of figures of speech, like their pro-forma or pedestrian employment, is a barren exercise, and students are encouraged to explore the reasons that the poet uses them and how effective the imagery is that the poet creates by that use. Critical terminology requires fuller explication than can be offered here, though you will find some basic definitions in the Glossary.

From *Beowulf*

Written between the eighth and tenth centuries and preserved in a tenth-century manuscript, this epic poem is the oldest of the long poems in English. Recording the history of the Germanic forebears of the English (the Danes and the Geats) and the heroism of Beowulf of the Geats (from Sweden), the poem draws on Christian values as well as non-Christian heroic ideals. "The Last Survivor's Speech" reflects on the treasure that is the legacy of a great clan now buried in the barrow and on the transience of earthly matter. For an imitation of Anglo-Saxon alliteration and accentual balance, see Earle Birney's "Anglosaxon Street" (p. 262).

The Last Survivor's Speech in Old English

"Heald þū nū, hrūse,   nū hæleð ne mostan,
eorla æthe!   Hwæt, hyt ær on ðē
gōde begēaton.   Guþ-dēað fornam,
2250   feorh-bealo frēcne   fyra gehwylcne
lēoda mīnra,   þāra ðe þis līf ofgeaf,
gesāwon sele-drēamas.   Nāh hwā sweord wege
oððe feormie   fæted wæge,
drync-fæt dēore;   duguð ellor scōc.
2255   Sceal se hearda helm   hyrsted golde
fætum befeallen;   feormynd swefað,
þā ðe beado-grīman   bywan sceoldon;
gē swylce sēo here-pād,   sīo æt hilde gebād
ofer borda gebræc   bite īrena,
2260   brosnað æfter beorne;   ne mæg byrnan hring
æfter wīg-fruman   wīde fēran
hæleðum be healfe.   Næs hearpan wyn
gomen glēo-bēames,   nē gōd hafoc
geond sæl swingeð,   nē se swifta mearh
2265   burh-stede bēateð.   Bealo-cwealm hafað
fela feorh-cynna   forð onsended!"

The Last Survivor's Speech[1]

For death of yore
had hurried all hence; and he alone
left to live, the last of the clan,
weeping his friends, yet wished to bide
2240 warding the treasure, his one delight,
though brief his respite. The barrow, new-ready,
to strand and sea-waves stood anear,
hard by the headland, hidden and closed;
there laid within it his lordly heirlooms
2245 and heaped hoard of heavy gold
that warden of rings. Few words he spake:

"Now hold thou, earth, since heroes may not,
what earls have owned! Lo, erst from thee
brave men brought it! But battle-death seized
2250 and cruel killing my clansmen all,
robbed them of life and a liegeman's joys.
None have I left to lift the sword,
or to cleanse the carven cup of price,
beaker bright. My brave are gone.
2255 And the helmet hard, all haughty with gold,
shall part from its plating. Polishers sleep
who could brighten and burnish the battle-mask;
and those weeds of war that were wont to brave
over bicker of shields the bite of steel
2260 rust with their bearer. The ringed mail
fares not far with famous chieftain,
at side of hero! No harp's delight,
no glee-wood's gladness! No good hawk now
flies through the hall! Nor horses fleet
2265 stamp in the burgstead! Battle and death
the flower of my race have reft away."
Mournful of mood, thus he moaned his woe,
alone, for them all, and unblithe wept
by day and by night, till death's fell wave
2270 o'erwhelmed his heart.

---

1. Translation by Frances B. Grummere; line numbers here correspond to lines of
the original.

Geoffrey Chaucer (c. 1343–1400)

Born into a prosperous merchant family in London, Geoffrey Chaucer became a page to an aristocratic household en route to a career in public service as administrator, diplomat, soldier, justice of the peace, Member of Parliament, and customs controller. Chaucer was schooled in Latin and fluent in French, turning early in his writing to French models and later to Italian models: Dante, Petrarch, and Boccaccio. In adapting French and Italian sources to native needs, Chaucer transformed English practice and helped establish English as a venerable poetic medium. The fictional frame of the pilgrimage is introduced in the General Prologue to his famous Canterbury Tales.

From *The Canterbury Tales*
The General Prologue

    Whan that April with his showres soote[1]
The droughte of March hath perced to the roote,
And bathed every veine in swich licour,
Of which vertu engendred is the flowr;
5 Whan Zephyrus[2] eek with his sweete breeth
Inspired hath in every holt and heeth[3]
The tendre croppes, and the yonge sonne[4]
Hath in the Ram his halve cours yronne,
And smale fowles maken melodye,
10 That sleepen al the night with open yë—
So priketh hem Nature in hir corages[5]—
Thanne longen folk to goon on pilgrimages,
And palmeres[6] for to seeken straunge strondes
To ferne halwes,[7] couthe in sondry londes;

---

1. Soote: fresh.
2. Zephyrus: the west wind.
3. Holt: copse or thicket; heeth: field.
4. The sun is only halfway through Aries, the Ram and first sign of the zodiac.
5. Hir corages: their hearts.
6. Palmeres: palmers, or pilgrims returning with palm branches from the "straunge strondes," or foreign shores, of the Holy Land.
7. Ferne halwes: far-off shrines.

15 And specially from every shires ende
    Of Engelond to Canterbury they wende,
    The holy blisful martyr[8] for to seeke,
    That hem hath holpen whan that they were seke.
      Bifel that in that seson on a day,
20 In Southwerk[9] at the Tabard as I lay,
    Redy to wenden on my pilgrimage
    To Canterbury with ful devout corage,
    At night was come into that hostelrye
    Wel nine and twenty in a compaignye
25 Of sondry folk, by aventure yfalle
    In felaweshipe, and pilgrimes were they alle
    That toward Canterbury wolden ride.
    The chambres and the stables weren wide,
    And wel we weren esed at the beste.
30 And shortly, whan the sonne was to reste,
    So hadde I spoken with hem everichoon
    That I was of hir felaweshipe anoon,
    And made forward[10] erly for to rise,
    To take oure way ther as I you devise.
35   But nathelees, whil I have time and space,
    Er that I ferther in this tale pace,
    Me thinketh it accordant to resoun
    To telle you al the condicioun
    Of eech of hem, so as it seemed me,
40 And whiche they were, and of what degree,[11]
    And eek in what array that they were inne:
    And at a knight thanne wol I first biginne.
      A Knight ther was, and that a worthy man,
    That fro the time that he first bigan
45 To riden out, he loved chivalrye,
    Trouthe and honour, freedom[12] and curteisye.
    Ful worthy was he in his lordes werre,
    And therto hadde he riden, no man ferre,
    As wel in Cristendom as hethenesse,
50 And evere honoured for his worthinesse.
      At Alisandre[13] he was whan it was wonne;

---

8. St. Thomas à Becket, who was murdered in Canterbury Cathedral, 1170.

9. Southwark, site of the Tabard Inn, a London suburb south of the River Thames.

10. Forward: forward planning.

11. Degree: social rank.

12. Freedom: generous spirit.

13. The Knight has battled threats to fourteenth-century Christian Europe: the Muslims at Alexandria; barbarians in Prussia, Lithuania, and Russia; and the Moors in North Africa. Battlegrounds are named in ll. 56–58.

Ful ofte time he hadde the boord bigonne[14]
Aboven alle nacions in Pruce;
In Lettou had he reised, and in Ruce,
55 No Cristen man so ofte of his degree;
In Gernade at the sege eek hadde he be
Of Algezir, and riden in Belmarye;
At Lyeis was he, and at Satalye,
Whan they were wonne; and in the Grete See[15]
60 At many a noble arivee hadde he be.
    At mortal batailes hadde he been fifteene,
And foughten for oure faith at Tramissene
In listes[16] thries, and ay slain his fo.
    This ilke worthy Knight hadde been also
65 Sometime with the lord of Palatye[17]
Again another hethen in Turkye;
And everemore he hadde a soverein pris.
And though that he were worthy, he was wis,
And of his port as meeke as is a maide.
70 He nevere yit no vilainye ne saide
In al his lif unto no manere wight:[18]
He was a verray, parfit, gentil knight.
But, for to tellen you of his array,
His hors were goode, but he was nat gay.[19]
75 Of fustian he wered a gipoun[20]
Al bismotered with his haubergeoun,[21]
For he was late come from his viage,
And wente for to doon his pilgrimage.
    With him ther was his sone, a yong Squier,[22]
80 A lovere and a lusty bacheler,
With lokkes crulle[23] as they were laid in presse.
Of twenty yeer of age he was, I gesse.
Of his stature he was of evene lengthe,
And wonderly delivere,[24] and of greet strengthe.

---

14. Taken the place of honour at military celebrations.
15. The Mediterranean.
16. Listes: tournaments.
17. Palatye: a Muslim with whom alliance was made.
18. No manere wight: any sort of person.
19. Gay: gaily dressed.
20. Gipoun: tunic worn under coat of mail.
21. Haubergeoun: hauberk or coat of mail.
22. Squier: a young knight in the service of a senior knight.
23. Crulle: curly.
24. Delivere: agile.

85 And he hadde been som time in chivachye[25]
In Flandres, in Artois, and Picardye,
And born him wel, as of so litel space,[26]
In hope to stonden in his lady grace.
    Embrouded was he as it were a mede,
90 Al ful of fresshe flowres, white and rede;
Singing he was, or floiting,[27] al the day:
He was as fressh as is the month of May.
Short was his gowne, with sleeves longe and wide.
Wel coude he sitte on hors, and faire ride;
95 He coude songes make, and wel endite,[28]
Juste and eek daunce, and wel portraye and write.
So hote he loved that by nightertale.[29]
He slepte namore than dooth a nightingale.
Curteis he was, lowely, and servisable,
100 And carf biforn his fader at the table.

. . . .

    Ther was also a Nonne, a Prioresse,
That of hir smiling was ful simple and coy.
Hir gretteste ooth was but by sainte Loy!
And she was cleped Madame Eglantine.
105 Ful weel she soong the service divine,
Entuned in hir nose ful semely;
And Frenssh she spak ful faire and fetisly,[30]
After the scole of Stratford at the Bowe[31]—
For Frenssh of Paris was to hir unknowe.
110 At mete wel ytaught was she withalle:
She leet no morsel from hir lippes falle,
Ne wette hir fingres in hir sauce deepe;
Wel coude she carye a morsel, and wel keepe
That no drope ne fille upon hir brest.
115 In curteisye was set ful muchel hir lest.[32]
Hir over-lippe wiped she so clene
That in hir coppe ther was no ferthing[33] seene

---

25. Chivachye: cavalry expeditions.
26. As of so litel space: in the short time of his service.
27. Floiting: whistling.
28. Endite: compose verse.
29. Nightertale: by night.
30. Fetisly: elegantly.
31. Stratford at the Bowe: a London suburb, where the convent school French did not meet Parisian standards.
32. In good manners she took great delight.
33. Ferthing: bit.

Of grece, whan she dronken hadde hir draughte;
Ful semely after hir mete she raughte.
120 And sikerly she was of greet disport,
And ful plesant, and amiable of port,
And pained hire to countrefete cheere
Of court, and to been statlich of manere,
And to been holden digne of reverence.
125 But, for to speken of hir conscience,
She was so charitable and so pitous
She wolde weepe if that she saw a mous
Caught in a trappe, if it were deed or bledde.
Of smale hounes hadde she that she fedde
130 With rosted flessh, or milk and wastelbreed;[34]
But sore wepte she if oon of hem were deed,
Or if men smoot it with a yerde smerte;
And al was conscience and tendre herte.
Ful semely hir wimpel pinched was,
135 Hir nose tretis, hir yën greye as glas,
Hir mouth ful smal, and therto softe and reed,
But sikerly she hadde a fair forheed:
It was almost a spanne brood,[35] I trowe,
For hardily, she was nat undergrowe.
140 Ful fetis[36] was hir cloke, as I was war;
Of smal coral aboute hir arm she bar
A paire of bedes, gauded all with greene,
And theron heeng a brooch of gold ful sheene,
On which ther was first writen a crowned A,
145 And after, *Amor vincit omnia.*[37]
      Another Nonne with hire hadde she,
That was hir chapelaine, and preestes three.

.   .   .   .

      A good Wif was ther of biside Bathe,
But she was somdeel deef, and that was scathe.
150 Of cloth-making she hadde swich an haunt,[38]
She passed hem of Ypres and of Gaunt.[39]
In al the parissh wif ne was ther noon
That to the offring bifore hire sholde goon,
And if ther dide, certain so wroth was she

---

34. Wastelbreed: fine white bread.
35. Spanne brood: handsbreadth in width.
36. Fetis: becoming.
37. Amor vincit omnia: Love conquers all. The "A" has an ornamental crown on it.
38. Haunt: skill.
39. Ypres and Ghent, Flemish centres of cloth-making.

155 That she was out of alle charitee.
Hir coverchiefs ful fine were of ground—
I dorste swere they weyeden ten pound
That on a Sonday weren upon hir heed.
Hir hosen weren of fin scarlet reed,
160 Ful straite yteyd, and shoes ful moiste and newe.
Bold was hir face and fair and reed of hewe.
She was a worthy womman al hir live:
Housbondes at chirche dore she hadde five,
Withouten other compaignye in youthe—
165 But therof needeth nought to speke as nouthe.
And thries hadde she been at Jerusalem;
She hadde passed many a straunge streem;
At Rome she hadde been, and at Boloigne,
In Galice at Saint Jame, and at Coloigne:[40]
170 She coude muchel of wandring by the waye:
Gat-toothed was she, soothly for to saye.
Upon an amblere[41] esily she sat,
Ywimpled wel, and on hir heed an hat
As brood as is a bokeler or a targe,
175 A foot-mantel aboute hir hipes large,
And on hir feet a paire of spores sharpe.
In felaweshipe wel coude she laughe and carpe:
Of remedies of love she knew parchaunce,
For she coude of that art the olde daunce.

(1387–1400)

---

40. Rome, Boulogne in France, St. James of Compostella in Spain, and Cologne in Germany were shrines visited by pilgrims.
41. Amblere: horse with easy gait.

Anonymous

Sir Patrick Spens

The king sits in Dumferling town,
    Drinking the blude-reid[1] wine:
"O whar will I get guid sailor,
    To sail this ship of mine?"

5 Up and spak an eldern knicht,
    Sat at the king's richt knee:
"Sir Patrick Spens is the best sailor
    That sails upon the sea."

The king has written a braid[2] letter
10   And signed it wi' his hand,
And sent it to Sir Patrick Spens,
    Was walking on the sand.

The first line that Sir Patrick read,
    A loud lauch[3] lauched he;
15 The next line that Sir Patrick read,
    The tear blinded his ee.

"O wha is this has done this deed,
    This ill deed done to me,
To send me out this time o' the year,
20   To sail upon the sea?

"Mak haste, mak haste, my mirry men all,
    Our guid ship sails the morn."
"O say na sae, my master dear,
    For I fear a deadly storm.

25 "Late, late yestre'en I saw the new moon
    Wi' the auld moon in hir arm,
And I fear, I fear, my dear master,
    That we will come to harm."

---

1. Blood red.
2. Literally "broad," possibly "official."
3. Laugh.

O our Scots nobles were richt laith[4]
30   To weet[5] their cork-heeled shoon,[6]
But lang or a' the play were played
        Their hats they swam aboon.[7]

O lang, lang may their ladies sit,
        Wi' their fans into their hand,
35 Or ere they see Sir Patrick Spens
        Come sailing to the land.

O lang, lang may the ladies stand
        Wi' their gold kems[8] in their hair,
Waiting for their ain dear lords,
40   For they'll see them na mair.

Half o'er, half o'er to Aberdour
        It's fifty fadom deep.
And there lies guid Sir Patrick Spens
        Wi' the Scots lords at his feet.

Lord Randal

"O where ha' you been, Lord Randal, my son?
And where ha' you been, my handsome young man?"
"I ha' been at the greenwood: mother, mak my bed soon,
For I'm wearied wi' huntin', and fain wad lie down."

5   "And wha met ye there, Lord Randal, my son?
And wha met you there, my handsome young man?"
"O I met wi' my true-love; mother, mak my bed soon,
For I'm wearied wi' huntin', and fain wad lie down."

"And what did she give you, Lord Randal, my son?
10 And what did she give you, my handsome young man?"
"Eels fried in a pan; mother, mak my bed soon,
For I'm wearied wi' huntin', and fain wad lie down."

---

4. Loath.
5. Wet.
6. Shoes.
7. Above.
8. Combs.

"And wha gat your leavin's, Lord Randal, my son?
And wha gat your leavin's, my handsome young man?"
15 "My hawks and my hounds; mother, mak my bed soon,
For I'm wearied wi' huntin', and fain wad lie down."

"And what becam of them, Lord Randal, my son?
And what becam of them, my handsome young man?"
"They stretched their legs out and died; mother, mak my bed soon,
20 For I'm wearied wi' huntin', and fain wad lie down."

"Oh I fear you are poisoned, Lord Randal, my son!
I fear you are poisoned, my handsome young man!"
"O yes, I am poisoned; mother, mak my bed soon,
For I'm sick at the heart, and I fain wad lie down."

25 "What d'ye leave to your mother, Lord Randal, my son?
What d'ye leave to your mother, my handsome young man?"
"Four and twenty milk kye;[1] mother, mak my bed soon,
For I'm sick at the heart, and I fain wad lie down."

"What d'ye leave to your sister, Lord Randal, my son?
30 What d'ye leave to your sister, my handsome young man?"
"My gold and my silver; mother, mak my bed soon,
For I'm sick at the heart, and I fain wad lie down."

"What d'ye leave to your brother, Lord Randal, my son?
What d'ye leave to your brother, my handsome young man?"
35 "My houses and my lands; mother, mak my bed soon,
For I'm sick at the heart, and I fain wad lie down."

"What d'ye leave to your true-love, Lord Randal, my son?
What d'ye leave to your true-love, my handsome young man?"
"I leave her hell and fire; mother, mak my bed soon,
40 For I'm sick at the heart, and I fain wad lie down."

1. Dairy cows.

The Twa Corbies[1]

(Version 1)

There were three ravens sat on a tree,
    Downe a downe, hay downe, hay downe
There were three ravens sat on a tree,
    With a downe
5 There were three ravens sat on a tree,
They were as blacke as they might be,
    With a downe derrie, derrie, derrie, downe, downe.

The one of them said to his mate,
"Where shall we our breakfast take?"

10 "Down in yonder greene field,
There lies a knight slain under his shield.

"His hounds they lie downe at his feete,
So well they can their master keepe.

"His haukes they flie so eagerly,
15 There's no fowle dare him come nie."

Downe there comes a fallow doe,
As great with yong as she might goe.

She lift up his bloudy hed,
And kist his wounds that were so red.

20 She got him up upon her backe,
And carried him to earthen lake.[2]

She buried him before the prime,
She was dead herself ere even-song time.

God send every gentleman
25 Such haukes, such hounds, and such a leman.[3]

---

1. Two crows.
2. Pit.
3. Sweetheart.

The Twa Corbies[1]

(Version 2)

As I was walking all alane,
I heard twa corbies making a mane;[2]
The tane[3] unto the t'other say,
"Where sall we gang and dine today?"

5   "In behint you auld fail dyke,[4]
I wot there lies a new-slain knight;
And naebody kens that he lies there,
But his hawk, his hound, and lady fair.

"His hound is to the hunting gane,
10   His hawk to fetch the wild-fowl hame,
His lady's ta'en another mate,
So we may mak our dinner sweet.

"Ye'll sit on his white hause-bane,[5]
And I'll pick out his bonny blue een;
15   Wi' ae lock o' his gowden hair
We'll theek[6] our nest when it grows bare.

"Mony a one for him makes mane,
But nane sall ken where he is gane;
O'er his white banes when they are bare,
20   The wind sall blaw for evermair."

Western Wind

Western wind, when will thou blow,
     The small rain down can rain?
Christ, if my love were in my arms
     And I in my bed again!

---

1. Two crows.
2. Moan.
3. One.
4. Old turf wall.
5. Neck.
6. Thatch.

Sir Thomas Wyatt (1503–1542)

A courtier and career diplomat, Wyatt travelled extensively in France,

Spain, the Netherlands, and Italy and is credited with introducing the Italian

sonnet form into English poetry.

They Flee from Me

They flee from me, that sometime did me seek,
With naked foot, stalking in my chamber:
I have seen them gentle, tame, and meek,
That now are wild, and do not remember
5   That sometime they put themselves in danger
To take bread at my hand; and now they range,
Busily seeking with a continual change.

Thanked be fortune, it hath been otherwise
Twenty times better; but once, in special,
10   In thin array, after a pleasant guise,
When her loose gown from her shoulders did fall,
And she me caught in her arms long and small,
Therewithal sweetly did me kiss,
And softly said, "Dear heart, how like you this?"

15   It was no dream; I lay broad waking.
But all is turned, thorough my gentleness,
Into a strange fashion of forsaking;
And I have leave to go of her goodness,
And she also to use new-fangledness.
20   But since that I so kindely[1] am served,
I would fain know what she hath deserved.

(1557)

---

1. In the normal way of women.

Description of the Contrarious Passions in a Lover

I find no peace, and all my war is done;
I fear and hope; I burn, and freeze like ice;
I fly above the wind, yet can I not arise;
And nought I have, and all the world I season.
5   That looseth nor locketh holdeth me in prison,
And holdeth me not, yet can I 'scape no wise;
Nor letteth me live, nor die, at my devise,[1]
And yet of death it giveth none occasion.
Without eyen, I see; and without tongue, I plain;
10   I desire to perish, and yet I ask for health;
I love another, and thus I hate myself;
I feed me in sorrow, and laugh in all my pain.
Likewise displeaseth me both death and life,
And my delight is causer of this strife.

(1557)

Edmund Spenser (1552–1599)

Known primarily for pastoral and love poetry, Spenser is the foremost
English non-dramatic poet of the Renaissance. His most famous work, The
Faerie Queene *(1590, 1596), is a moral allegory. The sonnets below are*
from the Amoretti, *a sonnet cycle.*

My Love Is Like to Ice

My love is like to ice, and I to fire:
How comes it then that this her cold so great
Is not dissolved through my so hot desire,
But harder grows the more I her entreat?

---

1. Will.

5　Or how comes it that my exceeding heat
　　Is not allayed by her heart-frozen cold:
　　But that I burn much more in boiling sweat,
　　And feel my flames augmented manifold?
　　What more miraculous thing may be told,
10　That fire, which all things melts, should harden ice,
　　And ice, which is congealed with senseless cold,
　　Should kindle fire by wonderful device?
　　Such is the power of love in gentle mind,
　　That it can alter all the course of kind.

(1595)

One Day I Wrote Her Name upon the Strand

One day I wrote her name upon the strand,
But came the waves and washèd it away.
Again I wrote it with a second hand,
But came the tide, and made my pains his prey.
5　Vain man, said she, that dost in vain assay
　　A mortal thing so to immortalize.

For I myself shall, like to this, decay,
And eke[1] my name be wipèd out likewise.
Not so, quoth I; let baser things devise[2]
10　To die in dust, but you shall live by fame:
　　My verse your virtues rare shall eternize,
　　And in the heavens write your glorious name.
　　Where, whenas death shall all the world subdue,
　　Our love shall live, and later life renew.

(1595)

---

1. Also.
2. Expect, plan.

Sir Walter Ralegh (c. 1552–1618)

Poet, explorer, and colonizer, Ralegh travelled extensively for the Crown in both the Old and New Worlds. His execution in 1618 followed a charge of treason. "The Nymph's Reply" is a response to Christopher Marlowe's "Passionate Shepherd," p. 132.

The Nymph's Reply to the Shepherd

If all the world and love were young
And truth in every shepherd's tongue,
These pretty pleasures might me move
To live with thee and be thy love.

5   Time drives the flocks from field to fold.
When rivers rage, and rocks grow cold,
And Philomel[1] becometh dumb;
The rest complain of cares to come.

The flowers do fade, and wanton fields
10   To wayward winter reckoning yields:
A honey tongue, a heart of gall,
Is fancy's spring, but sorrow's fall.

Thy gowns, thy shoes, thy beds of roses,
Thy cap, thy kirtle, and thy posies
15   Soon break, soon wither, soon forgotten;
In folly ripe, in reason rotten.

Thy belt of straw and ivy buds,
Thy coral clasps and amber studs,
All these in me no means can move
20   To come to thee and be thy love.

---

1. Poetic name for the nightingale.

But could youth last, and love still breed,
Had joys no date, nor age no need,
Then these delights my mind might move
To live with thee and be thy love.

(1600)

Sir Philip Sidney (1554–1586)

A courtier and soldier as well as patron of the arts and poet, Sidney is

known for his prose romance, Arcadia *(1590, 1593), which exists in two*

versions; his critical work, A Defence of Poetry *(1595); and his sonnet*

cycle, Astrophel and Stella *(1591). All of these works were published*

posthumously.

With How Sad Steps, O Moon

With how sad steps, O moon, thou climb'st the skies,
    How silently, and with how wan a face.
    What, may it be that even in heavenly place
    That busy archer[1] his sharp arrow tries?
5 Sure, if that long-with-love-acquainted eyes
    Can judge of love, thou feel'st a lover's case;
    I read it in thy looks; thy languished grace
    To me, that feel the like, thy state descries.
Then, even of fellowship, O moon, tell me,
10   Is constant love deemed there but want of wit?
    Are beauties there as proud as here they be?
Do they above love to be loved, and yet
    Those lovers scorn whom that love doth possess?
    Do they call virtue there ungratefulness?

(1591)

---

1. Cupid.

Christopher Marlowe (1564–1593)

Best known for his plays Dr. Faustus *(1604),* Tamburlaine *(1590), and*
The Jew of Malta *(1633), Marlowe is admired for his poetic as well as for*
his dramatic talent. "The Passionate Shepherd," a famous Elizabethan song,
elicits a poetic reply from Ralegh, and from C. Day Lewis. See "The Nymph's
Reply to the Shepherd," p. 130, and "Song," p. 259.

The Passionate Shepherd to His Love

Come live with me and be my love,
And we will all the pleasures prove
That valleys, groves, hills, and fields,
Woods, or steepy mountain yields.

5   And we will sit upon the rocks,
Seeing the shepherds feed their flocks,
By shallow rivers to whose falls
Melodious birds sing madrigals.

And I will make thee beds of roses
10   And a thousand fragrant posies,
A cap of flowers, and a kirtle[1]
Embroidered all with leaves of myrtle;

A gown made of the finest wool
Which from our pretty lambs we pull;
15   Fair lined slippers for the cold,
With buckles of the purest gold;

A belt of straw and ivy buds,
With coral clasps and amber studs:
And if these pleasures may thee move,
20   Come live with me, and be my love.

---

1. Gown.

The shepherd swains shall dance and sing
For thy delight each May morning:
If these delights thy mind may move,
Then live with me and be my love.

(1599)

William Shakespeare (1564–1616)

Dramatist, poet, and actor, Shakespeare is the best-known writer in the

English language. His Sonnets *(1609), which can be numbered with the*

finest poems in any language, exhibit various recurrent motifs of love,

beauty, and poetry.

Sonnet 18

Shall I compare thee to a summer's day?
Thou art more lovely and more temperate.
Rough winds do shake the darling buds of May,
And summer's lease[1] hath all too short a date.
5   Sometime too hot the eye of heaven shines,
And often is his gold complexion dimmed;
And every fair from fair sometime declines,
By chance, or nature's changing course, untrimmed;[2]
But thy eternal summer shall not fade,

---

1. Allotted time.
2. Stripped of ornament (*O.E.D.*), but also includes the sense of "trimming" a ship's sails to control its course.

10 Nor lose possession of that fair thou owest,[3]
    Nor shall death brag thou wanderest in his shade,[4]
    When in eternal lines to time thou growest.
    So long as men can breathe or eyes can see,
    So long lives this, and this gives life to thee.

                                                    (1609)

Sonnet 29

    When in disgrace with fortune and men's eyes
    I all alone beweep my outcast state,
    And trouble deaf heaven with my bootless[1] cries,
    And look upon myself, and curse my fate,
5   Wishing me like to one more rich in hope,
    Featured like him, like him with friends possessed,
    Desiring this man's art, and that man's scope,
    With what I most enjoy contented least;
    Yet in these thoughts myself almost despising,
10 Haply I think on thee, and then my state,
    Like to the lark at break of day arising
    From sullen earth, sings hymns at heaven's gate;
    For thy sweet love remembered such wealth brings
    That then I scorn to change my state with kings.

                                                    (1609)

Sonnet 116

    Let me not to the marriage of true minds
    Admit impediments. Love is not love
    Which alters when it alteration finds,
    Or bends with the remover to remove.
5   Oh, no! It is an ever-fixèd mark
    That looks on tempests and is never shaken.
    It is the star to every wand'ring bark,
    Whose worth's unknown, although his height be taken.
    Love's not Time's fool, though rosy lips and cheeks

---

3. Ownest.

4. Oblivion.

1. Useless, futile.

10   Within his bending sickle's compass come;
Love alters not with his brief hours and weeks,
But bears it out even to the edge of doom.
If this be error, and upon me proved,
I never writ, nor no man ever loved.

(1609)

Sonnet 130

My mistress' eyes are nothing like the sun;
Coral is far more red than her lips' red:
If snow be white, why then her breasts are dun;
If hairs be wires, black wires grow on her head.
5   I have seen roses damask'd,[1] red and white,
But no such roses see I in her cheeks;
And in some perfumes is there more delight
Than in the breath that from my mistress reeks.
I love to hear her speak, yet well I know
10   That music hath a far more pleasing sound:
I grant I never saw a goddess go;
My mistress, when she walks, treads on the ground:
And yet, by heaven, I think my love as rare
As any she belied[2] with false compare.

(1609)

---

1. Variegated.
2. Misrepresented.

John Donne (1572–1631)

Donne is usually identified with a group of poets known as the
Metaphysicals, including George Herbert, Richard Crashaw, Henry Vaughan,
Andrew Marvell, and Thomas Traherne, whose poetic images are sustained
by contrast and paradox. His themes are both religious and secular.

A Valediction Forbidding Mourning

As virtuous men pass mildly away,
    And whisper to their souls to go,
Whilst some of their sad friends do say,
    The breath goes now, and some say, no;

5   So let us melt and make no noise,
    No tear-floods nor sigh-tempests move;
'Twere profanation of our joys
    To tell the laity our love.

Moving of th'earth brings harms and fears;
10   Men reckon what it did and meant;
But trepidation of the spheres,
    Though greater far, is innocent.

Dull sublunary[1] lovers' love,
    Whose soul is sense, cannot admit
15 Absence, because it doth remove
    Those things which elemented it.

But we, by a love so much refined
    That ourselves know not what it is,
Inter-assurèd of the mind,
20   Care less eyes, lips, hands to miss.

Our two souls, therefore, which are one,
    Though I must go, endure not yet
A breach, but an expansion,
    Like gold to airy thinness beat.

---

1. Earthly.

25 If they be two, they are two so
        As stiff twin compasses are two;
Thy soul, the fixed foot, makes no show
        To move, but doth if th'other do.

And though it in the centre sit,
30   Yet when the other far doth roam,
It leans, and hearkens after it,
        And grows erect as that comes home.

Such wilt thou be to me, who must
        Like th'other foot, obliquely run:
35 Thy firmness makes my circle just,
        And makes me end where I begun.

(1633)

The Sun Rising

        Busy old fool, unruly sun,
        Why dost thou thus
Through windows and through curtains call on us?
Must to thy motions lovers' seasons run?
5   Saucy pedantic wretch, go chide
        Late schoolboys and sour prentices,
    Go tell court-huntsmen that the king will ride,
    Call country ants to harvest offices;
Love, all alike, no season knows, nor clime,
10 Nor hours, days, months, which are the rags of time.

        Thy beams, so reverend, and strong
        Why shouldst thou think?
I could eclipse and cloud them with a wink,
But that I would not lose her sight so long;
15   If her eyes have not blinded thine,
        Look, and tomorrow late tell me
    Whether both the Indias[1] of spice and mine
    Be where thou left'st them, or lie here with me.
Ask for those kings whom thou saw'st yesterday,
20 And thou shalt hear, all here in one bed lay.

---

1. Both India and the West Indies, noted, respectively, for spices and for gold.

NEL

> She is all states, and all princes I;
>   Nothing else is.
> Princes do but play us; compared to this,
> All honor's mimic, all wealth alchemy.[2]

25   Thou, sun, art half as happy as we,
>   In that the world's contracted thus;
>   Thine age asks ease, and since thy duties be
>   To warm the world, that's done in warming us.
> Shine here to us, and thou art everywhere;
30 This bed thy centre is, these walls thy sphere.

(1633)

Death, Be Not Proud (Holy Sonnet X)

Death, be not proud, though some have called thee
Mighty and dreadful, for thou art not so.
For those whom thou think'st thou dost overthrow
Die not, poor death; nor yet canst thou kill me.
5 From rest and sleep, which but thy pictures be,
Much pleasure; then from thee much more must flow;
And soonest our best men with thee do go,
Rest of their bones, and soul's delivery.
Thou'rt slave to fate, chance, kings, and desperate men,
10 And dost with poison, war, and sickness dwell;
And poppy or charms can make us sleep as well
And better than thy stroke. Why swell'st thou then?
One short sleep past, we wake eternally,
And death shall be no more: Death, thou shalt die.

(1633)

---

2. That is, a fraud.

Ben Jonson (c. 1572–1637)

Jonson wrote plays, poetry, and court masques and enjoyed both reputation and influence. A friend of Shakespeare and Donne and a court favourite, Jonson had a following of younger poets who styled themselves as the "sons of Ben."

On My First Son

Farewell, thou child of my right hand,[1] and joy.
My sin was too much hope of thee, loved boy;
Seven years thou wert lent to me, and I thee pay,
Exacted by thy fate, on the just day.
5   Oh, could I lose all father[2] now. For why
Will man lament the state he should envy?—
To have so soon 'scaped world's and flesh's rage,
And, if no other misery, yet age.
Rest in soft peace, and, asked, say here doth lie
10 Ben Jonson his best piece of poetry.
For whose sake, henceforth, all his vows be such
As what he loves may never like too much.

(*1616*)

---

1. The English translation of the Hebrew name "Benjamin." Jonson's son, Benjamin, died in 1603 on his seventh birthday, during a plague epidemic.
2. All fatherly qualities.

George Herbert (1593–1633)

Herbert wrote short, highly structured poems, some of which are shaped verses.
They are almost all devotional and they trace, in Herbert's words, "a picture of
the many spiritual conflicts that have passed betwixt God and my soul."

The Collar

        I struck the board and cried, No more!
              I will abroad.
        What? Shall I ever sigh and pine?
      My lines and life are free, free as the road,
5   Loose as the wind, as large as store.¹
            Shall I be still in suit?²
        Have I no harvest but a thorn
        To let me blood, and not restore
      What I have lost with cordial³ fruit?
10   Sure there was wine
       Before my sighs did dry it; there was corn
         Before my tears did drown it.
       Is the year only lost to me?
         Have I no bays⁴ to crown it?
15 No flowers, no garlands gay? All blasted?
            All wasted?
       No so, my heart! But there is fruit,
          And thou hast hands.
        Recover all thy sigh-blown age
20 On double pleasures. Leave thy cold dispute
    Of what is fit and not. Forsake thy cage,
          Thy rope of sands,
   Which petty thoughts have made, and made to thee
       Good cable, to enforce and draw,
25   And be thy law,
     While thou didst wink and wouldst not see.
         Away! Take heed!
         I will abroad.

---

1. Abundance.
2. Obligation.
3. Comforting, cheering.
4. A garland of laurel, symbolizing honour.

Call in thy death's head[5] there. Tie up thy fears.
30   He that forbears
              To suit and serve his need
              Deserves his load.
But as I raved and grew more fierce and wild
              At every word,
35   Me thoughts I heard one calling, Child!
              And I replied, My Lord.

(1633)

Easter Wings

Lord, who createdst man in wealth and store,[1]
Though foolishly he lost[2] the same,
Decaying more and more,
Till he became
5   Most poor:
       With thee
       O let me rise
As larks, harmoniously,
And sing this day thy victories:
10   Then shall the fall further the flight in me.

My tender age in sorrow did begin;
And still with sicknesses and shame
Thou didst so punish sin,
That I became
15   Most thin.
       With thee
       Let me combine,
And feel this day thy victory;
For, if I imp[3] my wing on thine,
20   Affliction shall advance the flight in me.

(1633)

5. A skull, symbolizing mortality.

1. Abundance.

2. Through the Fall.

3. The injured wings of falcons were strengthened by imping (grafting on) new feathers.

John Milton (1608–1674)

Milton was the most eminent Puritan poet of the seventeenth century. His

major works—Paradise Lost (1667), Paradise Regained (1671), and

Samson Agonistes (1671)—were all written after the poet lost his sight in

1652. "When I Consider How My Light Is Spent" attempts an intellectual

and spiritual reconciliation with his blindness.

When I Consider How My Light Is Spent

When I consider how my light is spent,
Ere half my days, in this dark world and wide,
And that one talent[1] which is death to hide
Lodged with me useless, though my soul more bent
5 To serve therewith my Maker, and present
My true account, lest he returning chide;
"Doth God exact day labour, light denied?"
I fondly[2] ask; but Patience, to prevent
That murmur, soon replies: "God doth not need
10 Either man's work or his own gifts; who best
Bear his mild yoke, they serve him best. His state
Is kingly: thousands at his bidding speed
And post[3] o'er land and ocean without rest.
They also serve who only stand and wait."

(1673)

---

1. See the Parable of the Talents, Matt. 25:14–30.
2. Foolishly.
3. Travel quickly.

From *Paradise Lost*

BOOK 1

Of man's first disobedience, and the fruit
Of that forbidden tree whose mortal taste
Brought death into the world, and all our woe,
With loss of Eden, till one greater Man[1]
5 Restore us, and regain the blissful seat,
Sing, Heavenly Muse,[2] that on the secret top
Of Oreb, or of Sinai, didst inspire
That shepherd who first taught the chosen seed
In the beginning how the heavens and earth
10 Rose out of Chaos: or, if Sion hill
Delight thee more, and Siloa's brook that flowed
Fast by the oracle of God, I thence
Invoke thy aid to my adventurous song,
That with no middle flight intends to soar
15 Above th' Aonian mount,[3] while it pursues
Things unattempted yet in prose or rhyme.
And chiefly thou, O Spirit,[4] that dost prefer
Before all temples th' upright heart and pure,
Instruct me, for thou know'st; thou from the first
20 Wast present, and with mighty wings outspread
Dovelike sat'st brooding[5] on the vast abyss,
And mad'st it pregnant: what in me is dark
Illumine; what is low, raise and support;
That to the height of this great argument
25 I may assert Eternal Providence,
And justify the ways of God to men.

Say first (for Heaven hides nothing from thy view,
Nor the deep tract of Hell) say first what cause

---

1. Christ, the second Adam.

2. Urania, Muse of astronomy, but the references to Oreb and Sinai suggest the Holy Spirit of the Bible, which inspired Moses to write Genesis and the other four books of the Pentateuch.

3. "Th' Aonian mount": Helicon, home of the Muses. The line "Things unattempted yet in prose or rhyme" translates a line from Ariosto's *Orlando Furioso*.

4. The Spirit is an impulse of God, inspiring the Hebrew prophets.

5. Milton's words echo Genesis 1.2 ("And the earth was without form, and void; and darkness was upon the face of the deep. And the Spirit of God moved upon the face of the waters"); Matthew 3.16 ("and he saw the Spirit of God descending like a dove, and lighting upon him"); and Luke 3.22 ("and the Holy Ghost descended in a bodily shape like a dove upon him").

Moved our grand parents, in that happy state,
30 Favored of Heaven so highly, to fall off
From their Creator, and transgress his will
For one restraint, lords of the world besides?
Who first seduced them to that foul revolt?

Th' infernal serpent; he it was, whose guile,
35 Stirred up with envy and revenge, deceived
The mother of mankind, what time his pride
Had cast him out from Heaven, with all his host
Of rebel angels, by whose aid aspiring
To set himself in glory above his peers,
40 He trusted to have equaled the Most High,
If he opposed; and with ambitious aim
Against the throne and monarchy of God
Raised impious war in Heaven and battle proud,
With vain attempt. Him the Almighty Power
45 Hurled headlong flaming from th' ethereal sky
With hideous ruin and combustion down
To bottomless perdition, there to dwell
In adamantine chains and penal fire,
Who durst defy th' Omnipotent to arms.

50 Nine times the space that measures day and night
To mortal men, he with his horrid crew
Lay vanquished, rowling in the fiery gulf
Confounded though immortal. But his doom
Reserved him to more wrath; for now the thought
55 Both of lost happiness and lasting pain
Torments him; round he throws his baleful eyes,
That witnessed huge affliction and dismay,
Mixed with obdùrate pride and steadfast hate.
At once, as far as angel's ken, he views
60 The dismal situation waste and wild:
A dungeon horrible, on all sides round
As one great furnace flamed; yet from those flames
No light, but rather darkness visible
Served only to discover sights of woe,
65 Regions of sorrow, doleful shades, where peace
And rest can never dwell, hope never comes
That comes to all,[6] but torture without end
Still urges,[7] and a fiery deluge, fed
With ever-burning sulphur unconsumed:

---

6. The phrase echoes an expression in Dante ("All hope abandon, ye who enter here").

7. Afflicts.

70 Such place Eternal Justice had prepared
For those rebellious; here their prison ordained
In utter darkness and their portion set
As far removed from God and light of Heaven
As from the center thrice to th' utmost pole.[8]
75 Oh how unlike the place from whence they fell!
There the companions of his fall, o'erwhelmed
With floods and whirlwinds of tempestuous fire,
He soon discerns; and, weltering by his side,
One next himself in power, and next in crime,
80 Long after known in Palestine, and named
Beëlzebub.[9] To whom th' arch-enemy,
And thence in Heaven called Satan,[10] with bold words
Breaking the horrid silence, thus began:

"If thou beëst he—but O how fallen! how changed
85 From him who in the happy realms of light
Clothed with transcendent brightness didst outshine
Myriads, though bright! if he whom mutual league,
United thoughts and counsels, equal hope
And hazard in the glorious enterprise,
90 Joined with me once, now misery hath joined
In equal ruin; into what pit thou seest
From what height fallen, so much the stronger proved
He with his thunder:[11] and till then who knew
The force of those dire arms? Yet not for those,
95 Nor what the potent Victor in his rage
Can else inflict, do I repent or change,
Though changed in outward luster, that fixed mind
And high disdain, from sense of injured merit,
That with the Mightiest raised me to contend,
100 And to the fierce contention brought along
Innumerable force of spirits armed,
That durst dislike his reign, and me preferring,
His utmost power with adverse power opposed
In dubious battle on the plains of Heaven,
105 And shook his throne. What though the field be lost?
All is not lost: the unconquerable will,
And study of revenge, immortal hate,

---

8. The earth is the centre of the Ptolemaic cosmos of ten concentric spheres, but the earth and the whole created cosmos are also a mere appendage, hanging from Heaven by a golden chain. The fall from Heaven to Hell is described as thrice as far as the distance from the centre to the outermost sphere.

9. The devil, or Lord of the Flies.

10. Hebrew for adversary.

11. God with his thunderbolts.

And courage never to submit or yield:
And what is else not to be overcome?
110 That glory never shall his wrath or might
Extort from me. To bow and sue for grace
With suppliant knee, and deify his power
Who, from the terror of this arm so late
Doubted his empire—that were low indeed;
115 That were an ignominy and shame beneath
This downfall; since, by fate, the strength of gods
And this empyreal substance cannot fail;[12]
Since, through experience of this great event,
In arms not worse, in foresight much advanced,
120 We may with more successful hope resolve
To wage by force or guile eternal war,
Irreconcilable to our grand Foe,
Who now triumphs, and in th' excess of joy
Sole reigning holds the tyranny of Heaven."

BOOK 5

(Eve's Dream: Trouble in Paradise)

Now Morn her rosy steps in th' eastern clime
Advancing, sowed the earth with orient pearl,
When Adam waked, so customed, for his sleep
Was airy light, from pure digestion bred
5 And temperate vapors bland, which the only sound
Of leaves and fuming rills, Aurora's fan,[13]
Lightly dispersed, and the shrill matin song
Of birds on every bough; so much the more
His wonder was to find unwakened Eve
10 With tresses discomposed and glowing cheek
As through unquiet rest; he on his side
Leaning half-raised with looks of cordial love
Hung over her enamored, and beheld
Beauty which whether waking or asleep
15 Shot forth peculiar graces; then with voice
Mild as when Zephyrus on Flora[14] breathes,
Her hand soft touching, whispered thus. "Awake,

---

12. Satan's substance is "empyreal" (heavenly) and cannot be destroyed, but he learns it can be confounded by God's greater power and corrupted by his own contradictions.

13. The fan of Aurora (goddess of dawn) is the rustling leaves; the "orient pearl" is dewdrops.

14. Zephyrus is god of the west wind, Flora goddess of flowers.

My fairest, my espoused, my latest found,
Heaven's last best gift, my ever new delight,
20 Awake, the morning shines, and the fresh field
Calls us: we lose the prime, to mark how spring
Our tended plants, how blows the citron grove,
What drops the myrrh and what the balmy reed,
How nature paints her colors, how the bee
25 Sits on the bloom extracting liquid sweet."

Such whispering waked her, but with startled eye
On Adam, whom embracing, thus she spake:

"O sole in whom my thoughts find all repose,
My glory, my perfection, glad I see
30 Thy face, and morn returned, for I this night—
Such night till this I never passed—have dreamed,
If dreamed, not as I oft am wont, of thee,
Works of day past or morrow's next design,
But of offense and trouble, which my mind
35 Knew never till this irksome night. Methought
Close at mine ear one called me forth to walk
With gentle voice; I thought it thine; it said,
'Why sleep'st thou, Eve? Now is the pleasant time,
The cool, the silent, save where silence yields
40 To the night-warbling bird, that now awake
Tunes sweetest his love-labored song; now reigns
Full-orbed the moon, and with more pleasing light
Shadowy sets off the face of things—in vain
If none regard. Heaven wakes with all his eyes,
45 Whom to behold but thee, nature's desire,
In whose sight all things joy with ravishment
Attracted by thy beauty still to gaze.'
I rose as at thy call, but found thee not;
To find thee I directed then my walk;
50 And on, methought, alone I passed through ways
That brought me on a sudden to the tree
Of interdicted knowledge: fair it seemed,
Much fairer to my fancy than by day;
And as I wondering looked, beside it stood
55 One shaped and winged like one of those from Heaven
By us oft seen. His dewy locks distilled
Ambrosia;[15] on that tree he also gazed:
And 'O fair plant,' said he, 'with fruit surcharged,
Deigns none to ease thy load and taste thy sweet,

---

15. The food of the gods.

60 Nor god nor man? is knowledge so despised?
Or envy or what reserve forbids to taste?
Forbid who will, none shall from me withhold
Longer thy offered good, why else set here?'
This said, he paused not, but with venturous arm
65 He plucked, he tasted; me damp horror chilled
At such bold words vouched with a deed so bold.
But he thus overjoyed: 'O fruit divine,
Sweet of thyself, but much more sweet thus cropped,
Forbidden here, it seems, as only fit
70 For gods, yet able to make gods of men:
And why not gods of men, since good, the more
Communicated, more abundant grows,
The author not impaired, but honored more?
Here, happy creature, fair angelic Eve,
75 Partake thou also; happy though thou art,
Happier thou may'st be, worthier canst not be.
Taste this, and be henceforth among the gods
Thyself a goddess, not to earth confined,
But sometimes in the air, as we, sometimes
80 Ascend to Heaven, by merit thine, and see
What life the gods live there, and such live thou.'
So saying, he drew nigh, and to me held,
Even to my mouth of that same fruit held part
Which he had plucked; the pleasant savory smell
85 So quickened appetite that I, methought,
Could not but taste. Forthwith up to the clouds
With him I flew, and underneath beheld
The earth outstretched immense, a prospect wide
And various: wondering at my flight and change
90 To this high exaltation, suddenly
My guide was gone, and I, methought, sunk down
And fell asleep. But O how glad I waked
To find this but a dream!" Thus Eve her night
Related, and thus Adam answered sad:

95 "Best image of myself and dearer half,
The trouble of thy thoughts this night in sleep
Affects me equally; nor can I like
This uncouth dream, of evil sprung, I fear;
Yet evil whence? In thee can harbor none,
100 Created pure. But know that in the soul
Are many lesser faculties that serve
Reason as chief; among these fancy next
Her office holds. Of all external things
Which the five watchful senses represent,
105 She forms imaginations, airy shapes

Which reason, joining or disjoining, frames
All what we affirm or what deny, and call
Our knowledge or opinion; then retires
Into her private cell when nature rests.
110 Oft in her absence mimic fancy wakes
To imitate her; but, misjoining shapes,
Wild work produces oft, and most in dreams,
Ill matching words and deeds long past or late.
Some such resemblances methinks I find
115 Of our last evening's talk in this thy dream,
But with addition strange. Yet be not sad,
Evil into the mind of god or man
May come and go, so unapproved, and leave
No spot or blame behind; which gives me hope
120 That what in sleep thou didst abhor to dream,
Waking thou never wilt consent to do.
Be not disheartened then, nor cloud those looks
That wont to be more cheerful and serene
Than when fair morning first smiles on the world;
125 And let us to our fresh employments rise
Among the groves, the fountains, and the flowers
That open now their choicest bosomed smells
Reserved from night, and kept for thee in store."

So cheered he his fair spouse, and she was cheered,
130 But silently a gentle tear let fall
From either eye, and wiped them with her hair;
Two other precious drops that ready stood,
Each in their crystal sluice, he ere they fell
Kissed as the gracious signs of sweet remorse
135 And pious awe that feared to have offended.

(1667, 1674)

Anne Bradstreet (c. 1612–1672)

Bradstreet, an American poet who was born in England, moved to Massachusetts in 1630. A devout Puritan, she combined theological and domestic themes in her poetry and produced the first volume of verse in America, The Tenth Muse Lately Sprung Up in America *(1650).*

To My Dear and Loving Husband

If ever two were one, then surely we.
If ever man were loved by wife, then thee;
If ever wife was happy in a man,
Compare with me, ye women, if you can.
5   I prize thy love more than whole mines of gold,
Or all the riches that the East doth hold.
My love is such that rivers cannot quench,
Nor aught but love from thee give recompense.
Thy love is such I can no way repay,
10   The heavens reward thee manifold, I pray.
Then while we live, in love let's so perséver
That when we live no more, we may live ever.

(1678)

Richard Lovelace (1618–1658)

Richard Lovelace was a wealthy and talented courtier, soldier, and poet who became involved in the political strife of the English Civil War. Loyal to the king, he presented to Parliament a petition deemed seditious and was imprisoned. "To Althea, from Prison" is thought to have been written during his imprisonment.

To Althea, from Prison

When Love with unconfinèd wings
    Hovers within my gates,
And my divine Althea brings
    To whisper at the grates;
5 When I lie tangled in her hair,
    And fettered to her eye,
The gods[1] that wanton[2] in the air
    Know no such liberty.

When flowing cups run swiftly round
10   With no allaying Thames,[3]
Our careless heads with roses bound,
    Our hearts with loyal flames;
When thirsty grief in wine we steep,
    When healths and draughts go free,
15 Fishes that tipple in the deep
    Know no such liberty.

When, like committed[4] linnets, I
    With shriller throat shall sing
The sweetness, mercy, majesty,
20   And glories of my King;
When I shall voice aloud, how good
    He is, how great should be,
Enlargèd[5] winds that curl the flood
    Know no such liberty.

25 Stone walls do not a prison make,
    Nor iron bars a cage;
Minds innocent and quiet take
    That for an hermitage;
If I have freedom in my love,
30   And in my soul am free,
Angels alone that soar above
    Enjoy such liberty.

(1649)

---

1. Most seventeenth-century printings of this poem substitute "birds" for "gods."
2. Play.
3. That is, with no water to dilute them.
4. Caged.
5. Freed, unconfined.

Andrew Marvell (1621–1678)

Known during his lifetime as a satirist and a patriot, Marvell, Member of
Parliament for Hull in northern England from 1659 to his death, is recog-
nized today as a political and lyric poet of considerable skill. His lyric
poems were published three years after his death.

To His Coy Mistress

      Had we but world enough, and time,
This coyness, lady, were no crime.
We would sit down, and think which way
To walk, and pass our long love's day.
5   Thou by the Indian Ganges' side
Shouldst rubies[1] find; I by the tide
Of Humber[2] would complain. I would
Love you ten years before the flood,
And you should, if you please, refuse
10 Till the conversion of the Jews.[3]
My vegetable love should grow
Vaster than empires and more slow;
An hundred years should go to praise
Thine eyes, and on thy forehead gaze;
15 Two hundred to adore each breast,
But thirty thousand to the rest;
An age at least to every part,
And the last age should show your heart.
For, lady, you deserve this state,
20 Nor would I love at lower rate.
      But at my back I always hear
Time's wingèd chariot[4] hurrying near;
And yonder all before us lie
Deserts of vast eternity.

---

1. Because of its colour, the ruby reputedly removed evil thoughts, banished sadness, gave protection against the plague, and controlled amorous desires.
2. River in northern England.
3. Christians in Marvell's time believed that the conversion of the Jews to
   Christianity would be the final historical event before the Second Coming of
   Christ and the Last Judgment.
4. Apollo, the sun god, drove a winged chariot, one of whose steeds was Chronos
   (time).

25 Thy beauty shall no more be found;
Nor, in thy marble vault, shall sound
My echoing song; then worms shall try
That long-preserved virginity,
And your quaint honour turn to dust,
30 And into ashes all my lust:
The grave's a fine and private place,
But none, I think, do there embrace.
       Now therefore, while the youthful hue
Sits on thy skin like morning dew,
35 And while thy willing soul transpires
At every pore with instant fires,
Now let us sport us while we may,
And now, like amorous birds of prey,
Rather at once our time devour
40 Than languish in his slow-chapped[5] power.
Let us roll all our strength and all
Our sweetness up into one ball,
And tear our pleasures with rough strife
Thorough the iron gates of life:
45 Thus, though we cannot make our sun
Stand still, yet we will make him run.

(1681)

Aphra Behn (c. 1640–1689)

English playwright, novelist, and poet Aphra Behn was the first professional woman writer in England. "Forced to write for Bread, and not ashamed to own it," Behn was possibly unable to do justice to her poetic gifts, which did not bring the money that drama and novels did.

---

5. Slow-jawed (i.e., slowly devouring).

A Thousand Martyrs I Have Made

A thousand martyrs I have made,
    All sacrific'd to my desire;
A thousand beauties have betray'd,
    That languish in resistless fire.
5   The untam'd heart to hand I brought,
And fixed the wild and wandering thought.

I never vow'd nor sigh'd in vain,
    But both, tho' false, were well receiv'd.
The fair are pleas'd to give us pain,
10   And what they wish is soon believ'd.
And tho' I talk'd of wounds and smart,
Love's pleasures only touched my heart.

Alone the glory and the spoil
    I always laughing bore away;
15 The triumphs, without pain or toil,
    Without the hell, the heav'n of joy.
And while I thus at random rove
Despis'd the fools that whine for love.

(1688)

Lady Mary Chudleigh (1656–1710)

Chudleigh's unusually advanced views on women are suggested by both the poem below and the title of her 1701 publication, The Female Advocate: Or a Plea for the Just Liberty of the Tender Sex and Particularly of Married Women.

To the Ladies

Wife and servant are the same,
But only differ in the name:
For when the fatal knot is tied,

Which nothing, nothing can divide:
5   When she the word *obey* has said,
And man by law supreme has made,
Then all that's kind[1] is laid aside,
And nothing left but state[2] and pride:
Fierce as an Eastern prince he grows,
10   And all his innate rigour shows:
Then but to look, to laugh, or speak,
Will the nuptial contract break.
Like mutes she signs alone must make,
And never any freedom take:
15   But still be governed by a nod,
And fear her husband as her God:
Him still must serve, him still obey,
And nothing act, and nothing say,
But what her haughty lord thinks fit,
20   Who with the power, has all the wit.
Then shun, oh! shun that wretched state,
And all the fawning flatt'rers hate:
Value your selves, and men despise,
You must be proud, if you'll be wise.

(1703)

Anne Finch (1661–1720)

Anne Finch, Countess of Winchilsea, wrote her poetry from an estate in Kent, England. Her poetic observations of nature led William Wordsworth to admire her writing. She was acutely aware of the restrictions placed on women. Miscellany Poems on Several Occasions *appeared anonymously in 1713 and was reissued with her name in 1714.*

---

1. Natural.
2. Pomp.

The Unequal Fetters

Could we stop the time that's flying
    Or recall it when 'tis past,
Put far off the day of dying
    Or make youth for ever last,
5   To love would then be worth our cost.

But since we must lose those graces
    Which at first your hearts have won
And you seek for in new faces
    When our spring of life is done,
10   It would but urge our ruin on.

Free as Nature's first intention
    Was to make us, I'll be found,
Nor by subtle man's invention
    Yield to be in fetters bound
15   By one that walks a freer round.

Marriage does but slightly tie men
    Whilst close prisoners we remain,
They the larger slaves of Hymen[1]
    Still are begging love again
20   At the full length of all their chain.

(1713)

Alexander Pope (1688–1744)

Pope's Essay on Criticism *(1711), the poet's first success, brought forth his metrical virtuosity, but* The Rape of the Lock *(1712) earned his reputation as an urbane and witty satirist. Pope's satirical voice could be as vicious as it was funny.*

---

1. Greek god of marriage.

From *An Essay on Criticism*

PART 1

'Tis hard to say, if greater want of skill
Appear in writing or in judging ill;
But of the two less dangerous is the offense
To tire our patience than mislead our sense.
5 Some few in that, but numbers err in this,
Ten censure wrong for one who writes amiss;
A fool might once himself alone expose,
Now one in verse makes many more in prose.

'Tis with our judgments as our watches, none
10 Go just alike, yet each believes his own.
In poets as true genius is but rare,
True taste as seldom is the critic's share;
Both must alike from Heaven derive their light,
These born to judge, as well as those to write.
15 Let such teach others who themselves excel,
And censure freely who have written well.
Authors are partial to their wit, 'tis true,
But are not critics to their judgment too?

Yet if we look more closely, we shall find
20 Most have the seeds of judgment in their mind:
Nature affords at least a glimmering light;
The lines, though touched but faintly, are drawn right.
But as the slightest sketch, if justly traced,
Is by ill coloring but the more disgraced,
25 So by false learning is good sense defaced:
Some are bewildered in the maze of schools,
And some made coxcombs Nature meant but fools.
In search of wit these lose their common sense,
And then turn critics in their own defense:
30 Each burns alike, who can, or cannot write,
Or with a rival's or an eunuch's spite.
All fools have still an itching to deride,
And fain would be upon the laughing side.
If Mævius[1] scribble in Apollo's spite,
35 There are who judge still worse than he can write.

---

1. A poet disdained by Virgil in *Eclogue* 3 and by Horace in *Epode* 10.

Some have at first for wits, then poets passed,
Turned critics next, and proved plain fools at last.
Some neither can for wits nor critics pass,
As heavy mules are neither horse nor ass.
40 Those half-learn'd witlings, numerous in our isle,
As half-formed insects on the banks of Nile;[2]
Unfinished things, one knows not what to call,
Their generation's so equivocal:
To tell them would a hundred tongues require,
45 Or one vain wit's, that might a hundred tire.

But you who seek to give and merit fame,
And justly bear a critic's noble name,
Be sure yourself and your own reach to know,
How far your genius, taste, and learning go;
50 Launch not beyond your depth, but be discreet,
And mark that point where sense and dullness meet.

Nature to all things fixed the limits fit,
And wisely curbed proud man's pretending wit.
As on the land while here the ocean gains,
55 In other parts it leaves wide sandy plains;
Thus in the soul while memory prevails,
The solid power of understanding fails;
Where beams of warm imagination play,
The memory's soft figures melt away.
60 One science only will one genius fit,
So vast is art, so narrow human wit.
Not only bounded to peculiar arts,
But oft in those confined to single parts.
Like kings we lose the conquests gained before,
65 By vain ambition still to make them more;
Each might his several province well command,
Would all but stoop to what they understand.

First follow Nature, and your judgment frame
By her just standard, which is still the same;
70 Unerring Nature, still divinely bright,
One clear, unchanged, and universal light,
Life, force, and beauty must to all impart,
At once the source, and end, and test of art.
Art from that fund each just supply provides,
75 Works without show, and without pomp presides.
In some fair body thus the informing soul
With spirits feeds, with vigor fills the whole,

---

2. The ancients believed forms of life were generated in the mud of the Nile.

Each motion guides, and every nerve sustains;
Itself unseen, but in the effects remains.
80 Some, to whom Heaven in wit has been profuse,
Want as much more to turn it to its use;
For wit and judgment often are at strife,
Though meant each other's aid, like man and wife.
'Tis more to guide than spur the Muse's steed,
85 Restrain his fury than provoke his speed;
The wingèd courser, like a generous horse,
Shows most true mettle when you check his course.

Those rules of old discovered, not devised,
Are Nature still, but Nature methodized;
90 Nature, like liberty, is but restrained
By the same laws which first herself ordained.

(1711)

From *An Essay on Man*
From *Epistle 2. Of the Nature and State of Man with Respect to Himself, as an Individual*

Know then thyself, presume not God to scan;
The proper study of mankind is Man.
Placed on this isthmus of a middle state,
A being darkly wise, and rudely great:
5 With too much knowledge for the skeptic side,
With too much weakness for the Stoic's pride,
He hangs between; in doubt to act, or rest,
In doubt to deem himself a god, or beast;
In doubt his mind or body to prefer,
10 Born but to die, and reasoning but to err;
Alike in ignorance, his reason such,
Whether he thinks too little, or too much:
Chaos of thought and passion, all confused;
Still by himself abused, or disabused;
15 Created half to rise, and half to fall;
Great lord of all things, yet a prey to all;
Sole judge of truth, in endless error hurled:
The glory, jest, and riddle of the world!

(1733)

Samuel Johnson (1709–1784)

A reviewer, essayist, critic, lexicographer, editor, and poet, Johnson was a leading literary figure of his day. He is best known for his Dictionary *(1755), his edition of Shakespeare (1765), and the* Lives of the English Poets *(1779–81), a work of criticism and biography. Dr. Levet, an unlicensed physician, lived in Johnson's house and worked with the poor.*

On the Death of Dr. Robert Levet

Condemn'd to hope's delusive mine,
    As on we toil from day to day,
By sudden blasts, or slow decline,
    Our social comforts drop away.

5   Well tried through many a varying year,
    See LEVET to the grave descend;
Officious,[1] innocent, sincere,
    Of ev'ry friendless name the friend.

Yet still he fills affection's eye,
10   Obscurely wise, and coarsely kind;
Nor, letter'd arrogance, deny
    Thy praise to merit unrefin'd.

When fainting nature call'd for aid,
    And hov'ring death prepar'd the blow,
15   His vig'rous remedy display'd
    The power of art without the show.

In misery's darkest cavern known,
    His useful care was ever nigh,
Where hopeless anguish pour'd his groan,
20   And lonely want retir'd to die.

No summons mock'd by chill delay,
    No petty gain disdain'd by pride,

---

1. Dutiful.

The modest wants of ev'ry day
  The toil of ev'ry day supplied.

25 His virtues walk'd their narrow round,
  Nor made a pause, nor left a void;
And sure th'Eternal Master found
  The single talent[2] well employ'd.

The busy day, the peaceful night,
30   Unfelt, uncounted, glided by;
His frame was firm, his powers were bright,
  Tho' now his eightieth year was nigh.

Then with no throbbing fiery pain,
  No cold gradations of decay,
35 Death broke at once the vital chain,
  And free'd his soul the nearest way.

(1783)

Thomas Gray (1716–1771)

London-born, Gray lived and wrote in Cambridge for most of his life. The melancholy tone of his "Elegy Written in a Country Churchyard," one of the most famous poems in the English language, is entirely absent from Gray's good-humoured "Ode on the Death of a Favourite Cat," offered here.

Ode on the Death of a Favourite Cat, Drowned in a Tub of Gold Fishes

'Twas on a lofty vase's side,
Where China's gayest art had dy'd
  The azure flowers that blow;
Demurest of the tabby kind,

---

2. See the Parable of the Talents, Matt. 25:14–30.

5   The pensive Selima reclin'd,
          Gazed on the lake below.

       Her conscious tail her joy declar'd;
       The fair round face, the snowy beard,
          The velvet of her paws,
10   Her coat, that with the tortoise vies,
       Her ears of jet, and emerald eyes,
          She saw; and purr'd applause.

       Still had she gaz'd; but 'midst the tide
       Two angel forms were seen to glide,
15   The Genii of the stream:
       Their scaly armour's Tyrian hue[1]
       Thro' richest purple to the view
          Betray'd a golden gleam.

       The hapless Nymph with wonder saw:
20   A whisker first and then a claw,
          With many an ardent wish,
       She stretch'd in vain to reach the prize.
       What female heart can gold despise?
          What Cat's averse to fish?

25   Presumptuous Maid! with looks intent
       Again she stretch'd, again she bent,
          Nor knew the gulf between.
       (Malignant Fate sat by, and smil'd.)
       The slipp'ry verge her feet beguil'd.
30   She tumbled headlong in.

       Eight times emerging from the flood
       She mew'd to ev'ry wat'ry God,
          Some speedy aid to send.
       No Dolphin[2] came, no Nereid[3] stirr'd:
35   Nor cruel Tom, nor Susan heard.
          A Fav'rite has no friend!

       From hence, ye Beauties, undeceiv'd,
       Know, one false step is ne'er retriev'd,
          And be with caution bold.

---

1. A purple dye of great importance in antiquity, obtained from the secretion of the Mediterranean sea snail.
2. A reference to the story of Arion, a seventh-century B.C. Greek poet and musician, who was rescued from the sea by a dolphin.
3. Water nymph.

40 Not all that tempts your wand'ring eyes
And heedless hearts, is lawful prize;
   Nor all, that glisters, gold.

(1748)

Mary Leapor (1722–1746)

Born to a working-class family in Northamptonshire, England, Mary Leapor
was put to work as a kitchen maid at Weston Hall before her mother's death
returned her to the family home and responsibilities. She read assiduously
and showed at a young age her talent for writing and for ironic reflection on
issues of class and gender. After Leapor's death from measles at the age of
twenty-four, her patron, Bridget Freemantle, helped ensure publication of
two volumes of her work in 1748 and 1751.

An Essay on Woman

Woman, a pleasing but short-lived flower,
Too soft for business and too weak for power:
A wife in bondage, or neglected maid;
Despised, if ugly; if she's fair, betrayed.
5 'Tis wealth alone inspires every grace,
And calls the raptures to her plenteous face.
What numbers for those charming features pine,
If blooming acres round her temples twine!
Her lip the strawberry, and her eyes more bright
10 Than sparkling Venus[1] in a frosty night;
Pale lilies fade and, when the fair appears,
Snow turns a negro and dissolves in tears,
And, where the charmer treads her magic toe,
On English ground Arabian odours grow;

---

1. The Roman goddess of love (in Greek myth, Aphrodite).

15   Till mighty Hymen[2] lifts his sceptred rod,
     And sinks her glories with a fatal nod,
     Dissolves her triumphs, sweeps her charms away,
     And turns the goddess to her native clay.

     But, Artemisia,[3] let your servant sing
20   What small advantage wealth and beauties bring.
     Who would be wise, that knew Pamphilia's[4] fate?
     Or who be fair, and joined to Sylvia's mate?
     Sylvia, whose cheeks are fresh as early day,
     As evening mild, and sweet as spicy May:
25   And yet that face her partial husband tires,
     And those bright eyes, that all the world admires.
     Pamphilia's wit who does not strive to shun,
     Like death's infection or a dog-day's sun?
     The damsels view her with malignant eyes,
30   The men are vexed to find a nymph so wise:
     And wisdom only serves to make her know
     The keen sensation of superior woe.
     The secret whisper and the listening ear,
     The scornful eyebrow and the hated sneer,
35   The giddy censures of her babbling kind,
     With thousands ills that grate a gentle mind,
     By her are tasted in the first degree,
     Though overlooked by Simplicus and me.
     Does thirst of gold a virgin's heart inspire,
40   Instilled by nature or a careful sire?
     Then let her quit extravagance and play,
     The brisk companion and expensive tea,
     To feast with Cordia in her filthy sty
     On stewed potatoes or on mouldy pie;
45   Whose eager eyes stare ghastly at the poor,
     And fright the beggars from her hated door;
     In greasy clouts she wraps her smoky chin,
     And holds that pride's a never-pardoned sin.

---

2. The Greek god of marriage.

3. Artemisia Gentileschi (1593–1652/53), Baroque artist and daughter of Roman artist Orazio Gentileschi (1563–1639). One of the first recognized women artists, Artemisia's experience of rape and a humiliating public trial greatly influenced her work.

4. Pamphilia ("all-loving") is the subject of a sonnet sequence *Pamphilia to Amphilanthus* and protagonist of the prose fiction *The Countess of Montgomery's Urania* (1621) by Lady Mary Wroth (1587–1651). Amphilanthus ("lover of two") is Pamphilia's unfaithful lover.

If this be wealth, no matter where it falls;
50   But save, ye Muses, save your Mira's[5] walls:
Still give me pleasing indolence and ease,
A fire to warm me and a friend to please.

Since, whether sunk in avarice or pride,
A wanton virgin or a starving bride,
55   Or wondering crowds attend her charming tongue,
Or, deemed an idiot, ever speaks the wrong;
Though nature armed us for the growing ill
With fraudful cunning and a headstrong will;
Yet, with ten thousand follies to her charge,
60   Unhappy woman's but a slave at large.

(1751)

Mary Alcock (c. 1742–1798)

Daughter of Joanna Bentley and the Reverend Denison Cumberland, Mary Alcock came of literary stock—her grandfather was Richard Bentley, the classical scholar, and her brother, Richard Cumberland, a dramatist. She went to Ireland in 1763, where she married and spent her widowhood. The collection of her poems published posthumously by her niece in 1799 reveals technical accomplishment and an interest in social reform. "Instructions" reflects anxieties in the wake of the French Revolution.

Instructions, Supposed to be Written in Paris, for the Mob in England

Of liberty, reform, and rights I sing—
Freedom I mean, without or church or king;
Freedom to seize and keep whate'er I can,

---

5. Mira = Leapor's pen name.

And boldly claim my right—The Rights of Man!
5   Such is the blessed liberty in vogue,
The envied liberty to be a rogue,
The right to pay no taxes, tithes or dues,
The liberty to do whate'er I choose;
The right to take by violence and strife
10 My neighbour's goods, and (if I please) his life;
The liberty to raise a mob or riot
(For spoil and plunder ne'er were got by quiet);
The right to level and reform the great;
The liberty to overturn the state;
15 The right to break through all the nation's laws
And boldly dare to take rebellion's cause:
Let all be equal, every man my brother—
Why have one property and not another?
Why suffer titles to give awe and fear?
20 There shall not long remain one British peer—
Nor shall the criminal appalled stand
Before the mighty judges of the land;
Nor judge nor jury shall there longer be,
Nor any jail, but ev'ry pris'ner free;
25 All law abolished, and with sword in hand
We'll seize the property of all the land.
Then hail to liberty, reform and riot!—
Adieu contentment, safety, peace and quiet!

(1799)

Anna Laetitia Barbauld (1743–1825)

English poet, prose writer, and editor Barbauld published her Poems *in
1773. She is best known today for her devotional and instructional works
for children. Barbauld worked actively to abolish the slave trade and repeal
the laws that excluded all but members of the Established Church from
holding public office.*

Washing-Day

... and their voice,
Turning again towards childish treble, pipes
And whistles in its sound.—— [1]

The Muses are turned gossips; they have lost
The buskined step,[2] and clear high-sounding phrase,
Language of gods. Come then, domestic Muse,
In slipshod measure loosely prattling on
5   Of farm or orchard, pleasant curds and cream,
Or drowning flies, or shoe lost in the mire
By little whimpering boy, with rueful face;
Come, Muse, and sing the dreaded Washing-Day.
Ye who beneath the yoke of wedlock bend,
10   With bowèd soul, full well ye ken the day
Which week, smooth sliding after week, brings on
Too soon—for to that day nor peace belongs
Nor comfort; ere the first gray streak of dawn,
The red-armed washers come and chase repose.
15   Nor pleasant smile, nor quaint device of mirth,
E'er visited that day: the very cat,
From the wet kitchen scared and reeking hearth,
Visits the parlor—an unwonted guest.
The silent breakfast-meal is soon dispatched;
20   Uninterrupted, save by anxious looks
Cast at the lowering sky, if sky should lower.
From the last evil, O preserve us, heavens!
For should the skies pour down, adieu to all
Remains of quiet: then expect to hear
25   Of sad disasters—dirt and gravel stains
Hard to efface, and loaded lines at once
Snapped short—and linen-horse[3] by dog thrown down,
And all the petty miseries of life.
Saints have been calm while stretched upon the rack,
30   And Guatimozin smiled on burning coals;[4]
But never yet did housewife notable

---

1. Shakespeare, *As You Like It*, II, vii, 161–63.
2. Tragic style. Greek tragic actors wore thick-soled boots to make them look taller and more impressive.
3. Frame on which washing is hung to dry.
4. Guatimozin, last Aztec emperor of Mexico, whose stoicism while being tortured to death (by Cortez) had become legendary in Europe.

Greet with a smile a rainy washing-day.
—But grant the welkin[5] fair, require not thou
Who call'st thyself perchance the master there,
35 Or study swept, or nicely dusted coat,
Or usual 'tendance; ask not, indiscreet,
Thy stockings mended, though the yawning rents
Gape wide as Erebus;[6] nor hope to find
Some snug recess impervious: shouldst thou try
40 The 'customed garden walks, thine eye shall rue
The budding fragrance of thy tender shrubs,
Myrtle or rose, all crushed beneath the weight
Of coarse checked apron—with impatient hand
Twitched off when showers impend: or crossing lines
45 Shall mar thy musings, as the wet cold sheet
Flaps in thy face abrupt. Woe to the friend
Whose evil stars have urged him forth to claim
On such a day the hospitable rites!
Looks, blank at best, and stinted courtesy,
50 Shall he receive. Vainly he feeds his hopes
With dinner of roast chicken, savory pie,
Or tart or pudding: pudding he nor tart
That day shall eat; nor, though the husband try,
Mending what can't be helped, to kindle mirth
55 From cheer deficient, shall his consort's brow
Clear up propitious: the unlucky guest
In silence dines, and early slinks away.
I well remember, when a child, the awe
This day struck into me; for then the maids,
60 I scarce knew why, looked cross, and drove me from them:
Nor soft caress could I obtain, nor hope
Usual indulgences; jelly or creams,
Relic of costly suppers, and set by
For me their petted one; or buttered toast,
65 When butter was forbid; or thrilling tale
Of ghost or witch, or murder—so I went
And sheltered me beside the parlor fire:
There my dear grandmother, eldest of forms,
Tended the little ones, and watched from harm,
70 Anxiously fond, though oft her spectacles
With elfin cunning hid, and oft the pins
Drawn from her ravelled stocking, might have soured
One less indulgent.

---

5. Poetic name for the sky.

6. In Greek mythology, the son of Chaos and brother of Night, and thus darkness personified. His name was given to the gloomy underworld cavern that led to Hades.

At intervals my mother's voice was heard,
75 Urging dispatch: briskly the work went on,
All hands employed to wash, to rinse, to wring,
To fold, and starch, and clap, and iron, and plait.
Then would I sit me down, and ponder much
Why washings were. Sometimes through hollow bowl
80 Of pipe amused we blew, and sent aloft
The floating bubbles; little dreaming then
To see, Montgolfier,[7] thy silken ball
Ride buoyant through the clouds—so near approach
The sports of children and the toils of men.
85 Earth, air, and sky, and ocean, hath its bubbles,
And verse is one of them—this most of all.

(1797)

Charlotte Smith (1748–1806)

Charlotte Smith wrote novels, short stories, sketches, and poetry. She had her first success with Elegaic Sonnets *in 1784. The* Old Manor House *(1793), praised by Sir Walter Scott, is considered her best novel.*

Thirty-eight

Addressed to Mrs. H—— y

In early youth's unclouded scene,
The brilliant morning of eighteen,
With health and sprightly joy elate
    We gazed on life's enchanting spring,
5   Nor thought how quickly time would bring
The mournful period—Thirty-eight.

---

7. The Montgolfier brothers, Joseph Michel (1740–1810) and Jacques-Étienne (1745–1799), invented the hot-air balloon, a huge linen globe fuelled by bundles of burning straw, which they demonstrated before a large crowd in 1783.

Then the starch maid or matron sage,
Already of that sober age,
We viewed with mingled scorn and hate,
10   In whose sharp words or sharper face
    With thoughtless mirth we loved to trace
The sad effects of—Thirty-eight.

Till saddening, sickening at the view,
We learned to dread what time might do;
15   And then preferred[1] a prayer to fate
    To end our days ere that arrived,
    When (power and pleasure long survived)
We met neglect and—Thirty-eight.

But time, in spite of wishes, flies,
20   And fate our simplest prayer denies,
And bids us death's own hour await:
    The auburn locks are mixed with grey,
    The transient roses fade away,
But reason comes at—Thirty-eight.

25   Her voice the anguish contradicts
That dying vanity inflicts;
Her hand new pleasures can create.
    For us she opens to the view
    Prospects less bright—but far more true,
30   And bids us smile at—Thirty-eight.

No more shall scandal's breath destroy
The social converse we enjoy
With bard or critic tête à tête;
    O'er youth's bright blooms her blights shall pour,
35   But spare the improving friendly hour
That science[2] gives to—Thirty-eight.

Stripped of their gaudy hues by truth,
We view the glitt'ring toys of youth,
And blush to think how poor the bait
40   For which to public scenes we ran
    And scorned of sober sense the plan
Which gives content at—Thirty-eight.

---

1. Offered.
2. Knowledge.

Though time's inexorable sway
Has torn the myrtle bands away,
45 For other wreaths 'tis not too late;
        The amaranth's purple glow survives.
        And still Minerva's olive lives[3]
On the calm brow of—Thirty-eight.

With eye more steady we engage
50 To contemplate approaching age,
And life more justly estimate.
        With firmer souls and stronger powers,
        With reason, faith, and friendship ours,
        We'll not regret the stealing hours
55 That lead from Thirty—even to Forty-eight.

(1786)

Phillis Wheatley (1753–1784)

Born in Africa and brought to slavery in Boston, Phillis Wheatley was bought by John Wheatley in 1761 and became the servant of Mrs. Susannah Wheatley. Phillis Wheatley learned English and Latin and started writing religious verse at thirteen, publishing her first poem when she was about seventeen years old. In 1773, for health reasons, she was sent to England where her Poems on Various Subjects, Religious and Moral *was published. After the death of the Wheatleys, she was freed and married John Peters, a freedman, in 1778. Margaret Odell's memoir in an 1834 edition of* Poems *established Wheatley as the first black American woman poet.*

---

3. The myrtle was sacred to Venus, goddess of love; the amaranth was a legendary flower that never faded; the olive was sacred to Minerva, goddess of wisdom, and olive wreaths came to symbolize peace.

On Being Brought from Africa to America

'Twas mercy brought me from my *Pagan* land,
Taught my benighted soul to understand
That there's a God, that there's a *Saviour* too:
Once I redemption neither sought nor knew.
5   Some view our sable race with scornful eye,
"Their colour is a diabolic dye."
Remember, *Christians*, *Negroes*, black as *Cain*,
May be refined, and join th' angelic train.

(1773)

William Blake (1757–1827)

Among the distinctive works written by this gifted poet and visionary are
Songs of Innocence *(1789) and its correlative,* Songs of Experience
(1794), samples from which are included here. Blake rejected both conventional thought and conventional versification.

The Lamb

Little Lamb, who made thee?
Dost thou know who made thee?
Gave thee life & bid thee feed,
By the stream & o'er the mead;
5   Gave thee clothing of delight,
Softest clothing wooly bright;
Gave thee such a tender voice,
Making all the vales rejoice!
Little Lamb who made thee?
10   Dost thou know who made thee?

Little Lamb I'll tell thee,
Little Lamb I'll tell thee!
He is callèd by thy name,
For he calls himself a Lamb:

15 He is meek & he is mild.
He became a little child:
I a child & thou a lamb,
We are callèd by his name.
    Little Lamb God bless thee.
20   Little Lamb God bless thee.

(1789)

London

I wander thro' each charter'd[1] street,
Near where the charter'd Thames does flow,
And mark in every face I meet
Marks of weakness, marks of woe.

5 In every cry of every Man,
In every Infant's cry of fear,
In every voice, in every ban,[2]
The mind-forg'd manacles I hear.

How the Chimney-sweeper's cry
10 Every black'ning Church appalls;
And the hapless Soldier's sigh
Runs in blood down Palace walls.

But most thro' midnight streets I hear
How the youthful Harlot's curse
15 Blasts the new-born Infant's tear,
And blights with plagues the Marriage hearse.

(1794)

---

1. Mapped, legally restricted. The Charter of the City of London once represented its source of freedom, by which citizens held certain liberties and privileges.

2. A ban is a political or legal prohibition but can also be a public condemnation or a curse. Also "banns" in the sense of a marriage proclamation.

The Sick Rose

O rose, thou art sick.
The invisible worm
That flies in the night
In the howling storm

5   Has found out thy bed
Of crimson joy,
And his dark secret love
Does thy life destroy.

(1794)

The Tyger

Tyger! Tyger! burning bright
In the forests of the night.
What immortal hand or eye
Could frame thy fearful symmetry?

5   In what distant deeps or skies
Burnt the fire of thine eyes?
On what wings dare he aspire?
What the hand, dare seize the fire?

And what shoulder, & what art,
10   Could twist the sinews of thy heart?
And when thy heart began to beat,
What dread hand? & what dread feet?

What the hammer? what the chain?
In what furnace was thy brain?
15   What the anvil? what dread grasp
Dare its deadly terrors clasp?

When the stars threw down their spears,
And water'd heaven with their tears,
Did he smile his work to see?
20   Did he who made the Lamb make thee?

Tyger! Tyger! burning bright
In the forests of the night,
What immortal hand or eye
Dare frame thy fearful symmetry?

(1794)

Robert Burns (1759–1796)

Burns's talent for writing verse in common language (some in Scots dialect) and his labouring roots led to his considerable popularity. His most ambitious project was a collection of Scottish lyrics, The Scots Musical Museum *(1787–1803).*

Auld Lang Syne[1]

Should auld acquaintance be forgot,
    And never brought to mind?
Should auld acquaintance be forgot,
    And auld lang syne!

CHORUS

5   For auld lang syne, my dear.
          For auld lang syne,
      We'll tak a cup o' kindness yet
          For auld lang syne.

And surely ye'll be your pint-stowp![2]
10   And surely I'll be mine!
And we'll tak a cup o' kindness yet,
    For auld lang syne.

We twa hae run about the braes,
    And pou'd the gowans[3] fine;
15 But we've wander'd mony a weary fitt[4]
    Sin' auld lang syne.

We twa hae paidl'd[5] in the burn,
    Frae morning sun till dine;[6]

---

1. Long ago.
2. Pay for your tankard.
3. Daisies.
4. Foot.
5. Waded.
6. Dinner-time.

But seas between us braid hae roar'd,
20   Sin' auld lang syne.

And there's a hand, my trusty fiere![7]
    And gie's a hand o' thine!
And we'll tak a right guid-willie-waught,[8]
    For auld lang syne.

(1796)

William Wordsworth (1770–1850)

Wordsworth greatly influenced the subject matter of poetry and poetic diction.

His friendship with Coleridge culminated in the Lyrical Ballads *(1798), a*

landmark in the history of the Romantic Movement in English poetry.

Lines Composed a Few Miles above Tintern Abbey,[1] on Revisiting the Banks of the Wye during a Tour, July 13, 1798

Five years have past; five summers, with the length
Of five long winters! and again I hear
These waters, rolling from their mountain-springs
With a soft inland murmur.—Once again
5 Do I behold these steep and lofty cliffs,
That on a wild secluded scene impress
Thoughts of more deep seclusion; and connect
The landscape with the quiet of the sky.
The day is come when I again repose
10 Here, under this dark sycamore, and view
These plots of cottage-ground, these orchard-tufts,
Which at this season, with their unripe fruits,

---

7. Friend.

8. Good-will draught.

1. Ruins of a medieval abbey on the River Wye near the southern border of Wales.

Are clad in one green hue, and lose themselves
'Mid groves and copses. Once again I see
15 These hedge-rows, hardly hedge-rows, little lines
Of sportive wood run wild: these pastoral farms,
Green to the very door; and wreaths of smoke
Sent up, in silence, from among the trees!
With some uncertain notice, as might seem
20 Of vagrant dwellers in the houseless woods,
Or of some Hermit's cave, where by his fire
The Hermit sits alone.
                These beauteous forms,
Through a long absence, have not been to me
25 As is a landscape to a blind man's eye:
But oft, in lonely rooms, and 'mid the din
Of towns and cities, I have owed to them
In hours of weariness, sensations sweet,
Felt in the blood, and felt along the heart;
30 And passing even into my purer mind,
With tranquil restoration:—feelings too
Of unremembered pleasure: such, perhaps,
As have no slight or trivial influence
On that best portion of a good man's life,
35 His little, nameless, unremembered acts
Of kindness and of love. Nor less, I trust,
To them I may have owed another gift,
Of aspect more sublime; that blessed mood,
In which the burthen of the mystery,
40 In which the heavy and the weary weight
Of all this unintelligible world,
Is lightened:—that serene and blessed mood,
In which the affections gently lead us on,—
Until, the breath of this corporeal frame
45 And even the motion of our human blood
Almost suspended, we are laid asleep
In body, and become a living soul:
While with an eye made quiet by the power
Of harmony, and the deep power of joy,
50 We see into the life of things.
                        If this
Be but a vain belief, yet, oh! how oft—
In darkness and amid the many shapes
Of joyless daylight; when the fretful stir
55 Unprofitable, and the fever of the world,
Have hung upon the beatings of my heart—
How oft, in spirit, have I turned to thee,
O sylvan Wye! thou wanderer thro' the woods,
How often has my spirit turned to thee!

60   And now, with gleams of half-extinguished thought,
With many recognitions dim and faint,
And somewhat of a sad perplexity,
The picture of the mind revives again:
While here I stand, not only with the sense
65 Of present pleasure, but with pleasing thoughts
That in this moment there is life and food
For future years. And so I dare to hope,
Though changed, no doubt, from what I was when first
I came along these hills; when like a roe
70 I bounded o'er the mountains, by the sides
Of the deep rivers, and the lonely streams,
Wherever nature led: more like a man
Flying from something that he dreads, than one
Who sought the thing he loved. For nature then
75 (The coarser pleasures of my boyish days,
And their glad animal movements all gone by)
To me was all in all.—I cannot paint
What then I was. The sounding cataract
Haunted me like a passion: the tall rock,
80 The mountain, and the deep and gloomy wood,
Their colours and their forms, were then to me
An appetite; a feeling and a love,
That had no need of a remoter charm,
By thought supplied, nor any interest
85 Unborrowed from the eye.—That time is past,
And all its aching joys are now no more,
And all its dizzy raptures. Not for this
Faint I, nor mourn nor murmur; other gifts
Have followed; for such loss, I would believe,
90 Abundant recompense. For I have learned
To look on nature, not as in the hour
Of thoughtless youth; but hearing oftentimes
The still, sad music of humanity,
Nor harsh nor grating, though of ample power
95 To chasten and subdue. And I have felt
A presence that disturbs me with the joy
Of elevated thoughts; a sense sublime
Of something far more deeply interfused,
Whose dwelling is the light of setting suns,
100 And the round ocean and the living air,
And the blue sky, and in the mind of man;
A motion and a spirit, that impels
All thinking things, all objects of all thought,
And rolls through all things. Therefore I am still
105 A lover of the meadows and the woods,
And mountains; and of all that we behold

From this green earth; of all the mighty world
Of eye, and ear,—both what they half create,
And what perceive; well pleased to recognise
110 In nature and the language of the sense,
The anchor of my purest thoughts, the nurse,
The guide, the guardian of my heart, and soul
Of all my moral being.
      Nor perchance,
115 If I were not thus taught, should I the more
Suffer my genial spirits to decay:
For thou art with me here upon the banks
Of this fair river; thou my dearest Friend,[2]
My dear, dear Friend; and in thy voice I catch
120 The language of my former heart, and read
My former pleasures in the shooting lights
Of thy wild eyes. Oh! yet a little while
May I behold in thee what I was once,
My dear, dear Sister! and this prayer I make,
125 Knowing that Nature never did betray
The heart that loved her; 'tis her privilege,
Through all the years of this our life, to lead
From joy to joy: for she can so inform
The mind that is within us, so impress
130 With quietness and beauty, and so feed
With lofty thoughts, that neither evil tongues,
Rash judgments, nor the sneers of selfish men,
Nor greetings where no kindness is, nor all
The dreary intercourse of daily life,
135 Shall e'er prevail against us, or disturb
Our cheerful faith, that all which we behold
Is full of blessings. Therefore let the moon
Shine on thee in thy solitary walk;
And let the misty mountain-winds be free
140 To blow against thee: and, in after years,
When these wild ecstasies shall be matured
Into a sober pleasure; when thy mind
Shall be a mansion for all lovely forms,
Thy memory be as a dwelling-place
145 For all sweet sounds and harmonies; oh! then,
If solitude, or fear, or pain, or grief,
Should be thy portion, with what healing thoughts
Of tender joy wilt thou remember me,
And these my exhortations! Nor, perchance—
150 If I should be where I no more can hear

---

2. His sister, Dorothy, with whom he was on a walking tour when he composed the
poem.

Thy voice, nor catch from thy wild eyes these gleams
Of past existence—wilt thou then forget
That on the banks of this delightful stream
We stood together; and that I, so long
155 A worshipper of Nature, hither came
Unwearied in that service: rather say
With warmer love—oh! with far deeper zeal
Of holier love. Nor wilt thou then forget,
That after many wanderings, many years
160 Of absence, these steep woods and lofty cliffs,
And this green pastoral landscape, were to me
More dear, both for themselves and for thy sake!

(1798)

Composed upon Westminster Bridge, 3 September 1802

Earth has not any thing to show more fair:
Dull would he be of soul who could pass by
A sight so touching in its majesty.
This city now doth like a garment wear
5 The beauty of the morning—silent, bare,
Ships, towers, domes, theatres, and temples lie
Open unto the fields, and to the sky,
All bright and glittering in the smokeless air.
Never did sun more beautifully steep
10 In his first splendour valley, rock, or hill;
Ne'er saw I, never felt, a calm so deep.
The river glideth at his own sweet will—
Dear God! the very houses seem asleep;
And all that mighty heart is lying still.

(1807)

Samuel Taylor Coleridge (1772–1834)

Coleridge worked closely with William and Dorothy Wordsworth for over a year, their work laying the foundation for the English Romantic Movement. A critic, political philosopher, and poet, he was an influential and imaginative thinker.

Kubla Khan

Or a Vision in a Dream. A Fragment[1]

In Xanadu did Kubla Khan
A stately pleasure dome decree:
Where Alph, the sacred river, ran
Through caverns measureless to man
5   Down to a sunless sea.
So twice five miles of fertile ground
With walls and towers were girdled round:
And there were gardens bright with sinuous rills,
Where blossomed many an incense-bearing tree;

---

1. Kubla Khan was a Mongol emperor in thirteenth-century China. In an introductory note to the poem, Coleridge gave the following explanation of its composition: "In the summer of the year 1797, the Author, then in ill health, had retired to a lonely farmhouse between Porlock and Linton, on the Exmoor confines of Somerset and Devonshire. In consequence of a slight indisposition, an anodyne had been prescribed, from the effects of which he fell asleep in his chair at the moment that he was reading the following sentence, or words of the same substance, in *Purchas's Pilgrimage*: 'Here the Khan Kubla commanded a palace to be built, and a stately garden thereunto. And thus ten miles of fertile ground were inclosed with a wall.' The Author continued for about three hours in a profound sleep, at least of the external senses, during which time he has the most vivid confidence that he could not have composed less than from two to three hundred lines; if that indeed can be called composition in which all the images rose up before him as *things*, with a parallel production of the correspondent expressions, without any sensation or consciousness of effort. On awakening he appeared to himself to have a distinct recollection of the whole, and taking his pen, ink, and paper, instantly and eagerly wrote down the lines that here are preserved. At this moment he was unfortunately called out by a person on business from Porlock, and detained by him above an hour, and on his return to his room, found, to his no small surprise and mortification, that though he still retained some vague and dim recollection of the general purport of this vision, yet, with the exception of some eight or ten scattered lines and images, all the rest had passed away like the images on the surface of a stream into which a stone has been cast, but, alas! without the after restoration of the latter." See Stevie Smith, "Thoughts about the Person from Porlock," p. 257.

10 And here were forests ancient as the hills,
Enfolding sunny spots of greenery.
But oh! that deep romantic chasm which slanted
Down the green hill athwart a cedarn cover!
A savage place! as holy as enchanted
15 As e'er beneath a waning moon was haunted
By woman wailing for her demon lover!
And from this chasm, with ceaseless turmoil seething,
As if this earth in fast thick pants were breathing,
A mighty fountain momently was forced:
20 Amid whose swift half-intermitted burst
Huge fragments vaulted like rebounding hail,
Or chaffy grain beneath the thresher's flail:
And 'mid these dancing rocks at once and ever
It flung up momently the sacred river.
25 Five miles meandering with a mazy motion
Through wood and dale the sacred river ran,
Then reached the caverns measureless to man,
And sank in tumult to a lifeless ocean:
And 'mid this tumult Kubla heard from far
30 Ancestral voices prophesying war!
  The shadow of the dome of pleasure
  Floated midway on the waves;
  Where was heard the mingled measure
  From the fountain and the caves.
35 It was a miracle of rare device,
A sunny pleasure-dome with caves of ice!
  A damsel with a dulcimer
  In a vision once I saw:
  It was an Abyssinian maid,
40   And on her dulcimer she played,
  Singing of Mount Abora.
  Could I revive within me
  Her symphony and song,
  To such a deep delight 'twould win me,
45 That with music loud and long,
I would build that dome in air,
That sunny dome! those caves of ice!
And all who heard should see them there,
And all should cry, Beware! Beware!
50 His flashing eyes, his floating hair!
Weave a circle round him thrice,
And close your eyes with holy dread,
For he on honey-dew hath fed,
And drunk the milk of Paradise.

(1816)

George Gordon, Lord Byron (1788–1824)

Dramatist, poet, incomparable letter writer, and political activist, Byron contributed to the Romantic Movement the figure of the Byronic hero—a passionate, moody, and rebellious character who remains proudly unrepentant.

Song for the Luddites[1]

As the Liberty lads o'er the sea
Bought their freedom, and cheaply, with blood,
So we, boys, we
Will *die* fighting, or *live* free,
5 And down with all kings by King Ludd!

When the web that we weave is complete,
And the shuttle exchanged for the sword,
We will fling the winding sheet
O'er the despot at our feet,
10 And dye it deep in the gore he has pour'd.

Though black as his heart its hue,
Since his veins are corrupted to mud,
Yet this is the dew
Which the tree shall renew
15 Of Liberty, planted by Ludd!

(1816)

---

1. During the economic slump resulting from Britain's wars in Europe and America, the introduction of machinery for textile manufacture caused mass unemployment in the north of England. Organized bands destroyed the machines at night, often leaving notes signed by the (probably fictitious) "Ned" or "King Ludd." The government introduced legislation to apply savage penalties to the Luddites' protests. Byron's first speech in the House of Lords in February 1812 was a bitter and eloquent attack on the proposed Framebreaking Bill.

Percy Bysshe Shelley (1792–1822)

One of the major poets of the Romantic Movement, Shelley built his reputa-
tion on a vigorous intellectual curiosity in combination with a powerful lyric
voice. The poems below demonstrate Shelley's characteristic idealism as well
as his energy.

England in 1819

An old, mad, blind, despised, and dying king,[1]—
Princes, the dregs of their dull race, who flow
Through public scorn—mud from a muddy spring—
Rulers who neither see, nor feel, nor know,
5   But leech-like to their fainting country cling,
Till they drop, blind in blood, without a blow,—
A people starved and stabbed in the untilled field,[2]—
An army, which liberticide and prey
Makes as a two-edged sword to all who wield,—
10   Golden and sanguine laws which tempt and slay;
Religion Christless, Godless—a book sealed;
A Senate,—Time's worst statute unrepealed,[3]—
Are graves, from which a glorious Phantom may
Burn, to illume our tempestuous day.

(1839)

1. George III (1738–1820), successor to the British throne in 1760, suffered from periodic bouts of insanity from 1788 until his death.
2. On August 16, 1819, government troops charged a peaceful demonstration of 60 000 people gathered at St. Peter's Field, Manchester. With eleven killed and 400 wounded, the event became known as the "Peterloo" massacre.
3. The Test Act, which restricted the civil rights of Roman Catholics and religious dissenters.

Ode to the West Wind

1

O wild West Wind, thou breath of Autumn's being,
Thou, from whose unseen presence the leaves dead
Are driven, like ghosts from an enchanter fleeing,

Yellow, and black, and pale, and hectic red,
5   Pestilence-stricken multitudes: O thou,
Who chariotest to their dark wintry bed

The wingèd seeds, where they lie cold and low,
Each like a corpse within its grave, until
Thine azure sister of the Spring shall blow

10 Her clarion o'er the dreaming earth, and fill
(Driving sweet buds like flocks to feed in air)
With living hues and odours plain and hill:

Wild Spirit, which art moving everywhere;
Destroyer and preserver; hear, oh, hear!

2

15 Thou on whose stream, mid the steep sky's commotion,
Loose clouds like earth's decaying leaves are shed,
Shook from the tangled boughs of Heaven and Ocean,

Angels of rain and lightning: there are spread
On the blue surface of thine aëry surge,
20 Like the bright hair uplifted from the head

Of some fierce Maenad,[1] even from the dim verge
Of the horizon to the zenith's height,
The locks of the approaching storm. Thou dirge

Of the dying year, to which this closing night
25 Will be the dome of a vast sepulchre,
Vaulted with all thy congregated might

---

1. In Greek mythology, the Maenads were female worshippers of Dionysus who took part in frenzied orgiastic festivals. They were also responsible for dismembering the poet Orpheus.

Of vapours, from whose solid atmosphere
Black rain, and fire, and hail will burst: oh, hear!

3

Thou who didst waken from his summer dreams
30 The blue Mediterranean, where he lay,
Lulled by the coil of his crystàlline streams,

Beside a pumice isle on Baiae's bay,[2]
And saw in sleep old palaces and towers
Quivering within the wave's intenser day,

35 All overgrown with azure moss and flowers
So sweet, the sense faints picturing them! Thou
For whose path the Atlantic's level powers

Cleave themselves into chasms, while far below
The sea-blooms and the oozy woods which wear
40 The sapless foliage of the ocean, know

Thy voice, and suddenly grow gray with fear,
And tremble and despoil themselves: oh, hear!

4

If I were a dead leaf thou mightest bear,
If I were a swift cloud to fly with thee;
45 A wave to pant beneath thy power, and share

The impulse of thy strength, only less free
Than thou, O uncontrollable! If even
I were as in my boyhood, and could be

The comrade of thy wanderings over Heaven,
50 As then, when to outstrip thy skyey speed
Scarce seemed a vision; I would ne'er have striven

As thus with thee in prayer in my sore need.
Oh, lift me as a wave, a leaf, a cloud!
I fall upon the thorns of life! I bleed!

---

2. Near Naples, Italy.

55 A heavy weight of hours has chained and bowed
    One too like thee: tameless, and swift, and proud.

5

    Make me thy lyre, even as the forest is:
    What if my leaves are falling like its own!
    The tumult of thy mighty harmonies

60 Will take from both a deep, autumnal tone,
    Sweet though in sadness. Be thou, Spirit fierce,
    My spirit! Be thou me, impetuous one!

    Drive my dead thoughts over the universe
    Like withered leaves to quicken a new birth!
65 And, by the incantation of this verse,

    Scatter, as from an unextinguished hearth
    Ashes and sparks, my words among mankind!
    Be through my lips to unawakened earth

    The trumpet of a prophecy! O Wind,
70 If Winter comes, can Spring be far behind?

(1820)

John Keats (1795–1821)

Keats is considered one of the principal poets of the Romantic Movement, a reputation that is the more remarkable when one thinks of the poet's brief life. Keats is unparalleled in his evocation of sensuous experience.

Ode to a Nightingale

1

My heart aches, and a drowsy numbness pains
    My sense, as though of hemlock[1] I had drunk,
Or emptied some dull opiate to the drains
    One minute past, and Lethe-wards[2] had sunk:
5   'Tis not through envy of thy happy lot,
        But being too happy in thine happiness—
            That thou, light-wingèd Dryad[3] of the trees,
                In some melodious plot
        Of beechen green, and shadows numberless,
10   Singest of summer in full-throated ease.

2

O, for a draught of vintage! that hath been
    Cooled a long age in the deep-delvèd earth,
Tasting of Flora[4] and the country green,
    Dance, and Provençal song,[5] and sunburnt mirth!
15 O for a beaker full of the warm South,
        Full of the true, the blushful Hippocrene,[6]
            With beaded bubbles winking at the brim,
                And purple-stainèd mouth;
        That I might drink, and leave the world unseen,
20   And with thee fade away into the forest dim:

3

Fade far away, dissolve, and quite forget
    What thou among the leaves has never known,
The weariness, the fever, and the fret
    Here, where men sit and hear each other groan;

---

1. Poisonous plant used as a powerful sedative.
2. Toward the river of forgetfulness, Lethe, in Hades.
3. Wood nymph.
4. Roman goddess of springtime and flowers.
5. The medieval troubadours of Provence, in southern France, were famous for their elaborate and often improvised songs.
6. Fountain on Mount Helicon in Greece sacred to the Muses (goddesses of poetry and the arts); its waters provide poetic inspiration.

25 Where palsy shakes a few, sad, last gray hairs,
    Where youth grows pale, and spectre-thin, and dies,
      Where but to think is to be full of sorrow
        And leaden-eyed despairs,
    Where Beauty cannot keep her lustrous eyes,
30   Or new Love pine at them beyond tomorrow.

    4

Away! away! for I will fly to thee,
    Not charioted by Bacchus and his pards,[7]
But on the viewless wings of Poesy,
    Though the dull brain perplexes and retards;
35 Already with thee! tender is the night,
    And haply the Queen-Moon is on her throne,
      Clustered around by all her starry Fays;
        But here there is no light,
Save what from heaven is with the breezes blown
40   Through verdurous glooms and winding mossy ways.

    5

I cannot see what flowers are at my feet,
    Nor what soft incense hangs upon the boughs,
But, in embalmèd darkness, guess each sweet
    Wherewith the seasonable month endows
45 The grass, the thicket, and the fruit tree wild;
    White hawthorn, and the pastoral eglantine;
      Fast fading violets covered up in leaves;
        And mid-May's eldest child.
The coming musk-rose, full of dewy wine,
50   The murmurous haunt of flies on summer eves.

    6

Darkling I listen; and for many a time
    I have been half in love with easeful Death,
Called him soft names in many a musèd rhyme,
    To take into the air my quiet breath;
55 Now more than ever seems it rich to die,

---

7. Bacchus, Roman god of wine and fertility, was sometimes portrayed in a chariot
   drawn by leopards.

To cease upon the midnight with no pain,
    While thou art pouring forth thy soul abroad
        In such an ecstasy!
Still wouldst thou sing, and I have ears in vain—
60   To thy high requiem become a sod.

7

Thou was not born for death, immortal bird!
    No hungry generations tread thee down;
The voice I hear this passing night was heard
    In ancient days by emperor and clown:
65 Perhaps the selfsame song that found a path
    Through the sad heart of Ruth,[8] when, sick for home,
        She stood in tears amid the alien corn;
            The same that ofttimes hath
    Charmed magic casements, opening on the foam
70   Of perilous seas, in faery lands forlorn.

8

Forlorn! the very word is like a bell
    To toll me back from thee to my sole self!
Adieu! the fancy cannot cheat so well
    As she is famed to do, deceiving elf.
75 Adieu! adieu! thy plaintive anthem fades
    Past the near meadows, over the still stream,
        Up the hill side; and now 'tis buried deep
            In the next valley-glades:
    Was it a vision, or a waking dream?
80   Fled is that music:—Do I wake or sleep?

(1820)

---

8. See Ruth 2.

To Autumn

1

Season of mists and mellow fruitfulness,
   Close bosom-friend of the maturing sun;
Conspiring with him how to load and bless
   With fruit the vines that round the thatch-eves run;
5 To bend with apples the mossed cottage-trees,
   And fill all fruit with ripeness to the core;
     To swell the gourd, and plump the hazel shells
   With a sweet kernel; to set budding more,
And still more, later flowers for the bees,
10 Until they think warm days will never cease,
     For Summer has o'er-brimmed their clammy cells.

2

Who hath not seen thee oft amid thy store?
   Sometimes whoever seeks abroad may find
Thee sitting careless on a granary floor,
15   Thy hair soft-lifted by the winnowing wind;
Or on a half-reaped furrow sound asleep,
   Drowsed with the fume of poppies, while thy hook
     Spares the next swath and all its twinèd flowers:
   And sometimes like a gleaner thou dost keep
20 Steady thy laden head across a brook;
Or by a cider-press, with patient look,
     Thou watchest the last oozings hours by hours.

3

Where are the songs of Spring? Ay, where are they?
   Think not of them, thou hast thy music too—
25 While barrèd clouds bloom the soft-dying day,
   And touch the stubble-plains with rosy hue;
Then in a wailful choir the small gnats mourn
   Among the river sallows,[1] borne aloft
     Or sinking as the light wind lives or dies;

---

1. Low-growing willows.

30   And full-grown lambs loud bleat from hilly bourn;
      Hedge-crickets sing; and now with treble soft
      The red-breast whistles from a garden-croft;
            And gathering swallows twitter in the skies.

                                                    (1820)

Elizabeth Barrett Browning (1806–1861)

Once known for her support of liberal causes as well as for her poetry,
Elizabeth Barrett Browning is today most often remembered for Sonnets
from the Portuguese *(1850), a sequence of love poems dedicated to poet*
Robert Browning, her husband. Sonnet 18 is from this sonnet sequence.

Sonnet 18

      I never gave a lock of hair away
      To a man, dearest, except this to thee,
      Which now upon my fingers thoughtfully,
      I ring out to the full brown length and say
5   "Take it." My day of youth went yesterday;
      My hair no longer bounds to my foot's glee,
      Nor plant I it from rose or myrtle-tree,
      As girls do, any more: it only may
      Now shade on two pale cheeks the mark of tears,
10   Taught drooping from the head that hangs aside
      Through sorrow's trick. I thought the funeral-shears[1]
      Would take this first, but love is justified:
      Take it thou—finding pure, from all those years,
      The kiss my mother left there when she died.

                                                    (1850)

---

1. Nineteenth-century mourners often kept a lock of hair from a dead lover or relative as a treasured memento.

A Musical Instrument

What was he doing, the great god Pan,[1]
    Down in the reeds by the river?
Spreading ruin and scattering ban,[2]
Splashing and paddling with hoofs of a goat,
5   And breaking the golden lilies afloat
    With the dragonfly on the river.

He tore out a reed, the great god Pan,
    From the deep cool bed of the river;
The limpid water turbidly ran,
10   And the broken lilies a-dying lay,
And the dragonfly had fled away,
    Ere he brought it out of the river.

High on the shore sat the great god Pan
    While turbidly flowed the river;
15   And hacked and hewed as a great god can,
With his hard bleak steel at the patient reed,
Till there was not a sign of the leaf indeed
    To prove it fresh from the river.

He cut it short, did the great god Pan
20   (How tall it stood in the river!),
Then drew the pith, like the heart of a man,
Steadily from the outside ring,
And notched the poor dry empty thing
    In holes, as he sat by the river.

25   "This is the way," laughed the great god Pan
    (Laughed while he sat by the river),
"The only way, since gods began
To make sweet music, they could succeed."
Then, dropping his mouth to a hole in the reed,
30   He blew in power by the river.

Sweet, sweet, sweet, O Pan!
    Piercing sweet by the river!
Blinding sweet, O great god Pan!
The sun on the hill forgot to die,

---

1. In Greek mythology, an Arcadian god of shepherds and flocks, in shape half goat, half human, son of Hermes. One of his loves was the nymph Syrinx who, trying to escape Pan, was turned into a reed from which Pan made his flute. Pastoral poets made him the patron of their art.

2. Curses, evil influence.

35 And the lilies revived, and the dragonfly
        Came back to dream on the river.

Yet half a beast is the great god Pan,
        To laugh as he sits by the river,
Making a poet out of a man;
40 The true gods sigh for the cost and pain—
For the reed which grows nevermore again
        As a reed with the reeds in the river.

(1862)

Alfred, Lord Tennyson (1809–1892)

*One of the most popularly acclaimed poets of the Victorian period, Tennyson
was frequently inspired by heroic figures from an imaginary, classical, or
medieval past. This element of heroic fantasy is often combined with an
acute sense of the natural landscape.*

Ulysses[1]

It little profits that an idle king,
By this still hearth, among these barren crags,
Matched with an aged wife, I mete and dole
Unequal laws unto a savage race,
5 That hoard, and sleep, and feed, and know not me.

        I cannot rest from travel; I will drink
Life to the lees. All times I have enjoyed
Greatly, have suffered greatly, both with those
That loved me, and alone; on shore, and when

---

1. The figure in the poem is probably inspired less by Homer's *Odyssey* than by
   Canto XXVI of Dante's *Inferno* in which Ulysses goes forth on a last voyage to
   "explore the world, and search the ways of life, / Man's evil and his virtue."

10 Thro' scudding drifts the rainy Hyades[2]
Vext the dim sea. I am become a name;
For always roaming with a hungry heart
Much have I seen and known,—cities of men
And manners, climates, councils, governments,
15 Myself not least, but honoured of them all,—
And drunk delight of battle with my peers,
Far on the ringing plains of windy Troy.
I am a part of all that I have met;
Yet all experience is an arch wherethro'
20 Gleams that untravelled world whose margin fades
For ever and for ever when I move.
How dull it is to pause, to make an end,
To rust unburnished, not to shine in use!
As tho' to breathe were life! Life piled on life
25 Were all too little, and of one to me
Little remains; but every hour is saved
From that eternal silence, something more,
A bringer of new things; and vile it were
For some three suns[3] to store and hoard myself,
30 And this gray spirit yearning in desire
To follow knowledge like a sinking star,
Beyond the utmost bound of human thought.

This is my son, mine own Telemachus,
To whom I leave the sceptre and the isle,—
35 Well-loved of me, discerning to fulfil
This labour, by slow prudence to make mild
A rugged people, and thro' soft degrees
Subdue them to the useful and the good.
Most blameless is he, centred in the sphere
40 Of common duties, decent not to fail
In offices of tenderness, and pay
Meet[4] adoration to my household gods,
When I am gone. He works his work, I mine.

There lies the port; the vessel puffs her sail;
45 There gloom the dark broad seas. My mariners,
Souls that have toiled, and wrought, and thought with me,—
That ever with a frolic welcome took
The thunder and the sunshine, and opposed
Free hearts, free foreheads,—you and I are old;

---

2. Five stars in the constellation Taurus, named "the rainy ones" for the notion that
they indicated rain when they rose with the sun in spring.

3. Three years.

4. Appropriate.

50 Old age hath yet his honour and his toil.
    Death closes all; but something ere the end.
    Some work of noble note, may yet be done,
    Not unbecoming men that strove with Gods.
    The lights begin to twinkle from the rocks;
55 The long day wanes; the slow moon climbs; the deep
    Moans round with many voices. Come, my friends.
    'Tis not too late to seek a newer world.
    Push off, and sitting well in order smite
    The sounding furrows; for my purpose holds
60 To sail beyond the sunset, and the baths
    Of all the western stars, until I die.
    It may be that the gulfs will wash us down;
    It may be we shall touch the Happy Isles,[5]
    And see the great Achilles,[6] whom we knew.
65 Tho' much is taken, much abides; and tho'
    We are not now that strength which in old days
    Moved earth and heaven, that which we are, we are,—
    One equal temper of heroic hearts,
    Made weak by time and fate, but strong in will
70 To strive, to seek, to find, and not to yield.

(1842)

Robert Browning (1812–1889)

As in the poem reproduced here, Browning's most successful work depends upon a dramatic speaker. Browning established his reputation with the volume Men and Women *(1855), written while living in Italy with his wife, poet Elizabeth Barrett.*

---

5. In classical mythology, the souls of the virtuous inhabited the Happy Isles or Isles of the Blessed, thought to lie just west of the Strait of Gibraltar.
6. Greek hero in classical mythology who killed Hector and was himself killed in battle.

My Last Duchess

Ferrara¹

That's my last duchess painted on the wall,
Looking as if she were alive. I call
That piece a wonder, now: Frà Pandolf's hands
Worked busily a day, and there she stands.
5 Will't please you sit and look at her? I said
"Frà Pandolf" by design, for never read
Strangers like you that pictured countenance,
The depth and passion of its earnest glance,
But to myself they turned (since none puts by
10 The curtain I have drawn for you, but I)
And seemed as they would ask me, if they durst,
How such a glance came there; so, not the first
Are you to turn and ask thus. Sir, 'twas not
Her husband's presence only, called that spot
15 Of joy into the Duchess' cheek: perhaps
Frà Pandolf chanced to say "Her mantle laps
Over my lady's wrist too much," or "Paint
Must never hope to reproduce the faint
Half-flush that dies along her throat": such stuff
20 Was courtesy, she thought, and cause enough
For calling up that spot of joy. She had
A heart—how shall I say?—too soon made glad,
Too easily impressed; she liked whate'er
She looked on, and her looks went everywhere.
25 Sir, 'twas all one! My favor at her breast,
The dropping of the daylight in the West,
The bough of cherries some officious fool
Broke in the orchard for her, the white mule
She rode with round the terrace—all and each
30 Would draw from her alike the approving speech,
Or blush, at least. She thanked men—good! but thanked
Somehow—I know not how—as if she ranked
My gift of a nine-hundred-years-old name
With anybody's gift. Who'd stoop to blame
35 This sort of trifling? Even had you skill
In speech—which I have not—to make your will
Quite clear to such an one, and say, "Just this
Or that in you disgusts me; here you miss,
Or there exceed the mark"—and if she let

---

1. In 1564, Alfonso II, duke of Ferrara in Italy, was negotiating through an agent for
the hand of the niece of the Count of Tyrol. His previous wife had died three
years earlier at age seventeen, apparently as the result of poisoning.

40   Herself be lessoned so, nor plainly set
     Her wits to yours, forsooth, and made excuse,
     —E'en then would be some stooping; and I choose
     Never to stoop. Oh sir, she smiled, no doubt,
     Whene'er I passed her; but who passed without
45   Much the same smile? This grew; I gave commands;
     Then all smiles stopped together. There she stands
     As if alive. Will't please you rise? We'll meet
     The company below, then. I repeat,
     The Count your master's known munificence
50   Is ample warrant that no just pretence
     Of mine for dowry will be disallowed;
     Though his fair daughter's self, as I avowed
     At starting, is my object. Nay, we'll go
     Together down, sir. Notice Neptune, though.
55   Taming a sea-horse, thought a rarity,
     Which Claus of Innsbruck[2] cast in bronze for me!

                                                        (1842)

Emily Brontë (1818–1848)

Emily Brontë and her famous sisters, Charlotte and Anne, first published
their poetry pseudonymously. Although she is better known for the novel
Wuthering Heights (1847) *than for her poetry, Brontë's lyrics are both orig-*
inal and memorable.

Remembrance

Cold in the earth—and the deep snow piled above thee,
Far, far removed, cold in the dreary grave!
Have I forgot, my only love, to love thee,
Severed at last by time's all-severing wave?

---

2. Claus of Innsbruck, like Frà Pandolf (l. 3), is a fictitious artist.

5   Now, when alone, do my thoughts no longer hover
Over the mountains, on that northern shore;
Resting their wings where heath and fern-leaves cover
Thy noble heart for ever, ever more?

Cold in the earth—and fifteen wild Decembers,
10 From those brown hills, have melted into spring:
Faithful, indeed, is the spirit that remembers
After such years of change and suffering!

Sweet love of youth, forgive, if I forget thee
While the world's tide is bearing me along;
15 Other desires and other hopes beset me,
Hopes which obscure, but cannot do thee wrong.

No later light has lightened up my heaven,
No second morn has ever shone for me;
All my life's bliss from thy dear life was given,
20 All my life's bliss is in the grave with thee.

But when the days of golden dreams had perished,
And even despair was powerless to destroy,
Then did I learn how existence could be cherished,
Strengthened, and fed without the aid of joy.

25 Then did I check the tears of useless passion—
Weaned my young soul from yearning after thine;
Sternly denied its burning wish to hasten
Down to that tomb already more than mine.

And, even yet, I dare not let it languish,
30 Dare not indulge in memory's rapturous pain;
Once drinking deep of that divinest anguish,
How could I seek the empty world again?

(1846)

Walt Whitman (1819–1892)

Whitman's efforts to discover a poetic language that was uniquely American resulted in innovative content and form. His images and themes stress the common experience of American life, and his verse is freely expansive.

When I Heard the Learn'd Astronomer

When I heard the learn'd astronomer,
When the proofs, the figures, were ranged in columns before me,
When I was shown the charts and diagrams, to add, divide, and
    measure them,
When I sitting heard the astronomer where he lectured with much
    applause in the lecture-room,
5   How soon unaccountable I became tired and sick,
Till rising and gliding out I wander'd off by myself,
In the mystical moist night-air, and from time to time,
Look'd up in perfect silence at the stars.

(1865)

Reconciliation

Word over all, beautiful as the sky,
Beautiful that war and all its deeds of carnage must in time be
    utterly lost,
That the hands of the sisters of Death and Night incessantly softly
    wash again, and ever again, this soil'd world;
For my enemy is dead, a man divine as myself is dead,
5   I look where he lies white-faced and still in the coffin—I draw near,
Bend down and touch lightly with my lips the white face in the coffin.

(1881)

Matthew Arnold (1822–1888)

Many people think of Arnold first as a critic, his literary and social criti-cism being largely the result of his years as inspector of schools. His poetry expresses many of the religious doubts common to intellectuals of the Victorian period.

Dover Beach[1]

The sea is calm to-night.
The tide is full, the moon lies fair
Upon the straits;—on the French coast, the light
Gleams, and is gone; the cliffs of England stand,
5 Glimmering and vast, out in the tranquil bay.
Come to the window, sweet is the night air!
Only, from the long line of spray
Where the sea meets the moon-blanched land,
Listen! you hear the grating roar
10 Of pebbles which the waves draw back, and fling,
At their return, up the high strand,
Begin, and cease, and then again begin,
With tremulous cadence slow, and bring
The eternal note of sadness in.

15 Sophocles[2] long ago
Heard it on the Ægean, and it brought
Into his mind the turbid ebb and flow
Of human misery; we
Find also in the sound a thought,
20 Hearing it by this distant northern sea.

The Sea of Faith
Was once, too, at the full, and round earth's shore
Lay like the folds of a bright girdle furled.
But now I only hear
25 Its melancholy, long, withdrawing roar,

---

1. The Strait of Dover is a narrow channel that connects the North Sea with the English Channel and separates England and France at their closest points. The lights on the French coast (see ll. 3–4) would be almost 34 kilometres away.

2. Greek writer of tragedies of the fifth century B.C.

Retreating, to the breath
Of the night-wind down the vast edges drear
And naked shingles of the world.

Ah, love, let us be true
30   To one another! for the world, which seems
To lie before us like a land of dreams,
So various, so beautiful, so new,
Hath really neither joy, nor love, nor light,
Nor certitude, nor peace, nor help for pain;
35   And we are here as on a darkling plain
Swept with confused alarms of struggle and flight,
Where ignorant armies clash by night.

(1867)

Emily Dickinson (1830–1886)

Dickinson lived as a virtual recluse for most of her adult life, and her com-
pressed and often radically elliptical style seems to reflect her legendary
seclusion. She constantly surprises readers with her ability to enlist an
everyday vocabulary to explore intense spiritual or mystical experiences.

There's a certain Slant of light

There's a certain Slant of light,
Winter Afternoons—
That oppresses, like the Heft[1]
Of Cathedral Tunes—

5   Heavenly Hurt, it give us—
We can find no scar,
But internal difference,
Where the Meanings, are—

---

1. Weight.

None may teach it—Any—
10   'Tis the Seal Despair—
An imperial affliction
Sent us of the Air—

When it comes, the Landscape listens—
Shadows—hold their breath—
15   When it goes, 'tis like the Distance
On the look of Death—

(1890)

After great pain, a formal feeling comes

After great pain, a formal feeling comes—
The Nerves sit ceremonious, like Tombs—
The stiff Heart questions was it He, that bore,
And Yesterday, or Centuries before?

5   The Feet, mechanical, go round—
Of Ground, or Air, or Ought—
A Wooden way
Regardless grown,
A Quartz contentment, like a stone—

10   This is the Hour of Lead—
Remembered, if outlived,
As Freezing persons, recollect the Snow—
First—Chill—then Stupor—then the letting go—

(1929)

The Bustle in a House

The Bustle in a House
The Morning after Death
Is solemnest of industries
Enacted upon Earth—

5   The Sweeping up the Heart
And putting Love away
We shall not want to use again
Until Eternity.

(1890)

Tell all the Truth but tell it slant

Tell all the Truth but tell it slant—
Success in Circuit lies
Too bright for our infirm Delight
The Truth's superb surprise

5   As Lightning to the Children eased
With explanation kind
The Truth must dazzle gradually
Or every man be blind—

(1945)

Presentiment

Presentiment—is that long Shadow—on the Lawn—
Indicative that Suns go down

The Notice to the startled Grass
That Darkness—is about to pass

(1890)

Christina Rossetti (1830–1894)

Rossetti was part of a circle of avant-garde artists that included her famous brother, poet and painter Dante Gabriel Rossetti. Her work is distinguished by both its spiritual austerity and its technical skill.

In an Artist's Studio

One face looks out from all his canvases,
    One selfsame figure sits or walks or leans:
    We found her hidden just behind those screens,

That mirror gave back all her loveliness.
5　A queen in opal or in ruby dress,
　　A nameless girl in freshest summer-greens,
　　A saint, an angel—every canvas means
The same one meaning, neither more nor less.
He feeds upon her face by day and night,
10　And she with true kind eyes looks back on him,
Fair as the moon and joyful as the light:
　　Not wan with waiting, not with sorrow dim;
Not as she is, but was when hope shone bright;
　　Not as she is, but as she fills his dream.

(1896)

Lewis Carroll (1832–1898)

Charles Lutwidge Dodgson, who wrote under the pseudonym Lewis Carroll, was born in Cheshire, England, and educated at Rugby School and Christ Church, Oxford. A lecturer in mathematics at Oxford, he published widely on mathematics, though he is best known for his Alice in Wonderland *(1865) and* Through the Looking-Glass *(1871). "Jabberwocky" shows Carroll's delight in puzzles and word play.*

Jabberwocky

'Twas brillig, and the slithy toves
　　Did gyre and gimble in the wabe:
All mimsy were the borogoves,
　　And the mome raths outgrabe.

5　"Beware the Jabberwock, my son!
　　The jaws that bite, the claws that catch!
Beware the Jubjub bird, and shun
　　The frumious Bandersnatch!"

He took his vorpal sword in hand;
10   Long time the manxome foe he sought—
So rested he by the Tumtum tree
        And stood awhile in thought.

And, as in uffish thought he stood,
        The Jabberwock, with eyes of flame,
15   Came whiffling through the tulgey wood,
        And burbled as it came!

One, two! One, two! And through and through
        The vorpal blade went snicker-snack!
He left it dead, and with its head
20   He went galumphing back.

"And hast thou slain the Jabberwock?
        Come to my arms, my beamish boy!
O frabjous day! Callooh! Callay!"
        He chortled in his joy.

25   'Twas brillig, and the slithy toves
        Did gyre and gimble in the wabe:
All mimsy were the borogoves,
        And the mome raths outgrabe.

(1871)

Thomas Hardy (1840–1928)

Hardy wrote novels and short stories before giving up fiction for poetry.
Reflecting Hardy's loss of religious faith, much of his work deals with
humanity's struggle against an indifferent and often violent ruling deity.

The Darkling Thrush

I leaned upon a coppice gate
    When Frost was spectre-gray,
And Winter's dregs made desolate
    The weakening eye of day.
5 The tangled bine-stems scored the sky
    Like strings from broken lyres,
And all mankind that haunted nigh
    Had sought their household fires.

The land's sharp features seemed to be
10   The Century's corpse outleant;
His crypt the cloudy canopy,
    The wind his death-lament.
The ancient pulse of germ and birth
    Was shrunken hard and dry,
15 And every spirit upon earth
    Seemed fervourless as I.

At once a voice burst forth among
    The bleak twigs overhead
In a full-hearted evensong
20   Of joy illimited;
An aged thrush, frail, gaunt, and small,
    In blast-beruffled plume,
Had chosen thus to fling his soul
    Upon the growing gloom.

25 So little cause for carollings
    Of such ecstatic sound
Was written on terrestrial things
    Afar or nigh around,
That I could think there trembled through
30   His happy good-night air
Some blessed hope, whereof he knew
    And I was unaware.

December 31, 1900

(1902)

In Time of "The Breaking of Nations"[1]

(1915)

1

Only a man harrowing clods
   In a slow silent walk
With an old horse that stumbles and nods
   Half asleep as they stalk.

2

5   Only thin smoke without flame
      From the heaps of couch-grass:
    Yet this will go onward the same
      Though Dynasties pass.

3

    Yonder a maid and her wight
10   Come whispering by:
    War's annals will cloud into night
      Ere their story die.

(1916)

Gerard Manley Hopkins (1844–1889)

A poet and Jesuit priest, Hopkins had a deep sense of vocation to both call-
ings. He wrote of the beauty of the natural and human world. Much of his
effort went into innovative experiments in the use of language and rhythm.

---

1. See Jer. 51:20: "Thou art my battle axe and weapons of war: for with thee will I
    break in pieces the nations, and with thee will I destroy kingdoms."

God's Grandeur

The world is charged with the grandeur of God.
    It will flame out, like shining from shook foil;[1]
    It gathers to a greatness, like the ooze of oil
Crushed. Why do men then now not reck his rod?
5 Generations have trod, have trod, have trod;
    And all is seared with trade; bleared, smeared with toil;
    And wears man's smudge and shares man's smell: the soil
Is bare now, nor can foot feel, being shod.

And for all this, nature is never spent;
10   There lives the dearest freshness deep down things;
And though the last lights off the black West went
    Oh, morning, at the brown brink eastward, springs—
Because the Holy Ghost over the bent
    World broods with warm breast and with ah! bright wings.

                                 (1895)

The Windhover[1]

To Christ Our Lord

I caught this morning morning's minion, king-
    dom of daylight's dauphin, dapple-dawn-drawn Falcon, in his riding
    Of the rolling level underneath him steady air, and striding
High there, how he rung upon the rein of a wimpling wing
5 In his ecstasy! then off, off forth on swing,
    As a skate's heel sweeps smooth on a bow-bend: the hurl and gliding
    Rebuffed the big wind. My heart in hiding
Stirred for a bird,—the achieve of, the mastery of the thing!

Brute beauty and valor and act, oh, air, pride, plume, here
10   Buckle! AND the fire that breaks from thee then, a billion
Times told lovelier, more dangerous, O my chevalier!

---

1. "I mean foil in its sense of leaf or tinsel.... Shaken goldfoil gives off broad glares like sheet lightning and also, and this is true of nothing else, owing to its zigzag dents and creasings and network of small many cornered facets, a sort of fork lightning too" (Hopkins, *Letters*).
1. Name for a small falcon, the kestrel, from its habit of hovering or hanging in the air with its head to the wind.

No wonder of it: shéer plód makes plough down sillion[2]
Shine, and blue-bleak embers, ah my dear,
    Fall, gall themselves, and gash gold-vermilion.

                                        (1918)

Pied Beauty

Glory be to God for dappled things—
    For skies of couple-colour as a brinded cow:
        For rose-moles all in stipple upon trout that swim;
Fresh-firecoal chestnut-falls; finches' wings;
5   Landscape plotted and pieced—fold, fallow, and plow;
        And áll trádes, their gear and tackle and trim.
All things counter, original, spare, strange;
    Whatever is fickle, freckled (who knows how?)
        With swift, slow; sweet, sour; adazzle, dim;
10 He fathers-forth whose beauty is past change:
        Praise him.

                                          (1918)

A.E. Housman (1859–1936)

Although he had been a first-rate scholar in classics, Housman failed his

final examinations at Oxford. Continuing his studies on his own while

working for ten years in the civil service, he went on to become a professor

of Latin at University College, London. His A Shropshire Lad (1896), from

which the selection is taken, became enormously popular during World War

I. His poems are as influenced by the popular ballad as by the classical lyric

and are marked by balance and opposition, melancholy and irony.

---

2. A ridge or narrow strip lying between two furrows formed in dividing an open
   field.

To an Athlete Dying Young

The time you won your town the race
We chaired you through the market-place;
Man and boy stood cheering by,
And home we brought you shoulder-high.

5   Today, the road all runners come,
Shoulder-high we bring you home,
And set you at your threshold down,
Townsman of a stiller town.

Smart lad, to slip betimes away
10   From fields where glory does not stay
And early though the laurel grows
It withers quicker than the rose.

Eyes the shady night has shut
Cannot see the record cut,
15   And silence sounds no worse than cheers
After earth has stopped the ears:

Now you will not swell the rout
Of lads that wore their honours out,
Runners whom renown outran
20   And the name died before the man.

So set, before its echoes fade,
The fleet foot on the sill of shade,
And hold to the low lintel up
The still-defended challenge-cup.

25   And round that early-laurelled head
Will flock to gaze the strengthless dead
And find unwithered on its curls
The garland briefer than a girl's.

(1896)

Sir Charles G.D. Roberts (1860–1943)

As a young poet, Roberts inspired his generation of Canadian writers with his ability to observe natural landscape. Later he became a prolific author of a variety of prose works. His reputation now rests as much on his contribution to the development of the animal story as on his poetry.

The Tantramar[1] Revisited

Summers and summers have come, and gone with the flight of the
    swallow;
Sunshine and thunder have been, storm, and winter, and frost;
Many and many a sorrow has all but died from remembrance,
Many a dream of joy fall'n in the shadow of pain.
5 Hands of chance and change have marred, or moulded, or broken,
Busy with spirit or flesh, all I most have adored;
Even the bosom of Earth is strewn with heavier shadows,—
Only in these green hills, aslant to the sea, no change!
Here where the road that has climbed from the inland valleys and
    woodlands,
10 Dips from the hill-tops down, straight to the base of the hills,—
Here, from my vantage-ground,[2] I can see the scattering houses,
Stained with time, set warm in orchards, and meadows, and wheat,
Dotting the broad bright slopes outspread to southward and eastward,
Wind-swept all day long, blown by the south-east wind.

15 Skirting the sunbright uplands stretches a riband of meadow,
Shorn of the labouring grass, bulwarked well from the sea,
Fenced on its seaward border with long clay dikes from the turbid
Surge and flow of the tides vexing the Westmoreland shores.
Yonder, toward the left, lie broad the Westmoreland marshes,—
20 Miles on miles they extend, level, and grassy, and dim,
Clear from the long red sweep of flats to the sky in the distance,
Save for the outlying heights, green-rampired[3] Cumberland Point;

---

1. The Tantramar Marshes are located at the head of Cumberland Basin, a body of
   water bounded by Westmoreland County, New Brunswick, on the north, and
   Cumberland County, Nova Scotia, on the south.
2. Westcock, New Brunswick, near Sackville. Minudie, Nova Scotia (see l. 25) is
   directly across the Cumberland Basin from this location.
3. Fortified (against an attack).

Miles on miles outrolled, and the river-channels divide them,—
Miles on miles of green barred by the hurtling gusts.

25 Miles on miles beyond the tawny bay is Minudie.
There are the low blue hills; villages gleam at their feet.
Nearer a white sail shines across the water, and nearer
Still are the slim, grey masts of fishing boats dry on the flats.
Ah, how well I remember those wide red flats, above tide-mark
30 Pale with scurf of the salt, seamed and baked in the sun!
Well I remember the piles of blocks and ropes, and the net-reels
Wound with the beaded nets, dripping and dark from the sea!
Now at this season the nets are unwound; they hang from the rafters
Over the fresh-stowed hay in upland barns, and the wind
35 Blows all day through the chinks, with the streaks of sunlight, and
     sways them
Softly at will; or they lie heaped in the gloom of a loft.

Now at this season the reels are empty and idle; I see them
Over the lines of the dikes, over the gossiping grass.
Now at this season they swing in the long strong wind, thro' the
     lonesome
40 Golden afternoon, shunned by the foraging gulls.
Near about sunset the crane will journey homeward above them;
Round them, under the moon, all the calm night long,
Winnowing soft grey wings of marsh-owls wander and wander,
Now to the broad, lit marsh, now to the dusk of the dike.
45 Soon, thro' their dew-wet frames, in the live keen freshness of morning,
Out of the teeth of the dawn blows back the awakening wind.
Then, as the blue day mounts, and the low-shot shafts of the sunlight
Glance from the tide to the shore, gossamers jewelled with dew
Sparkle and wave, where late sea-spoiling fathoms of drift-net
50 Myriad-meshed, uploomed sombrely over the land.

Well I remember it all. The salt, raw scent of the margin;[4]
While, with men at the windlass, groaned each reel, and the net,
Surging in ponderous lengths, uprose and coiled in its station;
Then each man to his home,—well I remember it all!

55 Yet, as I sit and watch, this present peace of the landscape,—
Stranded boats, these reels empty and idle, the hush,
One grey hawk slow-wheeling above yon cluster of haystacks,—
More than the old-time stir this stillness welcomes me home.
Ah the old-time stir, how once it slung me with rapture,—
60 Old-time sweetness, the winds freighted with honey and salt!
Yet will I stay my steps and not go down to the marshland,—

---

4. The beach immediately adjacent to the water.

Muse and recall far off, rather remember than see,—
Lest on too close sight I miss the darling illusion,
Spy at their task even here the hands of chance and change.

(1883)

Bliss Carman (1861–1929)

While in the United States, Carman worked as a literary journalist and saw other Canadian writers into print. Carman's poetry illustrates various emotional states in impressionistic Maritime and New England landscapes.

Low Tide on Grand Pré[1]

The sun goes down, and over all
    These barren reaches by the tide
Such unelusive glories fall,
    I almost dream they yet will abide
5   Until the coming of the tide.

And yet I know that not for us,
    By any ecstasy of dream,
He lingers to keep luminous
    A little while the grievous stream,
10   Which frets, uncomforted of dream—

A grievous stream, that to and fro
    Athrough the fields of Acadie
Goes wandering, as if to know
    Why one beloved face should be
15   So long from home and Acadie.

---

1. Marshlands near Wolfville, Nova Scotia, reclaimed by the Acadians in the seventeenth century.

Was it a year or lives ago
    We took the grasses in our hands,
And caught the summer flying low
    Over the waving meadow lands,
20   And held it there between our hands?

The while the river at our feet—
    A drowsy inland meadow stream—
At set of sun and after-heat
    Made running gold, and in the gleam
25   We freed our birch upon the stream.

There down along the elms at dusk
    We lifted dripping blade to drift,
Through twilight scented fine like musk,
    Where night and gloom awhile uplift,
30   Nor sunder soul and soul adrift.

And that we took into our hands
    Spirit of life or subtler thing—
Breathed on us there, and loosed the bands
    Of death, and taught us, whispering,
35   The secret of some wonder-thing.

Then all your face grew light, and seemed
    To hold the shadow of the sun;
The evening faltered, and I deemed
    That time was ripe, and years had done
40   Their wheeling underneath the sun.

So all desire and all regret,
    And fear and memory, were naught;
One to remember or forget
    The keen delight our hands had caught;
45   Morrow and yesterday were naught.

The night has fallen, and the tide …
    Now and again comes drifting home,
Across these aching barrens wide,
    A sigh like driven wind or foam:
50   In grief the flood is bursting home.

(1886)

E. Pauline Johnson (1861–1913)

Born on the Six Nations Reserve near Brantford, Ontario, Johnson was the
child of a Mohawk chief and an English woman. She made national and
international reading tours and became a well-known figure, thus giving the
Native voice a popular audience. Johnson wrote both poetry and prose. Her
most famous book is Flint and Feather *(1912).*

Silhouette

The sky-line melts from the russet into blue,
Unbroken the horizon, saving where
A wreath of smoke curls up the far, thin air,
And points the distant lodges of the Sioux.

5   Etched where the lands and cloudlands touch and die
A solitary Indian tepee stands,
The only habitation of these lands,
That roll their magnitude from sky to sky.

The tent poles lift and loom in thin relief,
10 The upward floating smoke ascends between,
And near the open doorway, gaunt and lean,
And shadow-like, there stands an Indian Chief.

With eyes that lost their lustre long ago,
With visage fixed and stern as fate's decree,
15 He looks towards the empty west, to see
The never-coming herd of buffalo.

Only the bones that bleach upon the plains,
Only the fleshless skeletons that lie
In ghastly nakedness and silence, cry
20 Out mutely that naught else to him remains.

(1903)

William Butler Yeats (1865–1939)

Poet, mystic, spiritualist, and Irish nationalist, Yeats helped found an Irish
national theatre and often worked with traditional and nationalist Irish
themes. A major poet of the twentieth century, he won the Nobel Prize for
literature in 1923.

Easter 1916[1]

I have met them at close of day
Coming with vivid faces
From counter or desk among grey
Eighteenth-century houses.
5   I have passed with a nod of the head
Or polite meaningless words,
Or have lingered awhile and said
Polite meaningless words,
And thought before I had done
10 Of a mocking tale or a gibe
To please a companion
Around the fire at the club,
Being certain that they and I
But lived where motley is worn:
15 All changed, changed utterly:
A terrible beauty is born.

That woman's[2] days were spent
In ignorant good-will,
Her nights in argument
20 Until her voice grew shrill.
What voice more sweet than hers
When, young and beautiful,
She rode to harriers?

---

1. In the Easter Rebellion of April 24, 1916, Irish republicans occupied the Post
   Office and other buildings in central Dublin. They were forced to surrender to
   British troops after a week, and fifteen of the leaders were tried and executed the
   following month.
2. Constance Gore-Booth (Countess Markiewicz) (1868–1927), Irish nationalist,
   whom Yeats remembered as a beautiful young woman and daring rider. She was
   sentenced to death for her part in the uprising, but the sentence was later com-
   muted.

This man[3] had kept a school
25 And rode our wingèd horse;[4]
This other[5] his helper and friend
Was coming into his force;
He might have won fame in the end,
So sensitive his nature seemed,
30 So daring and sweet his thought.
This other man[6] I had dreamed
A drunken, vainglorious lout.
He had done most bitter wrong
To some who are near my heart,
35 Yet I number him in the song;
He, too, has resigned his part
In the casual comedy;
He, too, has been changed in his turn,
Transformed utterly:
40 A terrible beauty is born.

Hearts with one purpose alone
Through summer and winter seem
Enchanted to a stone
To trouble the living stream.
45 The horse that comes from the road,
The rider, the birds that range
From cloud to tumbling cloud,
Minute by minute they change;
A shadow of cloud on the stream
50 Changes minute by minute;
A horse-hoof slides on the brim,
And a horse plashes within it;
The long-legged moor-hens dive,
And hens to moor-cocks call;
55 Minute by minute they live:
The stone's in the midst of all.

Too long a sacrifice
Can make a stone of the heart.
O when may it suffice?

---

3. Patrick Pearse (1879–1916) founded St. Edna's School for Boys near Dublin and wrote poetry in Irish and English.

4. Pegasus is the symbolic winged charger of poetic inspiration.

5. Thomas MacDonagh (1878–1916), playwright and poet, who taught at University College, Dublin.

6. Major John MacBride (d. 1916). In 1903, he married Maud Gonne, with whom Yeats had been in love for many years. They separated after only two years because of MacBride's heavy drinking.

60 That is Heaven's part, our part
To murmur name upon name,
As a mother names her child
When sleep at last has come
On limbs that had run wild.
65 What is it but nightfall?
No, no, not night but death;
Was it needless death after all?
For England may keep faith
For all that is done and said.[7]
70 We know their dream; enough
To know they dreamed and are dead;
And what if excess of love
Bewildered them till they died?
I write it out in a verse—
75 MacDonagh and MacBride
And Connolly and Pearse
Now and in time to be,
Wherever green is worn,
Are changed, changed utterly:
80 A terrible beauty is born.

(1916)

The Second Coming[1]

Turning and turning in the widening gyre[2]
The falcon cannot hear the falconer;
Things fall apart; the centre cannot hold;
Mere anarchy is loosed upon the world,
5 The blood-dimmed tide is loosed, and everywhere
The ceremony of innocence is drowned;
The best lack all conviction, while the worst
Are full of passionate intensity.

---

7. Britain had promised Home Rule for Ireland, but the proposals were laid aside because of the outbreak of World War I.

1. In Matt. 24, Christ predicts "the coming of the Son of Man" after a time of war, famine, and natural disasters. Yeats combines this prophecy with the vision of the coming of the Antichrist in I John 2:18.

2. The cone shape made by the falcon's spiralling flight in ever-widening circles from the controlling falconer. In A Vision, Yeats uses the idea of the gyre to illustrate his view of the cyclical nature of history. He believed that the two-thousand-year cycle of Christianity was showing signs of ending and that it would be replaced by its opposite.

220 William Butler Yeats

Surely some revelation is at hand;
10 Surely the Second Coming is at hand.
The Second Coming! Hardly are those words out
When a vast image out of *Spiritus Mundi*[3]
Troubles my sight: somewhere in sands of the desert
A shape with lion body and the head of a man,
15 A gaze blank and pitiless as the sun,
Is moving its slow thighs, while all about it
Reel shadows of the indignant desert birds.
The darkness drops again; but now I know
That twenty centuries of stony sleep
20 Were vexed to nightmare by a rocking cradle,
And what rough beast, its hour come round at last,
Slouches towards Bethlehem to be born?

(1921)

A Prayer for My Daughter

Once more the storm is howling, and half hid
Under this cradle-hood and coverlid
My child sleeps on. There is no obstacle
But Gregory's wood and one bare hill
5 Whereby the haystack- and roof-levelling wind,
Bred on the Atlantic, can be stayed;
And for an hour I have walked and prayed
Because of the great gloom that is in my mind.

I have walked and prayed for this young child an hour
10 And heard the sea-wind scream upon the tower,
And under the arches of the bridge, and scream
In the elms above the flooded stream;
Imagining in excited reverie
That the future years had come,
15 Dancing to a frenzied drum,
Out of the murderous innocence of the sea.

---

3. Yeats believed in a psychic reservoir of images shared by all. "Before the mind's
    eye, whether in sleep or waking, came images that one was to discover presently
    in some book one had never read, and after looking in vain for explanation to
    the current theory of forgotten personal memory, I came to believe in a great
    memory passing on from generation to generation.... Our daily thought was cer-
    tainly but the line of foam at the shallow edge of a vast luminous sea" (*Per Amica
    Silentia Lunae*).

May she be granted beauty and yet not
Beauty to make a stranger's eye distraught,
Or hers before a looking-glass, for such,
20   Being made beautiful overmuch,
Consider beauty a sufficient end,
Lose natural kindness and maybe
The heart-revealing intimacy
That chooses right, and never find a friend.

25   Helen[1] being chosen found life flat and dull
And later had much trouble from a fool,
While that great Queen,[2] that rose out of the spray,
Being fatherless could have her way
Yet chose a bandy-leggèd smith for man.
30   It's certain that fine women eat
A crazy salad with their meat
Whereby the Horn of Plenty is undone.

In courtesy I'd have her chiefly learned;
Hearts are not had as a gift but hearts are earned
35   By those that are not entirely beautiful;
Yet many, that have played the fool
For beauty's very self, has charm made wise,
And many a poor man that has roved,
Loved and thought himself beloved,
40   From a glad kindness cannot take his eyes.

May she become a flourishing hidden tree
That all her thoughts may like the linnet[3] be,
And have no business but dispensing round
Their magnanimities of sound,
45   Nor but in merriment begin a chase,
Nor but in merriment a quarrel.
O may she live like some green laurel
Rooted in one dear perpetual place.

My mind, because the minds that I have loved,
50   The sort of beauty that I have approved,
Prosper but little, has dried up of late,
Yet knows that to be choked with hate
May well be of all evil chances chief.

---

1. Helen of Troy, wife of Menelaus, King of Sparta, whose abduction by the Trojan prince, Paris, was reputed to have caused the Trojan War.
2. Aphrodite, goddess of love and beauty, who was born out of the sea foam and married to the crippled and ugly god of fire, Hephaestus.
3. Songbird.

If there's no hatred in a mind
55 Assault and battery of the wind
Can never tear the linnet from the leaf.

An intellectual hatred is the worst,
So let her think opinions are accursed.
Have I not seen the loveliest woman[4] born
60 Out of the mouth of Plenty's horn,
Because of her opinionated mind
Barter that horn and every good
By quiet natures understood
For an old bellows full of angry wind?

65 Considering that, all hatred driven hence,
The soul recovers radical innocence
And learns at last that it is self-delighting,
Self-appeasing, self-affrighting,
And that its own sweet will is Heaven's will;
70 She can, though every face should scowl
And every windy quarter howl
Or every bellows burst, be happy still.

And may her bridegroom bring her to a house
Where all's accustomed, ceremonious;
75 For arrogance and hatred are the wares
Peddled in the thoroughfares.
How but in custom and in ceremony
Are innocence and beauty born?
Ceremony's a name for the rich horn,
80 And custom for the spreading laurel tree.

(1919)

---

4. Maud Gonne, with whom Yeats had been romantically in love for many years and
who became deeply involved in Irish nationalist politics.

Robert Frost (1874–1963)

Frost was a poet, teacher, and farmer. Although the colloquial style and homely New England landscape of his poems assure his popularity as a modern American poet, his work is often both darker and more complex than it appears.

Home Burial

He saw her from the bottom of the stairs
Before she saw him. She was starting down,
Looking back over her shoulder at some fear.
She took a doubtful step and then undid it
5   To raise herself and look again. He spoke
Advancing toward her: "What is it you see
From up there always?—for I want to know."
She turned and sank down upon her skirts at that,
And her face changed from terrified to dull.
10   He said to gain time: "What is it you see?"
Mounting until she cowered under him.
"I will find out now—you must tell me, dear."
She, in her place, refused him any help,
With the least stiffening of her neck and silence.
15   She let him look, sure that he wouldn't see,
Blind creature; and awhile he didn't see.
But at last he murmered, "Oh," and again, "Oh."

"What is it—what?" she said.

                  "Just that I see."

20   "You don't," she challenged. "Tell me what it is."

"The wonder is I didn't see at once.
I never noticed it from here before.
I must be wonted to it—that's the reason.
The little graveyard where my people are!
25   So small the window frames the whole of it.
Not so much larger than a bedroom, is it?
There are three stones of slate and one of marble,
Broad-shouldered little slabs there in the sunlight

On the sidehill. We haven't to mind *those*.
30   But I understand; it is not the stones,
But the child's mound——"

                           "Don't, don't, don't, don't," she cried.

She withdrew, shrinking from beneath his arm
That rested on the banister, and slid downstairs;
35   And turned on him with such a daunting look,
He said twice over before he knew himself:
"Can't a man speak of his own child he's lost?"

"Not you!—Oh, where's my hat? Oh, I don't need it!
I must get out of here. I must get air.—
40   I don't know rightly whether any man can."

"Amy! Don't go to someone else this time
Listen to me. I won't come down the stairs."
He sat and fixed his chin between his fists.
"There's something I should like to ask you, dear."

45   "You don't know how to ask it."

                           "Help me, then."

Her fingers moved the latch for all reply.

"My words are nearly always an offense.
I don't know how to speak of anything
50   So as to please you. But I might be taught,
I should suppose. I can't say I see how.
A man must partly give up being a man
With womenfolk. We could have some arrangement
By which I'd bind myself to keep hands off
55   Anything special you're a-mind to name.
Though I don't like such things 'twixt those that love.
Two that don't love can't live together without them.
But two that do can't live together with them."
She moved the latch a little. "Don't—don't go.
60   Don't carry it to someone else this time.
Tell me about it if it's something human.
Let me into your grief. I'm not so much
Unlike other folks as your standing there
Apart would make me out. Give me my chance.
65   I do think, though, you overdo it a little.
What was it brought you up to think it the thing
To take your mother-loss of a first child

So inconsolably—in the face of love.
You'd think this memory might be satisfied——"

70   "There you go sneering now!"

                              "I'm not, I'm not!
You make me angry. I'll come down to you.
God, what a woman! And it's come to this.
A man can't speak of his own child that's dead."

75   "You can't because you don't know how to speak.
If you had any feelings, you that dug
With your own hand—how could you?—his little grave;
I saw you from that very window there,
Making the gravel leap and leap in air,
80   Leap up, like that, like that, and land so lightly
And roll back down the mound beside the hole.
I thought, Who is that man? I didn't know you.
And I crept down the stairs and up the stairs
To look again, and still your spade kept lifting.
85   Then you came in. I heard your rumbling voice
Out in the kitchen, and I don't know why,
But I went near to see with my own eyes.
You could sit there with the stains on your shoes
Of the fresh earth from your own baby's grave
90   And talk about your everyday concerns.
You had stood the spade up against the wall
Outside there in the entry, for I saw it."

"I shall laugh the worst laugh I ever laughed.
I'm cursed. God, if I don't believe I'm cursed."

95   "I can repeat the very words you were saying:
'Three foggy mornings and one rainy day
Will rot the best birch fence a man can build.'
Think of it, talk like that at such a time!
What had how long it takes a birch to rot
100 To do with what was in the darkened parlor?
You *couldn't* care! The nearest friends can go
With anyone to death, comes so far short
They might as well not try to go at all.
No, from the time when one is sick to death,
105 One is alone, and he dies more alone.
Friends make pretense of following to the grave,
But before one is in it, their minds are turned
And making the best of their way back to life
And living people, and things they understand.

110 But the world's evil. I won't have grief so
     If I can change it. Oh, I won't, I won't!"

"There, you have said it all and you feel better.
You won't go now. You're crying. Close the door.
The heart's gone out of it: why keep it up?
115 Amy! There's someone coming down the road!"

"*You*—oh, you think the talk is all. I must go—
Somewhere out of this house. How can I make you——"

"If—you—do!" She was opening the door wider.
"Where do you mean to go? First tell me that.
120 I'll follow and bring you back by force. I *will!*—"

(1914)

"Out, Out—"[1]

The buzz saw snarled and rattled in the yard
And made dust and dropped stove-length sticks of wood,
Sweet-scented stuff when the breeze drew across it.
And from there those that lifted eyes could count
5 Five mountain ranges one behind the other
Under the sunset far into Vermont.
And the saw snarled and rattled, snarled and rattled,
As it ran light, or had to bear a load.
And nothing happened: day was all but done.
10 Call it a day, I wish they might have said
To please the boy by giving him the half hour
That a boy counts so much when saved from work.
His sister stood beside them in her apron
To tell them "Supper." At the word, the saw,
15 As if to prove saws knew what supper meant,
Leaped out of the boy's hand, or seemed to leap—
He must have given the hand. However it was,
Neither refused the meeting. But the hand!
The boy's first outcry was a rueful laugh,
20 As he swung toward them holding up the hand
Half in appeal, but half as if to keep
The life from spilling. Then the boy saw it all—
Since he was old enough to know, big boy
Doing a man's work, though a child at heart—

---

1. See Shakespeare's *Macbeth*, V, v, 19–28.

25 He saw all spoiled. "Don't let him cut my hand off—
The doctor, when he comes. Don't let him, sister!"
So. But the hand was gone already.
The doctor put him in the dark of ether.
He lay and puffed his lips out with his breath.
30 And then—the watcher at his pulse took fright.
No one believed. They listened at his heart.
Little—less—nothing!—and that ended it.
No more to build on there. And they, since they
Were not the one dead, turned to their affairs.

(1916)

Wallace Stevens (1879–1955)

Wallace Stevens was a lawyer, insurance company executive, and highly respected American poet. He believed that the structure of art mirrored the order of the natural universe. This idea is reflected in the titles of his works, such as Harmonium *(1923) and* Ideas of Order *(1935).*

Anecdote of the Jar

I placed a jar in Tennessee,
And round it was, upon a hill.
It made the slovenly wilderness
Surround that hill.

5 The wilderness rose up to it,
And sprawled around, no longer wild.
The jar was round upon the ground
And tall and of a port in air.

It took dominion everywhere.
10 The jar was gray and bare.
It did not give of bird or bush,
Like nothing else in Tennessee.

(1923)

The Snow Man

One must have a mind of winter
To regard the frost and the boughs
Of the pine-trees crusted with snow;

And have been cold a long time
5   To behold the junipers shagged with ice,
The spruces rough in the distant glitter

Of the January sun; and not to think
Of any misery in the sound of the wind,
In the sound of a few leaves,

10   Which is the sound of the land
Full of the same wind
That is blowing in the same bare place

For the listener, who listens in the snow,
And, nothing himself, beholds
15   Nothing that is not there and the nothing that is.

(1923)

E.J. Pratt (1882–1964)

Although he spent much of his professional life at the University of Toronto, where he first studied for the Methodist ministry and later taught English, much of Pratt's poetry reflects his Newfoundland outport childhood.

The Shark

He seemed to know the harbour,
So leisurely he swam;
His fin,
Like a piece of sheet-iron,
5   Three-cornered,

And with knife-edge,
Stirred not a bubble
As it moved
With its base-line on the water.

10 His body was tubular
And tapered
And smoke-blue,
And as he passed the wharf
He turned,
15 And snapped at a flat-fish
That was dead and floating.
And I saw the flash of a white throat,
And a double row of white teeth,
And eyes of metallic grey,
20 Hard and narrow and slit.

Then out of the harbour,
With that three-cornered fin
Shearing without a bubble the water
Lithely,
25 Leisurely,
He swam—
That strange fish,
Tubular, tapered, smoke-blue,
Part vulture, part wolf,
30 Part neither—for his blood was cold.

(1923)

Silences

There is no silence upon the earth or under the earth like the
    silence under the sea;
No cries announcing birth,
No sounds declaring death.
There is silence when the milt is laid on the spawn in the weeds
    and fungus of the rock-clefts;
5   And silence in the growth and struggle for life.
The bonitoes pounce upon the mackerel,
And are themselves caught by the barracudas,
The sharks kill the barracudas
And the great molluscs rend the sharks,
10 And all noiselessly—
Though swift be the action and final the conflict,

NEL

The drama is silent.
There is no fury upon the earth like the fury under the sea.
For growl and cough and snarl are the tokens of spendthrifts who
    know not the ultimate economy of rage.
15 Moreover, the pace of the blood is too fast.
But under the waves the blood is sluggard and has the same
    temperature as that of the sea.
There is something pre-reptilian about a silent kill.

Two men may end their hostilities just with their battle-cries.
"The devil take you," says one.
20 "I'll see you in hell first," says the other.
And these introductory salutes followed by a hail of gutturals and
    sibilants are often the beginning of friendship, for who would not
    prefer to be lustily damned than to be half-heartedly blessed?
No one need fear oaths that are properly enunciated, for they
    belong to the inheritance of just men made perfect, and, for all
    we know, of such may be the Kingdom of Heaven.
But let silent hate be put away for it feeds upon the heart of the hater.
Today I watched two pairs of eyes. One pair was black and the other
    grey. And while the owners thereof, for the space of five seconds
    walked past each other, the grey snapped at the black and the
    black riddled the grey.
25 One looked to say—"The cat,"
And the other—"The cur."
But no words were spoken;
No so much as a hiss or a murmur came through the perfect enamel
    of the teeth; not so much as a gesture of enmity.
If the right upper lip curled over the canine, it went unnoticed.
30 The lashes veiled the eyes not for an instant in the passing.
And as between the two in respect to candour of intention or
    eternity of wish, there was no choice, for the stare was mutual
    and absolute.
A word would have dulled the exquisite edge of the feeling,
An oath would have flawed the crystallization of the hate.
For only such culture could grow in a climate of silence,—
35 Away back before the emergence of fur or feather, back to the
    unvocal sea and down deep where the darkness spills its wash on
    the threshold of light, where the lids never close upon the eyes,
    where the inhabitants slay in silence and are as silently slain.

(1936)

William Carlos Williams (1883–1963)

An American physician, poet, and short-story and prose writer, Williams makes powerful what is plain and usual. He was concerned that his poetry reflect "those things which lie under the direct scrutiny of the sense, close to the nose."

The Red Wheelbarrow

so much depends
upon

a red wheel
barrow

5   glazed with rain
water

beside the white
chickens

(1923)

D.H. Lawrence (1885–1930)

The son of a miner, David Herbert Lawrence was educated at Nottingham University College and gave up teaching to pursue his writing. Lawrence travelled extensively and wrote prolifically in a range of genres despite frequent ill health. Although better known for his fiction (and the obscenity charges it occasioned), Lawrence's first published work was poetry. See his short story "You Touched Me," p. 411.

Piano

Softly, in the dusk, a woman is singing to me;
Taking me back down the vista of years, till I see
A child sitting under the piano, in the boom of the tingling strings
And pressing the small, poised feet of a mother who smiles as she sings.

5   In spite of myself, the insidious mastery of song
Betrays me back, till the heart of me weeps to belong
To the old Sunday evenings at home, with winter outside
And hymns in the cosy parlour, the tinkling piano our guide.

So now it is vain for the singer to burst into clamour
10   With the great black piano appassionato. The glamour
Of childish days is upon me, my manhood is cast
Down in the flood of remembrance, I weep like a child for the past.

(1918)

Ezra Pound (1885–1972)

Pound was a prominent American expatriate in early twentieth-century literary circles that included H.D. (Hilda Doolittle) and T.S. Eliot. His virtuosity ranged from poetry and translation to criticism. His sympathy with fascism has clouded his reputation.

The River-Merchant's Wife: A Letter[1]

While my hair was still cut straight across my forehead
I played about the front gate, pulling flowers.
You came by on bamboo stilts, playing horse,
You walked about my seat, playing with blue plums.

---

1. Pound based this version of a poem by the eighth-century poet Li Po (Rihaku) on the English notes of American scholar Ernest Fenollosa. In these notes, all names were rendered according to the Japanese manner of pronunciation. Pound repeats this convention with the place names in his poem.

5 And we went on living in the village of Chokan:
   Two small people, without dislike or suspicion.

   At fourteen I married My Lord you.
   I never laughed, being bashful.
   Lowering my head, I looked at the wall.
10 Called to, a thousand times, I never looked back.

   At fifteen I stopped scowling,
   I desired my dust to be mingled with yours
   Forever and forever and forever.
   Why should I climb the look out?

15 At sixteen you departed,
   You went into far Ku-to-yen, by the river of swirling eddies,
   And you have been gone five months.
   The monkeys make sorrowful noise overhead.

   You dragged your feet when you went out.
20 By the gate now, the moss is grown, the different mosses,
   Too deep to clear them away!
   The leaves fall early this autumn, in wind.
   The paired butterflies are already yellow with August
   Over the grass in the West garden;
25 They hurt me. I grow older.
   If you are coming down through the narrows of the river Kiang,
   Please let me know beforehand,
   And I will come out to meet you
           As far as Cho-fu-Sa.

By Rihaku

(1915)

In a Station of the Metro

The apparition of these faces in the crowd;
Petals on a wet, black bough.

(1913)

NEL

(Hilda Doolittle) H.D. (1886–1961)

H.D., as she is known, and Ezra Pound led the Imagist movement in poetry. Imagist poems, like the poem reproduced here, are usually lean and musical representations of clear and concrete subjects.

Heat

O wind, rend open the heat,
cut apart the heat,
rend it to tatters.

Fruit cannot drop
5 through this thick air—
fruit cannot fall into heat
that presses up and blunts
the points of pears
and rounds the grapes.

10 Cut the heat—
plough through it,
turning it on either side
of your path.

(1916)

Siegfried Sassoon (1886–1967)

One of the major poets of World War I, Sassoon began writing in the trenches and skillfully reflected his own experience at the Front. The realism of his verse contrasted starkly with the patriotic idealism of the early war period.

Counter-Attack

We'd gained our first objective hours before
While dawn broke like a face with blinking eyes,
Pallid, unshaved and thirsty, blind with smoke.
Things seemed all right at first. We held their line,
5   With bombers posted, Lewis guns[1] well placed,
And clink of shovels deepening the shallow trench.
    The place was rotten with dead; green clumsy legs
    High-booted, sprawled and grovelled along the saps
    And trunks, face downward, in the sucking mud,
10   Wallowed like trodden sand-bags loosely filled;
    And naked sodden buttocks, mats of hair,
    Bulged, clotted heads slept in the plastering slime,
    And then the rain began,—the jolly old rain!

A yawning soldier knelt against the bank,
15 Staring across the morning blear with fog;
He wondered when the Allemands[2] would get busy;
And then, of course, they started with five-nines[3]
Traversing, sure as fate, and never a dud.
Mute in the clamour of shells he watched them burst
20 Spouting dark earth and wire with gusts from hell,
While posturing giants dissolved in drifts of smoke.
He crouched and flinched, dizzy with galloping fear,
Sick for escape,—loathing the strangled horror
And butchered, frantic gestures of the dead.

25 An officer came blundering down the trench:
"Stand-to and man the fire-step!" On he went ...
Gasping and bawling, "Fire-step ... counter-attack!"
Then the haze lifted. Bombing on the right
Down the old sap:[4] Machine-guns on the left;
30 And stumbling figures looming out in front.
"O Christ, they're coming at us!" Bullets spat,
And he remembered his rifle ... rapid fire ...
And started blazing wildly ... then a bang
Crumpled and spun him sideways, knocked him out
35 To grunt and wriggle: none heeded him; he choked
And fought the flapping veils of smothering gloom,
Lost in a blurred confusion of yells and groans ...

---

1. A light machine gun adopted by the British Army during World War I.
2. That is, the Germans.
3. I.e., 5.9-inch calibre shells.
4. Trench.

Down, and down, and down, he sank and drowned,
Bleeding to death. The counter-attack had failed.

(1918)

Marianne Moore (1887–1972)

A poet and editor, Moore was born in Missouri but spent most of her life in Brooklyn. Poet and critic Randall Jarrell wrote that Moore "has made a principle out of refusing to believe that there is any such thing as the antipoetic." The poems included here capture her typically conversational tone and precisely observed detail.

Poetry

I, too, dislike it: there are things that are important beyond all this fiddle.
    Reading it, however, with a perfect contempt for it, one discovers in
    it after all, a place for the genuine.
        Hands that can grasp, eyes
5   that can dilate, hair that can rise
            if it must, these things are important not because a

high-sounding interpretation can be put upon them but because they are
    useful. When they become so derivative as to become unintelligible,
    the same thing may be said for all of us, that we
10   do not admire what
        we cannot understand: the bat
            holding on upside down or in quest of something to

eat, elephants pushing, a wild horse taking a roll, a tireless wolf under
    a tree, the immovable critic twitching his skin like a horse that feels
15   a flea, the base-
        ball fan, the statistician—
        nor is it valid
            to discriminate against "business documents and

school-books";[1] all these phenomena are important. One must make a
   distinction
20   however: when dragged into prominence by half poets, the result is
       not poetry,
     nor till the poets among us can be
        "literalists of
        the imagination"[2]—above
           insolence and triviality and can present

25   for inspection, "imaginary gardens with real toads in them," shall we have
     it. In the meantime, if you demand on the one hand,
     the raw material of poetry in
        all its rawness and
        that which is on the other hand
30   genuine, you are interested in poetry.

                                                        (1921)

The Fish

wade
through black jade.
   of the crow-blue mussel-shells, one keeps
   adjusting the ash-heaps;
5   opening and shutting itself like

an
injured fan.
   The barnacles which encrust the side
   of the wave, cannot hide
10   there for the submerged shafts of the

---

1. *Diary of Tolstoy* (Dutton), p. 84. "Where the boundary between prose and poetry
   lies, I shall never be able to understand. The question is raised in manuals of
   style, yet the answer to it lies beyond me. Poetry is verse: prose is not verse. Or
   else poetry is everything with the exception of business documents and school
   books." [Moore's note.]

2. "Literalists of the imagination." Yeats: *Ideas of Good and Evil*, London, 1903, p.
   182. "The limitation of his [Blake's] view was from the very intensity of his
   vision; he was a too literal realist of imagination, as others are of nature; and
   because he believed that the figures seen by the mind's eye, when exalted by
   inspiration, were 'external existences,' symbols of divine essences, he hated every
   grace of style that might obscure their lineaments." [Moore's note.]

sun,
split like spun
    glass, move themselves with spotlight swiftness
    into the crevices—
15   in and out, illuminating

the
turquoise sea
    of bodies. The water drives a wedge
    of iron through the iron edge
20   of the cliff; whereupon the stars,

pink
rice-grains, ink-
    bespattered jelly-fish, crabs like green
    lilies, and submarine
25   toadstools, slide each on the other.

All
external
    marks of abuse are present on this
    defiant edifice—
30   all the physical features of

ac-
cident—lack
    of cornice, dynamite grooves, burns, and
    hatchet strokes, these things stand
35   out on it; the chasm-side is

dead.
Repeated
    evidence has proved that it can live
    on what can not revive
40   its youth. The sea grows old in it.

(1921)

Edwin Muir (1887–1959)

Best known as a poet, Edwin Muir was also a novelist, translator, critic,
and literary journalist. A move from the Orkney Islands of Scotland to
industrial Glasgow at age fourteen had a considerable influence on his
literary sensibility.

The Wayside Station

Here at the wayside station, as many a morning,
I watch the smoke torn from the fumy engine
Crawling across the fields in serpent sorrow.
Flat in the east, held down by stolid clouds,
5   The struggling day is born and shines already
On its warm hearth far off. Yet something here
Glimmers along the ground to show the seagulls
White on the furrows' black unturning waves.

But now the light has broadened.
10   I watch the farmstead on the little hill,
That seems to mutter: "Here is day again"
Unwillingly. Now the sad cattle wake
In every byre and stall,
The ploughboy stirs in the loft, the farmer groans
15   And feels the day like a familiar ache
Deep in his body, though the house is dark.
The lovers part
Now in the bedroom where the pillows gleam
Great and mysterious as deep hills of snow,
20   An inaccessible land. The wood stands waiting
While the bright snare slips coil by coil around it,
Dark silver on every branch. The lonely stream
That rode through darkness leaps the gap of light,
Its voice grown loud, and starts its winding journey
25   Through the day and time and war and history.

(1943)

T.S. Eliot (1888–1965)

With his poetic representations of the ennui and quiet desperation of the twentieth century, Eliot secured his reputation as the eminent modern poet. His critical attitudes were as influential as his verse rhythms and subtle ironies. Born in Missouri, Eliot lived in England for many years, becoming a British citizen in 1927.

The Love Song of J. Alfred Prufrock

> *S'io credessi che mia riposta fosse*
> *a persona che mai tornasse al mondo,*
> *questa fiamma staria senzi più scosse.*
> *Ma per ciò che giammai di questo fondo*
> *non tornò vivo alcun, s'i'odo il vero,*
> *senza tema d'infamia ti rispondo.*[1]

Let us go then, you and I,
When the evening is spread out against the sky
Like a patient etherized upon a table;
Let us go, through certain half-deserted streets,
5   The muttering retreats
Of restless nights in one-night cheap hotels
And sawdust restaurants with oyster-shells:
Streets that follow like a tedious argument
Of insidious intent
10   To lead you to an overwhelming question …
Oh, do not ask, "What is it?"
Let us go and make our visit.

In the room the women come and go
Talking of Michelangelo.

---

1. The epigraph is taken from Dante's *Inferno* (XXVII, 61–66), where the poet encounters a fraudulent papal counsellor, Guido Da Montefeltro. In responding to the request to reveal his identity, the man, having sinned with his tongue in life, is now obliged to speak through the tongue of flame that encircles him: "If I thought that my reply were to one who would ever go back to the world, this flame would rest from further movement. But since no one, if what I hear is true, has ever returned alive from this abyss, I answer you without fear of infamy."

15   The yellow fog that rubs its back upon the window-panes,
     The yellow smoke that rubs its muzzle on the window-panes,
     Licked its tongue into the corners of the evening,
     Lingered upon the pools that stand in drains,
     Let fall upon its back the soot that falls from chimneys,
20   Slipped by the terrace, made a sudden leap,
     And seeing that it was a soft October night,
     Curled once about the house, and fell asleep.

     And indeed there will be time
     For the yellow smoke that slides along the street,
25   Rubbing its back upon the window-panes;
     There will be time, there will be time
     To prepare a face to meet the faces that you meet;
     There will be time to murder and create,
     And time for all the works and days² of hands
30   That lift and drop a question on your plate;
     Time for you and time for me.
     And time yet for a hundred indecisions,
     And for a hundred visions and revisions,
     Before the taking of a toast and tea.

35   In the room the women come and go
     Talking of Michelangelo.

     And indeed there will be time
     To wonder, "Do I dare?" and, "Do I dare?"
     Time to turn back and descend the stair,
40   With a bald spot in the middle of my hair—
     (They will say: "How his hair is growing thin!")
     My morning coat, my collar mounting firmly to the chin,
     My necktie rich and modest, but asserted by a simple pin—
     (They will say: "But how his arms and legs are thin!")
45   Do I dare
     Disturb the universe?
     In a minute there is time
     For decisions and revisions which a minute will reverse.

     For I have known them all already, known them all—
50   Have known the evenings, mornings, afternoons,
     I have measured out my life with coffee spoons;
     I know the voices dying with a dying fall
     Beneath the music from a farther room.
     So how should I presume?

---

2. Title of a poem by the eighth-century B.C. writer Hesiod, containing a practical account of farming and rural life, as well as fable, allegory, and autobiography.

55   And I have known the eyes already, known them all—
The eyes that fix you in a formulated phrase,
And when I am formulated, sprawling on a pin,
When I am pinned and wriggling on the wall,
Then how should I begin
60   To spit out all the butt-ends of my days and ways?
    And how should I presume?

    And I have known the arms already, known them all—
Arms that are braceleted and white and bare
(But in the lamplight, downed with light brown hair!)
65   Is it perfume from a dress
That makes me so digress?
Arms that lie along a table, or wrap about a shawl.
    And should I then presume?
    And how should I begin?

                .   .   .   .   .

70   Shall I say, I have gone at dusk through narrow streets
And watched the smoke that rises from the pipes
Of lonely men in shirt-sleeves, leaning out of windows? ...

    I should have been a pair of ragged claws
Scuttling across the floors of silent seas.

                .   .   .   .   .

75   And the afternoon, the evening, sleeps so peacefully!
Smoothed by long fingers,
Asleep ... tired ... or it malingers,
Stretched on the floor, here beside you and me.
Should I, after tea and cakes and ices,
80   Have the strength to force the moment to a crisis?
But though I have wept and fasted, wept and prayed,
Though I have seen my head (grown slightly bald) brought in upon
    a platter,[3]
I am no prophet—and here's no great matter;
I have seen the moment of my greatness flicker,
85   And I have seen the eternal Footman hold my coat, and snicker,
And in short, I was afraid.

    And would it have been worth it, after all,
After the cups, the marmalade, the tea,

---

3. Salome, rejected in love by John the Baptist, persuaded Herod to have John's severed head brought to her (Matt. 14:3–11).

Among the porcelain, among some talk of you and me,
90 Would it have been worth while,
To have bitten off the matter with a smile,
To have squeezed the universe into a ball[4]
To roll it toward some overwhelming question,
To say: "I am Lazarus,[5] come from the dead,
95 Come back to tell you all, I shall tell you all"—
If one, settling a pillow by her head,
    Should say: "That is not what I meant at all.
    That is not it, at all."

    And would it have been worth it, after all,
100 Would it have been worth while,
After the sunsets and the dooryards and the sprinkled streets,
After the novels, after the teacups, after the skirts that trail along
    the floor—
And this, and so much more?—
It is impossible to say just what I mean!
105 But as if a magic lantern threw the nerves in patterns on a screen:
Would it not have been worth while
If one, settling a pillow or throwing off a shawl,
And turning toward the window, should say:
    "That is not it at all,
110   That is not what I meant, at all."

                .   .   .   .   .

    No! I am not Prince Hamlet, nor was meant to be;
Am an attendant lord, one that will do
To swell a progress, start a scene or two,
Advise the prince; no doubt, an easy tool,
115 Deferential, glad to be of use,
Politic, cautious, and meticulous;
Full of high sentence, but a bit obtuse;
At times, indeed, almost ridiculous—
Almost, at times, the Fool.

120   I grow old ... I grow old ...
I shall wear the bottoms of my trousers rolled.

---

4. See Marvell, "To His Coy Mistress" (ll. 41–42), p. 152.

5. This reference may not be only to the Lazarus whom Christ raised from the dead (John 11:1–44) but also to the beggar Lazarus (Luke 16:19–31), who was not permitted to return from the dead to warn the wealthy about hell.

Shall I part my hair behind? Do I dare to eat a peach?
I shall wear white flannel trousers, and walk upon the beach.
I have heard the mermaids singing, each to each.

125 I do not think that they will sing to me.

I have seen them riding seaward on the waves
Combing the white hair of the waves blown back
When the wind blows the water white and black.

We have lingered in the chambers of the sea
130 By sea-girls wreathed with seaweed red and brown
Till human voices wake us, and we drown.

(1917)

Journey of the Magi[1]

"A cold coming we had of it,
Just the worst time of the year
For a long journey, and such a long journey:
The ways deep and the weather sharp,
5   The very dead of winter."[2]
And the camels galled, sore-footed, refractory,
Lying down in the melting snow.
There were times we regretted
The summer palaces on the slopes, the terraces,
10   And the silken girls bringing sherbet.
Then the camel men cursing and grumbling
And running away, and wanting their liquor and women,
And the night-fires going out, and the lack of shelters,
And the cities hostile and the towns unfriendly
15   And the villages dirty and charging high prices:
A hard time we had of it.
At the end we preferred to travel all night,
Sleeping in snatches,
With the voices singing in our ears, saying
20   That this was all folly.

---

1. Three kings or wise men of the East who followed the star of Bethlehem and
   brought gifts to the infant Jesus.

2. Adapted from a passage in a Nativity sermon by the seventeenth-century divine
   Lancelot Andrewes: "A cold coming they had of it at this time of the year, just the
   worst time of the year to take a journey, and specially a long journey in. The ways
   deep, the weather sharp, the days short, the sun farthest off, in *solstitio brumali*,
   'the very dead of winter.'"

Then at dawn we came down to a temperate valley,
Wet, below the snow line, smelling of vegetation,
With a running stream and water-mill beating the darkness,
And three trees on the low sky.
25 And an old white horse galloped away in a meadow.
Then we came to a tavern with vine-leaves over the lintel,
Six hands at an open door dicing for pieces of silver,
And feet kicking the empty wine-skins.
But there was no information, and so we continued
30 And arrived at evening, not a moment too soon
Finding the place; it was (you may say) satisfactory.

All this was a long time ago, I remember,
And I would do it again, but set down
This set down
35 This: were we led all the way for
Birth or Death? There was a Birth, certainly,
We had evidence and no doubt. I had seen birth and death,
But had thought they were different; this Birth was
Hard and bitter agony for us, like Death, our death.
40 We returned to our places, these Kingdoms,
But no longer at ease here, in the old dispensation,
With an alien people clutching their gods.
I should be glad of another death.

(1927)

Kenneth Leslie (1892–1974)

*Leslie was a strong advocate of Christian socialism, which is reflected in his
poetry. In addition to his political verse, he also wrote a good deal of poetry
that draws its strength from his powerful ties to Nova Scotia and the sea.*

Harlem Preacher

To Martin Luther King[1]

The gospel song, hushed suddenly to a hum,
dies in vibrating silence; a child clings
to its mother, wondering what is to come.
The preacher closes his eyes and waits till wings
5   have winnowed the world of guile, then lifts his head
with flash of power and grace no art can teach,
now softly repeats the text that he had read,
and, throwing himself away, begins to preach.
Not arguments but God Himself, the Maker,
10   worlds for His whims, the Dreamer and the Doer,
the Lover, cruel and kind, the Heart-breaker,
wayward and jealous, the mad and mighty Wooer,
God in the flesh is what this black man brings,
into the hungry throng it is himself he flings.

(1934)

Wilfred Owen (1893–1918)

*A highly esteemed war poet whose work combines compassion and realism,
Owen was killed a week before the end of World War I. The sombre, acerbic,
and often ironic tone of his poems is complemented by his use of half, or
"slant," rhymes.*

Anthem for Doomed Youth

What passing-bells for these who die as cattle?
  Only the monstrous anger of the guns.

---

1. Martin Luther King, Sr. (1899–1984), pastor of the Ebenezer Baptist Church, Atlanta, Georgia, who preached non-violence. Father of civil-rights leader Martin Luther King, Jr. (1929–1968).

Only the stuttering rifles' rapid rattle
Can patter out their hasty orisons.
5 No mockeries for them; no prayers or bells,
Nor any voice of mourning save the choirs,—
The shrill demented choirs of wailing shells;
And bugles calling for them from sad shires.

What candles may be held to speed them all?
10   Not in the hands of boys, but in their eyes
Shall shine the holy glimmers of good-byes.
The pallor of girls' brows shall be their pall;
Their flowers the tenderness of patient minds,
And each slow dusk a drawing-down of blinds.

(1920)

Disabled

He sat in a wheeled chair, waiting for dark,
And shivered in his ghastly suit of grey,
Legless, sewn short at elbow. Through the park
Voices of boys rang saddening like a hymn,
5 Voices of play and pleasure after day,
Till gathering sleep had mothered them from him.

. . .

About this time Town used to swing to gay
When glow-lamps budded in the light blue trees,
And girls glanced lovelier as the air grew dim,—
10 In the old times, before he threw away his knees.
Now he will never feel again how slim
Girls' waists are, or how warm their subtle hands;
All of them touch him like some queer disease.

. . .

There was an artist silly for his face,
15 For it was younger than his youth, last year.
Now, he is old; his back will never brace;
He's lost his color very far from here,
Poured it down shell-holes till the veins ran dry,
And half his lifetime lapsed in the hot race,
20 And leap of purple spurted from his thigh.

. . .

One time he liked a blood-smear down his leg,
After the matches, carried shoulder-high
It was after football, when he'd drunk a peg.[1]
He thought he'd better join.—He wonders why.
25 Someone had said he'd look a god in kilts,
That's why; and may be, too, to please his Meg;
Aye, that was it, to please the giddy jilts
He asked to join. He didn't have to beg;
Smiling they wrote his lie; aged nineteen years.
30 Germans he scarcely thought of; all their guilt,
And Austria's, did not move him. And no fears
Of Fear came yet. He thought of jeweled hilts
For daggers in plaid socks; of smart salutes;
And care of arms; and leave; and pay arrears;
35 *Esprit de corps*; and hints for young recruits.
And soon, he was drafted out with drums and cheers.

· · ·

Some cheered him home, but not as crowds cheer Goal.
Only a solemn man who brought him fruits
Thanked him; and then inquired about his soul.
40 Now, he will spend a few sick years in Institutes,
And do what things the rules consider wise,
And take whatever pity they may dole.
Tonight he noticed how the women's eyes
Passed from him to the strong men that were whole.
45 How cold and late it is! Why don't they come
And put him to bed? Why don't they come?

(1920)

E.E. Cummings (1894–1962)

Cummings's iconoclasm is shown in his disregard of standard grammar and syntax, matched by his concern for freely led and unconventional life. A fine lyric (and satiric) poet, he expresses a profound love of both people and nature.

---

1. Anglo-Indian slang for a drink, usually of brandy and soda.

since feeling is first

since feeling is first
who pays any attention
to the syntax of things
will never wholly kiss you;

5   wholly to be a fool
while Spring is in the world

my blood approves,
and kisses are a better fate
than wisdom
10   lady i swear by all flowers.   Don't cry
—the best gesture of my brain is less than
your eyelids' flutter which says

we are for each other:then
laugh,leaning back in my arms
15   for life's not a paragraph

And death i think is no parenthesis

(1926)

somewhere i have never travelled

somewhere i have never travelled,gladly beyond
any experience,your eyes have their silence:
in your most frail gesture are things which enclose me,
or which i cannot touch because they are too near

5   your slightest look easily will unclose me
though i have closed myself as fingers,
you open always petal by petal myself as Spring opens
(touching skilfully,mysteriously)her first rose

or if your wish be to close me,i and
10   my life will shut very beautifully,suddenly,
as when the heart of this flower imagines
the snow carefully everywhere descending;

nothing which we are to perceive in this world equals
the power of your intense fragility:whose texture
15   compels me with the colour of its countries,
rendering death and forever with each breathing

(i do not know what it is about you that closes
and opens;only something in me understands
the voice of your eyes is deeper than all roses)
20 nobody,not even the rain,has such small hands

(1931)

O sweet spontaneous

O sweet spontaneous
earth how often have
the
doting

5   fingers of
prurient philosophers pinched
and
poked

thee
10 ,has the naughty thumb
of science prodded
thy

   beauty   .how
often have religions taken
15 thee upon their scraggy knees
squeezing and

buffeting thee that thou mightest conceive
gods
    (but
20 true

to the incomparable
couch of death thy
rhythmic
lover

25   thou answerest

them only with

     spring)

(1923)

F.R. Scott (1899–1985)

A Canadian poet, social philosopher, and professor of law, Scott received a
Governor General's Award for The Collected Poems of F.R. Scott *(1981).*
His poetry is often satirical and usually reflects Scott's social concerns.

Spain: 1937

For these our hearts are bleeding: the homes burning,
The schools broken and ended, the vision thwarted,
The youths, their backs to the wall, awaiting the volley,
The child staring at the huddled form.

5   And Guernica,[1] more real than our daily bread.

For these our hurt and hate, sharp couriers,
Arouse a waking world: the black crusade,
Pious brutality, mass massacre,
Sudden cohesion of class, wealth and creed,
10   Behind the gilded cross, the swastika,
Behind neutrality, the will to kill.

And Lorca,[2] rising godlike from the fascist guns.

In the spring of ideas they were, the rare spring
That breaks historic winters. Street and field
15   Stirring with hope and green with new endeavour,
The crackling husks copious with sprouting seed.
Here was destruction before flowering,
Here freedom was cut in its first tendrils.

This issue is not ended with defeat.

(1945)

---

1. During the Spanish Civil War of 1936–39, Nationalist forces used German planes
    and pilots to obliterate the Basque town of Guernica, killing between 1000 and
    2000 civilians. Commemorated in Picasso's famous painting *Guernica*, the assault
    also marks the first time that indiscriminate terror bombing of civilians was used
    as an instrument of war.
2. Federico García Lorca (1898–1936), Spanish poet and dramatist assassinated by
    Nationalists in the Spanish Civil War.

Calamity

A laundry truck
Rolled down the hill
And crashed into my maple tree.
It was a truly North American calamity.
5   Three cans of beer fell out
(Which in itself was revealing)
And a jumble of skirts and shirts
Spilled onto the ploughed grass.
Dogs barked, and the children
10   Sprouted like dandelions in my lawn.
Normally we do not speak to one another on this avenue,
But the excitement made us suddenly neighbours.
People exchanged remarks
Who had never been introduced
15   And for a while we were quite human.
Then the policeman came—
Sedately, for this was Westmount—
And carefully took down all names and numbers.
The towing truck soon followed,
20   Order was restored.
The starch came raining down.

(1954)

Langston Hughes (1902–1967)

The literary career of Missouri-born Langston Hughes began with poetry.
The Weary Blues (1926) was followed by more than ten books and pam-
phlets of poetry. The poems below address the experience of African
Americans, a major concern of his work. See also his "On the Road," p. 446.

The Negro Speaks of Rivers

(To W.E.B. DuBois)[1]

I've known rivers:
I've known rivers ancient as the world and older than the
    flow of human blood in human veins.

My soul has grown deep like the rivers.

     I bathed in the Euphrates when dawns were young.
5   I built my hut near the Congo and it lulled me to sleep.
     I looked upon the Nile and raised the pyramids above it.
     I heard the singing of the Mississippi when Abe Lincoln
        went down to New Orleans, and I've seen its muddy
        bosom turn all golden in the sunset.

I've known rivers:
Ancient, dusky rivers.

10 My soul has grown deep like the rivers.

(1926)

Theme for English B

The instructor said,

    Go home and write
    a page tonight.
    And let that page come out of you—
5   *Then, it will be true.*

I wonder if it's that simple?
I am twenty-two, colored, born in Winston-Salem.
I went to school there, then Durham, then here
to this college on the hill above Harlem.
10 I am the only colored student in my class
The steps from the hill lead down into Harlem,
through a park, then I cross St. Nicholas,
Eighth Avenue, Seventh, and I come to the Y,

---

1. William Edward Burghardt DuBois (1868–1963). American author and civil
   rights activist who helped found the National Association for the Advancement
   of Colored People (NAACP) in 1909.

the Harlem Branch Y, where I take the elevator
15 up to my room, sit down, and write this page:

It's not easy to know what is true for you or me
at twenty-two, my age. But I guess I'm what
I feel and see and hear. Harlem, I hear you:
hear you, hear me—we two—you, me, talk on this page.
20 (I hear New York, too.) Me—who?

Well, I like to eat, sleep, drink, and be in love.
I like to work, read, learn, and understand life.
I like a pipe for a Christmas present,
or records—Bessie,[1] bop, or Bach.
25 I guess being colored doesn't make me not like
the same things other folks like who are other races.
So will my page be colored that I write?

Being me, it will not be white.
But it will be
30 a part of you, instructor.
You are white—
yet a part of me, as I am part of you.
That's American.
Sometimes perhaps you don't want to be a part of me.
35 Nor do I often want to be a part of you.
But we are, that's true!

As I learn from you,
I guess you learn from me—
although you're older—and white—
40 and somewhat more free.

This is my page for English B.

(1951)

Harlem

What happens to a dream deferred?

Does it dry up
like a raisin in the sun?
Or fester like a sore—

---

1. That is, Bessie Smith (1894–1937), known as the "Empress of the Blues."

5   And then run?
     Does it stink like rotten meat?
     Or crust and sugar over—
     like a syrupy sweet?

     Maybe it just sags
10   like a heavy load.

     Or does it explode?

                                              (1951)

A.J.M. Smith (1902–1980)

Critic, anthologist, and poet, Smith was a highly influential figure

in Canadian poetry. His poetry is well crafted and wide-ranging in style.

Smith contributed to New Provinces *(1936), a landmark anthology of*

Canadian verse.

The Lonely Land

     Cedar and jagged fir
     uplift sharp barbs
     against the gray
     and cloud-piled sky;
5   and in the bay
     blown spume and windrift
     and thin, bitter spray
     snap
     at the whirling sky;
10   and the pine trees
     lean one way.

     A wild duck calls
     to her mate,
     and the ragged
15   and passionate tones

stagger and fall,
and recover,
and stagger and fall,
on these stones—
20 are lost
in the lapping of water
on smooth, flat stones.

This is a beauty
of dissonance,
25 this resonance
of stony strand,
this smoky cry
curled over a black pine
like a broken
30 and wind-battered branch
when the wind
bends the tops of the pines
and curdles the sky
from the north.

35 This is the beauty
of strength
broken by strength
and still strong.

(1936)

Stevie Smith (1902–1971)

Smith, who lived in London, England, for most of her life, wrote three novels but is better known for her verse, which she illustrated with what she called "something like doodling." Smith's witty verse is often subtle and enigmatic.

Thoughts about the Person from Porlock[1]

Coleridge received the Person from Porlock
And ever after called him a curse,
Then why did he hurry to let him in?
He could have hid in the house.

5 It was not right of Coleridge in fact it was wrong
(But often we all do wrong)
As the truth is I think he was already stuck
With Kubla Khan.

He was weeping and wailing: I am finished, finished,
10 I shall never write another word of it,
When along comes the Person from Porlock
And takes the blame for it.

It was not right, it was wrong,
But often we all do wrong.

15 May we enquire the name of the Person from Porlock?
Why, Porson, didn't you know?
He lived at the bottom of Porlock Hill
So had a long way to go,

He wasn't much in the social sense
20 Though his grandmother was a Warlock,
One of the Rutlandshire ones I fancy
And nothing to do with Porlock,

And he lived at the bottom of the hill as I said
And had a cat named Flo,
25 And had a cat named Flo.

I long for the Person from Porlock
To bring my thoughts to an end,
I am becoming impatient to see him
I think of him as a friend,

30 Often I look out the window
Often I run to the gate

---

1. Coleridge attributed the fact that his poem "Kubla Khan" was left unfinished to his having been interrupted, while writing it, by "a person on business from Porlock," to having been "detained by him for above an hour," and then having been unable to recapture the vision that was the substance of the poem. See the note to "Kubla Khan," p. 181.

I think, He will come this evening,
I think it is rather late.

I am hungry to be interrupted
35 For ever and ever amen
O Person from Porlock come quickly
And bring my thoughts to an end.

I felicitate the people who have a Person from Porlock
To break up everything and throw it away
40 Because then there will be nothing to keep them
And they need not stay.

Why do they grumble so much?
He comes like a benison[2]
They should be glad he has not forgotten them
45 They might have had to go on.

These thoughts are depressing I know. They are depressing,
I wish I was more cheerful, it is more pleasant,
Also it is a duty, we should smile as well as submitting
To the purpose of the One Above who is experimenting
50 With various mixtures of human character which goes best,
All is interesting for him it is exciting, but not for us.
There I go again. Smile, smile, and get some work to do
Then you will be practically unconscious without positively having to go.

(1962)

C. Day Lewis (1904–1972)

C. Day Lewis, often linked with a group of socially concerned poets of the thirties that included W.H. Auden, Stephen Spender, and Louis MacNeice, wrote, in "Song," a politicized version of Marlowe's "Passionate Shepherd," p. 132.

---

2. Blessing.

Song

Come, live with me and be my love,
And we will all the pleasures prove
Of peace and plenty, bed and board,
That chance employment may afford.

5   I'll handle dainties on the docks
And thou shalt read of summer frocks:
At evening by the sour canals
We'll hope to hear some madrigals.

Care on thy maiden brow shall put
10 A wreath of wrinkles, and thy foot
Be shod in pain: not silken dress
But toil shall tire thy loveliness.

Hunger shall make thy modest zone
And cheat fond death of all but bone—
15 If these delights thy mind may move,
Then live with me and be my love.

(1938)

Earle Birney (1904–1995)

An experimental and technically innovative poet who won Governor General's awards for his first published collection in 1942 and for Now Is Time *(1945), Birney uses colloquial language to make his poems highly accessible to the ordinary reader. His "Anglosaxon Street" imitates the style of Anglo-Saxon poems such as* Beowulf *(p. 114). He also wrote novels and short stories.*

The Road to Nijmégen¹

December my dear on the road to Nijmégen
between the stones and the bitten sky was your face

Not yours at first but only the countenance of lank canals
and gathered stares   too rapt to note my passing
5   of graves with frosted billy-tins for hats
of bones of tanks beside the stoven bridges
of old men in the mist who hacked at roots
knifing the final chips from a boulevard of stumps.

These for miles and the fangs of homes but more the women
10   wheeling into the wind on the tireless rims of their cycles
like tattered sailboats tossing over the cobbles
and the children groping in gravel for knobs of coal
or clustered like wintered flies at the back of messhuts
their legs standing like dead stems out of their clogs

15   Numbed on the long road to mangled Nijmégen
I thought that only the living of others assures us
the gentle and true we remember as trees walking
Their arms reach down from the light of kindness
into this Lazarus² tomb

20   So peering through sleet as we neared Nijmégen
I glimpsed the rainbow arch of your eyes
Over the clank of the jeep   your quick grave laughter
outrising at last the rockets
brought me what spells I repeat as I travel this road
25   that arrives at no future

and what creed I bring to our daily crimes
to this guilt
in the griefs of the old and the tombs of the young

Holland, January 1945

(1945)

---

1. Nijmégen was in 1944–45 the town at the tip of the Canadian salient in Holland, connected with rearward troops by a single much-bombed highway. The area had been
   the scene of tank battles, artillery duels, air raids, buzz-bombs, and V-2 rocket attacks.
   It had also been denuded of trees, coal, and foodstocks by the retreating Germans. The
   winter was in all Europe one of the coldest of the century. [Author's note.]
2. According to John 11, Christ raised Lazarus from the dead after he had been
   buried for four days.

The Bear on the Delhi Road

Unreal   tall as a myth
by the road the Himalayan bear
is beating the brilliant air
with his crooked arms
5   About him two men   bare
spindly as locusts   leap

One pulls on a ring
in the great soft nose   His mate
flicks   flicks with a stick
10   up at the rolling eyes

They have not led him here
down from the fabulous hills
to this bald alien plain
and the clamorous world   to kill
15   but simply to teach him to dance

They are peaceful both   these spare
men of Kashmir   and the bear
alive is their living   too
If   far on the Delhi way
20   around him galvanic they dance
it is merely to wear   wear
from his shaggy body the tranced
wish forever to stay
only an ambling bear
25   four-footed in berries

It is no more joyous for them
in this hot dust to prance
out of reach of the praying claws
sharpened to paw for ants
30   in the shadows of deodars
It is not easy to free
myth from reality
or rear this fellow up
to lurch   lurch with them
35   in the tranced dancing of men

(1962)

Anglosaxon Street

Dawndrizzle ended   dampness steams from
blotching brick and   blank plasterwaste
Faded housepatterns   hoary and finicky
unfold stuttering   stick like a phonograph

5   Here is a ghetto   gotten for goyim[1]
O with care denuded   of nigger and kike
No coonsmell rankles   reeks only cellarrot
attar of carexhaust   catcorpse and cookinggrease
Imperial hearts   heave in this haven
10   Cracks across windows   are welded with slogans
There'll Always Be An England   enhances geraniums
and V's for Victory   vanquish the housefly

Ho! with climbing sun   march the bleached beldames
festooned with shopping bags   farded[2] flatarched
15   bigthewed Saxonwives[3]   stepping over buttrivers
waddling back wienerladen   to suckle smallfry

Hoy! with sunslope   shrieking over hydrants
flood from learninghall   the lean fingerlings
Nordic nobblecheeked[4]   not all clean of nose
20   leaping Commandowise   into leprous lanes

What! after whistleblow!   spewed from wheelboat
after daylong doughtiness   dire handplay
in sewertrench or sandpit   come Saxonthegns[5]
Junebrown Jutekings   jawslack for meat

25   Sit after supper   on smeared doorsteps
not humbly swearing   hatedeeds on Huns[6]
profiteers politicians   pacifists Jews

Then by twobit magic   to muse in movie
unlock picturehoard   or lope to alehall
30   soaking bleakly   in beer skittleless

---

1. Gentiles. Along with "nigger" (black) and "kike" (Jew), a term of abuse.
2. Painted with cosmetics.
3. The Saxons, the Jutes, and the Angles were three Germanic tribes who conquered
   Britain in the fifth century.
4. Pimpled.
5. A freeman who held land by virtue of military service.
6. Warlike Asiatic tribe of nomads who conquered much of Europe in the fourth and
   fifth centuries; a derogatory appellation for Germans during the two world wars.

Home again to hotbox   and humid husbandhood
in slumbertrough adding   sleepily to Anglekin
Alongside the lanenooks   carling[7] and leman[8]
caterwaul and clip   careless of Saxonry
35   with moonglow and haste   and a higher heartbeat

Slumbers now slumtruck   unstinks cooling
waiting brief for milkmaid   mornstar and worldrise

(Toronto 1942)

(1966)

Sir John Betjeman (1906–1984)

Betjeman's verse is often a witty and urbane examination of the manners of bourgeois English society. Appointed poet laureate in 1972, Betjeman was an unusually popular public figure.

In Westminster Abbey

Let me take this other glove off
    As the *vox humana*[1] swells,
And the beauteous fields of Eden
    Bask beneath the Abbey bells.
5   Here, where England's statesmen lie,
Listen to a lady's cry.

Gracious Lord, oh bomb the Germans.
    Spare their women for Thy Sake,
And if that is not too easy
10   We will pardon Thy Mistake.

---

7. Woman.
8. Lover.
1. The organ stop that produces a sound imitative of the human voice.

But, gracious Lord, whate'er shall be,
Don't let anyone bomb me.

Keep our Empire undismembered
    Guide our Forces by Thy Hand,
15 Gallant blacks from far Jamaica,
    Honduras and Togoland;
Protect them Lord in all their fights,
And, even more, protect the whites.

Think of what our Nation stands for,
20   Books from Boots'[2] and country lanes,
Free speech, free passes, class distinction,
    Democracy and proper drains.
Lord, put beneath Thy special care
One-eighty-nine Cadogan Square.[3]

25 Although dear Lord I am a sinner,
    I have done no major crime;
Now I'll come to Evening Service
    Whensoever I have the time.
So, Lord, reserve for me a crown,
30 And do not let my shares go down.

I will labour for Thy Kingdom,
    Help our lads to win the war,
Send white feathers to the cowards
    Join the Women's Army Corps,
35 Then wash the Steps around Thy Throne
In the Eternal Safety Zone.

Now I feel a little better,
    What a treat to hear Thy Word,
Where the bones of leading statesmen,
40   Have so often been interr'd.
And now, dear Lord, I cannot wait
Because I have a luncheon date.

(1940)

---

2. A chain drugstore. At one time, branches in English country towns had lending
   libraries patronized mainly by the genteel.
3. A fashionable square near Knightsbridge, London, not far from Hyde Park.

W.H. Auden (1907–1973)

Although Auden was born in England, he moved to the United States in
1939 and became an American citizen in 1946. His poetry ranges from con-
cise, politically engaged verse to lengthy, reflective poems. As one of the
most versatile and influential figures of his century, he analyzes with symp-
tomatic incisiveness yet sympathy his generation's pains and powers.

Musée des Beaux Arts

About suffering they were never wrong,
The Old Masters: How well they understood
Its human position; how it takes place
While someone else is eating or opening a window or just walking
    dully along;
5 How, when the aged are reverently, passionately waiting
For the miraculous birth, there always must be
Children who did not specially want it to happen, skating
On a pond at the edge of the wood:
They never forgot
10 That even the dreadful martyrdom must run its course
Anyhow in a corner, some untidy spot
Where the dogs go on with their doggy life and the torturer's horse
Scratches its innocent behind on a tree.

In Brueghel's *Icarus*,[1] for instance: how everything turns away
15 Quite leisurely from the disaster; the ploughman may
Have heard the splash, the forsaken cry,
But for him it was not an important failure; the sun shone
As it had to on the white legs disappearing into the green
Water; and the expensive delicate ship that must have seen
20 Something amazing, a boy falling out of the sky,
Had somewhere to get to and sailed calmly on.

(1940)

---

1. *The Fall of Icarus*, by Pieter Brueghel (c. 1525–1569), hangs in the Palace of the
   Royal Museum of Painting and Sculpture in Brussels. Icarus was the son of
   Daedalus, a skilled Athenian craftsman who built the labyrinth for Minos, King
   of Crete. Later, when Daedalus was imprisoned there with his son, he made
   wings of wax and feathers with which they flew away. Icarus, however, flew too
   close to the sun, melted the wax, and fell into the sea.

One Evening

As I walked out one evening,
    Walking down Bristol Street,
The crowds upon the pavement
    Were fields of harvest wheat.

5   And down by the brimming river
    I heard a lover sing
Under an arch of the railway:
    "Love has no ending.

"I'll love you, dear, I'll love you
10   Till China and Africa meet,
And the river jumps over the mountain
    And the salmon sing in the street.

"I'll love you till the ocean
    Is folded and hung up to dry,
15   And the seven stars go squawking
    Like geese about the sky.

"The years shall run like rabbits,
    For in my arms I hold
The Flower of the Ages,
20   And the first love of the world."

But all the clocks in the city
    Began to whirr and chime:
"O let not Time deceive you,
    You cannot conquer Time.

25   "In the burrows of the Nightmare
    Where Justice naked is,
Time watches from the shadow
    And coughs when you would kiss.

"In headaches and in worry
30   Vaguely life leaks away,
And Time will have his fancy
    To-morrow or to-day.

"Into many a green valley
    Drifts the appalling snow;
35   Time breaks the threaded dances
    And the diver's brilliant bow.

"O plunge your hands in water,
    Plunge them in up to the wrist;
Stare, stare in the basin
40   And wonder what you've missed.

"The glacier knocks in the cupboard,
    The desert sighs in the bed,
And the crack in the tea-cup opens
    A lane to the land of the dead.

45   "Where the beggars raffle the banknotes
    And the Giant is enchanting to Jack,
And the Lily-white Boy[1] is a Roarer,
    And Jill goes down on her back.

"O look, look in the mirror,
50   O look in your distress;
Life remains a blessing
    Although you cannot bless.

"O stand, stand at the window
    As the tears scald and start;
55 You shall love your crooked neighbour
    With your crooked heart."

It was late, late in the evening
    The lovers they were gone;
The clocks had ceased their chiming,
60   And the deep river ran on.

(1940)

---

1. Like the "seven stars" (l. 15), this is derived from the folk song "Green Grow the Rushes," which Auden included in his edition of *The Oxford Book of Light Verse*.

Louis MacNeice (1907–1963)

MacNeice went to Oxford, where he met poets Auden and Spender. He subsequently lectured in classics and worked for the BBC. His technically skillful poetry, like "Snow," renders intelligible the "drunkenness of things being various."

Snow

The room was suddenly rich and the great bay-window was
Spawning snow and pink roses against it
Soundlessly collateral and incompatible:
World is suddener than we fancy it.

5   World is crazier and more of it than we think,
Incorrigibly plural. I peel and portion
A tangerine and spit the pips and feel
The drunkenness of things being various.

And the fire flames with a bubbling sound for world
10   Is more spiteful and gay than one supposes—
On the tongue on the eyes on the ears in the palms of one's hands—
There is more than glass between the snow and the huge roses.

(1935)

Theodore Roethke (1908–1963)

Born in Michigan, Roethke taught at a number of American colleges. Intensely experienced and very specific images from the world of nature dominate his work. Roethke recognized Blake and Whitman as his literary influences.

My Papa's Waltz

The whiskey on your breath
Could make a small boy dizzy;
But I hung on like death:
Such waltzing was not easy.

5   We romped until the pans
Slid from the kitchen shelf;
My mother's countenance
Could not unfrown itself.

That hand that held my wrist
10   Was battered on one knuckle;
At every step you missed
My right ear scraped a buckle.

You beat time on my head
With a palm caked hard by dirt,
15   Then waltzed me off to bed
Still clinging to your shirt.

(1948)

A.M. Klein *(1909–1972)*

*Klein was a Canadian poet, short-story writer, novelist, and lawyer. His
poetry frequently focuses on his Jewish background. "The Rocking Chair" is
from* The Rocking Chair and Other Poems *(1948), which received a
Governor General's Award.*

The Rocking Chair

It seconds the crickets of the province. Heard
in the clean lamplit farmhouses of Quebec,—
wooden,—it is no less a national bird;
and rivals, in its cage, the mere stuttering clock.

5 To its time, the evenings are rolled away;
   and in its peace the pensive mother knits
   contentment to be worn by her family,
   grown-up, but still cradled by the chair in which she sits.

   It is also the old man's pet, pair to his pipe,
10 the two aids of his arithmetic and plans,
   plans rocking and puffing into market-shape;
   and it is the toddler's game and dangerous dance.
   Moved to the verandah, on summer Sundays, it is,
   among the hanging plants, the girls, the boy-friends,
15 sabbatical and clumsy, like the white haloes
   dangling above the blue serge suits of the young men.

   It has a personality of its own;
   is a character (like that old drunk Lacoste,
   exhaling amber, and toppling on his pins);
20 it is alive; individual; and no less
   an identity than those about it. And
   it is tradition. Centuries have been flicked
   from its arcs, alternately flicked and pinned.
   It rolls with the gait of St. Malo.[1] It is act

25 and symbol, symbol of this static folk
   which moves in segments, and returns to base,—
   a sunken pendulum: *invoke, revoke*;
   loosed yon, leashed hither, motion on no space.
   O, like some Anjou ballad, all refrain,
30 which turns about its longing, and seems to move
   to make a pleasure out of repeated pain,
   its music moves, as if always back to a first love.

                                                    (1945)

---

1. Seaport in western France and birthplace of Jacques Cartier, who led an expedi-
    tion to look for a Northwest Passage to the East. He left St. Malo with two ships
    and 62 men in April 1524, and reached Newfoundland and the Bay of Chaleur.
    On a second expedition, two years later, Cartier sailed up the St. Lawrence as far
    as what is now Montreal.

Dorothy Livesay (1909–1996)

Dorothy Livesay, born in Winnipeg and educated at the University of Toronto and the Sorbonne, combined her interests in politics, women's issues, and poetry. During the Depression years, she was a social worker and joined the Communist Party. She twice won the Governor General's Award for her poetry.

Lament

for J.F.B.L.

What moved me, was the way your hand
Lay in my hand, not withering,
But warm, like a hand cooled in a stream
And purling still; or a bird caught in a snare
5   Wings folded stiff, eyes in a stare,
But still alive with the fear,
Heart hoarse with hope—
So your hand, your dead hand, my dear.

And the veins, still mounting as blue rivers,
10 Mounting towards the tentative finger-tips,
The delta where four seas come in—
Your fingers promontories into colourless air
Were rosy still—not chalk (like cliffs
You knew in boyhood, Isle of Wight):
15 But blushed with colour from the sun you sought
And muscular from garden toil;
Stained with the purple of an iris bloom,
Violas grown for a certain room;
Hands seeking faïence, filagree,
20 Chinese lacquer and ivory—
Brussels lace: and a walnut piece
Carved by a hand now phosphorus.

What moved me, was the way your hand
Held life, although the pulse was gone.
25 The hand that carpentered a children's chair,
Carved out a stair
Held leash upon a dog in strain
Gripped wheel, swung sail,

Flicked horse's rein
30 And then again
Moved kings and queens meticulous on a board,
Slashed out the cards, cut bread, and poured
A purring cup of tea;
The hand so neat and nimble
35 Could make a tennis partner tremble,
Write a resounding round
Of sonorous verbs and nouns—
Hand that would not strike a child, and yet
Could ring a bell and send a man to doom.

40 And now unmoving in this Spartan room
The hand still speaks:
After the brain was fogged
And the tight lips tighter shut,
After the shy appraising eyes
45 Relinquished the fire for the sea's green gaze—
The hand still breathes, fastens its hold on life;
Demands the whole, establishes the strife.
What moved me, was the way your hand
Lay cool in mine, not withering;
50 As bird still breathes, and stream runs clear—
So your hand; your dear hand, my dear.

(1953)

Without Benefit of Tape

The real poems are being written in outports
on backwoods farms
in passageways where pantries still exist
or where geraniums
5 nail light to the window
while out of the window boy in the flying field
is pulled to heaven on the keel of a kite.

Stories breed in the north:
men with snow in their mouths
10 trample and shake at the bit
kneading the woman down under blankets of snow
icing her breath, her eyes.

The living speech is shouted out
by men and women leaving railway lines

15 to trundle home, pack-sacked
just company for deer or bear—

    Hallooed
across the counter, in a corner store
it booms upon the river's shore:
20 on midnight roads where hikers flag you down
speech echoes from the canyon's wall
    resonant
    indubitable.

(1967)

Elizabeth Bishop (1911–1979)

Bishop was raised by her paternal and maternal grandparents in New England and Nova Scotia. After living in Brazil in the fifties and sixties, Bishop taught at the University of Washington in Seattle and at Harvard. She is known for her descriptive landscapes and her interest in travel and displacement.

Sestina

September rain falls on the house.
In the falling light, the old grandmother
sits in the kitchen with the child
beside the Little Marvel Stove,
5 reading the jokes from the almanac,
laughing and talking to hide her tears.

She thinks that her equinoctial tears
and the rain that beats on the roof of the house
were both foretold by the almanac,
but only known to a grandmother.
10 The iron kettle sings on the stove.
She cuts some bread and says to the child,

It's time for tea now; but the child
is watching the teakettle's small hard tears
15 dance like mad on the hot black stove,
the way the rain must dance on the house.
Tidying up, the old grandmother
hangs up the clever almanac

on its string. Birdlike, the almanac
20 hovers half open above the child,
hovers above the old grandmother
and her teacup full of dark brown tears.
She shivers and says she thinks the house
feels chilly, and puts more wood in the stove.

25 *It was to be*, says the Marvel Stove.
I know what I know, says the almanac.
With crayons the child draws a rigid house
and a winding pathway. Then the child
puts in a man with buttons like tears
30 and shows it proudly to the grandmother.

But secretly, while the grandmother
busies herself about the stove,
the little moons fall down like tears
from between the pages of the almanac
35 into the flower bed the child
has carefully placed in front of the house.

Time to plant tears, says the almanac.
The grandmother sings to the marvellous stove
and the child draws another inscrutable house.

(1965)

Irving Layton (b. 1912)

An extremely prolific poet born in Romania and raised in Montreal, Layton
has also worked as an editor to assist other Canadian poets into print.
Layton's poetry is remarkable for its vitality, its commitment to life, and its
aversion to the puritanically restrictive. For Layton, poets are akin to the
Hebrew prophets in their knowledge of truth.

Keine Lazarovitch[1]

1870–1959

When I saw my mother's head on the cold pillow,
Her white waterfalling hair in the cheeks' hollows,
I thought, quietly circling my grief, of how
She had loved God but cursed extravagantly his creatures.

5   For her final mouth was not water but a curse,
A small black hole, a black rent in the universe,
Which damned the green earth, stars and trees in its stillness
And the inescapable lousiness of growing old.

And I record she was comfortless, vituperative,
10   Ignorant, glad, and much else besides; I believe
She endlessly praised her black eyebrows, their thick weave,
Till plagiarizing Death leaned down and took them for his mould.

And spoiled a dignity I shall not again find,
And the fury of her stubborn limited mind;
15   Now none will shake her amber beads and call God blind,
Or wear them upon a breast so radiantly.

O fierce she was, mean and unaccommodating;
But I think now of the toss of her gold earrings,
Their proud carnal assertion, and her youngest sings,
20   While all the rivers of her red veins move into the sea.

                                                        (1961)

---

1. Poet's mother, who is identified here by the family's Romanian name.

Karl Shapiro (b. 1913)

American poet and literary critic Karl Shapiro won the Pulitzer Prize for
Poetry in 1945. One critic has said that Shapiro's poetry, remarkable for its
stylistic variability, is also "striking for its concrete but detached insights,"
an observation that seems especially applicable to "Auto Wreck."

Auto Wreck

Its quick soft silver bell beating, beating,
And down the dark one ruby flare
Pulsing out red light like an artery,
The ambulance at top speed floating down
5   Past beacons and illuminated clocks
Wings in a heavy curve, dips down,
And brakes speed, entering the crowd.

The doors leap open, emptying light;
Stretchers are laid out, the mangled lifted
10   And stowed into the little hospital.
Then the bell, breaking the hush, tolls once,
And the ambulance with its terrible cargo
Rocking, slightly rocking, moves away,
As the doors, an afterthought, are closed.
15   We are deranged, walking among the cops
Who sweep glass and are large and composed.
One is still making notes under the light.
One with a bucket douches ponds of blood
Into the street and gutter.
20   One hangs lanterns on the wrecks that cling,
Empty husks of locusts, to iron poles.

Our throats were tight as tourniquets,
Our feet were bound with splints, but now,
Like convalescents intimate and gauche,
25   We speak through sickly smiles and warn
With the stubborn saw of common sense,
The grim joke and the banal resolution.
The traffic moves around with care,
But we remain, touching a wound
30   That opens to our richest horror.

Already old, the question Who shall die?
Becomes unspoken Who is innocent?

For death in war is done by hands;
Suicide has cause and stillbirth, logic;
35 And cancer, simple as a flower, blooms.
But this invites the occult mind,
Cancels our physics with a sneer,
And spatters all we knew of denouement
Across the expedient and wicked stones.

(1942)

Henry Reed (1914–1986)

*Henry Reed was a British poet, radio dramatist, and translator. The poem
reprinted here is from his longer "Lessons of the War" (included in* A Map
of Verona, *1946) and draws on his own wartime experience in the army.*

Naming of Parts

Today we have naming of parts. Yesterday,
We had daily cleaning. And tomorrow morning,
We shall have what to do after firing. But today,
Today we have naming of parts. Japonica
5 Glistens like coral in all of the neighbouring gardens,
      And today we have naming of parts.

This is the lower sling swivel. And this
Is the upper sling swivel, whose use you will see,
When you are given your slings. And this is the piling swivel
10 Which in your case you have not got. The branches
Hold in the gardens their silent, eloquent gestures,
      Which in our case we have not got.

This is the safety-catch, which is always released
With an easy flick of the thumb. And please do not let me
15 See anyone using his finger. You can do it quite easy

If you have any strength in your thumb. The blossoms
Are fragile and motionless, never letting anyone see
    Any of them using their finger.

And this you can see is the bolt. The purpose of this
20 Is to open the breech, as you see. We can slide it
Rapidly backwards and forwards: we call this
Easing the spring. And rapidly backwards and forwards
The early bees are assaulting and fumbling the flowers:
    They call it easing the Spring.

25 They call it easing the Spring: it is perfectly easy
If you have any strength in your thumb: like the bolt,
And the breech, and the cocking-piece, and the point of balance,
Which in our case we have not got; and the almond-blossom
Silent in all of the gardens and the bees going backwards and forwards,
30   For today we have naming of parts.

                                        (1946)

Dylan Thomas (1914–1953)

Born in Swansea, Wales, Thomas was a poet, dramatist, prose and short-
story writer as well as a successful reader and broadcaster of his work. His
poetry has had a wide audience and is notable for its energy, exuberance,
and affirmation of life.

Fern Hill

Now as I was young and easy under the apple boughs
About the lilting house and happy as the grass was green,
    The night above the dingle starry,
      Time let me hail and climb
5   Golden in the heydays of his eyes,
And honoured among wagons I was prince of the apple towns
And once below a time I lordly had the trees and leaves
      Trail with daisies and barley
    Down the rivers and the windfall light.

10　And as I was green and carefree, famous among the barns
　　About the happy yard and singing as the farm was home,
　　　　In the sun that is young once only,
　　　　　　Time let me play and be
　　　　Golden in the mercy of his means,
15　And green and golden I was huntsman and herdsman, the calves
　　Sang to my horn, the foxes on the hills barked clear and cold,
　　　　And the sabbath rang slowly
　　　　In the pebbles of the holy streams.

　　All the sun long it was running, it was lovely, the hay-
20　Fields high as the house, the tunes from the chimneys, it was air
　　　　And playing, lovely and watery
　　　　　　And fire green as grass.
　　　　And nightly under the simple stars
　　As I rode to sleep the owls were bearing the farm away,
25　All the moon long I heard, blessèd among stables, the night-jars
　　　　Flying with the ricks, and the horses
　　　　Flashing into the dark.

　　And then to awake, and the farm, like a wanderer white
　　With the dew, come back, the cock on his shoulder: it was all
30　　　Shining, it was Adam and maiden,
　　　　　　The sky gathered again
　　　　And the sun grew round that very day.
　　So it must have been after the birth of the simple light
　　In the first, spinning place, the spellbound horses walking warm
35　　　Out of the whinnying green stable
　　　　On to the fields of praise.

　　And honoured among foxes and pheasants by the gay house
　　Under the new made clouds and happy as the heart was long,
　　　　In the sun born over and over,
40　　　　I ran my heedless ways,
　　　　My wishes raced through the house-high hay
　　And nothing I cared, at my sky blue trades, that time allows
　　In all this tuneful turning so few and such morning songs
　　　　Before the children green and golden
45　　Follow him out of grace,

　　Nothing I cared, in the lamb white days, that time would take me
　　Up to the swallow thronged loft by the shadow of my hand,
　　　　In the moon that is always rising,
　　　　　　Nor that riding to sleep
50　　I should hear him fly with the high fields
　　And wake to the farm forever fled from the childless land.
　　Oh as I was young and easy in the mercy of his means,

Time held me green and dying
Though I sang in my chains like the sea.

(1946)

Do Not Go Gentle into That Good Night

Do not go gentle into that good night,
Old age should burn and rave at close of day;
Rage, rage against the dying of the light.

Though wise men at their end know dark is right,
5   Because their words had forked no lightning they
Do not go gentle into that good night.

Good men, the last wave by, crying how bright
Their frail deeds might have danced in a green bay,
Rage, rage against the dying of the light.

10   Wild men who caught and sang the sun in flight,
And learn, too late, they grieved it on its way,
Do not go gentle into that good night.

Grave men, near death, who see with blinding sight
Blind eyes could blaze like meteors and be gay,
15   Rage, rage against the dying of the light.

And you, my father, there on the sad height,
Curse, bless, me now with your fierce tears, I pray.
Do not go gentle into that good night.
Rage, rage against the dying of the light.

(1952)

P.K. Page (b. 1916)

P.K. Page, whose The Metal and the Flower *(1946) won a Governor*

General's Award, has also worked as a scriptwriter and written a novel,

The Sun and the Moon (1944), and short stories. She lived abroad in several different countries before returning to Canada.

Stories of Snow

Those in the vegetable rain retain
an area behind their sprouting eyes
held soft and rounded with the dream of snow
precious and reminiscent at those globes—
5   souvenir of some never-never land—
which hold their snow-storms circular, complete,
high in a tall and teakwood cabinet.

In countries where the leaves are large as hands
where flowers protrude their fleshy chins
10   and call their colours,
an imaginary snow-storm sometimes falls
among the lilies.
And in the early morning one will waken
to think the glowing linen of his pillow
15   a northern drift, will find himself mistaken
and lie back weeping.
And there the story shifts from head to head,
of how in Holland, from their feather beds
hunters arise and part the flakes and go
20   forth to the frozen lakes in search of swans—
the snow-light falling white along their guns,
their breath in plumes.
While tethered in the wind like sleeping gulls
ice-boats wait the raising of their wings
25   to skim the electric ice at such a speed
they leap jet strips of naked water,
and how these flying, sailing hunters feel
air in their mouths as terrible as ether.
And on the story runs that even drinks
30   in that white landscape dare to be no colour;
how flasked and water clear, the liquor slips
silver against the hunters' moving hips.
And of the swan in death these dreamers tell
of its last flight and how it falls, a plummet,
35   pierced by the freezing bullet
and how three feathers, loosened by the shot,
descend like snow upon it.
While hunters plunge their fingers in its down
deep as a drift, and dive their hands

40   up to the neck of the wrist
in that warm metamorphosis of snow
as gentle as the sort that woodsmen know
who, lost in the white circle, fall at last
and dream their way to death.

45   And stories of this kind are often told
in countries where great flowers bar the roads
with reds and blues which seal the route to snow—
as if, in telling, raconteurs unlock
the colour with its complement and go
50   through to the area behind the eyes
where silent, unrefractive whiteness lies.

(1946)

Gwendolyn Brooks (1917–2000)

Gwendolyn Brooks, the first African-American poet to win a Pulitzer Prize (for Annie Allen, *1949), writes with humour, irony, and restraint. Her poetry, often invigorated with African-American colloquialisms, explores the lives of poor urban blacks. Brooks became increasingly concerned with racial politics in the late 1960s.*

We Real Cool

The Pool Players
Seven at the Golden Shovel

We real cool. We
Left school. We

Lurk late. We
Strike straight. We

5   Sing sin. We
Thin gin. We

Jazz June. We
Die soon.

(1960)

Margaret Avison (b. 1918)

Avison has been a librarian, lecturer, and social worker. She has also been writer-in-residence at the University of Western Ontario. Of her collections of poetry, Winter Sun *(1960) and* No Time *(1989) both won the Governor General's Award.*

In a Season of Unemployment

These green painted park benches are
all new. The Park Commissioner had them
planted.
Sparrows go on
5 having dust baths at the edge of
the park maple's shadow, just where
the bench is cemented down, planted
and then cemented.

    Not a breath moves
10 this newspaper.
I'd rather read it by the Lapland sun at midnight. Here we're
bricked in early by a
stifling dark.

On that bench a man in a
15 pencil-striped white shirt
keeps his head up and steady.

    The newspaper-astronaut says
"I feel excitement under the condition of weightlessness."
And from his bench a
20 scatter of black bands in the hollow-air

ray out—too quick for the eye—
and cease.

    "Ground observers watching him on a TV circuit said
    At the time of this report he
25   was smiling," Moscow ra-
    dio reported.

I glance across at him, and mark that
he is feeling
excellent too, I guess, and
30   weightless and
"smiling."

(1966)

Al Purdy (1918–2000)

Although he wrote about his travels throughout Canada and abroad, Purdy is largely recognized as a poet of his native rural Ontario. One of Canada's most recognized poets, Purdy won a Governor General's Award for Cariboo Horses *(1965).*

Wilderness Gothic

Across Roblin Lake, two shores away,
they are sheathing the church spire
with new metal. Someone hangs in the sky
over there from a piece of rope,
5   hammering and fitting God's belly-scratcher.
working his way up along the spire
until there's nothing left to nail on—
Perhaps the workman's faith reaches beyond:
touches intangibles, wrestles with Jacob,[1]

---

1. This reference alludes to the biblical account of Jacob wrestling with an angel (Gen. 32:22–32).

10 replacing rotten timber with pine thews,
pounds hard in the blue cave of the sky,
contends heroically with difficult problems
of gravity, sky navigation and mythopeia,
his volunteer time and labour donated to God.
15 minus sick benefits of course on a non-union job—

Fields around are yellowing into harvest,
nestling and fingerling are sky and water borne,
death is yodelling quiet in green woodlots,
and bodies of three young birds have disappeared
20 in the sub-surface of the new county highway—

That picture is incomplete, part left out
that might alter the whole Dürer[2] landscape:
gothic ancestors peer from medieval sky,
dour faces trapped in photograph albums escaping
25 to clop down iron roads with matched greys:
work-sodden wives groping inside their flesh
for what keeps moving and changing and flashing
beyond and past the long frozen Victorian day.
A sign of fire and brimstone? A two-headed calf
30 born in the barn last night? A sharp female agony?
An age and a faith moving into transition,
the dinner cold and new-baked bread a failure,
deep woods shiver and water drops hang pendant,
double yolked eggs and the house creaks a little—
35 Something is about to happen. Leaves are still.
Two shores away, a man hammering in the sky.
Perhaps he will fall.

(1968)

Philip Larkin (1922–1985)

One of a group of postwar British poets designated as "The Movement,"
Larkin was also a novelist and a librarian. The title of his 1955 volume of
poetry, The Less Deceived, *is indicative of his unsentimental and ironic style.*

---

2. Albrecht Dürer (1471–1528), a German painter, engraver, and writer.

The Explosion

On the day of the explosion
Shadows pointed towards the pithead:
In the sun the slagheap slept.

Down the lane came men in pitboots
5   Coughing oath-edged talk and pipe-smoke,
Shouldering off the freshened silence.

One chased after rabbits; lost them;
Came back with a nest of lark's eggs;
Showed them; lodged them in the grasses.

10   So they passed in beards and moleskins,[1]
Fathers, brothers, nicknames, laughter,
Through the tall gates standing open.

At noon, there came a tremor; cows
Stopped chewing for a second; sun,
15   Scarfed as in a heat-haze, dimmed.

The dead go on before us, they
Are sitting in God's house in comfort,
We shall see them face to face—

Plain as lettering in the chapels
20   It was said, and for a second
Wives saw men of the explosion

Larger than in life they managed—
Gold as on a coin, or walking
Somehow from the sun towards them,

25   One showing the eggs unbroken.

(1974)

Church Going

Once I am sure there's nothing going on
I step inside, letting the door thud shut.

---

1. A hard-wearing cotton fabric with the texture of leather.

Another church: matting, seats, and stone,
And little books; sprawlings of flowers, cut
5 For Sunday, brownish now; some brass and stuff
Up at the holy end; the small neat organ;
And a tense, musty, unignorable silence,
Brewed God knows how long. Hatless, I take off
My cycle-clips in awkward reverence,

10 Move forward, run my hand around the font.
From where I stand, the roof looks almost new—
Cleaned or restored? Someone would know: I don't.
Mounting the lectern, I peruse a few
Hectoring large-scale verses, and pronounce
15 "Here endeth" much more loudly than I meant.
The echoes snigger briefly. Back at the door
I sign the book, donate an Irish sixpence,
Reflect the place was not worth stopping for.

Yet stop I did: in fact I often do,
20 And always end much at a loss like this,
Wondering what to look for; wondering, too,
When churches fall completely out of use
What we shall turn them into, if we shall keep
A few cathedrals chronically on show,
25 Their parchment, plate and pyx in locked cases,
And let the rest rent-free to rain and sheep.
Shall we avoid them as unlucky places?

Or, after dark, will dubious women come
To make their children touch a particular stone;
30 Pick simples¹ for a cancer; or in some
Advised night see walking a dead one?
Power of some sort or other will go on
In games, in riddles, seemingly at random;
But superstition, like belief, must die,
35 And what remains when disbelief is gone?
Grass, weedy pavement, brambles, buttress, sky,

A shape less recognisable each week,
A purpose more obscure, I wonder who
Will be the last, the very last, to seek
40 This place for what it was: one of the crew
That tap and jot and know what rood-lofts were?
Some ruin-bibber,² randy for antique,

---

1. A medicinal plant.

2. A tippler, a drinker; here, someone addicted to ruins.

Or Christmas-addict, counting on a whiff
Of gown-and-bands and organ-pipes and myrrh?
45 Or will he be my representative,

Bored, uninformed, knowing the ghostly silt
Dispersed, yet tending to this cross of ground
Through suburb scrub because it held unspilt
So long and equably what since is found
50 Only in separation—marriage, and birth,
And death, and thoughts of these—for whom was built
This special shell? For, though I've no idea
What this accoutred frowsty barn is worth,
It pleases me to stand in silence here;

55 A serious house on serious earth it is,
In whose blent air all our compulsions meet,
Are recognized, and robed as destinies.
And that much never can be obsolete,
Since someone will forever be surprising
60 A hunger in himself to be more serious,
And gravitating with it to this ground,
Which, he once heard, was proper to grow wise in,
If only that so many dead lie round.

(1955)

Anthony Hecht (b. 1923)

Born in New York and educated at Bard College and Columbia University, Hecht taught at Kenyon College and Rochester and Georgetown universities. In addition to his poetry, Hecht has published three books of criticism and translations of Aeschylus and Joseph Brodsky. Often working in traditional forms and metres, Hecht is known for his wit, his erudition, and the allusiveness of his writing, as in the following parody of Matthew Arnold's "Dover Beach," p. 201.

The Dover Bitch

A Criticism of Life

For Andrews Wanning

So there stood Matthew Arnold and this girl
With the cliffs of England crumbling away behind them,
And he said to her, "Try to be true to me,
And I'll do the same for you, for things are bad
5 All over, etc., etc."
Well now, I knew this girl. It's true she had read
Sophocles in a fairly good translation
And caught the bitter allusion to the sea,
But all the time he was talking she had in mind
10 The notion of what his whiskers would feel like
On the back of her neck. She told me later on
That after a while she got to looking out
At the lights across the channel, and really felt sad,
Thinking of all the wine and enormous beds
15 And blandishments in French and the perfumes.
And then she got really angry. To have been brought
All the way down from London, and then be addressed
As a sort of mournful cosmic last resort
Is really tough on a girl, and she was pretty.
20 Anyway, she watched him pace the room
And finger his watch-chain and seem to sweat a bit,
And then she said one or two unprintable things.
But you mustn't judge her by that. What I mean to say is,
She's really all right. I still see her once in a while
25 And she always treats me right. We have a drink
And I give her a good time, and perhaps it's a year
Before I see her again, but there she is,
Running to fat, but dependable as they come.
And sometimes I bring her a bottle of *Nuit d'Amour*.

(1968)

Milton Acorn (1923–1986)

Often referred to as the "people's poet," Acorn is known for revealing his strongly held political beliefs, even in his poems about love and nature. This Island Means Minago (1975) won him the Governor General's Award.

I've Tasted My Blood

If this brain's over-tempered
consider that the fire was want
and the hammers were fists.
I've tasted my blood too much
5   to love what I was born to.

But my mother's look
was a field of brown oats, soft-bearded;
her voice rain and air rich with lilacs:
and I loved her too much to like
10   how she dragged her days like a sled over gravel.

Playmates? I remember where their skulls roll!
One died hungry, gnawing grey perch-planks;
one fell, and landed so hard he splashed;
and many and many
15   come up atom by atom
in the worm-casts of Europe.

My deep prayer a curse.
My deep prayer the promise that this won't be.
My deep prayer my cunning,
20   my love, my anger,
and often even my forgiveness
that this won't be and be.
I've tasted my blood too much
to abide what I was born to.

(1963)

A.R. Ammons (b. 1926)

Influenced by the world of his rural North Carolina youth as well as by the poets Browning, Whitman, and Dickinson, Ammons is one of the most prolific American poets of the twentieth century (with something like seventeen volumes of poetry). The conversational tone and specificity of "Needs" typify his work, both reflecting his poetic statement, "Overall is beyond me: is the sum of these events / I cannot draw."

Needs

I want something suited to my special needs
I want chrome hubcaps, pin-on attachments
and year round use year after year
I want a workhorse with smooth uniform cut,
5   dozer blade and snow blade & deluxe steering
wheel
I want something to mow, throw snow, tow
and sow with
I want precision reel blades
10 I want a console styled dashboard
I want an easy spintype recoil starter
I want combination bevel and spur gears, 14
gauge stamped steel housing and
washable foam element air cleaner
15 I want a pivoting front axle and extrawide
turf tires
I want an inch of foam rubber inside a vinyl
covering
and especially if it's not too much, if I
20 can deserve it, even if I can't pay for it
I want to mow while riding.

(1968)

Robert Bly (b. 1926)

Minnesota-born poet and translator Bly won a National Book Award for
The Light Around the Body (1967). Bly's poems have a strong sense of
landscape and space, often used as measures of psychic distance. They
attempt to examine public and political concerns as well as to explore pri-
vate and interior worlds. Bly's work focuses on the image, the central, asso-
ciative element of the prose poem.

Visiting Emily Dickinson's Grave with Robert Francis[1]

1   A black iron fence closes the graves in, its ovals delicate as wine stems. They resemble those chapel windows on the main Aran island,[2] made narrow in the 4th century so that not too much rain would drive in … It is April, clear and dry. Curls of grass rise around the nearby gravestones.

2   The Dickinson house is not far off. She arrived here one day, at 56, Robert says, carried over the lots between by six Irish laboring men, when her brother refused to trust her body to a carriage. The coffin was darkened with violets and pine boughs, as she covered the immense distance between the solid Dickinson house and this plot.

3   The distance is immense, the distances through which Satan and his helpers rose and fell, oh vast areas, the distances between stars, between the first time love is felt in the sleeves of the dress, and the death of the person who was in that room … the distance between the feet and head as you lie down, the distance between the mother and father, through which we pass reluctantly.

4   My family "address an Eclipse every morning, which they call their 'Father.'" Each of us crosses that distance at night, arriving out of sleep

---

1. American poet (1901–1987). Like Emily Dickinson, Francis was a long-time resident of the Amherst, Massachusetts area.

2. The three Aran islands of Inishmore (or Aranmore), Inishmaan, and Inisheer lie off the west coast of Ireland in Galway Bay. The main island is also known as "Ára na Naomh," or Aran of the Saints, because of the number of religious recluses who lived there during the fifth century. Remains of numerous early religious shrines, holy wells, and monastic buildings are scattered over all three islands.

on hands and knees, astonished we see a hump in the ground where
we thought a chapel would be ... it is a grassy knoll. And we clamber
out of sleep, holding on to it with our hands ...

(1981)

Phyllis Webb (b. 1927)

Born in British Columbia, Webb has been publishing her finely controlled
poetry since the 1950s. The Vision Tree: Selected Poems *(1982) won a*
Governor General's Award. She has worked for the CBC and taught at
various universities.

Treblinka Gas Chamber[1]

Klostermayer ordered another count of the children.
Then their stars were snipped off and thrown into
the center of the courtyard. It looked like a field of
buttercups.
　　　　　　— Joseph Hyams, *A Field of Buttercups*

fallingstars
　　　　　"a field of
　　　　　　　　buttercups"

　　　　　yellow stars
　　　　　　　　of David
　　　　　　　　　　falling

the prisoners
　　　　　　the children
　　　　　　　　falling

---

1. Treblinka was a Nazi death camp in which more than 700 000 people were killed
    from 1941 to 1944. After World War II, only 50 survivors could be found.

10   in heaps
                        on one another
                                    they go down
Thanatos²
            showers
15   his dirty breath
                            they must breathe
                                        him in
                they see stars
                        behind their
20   eyes
David's
        "a field of
                buttercups"

        a metaphor
25   where all that's
                            left lies down

                                            (1980)

Composed Like Them

(November 11, 1978)

A pair of strange old birds
flew right into my dream,
Orville's and Wilbur's¹ crates
waking me up with a start,
5   knocking my ivory gate,
calling me up to see
some old-time movie I knew
I never wanted to be.

Out of my past they came
10 creaking above Pat Bay,²
come from a small backyard
in Kitty Hawk, USA. Or come
from farther away. Come from

---

2. The death instinct; here, the personification of death.
1. Orville and Wilbur Wright were the first to accomplish the flight of power-driven heavier-than-air machines at Kitty Hawk, North Carolina, in December 1903.
2. Patricia Bay is off the southeastern tip of Vancouver Island.

the Ancient of Days.[3] Tacky
15 old spiritual pair,
idle, extinct, and adored.

Am I the one with wings
fixed on with faulty glue?
Or am I the angelic form
20 doting, unfaithful, and true?
No matter who I am,
I'm sure they're here to stay,
I swear their corruption's done,
their wings now silvery-grey;
25 moth-eaten skeletons,
odd awkwardness at play.

Out of the fire they came
into Comedic light,
dragonflight spheres of thought,
30 filigreed lace for my sight.
But living together so long,
aloft in the petalled night,
has muted their loon-like song
to which they had every right.

35 Is that what Auden[4] knew,
that the pair are secretly bored,
cruising the River of Light,
scaring the illiterate horde?
Too old to mate, do they get
40 from Alighieri's[5] shore
a voyeuristic view of this
small round polished floor
which makes us passionate,
or leaves us cold—and late?

45 A few feet above Pat Bay,
Dear lovers, you float upon
my childhood's airforce base,
my obsolescent song.

---

3. One of the names for God used in the Old Testament (see Dan. 7:9).

4. W.H. Auden (1907–1973), British poet who immigrated to the United States and became one of the twentieth century's most influential poets. See p. 265.

5. Dante Alighieri (1265–1321), most revered of all Italian poets, wrote *The Divine Comedy*, in which he describes his dream-journey through Hell, Purgatory, and Paradise led by the Roman poet Virgil. Among the damned souls Dante meets in his journey through Hell are the lovers Paolo and Francesca, who are condemned to fly through the air together forever.

Old combatants up there,
50   hang-gliding Gemini,
yet sombre, home at last,
mechanically free,
steering your time machine
all for the likes of me.

55   I the dreamer dream
this flight at 51,
I, astonished and awed
under the moon and sun;
I, under the supernova,
60   asleep on the small round floor,
hear cackles of Zennish[6] laughter
riming ecstatic puns.
I with my *Vita Nuova*,[7]
I with my lines undone.

(1978)

Anne Sexton (1928–1974)

Born in Massachusetts, Sexton wrote frank, confessional poetry, often about her bouts of severe depression. Poet Maxine Kumin speaks of Sexton as a woman "writing poetry that confronts issues of gender, social role, and female life." Her Transformations *(1971) contains reworkings of fairy tales, including "Cinderella."*

Cinderella

You always read about it:
the plumber with twelve children

---

6. Zen Buddhism is a Japanese form of mysticism that emphasizes austerity, mental tranquillity, and the achievement of a perception of reality transcending reason.
7. Literally, "young life" or "new life." The title given by Dante to his long poem describing his love for Beatrice.

who wins the Irish Sweepstakes.
From toilets to riches.
5   That story.

Or the nursemaid,
some luscious sweet from Denmark
who captures the oldest son's heart.
From diapers to Dior.
10 That story.

Or a milkman who serves the wealthy,
eggs, cream, butter, yogurt, milk,
the white truck like an ambulance
who goes into real estate
15 and makes a pile.
From homogenized to martinis at lunch.

Or the charwoman
who is on the bus when it cracks up
and collects enough from the insurance.
20 From mops to Bonwit Teller.
That story.

Once
the wife of a rich man was on her deathbed
and she said to her daughter Cinderella:
25 Be devout. Be good. Then I will smile
down from heaven in the seam of a cloud.
The man took another wife who had
two daughters, pretty enough
But with hearts like blackjacks.
30 Cinderella was their maid.
She slept on the sooty hearth each night
and walked around looking like Al Jolson.
Her father brought presents home from town,
jewels and gowns for the other women
35 but the twig of a tree for Cinderella.
She planted that twig on her mother's grave
and it grew to a tree where a white dove sat.
Whenever she wished for anything the dove
would drop it like an egg upon the ground.
40 The bird is important, my dears, so heed him.

Next came the ball, as you all know.
It was a marriage market.
The prince was looking for a wife.
All but Cinderella were preparing

45 and gussying up for the big event.
Cinderella begged to go too.
Her stepmother threw a dish of lentils
into the cinders and said: Pick them
up in an hour and you shall go.
50 The white dove brought all his friends;
all the warm wings of the fatherland came,
and picked up the lentils in a jiffy.
No, Cinderella, said the stepmother,
you have no clothes and cannot dance.
55 That's the way with stepmothers.

Cinderella went to the tree at the grave
and cried forth like a gospel singer:
Mama! Mama! My turtledove,
send me to the prince's ball!
60 The bird dropped down a golden dress
and delicate little gold slippers.
Rather a large package for a simple bird.
So she went. Which is no surprise.
Her stepmothers and sisters didn't
65 recognize her without her cinder face
and the prince took her hand on the spot
and danced with no other the whole day.

As nightfall came she thought she'd better
get home. The prince walked her home
70 and she disappeared into the pigeon house
and although the prince took an axe and broke
it open she was gone. Back to her cinders.
These events repeated themselves for three days.
However on the third day the prince
75 covered the palace steps with cobbler's wax
and Cinderella's gold shoe stuck upon it.

Now he would find whom the shoe fit
and find his strange dancing girl for keeps.
He went to their house and the two sisters
80 were delighted because they had lovely feet.
The eldest went into a room to try the slipper on
but her big toe got in the way so she simply
sliced it off and put on the slipper.
The prince rode away with her until the white dove
85 told him to look at the blood pouring forth.
That is the way with amputations.
They don't just heal up like a wish.
The other sister cut off her heel

but the blood told as blood will.
90 The prince was getting tired.
He began to feel like a shoe salesman.
But he gave it one last try.
This time Cinderella fit into the shoe
like a love letter into its envelope.

95 At the wedding ceremony
the two sisters came to curry favor
and the white dove pecked their eyes out.
Two hollow spots were left
like soup spoons.

100 Cinderella and the prince
lived, they say, happily ever after,
like two dolls in a museum case
never bothered by diapers or dust,
never arguing over the timing of an egg,
105 never telling the same story twice,
never getting a middle-aged spread,
their darling smiles pasted on for eternity
Regular Bobbsey Twins.[1]
That story.

(1971)

Adrienne Rich (b. 1929)

American poet, teacher, editor, prose writer, and feminist, Rich published her first volume of poems, introduced by W.H. Auden, when she was still an undergraduate. Since the 1970s, her own and other women's experiences have shaped her writing.

---

1. The central characters in a series of books for children, they are synonymous with an idyllic life, too good to be true.

Aunt Jennifer's Tigers

Aunt Jennifer's tigers prance across a screen,
Bright topaz denizens of a world of green.
They do not fear the men beneath the tree;
They pace in sleek chivalric certainty.

5   Aunt Jennifer's fingers fluttering through her wool
Find even the ivory needle hard to pull.
The massive weight of Uncle's wedding band
Sits heavily upon Aunt Jennifer's hand.

When Aunt is dead, her terrified hands will lie
10   Still ringed with ordeals she was mastered by.
The tigers on the panel that she made
Will go on prancing, proud and unafraid.

(1951)

What Kind of Times Are These[1]

There's a place between two stands of trees where the grass grows uphill
and the old revolutionary road breaks off into shadows
near a meeting-house abandoned by the persecuted
who disappeared into those shadows.

5   I've walked there picking mushrooms at the edge of dread, but don't
be fooled,
this isn't a Russian poem, this is not somewhere else but here,
our country moving closer to its own truth and dread,[2]
its own way of making people disappear.

I won't tell you where the place is, the dark mesh of the woods
10   meeting the unmarked strip of light—
ghost-ridden crossroads, leafmold paradise:
I know already who wants to buy it, sell it, make it disappear.

---

1. In her note to this poem, Rich says, "The title is from Bertolt Brecht's poem 'An Die Nachgebornen' ('For Those Born Later'): *What kinds of times are these / When it's almost a crime to talk about trees / Because it means keeping still about so many evil deeds?*"

2. Rich explains that this line "echoes Osip Mandelstam's 1921 poem that begins *I was washing outside in the darkness* and ends *The earth's moving closer to truth and to dread....* Mandelstam was forbidden to publish, then exiled and sentenced to five years of hard labor for a poem caricaturing Stalin; he died in a transit camp in 1938."

And I won't tell you where it is, so why do I tell you
anything? Because you still listen, because in times like these
15   to have you listen at all, it's necessary
to talk about trees.

(1995)

Derek Walcott (b. 1930)

Born in St. Lucia, Walcott published his first poetry collection at the age of
eighteen, had his first play produced at twenty, and received the Nobel Prize
for literature in 1992. Walcott typically explores his Caribbean heritage, a
history of colonialism, and conflicted relations to European culture.

A Far Cry from Africa

A wind is ruffling the tawny pelt
Of Africa. Kikuyu,[1] quick as flies,
Batten upon the bloodstreams of the veldt.[2]
Corpses are scattered through a paradise.
5   Only the worm, colonel of carrion, cries:
"Waste no compassion on these separate dead!"
Statistics justify and scholars seize
The salients of colonial policy.
What is that to the white child hacked in bed?
10   To savages, expendable as Jews?

Threshed out by beaters,[3] the long rushes break
In a white dust of ibises[4] whose cries
Have wheeled since civilization's dawn
From the parched river or beast-teeming plain.

---

1. Bantu-speaking tribe in Kenya whose members formed the Mau Mau, a secret
   revolutionary organization that operated to drive out British colonialists.
2. Open country; grassland.
3. Natives hired to drive game from cover.
4. Wading birds with downward-curving bills.

15　The violence of beast on beast is read
As natural law, but upright man
Seeks his divinity by inflicting pain.
Delirious as these worried beasts, his wars
Dance to the tightened carcass of a drum,
20　While he calls courage still that native dread
Of the white peace contracted by the dead.

Again brutish necessity wipes its hands
Upon the napkin of a dirty cause, again
A waste of our compassion, as with Spain,[5]
25　The gorilla wrestles with the superman.
I who am poisoned with the blood of both,[6]
Where shall I turn, divided to the vein?
I who have cursed
The drunken officer of British rule, how choose
30　Between this Africa and the English tongue I love?
Betray them both, or give back what they give?
How can I face such slaughter and be cool?
How can I turn from Africa and live?

(1962)

Ted Hughes (1930–1998)

In Hughes's poetry, animals and the natural world provide the focus for his uniquely conceived and powerful attempts to comprehend the human and natural order of things. He became the British poet laureate in 1984.

The Horses

I climbed through woods in the hour-before-dawn dark.
Evil air, a frost-making stillness.

---

5. In the Spanish Civil War (1936–39), the Loyalists, supported by intellectuals and communists, were defeated by the insurgents of Generalissimo Francisco Franco (1892–1975).

6. Walcott is of mixed ancestry: his grandfathers were white, and his grandmothers were black.

Not a leaf, not a bird,—
A world cast in frost. I came out above the wood

5 Where my breath left tortuous statues in the iron light.
But the valleys were draining the darkness

Till the moorline—blackening dregs of the brightening grey—

Halved the sky ahead. And I saw the horses:

Huge in the dense grey—ten together—
10 Megalith-still. They breathed, making no move.

With draped manes and tilted hind-hooves,
Making no sound.

I passed: not one snorted or jerked its head.
Grey silent fragments

15 Of a grey silent world.

I listened in emptiness on the moor-ridge.
The curlew's tear turned its edge on the silence.

Slowly detail leafed from the darkness. Then the sun
Orange, red, red erupted.

20 Silently, and splitting to its core tore and flung cloud,
Shook the gulf open, showed blue,

And the big planets hanging—
I turned

Stumbling in the fever of a dream, down towards
25 The dark woods, from the kindling tops,

And came to the horses.
                    There, still they stood,
But now steaming and glistening under the flow of light,

Their draped stone manes, their tilted hind-hooves
30 Stirring under a thaw while all around them

The frost showed its fires. But still they made no sound.
Not one snorted or stamped,

Their hung heads patient as the horizons,
High over valleys, in the red levelling rays—

35 In din of the crowded streets, going among the years, the faces,
May I still meet my memory in so lonely a place

Between the streams and the red clouds, hearing curlews,
Hearing the horizons endure.

(1957)

Hawk Roosting

I sit in the top of the wood, my eyes closed.
Inaction, no falsifying dream
Between my hooked head and hooked feet:
Or in sleep rehearse perfect kills and eat.

5 The convenience of the high trees!
The air's buoyancy and the sun's ray
Are of advantage to me;
And the earth's face upward for my inspection.

My feet are locked upon the rough bark.
10 It took the whole of Creation
To produce my foot, my each feather:
Now I hold Creation in my foot

Or fly up, and revolve it all slowly—
I kill where I please because it is all mine.
15 There is no sophistry in my body:
My manners are tearing off heads—

The allotment of death.
For the one path of my flight is direct
Through the bones of the living.
20 No arguments assert my right:

The sun is behind me.
Nothing has changed since I began.
My eye has permitted no change.
I am going to keep things like this.

(1960)

Sylvia Plath (1932–1963)

In her lifetime, American poet Sylvia Plath published only The Colossus *(1960), a volume of poetry, and* The Bell Jar *(1963), a novel. Married to Ted Hughes, p. 302, and mother of two young children, she committed suicide at thirty. After her suicide, other collections of her often highly anguished, yet sometimes gentle and witty, poetry were published.*

Morning Song

Love set you going like a fat gold watch.
The midwife slapped your footsoles, and your bald cry
Took its place among the elements.

Our voices echo, magnifying your arrival. New statue.
5   In a drafty museum, your nakedness
Shadows our safety. We stand round blankly as walls.

I'm no more your mother
Than the cloud that distils a mirror to reflect its own slow
Effacement at the wind's hand.

10   All night your moth-breath
Flickers among the flat pink roses. I wake to listen:
A far sea moves in my ear.

One cry, and I stumble from bed, cow-heavy and floral
In my Victorian nightgown.
15   Your mouth opens clean as a cat's. The window square

Whitens and swallows its dull stars. And now you try
Your handful of notes;
The clear vowels rise like balloons.

(1965)

Mirror

I am silver and exact. I have no preconceptions.
Whatever I see I swallow immediately
Just as it is, unmisted by love or dislike.
I am not cruel, only truthful—
5   The eye of a little god, four-cornered.
Most of the time I meditate on the opposite wall.
It is pink, with speckles. I have looked at it so long
I think it is a part of my heart. But it flickers.
Faces and darkness separate us over and over.

10   Now I am a lake. A woman bends over me,
Searching my reaches for what she really is.
Then she turns to those liars, the candles or the moon.
I see her back, and reflect it faithfully.
She rewards me with tears and an agitation of hands.
15   I am important to her. She comes and goes.
Each morning it is her face that replaces the darkness.
In me she has drowned a young girl, and in me an old woman
Rises toward her day after day, like a terrible fish.

(1963)

Lady Lazarus[1]

I have done it again.
One year in every ten
I manage it—

A sort of walking miracle, my skin
5   Bright as a Nazi lampshade,
My right foot

A paperweight,
My face a featureless, fine
Jew linen.

10   Peel off the napkin
O my enemy.
Do I terrify?—

The nose, the eye pits, the full set of teeth?
The sour breath
15   Will vanish in a day.

---

1. Lazarus brought back from death by Jesus (John 11).

Soon, soon the flesh
The grave cave ate will be
At home on me

And I a smiling woman.
20 I am only thirty.
And like the cat I have nine times to die.

This is Number Three.
What a trash
To annihilate each decade.

25 What a million filaments.
The peanut-crunching crowd
Shoves in to see

Them unwrap me hand and foot—
The bit strip tease.
30 Gentlemen, ladies

These are my hands
My knees.
I may be skin and bone,

Nevertheless, I am the same, identical woman.
35 The first time it happened I was ten.
It was an accident.

The second time I meant
To last it out and not come back at all.
I rocked shut

40 As a seashell.
They had to call and call
And pick the worms off me like sticky pearls.

Dying
Is an art, like everything else.
45 I do it exceptionally well.

I do it so it feels like hell.
I do it so it feels real.
I guess you could say I've a call.

It's easy enough to do it in a cell.
50 It's easy enough to do it and stay put.
It's the theatrical

Comeback in broad day
To the same place, the same face, the same brute
Amused shout:

55 "A miracle!"
That knocks me out.
There is a charge

For the eying of my scars, there is a charge
For the hearing of my heart—
60 It really goes.

And there is a charge, a very large charge
For a word or a touch
Or a bit of blood

Or a piece of my hair on my clothes.
65 So, so, Herr Doktor.
So, Herr Enemy.

I am your opus,
I am your valuable,
The pure gold baby

70 That melts to a shriek.
I turn and burn.
Do not think I underestimate your great concern.

Ash, ash—
You poke and stir.
75 Flesh, bone, there is nothing there—

A cake of soap,
A wedding ring,
A gold filling.

Herr God, Herr Lucifer
80 Beware.
Beware.

Out of the ash
I rise with my red hair
And I eat men like air.

(1965)

Alden Nowlan (1933–1983)

Nowlan was born in Nova Scotia but lived in and wrote about
New Brunswick for most of his life. In addition to twelve volumes
of verse, Nowlan wrote short stories and an autobiographical novel and col-
laborated on three plays. He received the Governor General's Award for
Bread, Wine and Salt *(1967).*

Warren Pryor

When every pencil meant a sacrifice
his parents boarded him at school in town,
slaving to free him from the stony fields,
the meagre acreage that bore them down.

5 They blushed with pride when, at his graduation,
they watched him picking up the slender scroll,
his passport from the years of brutal toil
and lonely patience in a barren hole.

When he went in the Bank their cups ran over.
10 They marvelled at how he wore a milk-white shirt
work days and jeans on Sundays. He was saved
from their thistle-strewn farm and its red dirt.

And he said nothing. Hard and serious
like a young bear inside his teller's cage,
15 his axe-hewn hands upon the paper bills
aching with empty strength and throttled rage.

(1961)

Wole Soyinka (b. 1934)

Born in Nigeria and educated at University College, Ibadan, and Leeds
University, Wole Soyinka, writer, filmmaker, and academic, received the
Nobel Prize for literature in 1986. Soyinka's struggles for human dignity
and justice have led to imprisonment (in his native Nigeria) and, since
1994, a life of exile from his homeland.

Telephone Conversation

The price seemed reasonable, location
Indifferent. The landlady swore she lived
Off premises. Nothing remained
But self-confession. "Madam," I warned,
5   "I hate a wasted journey—I am African."
Silence. Silenced transmission of
Pressurized good-breeding. Voice, when it came
Lipstick coated, long gold-rolled
Cigarette-holder pipped. Caught I was, foully.
10 "HOW DARK?" ... I had not misheard ... "ARE YOU LIGHT
OR VERY DARK?" Button B. Button A.[1] Stench
Of rancid breath of public hide-and-speak.
Red booth. Red pillar-box.[2] Red double-tiered
Omnibus squelching tar. It *was* real! Shamed
15 By ill-mannered silence, surrender
Pushed dumbfoundment to beg simplification.
Considerate she was, varying the emphasis—
"ARE YOU DARK? OR VERY LIGHT?" Revelation came.
"You mean—like plain or milk chocolate?"
20 Her assent was clinical, crushing in its light
Impersonality. Rapidly, wave-length adjusted,
I chose. "West African sepia"—and as afterthought,
"Down in my passport." Silence for spectroscopic[3]
Flight of fancy, till truthfulness clanged her accent
25 Hard on the mouthpiece. "WHAT'S THAT?" conceding

---

1. At the time, on coin-operated telephones in Britain the caller pressed Button A to make a connection and Button B to cancel the call.
2. Cylindrical postal box.
3. A spectroscope is an instrument for analysis of a range of colours.

"DON'T KNOW WHAT THAT IS." "Like brunette."
"THAT'S DARK, ISN'T IT?" "Not altogether.
Facially, I am brunette, but madam, you should see
The rest of me. Palm of my hand, soles of my feet
30 Are a peroxide blonde. Friction, caused—
Foolishly madam—by sitting down, has turned
My bottom raven black—One moment madam!"—sensing
Her receiver rearing on the thunderclap
About my ears—"Madam," I pleaded, "wouldn't you rather
35 See for yourself?"

(1960)

Leonard Cohen (b. 1934)

*Born and educated in Montreal, Cohen combines careers as popular singer
and poet. He refused to accept the Governor General's Award for* Selected
Poems *(1968) and in his poetry challenges old mythologies and conventional wisdom. In 1993 he received a Governor General's Performing Arts
Award in recognition of his lifetime achievement.*

For E.J.P.[1]

I once believed a single line
        in a Chinese poem could change
            forever how blossoms fell
and that the moon itself climbed on
5   the grief of concise weeping men
            to journey over cups of wine
I thought invasions were begun for crows
        to pick at a skeleton
            dynasties sown and spent
10 to serve the language of a fine lament
        I thought governors ended their lives

---

1. See E.J. Pratt, p. 228.

     as sweetly drunken monks
telling time by rain and candles
     instructed by an insect's pilgrimage
15   across the page—all this
so one might send an exile's perfect letter
to an ancient home-town friend

I chose a lonely country
     broke from love
20   scorned the fraternity of war
I polished my tongue against the pumice moon
     floated my soul in cherry wine
        a perfumed barge for Lords of Memory
to languish on to drink to whisper out
25   their store of strength
        as if beyond the mist along the shore
their girls their power still obeyed
     like clocks wound for a thousand years
I waited until my tongue was sore

30   Brown petals wind like fire around my poems
     I aimed them at the stars but
        like rainbows they were bent
before they sawed the world in half
     Who can trace the canyoned paths
35   cattle have carved out of time
wandering from meadowlands to feasts
     Layer after layer of autumn leaves
        Are swept away
Something forgets us perfectly

(1964)

Audre Lorde (1934–1992)

Born in New York, Lorde was a poet, editor, and teacher whose poetry derived from her feminism, her lesbianism, and her African-American roots; "I am Black, Woman, and Poet," she has written, "—all three are facts outside the realm of choice."

Hanging Fire

I am fourteen
and my skin has betrayed me
the boy I cannot live without
still sucks his thumb
5 in secret
how come my knees are
always so ashy
what if I die
before morning
10 and momma's in the bedroom
with the door closed.

I have to learn how to dance
in time for the next party
my room is too small for me
15 suppose I die before graduation
they will sing sad melodies
but finally
tell the truth about me
There is nothing I want to do
20 and too much
that has to be done
and momma's in the bedroom
with the door closed.

Nobody even stops to think
25 about my side of it
I should have been on Math Team
my marks were better than his
why do I have to be
the one
30 wearing braces
I have nothing to wear tomorrow
will I live long enough
to grow up
and momma's in the bedroom
35 with the door closed.

(1978)

George Bowering (b. 1935)

Canadian university professor, critic, and writer of both poetry and prose
fiction (as well as twice winning the Governor General's Award), Bowering
strives for a spare simplicity of language to create the taut intensity and
immediacy of his work.

Grandfather

Grandfather
        Jabez Harry Bowering
strode across the Canadian prairie
hacking down trees
            and building churches
delivering personal baptist sermons in them
leading Holy holy holy lord god almighty songs in them
red haired man squared off in the pulpit
reading Saul on the road to Damascus[1] at them

Left home
        big walled Bristol town
at age eight
        to make a living
buried his stubby fingers in root snarled earth
for a suit of clothes and seven hundred gruelly meals a year
taking an anabaptist cane across the back every day
for four years till he was whipt out of England

Twelve years old
        and across the ocean alone
to apocalyptic Canada
        Ontario of bone bending labor
six years on the road to Damascus till his eyes were blinded
with the blast of Christ and he wandered west
to Brandon among wheat kings and heathen Saturday nights
young red haired Bristol boy shovelling coal
in the basement of Brandon college five in the morning

---

1. Saul, who later became the apostle Paul, experienced a religious conversion that temporarily blinded him on the road to Damascus. See Acts 9.

Then built his first wooden church and married
a sick girl who bore two live children and died
leaving several pitiful letters and the Manitoba night

30   He moved west with another wife and built children and churches
Saskatchewan Alberta British Columbia Holy holy holy
lord god almighty
          struck his labored bones with pain
and left him a postmaster prodding grandchildren with crutches
35   another dead wife and a glass bowl of photographs
and holy books unopened save the bible by the bed

Till he died the day before his eighty fifth birthday
in a Catholic hospital of sheets white as his hair

                           (1962)

Marge Piercy (b. 1936)

American poet and novelist Marge Piercy is known for writing with a pronounced political edge. Her work has addressed such issues as poverty, racism, the environment, and women's rights. Her books include The Art of Blessing the Day: Poems with a Jewish Theme *(1999) and* Sleeping with Cats: A Memoir *(2002). "To Be of Use," typical in its energy and strength, celebrates those people who "move in a common rhythm" and whose work has a purpose.*

To Be of Use

The people I love the best
jump into work head first
without dallying in the shallows
and swim off with sure strokes almost out of sight.
5   They seem to become natives of that element,
the black sleek heads of seals
bouncing like half-submerged balls.

I love people who harness themselves, an ox to a heavy cart,
who pull like water buffalo, with massive patience,
10 who strain in the mud and the muck to move things forward,
who do what has to be done, again and again.

I want to be with people who submerge
in the task, who go into the fields to harvest
and work in a row and pass the bags along,
15 who are not parlor generals and field deserters
but move into a common rhythm
when the food must come in or the fire be put out.

The work of the world is common as mud.
Botched, it smears the hands, crumbles to dust.
20 But the thing worth doing well done
has a shape that satisfies, clean and evident.
Greek amphoras for wine or oil,
Hopi vases that held corn, are put in museums
but you know they were made to be used.
25 The pitcher cries for water to carry
and a person for work that is real.

(1973)

Barbie Doll

This girlchild was born as usual
and presented dolls that did pee-pee
and miniature GE stoves and irons
and wee lipsticks the color of cherry candy.
5 Then in the magic of puberty, a classmate said:
You have a great big nose and fat legs.

She was healthy, tested intelligent,
possessed strong arms and back,
abundant sexual drive and manual dexterity.
10 She went to and fro apologizing.
Everyone saw a fat nose on thick legs.

She was advised to play coy,
exhorted to come on hearty,
exercise, diet, smile and wheedle.
15 Her good nature wore out
like a fan belt.

So she cut off her nose and her legs
and offered them up.
In the casket displayed on satin she lay
20 with the undertaker's cosmetics painted on,
a turned-up putty nose,
dressed in a pink and white nightie.
Doesn't she look pretty? everyone said.
Consummation at last.
25 To every woman a happy ending.

(1969)

Margaret Atwood (b. 1939)

Atwood's poetry, novels, and short stories have earned her an international
reputation. Often using landscape and animals to explore human truths, she
works with images that juxtapose and occasionally blend human and nat-
ural worlds. See "Through the One-Way Mirror," p. 58, and "Happy
Endings," p. 511.

This Is a Photograph of Me

It was taken some time ago.
At first it seems to be
a smeared
print: blurred lines and grey flecks
5 blended with the paper;

then, as you scan
it, you see in the left-hand corner
a thing that is like a branch: part of a tree
(balsam or spruce) emerging
10 and, to the right, halfway up
what ought to be a gentle
slope, a small frame house.

In the background there is a lake,
and beyond that, some low hills.

15 (The photograph was taken
the day after I drowned.

I am in the lake, in the centre
of the picture, just under the surface.

It is difficult to say where
20 precisely, or to say
how large or small I am:
the effect of water
on light is a distortion

but if you look long enough,
25 eventually
you will be able to see me.)

(1966)

The animals in that country

In that country the animals
have the faces of people:

the ceremonial
cats possessing the streets

5 the fox run
politely to earth, the huntsmen
standing around him, fixed
in their tapestry of manners

the bull, embroidered
10 with blood and given
an elegant death, trumpets, his name
stamped on him, heraldic brand
because

(when he rolled
15 on the sand, sword in his heart, the teeth
in his blue mouth were human)

he is really a man

even the wolves, holding resonant
conversation in their
20   forests thickened with legend.

In this country the animals
have the faces of
animals.

Their eyes
25   flash once in car headlights
and are gone.

Their deaths are not elegant.

They have the faces of
no-one.

(1968)

Seamus Heaney (b. 1939)

*Born in Northern Ireland and preoccupied with the Troubles, Heaney began to
publish his evocative, highly concentrated, and thoughtful poetry in the
1960s. He subsequently lectured on poetry at Queen's University, Belfast, and
at Harvard University before winning the Nobel Prize for literature in 1995.*

The Tollund Man[1]

I

Some day I will go to Aarhus
To see his peat-brown head,
The mild pods of his eye-lids,
His pointed skin cap.

5 In the flat country nearby
Where they dug him out,
His last gruel of winter seeds
Caked in his stomach,

Naked except for
10 The cap, noose and girdle,
I will stand a long time.
Bridegroom to the goddess,

She tightened her torc[2] on him
And opened her fen.
15 Those dark juices working
Him to a saint's kept body,

Trove of the turfcutters'
Honeycombed workings.
Now his stained face
20 Reposes at Aarhus.

II

I could risk blasphemy,
Consecrate the cauldron bog
Our holy ground and pray
Him to make germinate

---

1. In 1950, the corpse of an Iron Age man who had been hanged was found in a Danish peat bog. The body was so perfectly preserved that scientists were able to deduce what he had eaten for his last meal from the contents of his stomach. The head is displayed in a museum in Aarhus, Denmark.

2. Also *torque*. A collar, necklace, or bracelet of twisted metal, worn by the ancient Gauls and Britons.

25 The scattered, ambushed
Flesh of labourers,
Stockinged corpses
Laid out in the farmyards,

Tell-tale skin and teeth
30 Flecking the sleepers
Of four young brothers, trailed
For miles along the lines.

III

Something of his sad freedom
As he rode the tumbril
35 Should come to me, driving,
Saying the names

Tollund, Grabaulle, Nebelgard,
Watching the pointing hands
Of country people,
40 Not knowing their tongue.

Out there in Jutland
In the old man-killing parishes
I will feel lost,
Unhappy and at home.

(1972)

After a Killing

There they were, as if our memory hatched them,
As if the unquiet founders walked again:
Two young men with rifles on the hill,
Profane and bracing as their instruments.

5 Who's sorry for our trouble?
Who dreamt that we might dwell among ourselves
In rain and scoured light and wind-dried stones?
Basalt, blood, water, headstones, leeches.

In that neuter original loneliness
10 From Brandon to Dunseverick[1]
I think of small-eyed survivor flowers,
The pined-for, unmolested orchid.

I see a stone house by a pier.
Elbow room. Broad window light.
15 The heart lifts. You walk twenty yards
To the boats and buy mackerel.

And to-day a girl walks in home to us
Carrying a basket full of new potatoes,
Three light green cabbages, and carrots
20 With the tops and mould still fresh on them.

(1979)

Digging

Between my finger and my thumb
The squat pen rests; snug as a gun.

Under my window, a clean rasping sound
When the spade sinks into gravelly ground:
5 My father, digging. I look down

Till his straining rump among the flowerbeds
Bends low, comes up twenty years away
Stooping in rhythm through potato drills
Where he was digging.

10 The coarse boot nestled on the lug, the shaft
Against the inside knee was levered firmly.
He rooted out tall tops, buried the bright edge deep
To scatter new potatoes that we picked
Loving their cool hardness in our hands.
15 By God, the old man could handle a spade.
Just like his old man.

My grandfather cut more turf in a day
Than any other man on Toner's bog.
Once I carried him milk in a bottle
20 Corked sloppily with paper. He straightened up

---

1. Locations in the extreme southwest and northeast of Ireland.

To drink it, then fell to right away
Nicking and slicing neatly, heaving sods
Over his shoulder, going down and down
For the good turf. Digging.

25 The cold smell of potato mould, the squelch and slap
Of soggy peat, the curt cuts of an edge
Through living roots awaken in my head.
But I've no spade to follow men like them.

Between my finger and my thumb
30 The squat pen rests.
I'll dig with it.

(1966)

Gwendolyn MacEwen (1941–1987)

Although Toronto-born Gwendolyn MacEwen wrote novels, plays, and short stories, she is known chiefly for her poetry. Both The Shadow-Maker *(1969) and* Afterworlds *(1987) won Governor General's awards. MacEwen once remarked that she wrote to communicate joy, "not the joy that naively exists without knowledge of pain, but that joy which arises out of and conquers pain. I want to construct a myth."*

A Breakfast for Barbarians

my friends, my sweet barbarians,
there is that hunger which is not for food—
but an eye at the navel turns the appetite
round
5 with visions of some fabulous sandwich,
the brain's golden breakfast
eaten with beasts
with books on plates

let us make an anthology of recipes,
10 let us edit for breakfast
our most unspeakable appetites—
let us pool spoons, knives
and all cutlery in a cosmic cuisine,
let us answer hunger
15 with boiled chimera[1]
and apocalyptic tea,
an arcane salad of spiced bibles,
tossed dictionaries—
        (O my barbarians
20   we will consume our mysteries)

and can we, can we slake the gaping eye of our desires?
we will sit around our hewn wood table
until our hair is long and our eyes are feeble,
eating, my people, O my insatiates,
25 eating until we are no more able
to jack up the jaws any longer—
to no more complain of the soul's vulgar cavities,
to gaze at each other over the rust-heap of cutlery,
drinking a coffee that takes an eternity—
30 till, bursting, bleary,
we laugh, barbarians, and rock the universe—
and exclaim to each other over the table
over the table of bones and scrap metal
over the gigantic junk-heaped table:

35 by God that was a meal

                                        (1966)

Dark Pines under Water

This land like a mirror turns you inward
And you become a forest in a furtive lake;
The dark pines of your mind reach downward,
You dream in the green of your time,
5 Your memory is a row of sinking pines.

---

1. In Greek mythology, the Chimera was a monster with a goat's body, lion's head,
   and dragon's tail. Its name has come to be used for any wild flight of fancy.

Explorer, you tell yourself this is not what you came for
Although it is good here, and green;
You had meant to move with a kind of largeness,
You had planned a heavy grace, an anguished dream.

10   But the dark pines of your mind dip deeper
And you are sinking, sinking, sleeper
In an elementary world;
There is something down there and you want it told.

(1969)

Daphne Marlatt (b. 1942)

Daphne Marlatt is a British Columbia poet who started writing and editing poetry in the late 1960s and continues her work in both areas. Her technical experiments with poetic voice and line lengths are apparent in the following two poems.

New Moon

for Roy

A windowpane fingernail moon last night, coming into the dark room
   for something
outside light, where I'd left him   in the bath   having clipt tiny
   fingernails all
over the blue carpet—all over the blue so black stars shine
   moon mostly a
finger of light appears at the crack of the door, dark, dark circle a child
5   sits arm around knees—listens to their voices in the other room, promise
time holds, or light (see to the full like some pencil mark in the night sky
so faint it is the reverse of night) imagining the other side of where he sits
hugging himself in a shoe or moon, in a funny clog he sails off in,
   wishing …
briars, wishing a gate, a way *into* what remains dark for you, the

10 nave of an abandoned church like the belly of some whale you call me
     on the
phone in full daylight full of the excitement of. This is a ship beached in
quiet halfway up a hill overlooking the sea. This is the architrave[1] of
sleep, "reaching 25 feet up," into invisible light on the other side
     of dream.
"I've found the place I want to live in"
15   (briar rose)
                                                    & does it sleep
at night on an empty road? do you? Nothing sleeps, not even that
     briar which buds
inside you, waiting spellbound for the door to open, your door,
     your hand on it.
Here, I have just finished planting beans & marigolds, those flowers
     of the sun.
20 New moon, our neighbour said, I been waiting all month for this,
     new moon & moon
in taurus, figure you can't get more earthy than that. Here is an
     architecture
of gardens, a block whose visible fences hide, under the night, the
     invisible
sympathy of seeds & moon. The same you, across a sea, wake
     under, walk in my
imagining that white expanse of beach, dark ribs, white whale or
     white reflected
25 walls this moon a door we can't afford to look at, opens, in reverse,
     onto a
brilliant terrain love lives inside of, dwarfed by a rising earth, its
     changes.

                                                    (1980)

coming home

if it's to
get lost, lose
way as a wave
breaks
5   "goodbye"

i am not speaking of
a path, the "right"

---

1. Architectural term for the parts surrounding a doorway or a window.

road, no such
wonderlust

10   weigh all steps
shift weight
to left or right to

a place where one
steps thru all erratic
15   wanderings down to
touch:

i am here, feel
my weight on the wet
ground

(1980)

Sharon Olds (b. 1942)

American poet Sharon Olds has written intensely personal and highly phys-
ical poetry about her family and childhood suffering as well as about global
violence and death. She has taught creative writing throughout the United
States and won the National Book Critics Circle Award for The Dead and
the Living *(1984).*

Leningrad Cemetery, Winter of 1941[1]

That winter, the dead could not be buried.
The ground was frozen, the gravediggers weak from hunger,
the coffin wood used for fuel. So they were covered with something
and taken on a child's sled to the cemetery

---

1. During World War II, the city of Leningrad (St. Petersburg) was besieged by the
   German army from August 1941 to January 1944. During the 900-day siege,
   more than a million people died, mostly from starvation, particularly during the
   first winter.

5   in the sub-zero air. They lay on the soil,
     some of them wrapped in dark cloth
     bound with rope like the tree's ball of roots
     when it waits to be planted; others wound in sheets,
     their pale, gauze, tapered shapes
10   stiff as cocoons that will split down the center
     when the new life inside is prepared;
     but most lay like corpses, their coverings
     coming undone, naked calves
     hard as corded wood spilling
15   from under a cloak, a hand reaching out
     with no sign of peace, wanting to come back
     even to the bread made of glue and sawdust,
     even to the icy winter, and the siege.

(1979)

Michael Ondaatje (b. 1943)

*Born in Ceylon (now Sri Lanka), Canadian poet, novelist, dramatist, editor,
and filmmaker Ondaatje enjoys an international reputation for his work. He
has won the Governor General's Award three times, twice for poetry and
most recently for his novel* The English Patient *(1992), which also won the
Booker Prize.*

Bearhug

Griffin calls to come and kiss him goodnight
I yell ok. Finish something I'm doing,
then something else, walk slowly round
the corner to my son's room.
5   He is standing arms outstretched
waiting for a bearhug. Grinning.

Why do I give my emotion an animal's name,
give it that dark squeeze of death?
This is the hug which collects

10 all his small bones and his warm neck against me.
The thin tough body under the pyjamas
locks to me like a magnet of blood.

How long was he standing there
like that, before I came?

(1979)

The Cinnamon Peeler[1]

If I were a cinnamon peeler
I would ride your bed
and leave the yellow bark dust
on your pillow.

5   Your breasts and shoulders would reek
you could never walk through markets
without the profession of my fingers
floating over you. The blind would
stumble certain of whom they approached
10 though you might bathe
under rain gutters, monsoon.

Here on the upper thigh
at this smooth pasture
neighbour to your hair
15 or the crease
that cuts your back. This ankle.
you will be known among strangers
as the cinnamon peeler's wife.

I could hardly glance at you
20 before marriage
never touch you
—your keen nosed mother, your rough brothers.
I buried my hands
in saffron, disguised them
25 over smoking tar,
helped the honey gatherers ...

. . . .

---

1. One who peels from the cinnamon tree the bark whose inner layer provides the
aromatic spice.

When we swam once
I touched you in water
and our bodies remained free,
30 you could hold me and be blind of smell.
You climbed the bank and said

            this is how you touch other women
the grass cutter's wife, the lime burner's daughter.
And you searched your arms
35 for the missing perfume
                    and knew

            what good is it
to be the lime burner's daughter
left with no trace
40 as if not spoken to in the act of love
as if wounded without the pleasure of a scar.

You touched
your belly to my hands
in the dry air and said
45 I am the cinnamon
peeler's wife. Smell me.

                                        (1982)

Bronwen Wallace (1945–1989)

Bronwen Wallace was born in Ontario and educated at Queen's University, where she taught creative writing. Her books include Marrying into the Family *(1980),* Signs of the Former Tenant *(1983),* Common Magic *(1985), and* The Stubborn Particulars of Grace *(1987). A book of short stories was published posthumously.*

Stunts

(a poem inspired by The Guinness Book of World Records *and an interview with Philippe Petit in* People *magazine)*

The ones they can't pull off
bring us nothing. Houdini's[1] dying promise
to return. How he must have climbed into his death
with the simple faith he'd demonstrated
5   all his life: if there's a way in
there's a way out. Counting on us
to believe it this time too, forgetting
the fist in his gut, the abrupt fall
into what it made of him.

10   Forgetting his body like that, though the trick's
there or nowhere, doing it over and over again
until it comes, another way of talking.
What the high-wire artist means
when he says that running is the acrobat's laughter.
15   "When my heart is open to the wind," he tells us,
"I am next to the gates of Paradise. Our domain
is bounded by death, not props."
And we can see how he holds to that,
the balance pole that gives him
20   the patience of one who has fallen before
and believes he will get
what he deserves.

As we all want to.
So that when Annie Edson Taylor,
25   first person down Niagara Falls in a barrel,
climbed out and said, "Nobody ought ever
to do that again," nobody listened.
It wasn't her advice
that got her over, any more than it's the air
30   that keeps the divers from the rocks
at La Quebrada or the roar of the cannon
that Zacchini flies with, at 54 m.p.h.
When the wind cuts through our overcoats
as we walk home from work, we know
35   Petit feels it too
as he steps out between the towers

---

1. Harry Houdini (born Erich Weiss, 1874–1926), celebrated magician, famous for his escapes, many of which have never been duplicated.

of the World Trade Center,
1350 feet above our heads;
and as our fingers fumble for our keys
40 we are glad for the ones
that keep a yo-yo going, 5 days
non-stop, or write the Lord's Prayer
34 times on a postage stamp.
We know what they look like,
45 no further escaped from a fin or a claw
than our own; so that it pleases us,
when the day boils up
smelling of burnt milk, when we're out of coffee
and the egg runs down our chins,
50 to know that someone's out there, for us,
making omelettes while dangling from a helicopter,
catching a grape in their mouth at 319 feet
or climbing a 30-foot coconut tree
in 4.88 seconds, barefoot.
55 To know we're deserving sometimes
as Petit steps out
into that instant, bounded by air
at the edge of the crowd's hope,
where everything comes easy
60 and the body fits.

(1987)

Tom Wayman (b. 1945)

Born in Hawkesbury, Ontario, Tom Wayman moved with his family first to Prince Rupert and then to Vancouver, British Columbia. Educated at the University of British Columbia (B.A. in English) and the University of California at Irvine (M.F.A.), he has worked in journalism as well as in manual and academic jobs. He has been writer-in-residence at the universities of Windsor, Alberta, Winnipeg, Toronto, and at Simon Fraser University

and has published thirteen collections of poems. Cofounder of the Vancouver
Industrial Writers' Union, Wayman has an abiding interest in work and
workplace issues.

Factory Time

The day divides neatly into four parts
marked off by the breaks. The first quarter
is a full two hours, 7:30 to 9:30, but that's okay
in theory, because I'm supposed to be fresh, but in fact
5   after some evenings it's a long first two hours.
Then, a ten-minute break. Which is good
another way, too: the second quarter
thus has ten minutes knocked off, 9:40 to 11:30
which is only 110 minutes, or
10   to put it another way, if I look at my watch
and it says 11:10
I can cheer up because if I had still been in the first quarter
and had worked for 90 minutes there would be
30 minutes to go, but now there is only
15   20. If it had been the first quarter, I could expect
the same feeling at 9 o'clock as here I have
when it is already ten minutes after 11.

Then it's lunch: a stretch, and maybe a little walk around.
And at 12 sharp the endless quarter begins:
20   a full two afternoon hours. And it's only the start
of the afternoon. Nothing to hope for the whole time.
Come to think of it, today
is probably only Tuesday. Or worse, Monday,
with the week barely begun and the day
25   only just half over, four hours down
and 36 to go this week
(if the foreman doesn't come padding by about 3
some afternoon and ask us all to work overtime).

Now while I'm trying to get through this early Tuesday afternoon
30   maybe this is a good place to say
Wednesday, Thursday and Friday have their personalities too.
As a matter of fact, Wednesday after lunch
I could be almost happy
because when that 12 noon hooter blast goes
35   the week is precisely and officially half over.
All downhill from here: Thursday, as you know

is the day before Friday
which means a little celebrating Thursday night
—perhaps a few rounds in the pub after supper—
40 won't do me any harm. If I don't get much sleep
Thursday night, so what? I can sleep in Saturday.
And Friday right after lunch Mike the foreman appears
with the long cheques dripping out of his hands
and he is so polite to each of us as he passes them over
45 just like they taught him in foreman school.
After that, not too much gets done.
People go away into a corner and add and subtract like crazy
trying to catch the Company in a mistake
or figuring out what incredible percentage the government
50 has taken this week, or what the money will actually mean
in terms of savings or payments—and me, too.

But wait. It's still Tuesday afternoon.
And only the first half of that: all the minutes
until 2—which comes at last
55 and everyone drops what they are doing
if they hadn't already begun drifting toward
their lunchboxes, or edging between the parts-racks
in the direction of the caterer's carts
which always appear a few minutes before the hooter
60 and may be taken on good authority as incontrovertible proof
that 2 o'clock is actually going to arrive.

And this last ten minute break of the day
is when I finally empty my lunchbox and the thermos inside
and put the now lightweight container back on its shelf
65 and dive into the day's fourth quarter: only 110 minutes.
Also, 20 to 30 minutes before the end I stop
and push a broom around, or just fiddle with something
or maybe fill up various parts-trays with washers
and bolts, or talk to the partsman, climb out of my
70 coveralls, and generally slack off.
Until the 4 p.m. hooter of hooters
when I dash to the timeclock, a little shoving and pushing
in line, and I'm done. Whew.

But even when I quit
75 the numbers of the minutes and hours from this shift
stick with me: I can look at a clock some morning
months afterwards, and see it is 20 minutes to 9

—that is, if I'm ever out of bed that early—
and the automatic computer in my head
80 starts to type out: *20 minutes to 9, that means*
30 minutes to work after 9: you are
50 minutes from the break; 50 minutes
of work, and it is only morning, and it is only
Monday, you poor dumb bastard . . .

85 And that's how it goes, round the clock, until a new time
from another job bores its way into my brain.

(*1993*)

Marlene Nourbese Philip (b. 1947)

Born in Tobago and educated at the University of the West Indies, in 1968
Nourbese Philip immigrated to Canada and attained an M.A. in political
science and an L.L.B. from the University of Western Ontario. She practised
law until she decided to become a full-time poet, novelist, and critic. Winner
of many awards, she is the author of Thorns (1980), Salmon Courage
(1983), She Tries Her Tongue, Her Silence Softly (1989), Looking for
Livingstone: An Odyssey of Silence (1991), *and* Frontiers: Essays and
Writings on Racism and Culture (1992).

Discourse on the Logic of Language

WHEN IT WAS BORN, THE MOTHER HELD HER NEWBORN CHILD CLOSE: SHE BEGAN THEN TO LICK IT ALL OVER. THE CHILD WHIMPERED A LITTLE, BUT AS THE MOTHER'S TONGUE MOVED FASTER AND STRONGER OVER ITS BODY, IT GREW SILENT—THE MOTHER TURNING IT THIS WAY AND THAT UNDER HER TONGUE, UNTIL SHE HAD TONGUED IT CLEAN OF THE CREAMY WHITE SUBSTANCE COVERING ITS BODY.

English
is my mother tongue.
A mother tongue is not
not a foreign lan lan lang
language
l/anguish
anguish
—a foreign anguish.

English is
my father tongue.
A father tongue is
a foreign language,
therefore English is
a foreign language
not a mother tongue.

What is my mother
tongue
my mammy tongue
my mummy tongue
my momsy tongue
my modder tongue
my ma tongue?

I have no mother
tongue
no mother tongue
no tongue to mother
to mother
tongue
me

I must therefore be tongue
dumb
dumb-tongued
dub-tongued
damn dumb
tongue

EDICT I

*Every owner of slaves
shall, wherever possible,
ensure that his slaves
belong to as many ethno-
linguistic groups as
possible. If they can-
not speak to each other, they
cannot then foment
rebellion and revolution.*

Those parts of the brain chiefly responsible for speech are named after two learned nineteenth century doctors, the eponymous Doctors Wernicke and Broca respectively.

Dr Broca believed the size of the brain determined intelligence; he devoted much of his time to "proving" that white males of the Caucasian race had larger brains than, and were therefore superior to, women, Blacks and other peoples of colour.

Understanding and recognition of the spoken word takes place in Wernicke's area—the left temporal lobe, situated next to the auditory cortex; from there relevant information passes to Broca's area—situated in the left frontal cortex—which then forms the response and passes it on to the motor cortex. The motor cortex controls the muscles of speech.

THE MOTHER THEN PUT HER FINGERS INTO HER CHILD'S MOUTH—GENTLY FORCING IT OPEN; SHE TOUCHES HER TONGUE TO THE CHILD'S TONGUE, AND HOLDING THE TINY MOUTH OPEN, SHE BLOWS INTO IT—HARD. SHE WAS BLOWING WORDS—HER WORDS, HER MOTHER'S WORDS, THOSE OF HER MOTHER'S MOTHER, AND ALL THEIR MOTHERS BEFORE—INTO HER DAUGHTER'S MOUTH.

but I have
a dumb tongue
tongue dumb
father tongue
and english is
my mother tongue
is
my father tongue
is a foreign lan lan lang
language/
l/anguish
  anguish
a foreign anguish
is english—
another tongue
my mother
    mammy
    mummy
    moder
    mater
    macer
    moder
tongue
mothertongue

tongue mother
tongue me
mothertongue me
mother me
touch me
with the tongue of your
lan lan lang
language
l/anguish
  anguish
english
is a foreign anguish

EDICT II

Every slave caught
speaking his native
language shall be severely
punished. Where
necessary, removal of the
tongue is recommended.
The offending organ, when
removed, should be hung
on high in a central place,
so that all may see and tremble.

A tapering, blunt-tipped, muscular, soft and fleshy organ describes
(a) the penis.
(b) the tongue.
(c) neither of the above.
(d) both of the above.

In man the tongue is
(a) the principal organ of taste.
(b) the principal organ of articulate speech.
(c) the principal organ of oppression and exploitation.
(d) all of the above.

The tongue
(a) is an interwoven bundle of striated muscle running in three planes.
(b) is fixed to the jawbone.
(c) has an outer covering of a mucous membrane covered with papillae.
(d) contains ten thousand taste buds, none of which is sensitive to the taste of foreign words.

Air is forced out of the lungs up the throat to the larynx where it causes the vocal cords to vibrate and create sound. The metamorphosis from sound to intelligible word requires
(a) the lip, tongue and jaw all working together.
(b) a mother tongue.
(c) the overseer's whip.
(d) all of the above or none.

(1989)

Jeannette Armstrong (b. 1948)

*A member of the Okanagan people of the Penticton Indian Reserve,
Armstrong is a writer and researcher, educator and activist for En'owkin
Centre, directed by the Okanagan Nation. Her writings, which draw on
oral and written traditions, include* Enwhisteetkwa *(1982),* Neekna and
Chemai *(1983),* Slash *(1985),* Breathtracks *(1991), and* The Native
Creative Process: A Collaborative Discourse between Douglas Cardinal
and Jeannette Armstrong *(1991).*

History Lesson

Out of the belly of Christopher's ship
a mob bursts
Running in all directions
Pulling furs off animals
5   Shooting buffalo
Shooting each other
left and right

Father mean well
waves his makeshift wand
10   forgives saucer-eyed Indians

Red coated knights
gallop across the prairie
to get their men
and to build a new world

15   Pioneers and traders
bring gifts
Smallpox, Seagrams
and rice krispies

Civilization has reached
20   the promised land

Between the snap crackle pop
of smoke stacks
and multicolored rivers

swelling with flower powered zee
25 and farmers sowing skulls and bones
and miners
pulling from gaping holes
green paper faces
of a smiling English lady

30 The colossi
in which they trust
while burying
breathing forests and fields
beneath concrete and steel
35 stand shaking fists
waiting to mutilate
whole civilizations
ten generations at a blow

Somewhere among the remains
40 of skinless animals
is the termination
to a long journey
and unholy search
for the power
45 glimpsed in a garden
forever closed
forever lost

(1991)

Lorna Crozier (b. 1948)

Born in Swift Current, Saskatchewan, Crozier has taught at the universities of Saskatchewan and Victoria and has won many awards, including the Governor General's, for her poetry. Her collections include The Garden Going on without Us *(1985),* Angels of Flesh, Angels of Silence *(1988),* Everything Arrives at the Light *(1995), and* A Saving Grace: The Collected Poems of Mrs. Bentley *(1996), a tribute to Sinclair Ross's* As For Me and My House.

Marriage: Getting Used To

It did not take me long
to get used to his leather
wings, no, they felt good
like an old, much-loved coat
5   draped over my shoulders
It was his feet I couldn't stand,
his horny feet, ugly as a bird's,
the yellow claws and the pride
he took in them:
10   how he oiled the scales
        and saved the clippings
        making me a necklace
        from the broken claws
        sewing flakes of skin
15   like sequins in my clothes.

Even his tricks were okay
the way his words turned
to flames at parties
sizzling flies from the air,
20   lighting cigarettes for ladies
with his tongue. It wasn't that
that bothered me.

It was waking to find him
with a flashlight and a mirror
25   staring under the covers at his feet.

It was his nails
clicking across linoleum
(he was too vain to wear slippers)
and after he had gone to work,
30   it was the fallen gold scales
that lay on the sheet like scattered coins.

(1980)

Medbh McGuckian (b. 1950)

*Medbh McGuckian was born of Catholic parents in Belfast and educated at
Queen's University, Belfast, where she became associated with the Northern
Irish poets Seamus Heaney and Paul Muldoon, among others. She has been
a writer-in-residence at Queen's University, Belfast, and at the University of
California, Berkeley. McGuckian is winner of the Cheltenham Award, the
Alice Hunter Bartlett Prize, and the Bass Ireland Award for Literature. Her
many books include* The Flower Master *(1982),* Marconi's Cottage *(1991),*
Drawing Ballerinas *(2001), and* The Face of the Earth *(2002).*

Slips

The studied poverty of a moon roof,
The earthenware of dairies cooled by apple trees,
The apple tree that makes the whitest wash ...

But I forget names, remembering them wrongly
5 Where they touch upon another name,
A town in France like a woman's Christian name.

My childhood is preserved as a nation's history,
My favourite fairy tales the shells
Leased by the hermit crab.

10 I see my grandmother's death as a piece of ice,
My mother's slimness restored to her,
My own key slotted in your door—

Tricks you might guess from this unfastened button,
A pen mislaid, a word misread,
15 My hair coming down in the middle of a conversation.

(1982)

The War Ending

In the still world
Between the covers of a book,
Silk glides through your name
Like a bee sleeping in a flower
5   Or a seal that turns its head to look
At a boy rowing a boat.

The fluttering motion of your hands
Down your body presses into my thoughts
As an enormous broken wave,
10   A rainbow or a painting being torn
Within me. I remove the hand
And order it to leave.

Your passion for light
Is so exactly placed,
15   I read them as eyes, mouth, nostrils,
Disappearing back into their mystery
Like the war that has gone
Into us ending;

There you have my head,
20   A meeting of Irish eyes
With something English:
And now,
Today,
It bursts

(1991)

Louise Bernice Halfe (b. 1953)

A Plains Cree woman, whose Cree name is Sky Dancer, Halfe draws on Aboriginal spirituality, black humour, and memory as instruments of healing. In her award-winning poetry, Halfe uncovers the powers and pain of her people, weaving together public and private stories. She won the Milton Acorn Award for her first collection, Bear Bones and Feathers *(1994).*

Valentine Dialogue

I got bit.

By what?

A snake bite.

Where?

5   In my spoon. Gon er eeah.

Wholee sheeit.

Love he dold me.

I have a pain in my heart.

Fuckin liar.

10   Hate all of them
Dink day can hang dair
balls all over da place.

Cross my legs next dime.

Mudder says day all alike.

15   Snake in dair mouth
snake in dair pants.
Guess dat's a forked dongue.

Mudder says I'll never lift it down.
Fadder says I'm nothin but a cheap dramp.

20   Shame, shame
Da pain in my heart hurts, hurts.

My brown tits
day shame me
My brown spoon
25   fails me.

Tired of sinning.
Dew ya dink confession will help?
Dew ya dink prayers will clean me?

NEL

Maybe I be born again.
30   Da pain in my heart hurts, hurts.

Durty priest
Jest wants da durty story
Needs to shine his rocks.

Fuckin men.

35   Day dink I a cheap badge
to hang on dair sleeve, as if
I an easy spoon.

A dongue in dair mouth.
A dongue in dair pants.
40   No nothin 'bout the heart.
No nothin 'bout my soul.

Day lookit my mouth.
Must be a nice mouth
cuz I see da look
45   in dair eyes.

And my mouth
wants
to feel dair wet lips.

It's mudder's fault
50   never told me right from wrong
Fadder's fault
always say mudder a slut.
Guess I must be one too.
Guess I showed dem.

55   Meet nice man one day.
Maybe brown.
Maybe white.
Maybe black.
Maybe yellow.

60   Won't show
my body talks.
Won't tell
'bout the snake bite.

(1994)

My Ledders

dear pope
i no, i no, you dired of my ledders
i couldn't let dis one go
i dought you could do somedin 'bout it.
5   years ago you stopped *nōhkom* and *nimosōm*[1]
from prayin in da sweatlodge and sundance,
drummin, singin and dancin.
you even stopped dem from Indian speakin
and storydellin.
10 well you must had some kind of bower
cuz da govment sure listen.

well, pope
last night on DV
i watched some whitemen
15 sweat in da lodge, and at
dinner dime on da radio
i heard dat man dell us
dat some darafist was havin a retreat
and to register.
20 what dat mean, i not sure.
anyway he is buildin' a sweatlodge.
i never hear anybody before on da radio
dell da whole world dat.
i sure surprise and kinda make me mad.

25 i wonder if you could dell da govment
to make dem laws dat stop dat
whiteman from dakin our *isistāwina*[2]
cuz i dell you pope
i don't dink you like it
30 if i dook you
gold cup and wine
pass it 'round our circles
cuz i don't have you drainin
from doze schools.
35 i haven't married you jeesuz
and i don't kneel to him,
cuz he ain't my god.

---

1. *Nōhkom*: my grandmother; *nimosōm*: my grandfather.
2. Rituals.

dese men, pope, don't know what
tobacco mean, what suffer mean,
40   alls dey no is you jeesuz die for dem
dey don't no what fastin' mean
dey jist dake and gobble our *mātotsān*[3]
as if dey own it.
dey don't know what it mean to dake
45   from da earth and give somedin' back
i so dired of all dis *kimoti*,[4] pope
deach your children.
eat your jeezuz body.
drink his blood.
50   dell dem to go back to dere own deachings,
pope.

(1994)

Dionne Brand (b. 1953)

Born in Trinidad, Dionne Brand immigrated to Canada in 1970. Her books include 'Fore Day Morning *(1979),* Earth Magic *(1980),* Primitive Offensive *(1982),* Winter Epigrams and Epigrams to Ernesto Cardenal in Defense of Claudia *(1983), and* Chronicles of the Hostile Sun *(1984).*

Amelia still

Mama must have left then
that day when I hung out the window
and saw the drabness of the street
and felt that no one lived in the house
5   any longer, she must have carried herself off to the
bush, grabbed up her own ghost and ran all the way

---

3. Sweatlodge.
4. Stealing.

to Toco,[1] ran all the way out of the hell of us
tied to her breasts and sweeping her brain
for answers. Mama must have fled that day
10 when I noticed that her shadow
left the veranda and understood that sweet water was
only lyrical in a girl child's wild undertakings
she must have gone hunting for her heart
where she had dropped it as she buried each navel
15 string hunting, hunting her blood and milk
spread over our stained greedy faces.
Mama must have gone crazy
trying to wrench herself away
from my memory burning around her
20 and denying her the bread of her death
as food from her mouth
she must have hurried to the Ortoire river
to wash her own hair, take her sweet time
waking up, pitch stones over water,
25 eat a little sugar, in peace.

(1990)

Blues Spiritual for Mammy Prater

*On looking at "the photograph of Mammy Prater an ex-slave,
115 years old when her photograph was taken"*

she waited for her century to turn
she waited until she was one hundred and fifteen
years old to take a photograph
to take a photograph and to put those eyes in it
5 she waited until the technique of photography was
suitably developed
to make sure the picture would be clear
to make sure no crude daguerreotype would lose
her image
10 would lose her lines and most of all her eyes
and her hands
she knew the patience of one hundred and fifteen years
she knew that if she had the patience,
to avoid killing a white man

---

1. Toco Bay is on the north coast of Trinidad, and the Ortoire River cuts through the
central-southern area.

15 that I would see this photograph
she waited until it suited her
to take this photograph and to put those eyes in it.
in the hundred and fifteen years which it took her to
wait for this photograph she perfected this pose
20 she sculpted it over a shoulder of pain,
a thing like despair which she never called
this name for she would not have lasted
the fields, the ones she ploughed
on the days that she was a mule, left
25 their etching on the gait of her legs
deliberately and unintentionally
she waited, not always silently, not always patiently,
for this self portrait
by the time she sat in her black dress, white collar,
30 white handkerchief, her feet had turned to marble,
her heart burnished red,
and her eyes.

she waited one hundred and fifteen years
until the science of photography passed tin and
35 talbotype[1] for a surface sensitive enough
to hold her eyes
she took care not to lose the signs
to write in those eyes what her fingers could not script
a pact of blood across a century, a decade and more
40 she knew then that it would be me who would find
her will, her meticulous account, her eyes,
her days when waiting for this photograph
was all that kept her sane
she planned it down to the day,
45 the light,
the superfluous photographer
her breasts,
her hands
this moment of
50 my turning the leaves of a book,
noticing, her eyes.

(1990)

---

1. The Talbotype was named after its inventor, William Henry Fox Talbot (1800–1877), who, in 1841, patented a process for producing photographic images on sensitized paper.

Rhea Tregebov (b. 1953)

*Born in Saskatoon, Saskatchewan, Rhea Tregebov was raised in Winnipeg
and now lives in Toronto. She has published* Remembering History *(1982)
and* No One We Know *(1986). "What Makes You Sure" gives an impression of the fragile and tenuous stability of life. See "Some Notes on the Story
of Esther," p. 87.*

What Makes You Sure

What makes you sure
one thing is better than another?
I can walk down this sidewalk
with a bag full of groceries—
5   milk, butter, eggs, oranges, grapes—
I can walk all the way home
and never believe they were ever touched
by a single pair of human hands.
It's two days to Easter
10 and I can not buy lilies.
I can't quite place her death.
Walking back from the supermarket
I'm very careful of the eggs,
I was taught to be careful of the eggs,
15 never to break anything.
I'll break the skin of the grapes
against my tongue but the eggs
I'll swallow whole.
What makes you sure?
20 I can live in one house my whole life
and never look out onto the yard
and see the bushes pressing their green paws
against the wind, avid, angry as I am.
Everything wants to live.
25 Me too.
Everything wants to live forever.

(1982)

Marilyn Dumont (b. 1955)

Born in Olds, Alberta, and a descendant of Gabriel Dumont, Marilyn
Dumont celebrates her Cree-Métis heritage while probing colonial categories
of identity in her first book, A Really Good Brown Girl *(1996), winner of*
the Gerald Lampert Memorial Award for the best first collection of poetry by
a Canadian writer. She has taught creative writing at Simon Fraser
University as well as at Kwantlen University College in Vancouver and has
been writer-in-residence at the University of Alberta (2000/01).

Letter to Sir John A. Macdonald

Dear John: I'm still here and halfbreed,
after all these years
you're dead, funny thing,
that railway you wanted so badly,
5   there was talk a year ago
of shutting it down
and part of it was shut down,
the dayliner at least,
'from sea to shining sea,'
10   and you know, John,
after all that shuffling us around to suit the settlers,
we're still here and Métis.

We're still here
after Meech Lake and
15   one no-good-for-nothin-Indian
holdin-up-the-train,
stalling the 'Cabin syllables /Nouns of settlement,
/ ... steel syntax [and] /The long sentence of its exploitation'[1]
and John, that goddamned railroad never made this a great nation,
20   cause the railway shut down
and this country is still quarreling over unity,
and Riel is dead
but he just keeps coming back
in all the Bill Wilsons yet to speak out of turn or favour

---

1. Lines from F.R. Scott's "Laurentian Shield."

25 because you know as well as I
   that we were railroaded
   by some steel tracks that didn't last
   and some settlers who wouldn't settle
   and it's funny we're still here and callin ourselves halfbreed.

(1996)

Armand Garnet Ruffo (b. 1955)

*Born and raised in northern Ontario, Armand Garnet Ruffo is from the
Ojibway Nation. A graduate of the universities of Ottawa and Windsor,
Ruffo teaches Native literature at Carleton University. Ruffo writes poetry,
plays, essays, and fiction and publishes widely in literary periodicals. The
poems below are from his second book,* Grey Owl: The Mystery of Archie
Belaney, *about Archibald Belaney (1888–1938), an English-born naturalist
who passed himself off as the half-Apache Grey Owl.*

Why I Write

So I can live in the past,
earn a living,
protect the beaver,
publicize conservation,
5 attract attention,
sell 35,000 copies in 3 months,
give 138 lectures in 88 days,
travel over 4350 miles,
wear feathers,
10 wear make-up,
play Indian—no
be Indian,
get to go to pow wows,
get to tour Britain,
15 meet the King & Queen,

become famous,
become alcoholic,
leave a legacy,
lose a wife,
20   be lonely.

(1997)

Archie Belaney,[1] 1935

You in the audience who sit in expectation cannot know.

This fear, this inexorable fear, I take with me,
so much a part of me I carry it in my blood. Picture me
stepping onto the stage and into a beam of light.
5   I look out to the audience, to you,
but I see only a curtain of black. Certainly I hear
your applause, the rumble of voices, the clapping of hands,

and I greet this not without a small degree of satisfaction,
but I am far from at ease (though this air I try to assume)
10 as I make my way to the podium, for here darkness is no forest
sanctuary but more a murky abyss, ready to open greedily
like the mouth that it is, with a sharp, accusing shriek.

The music has come to an end: Beethoven's Moonlight Sonata,
an echo of my childhood, of Highbury Villa, of Aunt Ada
15 towering over me, a music that continues to swell my past
inside me but which for some unknown reason—Call it love
—I continue to use as a prelude to my entrance.

Call it affliction.

The film is rolling; no, correction, I haven't yet given the cue.
20 After a prefatory greeting in which I tell you I come in peace,

---

1. These two poems are from a longer sequence by Ruffo focusing on real and imaginary events in the life of "Grey Owl," Archibald Stansfeld Belaney (1888–1938).
Belaney was born in Hastings, England, and became fascinated with what he read
about North American Aboriginal peoples. He immigrated to Canada, learned
wilderness lore from the Ojibwa in northern Ontario, and began presenting himself as the son of a Scot and an Apache, calling himself Grey Owl. His Iroquois
wife convinced him of the need for conservation, and he wrote numerous books
on the subject. He became a well-known public figure, making two lecture tours
of Britain, where he was very popular. After his death, the British press discovered his English birth, and in the ensuing uproar about his fraudulent public persona, his work on conservation was largely forgotten.

I'm now launched into a story of my early days as a riverman,
or maybe I'm mentioning how different it was for me to move
to northern Ontario from the southern United States, to learn
the still-hunt of the Ojibway as compared to the whoop
25 and holler of the Apache buffalo hunt.

What I do know is that I'm in the middle of a sentence when
as though by lightning my words are struck down.
Without warning. From behind the black curtain
where you sit, someone is shouting: Liar! Liar!

30 Nothing but a liar.

Immediately the house lights come on with a hush as blinding
and as penetrating as the darkness which has now accumulated
in the person of the woman who stands in front of me
dressed in black with a veil masking her face,
35 as though she were in mourning. Is she?
All heads are turned towards her,
as she extends her arm and points to me.

You and the rest of the audience are aghast, struck dumb.
No one knows what to do. In the room's startled breath,
40 you could hear a leaf drop, except there are no leaves,
for this is a London auditorium, no leaves, no trees,
no place to hide.

The woman is now addressing those seated around her.
She tells you that she knows me.
45 Her? Me? Yes, me. She slowly nods,
as she raises her veil and looks me in the eye.
She is close, so close I can see the tears,
the torn smile, her emotions mixed and ravenous,
as she fulfils her dream come true of confronting me.

50 He's both a liar and a scoundrel.
I know, I'm his wife. Here, look! She screams,
and raises her left hand to show off a wedding ring,
and then from her handbag pulls out a couple of photographs:
Ask him about these, she says amid the flashing cameras
55 to the photographers who have managed to shove their way
towards her, while two ushers try to grab hold of her.

But the audience is calling for her to continue. Continue.
And so she gives them dates and names,
the name of the church, the presiding minister,
60 witnesses, guests, and on and on.

It turns out she is not alone.
One by one others in the audience begin to stand,
begin to make their way towards me, all
bearing an accusing finger.

65 And you, whoever you are, are swept up among them.
Before I can even get off the stage, find a way to escape,
you have all encircled me and together
are pointing and chanting in unison:
Archibald, Archibald Stansfeld Belaney.
70 The photographers have also surrounded me, flashbulbs
explode in my face. Blinded. There is no escape.

The haunted has become the hunted.

I press my hands to my ears and implore everyone to stop,
to let me go: For you know now who I am.
75 Helpless, I fall to the knees. And above me, there she is, Ivy,
the young actress Belaney once loved and abandoned.
And beside her, all his old Hastings Grammar School class mates
laughing at odd-ball Archie who's still playing Indian
after all these years.

(1997)

Jo Carrillo (b. 1959)

Educated at Stanford and the University of New Mexico, Jo Carrillo is a professor at the University of California Hastings College of Law. She is editor of Readings in American Indian Law: Recalling the Rhythm of Survival *(1998) and is interested in indigenous populations and in adding a multicultural dimension to legal history. Her poetry appears in* This Bridge Called My Back: Writings by Radical Women of Color *(1983).*

And When You Leave, Take Your Pictures With You

Our white sisters
radical friends
love to own pictures of us
sitting at a factory machine
5   wielding a machete
in our bright bandanas
holding brown yellow black red children
reading books from literacy campaigns
holding machine guns bayonets bombs knives
10 Our white sisters
radical friends
should think
again.

Our white sisters
15 radical friends
love to own pictures of us
walking to the fields in hot sun
with straw hat on head if brown
bandana if black
20 in bright embroidered shirts
holding brown yellow black red children
reading books from literacy campaigns
smiling.
Our white sisters radical friends
25 should think again.
No one smiles
at the beginning of a day spent
digging for souvenir chunks of uranium
of cleaning up after
30 our white sisters
radical friends

And when our white sisters
radical friends see us
in the flesh
35 not as a picture they own,
they are not quite as sure
if
they like us as much.
We're not as happy as we look
40 on
their
wall.

(1983)

NEL

Chief Lindsay Marshall (b. 1960)

Chief of the Chapel Island First Nation on Bras d'Or Lake, Chief Lindsay Marshall is a frequent reader of his poetry at ceilidhs in Cape Breton. He won the Anne Marie Memorial Award for Creative Writing from the University College of Cape Breton. His Clay Pots and Bones/Pka'wo'qq aq Waqntal *was published in 1997. Reviewer George Elliott Clarke saluted "a new Mi'kmaq voice" determined "to interrogate history, denounce injustice and utter a poetry of utter clarity."*

Clay Pots and Bones

Dear successive fathers:
Explain to me please, when did the
change take place, from owners
to wards of the selfish state?
5 Write down the reasons why
the land under our feet became
foreign soil in perpetuity.
Say again how the signers of
1752 lost as much as they
10 gained while the ink from a
quill pen rested in its
blackened Royal well.
What justification exists that
allowed our mounds to be
15 desecrated, clay pots and bones.
Rock glyphs painted over by
cfc-propelled paint.
Our songs and stories protected
by copyright and law, not in the
20 bosom of our grandmothers or
grandfathers of yesterday.
The cost of keeping us does
not reflect the real cost.
How many ghostly sails with
25 reeking holds did English
ports comfort in early fog?

Have you much experience in
the destruction of people,
besides us?

(1997)

George Elliott Clarke (b. 1960)

A Nova Scotian whose first volume of poetry was published in 1983, Clarke
explores Canada from the vantage of what he calls an Africadian. He says
his "diction has been distilled from rural folk gospel and urban blues, from
Miltonic meditations and Eliotic intonations."

Hammonds Plains African Baptist Church

Drunk with light,
I think of maritime country.
I sing of Birchtown[1] blues, the stark,
sad beauty of that Kimmerian[2] land.
5   I dream of a dauntless dory
battling the blue, cruel combers
of a feral, runaway ocean—
a Trotskyite[3] ocean in permanent revolution,
turning fluid ideas over and over
10   in its leviathan mind,
turning driftwood, drums, and conundrums
over and over ...
Then, crazy with righteous anger,

---

1. A Black Loyalist settlement near Shelburne, Nova Scotia.
2. Cimmeria was a mythical land that Europeans thought of as in the far west and
   shrouded in darkness.
3. Leon Trotsky (1879–1940), Russian revolutionary who was briefly imprisoned in
   Halifax Citadel while returning to Russia for the 1917 revolution. His theory of
   "permanent revolution" led him into conflict with Stalin. He was expelled from
   the Soviet Union in 1929 and later murdered by Stalin's agents.

I think of Lydia Jackson,[4]
15   slave madonna, soon-rich with child,
whose Nova Scotian owner,
distinguished Dr. Bulman,
kicked her hard in the stomach,
struck her viciously with fire tongs,
20   and then went out upon the ocean
in his dory
to commune with God.

(1983 and 1994)

Crying the Beloved Country

Why can I not leave you
like a refugee?
Reluctantly, I abandon
your sea-bound beauty,
5   shale arms and red clay lips
sipping Fundy streams.
why can i not depart from you
like any proud, prodigal son,
ignoring your eyes'
10   Black Baptist churches?
what keeps me from easy going?
Mother, is it your death
I fear
or my life?

(1983 and 1994)

---

4. Lydia Jackson came to Nova Scotia from the United States in 1783 with the Black
Loyalists. She was indentured for life (in effect, a slave) to the household of a Dr.
Bulman, by whom she became pregnant. Bulman beat her so severely that she
miscarried. In 1790, with 1200 other Black Loyalists, Lydia Jackson left Nova
Scotia to settle in Sierra Leone, West Africa.

Salvation Army Blues

Seeking after hard things—
muscular work or sweat-swagger action—
I rip wispy, Help Wanted ads,
dream of water-coloured sailors
5   pulling apart insect wings of maps,
stagger down saxophone blues avenues
where blackbirds cry for crumbs.
I yearn to be Ulyssean,[1] to roam
foaming oceans or wrest
10   a wage from tough, mad adventure.
for now, I labour language,
earn a cigarette
for a poem, a coffee
for a straight answer,
15   and stumble, punch-drunk,
down these drawn and quartered streets,
tense hands manacled
by angry pockets.

(1992 and 1994)

---

1. In Greek legend, after the fall of Troy, Ulysses, King of Ithaca, wandered the seas
for ten years, going through many adventures.

Short Fiction

INTRODUCTION_____

The short story, in the broad sense of a relatively brief fictional narrative in prose, is a very old literary form. In Western literary tradition, it derives from ancient Egyptian storytelling, Old Testament stories and Christ's parables, fables, folk tales, myths, legends, ballads, tales, sketches, and anecdotes. The telling of stories is a basic human activity in all cultures that persists even in the many stories that circulate and help fashion our sense of the global village or our journey on the Information Highway. Short fiction (from the Latin *fictio*—shaping or feigning), story, or narrative, once broadly defined in opposition to history or truth-telling and associated with "primitive" and oral cultures, is now widely understood to be a priceless repository and living repertoire of cultural, historical, and other knowledge that extends narrative's power and value far beyond the literary domain. In the interests of a more humane, just, and equitable society, writers and researchers create new narratives as well as counter-narratives that challenge dominant views not only in literary studies but also in history, law, philosophy, psychology, anthropology, and sociology, for example. All of us, and not only the investigative reporters, "have the story."

As a quite distinctive literary genre, however, the short story dates only from the nineteenth century with practitioners such as Edgar Allan Poe, Nathaniel Hawthorne, Guy de Maupassant, Anton Chekhov, and E.T.W. Hoffmann. The short story, in this more defined sense, is associated with changes in society and print culture in the early decades of the century and, in the American context, with a culture trying to define itself by difference from the old world of European and specifically British models and practices. The legitimation of the novel as a literary form in early nineteenth-century Britain is closely related to the bulk of the three-decker (or three-volume) novel, which aspired to educate and entertain with its sweeping panoramas of historical and social change and detailed compendia of bourgeois manners. Since British novels had no copyright protection in America, they were widely pirated and dominated the market. Such considerations played no small part in Poe's efforts to promote the short story as a literary form designed for the growing magazine and annual market in the interests of cultural nationalism—and an audience concerned to make the most of its leisure time. The spread of literacy and an increasingly urban society created a wide and eager audience for weekly and monthly periodical literature, for which short fiction was ideally suited.

Poe's 1842 review of Hawthorne, by some accounts, marked the canonization of the American short story as a unified design with a single effect. Often focused on one character and/or episode, it typically deals with a single moment of crisis or conflict that reveals depths of character or makes a profound statement about life. The writing is characteristically intense and concentrated so that all aspects of the story—theme, character, setting, plot, point of view, tone, mood, and style—benefit from careful crafting. Poe's own "The Cask of Amontillado" is an effectively claustrophobic version of this aesthetic, in its intense focus on physical and mental interiors, on identifications and misidentifications, powers and powerlessness.

In Britain the short story gained prestige only gradually over the course of a nineteenth century concerned with the place and value of fiction more generally in debates on "the fiction question," "the art of fiction," and "candour in fiction." Given the dominance of the novel, the short story, "one of the blunders of the age," according to novelist Charles Reade, struggled in Britain to overcome its reputation as little more than a rest cure from the real labour of novel writing. With expanded audiences and developments in print technology as well as new magazines and the decline of the three-decker and the circulating library's control of household reading, the 1890s, however, proved a fertile period, when, as H.G. Wells put it, "short stories broke out everywhere." Because of the very different conditions of production, the British short story does not typically follow Poe's model of brevity or Henry James's valuing of proportion. In the case of Thomas Hardy, for example, as with many women writers, the short story is valued for "disproportioning" or "throwing out of proportion" and observing that which is typically overlooked or neglected.

It is an error, then, albeit a common one, to approach the short story as if it were a novel, or, still worse, the novel's poor relation. The short story, the product of a particular convergence of social, literary, economic, and other forces in the nineteenth century, has endured as a powerful and popular form of expression. Frank O'Connor is one writer who has found the short story remarkably receptive to the "romantic, individualistic, and intransigent," and undoubtedly it has proven a potent means for marginalized groups and individuals to speak the hitherto unspeakable and to challenge prevailing orthodoxies about, for example, human sexuality, racial difference, the decorum of public/private lives, and issues of human justice. Charlotte Perkins Gilman's "The Yellow Wallpaper," Alice Walker's "Nineteen Fifty-Five," and Evelyn Lau's "Marriage" are examples of women's stories as a form of resistance to a culture's grand narratives and habitual practices. The short story has proven a particularly valued form in Canada and postcolonial or anti-colonial contexts more generally. Alice Munro and Margaret Atwood, for example, figure largely in most collections of short stories.

Reading D.H. Lawrence, Katherine Mansfield, and others taught Nadine Gordimer how she might represent the realities of a divided South Africa. They and other short-story writers represented here are among the finest in the language, and it is our hope that their work will demonstrate the considerable richness, breadth, and potency of this literary form.

Before the age of mass literacy, it was common for the story to be used as a vehicle for teaching or preaching a specific moral. Fables, in general, narrate a simple story that exaggerates character and motive through the use of animal protagonists. They point to a highly specific moral that can usually be codified in a single sentence. The most widely known fables are traditionally ascribed to Aesop, a sixth-century B.C. Phrygian slave. However, surviving Egyptian papyri indicate that many of these fables were actually written nearly a thousand years earlier. They were retold many times by various writers, some of whom added their own original fables to the collection. A modern humorist, James Thurber, produced two volumes of fables that set out to parody the fable form while providing some sharp satiric comment. Ethel Wilson's "We Have to Sit Opposite" is a modern political fable of the struggles between civilization and barbarism and the implication of everybody in the "fear and folly" synonymous with Munich in the years leading to and during World War II.

The parable, like the fable, is a simple narrative that points the reader toward a specific interpretation of the story. Although its significance cannot always be codified in a single sentence, the parable nonetheless exists primarily as a "closed text" rather than one inviting a wide variety of readings. Early pre-literary story forms such as the parable, fable, and folk tale continue to surface in twentieth-century literary stories. For example, Langston Hughes's "On the Road" owes something of its structure to the biblical parable.

While the modern short story owes some of its origins to such early forms as the fable, the parable, and the folk tale, it could not have come into being without the rise of the popular literary magazine in the nineteenth century. Thus began an association between the short story and periodical publication that continues to the present day. (See, for example, Mavis Gallant's regular contributions to *The New Yorker*.) The majority of short stories are still published first in journals. Although it is usually much longer than either a fable or a parable, the nineteenth-century short story bears a closer resemblance to such forms than do its modern successors. For instance, Hawthorne's "The Birthmark" appears to point the reader toward rather clearer moral conclusions than do any of the more recent stories reprinted here. Also popular with the nineteenth-century short-story reader and writer was a significant authorial presence in the narrative voice. The narrator of "The Birthmark" comments on the action, philosophizes, and moralizes in a manner that has now been all but abandoned. Still, it is a mistake to attempt to reduce even those stories to a singular or unproblematic message since they probe without resolving cultural contradictions exposed in times of crisis and conflict. Hawthorne's story is as much about gender politics and domestic abuse as it is about science's presumption to master the environment and human reproduction.

In addition to such narrative control, the nineteenth-century short-story reader and writer liked a story that had a sharp twist of plot or sudden reversal at its conclusion. In this respect, many writers were influenced by the tales of de Maupassant and Poe—works that often concluded with a bitter or ironic twist. Gilman's "The Yellow Wallpaper" exploits the horror story to tell a woman's story of confinement in marriage, creativity, professional competence, and mental illness. Twentieth-century writers, such as Timothy Findley in his macabre story "Dreams" or William Faulkner in "A Rose for Emily," continue to be fascinated by the style of Gothic horror and the supernatural so favoured by Poe.

The unexpected ending, the pronounced authorial presence, and the story with a clear-cut moral have not remained very popular with more recent short-story writers. One source of this change was the psychoanalytic theories of Sigmund Freud and others. The "stream-of-consciousness" technique, developed by such writers as James Joyce (in his later works) and Virginia Woolf, depicts the subjective, often irrational, working of a character's mind, rather than the character's actions or motivations presented more or less objectively. Although Poe and Gilman already focus attention on the inner life, many twentieth-century writers divert interest from the external events to the inner life of thoughts, feelings, dreams, and fantasies—or elaborate connections between external circumstances and inner realities. James Joyce, D.H. Lawrence, Katherine Mansfield, Nadine Gordimer, and Margaret Laurence, for example, explore class, race, gender, religion, war, industrialization, and the contradictions of family as determinants of human emotion and behaviour.

The great complexity of the modern short story derives largely from the writer's handling of point of view, or the view from which the writer presents the action of the story. Examination of narrative technique often leads to fuller understanding. Of the stories included here, several ("The Cask of Amontillado," "The Yellow Wallpaper," "A Rose for Emily," "The Loons," "Boys and Girls," "The Lesson," "The One About Coyote Going West," "Nineteen Fifty-Five," "Yin Chin," "Drummer," "Swimming Lessons," "Automatic Timer," and "Marriage") use first-person narration. In each of these, the writer has invented a literary personage (or, as in Faulkner's case, a representative voice of the community) who speaks in character. These narrators have a limited point of view: they can tell readers only what they themselves know or what others tell them. The more mature narrator of "Boys and Girls," for example, reflects on her childhood view of her family while disclosing the gendering of identity, whereas when the narrator of

"Automatic Timer" tosses off a casual remark about Mexican whores, it is not the author who might be considered racist but a character in the story.

One way to probe characters' sense of reality is to provide the reader with a basis for suspicion or an ironic perspective. Generally, the authors of the first-person narrations included here develop some means whereby the narrator reveals himself or herself in ways that are not intended. Little inconsistencies, disparities between past and present, excessive self-justification, repetition, even trivial allusions to revealing details—all make one aware that what one is told is a compound of reliable and unreliable reportage. Such a method certainly presents interesting challenges to the reader's powers of interpretation. More than that, it reinforces, in a moving way, our sense of the relativity and frailty of the human perception of ourselves and others and of powerful differences of gender, of race and ethnicity, of age, and place.

An omniscient narrator is one who tells the story with a seemingly unlimited point of view or fund of knowledge about characters and their actions. Narrators are not necessarily omniscient, and even omniscience has its limits in "The Birthmark." Some writers prefer to limit the information they provide to the range of knowledge exhibited by the characters. While this kind of narrator does not take part in the action, objects and events are described from the perspective of someone inside the fictional world of the story. "The Boarding House" registers in turn the very different judgments of Mrs. Mooney, Mr. Doran, and Polly. Critics sometimes speak of such stories as having a central consciousness. In an increasing number of modern short stories, we are allowed only the characters' perspectives on the action. "On the Road" is told in the third person, but the reader understands the story from the viewpoint of its protagonist, Sargeant.

Our selection offers a wide variety of story lengths, which in their turn require a range of narrative techniques. On the one hand, there is the tale that the writer develops at a leisurely pace, which often allows for the filling in of minute details. "You Touched Me," for example, is developed at some length, with many detailed images. Other stories are very short. Writers like Joyce often rely on and focus attention on the stated and unstated, what is revealed and what concealed. Joyce does not reveal to his reader what passes between Mrs. Mooney and Mr. Doran at their climactic interview, leaving the outcome to the judgment and imagination of readers. Some authors focus vividly on a very few minutes in the lives of their characters: Sunday morning in Dublin in "The Boarding House" or the rail journey in "We Have to Sit Opposite." Brevity is the essence of "Automatic Timer."

Despite such variations, short-story writers must in general make the most of details of setting, character, plot, tone, mood, and diction. Stories such as Donna E. Smyth's "Red Hot" or Rudy Wiebe's "Where Is the Voice Coming From?" go further than those of Joyce and others in exploring the nature of evidence, considering the legal and other ramifications of gendered perception or the fragmented and contradictory remains of the past. In any case, writers must be able to shape an incident or set of incidents into a memorable scene immediately, without the luxury of lengthy development, drawing on such poetic devices as figurative and rhythmical language. Learning to swim is both a literal and a figurative concern for Rohinton Mistry. Like the essayists and poets, the short-story writers explore and exploit language's role in shaping identity and community. In stories like "The Lesson," "Drummer," "The One About Coyote Going West," "Nineteen Fifty-Five," "Swimming Lessons," or "Yin Chin," the distinct idioms of narrators and characters, the mix of oral and written, speak to the conundra of cultural exchange, the linking of past and present, and the complex construction of national and other identities.

Crucial in all stories, both for dramatic impact and for psychological insight, are sharply observed details. Sometimes they are inserted unexpectedly, characters sketched in a sentence with the right details. In "The Boarding House," Polly "had a habit of glancing upwards when she spoke with anyone, which made her look like a little perverse madonna." Carefully observed settings, such as the industrialized landscape of Lawrence's World War I England, often have a symbolic meaning. A symbolic significance may also be conveyed by the title of a story, as, for example, "The Birthmark," "The Boarding House," "The Fly," or "The Lesson." Is there a connection between the "touch" in the title of Lawrence's story and Matilda's sudden change of heart, or between the walls enclosing the Pottery House and the boundaries of class, gender, and family? Such symbols provide controlling images that help to establish a sense of order (and meaning) in the story.

The following selection of stories illustrates not only a diversity of techniques but also a wide variety of themes. Like essayists and poets, writers of fiction will often seek inspiration from personal or closely observed experiences. Mistry explores immigrant accommodations, while Maracle probes prejudice and uncovers human dignity and capacity to survive. "The Fly" focuses on problems of adjustment following war, in ways comparable to such poems as Owen's "Disabled" and Birney's "The Road to Nijmégen." Ideas about race, class, and culture emerge not only in a North American context, as in "On the Road," "The Lesson," "The Loons," "The One About Coyote Going West," and "Nineteen Fifty-Five," but in the South African background of apartheid in Gordimer's "Town and Country Lovers." While most of the stories are serious, they are not without humour. Writers such as Bambara, Wilson, and King explore themes that allow them to adopt a wryly humorous tone.

Given the variety of its historical origins and the diversity of literary modes and techniques that can be employed in the short story, it is best to approach the genre without fixed preconceptions or expectations. Indeed, many stories resist easy formulations, the clichéd and stereotyped, while others explore the realities of fiction and the fictions of reality. Margaret Atwood's "Happy Endings," for example, like King's "The One About Coyote Going West," focuses on the shaping power of stories; these stories do not allow the reader to forget that the writer is constantly involved in the technique of storytelling. The method is comparable to that of John Fowles, who constructs his novel *The French Lieutenant's Woman* in such a way that the action can move in a variety of different directions, or, in another medium, to the theatre of Bertolt Brecht, an influential playwright who insisted that viewers remain constantly aware that they are watching a play. Such playwrights as Luigi Pirandello and Thornton Wilder likewise experiment with the relationship between reality and illusion, when actors step out of the characters they are playing to discuss their roles; Woody Allen uses a comparable technique in his film *The Purple Rose of Cairo*. A story like "Red Hot" may upset preconceived notions about such a basic thing as plot: it partially concerns real people, uses quotations from actual newspaper reports, is divided into very short sections, and is narrated through a series of violently flashing images. This may suggest to the reader television channel surfing or the technique of the film docudrama, in which a fictitious story may be spliced with live footage to aid its authenticity. When such methods are employed, the reader never loses sight of the technique—or what it reveals about the connections between media representations and people's private behaviours. Similarly, stories as different from one another as "The Fly," "You Touched Me," and "Dreams" may deliberately provoke a framework of reader expectations only to demand a radical change in perception by the end of the story.

Experimentation with technique is only one of many aspects of short fiction by which an author may stimulate a reader's responses. Writers use multiple methods of amusing, exciting, or moving their readers by introducing them to the imagined worlds they create in their fiction. The selection that follows offers readers a wealth of styles and experiences; however much stories may have changed over the centuries, sharing stories remains at the heart of individual and collective life.

Nathaniel Hawthorne (1804–1864)

*Massachusetts-born novelist and short-story writer, Hawthorne is best
known for his examination of New England morality and consciousness.
His penchant for allegory is apparent in "The Birthmark" (1843), in which
science opposes nature.*

The Birthmark

1   In the latter part of the last century there lived a man of science, an
eminent proficient in every branch of natural philosophy, who not long
before our story opens had made experience of a spiritual affinity more
attractive than any chemical one. He had left his laboratory to the care
of an assistant, cleared his fine countenance from the furnace smoke,
washed the stain of acids from his fingers, and persuaded a beautiful
young woman to become his wife. In those days, when the compara-
tively recent discovery of electricity and other kindred mysteries of
Nature seemed to open paths into the region of miracle, it was not
unusual for the love of science to rival the love of woman in its depth
and absorbing energy. The higher intellect, the imagination, the spirit,
and even the heart might all find their congenial aliment in pursuits
which, as some of their ardent votaries believed, would ascend from
one step of powerful intelligence to another, until the philosopher
should lay his hand on the secret of creative force and perhaps make
new worlds for himself. We know not whether Aylmer possessed this
degree of faith in man's ultimate control over Nature. He had devoted
himself, however, too unreservedly to scientific studies ever to be
weaned from them by any second passion. His love for his young wife
might prove the stronger of the two; but it could only be by inter-
twining itself with his love of science and uniting the strength of the
latter to his own.

2   Such a union accordingly took place, and attended with truly
remarkable consequences and a deeply impressive moral. One day,
very soon after their marriage, Aylmer sat gazing at his wife with a
trouble in his countenance that grew stronger until he spoke.

3   "Georgiana," said he, "has it never occurred to you that the mark
upon your cheek might be removed?"

4   "No, indeed," said she, smiling; but, perceiving the seriousness of
his manner, she blushed deeply. "To tell you the truth, it has been so
often called a charm that I was simple enough to imagine it might
be so."

5   "Ah, upon another face perhaps it might," replied her husband; "but never on yours. No, dearest Georgiana, you came so nearly perfect from the hand of Nature that this slightest possible defect, which we hesitate whether to term a defect or a beauty, shocks me, as being the visible mark of earthly imperfection."

6   "Shocks you, my husband!" cried Georgiana, deeply hurt; at first reddening with momentary anger, but then bursting into tears. "Then why did you take me from my mother's side? You cannot love what shocks you!"

7   To explain this conversation it must be mentioned that in the centre of Georgiana's left cheek there was a singular mark, deeply interwoven, as it were, with the texture and substance of her face. In the usual state of her complexion—a healthy though delicate bloom—the mark wore a tint of deeper crimson, which imperfectly defined its shape amid the surrounding rosiness. When she blushed it gradually became more indistinct, and finally vanished amid the triumphant rush of blood that bathed the whole cheek with its brilliant glow. But if any shifting motion caused her to turn pale there was the mark again, a crimson stain upon the snow, in what Aylmer sometimes deemed an almost fearful distinctness. Its shape bore not a little similarity to the human hand, though of the smallest pygmy size. Georgiana's lovers were wont to say that some fairy at birth hour had laid her tiny hand upon the infant's cheek, and left this impress there in token of the magic endowments that were to give her such sway over all hearts. Many a desperate swain would have risked his life for the privilege of pressing his lips to the mysterious hand. It must not be concealed, however, that the impression wrought by this fairy sign manual varied exceedingly, according to the difference of temperament in the beholders. Some fastidious persons—but they were exclusively of her own sex—affirmed that the bloody hand, as they chose to call it, quite destroyed the effect of Georgiana's beauty, and rendered her countenance even hideous. But it would be as reasonable to say that one of those small blue stains which sometimes occur in the purest statuary marble would convert the Eve of Powers[1] to a monster. Masculine observers, if the birthmark did not heighten their admiration, contented themselves with wishing it away, that the world might possess one living specimen of ideal loveliness without the semblance of a flaw. After his marriage—for he thought little or nothing of the matter before,—Aylmer discovered that this was the case with himself.

8   Had she been less beautiful,—if Envy's self could have found aught else to sneer at,—he might have felt his affection heightened by the prettiness of this mimic hand, now vaguely portrayed, now lost, now stealing forth again and glimmering to and fro with every pulse of emotion that throbbed within her heart; but seeing her otherwise so perfect, he found this one defect grow more and more intolerable with

---

1. Hiram Powers (1805–1873), American sculptor. "Eve" refers to one of his statues.

every moment of their united lives. It was the fatal flaw of humanity which Nature, in one shape or another, stamps ineffaceably on all her productions, either to imply that they are temporary and finite, or that their perfection must be wrought by toil and pain. The crimson hand expressed the ineludible gripe in which mortality clutches the highest and purest of earthly mould, degrading them into kindred with the lowest, and even with the very brutes, like whom their visible frames return to dust. In this manner, selecting it as the symbol of his wife's liability to sin, sorrow, decay, and death, Aylmer's sombre imagination was not long in rendering the birthmark a frightful object, causing him more trouble and horror than ever Georgiana's beauty, whether of soul or sense, had given him delight.

9   At all the seasons which should have been their happiest he invariably, and without intending it, nay, in spite of a purpose to the contrary, reverted to this one disastrous topic. Trifling as it at first appeared, it so connected itself with innumerable trains of thought and modes of feeling that it became the central point of all. With the morning twilight Aylmer opened his eyes upon his wife's face and recognized the symbol of imperfection; and when they sat together at the evening hearth his eyes wandered stealthily to her cheek, and beheld, flickering with the blaze of the wood fire, the spectral hand that wrote mortality where he would fain have worshipped. Georgiana soon learned to shudder at his gaze. It needed but a glance with the peculiar expression that his face often wore to change the roses of her cheek into a deathlike paleness, amid which the crimson hand was brought strongly out, like a bas-relief of ruby on the whitest marble.

10   Late one night, when the lights were growing dim so as hardly to betray the stain on the poor wife's cheek, she herself, for the first time, voluntarily took up the subject.

11   "Do you remember, my dear Aylmer," said she, with a feeble attempt at a smile, "have you any recollection, of a dream last night about this odious hand?"

12   "None! none whatever!" replied Aylmer, starting; but then he added, in a dry, cold tone, affected for the sake of concealing the real depth of his emotion, "I might well dream of it; for, before I fell asleep, it had taken a pretty firm hold of my fancy."

13   "And you did dream of it?" continued Georgiana, hastily; for she dreaded lest a gush of tears should interrupt what she had to say. "A terrible dream! I wonder that you can forget it. Is it possible to forget this one expression?—'It is in her heart now; we must have it out!' Reflect, my husband; for by all means I would have you recall that dream."

14   The mind is in a sad state when Sleep, the all-involving, cannot confine her spectres within the dim region of her sway, but suffers them to break forth, affrighting this actual life with secrets that perchance belong to a deeper one. Aylmer now remembered his dream. He had fancied himself with his servant Aminadab, attempting an operation

for the removal of the birthmark; but the deeper went the knife, the deeper sank the hand, until at length its tiny grasp appeared to have caught hold of Georgiana's heart; whence, however, her husband was inexorably resolved to cut or wrench it away.

15 When the dream had shaped itself perfectly in his memory, Aylmer sat in his wife's presence with a guilty feeling. Truth often finds its way to the mind close muffled in robes of sleep, and then speaks with uncompromising directness, of matters in regard to which we practise an unconscious self-deception during our waking moments. Until now he had not been aware of the tyrannizing influence acquired by one idea over his mind, and of the lengths which he might find in his heart to go for the sake of giving himself peace.

16 "Aylmer," resumed Georgiana, solemnly, "I know not what may be the cost to both of us to rid me of this fatal birthmark. Perhaps its removal may cause cureless deformity; or it may be the stain goes as deep as life itself. Again: do we know that there is a possibility, on any terms, of unclasping the firm gripe of this little hand which was laid upon me before I came into the world?"

17 "Dearest Georgiana, I have spent much thought upon the subject," hastily interrupted Aylmer. "I am convinced of the perfect practicability of its removal."

18 "If there be the remotest possibility of it," continued Georgiana, "let the attempt be made at whatever risk. Danger is nothing to me; for life, while the hateful mark makes me the object of your horror and disgust,—life is a burden which I would fling down with joy. Either remove this dreadful hand, or take my wretched life! You have deep science. All the world bears witness of it. You have achieved great wonders. Cannot you remove this little, little mark, which I cover with the tips of two small fingers? Is this beyond your power, for the sake of your own peace, and to save your poor wife from madness?"

19 "Noblest, dearest, tenderest wife," cried Aylmer, rapturously, "doubt not my power. I have already given this matter the deepest thought—thought which might almost have enlightened me to create a being less perfect than yourself. Georgiana, you have led me deeper than ever into the heart of science. I feel myself fully competent to render this dear cheek as faultless as its fellow; and then, most beloved, what will be my triumph when I shall have corrected what Nature left imperfect in her fairest work! Even Pygmalion,[2] when his sculptured woman assumed life, felt not greater ecstasy than mine will be."

20 "It is resolved, then," said Georgiana, faintly smiling. "And, Aylmer, spare me not, though you should find the birthmark take refuge in my heart at last."

---

2. Sculptor and king of Cyprus in Greek legend who hated women but fell in love with his own ivory statue of a woman. The goddess Aphrodite answered his prayers and turned his statue into a live woman, Galatea, whom Pygmalion married.

21   Her husband tenderly kissed her cheek—her right cheek—not that which bore the impress of the crimson hand.

22   The next day Aylmer apprised his wife of a plan that he had formed whereby he might have opportunity for the intense thought and constant watchfulness which the proposed operation might require; while Georgiana, likewise, would enjoy the perfect repose essential to its success. They were to seclude themselves in the extensive apartments occupied by Aylmer as a laboratory, and where, during his toilsome youth, he had made discoveries in the elemental powers of Nature that had roused the admiration of all the learned societies in Europe. Seated calmly in this laboratory, the pale philosopher had investigated the secrets of the highest cloud region and of the profoundest mines; he had satisfied himself of the causes that kindled and kept alive the fires of the volcano; and had explained the mystery of fountains, and how it is that they gush forth, some so bright and pure, and others with such rich medicinal virtues, from the dark bosom of the earth. Here, too, at an earlier period, he had studied the wonders of the human frame, and attempted to fathom the very process by which Nature assimilates all her precious influences from earth and air, and from the spiritual world, to create and foster man, her masterpiece. The latter pursuit, however, Aylmer had long laid aside in unwilling recognition of the truth—against which all seekers sooner or later stumble—that our great creative Mother, while she amuses us with apparently working in the broadest sunshine, is yet severely careful to keep her own secrets, and, in spite of her pretended openness, shows us nothing but results. She permits us, indeed, to mar, but seldom to mend, and, like a jealous patentee, on no account to make. Now, however, Aylmer resumed these half-forgotten investigations; not, of course, with such hopes or wishes as first suggested them; but because they involved much physiological truth and lay in the path of his proposed scheme for the treatment of Georgiana.

23   As he led her over the threshold of the laboratory, Georgiana was cold and tremulous. Aylmer looked cheerfully into her face, with intent to reassure her, but was so startled with the intense glow of the birthmark upon the whiteness of her cheek that he could not restrain a strong convulsive shudder. His wife fainted.

24   "Aminadab! Aminadab!" shouted Aylmer, stamping violently on the floor.

25   Forthwith there issued from an inner apartment a man of low stature, but bulky frame, with shaggy hair hanging about his visage, which was grimed with the vapors of the furnace. This personage had been Aylmer's underworker during his whole scientific career, and was admirably fitted for that office by his great mechanical readiness, and the skill with which, while incapable of comprehending a single principle, he executed all the details of his master's experiments. With his vast strength, his shaggy hair, his smoky aspect, and the indescribable earthiness that incrusted him, he seemed to represent man's physical

nature; while Aylmer's slender figure, and pale, intellectual face, were no less apt a type of the spiritual element.

26 "Throw open the door of the boudoir, Aminadab," said Aylmer, "and burn a pastil."

27 "Yes, master," answered Aminadab, looking intently at the lifeless form of Georgiana; and then he muttered to himself, "If she were my wife, I'd never part with that birthmark."

28 When Georgiana recovered consciousness she found herself breathing an atmosphere of penetrating fragrance, the gentle potency of which had recalled her from her deathlike faintness. The scene around her looked like enchantment. Aylmer had converted those smoky, dingy, sombre rooms, where he had spent his brightest years in recondite pursuits, into a series of beautiful apartments not unfit to be the secluded abode of a lovely woman. The walls were hung with gorgeous curtains, which imparted the combination of grandeur and grace that no other species of adornment can achieve; and as they fell from the ceiling to the floor, their rich and ponderous folds, concealing all angles and straight lines, appeared to shut in the scene from infinite space. For aught Georgiana knew, it might be a pavilion among the clouds. And Aylmer, excluding the sunshine, which would have interfered with his chemical processes, had supplied its place with perfumed lamps, emitting flames of various hue, but all uniting in a soft, impurpled radiance. He now knelt by his wife's side, watching her earnestly, but without alarm; for he was confident in his science, and felt that he could draw a magic circle round her within which no evil might intrude.

29 "Where am I? Ah, I remember," said Georgiana, faintly; and she placed her hand over her cheek to hide the terrible mark from her husband's eyes.

30 "Fear not, dearest!" exclaimed he. "Do not shrink from me! Believe me, Georgiana, I even rejoice in this imperfection, since it will be such a rapture to remove it."

31 "Oh, spare me!" sadly replied his wife. "Pray do not look at it again. I can never forget that convulsive shudder."

32 In order to soothe Georgiana, and, as it were, to release her mind from the burden of actual things, Aylmer now put in practice some of the light and playful secrets which science had taught him among its profounder lore. Airy figures, absolutely bodiless ideas, and forms of unsubstantial beauty came and danced before her, imprinting their momentary footsteps on beams of light. Though she had some indistinct idea of the method of these optical phenomena, still the illusion was almost perfect enough to warrant the belief that her husband possessed sway over the spiritual world. Then again, when she felt a wish to look forth from her seclusion, immediately, as if her thoughts were answered, the procession of external existence flitted across a screen. The scenery and the figures of actual life were perfectly represented, but with that bewitching yet indescribable difference which

always makes a picture, an image, or a shadow so much more attractive than the original. When wearied of this, Aylmer bade her cast her eyes upon a vessel containing a quantity of earth. She did so, with little interest at first; but was soon startled to perceive the germ of a plant shooting upward from the soil. Then came the slender stalk; the leaves gradually unfolded themselves; and amid them was a perfect and lovely flower.

33   "It is magical!" cried Georgiana. "I dare not touch it."

34   "Nay, pluck it," answered Aylmer,—"pluck it, and inhale its brief perfume while you may. The flower will wither in a few moments and leave nothing save its brown seed vessels; but thence may be perpetuated with a race as ephemeral as itself."

35   But Georgiana had no sooner touched the flower than the whole plant suffered a blight, its leaves turning coal-black as if by the agency of fire.

36   "There was too powerful a stimulus," said Aylmer, thoughtfully.

37   To make up for this abortive experiment, he proposed to take her portrait by a scientific process of his own invention. It was to be effected by rays of light striking a polished plate of metal. Georgiana assented; but, on looking at the result, was affrighted to find the features of the portrait blurred and indefinable; while the minute figure of a hand appeared where the cheek should have been. Aylmer snatched the metallic plate and threw it into a jar of corrosive acid.

38   Soon, however, he forgot these mortifying failures. In the intervals of study and chemical experiment he came to her flushed and exhausted, but seemed invigorated by her presence, and spoke in glowing language of the resources of his art. He gave a history of the long dynasty of the alchemists, who spent so many ages in quest of the universal solvent by which the golden principle might be elicited from all things vile and base. Aylmer appeared to believe that, by the plainest scientific logic, it was altogether within the limits of possibility to discover this long-sought medium; "but," he added, "a philosopher who should go deep enough to acquire the power would attain too lofty a wisdom to stoop to the exercise of it." Not less singular were his opinions in regard to the elixir vitae. He more than intimated that it was at his option to concoct a liquid that should prolong life for years, perhaps interminably; but that it would produce a discord in Nature which all the world, and chiefly the quaffer of the immortal nostrum, would find cause to curse.

39   "Aylmer, are you in earnest?" asked Georgiana, looking at him with amazement and fear. "It is terrible to possess such power, or even to dream of possessing it."

40   "O, do not tremble, my love," said her husband. "I would not wrong either you or myself by working such inharmonious effects upon our lives; but I would have you consider how trifling, in comparison, is the skill requisite to remove this little hand."

41   At the mention of the birthmark, Georgiana, as usual, shrank as if a red-hot iron had touched her cheek.

42   Again Aylmer applied himself to his labors. She could hear his voice in the distant furnace room giving directions to Aminadab, whose harsh, uncouth, misshapen tones were audible in response, more like the grunt or growl of a brute than human speech. After hours of absence, Aylmer reappeared and proposed that she should now examine his cabinet of chemical products and natural treasures of the earth. Among the former he showed her a small vial, in which, he remarked, was contained the gentle yet most powerful fragrance, capable of impregnating all the breezes that blow across a kingdom. They were of inestimable value, the contents of that little vial; and, as he said so, he threw some of the perfume into the air and filled the room with piercing and invigorating delight.

43   "And what is this?" asked Georgiana, pointing to a small crystal globe containing a gold-colored liquid. "It is so beautiful to the eye that I could imagine it the elixir of life."

44   "In one sense it is," replied Aylmer, "or rather, the elixir of immortality. It is the most precious poison that ever was concocted in this world. By its aid I could apportion the lifetime of any mortal at whom you might point your finger. The strength of the dose would determine whether he were to linger out years, or drop dead in the midst of a breath. No king on his guarded throne could keep his life if I, in my private station, should deem the welfare of millions justified me in depriving him of it."

45   "Why do you keep such a terrific drug?" inquired Georgiana in horror.

46   "Do not mistrust me, dearest," said her husband, smiling; "its virtuous potency is yet greater than its harmful one. But see! here is a powerful cosmetic. With a few drops of this in a vase of water, freckles may be washed away as easily as the hands are cleansed. A stronger infusion would take the blood out of the cheek, and leave the rosiest beauty a pale ghost."

47   "Is it with this lotion that you intend to bathe my cheek?" asked Georgiana, anxiously.

48   "Oh, no," hastily replied her husband; "this is merely superficial. Your case demands a remedy that shall go deeper."

49   In his interviews with Georgiana, Aylmer generally made minute inquiries as to her sensations, and whether the confinement of the rooms and the temperature of the atmosphere agreed with her. These questions had such a particular drift that Georgiana began to conjecture that she was already subjected to certain physical influences, either breathed in with the fragrant air or taken with her food. She fancied likewise, but it might be altogether fancy, that there was a stirring up of her system—a strange, indefinite sensation creeping through her veins, and tingling, half painfully, half pleasurably, at her heart. Still, whenever she dared to look into the mirror, there she beheld herself pale as a

white rose and with the crimson birthmark stamped upon her cheek. Not even Aylmer now hated it so much as she.

50   To dispel the tedium of the hours which her husband found it necessary to devote to the process of combination and analysis, Georgiana turned over the volumes of his scientific library. In many dark old tomes she met with chapters full of romance and poetry. They were the works of the philosophers of the middle ages, such as Albertus Magnus, Cornelius Agrippa, Paracelsus, and the famous friar who created the prophetic Brazen Head.[3] All these antique naturalists stood in advance of their centuries, yet were imbued with some of their credulity, and therefore were believed, and perhaps imagined themselves to have acquired from the investigation of Nature a power above Nature, and from physics a sway over the spiritual world. Hardly less curious and imaginative were the early volumes of the Transactions of the Royal Society,[4] in which the members, knowing little of the limits of natural possibility, were continually recording wonders or proposing methods whereby wonders might be wrought.

51   But to Georgiana, the most engrossing volume was a large folio from her husband's own hand, in which he had recorded every experiment of his scientific career, its original aim, the methods adopted for its development, and its final success or failure, with the circumstances to which either event was attributable. The book, in truth, was both the history and emblem of his ardent, ambitious, imaginative, yet practical and laborious life. He handled physical details as if there were nothing beyond them; yet spiritualized them all and redeemed himself from materialism by his strong and eager aspiration towards the infinite. In his grasp the veriest clod of earth assumed a soul. Georgiana, as she read, reverenced Aylmer and loved him more profoundly than ever, but with a less entire dependence on his judgment than heretofore. Much as he had accomplished, she could not but observe that his splendid successes were almost invariably failures, if compared with the ideal at which he aimed. His brightest diamonds were the merest pebbles, and felt to be so by himself, in comparison with the inestimable gems which lay hidden beyond his reach. The volume, rich with achievements that had won renown for its author, was yet as melancholy a record as ever mortal hand had penned. It was the sad confession and

---

3. Albertus Magnus (1206–1280), German scholastic philosopher whose name was often associated with a book of alchemical "secrets." Heinrich Cornelius Agrippa von Nettesheim (1486–1535), German writer and physician who was reputed to be a magician. He was charged with heresy and his writings were suppressed by the Inquisition. Paracelsus (c. 1490–1541), German physician who devised a highly unconventional pharmaceutical system. The Brazen Head, a head of brass which knew all things and could speak, was supposed to have been created by Roger Bacon (c. 1214–1294?), the "famous friar," an English scholastic philosopher and scientist.

4. The Royal Society, founded in 1660, is the oldest scientific organization in Great Britain and one of the oldest in Europe. Its activities include the publication of its *Proceedings* and of *The Philosophical Transactions*.

continual exemplification of the shortcomings of the composite man, the spirit burdened with clay and working in matter, and of the despair that assails the higher nature at finding itself so miserably thwarted by the earthly part. Perhaps every man of genius, in whatever sphere, might recognize the image of his own experience in Aylmer's journal.

52   So deeply did these reflections affect Georgiana that she laid her face upon the open volume and burst into tears. In this situation she was found by her husband.

53   "It is dangerous to read in a sorcerer's books," said he with a smile, though his countenance was uneasy and displeased. "Georgiana, there are pages in that volume which I can scarcely glance over and keep my senses. Take heed lest it prove detrimental to you."

54   "It has made me worship you more than ever," said she.

55   "Ah, wait for this one success," rejoined he, "then worship me if you will. I shall deem myself hardly unworthy of it. But come, I have sought you for the luxury of your voice. Sing to me, dearest."

56   So she poured out the liquid music of her voice to quench the thirst of his spirit. He then took his leave with a boyish exuberance of gayety, assuring her that her seclusion would endure but a little longer, and that the result was already certain. Scarcely had he departed when Georgiana felt irresistibly impelled to follow him. She had forgotten to inform Aylmer of a symptom which for two or three hours past had begun to excite her attention. It was a sensation in the fatal birthmark, not painful, but which induced restlessness throughout her system. Hastening after her husband, she intruded for the first time into the laboratory.

57   The first thing that struck her eye was the furnace, that hot and feverish worker, with the intense glow of its fire, which by the quantities of soot clustered above it seemed to have been burning for ages. There was a distilling apparatus in full operation. Around the room were retorts, tubes, cylinders, crucibles, and other apparatus of chemical research. An electrical machine stood ready for immediate use. The atmosphere felt oppressively close, and was tainted with gaseous odors which had been tormented forth by the processes of science. The severe and homely simplicity of the apartment, with its naked walls and brick pavement, looked strange, accustomed as Georgiana had become to the fantastic elegance of her boudoir. But what chiefly, indeed almost solely, drew her attention, was the aspect of Aylmer himself.

58   He was pale as death, anxious and absorbed, and hung over the furnace as if it depended upon his utmost watchfulness whether the liquid which it was distilling should be the draught of immortal happiness or misery. How different from the sanguine and joyous mien that he had assumed for Georgiana's encouragement!

59   "Carefully now, Aminadab; carefully, thou human machine, carefully, thou man of clay," muttered Aylmer, more to himself than his assistant. "Now, if there be a thought too much or too little, it is all over!"

60   "Ho! ho!" mumbled Aminadab. "Look, master! look!"

61 Aylmer raised his eyes hastily, and at first reddened, then grew paler than ever, on beholding Georgiana. He rushed towards her and seized her arm with a gripe that left the print of his fingers upon it.

62 "Why do you come hither? Have you no trust in your husband?" cried he, impetuously. "Would you throw the blight of that fatal birth-mark over my labors? It is not well done. Go, prying woman! go!"

63 "Nay, Aylmer," said Georgiana with the firmness of which she possessed no stinted endowment, "it is not you that have a right to complain. You mistrust your wife; you have concealed the anxiety with which you watch the development of this experiment. Think not so unworthily of me, my husband. Tell me all the risk we run, and fear not that I shall shrink; for my share in it is far less than your own."

64 "No, no, Georgiana!" said Aylmer, impatiently; "it must not be."

65 "I submit," replied she, calmly. "And, Aylmer, I shall quaff whatever draught you bring me; but it will be on the same principle that would induce me to take a dose of poison if offered by your hand."

66 "My noble wife," said Aylmer, deeply moved, "I knew not the height and depth of your nature until now. Nothing shall be concealed. Know, then, that this crimson hand, superficial as it seems, has clutched its grasp into your being with a strength of which I had no previous conception. I have already administered agents powerful enough to do aught except to change your entire physical system. Only one thing remains to be tried. If that fail us we are ruined."

67 "Why did you hesitate to tell me this?" asked she.

68 "Because, Georgiana," said Aylmer, in a low voice, "there is danger."

69 "Danger? There is but one danger—that this horrible stigma shall be left upon my cheek!" cried Georgiana. "Remove it, remove it, whatever be the cost, or we shall both go mad!"

70 "Heaven knows your words are too true," said Aylmer, sadly. "And now, dearest, return to your boudoir. In a little while all will be tested."

71 He conducted her back and took leave of her with a solemn tenderness which spoke far more than his words how much was now at stake. After his departure Georgiana became rapt in musings. She considered the character of Aylmer and did it completer justice than at any previous moment. Her heart exulted, while it trembled, at his honorable love—so pure and lofty that it would accept nothing less than perfection nor miserably make itself contented with an earthlier nature than he had dreamed of. She felt how much more precious was such a sentiment than that meaner kind which would have borne with the imperfection for her sake, and have been guilty of treason to holy love by degrading its perfect idea to the level of the actual; and with her whole spirit she prayed that, for a single moment, she might satisfy his highest and deepest conception. Longer than one moment she well knew it could not be; for his spirit was ever on the march, ever ascending, and each instant required something that was beyond the scope of the instant before.

72   The sound of her husband's footsteps aroused her. He bore a crystal goblet containing a liquor colorless as water, but bright enough to be the draught of immortality. Aylmer was pale; but it seemed rather the consequence of a highly-wrought state of mind and tension of spirit than of fear or doubt.

73   "The concoction of the draught has been perfect," said he, in answer to Georgiana's look. "Unless all my science have deceived me, it cannot fail."

74   "Save on your account, my dearest Aylmer," observed his wife, "I might wish to put off this birthmark of mortality by relinquishing mortality itself in preference to any other mode. Life is but a sad possession to those who have attained precisely the degree of moral advancement at which I stand. Were I weaker and blinder, it might become happiness. Were I stronger, it might be endured hopefully. But, being what I find myself, methinks I am of all mortals the most fit to die."

75   "You are fit for heaven without tasting death!" replied her husband. "But why do we speak of dying? The draught cannot fail. Behold its effect upon this plant."

76   On the window seat there stood a geranium diseased with yellow blotches which had overspread all its leaves. Aylmer poured a small quantity of the liquid upon the soil in which it grew. In a little time, when the roots of the plant had taken up the moisture, the unsightly blotches began to be extinguished in a living verdure.

77   "There needed no proof," said Georgiana, quietly. "Give me the goblet. I joyfully stake all upon your word."

78   "Drink, then, thou lofty creature!" exclaimed Aylmer, with fervid admiration. "There is no taint of imperfection on thy spirit. Thy sensible frame, too, shall soon be all perfect."

79   She quaffed the liquid and returned the goblet to his hand.

80   "It is grateful," said she, with a placid smile. "Methinks it is like water from a heavenly fountain; for it contains I know not what of unobtrusive fragrance and deliciousness. It allays a feverish thirst that had parched me for many days. Now, dearest, let me sleep. My earthly senses are closing over my spirit like the leaves around the heart of a rose at sunset."

81   She spoke the last words with a gentle reluctance, as if it required almost more energy than she could command to pronounce the faint and lingering syllables. Scarcely had they loitered through her lips ere she was lost in slumber. Aylmer sat by her side, watching her aspect with the emotions proper to a man the whole value of whose existence was involved in the process now to be tested. Mingled with this mood, however, was the philosophic investigation characteristic of the man of science. Not the minutest symptom escaped him. A heightened flush of the cheek, a slight irregularity of breath, a quiver of the eyelid, a hardly perceptible tremor through the frame,—such were the details which, as the moments passed, he wrote down in his folio volume.

Intense thought had set its stamp upon every previous page of that volume; but the thoughts of years were all concentrated upon the last.

82   While thus employed, he failed not to gaze often at the fatal hand, and not without a shudder. Yet once, by a strange and unaccountable impulse, he pressed it with his lips. His spirit recoiled, however, in the very act; and Georgiana, out of the midst of her deep sleep, moved uneasily and murmured as if in remonstrance. Again Aylmer resumed his watch. Nor was it without avail. The crimson hand, which at first had been strongly visible upon the marble paleness of Georgiana's cheek, now grew more faintly outlined. She remained not less pale than ever; but the birthmark, with every breath that came and went lost somewhat of its former distinctness. Its presence had been awful; its departure was more awful still. Watch the stain of the rainbow fading out of the sky, and you will know how that mysterious symbol passed away.

83   "By Heaven! it is well nigh gone!" said Aylmer to himself, in almost irrepressible ecstasy. "I can scarcely trace it now. Success! success! And now it is like the faintest rose color. The lightest flush of blood across her cheek would overcome it. But she is so pale!"

84   He drew aside the window curtain and suffered the light of natural day to fall into the room and rest upon her cheek. At the same time he heard a gross, hoarse chuckle, which he had long known as his servant Aminadab's expression of delight.

85   "Ah, clod! ah, earthly mass!" cried Aylmer, laughing in a sort of frenzy, "you have served me well!" Matter and spirit—earth and heaven—have both done their part in this! Laugh, thing of the senses! You have earned the right to laugh."

86   These exclamations broke Georgiana's sleep. She slowly unclosed her eyes and gazed into the mirror which her husband had arranged for that purpose. A faint smile flitted over her lips when she recognized how barely perceptible was now that crimson hand which had once blazed forth with such disastrous brilliancy as to scare away all their happiness. But then her eyes sought Aylmer's face with a trouble and anxiety that he could by no means account for.

87   "My poor Aylmer!" murmured she.

88   "Poor? Nay, richest, happiest, most favored!" exclaimed he. "My peerless bride, it is successful! You are perfect!"

89   "My poor Aylmer," she repeated, with a more than human tenderness, "you have aimed loftily; you have done nobly. Do not repent that, with so high and pure a feeling, you have rejected the best the earth could offer. Aylmer, dearest Aylmer, I am dying!"

90   Alas! it was too true! The fatal hand had grappled with the mystery of life, and was the bond by which an angelic spirit kept itself in union with a mortal frame. As the last crimson tint of the birthmark—that sole token of human imperfection—faded from her cheek, the parting breath of the now perfect woman passed into the atmosphere, and her soul, lingering a moment near her husband, took its heavenward flight.

Then a hoarse, chuckling laugh was heard again! Thus ever does the gross fatality of earth exult in its invariable triumph over the immortal essence which, in this dim sphere of half development, demands the completeness of a higher state. Yet, had Aylmer reached a profounder wisdom, he need not thus have flung away the happiness which would have woven his mortal life of the selfsame textures with the celestial. The momentary circumstance was too strong for him; he failed to look beyond the shadowy scope of time, and, living once for all in eternity, to find the perfect future in the present.

(1843)

Edgar Allan Poe (1809–1849)

Short-story writer, poet, critic, and essayist, this American author was a leading architect of the short fiction form. Poe's best-known tales are appreciated for their psychological intensity, an effect often created by a finely tuned first-person narrator. Poe valued the aesthetic over the didactic properties of literature.

The Cask of Amontillado

1   The thousand injuries of Fortunato I had borne as I best could, but when he ventured upon insult I vowed revenge. You, who so well know the nature of my soul, will not suppose, however, that I gave utterance to a threat. *At length* I would be avenged; this was a point definitely settled—but the very definitiveness with which it was resolved precluded the idea of risk. I must not only punish but punish with impunity. A wrong is unredressed when retribution overtakes its redresser. It is equally unredressed when the avenger fails to make himself felt as such to him who has done the wrong.

2   It must be understood that neither by word nor deed had I given Fortunato cause to doubt my good will. I continued, as was my wont, to smile in his face, and he did not perceive that my smile *now* was at the thought of his immolation.

3   He had a weak point—this Fortunato—although in other regards he was a man to be respected and even feared. He prided himself upon his connoisseurship in wine. Few Italians have the true virtuoso spirit. For the most part their enthusiasm is adopted to suit the time and opportunity, to practice imposture upon the British and Austrian *millionaires*. In painting and gemmary, Fortunato, like his countrymen, was a quack, but in the matter of old wines he was sincere. In this respect I did not differ from him materially;—I was skilful in the Italian vintages myself, and bought largely whenever I could.

4   It was about dusk, one evening during the supreme madness of the carnival season, that I encountered my friend. He accosted me with excessive warmth, for he had been drinking much. The man wore motley. He had on a tight-fitting parti-striped dress, and his head was surmounted by the conical cap and bells. I was so pleased to see him that I thought I should never have done wringing his hand.

5   I said to him—"My dear Fortunato, you are luckily met. How remarkably well you are looking to-day. But I have received a pipe[1] of what passes for Amontillado, and I have my doubts."

6   "How?" said he. "Amontillado? A pipe? Impossible! And in the middle of the carnival!"

7   "I have my doubts," I replied; "and I was silly enough to pay the full Amontillado price without consulting you in the matter. You were not to be found, and I was fearful of losing a bargain."

8   "Amontillado!"

9   "I have my doubts."

10   "Amontillado!"

11   "And I must satisfy them."

12   "Amontillado!"

13   "As you are engaged, I am on my way to Luchresi. If any one has a critical turn it is he. He will tell me—"

14   "Luchresi cannot tell Amontillado from Sherry."

15   "And yet some fools will have it that his taste is a match for your own."

16   "Come, let us go."

17   "Whither?"

18   "To your vaults."

19   "My friend, no; I will not impose upon your good nature. I perceive you have an engagement. Luchresi—"

20   "I have no engagement;—come."

21   "My friend, no. It is not the engagement, but the severe cold with which I perceive you are afflicted. The vaults are insufferably damp. They are encrusted with nitre."

22   "Let us go, nevertheless. The cold is merely nothing. Amontillado! You have been imposed upon. And as for Luchresi, he cannot distinguish Sherry from Amontillado."

23   Thus speaking, Fortunato possessed himself of my arm; and putting on a mask of black silk and drawing a *roquelaire*[2] closely about my person, I suffered him to hurry me to my palazzo.

24   There were no attendants at home; they had absconded to make merry in honour of the time. I had told them that I should not return until the morning, and had given them explicit orders not to stir from the house. These orders were sufficient, I well knew, to insure their immediate disappearance, one and all, as soon as my back was turned.

25   I took from their sconces two flambeaux, and giving one to Fortunato, bowed him through several suites of rooms to the archway that led into the vaults. I passed down a long and winding staircase, requesting him to be cautious as he followed. We came at length to the foot of the descent, and stood together upon the damp ground of the catacombs of the Montresors.

---

1. A cask holding 126 gallons.
2. Roquelaire: man's heavy, knee-length cloak.

26   The gait of my friend was unsteady, and the bells upon his cap jingled as he strode.

27   "The pipe," said he.

28   "It is farther on," said I; "but observe the white web-work which gleams from these cavern walls."

29   He turned towards me, and looked into my eyes with two filmy orbs that distilled the rheum of intoxication.

30   "Nitre?" he asked, at length.

31   "Nitre," I replied. "How long have you had that cough?"

32   "Ugh! ugh! ugh!—ugh! ugh! ugh!—ugh! ugh! ugh!—ugh! ugh! ugh!—ugh! ugh! ugh!"

33   My poor friend found it impossible to reply for many minutes.

34   "It is nothing," he said, at last.

35   "Come," I said, with decision, "we will go back; your health is precious. You are rich, respected, admired, beloved; you are happy, as once I was. You are a man to be missed. For me it is no matter. We will go back; you will be ill, and I cannot be responsible. Besides, there is Luchresi—"

36   "Enough," he said; "the cough is a mere nothing; it will not kill me. I shall not die of a cough."

37   "True—true," I replied; "and, indeed, I had no intention of alarming you unnecessarily—but you should use all proper caution. A draught of this Medoc[3] will defend us from the damps."

38   Here I knocked off the neck of a bottle which I drew from a long row of its fellows that lay upon the mould.

39   "Drink," I said, presenting him the wine.

40   He raised it to his lips with a leer. He paused and nodded to me familiarly, while his bells jingled.

41   "I drink," he said, "to the buried that repose around us."

42   "And I to your long life."

43   He again took my arm, and we proceeded.

44   "These vaults," he said, "are extensive."

45   "The Montresors," I replied, "were a great and numerous family."

46   "I forget your arms."

47   "A huge human foot d'or,[4] in a field azure; the foot crushes a serpent rampant whose fangs are imbedded in the heel."

48   "And the motto?"

49   *"Nemo me impune lacessit."*[5]

50   "Good!" he said.

51   The wine sparkled in his eyes and the bells jingled. My own fancy grew warm with the Medoc. We had passed through long walls of piled skeletons, with casks and puncheons intermingling, into the inmost

---

3. Medoc and De Grâve (below) are French wines.

4. Of gold.

5. "No one provokes me with impunity."

recesses of the catacombs. I paused again, and this time I made bold to seize Fortunato by an arm above the elbow.

52   "The nitre!" I said; "see, it increases. It hangs like moss upon the vaults. We are below the river's bed. The drops of moisture trickle among the bones. Come, we will go back ere it is too late. Your cough—"

53   "It is nothing," he said; "let us go on. But first, another draught of the Medoc."

54   I broke and reached him a flaçon of De Grâve. He emptied it at a breath. His eyes flashed with a fierce light. He laughed and threw the bottle upwards with a gesticulation I did not understand.

55   I looked at him in surprise. He repeated the movement—a grotesque one.

56   "You do not comprehend?" he said.

57   "Not I," I replied.

58   "Then you are not of the brotherhood."

59   "How?"

60   "You are not of the masons."[6]

61   "Yes, yes," I said; "yes, yes."

62   "You? Impossible! A mason?"

63   "A mason," I replied.

64   "A sign," he said, "a sign."

65   "It is this," I answered, producing from beneath the folds of my roquelaire a trowel.

66   "You jest," he exclaimed, recoiling a few paces. "But let us proceed to the Amontillado."

67   "Be it so," I said, replacing the tool beneath the cloak and again offering him my arm. He leaned upon it heavily. We continued our route in search of the Amontillado. We passed through a range of low arches, descended, passed on, and descending again, arrived at a deep crypt, in which the foulness of the air caused our flambeaux rather to glow than flame.

68   At the most remote end of the crypt there appeared another less spacious. Its walls had been lined with human remains, piled to the vault overhead, in the fashion of the great catacombs of Paris. Three sides of this interior crypt were still ornamented in this manner. From the fourth side the bones had been thrown down, and lay promiscuously upon the earth, forming at one point a mound of some size. Within the wall thus exposed by the displacing of the bones, we perceived a still interior crypt or recess, in depth about four feet, in width three, in height six or seven. It seemed to have been constructed for no especial use within itself, but formed merely the interval between two of the colossal supports of the roof of the catacombs, and was backed by one of their circumscribing walls of solid granite.

---

6. Masons or Freemasons, an international secret fraternity condemned by the Catholic Church. Also, one who builds with stone or brick.

69 It was in vain that Fortunato, uplifting his dull torch, endeavoured to pry into the depth of the recess. Its termination the feeble light did not enable us to see.

70 "Proceed," I said; "herein is the Amontillado. As for Luchresi—"

71 "He is an ignoramus," interrupted my friend, as he stepped unsteadily forward, while I followed immediately at his heels. In an instant he had reached the extremity of the niche, and finding his progress arrested by the rock, stood stupidly bewildered. A moment more and I had fettered him to the granite. In its surface were two iron staples, distant from each other about two feet, horizontally. From one of these depended a short chain, from the other a padlock. Throwing the links about his waist, it was but the work of a few seconds to secure it. He was too much astounded to resist. Withdrawing the key I stepped back from the recess.

72 "Pass your hand," I said, "over the wall; you cannot help feeling the nitre. Indeed, it is *very* damp. Once more let me *implore* you to return. No? Then I must positively leave you. But I must first render you all the little attentions in my power."

73 "The Amontillado!" ejaculated my friend, not yet recovered from his astonishment.

74 "True," I replied; "the Amontillado."

75 As I said these words I busied myself among the pile of bones of which I have before spoken. Throwing them aside, I soon uncovered a quantity of building stone and mortar. With these materials and with the aid of my trowel, I began vigorously to wall up the entrance of the niche.

76 I had scarcely laid the first tier of the masonry when I discovered that the intoxication of Fortunato had in a great measure worn off. The earliest indication I had of this was a low moaning cry from the depth of the recess. It was *not* the cry of a drunken man. There was then a long and obstinate silence. I laid the second tier, and the third, and the fourth; and then I heard the furious vibration of the chain. The noise lasted for several minutes, during which, that I might hearken to it with the more satisfaction, I ceased my labours and sat down upon the bones. When at last the clanking subsided, I resumed the trowel, and finished without interruption the fifth, the sixth, and the seventh tier. The wall was now nearly upon a level with my breast. I again paused, and holding the flambeaux over the mason-work, threw a few feeble rays upon the figure within.

77 A succession of loud and shrill screams, bursting suddenly from the throat of the chained form, seemed to thrust me violently back. For a brief moment I hesitated, I trembled. Unsheathing my rapier, I began to grope with it about the recess; but the thought of an instant reassured me. I placed my hand upon the solid fabric of the catacombs, and felt satisfied. I reapproached the wall; I replied to the yells of him who clamoured. I re-echoed, I aided, I surpassed them in volume and in strength. I did this, and the clamourer grew still.

78   It was now midnight, and my task was drawing to a close. I had completed the eighth, the ninth and the tenth tier. I had finished a portion of the last and the eleventh; there remained but a single stone to be fitted and plastered in. I struggled with its weight; I placed it partially in its destined position. But now there came from out the niche a low laugh that erected the hairs upon my head. It was succeeded by a sad voice, which I had difficulty in recognizing as that of the noble Fortunato. The voice said—

79   "Ha! ha! ha!—he! he! he!—a very good joke, indeed—an excellent jest. We will have many a rich laugh about it at the palazzo—he! he! he!—over our wine—he! he! he!"

80   "The Amontillado!" I said.

81   "He! he! he!—he! he! he!—yes, the Amontillado. But is it not getting late? Will not they be awaiting us at the palazzo, the Lady Fortunato and the rest? Let us be gone."

82   "Yes," I said, "let us be gone."

83   *"For the love of God, Montresor!"*

84   "Yes," I said, "for the love of God!"

85   But to these words I hearkened in vain for a reply. I grew impatient. I called aloud—

86   "Fortunato!"

87   No answer. I called again—

88   "Fortunato!"

89   No answer still. I thrust a torch through the remaining aperture and let it fall within. There came forth in return only a jingling of the bells. My heart grew sick; it was the dampness of the catacombs that made it so. I hastened to make an end of my labour. I forced the last stone into its position; I plastered it up. Against the new masonry I re-erected the old rampart of bones. For the half of a century no mortal has disturbed them. *In pace requiescat!*[7]

(1846)

---

7. May he rest in peace!

Charlotte Perkins Gilman (1860–1935)

Born in Hartford, Connecticut, and the great-niece of Harriet Beecher Stowe, Charlotte Perkins was brought up by her mother after her father deserted the family. Soon after the birth of her daughter in 1885, she suffered a nervous breakdown—and escaped her first marriage by moving to California where she later remarried and established herself as a lecturer and feminist writer. Faced with inoperable cancer, in 1935 she committed suicide.

The Yellow Wallpaper

1   It is very seldom that mere ordinary people like John and myself secure ancestral halls for the summer.

2   A colonial mansion, a hereditary estate, I would say a haunted house, and reach the height of romantic felicity—but that would be asking too much of fate!

3   Still I will proudly declare that there is something queer about it.

4   Else, why should it be let so cheaply? And why have stood so long untenanted?

5   John laughs at me, of course, but one expects that in marriage.

6   John is practical in the extreme. He has no patience with faith, an intense horror of superstition, and he scoffs openly at any talk of things not to be felt and seen and put down in figures.

7   John is a physician, and *perhaps*—(I would not say it to a living soul, of course, but this is dead paper and a great relief to my mind)—*perhaps* that is one reason I do not get well faster.

8   You see he does not believe I am sick!

9   And what can one do?

10   If a physician of high standing, and one's own husband, assures friends and relatives that there is really nothing the matter with one but temporary nervous depression—a slight hysterical tendency—what is one to do?

11   My brother is also a physician, and also of high standing, and he says the same thing.

12   So I take phosphates or phosphites—whichever it is, and tonics, and journeys, and air, and exercise, and am absolutely forbidden to "work" until I am well again.

13   Personally, I disagree with their ideas.

14   Personally, I believe that congenial work, with excitement and change, would do me good.

15   But what is one to do?

16   I did write for a while in spite of them; but it *does* exhaust me a good deal—having to be so sly about it, or else meet with heavy opposition.

17   I sometimes fancy that in my condition if I had less opposition and more society and stimulus—but John says the very worst thing I can do is think about my condition, and I confess it always makes me feel bad.

18   So I will let it alone and talk about the house.

19   The most beautiful place! It is quite alone, standing well back from the road, quite three miles from the village. It makes me think of English places that you read about, for there are hedges and walls and gates that lock, and lots of separate little houses for the gardeners and people.

20   There is a *delicious* garden! I never saw such a garden—large and shady, full of box-bordered paths, and lined with long grape-covered arbors with seats under them.

21   There were greenhouses, too, but they are all broken now.

22   There was some legal trouble, I believe, something about the heirs and coheirs; anyhow, the place has been empty for years.

23   That spoils my ghostliness, I am afraid, but I don't care—there is something strange about the house—I can feel it.

24   I even said so to John one moonlight evening, but he said what I felt was a *draught*, and shut the window.

25   I get unreasonably angry with John sometimes. I'm sure I never used to be so sensitive. I think it is due to this nervous condition.

26   But John says if I feel so, I shall neglect proper self-control; so I take pains to control myself—before him, at least, and that makes me very tired.

27   I don't like our room a bit. I wanted one downstairs that opened on the piazza and had roses all over the window, and such pretty old-fashioned chintz hangings! But John would not hear of it.

28   He said there was only one window and not room for two beds, and no near room for him if he took another.

29   He is very careful and loving, and hardly lets me stir without special direction.

30   I have a schedule prescription for each hour in the day; he takes all care from me, and I feel basely ungrateful not to value it more.

31   He said we came here solely on my account, that I was to have perfect rest and all the air I could get. "Your exercise depends on your strength, my dear," said he, "and your food somewhat on your appetite; but air you can absorb all the time." So we took the nursery at the top of the house.

32   It is a big, airy room, the whole floor nearly, with windows that look all ways, and air and sunshine galore. It was nursery first and then playroom and gymnasium, I should judge; for the windows are barred for little children, and there are rings and things in the walls.

33   The paint and paper look as if a boys' school had used it. It is stripped off—the paper—in great patches all around the head of my

bed, about as far as I can reach, and in a great place on the other side of the room low down. I never saw a worse paper in my life.

34 One of those sprawling flamboyant patterns committing every artistic sin.

35 It is dull enough to confuse the eye in following, pronounced enough to constantly irritate and provoke study, and when you follow the lame uncertain curves for a little distance they suddenly commit suicide—plunge off at outrageous angles, destroy themselves in unheard of contradictions.

36 The color is repellent, almost revolting; a smouldering unclean yellow, strangely faded by the slow-turning sunlight.

37 It is a dull yet lurid orange in some places, a sickly sulphur tint in others.

38 No wonder the children hated it! I should hate it myself if I had to live in this room long.

39 There comes John, and I must put this away,—he hates to have me write a word.

40 We have been here two weeks, and I haven't felt like writing before, since that first day.

41 I am sitting by the window now, up in this atrocious nursery, and there is nothing to hinder my writing as much as I please, save lack of strength.

42 John is away all day, and even some nights when his cases are serious.

43 I am glad my case is not serious!

44 But these nervous troubles are dreadfully depressing.

45 John does not know how much I really suffer. He knows there is no *reason* to suffer, and that satisfies him.

46 Of course it is only nervousness. It does weigh on me so not to do my duty in any way!

47 I meant to be such a help to John, such a real rest and comfort, and here I am a comparative burden already!

48 Nobody would believe what an effort it is to do what little I am able,—to dress and entertain, and order things.

49 It is fortunate Mary is so good with the baby. Such a dear baby!

50 And yet I *cannot* be with him, it makes me so nervous.

51 I suppose John never was nervous in his life. He laughs at me so about this wallpaper!

52 At first he meant to repaper the room, but afterwards he said that I was letting it get the better of me, and that nothing was worse for a nervous patient than to give way to such fancies.

53 He said that after the wallpaper was changed it would be the heavy bedstead, and then the barred windows, and then that gate at the head of the stairs, and so on.

54 "You know the place is doing you good," he said, "and really, dear, I don't care to renovate the house just for a three months' rental."

55   "Then do let us go downstairs," I said, "there are such pretty rooms there."

56   Then he took me in his arms and called me a blessed little goose, and said he would go down to the cellar, if I wished, and have it white-washed into the bargain.

57   But he is right enough about the beds and windows and things.

58   It is as airy and comfortable room as any one need wish, and, of course, I would not be so silly as to make him uncomfortable just for a whim.

59   I'm really getting quite fond of the big room, all but that horrid paper.

60   Out of one window I can see the garden, those mysterious deep-shaded arbors, the riotous old-fashioned flowers, and bushes and gnarly trees.

61   Out of another I get a lovely view of the bay and a little private wharf belonging to the estate. There is a beautiful shaded lane that runs down there from the house. I always fancy I see people walking in these numerous paths and arbors, but John has cautioned me not to give way to fancy in the least. He says that with my imaginative power and habit of story-making, a nervous weakness like mine is sure to lead to all manner of excited fancies, and that I ought to use my will and good sense to check the tendency. So I try.

62   I think sometimes that if I were only well enough to write a little it would relieve the press of ideas and rest me.

63   But I find I get pretty tired when I try.

64   It is so discouraging not to have any advice and companionship about my work. When I get really well, John says we will ask Cousin Henry and Julia down for a long visit; but he says he would as soon put fireworks in my pillow-case as to let me have those stimulating people about now.

65   I wish I could get well faster.

66   But I must not think about that. This paper looks to me as if it *knew* what a vicious influence it had!

67   There is a recurrent spot where the pattern lolls like a broken neck and two bulbous eyes stare at you upside down.

68   I get positively angry with the impertinence of it and the everlast-ingness. Up and down and sideways they crawl, and those absurd, unblinking eyes are everywhere. There is one place where two breadths didn't match, and the eyes go all up and down the line, one a little higher than the other.

69   I never saw so much expression in an inanimate thing before, and we all know how much expression they have! I used to lie awake as a child and get more entertainment and terror out of blank walls and plain furniture than most children could find in a toy-store.

70   I remember what a kindly wink the knobs of our big, old bureau used to have, and there was one chair that always seemed like a strong friend.

71   I used to feel that if any of the other things looked too fierce I could always hop into that chair and be safe.

72   The furniture in this room is no worse than inharmonious, however, for we had to bring it all from downstairs. I suppose when this was used as a playroom they had to take the nursery things out, and no wonder! I never saw such ravages as the children have made here.

73   The wallpaper, as I said before, is torn off in spots, and it sticketh closer than a brother—they must have had perseverance as well as hatred.

74   Then the floor is scratched and gouged and splintered, the plaster itself is dug out here and there, and this great heavy bed, which is all we found in the room, looks as if it had been through the wars.

75   But I don't mind it a bit—only the paper.

76   There comes John's sister. Such a dear girl as she is, and so careful of me! I must not let her find me writing.

77   She is a perfect and enthusiastic housekeeper, and hopes for no better profession. I verily believe she thinks it is the writing which made me sick!

78   But I can write when she is out, and see her a long way off from these windows.

79   There is one that commands the road, a lovely shaded winding road, and one that just looks off over the country. A lovely country, too, full of great elms and velvet meadows.

80   This wallpaper has a kind of sub-pattern in a different shade, a particularly irritating one, for you can only see it in certain lights, and not clearly then.

81   But in the places where it isn't faded and where the sun is just so— I can see a strange, provoking, formless sort of figure, that seems to skulk about behind that silly and conspicuous front design.

82   There's sister on the stairs!

83   Well, the Fourth of July is over! The people are all gone and I am tired out. John thought it might do me good to see a little company, so we just had Mother and Nellie and the children down for the week.

84   Of course I didn't do a thing. Jennie sees to everything now.

85   But it tired me all the same.

86   John says if I don't pick up faster he shall send me to Weir Mitchell in the fall.

87   But I don't want to go there at all. I had a friend who was in his hands once, and she says he is just like John and my brother, only more so!

88   Besides, it is such an undertaking to go so far.

89   I don't feel as if it was worth while to turn my hand over for anything, and I'm getting dreadfully fretful and querulous.

90   I cry at nothing, and cry most of the time.

91   Of course I don't when John is here, or anybody else, but when I am alone.

92   And I am alone a good deal just now. John is kept in town very often by serious cases, and Jennie is good and lets me alone when I want her to.

93   So I walk a little in the garden or down that lovely lane, sit on the porch under the roses, and lie down up here a good deal.

94   I'm getting really fond of the room in spite of the wallpaper. Perhaps *because* of the wallpaper.

95   It dwells in my mind so!

96   I lie here on this great immovable bed—it is nailed down, I believe—and follow that pattern about by the hour. It is as good as gymnastics, I assure you. I start, we'll say, at the bottom, down in the corner over there where it has not been touched, and I determine for the thousandth time that I *will* follow that pointless pattern to some sort of a conclusion.

97   I know a little of the principle of design, and I know this thing was not arranged on any laws of radiation, or alternation, or repetition, or symmetry, or anything else that I ever heard of.

98   It is repeated, of course, by the breadths, but not otherwise.

99   Looked at in one way each breadth stands alone, the bloated curves and flourishes—a kind of "debased Romanesque" with *delirium tremens*—go waddling up and down in isolated columns of fatuity.

100   But, on the other hand, they connect diagonally, and the sprawling outlines run off in great slanting waves of optic horror, like a lot of wallowing seaweeds in full chase.

101   The whole thing goes horizontally too, at least it seems so, and I exhaust myself in trying to distinguish the order of its going in that direction.

102   They have used a horizontal breadth for a frieze, and that adds wonderfully to the confusion.

103   There is one end of the room where it is almost intact, and there, when the crosslights fade and the low sun shines directly upon it, I can almost fancy radiation after all,—the interminable grotesques seem to form around a common center and rush off in headlong plunges of equal distraction.

104   It makes me tired to follow it. I will take a nap I guess.

105   I don't know why I should write this.

106   I don't want to.

107   I don't feel able.

108   And I know John would think it absurd. But I *must* say what I feel and think in some way—it is such a relief!

109   But the effort is getting to be greater than the relief.

110   Half the time now I am awfully lazy, and lie down ever so much.

111   John says I mustn't lose my strength, and has me take cod liver oil and lots of tonics and things, to say nothing of ale and wine and rare meat.

112   Dear John! He loves me dearly, and hates to have me sick. I tried to have a real earnest reasonable talk with him the other day, and tell him

how I wish he would let me go and make a visit to Cousin Henry and Julia.

113 But he said I wasn't able to go, nor able to stand it after I got there; and I did not make out a very good case for myself, for I was crying before I had finished.

114 It is getting to be a great effort for me to think straight. Just this nervous weakness I suppose.

115 And dear John gathered me in his arms, and just carried me upstairs and laid me on the bed, and sat by me and read to me till it tired my head.

116 He said I was his darling and his comfort and all he had, and that I must take care of myself for his sake, and keep well.

117 He says no one but myself can help me out of it, that I must use my will and self-control and not let any silly fancies run away with me.

118 There's one comfort, the baby is well and happy, and does not have to occupy this nursery with the horrid wallpaper.

119 If we had not used it, that blessed child would have! What a fortunate escape! Why, I wouldn't have a child of mine, an impressionable little thing, live in such a room for worlds.

120 I never thought of it before, but it is lucky that John kept me here after all, I can stand it so much easier than a baby, you see.

121 Of course I never mention it to him any more—I am too wise—but keep watch of it all the same.

122 There are things in that paper that nobody knows but me, or ever will.

123 Behind that outside pattern the dim shapes get clearer every day.

124 It is always the same shape, only very numerous.

125 And it is like a woman stooping down and creeping about behind that pattern. I don't like it a bit. I wonder—I begin to think—I wish John would take me away from here!

126 It is so hard to talk with John about my case, because he is so wise, and because he loves me so.

127 But I tried it last night.

128 It was moonlight. The moon shines all around just as the sun does.

129 I hate to see it sometimes, it creeps so slowly, and always comes in by one window or another.

130 John was asleep and I hated to waken him, so I kept still and watched the moonlight on that undulating wallpaper till I felt creepy.

131 The faint figure behind seemed to shake the pattern, just as if she wanted to get out.

132 I got up softly and went to feel and see if the paper *did* move, and when I came back John was awake.

133 "What is it, little girl?" he said. "Don't go walking about like that— you'll get cold."

134 I thought it was a good time to talk, so I told him that I really was not gaining here, and that I wished he would take me away.

135 "Why darling!" said he, "our lease will be up in three weeks, and I can't see how to leave before.

136   "The repairs are not done at home, and I cannot possibly leave town just now. Of course if you were in any danger, I could and would, but you really are better, dear, and I know. You are gaining flesh and color, your appetite is better, I feel really much easier about you."

137   "I don't weigh a bit more," said I, "nor as much; and my appetite may be better in the evening when you are here, but it is worse in the morning when you are away!"

138   "Bless her little heart!" said he with a big hug, "she shall be as sick as she pleases! But now let's improve the shining hours by going to sleep, and talk about it in the morning!"

139   "And you won't go away?" I asked gloomily.

140   "Why, how can I, dear? It is only three weeks more and then we will take a nice little trip of a few days while Jennie is getting the house ready. Really dear you are better!"

141   "Better in body perhaps—" I began, and stopped short, for he sat straight up and looked at me with such a stern, reproachful look that I could not say another word.

142   "My darling," said he, "I beg of you, for my sake and for our child's sake, as well as for your own, that you will never one instant let that idea enter your mind! There is nothing so dangerous, so fascinating, to a temperament like yours. It is a false and foolish fancy. Can you not trust me as a physician when I tell you so?"

143   So of course I said no more on that score, and we went to sleep before long. He thought I was asleep first, but I wasn't, and lay there for hours trying to decide whether that front pattern and the back pattern really did move together or separately.

144 On a pattern like this, by daylight, there is a lack of sequence, a defiance of law, that is a constant irritant to a normal mind.

145   The color is hideous enough, and reliable enough, and infuriating enough, but the pattern is torturing.

146   You think you have mastered it, but just as you get well underway in following, it turns a back-somersault and there you are. It slaps you in the face, knocks you down, and tramples upon you. It is like a bad dream.

147   The outside pattern is a florid arabesque, reminding one of a fungus. If you can imagine a toadstool in joints, an interminable string of toadstools, budding and sprouting in endless convolutions—why, that is something like it.

148   That is, sometimes!

149   There is one marked peculiarity about this paper, a thing nobody seems to notice but myself, and that is that it changes as the light changes.

150   When the sun shoots through the east window—I always watch for that first long, straight ray—it changes so quickly that I never can quite believe it.

151   That is why I watch it always.

152 By moonlight—the moon shines in all night when there is a moon—I wouldn't know it was the same paper.

153 At night any kind of light, in twilight, candle light, lamplight, and worst of all by moonlight, it becomes bars! The outside pattern I mean, and the woman behind it is as plain as can be.

154 I didn't realize for a long time what the thing was that showed behind, that dim sub-pattern, but now I am quite sure it is a woman.

155 By daylight she is subdued, quiet. I fancy it is the pattern that keeps her so still. It is so puzzling. It keeps me quiet by the hour.

156 I lie down ever so much now. John says it is good for me, and to sleep all I can.

157 Indeed he started the habit by making me lie down for an hour after each meal.

158 It is a very bad habit I am convinced, for you see I don't sleep.

159 And that cultivates deceit, for I don't tell them I'm awake—O no!

160 The fact is I am getting a little afraid of John.

161 He seems very queer sometimes, and even Jennie has an inexplicable look.

162 It strikes me occasionally, just as a scientific hypothesis,—that perhaps it is the paper!

163 I have watched John when he did not know I was looking, and come into the room suddenly on the most innocent excuses, and I've caught him several times *looking at the paper*! And Jennie too. I caught Jennie with her hand on it once.

164 She didn't know I was in the room, and when I asked her in a quiet, a very quiet voice, with the most restrained manner possible, what she was doing with the paper—she turned around as if she had been caught stealing, and looked quite angry—asked me why I should frighten her so!

165 Then she said that the paper stained everything it touched, that she had found yellow smooches on all my clothes and John's and she wished we would be more careful!

166 Did not that sound innocent? But I know she was studying that pattern, and I am determined that nobody shall find it out but myself!

167 Life is very much more exciting now than it used to be. You see I have something more to expect, to look forward to, to watch. I really do eat better, and am more quiet than I was.

168 John is so pleased to see me improve! He laughed a little the other day, and said I seemed to be flourishing in spite of my wallpaper.

169 I turned it off with a laugh. I had no intention of telling him it was *because* of the wallpaper—he would make fun of me. He might even want to take me away.

170 I don't want to leave now until I have found it out. There is a week more, and I think that will be enough.

171   I'm feeling ever so much better! I don't sleep much at night, for it is so interesting to watch developments; but I sleep a good deal in the daytime.

172   In the daytime it is tiresome and perplexing.

173   There are always new shoots on the fungus, and new shades of yellow all over it. I cannot keep count of them, though I have tried conscientiously.

174   It is the strangest yellow, that wallpaper! It makes me think of all the yellow things I ever saw—not beautiful ones like buttercups, but old foul, bad yellow things.

175   But there is something else about that paper—the smell! I noticed it the moment we came into the room, but with so much air and sun it was not bad. Now we have had a week of fog and rain, and whether the windows are open or not, the smell is here.

176   It creeps all over the house.

177   I find it hovering in the dining-room, skulking in the parlor, hiding in the hall, lying in wait for me on the stairs.

178   It gets into my hair.

179   Even when I go to ride, if I turn my head suddenly and surprise it—there is that smell!

180   Such a peculiar odor, too! I have spent hours in trying to analyze it, to find what it smelled like.

181   It is not bad—at first, and very gentle, but quite the subtlest, most enduring odor I ever met.

182   In this damp weather it is awful, I wake up in the night and find it hanging over me.

183   It used to disturb me at first. I thought seriously of burning the house—to reach the smell.

184   But now I am used to it. The only thing I can think of that it is like is the *color* of the paper! A yellow smell.

185   There is a very funny mark on this wall, low down, near the mopboard. A streak that runs round the room. It goes behind every piece of furniture, except the bed, a long, straight, even *smooch*, as if it had been rubbed over and over.

186   I wonder how it was done and who did it, and what they did it for. Round and round and round—round and round and round—it makes me dizzy!

187   I really have discovered something at last.

188   Through watching so much at night, when it changes so, I have finally found out.

189   The front pattern *does* move—and no wonder! The woman behind shakes it!

190   Sometimes I think there are a great many women behind, and sometimes only one, and she crawls around fast, and her crawling shakes it all over.

191   Then in the very bright spots she keeps still, and in the very shady spots she just takes hold of the bars and shakes them hard.

192   And she is all the time trying to climb through. But nobody could climb through that pattern—it strangles so; I think that is why it has so many heads.

193   They get through, and then the pattern strangles them off and turns them upside down, and makes their eyes white!

194   If those heads were covered or taken off it would not be half so bad.

195   I think that woman gets out in the daytime!

196   And I'll tell you why—privately—I've seen her!

197   I can see her out of every one of my windows!

198   It is the same woman, I know, for she is always creeping, and most women do not creep by daylight.

199   I see her on that long road under the trees, creeping along, and when a carriage comes she hides under the blackberry vines.

200   I don't blame her a bit. It must be very humiliating to be caught creeping by daylight!

201   I always lock the door when I creep by daylight. I can't do it at night, for I know John would suspect something at once.

202   And John is so queer now, that I don't want to irritate him. I wish he would take another room! Besides, I don't want anybody to get that woman out at night but myself.

203   I often wonder if I could see her out of all the windows at once.

204   But, turn as fast as I can, I can only see out of one at a time.

205   And though I always see her, she *may* be able to creep faster than I can turn!

206   I have watched her sometimes away off in the open country, creeping as fast as a cloud shadow in a high wind.

207   If only that top pattern could be gotten off from the under one! I mean to try it, little by little.

208   I have found out another funny thing, but I shan't tell it this time! It does not do to trust people too much.

209   There are only two more days to get this paper off, and I believe John is beginning to notice. I don't like the look in his eyes.

210   And I heard him ask Jennie a lot of professional questions about me. She had a very good report to give.

211   She said I slept a good deal in the daytime.

212   John knows I don't sleep very well at night, for all I'm so quiet!

213   He asked me all sorts of questions, too, and pretended to be very loving and kind.

214   As if I couldn't see through him!

215   Still, I don't wonder he acts so, sleeping under this paper for three months.

216   It only interests me, but I feel sure John and Jennie are secretly affected by it.

217 Hurrah! This is the last day, but it is enough. John had to stay in town over night, and won't be out until this evening.

218 Jennie wanted to sleep with me—the sly thing! but I told her I should undoubtedly rest better for a night all alone.

219 That was clever, for really I wasn't alone a bit! As soon as it was moonlight and that poor thing began to crawl and shake the pattern, I got up and ran to help her.

220 I pulled and she shook, I shook and she pulled, and before morning we had peeled off yards of that paper.

221 A strip about as high as my head and half around the room.

222 And then when the sun came and that awful pattern began to laugh at me, I declared I would finish it to-day!

223 We go away to-morrow, and they are moving all my furniture down again to leave things as they were before.

224 Jennie looked at the wall in amazement, but I told her merrily that I did it out of pure spite at the vicious thing.

225 She laughed and said she wouldn't mind doing it herself, but I must not get tired.

226 How she betrayed herself that time!

227 But I am here, and no person touches this paper but me,—not *alive*!

228 She tried to get me out of the room—it was too patent! But I said it was so quiet and empty and clean now that I believed I would lie down again and sleep all I could; and not to wake me even for dinner—I would call when I woke.

229 So now she is gone, and the servants are gone, and the things are gone, and there is nothing left but the great bedstead nailed down, with the canvas mattress we found on it.

230 We shall sleep downstairs to-night, and take the boat home to-morrow.

231 I quite enjoy the room, now it is bare again.

232 How those children did tear about here!

233 This bedstead is fairly gnawed!

234 But I must get to work.

235 I have locked the door and thrown the key down into the front path.

236 I don't want to go out, and I don't want to have anybody come in, till John comes.

237 I want to astonish him.

238 I've got a rope up here that even Jennie did not find. If that woman does get out, and tries to get away, I can tie her!

239 But I forgot I could not reach far without anything to stand on!

240 This bed will *not* move!

241 I tried to lift and push it until I was lame, and then I got so angry I bit off a little piece at one corner—but it hurt my teeth.

242 Then I peeled off all the paper I could reach standing on the floor. It sticks horribly and the pattern just enjoys it! All those strangled heads and bulbous eyes and waddling fungus growths just shriek with derision!

243   I am getting angry enough to do something desperate. To jump out of the window would be admirable exercise, but the bars are too strong even to try.

244   Besides I wouldn't do it. Of course not. I know well enough that a step like that is improper and might be misconstrued.

245   I don't like to *look* out of the windows even—there are so many of those creeping women, and they creep so fast.

246   I wonder if they all come out of that wallpaper as I did?

247   But I am securely fastened now by my well-hidden rope—you don't get *me* out in the road there!

248   I suppose I shall have to get back behind the pattern when it comes night, and that is hard!

249   It is so pleasant to be out in this great room and creep around as I please!

250   I don't want to go outside. I won't, even if Jennie asks me to.

251   For outside you have to creep on the ground, and everything is green instead of yellow.

252   But here I can creep smoothly on the floor, and my shoulder just fits in that long smooch around the wall, so I cannot lose my way.

253   Why there's John at the door!

254   It is no use, young man, you can't open it!

255   How he does call and pound!

256   Now he's crying for an axe.

257   It would be a shame to break down that beautiful door!

258   "John dear!" said I in the gentlest voice, "the key is down by the front steps, under a plantain leaf!"

259   That silenced him for a few moments.

260   Then he said—very quietly indeed, "Open the door, my darling!"

261   "I can't," said I. "The key is down by the front door under a plantain leaf!"

262   And then I said it again, several times, very gently and slowly, and said it so often that he had to go to see, and he got it of course, and came in. He stopped short by the door.

263   "What is the matter?" he cried. "For God's sake, what are you doing?"

264   I kept on creeping just the same, but I looked at him over my shoulder.

265   "I've got out at last," said I, "in spite of you and Jane. And I've pulled off most of the paper, so you can't put me back!"

266   Now why should that man have fainted? But he did, and right across my path by the wall, so that I had to creep over him every time!

(1892)

James Joyce (1882–1941)

With his innovative narrative methods and linguistic experimentation, Joyce changed the form of fiction. He not only devised new ways of shaping character and action, but also articulated the Irish consciousness of his era.

The Boarding House[1]

1   Mrs. Mooney was a butcher's daughter. She was a woman who was quite able to keep things to herself: a determined woman. She had married her father's foreman, and opened a butcher's shop near Spring Gardens. But as soon as his father-in-law was dead Mr. Mooney began to go to the devil. He drank, plundered the till, ran headlong into debt. It was no use making him take the pledge: he was sure to break out again a few days after. By fighting his wife in the presence of customers and by buying bad meat he ruined his business. One night he went for his wife with the cleaver, and she had to sleep in a neighbour's house.

2   After that they lived apart. She went to the priest and got a separation from him, with care of the children. She would give him neither money nor food nor house-room; and so he was obliged to enlist himself as a sheriff's man. He was a shabby stooped little drunkard with a white face and a white moustache and white eyebrows, pencilled above his little eyes, which were pink-veined and raw; and all day long he sat in the bailiff's room, waiting to be put on a job. Mrs. Mooney, who had taken what remained of her money out of the butcher business and set up a boarding house in Hardwicke Street, was a big imposing woman. Her house had a floating population made up of tourists from Liverpool and the Isle of Man and, occasionally, *artistes* from the music halls. Its resident population was made up of clerks from the city. She governed the house cunningly and firmly, knew when to give credit, when to be stern and when to let things pass. All the resident young men spoke of her as *The Madam*.

3   Mrs. Mooney's young men paid fifteen shillings a week for board and lodgings (beer or stout at dinner excluded). They shared in common tastes and occupations and for this reason they were very chummy with one another. They discussed with one another the chances of favourites and outsiders. Jack Mooney, the Madam's son, who was clerk to a commission agent in Fleet Street, had the reputation of being a hard case. He was fond of using soldiers' obscenities:

---

1. From Joyce's collection of short stories, *Dubliners* (1914). Place names all refer to the city of Dublin, Ireland.

usually he came home in the small hours. When he met his friends he had always a good one to tell them and he was always sure to be on to a good thing—that is to say, a likely horse or a likely *artiste*. He was also handy with the mits[2] and sang comic songs. On Sunday night there would often be a reunion in Mrs. Mooney's front drawingroom. The music-hall *artistes* would oblige; and Sheridan played waltzes and polkas and vamped accompaniments. Polly Mooney, the Madam's daughter, would also sing. She sang:

> *I'm a ... naughty girl.*
> *You needn't sham:*
> *You know I am.*

4   Polly was a slim girl of nineteen; she had light soft hair and a small full mouth. Her eyes, which were grey with a shade of green through them, had a habit of glancing upwards when she spoke with anyone, which made her look like a little perverse madonna. Mrs. Mooney had first sent her daughter to be a typist in a corn-factor's[3] office, but as a disreputable sheriff's man used to come every other day to the office, asking to be allowed to say a word to his daughter, she had taken her daughter home again and set her to do housework. As Polly was very lively, the intention was to give her the run of the young men. Besides, young men like to feel that there is a young woman not very far away. Polly, of course, flirted with the young men, but Mrs. Mooney, who was a shrewd judge, knew that the young men were only passing the time away: none of them meant business. Things went on so for a long time, and Mrs. Mooney began to think of sending Polly back to typewriting, when she noticed that something was going on between Polly and one of the young men. She watched the pair and kept her own counsel.

5   Polly knew that she was being watched, but still her mother's persistent silence could not be misunderstood. There had been no open complicity between mother and daughter, no open understanding, but though people in the house began to talk of the affair, still Mrs. Mooney did not intervene. Polly began to grow a little strange in her manner and the young man was evidently perturbed. At last, when she judged it to be the right moment, Mrs. Mooney intervened. She dealt with moral problems as a cleaver deals with meat: and in this case she had made up her mind.

6   It was a bright Sunday morning of early summer, promising heat, but with a fresh breeze blowing. All the windows of the boarding house were open and the lace curtains ballooned gently towards the street beneath the raised sashes. The belfry of George's Church sent out constant peals and worshippers, singly or in groups, traversed the little

---

2. A variant of "mitts" or "mittens." "Handy with the mits" is a colloquialism meaning "ready with his fists."

3. Corn-merchant.

circus[4] before the church, revealing their purpose by their self-contained demeanour no less than by the little volumes in their gloved hands. Breakfast was over in the boarding house, and the table of the breakfast-room was covered with plates on which lay yellow streaks of eggs with morsels of bacon-fat and bacon-rind. Mrs. Mooney sat in the straw armchair and watched the servant Mary remove the breakfast things. She made Mary collect the crusts and pieces of broken bread to help to make Tuesday's bread pudding. When the table was cleared, the broken bread collected, the sugar and butter safe under lock and key, she began to reconstruct the interview which she had had the night before with Polly. Things were as she had suspected: she had been frank in her questions and Polly had been frank in her answers. Both had been somewhat awkward, of course. She had been made awkward by her not wishing to receive the news in too cavalier a fashion or to seem to have connived, and Polly had been made awkward not merely because allusions of that kind always made her awkward, but also because she did not wish it to be thought that in her wise innocence she had divined the intention behind her mother's tolerance.

7   Mrs. Mooney glanced instinctively at the little gilt clock on the mantelpiece as soon as she had become aware through her reverie that the bells of George's Church had stopped ringing. It was seventeen minutes past eleven: she would have lots of time to have the matter out with Mr. Doran and then catch short twelve[5] at Marlborough Street. She was sure she would win. To begin with, she had all the weight of social opinion on her side: she was an outraged mother. She had allowed him to live beneath her roof, assuming that he was a man of honour, and he had simply abused her hospitality. He was thirty-four or thirty-five years of age, so that youth could not be pleaded as his excuse; nor could ignorance be his excuse, since he was a man who had seen something of the world. He had simply taken advantage of Polly's youth and inexperience: that was evident. The question was: What reparation would he make?

8   There must be reparation made in such case. It is all very well for the man: he can go his ways as if nothing had happened, having had his moment of pleasure, but the girl has to bear the brunt. Some mothers would be content to patch up such an affair for a sum of money; she had known cases of it. But she would not do so. For her only one reparation could make up for the loss of her daughter's honour: marriage.

9   She counted all her cards again before sending Mary up to Mr. Doran's room to say that she wished to speak with him. She felt sure she would win. He was a serious young man, not rakish or loud-voiced like the others. If it had been Mr. Sheridan or Mr. Meade or Bantam Lyons, her task would have been much harder. She did not think he

4. Semicircular street.
5. The shortest Sunday Mass, lasting only fifteen or twenty minutes.

would face publicity. All the lodgers in the house knew something of
the affair; details had been invented by some. Besides, he had been
employed for thirteen years in a great Catholic wine-merchant's office,
and publicity would mean for him, perhaps, the loss of his sit.[6]
Whereas if he agreed all might be well. She knew he had a good screw[7]
for one thing, and she suspected he had a bit of stuff put by.

10 Nearly the half-hour! She stood up and surveyed herself in the pier-
glass. The decisive expression on her great florid face satisfied her, and
she thought of some mothers she knew who could not get their daughters off their hands.

11 Mr. Doran was very anxious indeed this Sunday morning. He had
made two attempts to shave, but his hand had been so unsteady that
he had been obliged to desist. Three days' reddish beard fringed his
jaws, and every two or three minutes a mist gathered on his glasses so
that he had to take them off and polish them with his pocket-handkerchief. The recollection of his confession of the night before was a
cause of acute pain to him; the priest had drawn out every ridiculous
detail of the affair, and in the end had so magnified his sin that he was
almost thankful at being afforded a loophole of reparation. The harm
was done. What could he do now but marry her or run away? He could
not brazen it out. The affair would be sure to be talked of, and his
employer would be certain to hear of it. Dublin is such a small city:
everyone knows everyone else's business. He felt his heart leap warmly
in his throat as he heard in his excited imagination old Mr. Leonard
calling out in his rasping voice: "*Send Mr. Doran here, please.*"

12 All his long years of service gone for nothing! All his industry and
diligence thrown away! As a young man he had sown his wild oats, of
course; he had boasted of his free-thinking and denied the existence of
God to his companions in public-houses. But that was all passed and
done with ... nearly. He still bought a copy of *Reynolds Newspaper*[8]
every week, but he attended to his religious duties, and for nine-tenths
of the year lived a regular life. He had money enough to settle down
on; it was not that. But the family would look down on her. First of all
there was her disreputable father, and then her mother's boarding
house was beginning to get a certain fame. He had a notion that he was
being had. He could imagine his friends talking of the affair and
laughing. She *was* a little vulgar; sometimes she said "*I seen*" and "*If I
had've known.*" But what would grammar matter if he really loved her?
He could not make up his mind whether to like her or despise her for
what she had done. Of course he had done it too. His instinct urged
him to remain free, not to marry. Once you are married you are done
for, it said.

6. Situation, i.e., his job.
7. Salary.
8. A popular newspaper perceived as expressing radical political views.

13   While he was sitting helplessly on the side of the bed in shirt and trousers, she tapped lightly at his door and entered. She told him all, that she had made a clean breast of it to her mother and that her mother would speak to him that morning. She cried and threw her arms around his neck, saying:

14   "O, Bob! Bob! What am I to do? What am I to do at all?"

15   She would put an end to herself, she said.

16   He comforted her feebly, telling her not to cry, that it would be all right, never fear. He felt against his shirt the agitation of her bosom.

17   It was not altogether his fault that it had happened. He remembered well, with the curious patient memory of the celibate, the first casual caresses her dress, her breath, her fingers had given him. Then late one night as he was undressing for bed she had tapped at his door, timidly. She wanted to relight her candle at his, for hers had been blown out by a gust. It was her bath night. She wore a loose open combing-jacket of printed flannel. Her white instep shone in the opening of her furry slippers and the blood glowed warmly behind her perfumed skin. From her hands and wrists too as she lit and steadied her candle a faint perfume arose.

18   On nights when he came in very late it was she who warmed up his dinner. He scarcely knew what he was eating feeling her beside him alone, at night, in the sleeping house. And her thoughtfulness! If the night was anyway cold or wet or windy there was sure to be a little tumbler of punch ready for him. Perhaps they could be happy together....

19   They used to go upstairs together on tiptoe, each with a candle, and on the third landing exchange reluctant good nights. They used to kiss. He remembered well her eyes, the touch of her hand and his delirium....

20   But delirium passes. He echoed her phrase, applying it to himself: "*What am I to do?*" The instinct of the celibate warned him to hold back. But the sin was there; even his sense of honour told him that reparation must be made for such a sin.

21   While he was sitting with her on the side of the bed Mary came to the door and said that the missus wanted to see him in the parlour. He stood up to put on his coat and waistcoat, more helpless than ever. When he was dressed he went over to her to comfort her. It would be all right, never fear. He left her crying on the bed and moaning softly: "*O my God!*"

22   Going down the stairs his glasses became so dimmed with moisture that he had to take them off and polish them. He longed to ascend through the roof and fly away to another country where he would never hear again of his trouble, and yet a force pushed him downstairs step by step. The implacable faces of his employer and of the Madam stared upon his discomfiture. On the last flight of stairs he passed Jack Mooney who was coming up from the pantry nursing two bottles of *Bass*.[9] They

---

9. A brand of beer.

saluted coldly; and the lover's eyes rested for a second or two on a thick bulldog face and a pair of thick short arms. When he reached the foot of the staircase he glanced up and saw Jack regarding him from the door of the return-room.

23 Suddenly he remembered the night when one of the music-hall *artistes*, a little blond Londoner, had made a rather free allusion to Polly. The reunion had been almost broken up on account of Jack's violence. Everyone tried to quiet him. The music-hall *artiste*, a little paler than usual, kept smiling and saying that there was no harm meant; but Jack kept shouting at him that if any fellow tried that sort of game on with *his* sister he'd bloody well put his teeth down his throat, so he would.

24 Polly sat for a little time on the side of the bed, crying. Then she dried her eyes and went over to the looking-glass. She dipped the end of the towel in the water-jug and refreshed her eyes with the cool water. She looked at herself in profile and readjusted a hairpin above her ear. Then she went back to the bed again and sat at the foot. She regarded the pillows for a long time and the sight of them awakened in her mind secret amiable memories. She rested the nape of her neck against the cool iron bed-rail and fell into a reverie. There was no longer any perturbation visible on her face.

25 She waited on patiently, almost cheerfully, without alarm, her memories gradually giving place to hopes and visions of the future. Her hopes and visions were so intricate that she no longer saw the white pillows on which her gaze was fixed or remembered that she was waiting for anything.

26 At last she heard her mother calling. She started to her feet and ran to the banisters.

—Polly! Polly!

—Yes, mamma?

—Come down, dear. Mr. Doran wants to speak to you.

Then she remembered what she had been waiting for.

(1914)

D.H. Lawrence (1885–1930)

Lawrence's centrality as a modern literary figure is due largely to his attempts to free British fiction from the fetters of puritanism and class. He was a prolific and controversial author of fiction, poetry, plays, and literary criticism. The emotional relations of Lawrence's fictional characters are often intensely unsettling. See his poem "Piano," p. 232.

You Touched Me

1   The Pottery House was a square, ugly, brick house girt in by the wall that enclosed the whole grounds of the pottery itself. To be sure, a privet hedge partly masked the house and its ground from the pottery-yard and works: but only partly. Through the hedge could be seen the desolate yard, and the many-windowed, factory-like pottery, over the hedge could be seen the chimneys and the out-houses. But inside the hedge, a pleasant garden and lawn sloped down to a willow pool, which had once supplied the works.

2   The Pottery itself was now closed, the great doors of the yard permanently shut. No more the great crates with yellow straw showing through stood in stacks by the packing-shed. No more the drays drawn by great horses rolled down the hill with a high load. No more the pottery-lasses in their clay-coloured overalls, their faces and hair splashed with grey fine mud, shrieked and larked with the men. All that was over.

3   "We like it much better—oh, much better—quieter," said Matilda Rockley.

4   "Oh, yes," assented Emmie Rockley, her sister.

5   "I'm sure you do," agreed the visitor.

6   But whether the two Rockley girls really like it better, or whether they only imagined they did, is a question. Certainly their lives were much more grey and dreary now that the grey clay had ceased to spatter its mud and silt its dust over the premises. They did not quite realise how they missed the shrieking, shouting lasses, whom they had known all their lives and disliked so much.

7   Matilda and Emmie were already old maids. In a thorough industrial district, it is not easy for the girls who have expectations above the common to find husbands. The ugly industrial town was full of men, young men who were ready to marry. But they were all colliers or pottery-hands, mere workmen. The Rockley girls would have about ten thousand pounds each when their father died: ten thou-

sand pounds' worth of profitable house-property. It was not to be sneezed at: they felt so themselves, and refrained from sneezing away such a fortune on any mere member of the proletariat. Consequently, bank-clerks or non-conformist clergymen or even school-teachers having failed to come forward, Matilda had begun to give up all idea of ever leaving the Pottery House.

8   Matilda was a tall, thin, graceful, fair girl, with a rather large nose. She was the Mary to Emmie's Martha: that is, Matilda loved painting and music, and read a good many novels, whilst Emmie looked after the housekeeping. Emmie was shorter, plumper than her sister, and she had no accomplishments. She looked up to Matilda, whose mind was naturally refined and sensible.

9   In their quiet, melancholy way, the two girls were happy. Their mother was dead. Their father was ill also. He was an intelligent man who had had some education, but preferred to remain as if he were one with the rest of the working people. He had a passion for music and played the violin pretty well. But now he was getting old, he was very ill, dying of a kidney disease. He had been rather a heavy whisky-drinker.

10   This quiet household, with one servant-maid, lived on year after year in the Pottery House. Friends came in, the girls went out, the father drank himself more and more ill. Outside in the street there was a continual racket of the colliers and their dogs and children. But inside the pottery wall was a deserted quiet.

11   In all this ointment there was one little fly. Ted Rockley, the father of the girls, had had four daughters, and no son. As his girls grew, he felt angry at finding himself always in a household of women. He went off to London and adopted a boy out of a Charity Institution. Emmie was fourteen years old, and Matilda sixteen, when their father arrived home with his prodigy, the boy of six, Hadrian.

12   Hadrian was just an ordinary boy from a Charity Home, with ordinary brownish hair and ordinary bluish eyes and of ordinary rather Cockney speech. The Rockley girls—there were three at home at the time of his arrival—had resented his being sprung on them. He, with his watchful, charity-institution instinct, knew this at once. Though he was only six years old, Hadrian had a subtle, jeering look on his face when he regarded the three young women. They insisted he should address them as Cousin: Cousin Flora, Cousin Matilda, Cousin Emmie. He complied, but there seemed a mockery in his tone.

13   The girls, however, were kind-hearted by nature. Flora married and left home. Hadrian did very much as he pleased with Matilda and Emmie, though they had certain strictnesses. He grew up in the Pottery House and about the Pottery premises, went to an elementary school, and was invariably called Hadrian Rockley. He regarded Cousin Matilda and Cousin Emmie with a certain laconic indifference, was quiet and reticent in his ways. The girls called him sly, but

that was unjust. He was merely cautious, and without frankness. His uncle, Ted Rockley, understood him tacitly, their natures were somewhat akin. Hadrian and the elderly man had a real but unemotional regard for one another.

14   When he was thirteen years old the boy was sent to a High School in the County town. He did not like it. His Cousin Matilda had longed to make a little gentleman of him, but he refused to be made. He would give a little contemptuous curve to his lip, and take on a shy, charity-boy grin, when refinement was thrust upon him. He played truant from the High School, sold his books, his cap with its badge, even his very scarf and pocket-handkerchief, to his school-fellows, and went raking off heaven knows where with the money. So he spent two very unsatisfactory years.

15   When he was fifteen he announced that he wanted to leave England to go to the Colonies. He had kept touch with the Home. The Rockleys knew that, when Hadrian made a declaration, in his quiet, half-jeering manner, it was worse than useless to oppose him. So at last the boy departed, going to Canada under the protection of the Institution to which he had belonged. He said good-bye to the Rockleys, without a word of thanks, and parted, it seemed, without a pang. Matilda and Emmie wept often to think of how he left them: even on their father's face a queer look came. But Hadrian wrote fairly regularly from Canada. He had entered some electricity works near Montreal, and was doing well.

16   At last, however, the war came. In his turn, Hadrian joined up and came to Europe. The Rockleys saw nothing of him. They lived on, just the same, in the Pottery House. Ted Rockley was dying of a sort of dropsy, and in his heart he wanted to see the boy. When the Armistice was signed, Hadrian had a long leave, and wrote that he was coming home to the Pottery House.

17   The girls were terribly fluttered. To tell the truth, they were a little afraid of Hadrian. Matilda, tall and thin, was frail in her health, both girls were worn with nursing their father. To have Hadrian, a young man of twenty-one, in the house with them, after he had left them so coldly five years before, was a trying circumstance.

18   They were in a flutter. Emmie persuaded her father to have his bed made finally in the morning-room downstairs, whilst his room upstairs was prepared for Hadrian. This was done, and preparations were going on for the arrival, when, at ten o'clock in the morning, the young man suddenly turned up, quite unexpectedly. Cousin Emmie, with her hair bobbed up in absurd little bobs round her forehead, was busily polishing the stair-rods, while Cousin Matilda was in the kitchen washing the drawing-room ornaments in a lather, her sleeves rolled back on her thin arms, and her head tied up oddly and coquettishly in a duster.

19   Cousin Matilda blushed deep with mortification when the self-possessed young man walked in with his kit-bag, and put his cap on

the sewing-machine. He was little and self-confident, with a curious neatness about him that still suggested the Charity Institution. His face was brown, he had a small moustache, he was vigorous enough in his smallness.

20   "*Well*, it is Hadrian!" exclaimed Cousin Matilda, wringing the lather off her hand. "We didn't expect you till to-morrow."

21   "I got off Monday night," said Hadrian, glancing round the room.

22   "Fancy!" said Cousin Matilda. Then, having dried her hands, she went forward, held out her hand, and said:

23   "How are you?"

24   "Quite well, thank you," said Hadrian.

25   "You're quite a man," said Cousin Matilda.

26   Hadrian glanced at her. She did not look her best: so thin, so large-nosed, with that pink-and-white checked duster tied round her head. She felt her disadvantage. But she had had a good deal of suffering and sorrow, she did not mind any more.

27   The servant entered—one that did not know Hadrian.

28   "Come and see my father," said Cousin Matilda.

29   In the hall they roused Cousin Emmie like a partridge from cover. She was on the stairs pushing the bright stair-rods into place. Instinctively her hand went to the little knobs, her front hair bobbed on her forehead.

30   "Why!" she exclaimed, crossly. "What have you come today for?"

31   "I got off a day earlier," said Hadrian, and his man's voice so deep and unexpected was like a blow to Cousin Emmie.

32   "Well, you've caught us in the midst of it," she said, with resentment. Then all three went into the middle room.

33   Mr. Rockley was dressed—that is, he had on his trousers and socks—but he was resting on the bed, propped up just under the window, from whence he could see his beloved and resplendent garden, where tulips and apple trees were ablaze. He did not look as ill as he was, for the water puffed him up, and his face kept its colour. His stomach was much swollen.

34   He glanced round swiftly, turning his eyes without turning his head. He was the wreck of a handsome, well-built man.

35   Seeing Hadrian, a queer, unwilling smile went over his face. The young man greeted him sheepishly.

36   "You wouldn't make a life-guardsman," he said. "Do you want something to eat?"

37   Hadrian looked around—as if for the meal.

38   "I don't mind," he said.

39   "What shall you have—egg and bacon?" asked Emmie shortly.

40   "Yes, I don't mind," said Hadrian.

41   The sisters went down to the kitchen, and sent the servant to finish the stairs.

42   "Isn't he *altered*?" said Matilda, *sotto voce*.

43   "Isn't he!" said Cousin Emmie. "What a little man!"

44   They both made a grimace, and laughed nervously.

45   "Get the frying-pan," said Emmie to Matilda.

46   "But he's as cocky as ever," said Matilda, narrowing her eyes and shaking her head knowingly, as she handed the frying-pan.

47   "Mannie!" said Emmie sarcastically. Hadrian's new-fledged, cock-sure manliness evidently found no favour in her eyes.

48   "Oh, he's not bad," said Matilda. "You don't want to be prejudiced against him."

49   "I'm not prejudiced against him. I think he's all right for looks," said Emmie, "but there's too much of the little mannie about him."

50   "Fancy catching us like this," said Matilda.

51   "They've no thought for anything," said Emmie with contempt. "You go up and get dressed, our Matilda. I don't care about him. I can see to things, and you can talk to him. I shan't."

52   "He'll talk to my father," said Matilda, meaningful.

53   "Sly—!" exclaimed Emmie, with a grimace.

54   The sisters believed that Hadrian had come hoping to get something out of their father—hoping for a legacy. And they were not at all sure he would not get it.

55   Matilda went upstairs to change. She had thought it all out how she would receive Hadrian, and impress him. And he had caught her with her head tied up in a duster, and her thin arms in a basin of lather. But she did not care. She now dressed herself most scrupulously, carefully folded her long, beautiful, blonde hair, touched her pallor with a little rouge, and put her long string of exquisite crystal beads over her soft green dress. Now she looked elegant, like a heroine in a magazine illustration, and almost as unreal.

56   She found Hadrian and her father talking away. The young man was short of speech as a rule, but he could find tongue with his "uncle." They were both sipping a glass of brandy, and smoking, and chatting like a pair of old cronies. Hadrian was telling about Canada. He was going back there when his leave was up.

57   "You wouldn't like to stop in England, then?" said Mr. Rockley.

58   "No, I wouldn't stop in England," said Hadrian.

59   "How's that? There's plenty of electricians here," said Mr. Rockley.

60   "Yes. But there's too much difference between the men and the employers over here—too much of that for me," said Hadrian.

61   The sick man looked at him narrowly, with oddly smiling eyes.

62   "That's it, is it?" he replied.

63   Matilda heard and understood. "So that's your big idea, is it, my little man," she said to herself. She had always said of Hadrian that he had no proper *respect* for anybody or anything, that he was sly and *common*. She went down to the kitchen for a *sotto voce* confab with Emmie.

64   "He thinks a rare lot of himself!" she whispered.

65   "He's somebody, he is!" said Emmie with contempt.

66   "He thinks there's too much difference between masters and men over here," said Matilda.

67   "Is it any different in Canada?" asked Emmie.

68   "Oh yes—democratic," replied Matilda. "He thinks they're all on a level over there."

69   "Ay, well, he's over here now," said Emmie dryly, "so he can keep his place."

70   As they talked they saw the young man sauntering down the garden, looking casually at the flowers. He had his hands in his pockets, and his soldier's cap neatly on his head. He looked quite at his ease, as if in possession. The two women, fluttered, watched him through the window.

71   "We know what he's come for," said Emmie, churlishly. Matilda looked a long time at the neat khaki figure. It had something of the charity-box about it still; but now it was a man's figure, laconic, charged with plebeian energy. She thought of a derisive passion in his voice as he had declaimed against the propertied classes, to her father.

72   "You don't know, Emmie. Perhaps he's not come for that," she rebuked her sister. They were both thinking of the money.

73   They were still watching the young soldier. He stood away at the bottom of the garden, with his back to them, his hands in his pockets, looking into the water of the willow pond. Matilda's dark blue eyes had a strange, full look in them, the lids, with the faint blue veins showing, dropped rather low. She carried her head light and high, but she had a look of pain. The young man at the bottom of the garden turned and looked up the path. Perhaps he saw them through the window. Matilda moved into shadow.

74   That afternoon their father seemed weak or ill. He was easily exhausted. The doctor came, and told Matilda that the sick man might die at any moment—but then he might not. They must be prepared.

75   So the day passed, and the next. Hadrian made himself at home. He went about in the morning in his brownish jersey and his khaki trousers, collarless, his bare neck showing. He explored the pottery premises, as if he had some secret purpose in so doing, he talked with Mr. Rockley, when the sick man had strength. The two girls were always angry when the two men sat talking together like cronies. Yet it was chiefly a kind of politics they talked.

76   On the second day after Hadrian's arrival, Matilda sat with her father in the evening. She was drawing a picture which she wanted to copy. It was very still, Hadrian was gone out somewhere, no one knew where, and Emmie was busy. Mr. Rockley reclined on his bed, looking out in silence over his evening-sunny garden.

77   "If anything happens to me, Matilda," he said, "you won't sell this house—you'll stop here—"

78   Matilda's eyes took their slightly haggard look as she stared at her father.

79   "Well, we couldn't do anything else," she said.

80   "You don't know what you might do," he said. "Everything is left to you and Emmie, equally. You do as you like with it—only don't sell this house, don't part with it."

81   "No," she said.

82   "And give Hadrian my watch and chain, and a hundred pounds out of what's in the bank—and help him if he ever wants helping. I haven't put his name in the will."

83   "Your watch and chain, and a hundred pounds—yes. But you'll be here when he goes back to Canada, father."

84   "You never know what'll happen," said her father.

85   Matilda sat and watched him, with her full, haggard eyes, for a long time, as if tranced. She saw that he knew he must go soon—she saw like a clairvoyant.

86   Later on she told Emmie what her father had said about the watch and chain and the money.

87   "What right has *he*"—he—meaning Hadrian—"to my father's watch and chain—what has it to do with him? Let him have the money, and get off," said Emmie. She loved her father.

88   That night Matilda sat late in her room. Her heart was anxious and breaking, her mind seemed entranced. She was too much entranced even to weep, and all the time she thought of her father, only her father. At last she felt she must go to him.

89   It was near midnight. She went along the passage and to his room. There was a faint light from the moon outside. She listened at his door. Then she softly opened and entered. The room was faintly dark. She heard a movement on the bed.

90   "Are you asleep?" she said softly, advancing to the side of the bed.

91   "Are you asleep?" she repeated gently, as she stood at the side of the bed. And she reached her hand in the darkness to touch his forehead. Delicately, her fingers met the nose and the eyebrows, she laid her fine, delicate hand on his brow. It seemed fresh and smooth—very fresh and smooth. A sort of surprise stirred her, in her entranced state. But it could not waken her. Gently, she leaned over the bed and stirred her fingers over the low-growing hair on his brow.

92   "Can't you sleep to-night?" she said.

93   There was a quick stirring in the bed. "Yes, I can," a voice answered. It was Hadrian's voice. She started away. Instantly she was wakened from her late-at-night trance. She remembered that her father was downstairs, that Hadrian had his room. She stood in the darkness as if stung.

94   "Is it you, Hadrian?" she said. "I thought it was my father." She was so startled, so shocked, that she could not move. The young man gave an uncomfortable laugh, and turned in his bed.

95   At last she got out of the room. When she was back in her own room, in the light, and her door was closed, she stood holding up her hand that had touched him, as if it were hurt. She was almost too shocked, she could not endure.

96   "Well," said her calm and weary mind, "it was only a mistake, why take any notice of it."

97   But she could not reason her feelings so easily. She suffered, feeling herself in a false position. Her right hand, which she had laid so gently on his face, on his fresh skin, ached now, as if it were really injured. She could not forgive Hadrian for the mistake: it made her dislike him deeply.

98   Hadrian too slept badly. He had been awakened by the opening of the door, and had not realised what the question meant. But the soft, straying tenderness of her hand on his face startled something out of his soul. He was a charity boy, aloof and more or less at bay. The fragile exquisiteness of her caress startled him most, revealed unknown things to him.

99   In the morning she could feel the consciousness in his eyes, when she came downstairs. She tried to bear herself as if nothing at all had happened, and she succeeded. She had the calm self-control, self-indifference, of one who has suffered and borne her suffering. She looked at him from her darkish, almost drugged blue eyes, she met the spark of consciousness in his eyes, and quenched it. And with her long, fine hand she put the sugar in his coffee.

100   But she could not control him as she thought she could. He had a keen memory stinging his mind, a new set of sensations working in his consciousness. Something new was alert in him. At the back of his reticent, guarded mind he kept his secret alive and vivid. She was at his mercy, for he was unscrupulous, his standard was not her standard.

101   He looked at her curiously. She was not beautiful, her nose was too large, her chin was too small, her neck was too thin. But her skin was clear and fine, she had a high-bred sensitiveness. This queer, brave, high-bred quality she shared with her father. The charity boy could see it in her tapering fingers, which were white and ringed. The same glamour that he knew in the elderly man he now saw in the woman. And he wanted to possess himself of it, he wanted to make himself master of it. As he went about through the old pottery-yard, his secretive mind schemed and worked. To be master of that strange soft delicacy such as he had felt in her hand upon his face—this was what he set himself towards. He was secretly plotting.

102   He watched Matilda as she went about, and she became aware of his attention, as of some shadow following her. But her pride made her ignore it. When he sauntered near her, his hands in his pockets, she received him with that same commonplace kindliness which mastered him more than any contempt. Her superior breeding seemed to control him. She made herself feel towards him exactly as

she had always felt: he was a young boy who lived in the house with them, but was a stranger. Only, she dared not remember his face under her hand. When she remembered that, she was bewildered. Her hand had offended her, she wanted to cut it off. And she wanted, fiercely, to cut off the memory in him. She assumed she had done so.

103   One day, when he sat talking with his "uncle," he looked straight into the eyes of the sick man, and said:

104   "But I shouldn't like to live and die here in Rawsley."

105   "No—well—you needn't," said the sick man.

106   "Do you think Cousin Matilda likes it?"

107   "I should think so."

108   "I don't call it much of a life," said the youth. "How much older is she than me, Uncle?"

109   The sick man looked at the young soldier.

110   "A good bit," he said.

111   "Over thirty?" said Hadrian.

112   "Well, not much. She's thirty-two."

113   Hadrian considered a while.

114   "She doesn't look it," he said.

115   Again the sick father looked at him.

116   "Do you think she'd like to leave here?" said Hadrian.

117   "Nay, I don't know," replied the father, restive.

118   Hadrian sat still, having his own thoughts. Then in a small, quiet voice, as if he were speaking from inside himself, he said:

119   "I'd marry her if you wanted me to."

120   The sick man raised his eyes suddenly and stared. He stared for a long time. The youth looked inscrutably out of the window.

121   "*You!*" said the sick man, mocking, with some contempt. Hadrian turned and met his eyes. The two men had an inexplicable understanding.

122   "If you wasn't against it," said Hadrian.

123   "Nay," said the father, turning aside, "I don't think I'm against it. I've never thought of it. But—but Emmie's the youngest."

124   He had flushed, and looked suddenly more alive. Secretly he loved the boy.

125   "You might ask her," said Hadrian.

126   The elder man considered.

127   "Hadn't you better ask her yourself?" he said.

128   "She'd take more notice of you," said Hadrian.

129   They were both silent. Then Emmie came in.

130   For two days Mr. Rockley was excited and thoughtful. Hadrian went about quietly, secretly, unquestioning. At last the father and daughter were alone together. It was very early morning, the father had been in much pain. As the pain abated, he lay still thinking.

131   "Matilda!" he said suddenly, looking at his daughter.

132   "Yes, I'm here," she said.

133   "Ay! I want you to do something—"

134   She rose in anticipation.

135   "Nay, sit still. I want you to marry Hadrian—"

136   She thought he was raving. She rose, bewildered and frightened.

137   "Nay, sit you still, sit you still. You hear what I tell you."

138   "But you don't know what you're saying, father."

139   "Ay, I know well enough. I want you to marry Hadrian, I tell you."

140   She was dumbfounded. He was a man of few words.

141   "You'll do what I tell you," he said.

142   She looked at him slowly.

143   "What put such an idea in your mind?" she said proudly.

144   "He did."

145   Matilda almost looked her father down, her pride was so offended.

146   "Why, it's disgraceful," she said.

147   "Why?"

148   She watched him slowly.

149   "What do you ask me for?" she said. "It's disgusting."

150   "The lad's sound enough," he said testily.

151   "You'd better tell him to clear out," she said coldly.

152   He turned and looked out of the window. She sat flushed and erect for a long time. At length her father turned to her, looking really malevolent.

153   "If you won't," he said, "you're a fool, and I'll make you pay for your foolishness, do you see?"

154   Suddenly a cold fear gripped her. She could not believe her senses. She was terrified and bewildered. She stared at her father, believing him to be delirious, or mad, or drunk. What could she do?

155   "I tell you," he said. "I'll send for Whittle to-morrow if you don't. You shall neither of you have anything of mine."

156   Whittle was the solicitor. She understood her father well enough: he would send for his solicitor, and make a will leaving all his property to Hadrian: neither she nor Emmie should have anything. It was too much. She rose and went out of the room, up to her own room, where she locked herself in.

157   She did not come out for some hours. At last, late at night, she confided in Emmie.

158   "The sliving demon, he wants the money," said Emmie. "My father's out of his mind."

159   The thought that Hadrian merely wanted the money was another blow to Matilda. She did not love the impossible youth—but she had not yet learned to think of him as a thing of evil. He now became hideous to her mind.

160   Emmie had a little scene with her father the next day.

161   "You don't mean what you said to our Matilda yesterday, do you, father?" she asked aggressively.

162   "Yes," he replied.

163   "What, that you'll alter your will?"

164   "Yes."

165 "You won't," said his angry daughter.

166 But he looked at her with a malevolent little smile.

167 "Annie!" he shouted. "Annie!"

168 He had still power to make his voice carry. The servant maid came in from the kitchen.

169 "Put your things on, and go down to Whittle's office, and say I want to see Mr. Whittle as soon as he can, and will he bring a will-form."

170 The sick man lay back a while—he could not lie down. His daughter sat as if she had been struck. Then she left the room.

171 Hadrian was pottering about in the garden. She went straight down to him.

172 "Here," she said. "You'd better get off. You'd better take your things and go from here, quick."

173 Hadrian looked slowly at the infuriated girl.

174 "Who says so?" he asked.

175 "*We* say so—get off, you've done enough mischief and damage."

176 "Does Uncle say so?"

177 "Yes, he does."

178 "I'll go and ask him."

179 But like a fury Emmie barred his way.

180 "No, you needn't. You needn't ask him nothing at all. We don't want you, so you can go."

181 "Uncle's boss here."

182 "A man that's dying, and you crawling round and working on him for his money!—you're not fit to live."

183 "Oh!" he said. "Who says I'm working for his money?"

184 "I say. But my father told our Matilda, and *she* knows what you are. *She* knows what you're after. So you might as well clear out, for all you'll get—guttersnipe!"

185 He turned his back on her, to think. It had not occurred to him that they would think he was after the money. He *did* want the money—badly. He badly wanted to be an employer himself, not one of the employed. But he knew, in his subtle, calculating way, that it was not for the money he wanted Matilda. He wanted both the money and Matilda. But he told himself the two desires were separate, not one. He could not do with Matilda, *without* the money. But he did not want her *for* the money.

186 When he got this clear in his mind, he sought for an opportunity to tell it her, lurking and watching. But she avoided him. In the evening the lawyer came. Mr. Rockley seemed to have a new access of strength—a will was drawn up, making the previous arrangements wholly conditional. The old will held good, if Matilda would consent to marry Hadrian. If she refused then at the end of six months the whole property passed to Hadrian.

187 Mr. Rockley told this to the young man, with malevolent satisfaction. He seemed to have a strange desire, quite unreasonable, for

revenge upon the women who had surrounded him for so long, and served him so carefully.

188   "Tell her in front of me," said Hadrian.

189   So Mr. Rockley sent for his daughters.

190   At last they came, pale, mute, stubborn. Matilda seemed to have retired far off, Emmie seemed like a fighter ready to fight to the death. The sick man reclined on the bed, his eyes bright, his puffed hand trembling. But his face had again some of its old, bright handsomeness. Hadrian sat quiet, a little aside: the indomitable, dangerous charity boy.

191   "There's the will," said their father, pointing them to the paper.

192   The two women sat mute and immovable, they took no notice.

193   "Either you marry Hadrian, or he has everything," said the father with satisfaction.

194   "Then let him have everything," said Matilda coldly.

195   "He's not! He's not!" cried Emmie fiercely. "He's not going to have it. The guttersnipe!"

196   An amused look came on her father's face.

197   "You hear that, Hadrian," he said.

198   "I didn't offer to marry Cousin Matilda for the money," said Hadrian, flushing and moving on his seat.

199   Matilda looked at him slowly, with her dark blue, drugged eyes. He seemed a strange monster to her.

200   "Why, you liar, you know you did," cried Emmie.

201   The sick man laughed. Matilda continued to gaze strangely at the young man.

202   "She knows I didn't," said Hadrian.

203   He too had his courage, as a rat has indomitable courage in the end. Hadrian had some of the neatness, the reserve, the underground quality of the rat. But he had perhaps the ultimate courage, the most unquenched courage of all.

204   Emmie looked at her sister.

205   "Oh, well," she said. "Matilda—don't you bother. Let him have everything, we can look after ourselves."

206   "I know he'll take everything," said Matilda, abstractedly.

207   Hadrian did not answer. He knew in fact that if Matilda refused him he would take everything, and go off with it.

208   "A clever little mannie—!" said Emmie, with a jeering grimace.

209   The father laughed noiselessly to himself. But he was tired....

210   "Go on, then," he said. "Go on, let me be quiet."

211   Emmie turned and looked at him.

212   "You deserve what you've got," she said to her father bluntly.

213   "Go on," he answered mildly. "Go on."

214   Another night passed—a night nurse sat up with Mr. Rockley. Another day came. Hadrian was there as ever, in his woollen jersey and coarse khaki trousers and bare neck. Matilda went about, frail and distant, Emmie black-browed in spite of her blondness. They

were all quiet, for they did not intend the mystified servant to learn anything.

215   Mr. Rockley had very bad attacks of pain, he could not breathe. The end seemed near. They all went about quiet and stoical, all unyielding. Hadrian pondered within himself. If he did not marry Matilda he would go to Canada with twenty thousand pounds. This was itself a very satisfactory prospect. If Matilda consented he would have nothing—she would have her own money.

216   Emmie was the one to act. She went off in search of the solicitor and brought him home with her. There was an interview, and Whittle tried to frighten the youth into withdrawal—but without avail. The clergyman and relatives were summoned—but Hadrian stared at them and took no notice. It made him angry, however.

217   He wanted to catch Matilda alone. Many days went by, and he was not successful: she avoided him. At last, lurking, he surprised her one day as she came to pick gooseberries, and he cut off her retreat. He came to the point at once.

218   "You don't want me, then?" he said, in his subtle, insinuating voice.

219   "I don't want to speak to you," she said, averting her face.

220   "You put your hand on me, though," he said. "You shouldn't have done that, and then I should never have thought of it. You shouldn't have touched me."

221   "If you were anything decent, you'd know that was a mistake, and forget it," she said.

222   "I know it was a mistake—but I shan't forget it. If you wake a man up, he can't go to sleep again because he's told to."

223   "If you had any decent feeling in you, you'd have gone away," she replied.

224   "I didn't want to," he replied.

225   She looked away into the distance. At last she asked:

226   "What do you persecute me for, if it isn't for the money? I'm old enough to be your mother. In a way I've been your mother."

227   "Doesn't matter," he said. "You've been no mother to me. Let us marry and go to Canada—you might as well—you've touched me."

228   She was white and trembling. Suddenly she flushed with anger.

229   "It's so *indecent*," she said.

230   "How?" he retorted. "You touched me."

231   But she walked away from him. She felt as if he had trapped her. He was angry and depressed, he felt again despised.

232   That same evening she went into her father's room.

233   "Yes," she said suddenly. "I'll marry him."

234   Her father looked up at her. He was in pain, and very ill.

235   "You like him now, do you?" he said, with a faint smile.

236   She looked down into his face, and saw death not far off. She turned and went coldly out of the room.

237   The solicitor was sent for, preparations were hastily made. In all the interval Matilda did not speak to Hadrian, never answered him if he addressed her. He approached her in the morning.

238   "You've come round to it, then?" he said, giving her a pleasant look from his twinkling, almost kindly eyes. She looked down at him and turned aside. She looked down on him both literally and figuratively. Still he persisted, and triumphed.

239   Emmie raved and wept, the secret flew abroad. But Matilda was silent and unmoved. Hadrian was quiet and satisfied, and nipped with fear also. But he held out against his fear. Mr. Rockley was very ill, but unchanged.

240   On the third day the marriage took place, Matilda and Hadrian drove straight home from the registrar, and went straight into the room of the dying man. His face lit up with a clear twinkling smile.

241   "Hadrian—you've got her?" he said, a little hoarsely.

242   "Yes," said Hadrian, who was pale round the gills.

243   "Ay, my lad, I'm glad you're mine," replied the dying man. Then he turned his eyes closely on Matilda.

244   "Let's look at you, Matilda," he said. Then his voice went strange and unrecognisable. "Kiss me," he said.

245   She stooped and kissed him. She had never kissed him before, not since she was a tiny kid. But she was quiet, very still.

246   "Kiss him," the dying man said.

247   Obediently, Matilda put forward her mouth and kissed the young husband.

248   "That's right! That's right!" murmured the dying man.

(1922)

Katherine Mansfield (1888–1923)

New Zealand–born but very much a London literary figure, Mansfield is
admired for her discipline as a short-story writer. Her sharply observed
human portraits and her ability to penetrate the surface realities of life can
be found in her five volumes of short stories, three published during her
lifetime and two published posthumously.

The Fly

1   "Y'are very snug in here," piped old Mr. Woodifield and he peered out
of the great, green-leather armchair by his friend the boss's desk as a
baby peers out of its pram. His talk was over; it was time for him to be
off. But he did not want to go. Since he had retired, since his ... stroke,
the wife and the girls kept him boxed up in the house every day of the
week except Tuesday. On Tuesday he was dressed and brushed and
allowed to cut back to the City for the day. Though what he did there
the wife and the girls couldn't imagine. Made a nuisance of himself to
his friends, they supposed.... Well, perhaps so. All the same, we cling
to our last pleasures as the tree clings to its last leaves. So there sat old
Woodifield, smoking a cigar and staring almost greedily at the boss,
who rolled in his office chair, stout, rosy, five years older than he, and
still going strong, still at the helm. It did one good to see him.

2   Wistfully, admiringly, the old voice added, "It's snug in here, upon
my word!"

3   "Yes, it's comfortable enough," agreed the boss, and he flipped the
Financial Times with a paper-knife. As a matter of fact he was proud of
his room; he liked to have it admired, especially by old Woodifield. It
gave him a feeling of deep, solid satisfaction to be planted there in the
midst of it in full view of that frail old figure in the muffler.

4   "I've had it done up lately," he explained, as he had explained for the
past—how many?—weeks. "New carpet," and he pointed to the bright
red carpet with a pattern of large white rings. "New furniture," and he
nodded towards the massive bookcase and the table with legs like
twisted treacle. "Electric heating!" He waved almost exultantly
towards the five transparent, pearly sausages glowing so softly in the
tilted copper pan.

5   But he did not draw old Woodifield's attention to the photograph
over the table of a grave-looking boy in uniform standing in one of
those spectral photographers' parks with photographers' storm-clouds
behind him. It was not new. It had been there for over six years.

6   "There was something I wanted to tell you," said old Woodifield, and his eyes grew dim remembering. "Now what was it? I had it in my mind when I started out this morning." His hands began to tremble, and patches of red showed above his beard.

7   Poor old chap, he's on his last pins, thought the boss. And, feeling kindly, he winked at the old man, and said jokingly, "I tell you what. I've got a little drop of something here that'll do you good before you go out into the cold again. It's beautiful stuff. It wouldn't hurt a child." He took a key off his watch-chain, unlocked a cupboard below his desk, and drew forth a dark, squat bottle. "That's the medicine," said he. "And the man from whom I got it told me on the strict Q.T. it came from the cellars at Windsor Castle."

8   Old Woodifield's mouth fell open at the sight. He couldn't have looked more surprised if the boss had produced a rabbit.

9   "It's whisky, ain't it?" he piped feebly.

10   The boss turned the bottle and lovingly showed him the label. Whisky it was.

11   "D'you know," said he, peering up at the boss wonderingly, "they won't let me touch it at home." And he looked as though he was going to cry.

12   "Ah, that's where we know a bit more than the ladies," cried the boss, swooping across for two tumblers that stood on the table with the water-bottle, and pouring a generous finger into each. "Drink it down. It'll do you good. And don't put any water with it. It's sacrilege to tamper with stuff like this. Ah!" He tossed off his, pulled out his handkerchief, hastily wiped his moustaches, and cocked an eye at old Woodifield, who was rolling his in his chaps.[1]

13   The old man swallowed, was silent a moment, and then said faintly, "It's nutty!"

14   But it warmed him; it crept into his chill old brain—he remembered.

15   "That was it," he said, heaving himself out of his chair. "I thought you'd like to know. The girls were in Belgium last week having a look at poor Reggie's grave, and they happened to come across your boy's. They're quite near each other, it seems."

16   Old Woodifield paused, but the boss made no reply. Only a quiver in his eyelids showed that he heard.

17   "The girls were delighted with the way the place is kept," piped the old voice. "Beautifully looked after. Couldn't be better if they were at home. You've not been across, have yer?"

18   "No, no!" For various reasons the boss had not been across.

19   "There's miles of it," quavered old Woodifield, "and it's all as neat as a garden. Flowers growing on all the graves. Nice broad paths." It was plain from his voice how much he liked a nice broad path.

20   The pause came again. Then the old man brightened wonderfully.

---

1. Mouth or jaws.

21   "D'you know what the hotel made the girls pay for a pot of jam?" he piped. "Ten francs! Robbery, I call it. It was a little pot, so Gertrude says, no bigger than a half-crown. And she hadn't taken more than a spoonful when they charged her ten francs. Gertrude brought the pot away with her to teach 'em a lesson. Quite right, too; it's trading on our feelings. They think because we're over there having a look round we're ready to pay anything. That's what it is." And he turned towards the door.

22   "Quite right, quite right!" cried the boss, though what was quite right he hadn't the least idea. He came round by his desk, followed the shuffling footsteps to the door, and saw the old fellow out. Woodifield was gone.

23   For a long moment the boss stayed, staring at nothing, while the grey-haired office messenger, watching him, dodged in and out of his cubby-hole like a dog that expects to be taken for a run. Then: "I'll see nobody for half an hour, Macey," said the boss. "Understand? Nobody at all."

24   "Very good, sir."

25   The door shut, the firm heavy steps recrossed the bright carpet, the fat body plumped down in the spring chair, and leaning forward, the boss covered his face with his hands. He wanted, he intended, he had arranged to weep....

26   It had been a terrible shock to him when old Woodifield sprang that remark upon him about the boy's grave. It was exactly as though the earth had opened and he had seen the boy lying there with Woodifield's girls staring down at him. For it was strange. Although over six years had passed away, the boss never thought of the boy except as lying unchanged, unblemished in his uniform, asleep for ever. "My son!" groaned the boss. But no tears came yet. In the past, in the first months and even years after the boy's death, he had only to say those words to be overcome by such grief that nothing short of a violent fit of weeping could relieve him. Time, he had declared then, he had told everybody, could make no difference. Other men perhaps might recover, might live their loss down, but not he. How was it possible? His boy was an only son. Ever since his birth the boss had worked at building up this business for him; it had no other meaning if it was not for the boy. Life itself had come to have no other meaning. How on earth could he have slaved, denied himself, kept going all those years without the promise for ever before him of the boy's stepping into his shoes and carrying on where he left off?

27   And that promise had been so near being fulfilled. The boy had been in the office learning the ropes for a year before the war. Every morning they had started off together; they had come back by the same train. And what congratulations he had received as the boy's father! No wonder; he had taken to it marvellously. As to his popularity with the staff, every man jack of them down to old Macey couldn't make enough of the boy. And he wasn't in the least spoilt. No, he was just his

bright natural self, with the right word for everybody, with that boyish look and his habit of saying, "Simply splendid!"

28 But all that was over and done with as though it never had been. The day had come when Macey had handed him the telegram that brought the whole place crashing about his head. "Deeply regret to inform you ..." And he had left the office a broken man, with his life in ruins.

29 Six years ago, six years.... How quickly time passed! It might have happened yesterday. The boss took his hands from his face; he was puzzled. Something seemed to be wrong with him. He wasn't feeling as he wanted to feel. He decided to get up and have a look at the boy's photograph. But it wasn't a favourite photograph of his; the expression was unnatural. It was cold, even stern-looking. The boy had never looked like that.

30 At that moment the boss noticed that a fly had fallen into his broad inkpot, and was trying feebly but desperately to clamber out again. Help! Help! said those struggling legs. But the sides of the inkpot were wet and slippery; it fell back again and began to swim. The boss took up a pen, picked the fly out of the ink, and shook it on a piece of blotting-paper. For a fraction of a second it lay still on the dark patch that oozed round it. Then the front legs waved, took hold, and, pulling its small, sodden body up, it began the immense task of cleaning the ink from its wings. Over and under, over and under, went a leg along a wing as the stone goes over and under the scythe. Then there was a pause, while the fly, seeming to stand on the tips of its toes, tried to expand first one wing and then the other. It succeeded at last, and, sitting down, it began, like a minute cat, to clean its face. Now one could imagine that the little front legs rubbed against each other lightly, joyfully. The horrible danger was over; it had escaped; it was ready for life again.

31 But just then the boss had an idea. He plunged his pen back into the ink, leaned his thick wrist on the blotting-paper, and as the fly tried its wings down came a great heavy blot. What would it make of that? What indeed! The little beggar seemed absolutely cowed, stunned, and afraid to move because of what would happen next. But then, as if painfully, it dragged itself forward. The front legs waved, caught hold, and, more slowly this time, the task began from the beginning.

32 He's a plucky little devil, thought the boss, and he felt a real admiration for the fly's courage. That was the way to tackle things; that was the right spirit. Never say die; it was only a question of ... But the fly had again finished its laborious task, and the boss had just time to refill his pen, to shake fair and square on the new-cleaned body yet another dark drop. What about it this time? A painful moment of suspense followed. But behold, the front legs were again waving; the boss felt a rush of relief. He leaned over the fly and said to it tenderly, "You artful little b ..." And he actually had the brilliant notion of breathing on it to help the drying process. All the same, there was something timid

and weak about its efforts now, and the boss decided that this time should be the last, as he dipped the pen deep into the inkpot.

33   It was. The last blot fell on the soaked blotting-paper, and the draggled fly lay in it and did not stir. The back legs were stuck to the body; the front legs were not to be seen.

34   "Come on," said the boss. "Look sharp!" And he stirred it with his pen—in vain. Nothing happened or was likely to happen. The fly was dead.

35   The boss lifted the corpse on the end of the paper-knife and flung it into the waste-paper basket. But such a grinding feeling of wretchedness seized him that he felt positively frightened. He started forward and pressed the bell for Macey.

36   "Bring me some fresh blotting-paper," he said sternly, "and look sharp about it." And while the old dog padded away he fell to wondering what it was he had been thinking about before. What was it? It was ... He took out his handkerchief and passed it inside his collar. For the life of him he could not remember.

(1922)

Ethel Wilson (1888–1980)

A novelist as well as a short-story writer, Ethel Wilson moved to Vancouver in 1898. "We Have to Sit Opposite," included in Mrs. Golightly and Other Stories *(1961), builds on the image of opposition suggested by its title and demonstrates the importance of place in Wilson's work. Her best-known novel,* Swamp Angel *(1954), is set in British Columbia.*

We Have to Sit Opposite

1   Even in the confusion of entering the carriage at Salzburg, Mrs. Montrose and her cousin Mrs. Forrester noticed the man with the blue tooth. He occupied a corner beside the window. His wife sat next to him. Next to her sat their daughter of perhaps seventeen. People poured into the train. A look passed between Mrs. Montrose and Mrs. Forrester. The look said, "These people seem to have filled up the carriage pretty well, but we'd better take these seats while we can as the train is so full. At least we can have seats together." The porter, in his porter's tyrannical way, piled their suitcases onto the empty rack above the heads of the man with the blue tooth, and his wife, and his daughter, and departed. The opposite rack was full of baskets, bags, and miscellaneous parcels. The train started. Here they were. Mrs. Montrose and Mrs. Forrester smiled at each other as they settled down below the rack which was filled with miscellaneous articles. Clinging vines that they were, they felt adventurous and successful. They had travelled alone from Vienna to Salzburg, leaving in Vienna their doctor husbands to continue attending the clinics of Dr. Bauer and Dr. Hirsch. And now, after a week in Salzburg, they were happily on their way to rejoin their husbands, who had flown to Munich.

2   Both Mrs. Montrose and Mrs. Forrester were tall, slight and fair. They were dressed with dark elegance. They knew that their small hats were smart, suitable and becoming, and they rejoiced in the simplicity and distinction of their own costumes. The selection of these and other costumes, and of these and other hats in Vienna had, they regretted, taken from the study of art, music and history a great deal of valuable time. Mrs. Montrose and Mrs. Forrester were sincerely fond of art, music and history and longed almost passionately to spend their days in the Albertina Gallery and the Kunsthistorische Museum. But the modest shops and shop windows of the craftsmen of Vienna had rather diverted the two young women from the study of art and history, and it was easy to lay the blame for this on the museums and art galleries,

which, in truth, closed their doors at very odd times. After each day's enchanting pursuits and disappointments, Mrs. Montrose and Mrs. Forrester hastened in a fatigued state to the café where they had arranged to meet their husbands who by this time had finished their daily sessions with Dr. Bauer and Dr. Hirsch.

3   This was perhaps the best part of the day, to sit together happily in the sunshine, toying with the good Viennese coffee or a glass of wine, gazing and being gazed upon, and giving up their senses to the music that flowed under the chestnut trees. (Ah Vienna, they thought, Vienna, Vienna.)

4   No, perhaps the evenings had been the best time when after their frugal pension dinner they hastened out to hear opera or symphony or wild atavistic gypsy music. All was past now. They had been very happy. They were fortunate. Were they too fortunate?

5   Mrs. Montrose and Mrs. Forrester were in benevolent good spirits as they looked round the railway carriage and prepared to take their seats and settle down for the journey to Munich to meet their husbands. In their window corner, opposite the man with the blue tooth, was a large hamper. "*Do* you mind?" asked Mrs. Montrose, smiling sweetly at the man, his wife, and his daughter. She prepared to lift the hamper on which the charming view from the carriage window was of course wasted, intending to move it along the seat, and take its place. The man, his wife, and his daughter had never taken their eyes off Mrs. Montrose and Mrs. Forrester since they had entered the carriage.

6   "*If* you please," said the man loudly and slowly in German English, "*if* you please, that place belongs to my wife or to my daughter. For the moment they sit beside me, but I keep that place for my wife or my daughter. That seat is therefore reserved. It is our seat. You may of course use the two remaining seats."

7   "I'm sorry," said Mrs. Montrose, feeling snubbed, and she and Mrs. Forrester sat down side by side on the two remaining seats opposite the German family. Beside them the hamper looked out of the window at the charming view. Their gaiety and self-esteem evaporated. The train rocked along.

8   The three continued to stare at the two young women. Suddenly the mother leaned toward her daughter. She put up her hand to her mouth and whispered behind her hand, her eyes remaining fixed on Mrs. Montrose. The daughter nodded. She also stared at Mrs. Montrose. Mrs. Montrose flushed. The mother sat upright again, still looking at Mrs. Montrose, who felt very uncomfortable, and very much annoyed at blushing.

9   The man ceased staring at the two young women. He looked up at the rack above him, which contained their suitcases.

10   "Those are your suitcases," he asked, or rather announced.

11   "Yes," said Mrs. Montrose and Mrs. Forrester without smiles.

12   "They are large," said the man in a didactic manner, "they are too large. They are too large to be put on racks. A little motion, a very little motion, and they might fall. If they fall they will injure myself, my wife, or my daughter. It is better," he continued instructively, "that if they fall, they should fall upon your heads, not upon our heads. That is logical. They are not my suitcases. They are your suitcases. You admit it. Please to move your suitcases to the opposite rack, where, if they fall, they will fall upon your own heads." And he continued to sit there motionless. So did his wife. So did his daughter.

13   Mrs. Montrose and Mrs. Forrester looked at the suitcases in dismay. "Oh," said Mrs. Forrester, "they are so heavy to move. If you feel like that, please won't you sit on this side of the carriage, and we will move across, under our own suitcases, though I can assure you they will not fall. Or perhaps you will help us?"

14   "We prefer this side of the carriage," said the man with the blue tooth. "We have sat here because we prefer this side of the carriage. It is logical that you should move your suitcases. It is not logical that my wife, my daughter and I should give up our seats in this carriage, or remove your suitcases."

15   Mrs. Montrose and Mrs. Forrester looked at each other with rage in their hearts. All their self-satisfaction was gone. They got up and tugged and tugged as the train rocked along. They leaned resentfully across the erectly sitting man, and his wife and his daughter. They experienced with exasperation the realization that they had better make the best of it. The train, they knew, was crowded. They had to remain in this carriage with this disagreeable family. With much pulling and straining they hauled down the heavy suitcases. Violently they removed the parcels of the German family and lifted their own suitcases onto the rack above their heads, disposing them clumsily on the rack. Panting a little (they disliked panting), they settled down again side by side with high colour and loosened wisps of hair. They controlled their features so as to appear serene and unaware of the existence of anyone else in the railway carriage, but their hearts were full of black hate.

16   The family exchanged whispered remarks, and then resumed their scrutiny of the two young women, whose elegance had by this time a sort of tipsy quality. The girl leaned toward her mother. She whispered behind her hand to her mother, who nodded. Both of them stared at Mrs. Forrester. Then they laughed.

17   "Heavens!" thought the affronted Mrs. Forrester, "this is outrageous! Why can't Alice and I whisper behind our hands to each other about those people and make them feel simply awful! But they wouldn't feel awful. Well, we can't, just because we've been properly brought up, and it would be too childish. And perhaps they don't even know they're rude. They're just being natural." She breathed in frustration, and composed herself again.

18   Suddenly the man with the blue tooth spoke. "Are you English?" he said loudly.

19   "Yes—well—no," said Mrs. Forrester.

20   "No—well—yes," said Mrs. Montrose, simultaneously.

21   A derisive look came over the man's face. "You must know what you are," he said, "either you are English or you are not English. Are you, or are you not?"

22   "No," said Mrs. Montrose and Mrs. Forrester, speaking primly. Their chins were high, their eyes flashed, and they were ready for discreet battle.

23   "Then you are Americans?" said the man in the same bullying manner.

24   "No," said Mrs. Montrose and Mrs. Forrester.

25   "You can't deceive *me*, you know," said the man with the blue tooth, "I know well the English language. You *say* you are not English. You *say* you are not American. What, then, may I ask, are you? You must be something."

26   "We are Canadians," said Mrs. Forrester, furious at this catechism.

27   "*Canadians*," said the man.

28   "Yes, Canadians," said Mrs. Montrose.

29   "This," murmured Mrs. Forrester to Mrs. Montrose, "is more than I can bear!"

30   "What did you say?" said the man, leaning forward quickly, his hands on his knees.

31   "I spoke to my friend," said Mrs. Forrester coldly, "I spoke about my bear."

32   "Yes," said Mrs. Montrose, "she spoke about her bear."

33   "Your bear? Have you a bear? But you cannot have a bear!" said the man with some surprise.

34   "In Canada I have a bear. I have two bears," said Mrs. Forrester conceitedly.

35   "That is true," said Mrs. Montrose nodding, "she has two bears. I myself have five bears. My father has seven bears. That is nothing. It is the custom."

36   "What do you do with your bears?" asked the man.

37   "We eat them," said Mrs. Forrester.

38   "Yes," said Mrs. Montrose, "we eat them. It is the custom."

39   The man turned and spoke briefly to his wife and daughter, whose eyes opened wider than ever.

40   Mrs. Montrose and Mrs. Forrester felt pleased. This was better.

41   The man with the blue tooth became really interested. "Are you married?" he asked Mrs. Forrester.

42   "Yes," she replied. (We'll see what he'll say next, then we'll see what we can do.)

43   "And you?" he enquired of Mrs. Montrose. Mrs. Montrose seemed uncertain. "Well, yes, in a way, I suppose," she said.

44   The man with the blue tooth scrutinized Mrs. Montrose for a
moment. "*Then*," he said, as though he had at last found her out, "if
you are married, where is your husband?"

45   Mrs. Montrose took out her pocket handkerchief. She buried her
face in her hands, covering her eyes with her handkerchief. She shook.
Evidently she sobbed.

46   "Now you see what you've done!" said Mrs. Forrester. "You
shouldn't ask questions like that. Just look at what you've done."

47   The three gazed fascinated at Mrs. Montrose. "Is he dead or what is
he?" asked the man of Mrs. Forrester, making the words almost quietly
with his mouth.

48   "Sh!!" said Mrs. Forrester very loudly indeed. The three jumped a
little. So did Mrs. Montrose.

49   There was a silence while Mrs. Montrose wiped her eyes. She looked
over the heads opposite. The wife leaned toward her husband and
addressed him timidly behind her hand. He nodded, and spoke to Mrs.
Forrester.

50   "Well," he said, "at least you admit that *you* have a husband. If you
have a husband then, where is he?"

51   "Oh, I don't know," said Mrs. Forrester lightly.

52   "No, she doesn't know," said Mrs. Montrose.

53   The three on the opposite seat went into a conference. Mrs.
Montrose and Mrs. Forrester did not dare to look at each other. They
were enjoying themselves. Their self-esteem had returned. They had
impressed. Unfavourably, it is true. But still they had impressed.

54   The man with the blue tooth pulled himself together. He reasserted
himself. Across his waistcoat hung a watch chain. He took his watch
out of his pocket and looked at the time. Then to the surprise of Mrs.
Montrose and Mrs. Forrester he took another watch out of the pocket
at the other end of the chain. "You see," he said proudly, "I have two
watches."

55   Mrs. Montrose and Mrs. Forrester were surprised, but they had
themselves well in hand.

56   Mrs. Montrose looked at the watches disparagingly. "My husband
has six watches," she said.

57   "Yes, that is true," nodded Mrs. Forrester, "her husband *has* got six
watches, but my husband, like you, unfortunately has only two
watches."

58   The man put his watches back. Decidedly the battle was going in
favour of the two young women. How horrid of us, he was so pleased
with his watches, thought Mrs. Montrose. Isn't it true that horridness
just breeds horridness. We're getting horrider every minute. She
regarded the man, his wife and his daughter with distaste but with pity.

59   "You *say*," said the man, who always spoke as though their statements were open to doubt, which of course they were, "that you come
from Canada. Do you come from Winnipeg? I know about Winnipeg."

60   "No," said Mrs. Montrose, and she spoke this time quite truthfully, "I come from Vancouver." Mrs. Forrester remained silent.

61   "And you, where do you come from?" persisted the man in a hectoring tone, addressing Mrs. Forrester. Mrs. Forrester remained silent, she had almost decided to answer no more questions.

62   "Oh, do not tell, please do not tell," begged Mrs. Montrose in an anguished way.

63   "No," said Mrs. Forrester importantly, "I shall not tell. Rest assured. I shall not tell."

64   "Why will she not tell?" demanded the man. He was tortured by curiosity. So was his wife. So was his daughter.

65   "Sh!!" said Mrs. Montrose very loudly.

66   The man seemed ill at ease. By this time nothing existed in the world for him, or for his wife, or for his daughter but these two Canadian women who ate bears.

67   "How is it," asked the man, "that you no longer buy my trousers?"

68   "I beg your pardon?" faltered Mrs. Montrose. For a moment she lost ground.

69   "I said," replied the man, "why is it that you no longer buy my trousers?"

70   The ladies did not answer. They could not think of a good answer to that one.

71   "I," said the man, "am a manufacturer of trousers. I make the most beautiful trousers in Germany. Indeed in the world." (You do not so, thought Mrs. Forrester, picturing her husband's good London legs.) "For three years I receive orders from Winnipeg for my trousers. And now, since two years, yes, since 1929, I receive no more orders for my trousers. Why is that?" he asked, like a belligerent.

72   "Shall we tell him?" asked Mrs. Forrester, looking at Mrs. Montrose. Neither of them knew why he had received no more orders for his trousers, but they did not wish to say so. "Shall we tell him?" asked Mrs. Forrester.

73   "You tell him," said Mrs. Montrose.

74   "No, *you* tell him," said Mrs. Forrester.

75   "I do not like to tell him," said Mrs. Montrose, "I'd rather you told him."

76   The man with the blue tooth looked from one to the other.

77   "Very well. I shall tell him," said Mrs. Forrester. "The fact is," she said, looking downward, "that in Canada men no longer wear trousers."

78   "What are you saying? That is not true, never can that be true!" said the man in some confusion.

79   "Yes," said Mrs. Montrose, corroborating sombrely. "Yes, indeed that is true. When they go abroad they wear trousers, but in Canada, no. It is a new custom."

80   "It is the climate," said Mrs. Forrester.

81   "Yes, that is the reason, it is the climate," agreed Mrs. Montrose.

82 "But in Canada," argued the man with the blue tooth, "your climate is cold. Everyone knows your climate is cold."

83 "In the Arctic regions, yes, it is really intensely cold, we all find it so. But not in Winnipeg. Winnipeg is very salubrious." (That's a good one, thought Mrs. Montrose.)

84 The man turned and spoke rapidly to his wife. She also turned, and looked askance at her daughter. The expressions of the man, his wife, and his daughter were a blend of pleasure and shock. The two liars were delighted.

85 At last the man could not help asking, "But they *must* wear something! It is not logical."

86 "Oh, it's logical, all right!" said Mrs. Forrester.

87 "But what *do* they wear?" persisted the man.

88 "I never looked to see," said Mrs. Montrose. "*I* did, I looked," said Mrs. Forrester.

89 "Well?" asked the man.

90 "Oh, they just wear kilts," said Mrs. Forrester.

91 "Kilts? What are kilts? I do not know kilts," said the man.

92 "I would rather not tell you," said Mrs. Forrester primly.

93 "Oh," said the man.

94 Mrs. Montrose took out her vanity case, and inspected herself, powder puff in hand.

95 "I do not allow my wife and daughter to paint their faces so," said the man with the blue tooth.

96 "No?" said Mrs. Montrose.

97 "It is not good that women should paint their faces so. Good women do not do that. It is a pity."

98 (Oh, Alice, thought Mrs. Forrester in a fury, he shall not dare!) "It is a pity," she hissed, "that in your country there are no good dentists!"

99 "Be careful, be careful," whispered Mrs. Montrose.

100 "What do you mean?" demanded the man with the blue tooth.

101 (She will go too far, I know she will, thought Mrs. Montrose, alarmed, putting out her hand.)

102 "In our country," said the rash Mrs. Forrester "anyone needing attention is taken straight to the State Dentist by the Police. This is done for aesthetic reasons. It is logical."

103 "I am going to sleep," said Mrs. Montrose very loudly, and she shut her eyes tight.

104 "So am I," said Mrs. Forrester, in a great hurry, and she shut her eyes too. This had been hard work but good fun for Mrs. Montrose and Mrs. Forrester. They felt, though, that they had gone a bit too far. It might be as well if they slept, or pretended to sleep, until they reached Munich. They felt that outside their closed eyes was something frightening. The voice of the man with the blue tooth was saying, "I wish to tell you, I wish to tell you ..." but Mrs. Montrose was in a deep sleep, and so was Mrs. Forrester. They sat with their eyes tightly closed, beside the hamper which still occupied the seat with the view by the

darkening window. Mrs. Montrose had the inside corner, and so by reason of nestling down in the corner, and by reason of having an even and sensible temperament, she really and truly fell asleep at last.

105   Not so Mrs. Forrester. Her eyes were tightly closed, but her mind was greatly disturbed. Why had they permitted themselves to be baited? She pondered on the collective mentality that occupied the seat near to them (knees almost touching), and its results which now filled the atmosphere of the carriage so unpleasantly. She had met this mentality before, but had not been closely confined with it, as now. What of a world in which this mentality might ever become dominant? Then one would be confined with it without appeal or relief. The thought was shocking. She felt unreasonably agitated. She felt rather a fool, too, with her eyes shut tightly. But, if she opened them, she would have to look somewhere, presumably at the family, so it seemed safer to keep them closed. The train sped on. After what seemed to her a very long time, she peeped. The wife and daughter were busy. The husband sat back, hands on knees, chin raised, expectant, eyes closed. His wife respectfully undid his tie, his collar, and his top shirt button. By this time the daughter had opened the hamper, and had taken from it a bottle and a clean napkin. These she handed to her mother. The wife moistened the napkin from the bottle and proceeded to wash her husband, his face, his ears, round the back of his neck, and inside his shirt collar, with great care. "Like a cat," thought Mrs. Forrester, who had forgotten to shut her eyes.

106   The man with the blue tooth lowered his raised chin and caught her. "You see," he said loudly, "you see, wives should look properly after their husbands, instead of travelling alone and ..." But Mrs. Forrester was fast asleep again. The whole absurd encounter had begun to hold an element of terror. They had been tempted into folly. She knew—as she screwed up her closed eyes—that they were implicated in fear and folly.

107   The two young women took care to sleep until the train reached Munich. Then they both woke up.

108   Many people slept until they reached Munich. Then they all began to wake up.

(1945)

William Faulkner (1897–1962)

*Faulkner spent most of his life in his native Mississippi. Having left school
without graduating, he joined the Royal Canadian Air Force in 1918, lived
in New Orleans for a short time in the twenties, and clerked in a New York
bookstore for a few months, before publishing* The Marble Faun *(1924), a
book of poems. Many of his works focus on the fictional Yoknapatawpha
County and its characters and families. He won the Nobel Prize for literature in 1950.*

A Rose for Emily

1   When Miss Emily Grierson died, our whole town went to her funeral:
the men through a sort of respectful affection for a fallen monument,
the women mostly out of curiosity to see the inside of her house,
which no one save an old man-servant—a combined gardener and
cook—had seen in at least ten years.

2   It was a big, squarish frame house that had once been white, decorated with cupolas and spires and scrolled balconies in the heavily
lightsome style of the seventies, set on what had once been our most
select street. But garages and cotton gins had encroached and obliterated even the august names of that neighborhood; only Miss Emily's
house was left, lifting its stubborn and coquettish decay above the
cotton wagons and the gasoline pumps—an eyesore among eyesores.
And now Miss Emily had gone to join the representatives of those
august names where they lay in the cedar-bemused cemetery among
the ranked and anonymous graves of Union and Confederate soldiers
who fell at the battle of Jefferson.

3   Alive, Miss Emily had been a tradition, a duty, and a care; a sort of
hereditary obligation upon the town, dating from that day in 1894
when Colonel Sartoris, the mayor—he who fathered the edict that no
Negro woman should appear on the streets without an apron—
remitted her taxes, the dispensation dating from the death of her father
on into perpetuity. Not that Miss Emily would have accepted charity.
Colonel Sartoris invented an involved tale to the effect that Miss
Emily's father had loaned money to the town, which the town, as a
matter of business, preferred this way of repaying. Only a man of
Colonel Sartoris' generation and thought could have invented it, and
only a woman could have believed it.

4   When the next generation, with its more modern ideas, became mayors and aldermen, this arrangement created some little dissatisfaction. On the first of the year they mailed her a tax notice. February came, and there was no reply. They wrote her a formal letter, asking her to call at the sheriff's office at her convenience. A week later the mayor wrote her himself, offering to call or to send his car for her, and received in reply a note on paper of an archaic shape, in a thin, flowing calligraphy in faded ink, to the effect that she no longer went out at all. The tax notice was also enclosed, without comment.

5   They called a special meeting of the Board of Aldermen. A deputation waited upon her, knocked at the door through which no visitor had passed since she ceased giving her china-painting lessons eight or ten years earlier. They were admitted by the old Negro into a dim hall from which a stairway mounted into still more shadow. It smelled of dust and disuse—a close, dank smell. The Negro led them into the parlor. It was furnished in heavy, leather-covered furniture. When the Negro opened the blinds of one window, they could see that the leather was cracked; and when they sat down, a faint dust rose sluggishly about their thighs, spinning with slow motes in the single sun-ray. On a tarnished gilt easel before the fireplace stood a crayon portrait of Miss Emily's father.

6   They rose when she entered—a small, fat woman in black, with a thin gold chain descending to her waist and vanishing into her belt, leaning on an ebony cane with a tarnished gold head. Her skeleton was small and spare; perhaps that was why what would have been merely plumpness in another was obesity in her. She looked bloated, like a body long submerged in motionless water, and of that pallid hue. Her eyes, lost in the fatty ridges of her face, looked like two small pieces of coal pressed into a lump of dough as they moved from one face to another while the visitors stated their errand.

7   She did not ask them to sit. She just stood in the door and listened quietly until the spokesman came to a stumbling halt. They could hear the invisible watch ticking at the end of the gold chain.

8   Her voice was dry and cold. "I have no taxes in Jefferson. Colonel Sartoris explained it to me. Perhaps one of you can gain access to the city records and satisfy yourselves."

9   "But we have. We are the city authorities, Miss Emily. Didn't you get a notice from the sheriff, signed by him?"

10   "I received a paper, yes," Miss Emily said. "Perhaps he considers himself the sheriff ... I have no taxes in Jefferson."

11   "But there is nothing on the books to show that, you see. We must go by the—"

12   "See Colonel Sartoris. I have no taxes in Jefferson."

13   "But, Miss Emily—"

14   "See Colonel Sartoris." (Colonel Sartoris had been dead almost ten years.) "I have no taxes in Jefferson. Tobe!" The Negro appeared. "Show these gentlemen out."

II

15 So she vanquished them, horse and foot, just as she had vanquished their fathers thirty years before about the smell. That was two years after her father's death and a short time after her sweetheart—the one we believed would marry her—had deserted her. After her father's death she went out very little; after her sweetheart went away, people hardly saw her at all. A few of the ladies had the temerity to call, but were not received, and the only sign of life about the place was the Negro man—a young man then—going in and out with a market basket.

16 "Just as if a man—any man—could keep a kitchen properly," the ladies said; so they were not surprised when the smell developed. It was another link between the gross, teeming world and the high and mighty Griersons.

17 A neighbor, a woman, complained to the mayor, Judge Stevens, eighty years old.

18 "But what will you have me do about it, madam?" he said.

19 "Why, send her word to stop it," the woman said. "Isn't there a law?"

20 "I'm sure that won't be necessary," Judge Stevens said. "It's probably just a snake or a rat that nigger of hers killed in the yard. I'll speak to him about it."

21 The next day he received two more complaints, one from a man who came in diffident deprecation. "We really must do something about it, Judge. I'd be the last one in the world to bother Miss Emily, but we've got to do something." That night the Board of Aldermen met—three graybeards and one younger man, a member of the rising generation.

22 "It's simple enough," he said. "Send her word to have her place cleaned up. Give her a certain time to do it in, and if she don't ..."

23 "Dammit, sir," Judge Stevens said, "will you accuse a lady to her face of smelling bad?"

24 So the next night, after midnight, four men crossed Miss Emily's lawn and slunk about the house like burglars, sniffing along the base of the brickwork and at the cellar openings while one of them performed a regular sowing motion with his hand out of a sack slung from his shoulder. They broke open the cellar door and sprinkled lime there, and in all the outbuildings. As they recrossed the lawn, a window that had been dark was lighted and Miss Emily sat in it, the light behind her, and her upright torso motionless as that of an idol. They crept quietly across the lawn and into the shadow of the locusts that lined the street. After a week or two the smell went away.

25 That was when people had begun to feel really sorry for her. People in our town, remembering how old lady Wyatt, her great-aunt, had gone completely crazy at last, believed that the Griersons held themselves a little too high for what they really were. None of the young men were quite good enough for Miss Emily and such. We had long

thought of them as a tableau, Miss Emily a slender figure in white in the background, her father a spraddled[1] silhouette in the foreground, his back to her and clutching a horsewhip, the two of them framed by the back-flung front door. So when she got to be thirty and was still single, we were not pleased exactly, but vindicated; even with insanity in the family she wouldn't have turned down all of her chances if they had really materialized.

26   When her father died, it got about that the house was all that was left to her; and in a way, people were glad. At last they could pity Miss Emily. Being left alone, and a pauper, she had become humanized. Now she too would know the old thrill and the old despair of a penny more or less.

27   The day after his death all the ladies prepared to call at the house and offer condolence and aid, as is our custom. Miss Emily met them at the door, dressed as usual and with no trace of grief on her face. She told them that her father was not dead. She did that for three days, with the ministers calling on her, and the doctors, trying to persuade her to let them dispose of the body. Just as they were about to resort to law and force, she broke down, and they buried her father quickly.

28   We did not say she was crazy then. We believed she had to do that. We remembered all the young men her father had driven away, and we knew that with nothing left, she would have to cling to that which had robbed her, as people will.

III

29   She was sick for a long time. When we saw her again, her hair was cut short, making her look like a girl, with a vague resemblance to those angels in colored church windows—sort of tragic and serene.

30   The town had just let the contracts for paving and sidewalks, and in the summer after her father's death they began the work. The construction company came with niggers and mules and machinery, and a foreman named Homer Barron, a Yankee—a big, dark, ready man, with a big voice and eyes lighter than his face. The little boys would follow in groups to hear him cuss the niggers, and the niggers singing in time to the rise and fall of picks. Pretty soon he knew everybody in town. Whenever you heard a lot of laughing anywhere about the square, Homer Barron would be in the center of the group. Presently we began to see him and Miss Emily on Sunday afternoons driving in the yellow-wheeled buggy and the matched team of bays from the livery stable.

31   At first we were glad that Miss Emily would have an interest, because the ladies all said, "Of course a Grierson would not think seriously of a Northerner, a day laborer." But there were still others, older people, who said that even grief could not cause a real lady to forget

---

1. Sprawled.

noblesse oblige—without calling it *noblesse oblige*. They just said, "Poor Emily. Her kinsfolk should come to her." She had some kin in Alabama; but years ago her father had fallen out with them over the estate of old lady Wyatt, the crazy woman, and there was no communication between the two families. They had not even been represented at the funeral.

32 And as soon as the old people said, "Poor Emily," the whispering began. "Do you suppose it's really so?" they said to one another. "Of course it is. What else could …" This behind their hands; rustling of craned silk and satin behind jalousies closed upon the sun of Sunday afternoon as the thin, swift clop-clop-clop of the matched team passed: "Poor Emily."

33 She carried her head high enough—even when we believed that she was fallen. It was as if she demanded more than ever the recognition of her dignity as the last Grierson; as if it had wanted that touch of earthiness to reaffirm her imperviousness. Like when she bought the rat poison, the arsenic. That was over a year after they had begun to say "Poor Emily," and while two female cousins were visiting her.

34 "I want some poison," she said to the druggist. She was over thirty then, still a slight woman, though thinner than usual, with cold, haughty black eyes in a face the flesh of which was strained across the temples and about the eye-sockets as you imagine a lighthouse-keeper's face ought to look. "I want some poison," she said.

35 "Yes, Miss Emily. What kind? For rats and such? I'd recom—"

36 "I want the best you have. I don't care what kind."

37 The druggist named several. "They'll kill anything up to an elephant. But what you want is—"

38 "Arsenic," Miss Emily said. "Is that a good one?"

39 "Is … arsenic? Yes, ma'am. But what you want—"

40 "I want arsenic."

41 The druggist looked down at her. She looked back at him, erect, her face like a strained flag. "Why, of course," the druggist said. "If that's what you want. But the law requires you to tell what you are going to use it for."

42 Miss Emily just stared at him, her head tilted back in order to look him eye for eye, until he looked away and went and got the arsenic and wrapped it up. The Negro delivery boy brought her the package; the druggist didn't come back. When she opened the package at home there was written on the box, under the skull and bones: "For rats."

IV

43 So the next day we all said, "She will kill herself"; and we said it would be the best thing. When she had first begun to be seen with Homer Barron, we had said, "She will marry him." Then we said, "She will persuade him yet," because Homer himself had remarked—he liked

men, and it was known that he drank with the younger men in the Elks' Club—that he was not a marrying man. Later we said, "Poor Emily" behind the jalousies as they passed on Sunday afternoon in the glittering buggy, Miss Emily with her head high and Homer Barron with his hat cocked and a cigar in his teeth, reins and whip in a yellow glove.

44   Then some of the ladies began to say that it was a disgrace to the town and a bad example to the young people. The men did not want to interfere, but at last the ladies forced the Baptist minister—Miss Emily's people were Episcopal—to call upon her. He would never divulge what happened during the interview, but he refused to go back again. The next Sunday they again drove about the streets, and the following day the minister's wife wrote to Miss Emily's relations in Alabama.

45   So she had blood-kin under her roof again and we sat back to watch developments. At first nothing happened. Then we were sure that they were to be married. We learned that Miss Emily had been to the jeweler's and ordered a man's toilet set in silver, with the letters H.B. on each piece. Two days later we learned that she had bought a complete outfit of men's clothing, including a nightshirt, and we said, "They are married." We were really glad. We were glad because the two female cousins were even more Grierson than Miss Emily had been.

46   So we were surprised when Homer Barron—the streets had been finished some time since—was gone. We were a little disappointed that there was not a public blowing-off, but we believed that he had gone on to prepare for Miss Emily's coming, or to give her a chance to get rid of the cousins. (By that time it was a cabal, and we were all Miss Emily's allies to help circumvent the cousins.) Sure enough, after another week they departed. And, as we had expected all along, within three days Homer Barron was back in town. A neighbor saw the Negro man admit him at the kitchen door at dusk one evening.

47   And that was the last we saw of Homer Barron. And of Miss Emily for some time. The Negro man went in and out with the market basket, but the front door remained closed. Now and then we would see her at a window for a moment, as the men did that night when they sprinkled the lime, but for almost six months she did not appear on the streets. Then we knew that this was to be expected too; as if that quality of her father which had thwarted her woman's life so many times had been too virulent and too furious to die.

48   When we next saw Miss Emily, she had grown fat and her hair was turning gray. During the next few years it grew grayer and grayer until it attained an even pepper-and-salt iron-gray, when it ceased turning. Up to the day of her death at seventy-four it was still that vigorous iron-gray, like the hair of an active man.

49   From that time on her front door remained closed, save for a period of six or seven years, when she was about forty, during which she gave lessons in china-painting. She fitted up a studio in one of the down-

stairs rooms, where the daughters and granddaughters of Colonel Sartoris' contemporaries were sent to her with the same regularity and in the same spirit that they were sent to church on Sundays with a twenty-five-cent piece for the collection plate. Meanwhile her taxes had been remitted.

50 Then the newer generation became the backbone and the spirit of the town, and the painting pupils grew up and fell away and did not send their children to her with boxes of color and tedious brushes and pictures cut from the ladies' magazines. The front door closed upon the last one and remained closed for good. When the town got free postal delivery, Miss Emily alone refused to let them fasten the metal numbers above her door and attach a mailbox to it. She would not listen to them.

51 Daily, monthly, yearly we watched the Negro grow grayer and more stooped, going in and out with the market basket. Each December we sent her a tax notice, which would be returned by the post office a week later, unclaimed. Now and then we would see her in one of the downstairs windows—she had evidently shut up the top floor of the house—like the carven torso of an idol in a niche, looking or not looking at us, we could never tell which. Thus she passed from generation to generation—dear, inescapable, impervious, tranquil, and perverse.

52 And so she died. Fell ill in the house filled with dust and shadows, with only a doddering Negro man to wait on her. We did not even know she was sick; we had long since given up trying to get any information from the Negro. He talked to no one, probably not even to her, for his voice had grown harsh and rusty, as if from disuse.

53 She died in one of the downstairs rooms, in a heavy walnut bed with a curtain, her gray head propped on a pillow yellow and moldy with age and lack of sunlight.

V

54 The Negro met the first of the ladies at the front door and let them in, with their hushed, sibilant voices and their quick, curious glances, and then he disappeared. He walked right through the house and out the back and was not seen again.

55 The two female cousins came at once. They held the funeral on the second day, with the town coming to look at Miss Emily beneath a mass of bought flowers, with the crayon face of her father musing profoundly above the bier and the ladies sibilant and macabre; and the very old men—some in their brushed Confederate uniforms—on the porch and the lawn, talking of Miss Emily as if she had been a contemporary of theirs, believing that they had danced with her and courted her perhaps, confusing time with its mathematical progression, as the old do, to whom all the past is not a diminishing road but,

instead, a huge meadow which no winter ever quite touches, divided from them now by the narrow bottle-neck of the most recent decade of years.

56   Already we knew that there was one room in that region above stairs which no one had seen in forty years, and which would have to be forced. They waited until Miss Emily was decently in the ground before they opened it.

57   The violence of breaking down the door seemed to fill this room with pervading dust. A thin, acrid pall as of the tomb seemed to lie everywhere upon this room decked and furnished as for a bridal: upon the valance curtains of faded rose color, upon the rose-shaded lights, upon the dressing table, upon the delicate array of crystal and the man's toilet things backed with tarnished silver, silver so tarnished that the monogram was obscured. Among them lay a collar and tie, as if they had just been removed, which, lifted, left upon the surface a pale crescent in the dust. Upon a chair hung the suit, carefully folded; beneath it the two mute shoes and the discarded socks.

58   The man himself lay in the bed.

59   For a long while we just stood there, looking down at the profound and fleshless grin. The body had apparently once lain in the attitude of an embrace, but now the long sleep that outlasts love, that conquers even the grimace of love, had cuckolded him. What was left of him, rotted beneath what was left of the nightshirt, had become inextricable from the bed in which he lay; and upon him and upon the pillow beside him lay that even coating of the patient and biding dust.

60   Then we noticed that in the second pillow was the indentation of a head. One of us lifted something from it, and leaning forward, that faint and invisible dust dry and acrid in the nostrils, we saw a long strand of iron-gray hair.

(1930)

Langston Hughes (1902–1967)

A central figure of the Harlem Renaissance, Langston Hughes was an American poet, short-story writer, novelist, dramatist, children's writer, editor, and translator. Irony and humour characterize his work, which in large measure reflects the urban African-American culture of his time. See also Hughes's poems, p. 253.

On the Road

1   He was not interested in snow. When he got off the freight, one early evening during the depression, Sargeant never even noticed the snow. But he must have felt it seeping down his neck, cold, wet, sopping in his shoes. But if you had asked him, he wouldn't have known it was snowing. Sargeant didn't see the snow, not even under the bright lights of the main street, falling white and flaky against the night. He was too hungry, too sleepy, too tired.

2   The Reverend Mr. Dorset, however, saw the snow when he switched on his porch light, opened the front door of his parsonage, and found standing there before him a big black man with snow on his face, a human piece of night with snow on his face—obviously unemployed.

3   Said the Reverend Mr. Dorset before Sargeant even realized he'd opened his mouth: "I'm sorry. No! Go right on down this street four blocks and turn to your left, walk up seven and you'll see the Relief Shelter. I'm sorry. No!" He shut the door.

4   Sargeant wanted to tell the holy man that he had already been to the Relief Shelter, been to hundreds of relief shelters during the depression years, the beds were always gone and supper was over, the place was full, and they drew the color line anyhow. But the minister said, "No," and shut the door. Evidently he didn't want to hear about it. And he *had* a door to shut.

5   The big black man turned away. And even yet he didn't see the snow, walking right into it. Maybe he sensed it, cold, wet, sticking to his jaws, wet on his black hands, sopping in his shoes. He stopped and stood on the sidewalk hunched over—hungry, sleepy, cold—looking up and down. Then he looked right where he was—in front of a church. Of course! A church! Sure, right next to a parsonage, certainly a church.

6   It had *two* doors.

7   Broad white steps in the night all snowy white. Two high arched doors with slender stone pillars on either side. And way up, a round

lacy window with a stone crucifix in the middle and Christ on the crucifix in stone. All this was pale in the street light, solid and stony pale in the snow.

8   Sargeant blinked. When he looked up, the snow fell into his eyes. For the first time that night he *saw* the snow. He shook his head. He shook the snow from his coat sleeves, felt hungry, felt lost, felt not lost, felt cold. He walked up the steps of the church. He knocked at the door. No answer. He tried the handle. Locked. He put his shoulder against the door and his long black body slanted like a ramrod. He pushed. With loud rhythmic grunts, like the grunts in a chain-gang song, he pushed against the door.

9   "I'm tired … Huh! … Hongry … Uh! … I'm sleepy … Huh! I'm cold … I got to sleep somewheres," Sargeant said. "This is a church, ain't it? Well, uh!"

10   He pushed against the door.

11   Suddenly, with an undue cracking and screaking, the door began to give way to the tall black Negro who pushed ferociously against it.

12   By now two or three white people had stopped in the street, and Sargeant was vaguely aware of some of them yelling at him concerning the door. Three or four more came running, yelling at him.

13   "Hey!" they said. "Hey!"

14   "Uh-huh," answered the big tall Negro, "I know it's a white folks' church, but I got to sleep somewhere." He gave another lunge at the door. "Huh!"

15   And the door broke open.

16   But just when the door gave way, two white cops arrived in a car, ran up the steps with their clubs, and grabbed Sargeant. But Sargeant for once had no intention of being pulled or pushed away from the door.

17   Sargeant grabbed, but not for anything so weak as a broken door. He grabbed for one of the tall stone pillars beside the door, grabbed at it and caught it. And held it. The cops pulled and Sargeant pulled. Most of the people in the street got behind the cops and helped them pull.

18   "A big black unemployed Negro holding onto our church!" thought the people. "The idea!"

19   The cops began to beat Sargeant over the head, and nobody protested. But he held on.

20   And then the church fell down.

21   Gradually, the big stone front of the church fell down, the walls and the rafters, the crucifix and the Christ. Then the whole thing fell down, covering the cops and the people with bricks and stones and debris. The whole church fell down in the snow.

22   Sargeant got out from under the church and went walking on up the street with the stone pillar on his shoulder. He was under the impression that he had buried the parsonage and the Reverend Mr. Dorset who said, "No!" So he laughed, and threw the pillar six blocks up the street and went on.

23   Sargeant thought he was alone, but listening to the *crunch, crunch, crunch* on the snow of his own footsteps, he heard other footsteps, too, doubling his own. He looked around, and there was Christ walking beside him, the same Christ that had been on the cross on the church—still stone with a rough surface, walking along beside him just like he was broken off the cross when the church fell down.

24   "Well, I'll be dogged," said Sargeant. "This here's the first time I ever seed you off the cross."

25   "Yes," said Christ, crunching his feet in the snow. "You had to pull the church down to get me off the cross."

26   "You glad?" said Sargeant.

27   "I sure am," said Christ.

28   They both laughed.

29   "I'm a hell of a fellow, ain't I?" said Sargeant. "Done pulled the church down!"

30   "You did a good job," said Christ. "They have kept me nailed on a cross for nearly two thousand years."

31   "Whee-ee-e!" said Sargeant. "I know you are glad to get off."

32   "I sure am," said Christ.

33   They walked on in the snow. Sargeant looked at the man of stone.

34   "And you have been up there two thousand years?"

35   "I sure have," said Christ.

36   "Well, if I had a little cash," said Sargeant, "I'd show you around a bit."

37   "I been around," said Christ.

38   "Yeah, but that was a long time ago."

39   "All the same," said Christ, "I've been around."

40   They walked on in the snow until they came to the railroad yards. Sargeant was tired, sweating and tired.

41   "Where you goin'?" Sargeant said, stopping by the tracks. He looked at Christ. Sargeant said, "I'm just a bum on the road. How about you? Where you goin'?"

42   "God knows," Christ said, "but I'm leavin' here."

43   They saw the red and green lights of the railroad yard half veiled by the snow that fell out of the night. Away down the track they saw a fire in a hobo jungle.

44   "I can go there and sleep," Sargeant said.

45   "You can?"

46   "Sure," said Sargeant. "That place ain't got no doors."

47   Outside the town, along the tracks, there were barren trees and bushes below the embankment, snow-gray in the dark. And down among the trees and bushes there were makeshift houses made out of boxes and tin and old pieces of wood and canvas. You couldn't see them in the dark, but you knew they were there if you'd ever been on the road, if you had ever lived with the homeless and hungry in a depression.

48   "I'm side-tracking," Sargeant said. "I'm tired."

49   "I'm gonna make it on to Kansas City," said Christ.

50   "O.K.," Sargeant said. "So long!"

51   He went down into the hobo jungle and found himself a place to sleep. He never did see Christ no more. About 6:00 A.M. a freight train came by. Sargeant scrambled out of the jungle with a dozen or so more hobos and ran along the track, grabbing at the freight. It was dawn, early dawn, cold and gray.

52   "Wonder where Christ is by now?" Sargeant thought. "He musta gone on way on down the road. He didn't sleep in this jungle."

53   Sargeant grabbed the train and started to pull himself up into a moving coal car, over the edge of a wheeling coal car. But strangely enough, the car was full of cops. The nearest cop rapped Sargeant soundly across the knuckles with his night stick. Wham! Rapped his big black hands for clinging to the top of the car. Wham! But Sargeant did not turn loose. He clung on and tried to pull himself into the car. He hollered at the top of his voice, "Damn it, lemme in this car!"

54   "Shut up," barked the cop. "You crazy coon!" He rapped Sargeant across the knuckles and punched him in the stomach. "You ain't out in no jungle now. This ain't no train. You in jail."

55   Wham! across his bare black fingers clinging to the bars of his cell. Wham! between the steel bars low down against his shins.

56   Suddenly Sargeant realized that he really was in jail. He wasn't on no train. The blood of the night before had dried on his face, his head hurt terribly, and a cop outside in the corridor was hitting him across the knuckles for holding onto the door, yelling and shaking the cell door.

57   "They musta took me to jail for breaking down the door last night," Sargeant thought, "that church door."

58   Sargeant went over and sat on a wooden bench against the cold stone wall. He was emptier than ever. His clothes were wet, clammy cold wet, and shoes sloppy with snow water. It was just about dawn. There he was, locked up behind a cell door, nursing his bruised fingers.

59   The bruised fingers were his, but not the *door*.

60   Not the *club*, but the fingers.

61   "You wait," mumbled Sargeant, black against the jail wall. "I'm gonna break down this door, too."

62   "Shut up—or I'll paste you one," said the cop.

63   "I'm gonna break down this door," yelled Sargeant as he stood up in his cell.

64   Then he must have been talking to himself because he said, "I wonder where Christ's gone? I wonder if he's gone to Kansas City?"

(1935)

Mavis Gallant (b. 1922)

Born in Montreal, Mavis Gallant experienced painful loss when her father
died when she was ten and suffered significant dislocation, attending seven-
teen schools in Quebec before completing high school in New York City. She
returned to Montreal to become a reporter for The Montreal Standard
before turning to fiction writing. Though she has retained her Canadian citi-
zenship, Gallant has lived mainly in Paris since 1950. She is an Officer of
the Order of Canada and won the Governor General's Award in 1981.
Protective of her independence and privacy, she explores themes of identity,
relationships, loss, and isolation.

From the Fifteenth District

1   Although an epidemic of haunting, widely reported, spread through
the Fifteenth District of our city last summer, only three acceptable
complaints were lodged with the police.

2   Major Emery Travella, 31st Infantry, 1914–18, Order of the Leopard,
Military Beech Leaf, Cross of St. Lambert First Class, killed while
defusing a bomb in a civilian area 9 June, 1941, Medal of Danzig
(posthumous), claims he is haunted by the entire congregation of St.
Michael and All Angels on Bartholomew Street. Every year on the
Sunday falling nearest the anniversary of his death, Major Travella
attends Holy Communion service at St. Michael's, the church from
which he was buried. He stands at the back, close to the doors, waiting
until all the communicants have returned to their places, before he
approaches the altar rail. His intention is to avoid a mixed queue of
dead and living, the thought of which is disgusting to him. The congregation sits, hushed and expectant, straining to hear the Major's footsteps (he drags one foot a little). After receiving the Host, the Major
leaves at once, without waiting for the Blessing. For the past several
years, the Major has noticed that the congregation doubles in size as 9
June approaches. Some of these strangers bring cameras and tape
recorders with them; others burn incense under the pews and wave
amulets and trinkets in what they imagine to be his direction, muttering pagan gibberish all the while. References he is sure must be
meant for him are worked into the sermons: "And he that was dead sat
up, and began to speak" (Luke 7:15), or "So Job died, being old and
full of days" (Job 42:17). The Major points out that he never speaks

and never opens his mouth except to receive Holy Communion. He lived about sixteen thousand and sixty days, many of which he does not remember. On 23 September, 1914, as a young private, he was crucified to a cart wheel for five hours for having failed to salute an equally young lieutenant. One ankle was permanently impaired.

3   The Major wishes the congregation to leave him in peace. The opacity of the living, their heaviness and dullness, the moisture of their skin, and the dustiness of their hair are repellent to a man of feeling. It was always his habit to avoid civilian crowds. He lived for six years on the fourth floor in Block E, Stoneflower Gardens, without saying a word to his neighbors or even attempting to learn their names. An affidavit can easily be obtained from the former porter at the Gardens, now residing at the Institute for Victims of Senile Trauma, Fifteenth District.

***

4   Mrs. Ibrahim, aged thirty-seven, mother of twelve children, complains about being haunted by Dr. L. Chalmeton of Regius Hospital, Seventh District, and by Miss Alicia Fohrenbach, social investigator from the Welfare Bureau, Fifteenth District. These two haunt Mrs. Ibrahim without respite, presenting for her ratification and approval conflicting and unpleasant versions of her own death.

5   According to Dr. Chalmeton's account, soon after Mrs. Ibrahim was discharged as incurable from Regius Hospital he paid his patient a professional call. He arrived at a quarter past four on the first Tuesday of April, expecting to find the social investigator, with whom he had a firm appointment. Mrs. Ibrahim was discovered alone, in a windowless room, the walls of which were coated with whitish fungus a quarter of an inch thick, which rose to a height of about forty inches from the floor. Dr. Chalmeton inquired, "Where is the social investigator?" Mrs. Ibrahim pointed to her throat, reminding him that she could not reply. Several dark-eyed children peeped into the room and ran away. "How many are yours?" the Doctor asked. Mrs. Ibrahim indicated six twice with her fingers. "Where do they sleep?" said the Doctor. Mrs. Ibrahim indicated the floor. Dr. Chalmeton said, "What does your husband do for a living?" Mrs. Ibrahim pointed to a workbench on which the Doctor saw several pieces of finely wrought jewelry; he thought it a waste that skilled work had been lavished on what seemed to be plastics and base metals. Dr. Chalmeton made the patient as comfortable as he could, explaining that he could not administer drugs for the relief of pain until the social investigator had signed a receipt for them. Miss Fohrenbach arrived at five o'clock. It had taken her forty minutes to find a suitable parking space: the street appeared to be poor, but everyone living on it owned one or two cars. Dr. Chalmeton, who was angry at having been kept waiting, declared he would not be responsible for the safety of his patient in a room filled with mold. Miss

Fohrenbach retorted that the District could not resettle a family of fourteen persons who were foreign-born when there was a long list of native citizens waiting for accommodation. Mrs. Ibrahim had in any case relinquished her right to a domicile in the Fifteenth District the day she lost consciousness in the road and allowed an ambulance to transport her to a hospital in the Seventh. It was up to the hospital to look after her now. Dr. Chalmeton pointed out that housing of patients is not the business of hospitals. It was well known that the foreign poor preferred to crowd together in the Fifteenth, where they could sing and dance in the streets and attend one another's weddings. Miss Fohrenbach declared that Mrs. Ibrahim could easily have moved her bed into the kitchen, which was somewhat warmer and which boasted a window. When Mrs. Ibrahim died, the children would be placed in foster homes, eliminating the need for a larger apartment. Dr. Chalmeton remembers Miss Fohrenbach's then crying, "Oh, why do all these people come here, where nobody wants them?" While he was trying to think of an answer, Mrs. Ibrahim died.

6   In her testimony, Miss Fohrenbach recalls that she had to beg and plead with Dr. Chalmeton to visit Mrs. Ibrahim, who had been discharged from Regius Hospital without medicines or prescriptions or advice or instructions. Miss Fohrenbach had returned several times that April day to see if the Doctor had arrived. The first thing Dr. Chalmeton said on entering the room was "There is no way of helping these people. Even the simplest rules of hygiene are too complicated for them to follow. Wherever they settle, they spread disease and vermin. They have been responsible for outbreaks of aphthous stomatitis, hereditary hypoxia, coccidioidomycosis, gonorrheal arthritis, and scleroderma.[1] Their eating habits are filthy. They never wash their hands. The virus that attacks them breeds in dirt. We took in the patient against all rules, after the ambulance drivers left her lying in the courtyard and drove off without asking for a receipt. Regius Hospital was built and endowed for ailing Greek scholars. Now it is crammed with unteachable persons who cannot read or write." His cheeks and forehead were flushed, his speech incoherent and blurred. According to the social investigator, he was the epitome of the broken-down, irresponsible old rascals the Seventh District employs in its public services. Wondering at the effect this ranting of his might have on the patient, Miss Fohrenbach glanced at Mrs. Ibrahim and noticed she had died.

7   Mrs. Ibrahim's version of her death has the social investigator arriving first, bringing Mrs. Ibrahim a present of a wine-colored dressing gown made of soft, quilted silk. Miss Fohrenbach explained

---

1. Aphthous stomatitis: canker sores; hypoxia: deficiency of oxygen reaching the tissues; coccidioidomycosis: infectious influenza-like disease; gonorrheal arthritis: inflammation of joint(s) caused by venereal disease with inflammatory discharge from urethra or vagina; scleroderma: chronic hardening of the skin and connective tissue.

that the gown was part of a donation of garments to the needy. Large plastic bags, decorated with a moss rose, the emblem of the Fifteenth District, and bearing the words "Clean Clothes for the Foreign-Born," had been distributed by volunteer workers in the more prosperous streets of the District. A few citizens kept the bags as souvenirs, but most had turned them in to the Welfare Bureau filled with attractive clothing, washed, ironed, and mended, and with missing buttons replaced. Mrs. Ibrahim sat up and put on the dressing gown, and the social investigator helped her button it. Then Miss Fohrenbach changed the bed linen and pulled the bed away from the wall. She sat down and took Mrs. Ibrahim's hand in hers and spoke about a new, sunny flat containing five warm rooms which would soon be available. Miss Fohrenbach said that arrangements had been made to send the twelve Ibrahim children to the mountains for special winter classes. They would be taught history and languages and would learn to ski.

8   The Doctor arrived soon after. He stopped and spoke to Mr. Ibrahim, who was sitting at his workbench making an emerald patch box. The Doctor said to him, "If you give me your social-security papers, I can attend to the medical insurance. It will save you a great deal of trouble." Mr. Ibrahim answered, "What is social security?" The Doctor examined the patch box and asked Mr. Ibrahim what he earned. Mr. Ibrahim told him, and the Doctor said, "But that is less than the minimum wage." Mr. Ibrahim said, "What is a minimum wage?" The Doctor turned to Miss Fohrenbach, saying, "We really must try and help them." Mrs. Ibrahim died. Mr. Ibrahim, when he understood that nothing could be done, lay face down on the floor, weeping loudly. Then he remembered the rules of hospitality and got up and gave each of the guests a present—for Miss Fohrenbach a belt made of Syriac coins, a copy of which is in the Cairo Museum, and for the Doctor a bracelet of precious metal engraved with pomegranates, about sixteen pomegranates in all, that has lifesaving properties.

9   Mrs. Ibrahim asks that her account of the afternoon be registered with the police as the true version and that copies be sent to the Doctor and the social investigator, with a courteous request for peace and silence.

***

10   Mrs. Carlotte Essling, née Holmquist, complains of being haunted by her husband, Professor Augustus Essling, the philosopher and historian. When they were married, the former Miss Holmquist was seventeen. Professor Essling, a widower, had four small children. He explained to Miss Holmquist why he wanted to marry again. He said, "I must have one person, preferably female, on whom I can depend absolutely, who will never betray me even in her thoughts. A disloyal thought revealed, a betrayal even in fantasy, would be enough to destroy me. Knowing that I may rely upon some one person will leave

me free to continue my work without anxiety or distraction." The work was the Professor's lifelong examination of the philosopher Nicolas de Malebranche,[2] for whom he had named his eldest child. "If I cannot have the unfailing loyalty I have described, I would as soon not marry at all," the Professor added. He had just begun work on *Malebranche and Materialism*.

11   Mrs. Essling recalls that at seventeen this seemed entirely within her possibilities, and she replied something like "Yes, I see," or "I quite understand," or "You needn't mention it again."

12   Mrs. Essling brought up her husband's four children and had two more of her own, and died after thirty-six years of marriage at the age of fifty-three. Her husband haunts her with proof of her goodness. He tells people that Mrs. Essling was born an angel, lived like an angel, and is an angel in eternity. Mrs. Essling would like relief from this charge. "Angel" is a loose way of speaking. She is astonished that the Professor cannot be more precise. Angels are created, not born. Nowhere in any written testimony will you find a scrap of proof that angels are "good." Some are merely messengers; others have a paramilitary function. All are stupid.

13   After her death, Mrs. Essling remained in the Fifteenth District. She says she can go nowhere without being accosted by the Professor, who, having completed the last phase of his work *Malebranche and Mysticism*, roams the streets, looking in shopwindows, eating lunch twice, in two different restaurants, telling his life story to waiters and bus drivers. When he sees Mrs. Essling, he calls out, "There you are!" and "What have you been sent to tell me?" and "Is there a message?" In July, catching sight of her at the open-air fruit market on Dulac Street, the Professor jumped off a bus, upsetting barrows of plums and apricots, waving an umbrella as he ran. Mrs. Essling had to take refuge in the cold-storage room of the central market, where, years ago, after she had ordered twenty pounds of raspberries and currants for making jelly, she was invited by the wholesale fruit dealer, Mr. Lobrano, aged twenty-nine, to spend a holiday with him in a charming southern city whose Mediterranean Baroque churches he described with much delicacy of feeling. Mrs. Essling was too startled to reply. Mistaking her silence, Mr. Lobrano then mentioned a northern city containing a Gothic cathedral. Mrs. Essling said that such a holiday was impossible. Mr. Lobrano asked for one good reason. Mrs. Essling was at that moment four months pregnant with her second child. Three stepchildren waited for her out in the street. A fourth stepchild was at home looking after the baby. Professor Essling, working on his *Malebranche and Money*, was at home, too, expecting his lunch. Mrs. Essling realized she could not give Mr. Lobrano one good reason. She left the cold-storage room without another word and did not return to it in her lifetime.

---

2. Nicolas de Malebranche (1638–1715), one of the principal promoters of René Descartes (1596–1650), French philosopher, mathematician, and scientist.

14   Mrs. Essling would like to be relieved of the Professor's gratitude. Having lived an exemplary life is one thing; to have it thrown up at one is another. She would like the police to send for Professor Essling and tell him so. She suggests that the police find some method of keeping him off the streets. The police ought to threaten him; frighten him; put the fear of the Devil into him. Philosophy has made him afraid of dying. Remind him about how he avoided writing his *Malebranche and Mortality*. He is an old man. It should be easy.

(1978)

Nadine Gordimer (b. 1923)

A writer, critic, and editor, Nadine Gordimer is internationally known for her achievements in both the short story and the novel. Her work often focuses on the race relations and politics of her native South Africa. One critic has said that Gordimer "is one of the very few links between white and black in South Africa." Gordimer received the Nobel Prize for literature in 1991.

Town and Country Lovers

1   Dr. Franz-Josef von Leinsdorf is a geologist absorbed in his work; wrapped up in it, as the saying goes—year after year the experience of his work enfolds him, swaddling him away from the landscapes, the cities and the people, wherever he lives: Peru, New Zealand, the United States. He's always been like that, his mother could confirm from their native Austria. There, even as a handsome small boy he presented only his profile to her: turned away to his bits of rock and stone. His few relaxations have not changed much since then. An occasional skiing trip, listening to music, reading poetry—Rainer Maria Rilke once stayed in his grandmother's hunting lodge in the forests of Styria and the boy was introduced to Rilke's poems while very young.

2   Layer upon layer, country after country, wherever his work takes him—and now he has been almost seven years in Africa. First the Côte d'Ivoire, and for the past five years, South Africa. The shortage of skilled manpower brought about his recruitment here. He has no interest in the politics of the countries he works in. His private preoccupation-within-the-preoccupation of his work has been research into underground water-courses, but the mining company that employs him in a senior though not executive capacity is interested only in mineral discovery. So he is much out in the field—which is the veld, here—seeking new gold, copper, platinum and uranium deposits. When he is at home—on this particular job, in this particular country, this city—he lives in a two-roomed flat in a suburban block with a landscaped garden, and does his shopping at a supermarket conveniently across the street. He is not married—yet. That is how his colleagues, and the typists and secretaries at the mining company's head office, would define his situation. Both men and women would describe him as a good-looking man, in a foreign way, with the lower half of the face dark and middle-aged (his mouth is thin and curving, and no matter how close-shaven his beard shows like fine shot embedded in the skin round mouth and chin) and the upper half con-

tradictorily young, with deep-set eyes (some would say grey, some black), thick eyelashes and brows. A tangled gaze: through which concentration and gleaming thoughtfulness perhaps appear as fire and langour. It is this that the women in the office mean when they remark he's not unattractive. Although the gaze seems to promise, he has never invited any of them to go out with him. There is the general assumption he probably has a girl who's been picked for him, he's bespoken by one of his own kind, back home in Europe where he comes from. Many of these well-educated Europeans have no intention of becoming permanent immigrants; neither the remnant of white colonial life nor idealistic involvement with Black Africa appeals to them.

3   One advantage, at least, of living in underdeveloped or half-developed countries is that flats are serviced. All Dr. von Leinsdorf has to do for himself is buy his own supplies and cook an evening meal if he doesn't want to go to a restaurant. It is simply a matter of dropping in to the supermarket on his way from his car to his flat after work in the afternoon. He wheels a trolley up and down the shelves, and his simple needs are presented to him in the form of tins, packages, plastic-wrapped meat, cheeses, fruit and vegetables, tubes, bottles ... At the cashiers' counters where customers must converge and queue there are racks of small items uncategorized, for last-minute purchase. Here, as the coloured girl cashier punches the adding machine, he picks up cigarettes and perhaps a packet of salted nuts or a bar of nougat. Or razor-blades, when he remembers he's running short. One evening in winter he saw that the cardboard display was empty of the brand of blades he preferred, and he drew the cashier's attention to this. These young coloured girls are usually pretty unhelpful, taking money and punching their machines in a manner that asserts with the time-serving obstinacy of the half-literate the limit of any responsibility towards customers, but this one ran an alert glance over the selection of razor-blades, apologized that she was not allowed to leave her post, and said she would see that the stock was replenished "next time." A day or two later she recognized him, gravely, as he took his turn before her counter—"I ahssed them, but it's out of stock. You can't get it. I did ahss about it." He said this didn't matter. "When it comes in, I can keep a few packets for you." He thanked her.

4   He was away with the prospectors the whole of the next week. He arrived back in town just before nightfall on Friday, and was on his way from car to flat with his arms full of briefcase, suitcase and canvas bags when someone stopped him by standing timidly in his path. He was about to dodge round unseeingly on the crowded pavement but she spoke. "We got the blades in now. I didn't see you in the shop this week, but I kept some for you when you come. So ..."

5   He recognized her. He had never seen her standing before, and she was wearing a coat. She was rather small and finely-made, for one of them. The coat was skimpy but no big backside jutted. The cold brought an apricot-graining of warm colour to her cheekbones,

beneath which a very small face was quite delicately hollowed, and the skin was smooth, the subdued satiny colour of certain yellow wood. That crêpey hair, but worn drawn back flat and in a little knot pushed into one of the cheap wool chignons that (he recognized also) hung in the miscellany of small goods along with the razor-blades, at the supermarket. He said thanks, he was in a hurry, he'd only just got back from a trip—shifting the burdens he carried, to demonstrate. "Oh shame." She acknowledged his load. "But if you want I can run in and get it for you quickly. If you want."

6   He saw at once it was perfectly clear that all the girl meant was that she would go back to the supermarket, buy the blades and bring the packet to him there where he stood, on the pavement. And it seemed that it was this certainty that made him say, in the kindly tone of assumption used for an obliging underling, "I live just across there— *Atlantis*—that flat building. Could you drop them by, for me—number seven-hundred-and-eighteen, seventh floor—"

7   She had not before been inside one of these big flat buildings near where she worked. She lived a bus- and train-ride away to the West of the city, but this side of the black townships, in a township for people her tint. There was a pool with ferns, not plastic, and even a little waterfall pumped electrically over rocks, in the entrance of the building *Atlantis*; she didn't wait for the lift marked GOODS but took the one meant for whites and a white woman with one of those sausage-dogs on a lead got in with her but did not pay her any attention. The corridors leading to the flats were nicely glassed-in, not draughty.

8   He wondered if he should give her a twenty-cent piece for her trouble—ten cents would be right for a black; but she said, "Oh no— please, here—" standing outside his open door and awkwardly pushing back at his hand the change from the money he'd given her for the razor-blades. She was smiling, for the first time, in the dignity of refusing a tip. It was difficult to know how to treat these people, in this country; to know what they expected. In spite of her embarrassing refusal of the coin, she stood there, completely unassuming, fists thrust down the pockets of her cheap coat against the cold she'd come in from, rather pretty thin legs neatly aligned, knee to knee, ankle to ankle.

9   "Would you like a cup of coffee or something?"

10   He couldn't very well take her into his study-cum-living-room and offer her a drink. She followed him to his kitchen, but at the sight of her pulling out the single chair to drink her cup of coffee at the kitchen table, he said, "No—bring it in here—" and led the way into the big room where, among his books and his papers, his files of scientific correspondence (and the cigar boxes of stamps from envelopes) his racks of records, his specimens of minerals and rocks, he lived alone.

11   It was no trouble to her; she saved him the trips to the supermarket and brought him his groceries two or three times a week. All he had to

do was leave a list and the key under the doormat, and she would come up in her lunch-hour to collect them, returning to put his supplies in the flat after work. Sometimes he was home and sometimes not. He bought a box of chocolates and left it, with a note, for her to find; and that was acceptable, apparently, as a gratuity.

12   Her eyes went over everything in the flat although her body tried to conceal its sense of being out of place by remaining as still as possible, holding its contours in the chair offered her as a stranger's coat is set aside and remains exactly as left until the owner takes it up to go. "You collect?"

13   "Well, these are specimens—connected with my work."

14   "My brother used to collect. Miniatures. With brandy and whiskey and that, in them. From all over. Different countries."

15   The second time she watched him grinding coffee for the cup he had offered her she said, "You always do that? Always when you make coffee?"

16   "But of course. Is it no good, for you? Do I make it too strong?"

17   "Oh it's just I'm not used to it. We buy it ready—you know, it's in a bottle, you just add a bit to the milk or water."

18   He laughed, instructive: "That's not coffee, that's a synthetic flavouring. In my country we drink only real coffee, fresh, from the beans—you smell how good it is as it's being ground?"

19   She was stopped by the caretaker and asked what she wanted in the building? Heavy with the *bona fides* of groceries clutched to her body, she said she was working at number 718, on the seventh floor. The caretaker did not tell her not to use the whites' lift; after all, she was not black; her family was very light-skinned.

20   There was the item "grey button for trousers" on one of his shopping lists. She said as she unpacked the supermarket carrier "Give me the pants, so long, then," and sat on his sofa that was always gritty with fragments of pipe tobacco, sewing in and out through the four holds of the button with firm, fluent movements of the right hand, gestures supplying the articulacy missing from her talk. She had a little yokel's, peasant's (he thought of it) gap between her two front teeth when she smiled that he didn't much like, but, face ellipsed to three-quarter angle, eyes cast down in concentration with soft lips almost closed, this didn't much matter. He said, watching her sew, "You're a good girl"; and touched her.

21 She remade the bed every late afternoon when they left it and she dressed again before she went home. After a week there was a day when late afternoon became evening, and they were still in the bed.

22   "Can't you stay the night?"

23   "My mother," she said.

24   "Phone her. Make an excuse." He was a foreigner. He had been in the country five years, but he didn't understand that people don't usually have telephones in their houses, where she lived. She got up to

dress. He didn't want that tender body to go out in the night cold and kept hindering her with the interruption of his hands; saying nothing. Before she put on her coat, when the body had already disappeared, he spoke. "But you must make some arrangement."

25   "Oh my mother!" Her face opened to fear and vacancy he could not read.

26   He was not entirely convinced the woman would think of her daughter as some pure and unsullied virgin … "Why?"

27   The girl said, "S'e'll be scared. S'e'll be scared we get caught."

28   "Don't tell her anything. Say I'm employing you." In this country he was working in now there were generally rooms on the roofs of flat buildings for tenants' servants.

29   She said: "That's what I told the caretaker."

30   She ground fresh coffee beans every time he wanted a cup while he was working at night. She never attempted to cook anything until she had watched in silence while he did it the way he liked, and she learned to reproduce exactly the simple dishes he preferred. She handled his pieces of rock and stone, at first admiring the colours—"It'd make a beautiful ring or a necklace, ay." Then he showed her the striations, the formation of each piece, and explained what each was, and how, in the long life of the earth, it had been formed. He named the mineral it yielded, and what that was used for. He worked at his papers, writing, writing, every night, so it did not matter that they could not go out together to public places. On Sundays she got into his car in the basement garage and they drove to the country and picnicked away up in the Magaliesberg,[1] where there was no one. He read or poked about among the rocks; they climbed together, to the mountain pools. He taught her to swim. She had never seen the sea. She squealed and shrieked in the water, showing the gap between her teeth, as—it crossed his mind—she must do when among her own people. Occasionally he had to go out to dinner at the houses of colleagues from the mining company; she sewed and listened to the radio in the flat and he found her in bed, warm and already asleep, by the time he came in. He made his way into her body without speaking; she made him welcome without a word. Once he put on evening dress for a dinner at his country's consulate; watching him brush one or two fallen hairs from the shoulders of the dark jacket that sat so well on him, she saw a huge room all chandeliers and people dancing some dance from a costume film—stately, hand-to-hand. She supposed he was going to fetch, in her place in the car, a partner for the evening. They never kissed when either left the flat; he said, suddenly, kindly, pausing as he picked up cigarettes and keys, "Don't be lonely." And added, "Wouldn't you like to visit your family sometimes, when I have to go out?"

---

1. A mountain range north of Johannesburg.

31   He had told her he was going home to his mother in the forests and mountains of his country near the Italian border (he showed her on the map) after Christmas. She had not told him how her mother, not knowing there was any other variety, assumed he was a medical doctor, so she had talked to her about the doctor's children and the doctor's wife who was a very kind lady, glad to have someone who could help out in the surgery as well as the flat.

32   She remarked wonderingly on his ability to work until midnight or later, after a day at work. She was so tired when she came home from her cash register at the supermarket that once dinner was eaten she could scarcely keep awake. He explained in a way she could understand that while the work she did was repetitive, undemanding of any real response from her intelligence, requiring little mental or physical effort and therefore unrewarding, his work was his greatest interest, it taxed his mental capacities to their limit, exercised all his concentration, and rewarded him constantly as much with the excitement of a problem presented as with the satisfaction of a problem solved. He said later, putting away his papers, speaking out of a silence: "Have you done other kinds of work?" She said, "I was in a clothing factory before. Sportbeau shirts; you know? But the pay's better in the shop."

33   Of course. Being a conscientious newspaper-reader in every country he lived in, he was aware that it was only recently that the retail consumer trade in this one had been allowed to employ coloureds as shop assistants; even punching a cash register represented advancement. With the continuing shortage of semi-skilled whites a girl like this might be able to edge a little farther into the white-collar category. He began to teach her to type. He was aware that her English was poor, even though, as a foreigner, in his ears her pronunciation did not offend, nor categorize her as it would in those of someone of his education whose mother tongue was English. He corrected her grammatical mistakes but missed the less obvious ones because of his own sometimes exotic English usage—she continued to use the singular pronoun "it" when what was required was the plural "they." Because he was a foreigner (although so clever, as she saw) she was less inhibited than she might have been by the words she knew she misspelled in her typing. While she sat at the typewriter she thought how one day she would type notes for him, as well as making coffee that way he liked it, and taking him inside her body without saying anything, and sitting (even if only through the empty streets of quiet Sundays) beside him in his car, like a wife.

34   On a summer night near Christmas—he had already bought and hidden a slightly showy but nevertheless good watch he thought she would like—there was a knocking at the door that brought her out of the bathroom and him to his feet, at his work-table. No one ever came to the flat at night; he had no friends intimate enough to drop in without warning. The summons was an imperious banging that did not pause and clearly would not stop until the door was opened.

35   She stood in the open bathroom doorway gazing at him across the passage into the living-room; her bare feet and shoulders were free of a big bath-towel. She said nothing, did not even whisper. The flat seemed to shake with the strong unhurried blows.

36   He made as if to go to the door, at last, but now she ran and clutched him by both arms. She shook her head wildly; her lips drew back but her teeth were clenched, she didn't speak. She pulled him into the bedroom, snatched some clothes from the clean laundry laid out on the bed and got into the wall-cupboard, thrusting the key at his hand. Although his arms and calves felt weakly cold he was horrified, distastefully embarrassed at the sight of her pressed back crouching there under his suits and coat; it was horrible and ridiculous. *Come out!* he whispered. *No! Come out!* She hissed: *Where? Where can I go?*

37   *Never mind! Get out of there!*

38   He put out his hand to grasp her. At bay, she said with all the force of her terrible whisper, baring the gap in her teeth: *I'll throw myself out the window.*

39   She forced the key into his hand like the handle of a knife. He closed the door on her face and drove the key home in the lock, then dropped it among the coins in his trouser pocket.

40   He unslotted the chain that was looped across the flat door. He turned the serrated knob of the Yale lock. The three policemen, two in plain clothes, stood there without impatience although they had been banging on the door for several minutes. The big dark one with an elaborate moustache held out in a hand wearing a plaited gilt ring some sort of identity card.

41   Dr. von Leinsdorf said quietly, the blood coming strangely back to legs and arms, "What is it?"

42   The sergeant told him they knew there was a coloured girl in the flat. They had had information; "I been watching this flat three months, I know."

43   "I am alone here." Dr. von Leinsdorf did not raise his voice.

44   "I know, I know who is here. Come—" And the sergeant and his two assistants went into the living-room, the kitchen, the bathroom (the sergeant picked up a bottle of after-shave cologne, seemed to study the French label) and the bedroom. The assistants removed the clean laundry that was laid upon the bed and then turned back the bedding, carrying the sheets over to be examined by the sergeant under the lamp. They talked to one another in Afrikaans, which the Doctor did not understand. The sergeant himself looked under the bed, and lifted the long curtains at the window. The wall cupboard was of the kind that has no knobs; he saw that it was locked and began to ask in Afrikaans, then politely changed to English, "Give us the key."

45   Dr. von Leinsdorf said, "I'm sorry, I left it at my office—I always lock and take my keys with me in the mornings."

46   "It's no good, man, you better give me the key."

47   He smiled a little, reasonably. "It's on my office desk."

48   The assistants produced a screwdriver and he watched while they inserted it where the cupboard doors met, gave it quick, firm but not forceful leverage. He heard the lock give.

49   She had been naked, it was true, when they knocked. But now she was wearing a long-sleeved T-shirt with an appliquéd butterfly motif on one breast, and a pair of jeans. Her feet were still bare; she had managed, by feel, in the dark, to get into some of the clothing she had snatched from the bed, but she had no shoes. She had perhaps been weeping behind the cupboard door (her cheeks looked stained) but now her face was sullen and she was breathing heavily, her diaphragm contracting and expanding exaggeratedly and her breasts pushing against the cloth. It made her appear angry; it might simply have been that she was half-suffocated in the cupboard and needed oxygen. She did not look at Dr. von Leinsdorf. She would not reply to the sergeant's questions.

50   They were taken to the police station where they were at once separated and in turn led for examination by the district surgeon. The man's underwear was taken away and examined, as the sheets had been, for signs of his seed. When the girl was undressed, it was discovered that beneath her jeans she was wearing a pair of men's briefs with his name on the neatly-sewn laundry tag; in her haste, she had taken the wrong garment to her hiding-place.

51   Now she cried, standing there before the district surgeon in a man's underwear.

52   He courteously pretended not to notice. He handed briefs, jeans and T-shirt round the door, and motioned her to lie on a white-sheeted high table where he placed her legs apart, resting in stirrups, and put into her where the other had made his way so warmly a cold hard instrument that expanded wider and wider. Her thighs and knees trembled uncontrollably while the doctor looked into her and touched her deep inside with more hard instruments, carrying wafers of gauze.

53   When she came out of the examining room back to the charge office, Dr. von Leinsdorf was not there; they must have taken him somewhere else. She spent what was left of the night in a cell, as he must be doing; but early in the morning she was released and taken home to her mother's house in the coloured township by a white man who explained he was the clerk of the lawyer who had been engaged for her by Dr. von Leinsdorf. Dr. von Leinsdorf, the clerk said, had also been bailed out that morning. He did not say when, or if she would see him again.

54   A statement made by the girl to the police was handed in to Court when she and the man appeared to meet charges of contravening the Immorality Act in a Johannesburg flat on the night of — December, 19——. *I lived with the white man in his flat. He had intercourse with me sometimes. He gave me tablets to take to prevent me becoming pregnant.*

55   Interviewed by the Sunday papers, the girl said, "I'm sorry for the sadness brought to my mother." She said she was one of nine children of a female laundry worker. She had left school in Standard Three because there was no money at home for gym clothes or a school blazer. She had worked as a machinist in a factory and a cashier in a supermarket. Dr. von Leinsdorf taught her to type his notes.

56   Dr. Franz-Josef von Leinsdorf, described as the grandson of a baroness, a cultured man engaged in international mineralogical research, said he accepted social distinctions between people but didn't think they should be legally imposed. "Even in my own country it's difficult for a person from a higher class to marry one from a lower class."

57   The two accused gave no evidence. They did not greet or speak to each other in Court. The Defence argued that the sergeant's evidence that they had been living together as man and wife was hearsay. (The woman with the dachshund, the caretaker?) The magistrate acquitted them because the State failed to prove carnal intercourse had taken place on the night of — December, 19——.

58   The girl's mother was quoted, with photograph, in the Sunday papers: "I won't let my daughter work as a servant for a white man again."

(1980)

Margaret Laurence (1926–1987)

Born in Neepawa, Manitoba, and educated at United College, Winnipeg,
Margaret Laurence travelled in Africa with her husband in the 1950s, and
out of that experience came a novel, stories, a travel book, and translations
of folk tales. Her later writings focus on her prairie background and a world
she called Manawaka, in which she could explore generational, gender, and
ethnic tensions and elaborate her anti-colonial feelings. See "Where the
World Began," p. 41.

The Loons

1 Just below Manawaka, where the Wachakwa River ran brown and noisy over the pebbles, the scrub oak and grey-green willow and chokecherry bushes grew in a dense thicket. In a clearing at the centre of the thicket stood the Tonnerre family's shack. The basis of this dwelling was a small square cabin made of poplar poles and chinked with mud, which had been built by Jules Tonnerre some fifty years before, when he came back from Batoche with a bullet in his thigh, the year that Riel was hung and the voices of the Metis entered their long silence. Jules had only intended to stay the winter in the Wachakwa Valley, but the family was still there in the thirties, when I was a child. As the Tonnerres had increased, their settlement had been added to, until the clearing at the foot of the town hill was a chaos of lean-tos, wooden packing cases, warped lumber, discarded car tyres, ramshackle chicken coops, tangled strands of barbed wire and rusty tin cans.

2 The Tonnerres were French halfbreeds, and among themselves they spoke a *patois* that was neither Cree nor French. Their English was broken and full of obscenities. They did not belong among the Cree of the Galloping Mountain reservation, further north, and they did not belong among the Scots-Irish and Ukrainians of Manawaka, either. They were, as my Grandmother MacLeod would have put it, neither flesh, fowl, nor good salt herring. When their men were not working at odd jobs or as section hands on the C.P.R., they lived on relief. In the summers, one of the Tonnerre youngsters, with a face that seemed totally unfamiliar with laughter, would knock at the doors of the town's brick houses and offer for sale a lard-pail full of bruised wild strawberries, and if he got as much as a quarter he would grab the coin and run before the customer had time to change her mind. Sometimes old Jules, or his son Lazarus, would get mixed up in a Saturday-night

brawl, and would hit out at whoever was nearest, or howl drunkenly among the offended shoppers on Main Street, and then the Mountie would put them for the night in the barred cell underneath the Court House, and the next morning they would be quiet again.

3   Piquette Tonnerre, the daughter of Lazarus, was in my class at school. She was older than I, but she had failed several grades, perhaps because her attendance had always been sporadic and her interest in schoolwork negligible. Part of the reason she had missed a lot of school was that she had had tuberculosis of the bone, and had once spent many months in hospital. I knew this because my father was the doctor who had looked after her. Her sickness was almost the only thing I knew about her, however. Otherwise, she existed for me only as a vaguely embarrassing presence, with her hoarse voice and her clumsy limping walk and her grimy cotton dresses that were always miles too long. I was neither friendly nor unfriendly towards her. She dwelt and moved somewhere within my scope of vision, but I did not actually notice her very much until that peculiar summer when I was eleven.

4   "I don't know what to do about that kid," my father said at dinner one evening. "Piquette Tonnerre, I mean. The damn bone's flared up again. I've had her in hospital for quite a while now, and it's under control all right, but I hate like the dickens to send her home again."

5   "Couldn't you explain to her mother that she has to rest a lot?" my mother said.

6   "The mother's not there," my father replied. "She took off a few years back. Can't say I blame her. Piquette cooks for them, and she says Lazarus would never do anything for himself as long as she's there. Anyway, I don't think she'd take much care of herself, once she got back. She's only thirteen, after all. Beth, I was thinking—what about taking her up to Diamond Lake with us for the summer? A couple of months rest would give that bone a much better chance."

7   My mother looked stunned.

8   "But Ewen—what about Roddie and Vanessa?"

9   "She's not contagious," my father said. "And it would be company for Vanessa."

10   "Oh dear," my mother said in distress, "I'll bet anything she has nits in her hair."

11   "For Pete's sake," my father said crossly, "do you think Matron would let her stay in the hospital for all this time like that? Don't be silly, Beth."

12   Grandmother MacLeod, her delicately featured face as rigid as a cameo, now brought her mauve-veined hands together as though she were about to begin a prayer.

13   "Ewen, if that half-breed youngster comes along to Diamond Lake, I'm not going," she announced. "I'll go to Morag's for the summer."

14   I had trouble in stifling my urge to laugh, for my mother brightened visibly and quickly tried to hide it. If it came to a choice between

Grandmother MacLeod and Piquette, Piquette would win hands down, nits or not.

15   "It might be quite nice for you, at that," she mused. "You haven't seen Morag for over a year, and you might enjoy being in the city for a while. Well, Ewen dear, you do what you think is best. If you think it would do Piquette some good, then we'll be glad to have her, as long as she behaves herself."

16   So it happened that several weeks later, when we all piled into my father's old Nash, surrounded by suitcases and boxes of provisions and toys for my ten-month-old brother, Piquette was with us and Grandmother MacLeod, miraculously, was not. My father would only be staying at the cottage for a couple of weeks, for he had to get back to his practice, but the rest of us would stay at Diamond Lake until the end of August.

17   Our cottage was not named, as many were, "Dew Drop Inn" or "Bide-a-Wee," or "Bonnie Doon." The sign on the roadway bore in austere letters only our name, MacLeod. It was not a large cottage, but it was on the lakefront. You could look out the windows and see, through the filigree of the spruce trees, the water glistening greenly as the sun caught it. All around the cottage were ferns, and sharp-branched raspberry bushes, and moss that had grown over fallen tree trunks. If you looked carefully among the weeds and grass, you could find wild strawberry plants which were in white flower now and in another month would bear fruit, the fragrant globes hanging like miniature scarlet lanterns on the thin hairy stems. The two grey squirrels were still there, gossiping at us from the tall spruce beside the cottage, and by the end of the summer they would again be tame enough to take pieces of crust from my hands. The broad moose antlers that hung above the back door were a little more bleached and fissured after the winter, but otherwise everything was the same. I raced joyfully around my kingdom, greeting all the places I had not seen for a year. My brother, Roderick, who had not been born when we were here last summer, sat on the car rug in the sunshine and examined a brown spruce cone, meticulously turning it round and round in his small and curious hands. My mother and father toted the luggage from car to cottage, exclaiming over how well the place had wintered, no broken windows, thank goodness, no apparent damage from storm-felled branches or snow.

18   Only after I had finished looking around did I notice Piquette. She was sitting on the swing, her lame leg held stiffly out, and her other foot scuffling the ground as she swung slowly back and forth. Her long hair hung black and straight around her shoulders, and her broad coarse-featured face bore no expression—it was blank, as though she no longer dwelt within her own skull, as though she had gone elsewhere. I approached her very hesitantly.

19   "Want to come and play?"

20   Piquette looked at me with a sudden flash of scorn.

21   "I ain't a kid," she said.

22   Wounded, I stamped angrily away, swearing I would not speak to her for the rest of the summer. In the days that followed, however, Piquette began to interest me, and I began to interest her. My reasons did not appear bizarre to me. Unlikely as it may seem I had only just realised that the Tonnerre family, whom I had always heard called half-breeds, were actually Indians, or as near as made no difference. My acquaintance with Indians was not extensive. I did not remember ever having seen a real Indian, and my new awareness that Piquette sprang from the people of Big Bear and Poundmaker, of Tecumseh, of the Iroquois who had eaten Father Brebeuf's heart—all this gave her an instant attraction in my eyes. I was a devoted reader of Pauline Johnson[1] at this age, and sometimes would orate aloud in an exalted voice, *West Wind, blow from your prairie nest; Blow from the mountains, blow from the west*—and so on. It seemed to me that Piquette must be in some way a daughter of the forest, a kind of junior prophetess of the wilds, who might impart to me, if I took the right approach, some of the secrets which she undoubtedly knew—where the whippoorwill made her nest, how the coyote reared her young, or whatever it was that it said in Hiawatha.[2]

23   I set about gaining Piquette's trust. She was not allowed to go swimming, with her bad leg, but I managed to lure her down to the beach—or rather, she came because there was nothing else to do. The water was always icy, for the lake was fed by springs, but I swam like a dog, thrashing my arms and legs around at such a speed and with such an output of energy that I never grew cold. Finally, when I had had enough, I came out and sat beside Piquette on the sand. When she saw me approaching, her hand squashed flat the sand castle she had been building, and she looked at me sullenly, without speaking.

24   "Do you like this place?" I asked, after a while, intending to lead on from there into the question of forest lore.

25   Piquette shrugged. "It's okay. Good as anywhere."

26   "I love it," I said. "We come here every summer."

27   "So what?" Her voice was distant, and I glanced at her uncertainly, wondering what I could have said wrong.

28   "Do you want to come for a walk?" I asked her. "We wouldn't need to go far. If you just walk around the point there, you come to a bay where great big reeds grow in the water, and all kinds of fish hang around there. Want to? Come on."

29   She shook her head.

30   "Your dad said I ain't supposed to do no more walking than I got to."

31   I tried another line.

---

1. See p. 216.
2. *The Song of Hiawatha* (1855), a long narrative poem by Henry Wadsworth Longfellow.

32   "I bet you know a lot about the woods and all that, eh?" I began respectfully.

33   Piquette looked at me from her large dark unsmiling eyes.

34   "I don't know what in hell you're talkin' about," she replied. "You nuts or somethin'? If you mean where my old man, and me, and all them live, you better shut up, by Jesus, you hear?"

35   I was startled and my feelings were hurt, but I had a kind of dogged perseverance. I ignored her rebuff.

36   "You know something, Piquette? There's loons here, on this lake. You can see their nests just up the shore there, behind those logs. At night, you can hear them even from the cottage, but it's better to listen from the beach. My dad says we should listen and try to remember how they sound because in a few years when more cottages are built at Diamond Lake and more people come in, the loons will go away."

37   Piquette was picking up stones and snail shells and then dropping them again.

38   "Who gives a good goddamn?" she said.

39   It became increasingly obvious that, as an Indian, Piquette was a dead loss. That evening I went out by myself, scrambling through the bushes that overhung the steep path, my feet slipping on the fallen spruce needles that covered the ground. When I reached the shore, I walked along the firm damp sand to the small pier that my father had built, and sat down there. I heard someone else crashing through the undergrowth and the bracken, and for a moment I thought Piquette had changed her mind, but it turned out to be my father. He sat beside me on the pier and we waited, without speaking.

40   At night the lake was like black glass with a streak of amber which was the path of the moon. All around, the spruce trees grew tall and close-set, branches blackly sharp against the sky, which was lightened by a cold flickering of stars. Then the loons began their calling. They rose like phantom birds from the nests on the shore, and flew out onto the dark still surface of the water.

41   No one can ever describe that ululating sound, the crying of the loons, and no one who has heard it can ever forget it. Plaintive, and yet with a quality of chilling mockery, those voices belonged to a world separated by aeons from our neat world of summer cottages and the lighted lamps of home.

42   "They must have sounded just like that," my father remarked, "before any person ever set foot here."

43   Then he laughed. "You could say the same, of course, about sparrows, or chipmunks, but somehow it only strikes you that way with the loons."

44   "I know," I said.

45   Neither of us suspected that this would be the last time we would ever sit here together on the shore, listening. We stayed for perhaps half an hour, and then we went back to the cottage. My mother was

reading beside the fireplace. Piquette was looking at the burning birch log, and not doing anything.

46   "You should have come along," I said, although in fact I was glad she had not.

47   "Not me," Piquette said. "You wouldn' catch me walkin' way down there jus' for a bunch of squawkin' birds."

48   Piquette and I remained ill at ease with one another. I felt I had somehow failed my father, but I did not know what was the matter, nor why she would not or could not respond when I suggested exploring the woods or playing house. I thought it was probably her slow and difficult walking that held her back. She stayed most of the time in the cottage with my mother, helping her with the dishes or with Roddie, but hardly ever talking. Then the Duncans arrived at their cottage, and I spend my days with Mavis, who was my best friend. I could not reach Piquette at all, and I soon lost interest in trying. But all that summer she remained as both a reproach and a mystery to me.

49   That winter, my father died of pneumonia, after less than a week's illness. For some time I saw nothing around me, being completely immersed in my own pain and my mother's. When I looked outward once more, I scarcely noticed that Piquette Tonnerre was no longer at school. I do not remember seeing her at all until four years later, one Saturday night when Mavis and I were having Cokes in the Regal Café. The jukebox was booming like tuneful thunder, and beside it, leaning lightly on its chrome and its rainbow glass, was a girl.

50   Piquette must have been seventeen then, although she looked about twenty. I stared at her, astounded that anyone could have changed so much. Her face, so stolid and expressionless before, was animated now with a gaiety that was almost violent. She laughed and talked very loudly with the boys around her. Her lipstick was bright carmine, and her hair was cut short and frizzily permed. She had not been pretty as a child, and she was not pretty now, for her features were still heavy and blunt. But her dark and slightly slanted eyes were beautiful, and her skin-tight skirt and orange sweater displayed to enviable advantage a soft and slender body.

51   She saw me, and walked over. She teetered a little, but it was not due to her once-tubercular leg, for her limp was almost gone.

52   "Hi, Vanessa." Her voice still had the same hoarseness. "Long time no see, eh?"

53   "Hi," I said. "Where've you been keeping yourself, Piquette?"

54   "Oh, I been around," she said. "I been away almost two years now. Been all over the place—Winnipeg, Regina, Saskatoon. Jesus, what I could tell you! I come back this summer, but I ain't stayin'. You kids goin' to the dance?"

55   "No," I said abruptly, for this was a sore point with me. I was fifteen, and thought I was old enough to go to the Saturday-night dances at the Flamingo. My mother, however, thought otherwise.

56   "Y'oughta come," Piquette said. "I never miss one. It's just about the on'y thing in this jerkwater town that's any fun. Boy, you couldn' catch me stayin' here. I don' give a shit about this place. It stinks."

57   She sat down beside me, and I caught the harsh over-sweetness of her perfume.

58   "Listen, you wanna know something, Vanessa?" she confided, her voice only slightly blurred. "Your dad was the only person in Manawaka that ever done anything good to me."

59   I nodded speechlessly. I was certain she was speaking the truth. I knew a little more than I had that summer at Diamond Lake, but I could not reach her now any more than I had then. I was ashamed, ashamed of my own timidity, the frightened tendency to look the other way. Yet I felt no real warmth towards her—I only felt that I ought to, because of that distant summer and because my father had hoped she would be company for me, or perhaps that I would be for her, but it had not happened that way. At this moment, meeting her again, I had to admit that she repelled and embarrassed me, and I could not help despising the self-pity in her voice. I wished she would go away. I did not want to see her. I did not know what to say to her. It seemed that we had nothing to say to one another.

60   "I'll tell you something else," Piquette went on. "All the old bitches an' biddies in this town will sure be surprised. I'm gettin' married this fall—my boyfriend, he's an English fella, works in the stockyards in the city there, a very tall guy, got blond wavy hair. Gee, is he ever handsome. Got this real classy name. Alvin Gerald Cummings—some handle, eh? They call him Al."

61   For the merest instant, then, I saw her. I really did see her, for the first and only time in all the years we had both lived in the same town. Her defiant face, momentarily, became unguarded and unmasked, and in her eyes there was a terrifying hope.

62   "Gee, Piquette—" I burst out awkwardly, "that's swell. That's really wonderful. Congratulations—good luck—I hope you'll be happy—"

63   As I mouthed the conventional phrases, I could only guess how great her need must have been, that she had been forced to seek the very things she so bitterly rejected.

64   When I was eighteen, I left Manawaka and went away to college. At the end of my first year, I came back home for the summer. I spent the first few days in talking non-stop with my mother, as we exchanged all the news that somehow had not found its way into letters—what had happened in my life and what had happened here in Manawaka while I was away. My mother searched her memory for events that concerned people I knew.

65   "Did I ever write to you about Piquette Tonnerre, Vanessa?" she asked one morning.

66   "No, I don't think so," I replied. "Last I heard of her, she was going to marry some guy in the city. Is she still there?"

67   My mother looked perturbed, and it was a moment before she spoke, as though she did not know how to express what she had to tell and wished she did not need to try.

68   "She's dead," she said at last. Then, as I stared at her, "Oh, Vanessa, when it happened, I couldn't help thinking of her as she was that summer—so sullen and gauche and badly dressed. I couldn't help wondering if we could have done something more at that time—but what could we do? She used to be around in the cottage there with me all day, and honestly, it was all I could do to get a word out of her. She didn't even talk to your father very much, although I think she liked him, in her way."

69   "What happened?" I asked.

70   "Either her husband left her, or she left him," my mother said. "I don't know which. Anyway, she came back here with two youngsters, both only babies—they must have been born very close together. She kept house, I guess, for Lazarus and her brothers, down the valley there, in the old Tonnerre place. I used to see her on the street sometimes, but she never spoke to me. She'd put on an awful lot of weight, and she looked a mess, to tell you the truth, a real slattern, dressed any old how. She was up in court a couple of times—drunk and disorderly, of course. One Saturday night last winter, during the coldest weather, Piquette was alone in the shack with the children. The Tonnerres made home brew all the time, so I've heard, and Lazarus said later she'd been drinking most of the day when he and the boys went out that evening. They had an old woodstove there—you know the kind, with exposed pipes. The shack caught fire. Piquette didn't get out, and neither did the children."

71   I did not say anything. As so often with Piquette, there did not seem to be anything to say. There was a kind of silence around the image in my mind of the fire and the snow, and I wished I could put from my memory the look that I had seen once in Piquette's eyes.

72   I went up to Diamond Lake for a few days that summer, with Mavis and her family. The MacLeod cottage had been sold after my father's death, and I did not even go to look at it, not wanting to witness my long-ago kingdom possessed now by strangers. But one evening I went down to the shore by myself.

73   The small pier which my father had built was gone, and in its place there was a large and solid pier built by the government, for Galloping Mountain was now a national park, and Diamond Lake had been re-named Lake Wapakata, for it was felt that an Indian name would have a greater appeal to tourists. The one store had become several dozen, and the settlement had all the attributes of a flourishing resort—hotels, a dance-hall, cafés with neon signs, the penetrating odours of potato chips and hot dogs.

74   I sat on the government pier and looked out across the water. At night the lake at least was the same as it had always been, darkly shining and bearing within its black glass the streak of amber that was

the path of the moon. There was no wind that evening, and everything was quiet all around me. It seemed too quiet, and then I realized that the loons were no longer here. I listened for some time, to make sure, but never once did I hear that long-drawn call, half mocking and half plaintive, spearing through the stillness across the lake.

75 I did not know what had happened to the birds. Perhaps they had gone away to some far place of belonging. Perhaps they had been unable to find such a place, and had simply died out, having ceased to care any longer whether they lived or not.

76 I remembered how Piquette had scorned to come along, when my father and I sat there and listened to the lake birds. It seemed to me now that in some unconscious and totally unrecognised way, Piquette might have been the only one, after all, who had heard the crying of the loons.

                                                          (1966)

Timothy Findley (b. 1930–2002)

Once an actor, Timothy Findley became one of Canada's most celebrated authors of short stories, novels, plays, and screenplays. A most versatile and ambitious literary figure, he won the Governor General's Award in 1977 for his third novel, The Wars. *In "Dreams," as in much of his other work, Findley's characters move between the realms of the rational and the irrational.*

Dreams

For R.E. Turner

1   Doctor Menlo was having a problem: he could not sleep and his wife—the other Doctor Menlo—was secretly staying awake in order to keep an eye on him. The trouble was, in spite of her concern and in spite of all her efforts, Doctor Menlo—whose name was Mimi—was always nodding off because of her exhaustion.

2   She had tried drinking coffee, but this had no effect. She detested coffee and her system had a built-in rejection mechanism. She also prescribed herself a week's worth of Dexedrine to see if that would do the trick. *Five mg at bedtime*—all to no avail. And even though she put the plastic bottle of small orange hearts beneath her pillow and kept augmenting her intake, she would wake half an hour later with a dreadful start to discover the night was moving on to morning.

3   Everett Menlo had not yet declared the source of his problem. His restless condition had begun about ten days ago and had barely raised his interest. Soon, however, the time spent lying awake had increased from one to several hours and then, on Monday last, to all-night sessions. Now he lay in a state of rigid apprehension—eyes wide open, arms above his head, his hands in fists—like a man in pain unable to shut it out. His neck, his back and his shoulders constantly harried him with cramps and spasms. Everett Menlo had become a full-blown insomniac.

4   Clearly, Mimi Menlo concluded, her husband was refusing sleep because he believed something dreadful was going to happen the moment he closed his eyes. She had encountered this sort of fear in one or two of her patients. Everett, on the other hand, would not discuss the subject. If the problem had been hers, he would have said *such things cannot occur if you have gained control of yourself.*

5   Mimi began to watch for the dawn. She would calculate its approach by listening for the increase of traffic below the bedroom window. The

Menlos' home was across the road from the Manulife Centre—corner of Bloor and Bay streets. Mimi's first sight of daylight always revealed the high, white shape of its terraced storeys. Their own apartment building was of a modest height and colour—twenty floors of smoky glass and polished brick. The shadow of the Manulife would crawl across the bedroom floor and climb the wall behind her, grey with fatigue and cold.

6   The Menlo beds were an arm's length apart, and lying like a rug between them was the shape of a large, black dog of unknown breed. All night long, in the dark of his well, the dog would dream and he would tell the content of his dreams the way that victims in a trance will tell of being pursued by posses of their nameless fears. He whimpered, he cried and sometimes he howled. His legs and his paws would jerk and flail and his claws would scrabble desperately against the parquet floor. Mimi—who loved this dog—would lay her hand against his side and let her fingers dabble in his coat in vain attempts to soothe him. Sometimes, she had to call his name in order to rouse him from his dreams because his heart would be racing. Other times, she smiled and thought: *at least there's one of us getting some sleep.* The dog's name was Thurber and he dreamed in beige and white.

7   Everett and Mimi Menlo were both psychiatrists. His field was schizophrenia; hers was autistic children. Mimi's venue was the Parkin Institute at the University of Toronto; Everett's was the Queen Street Mental Health Centre. Early in their marriage they had decided never to work as a team and not—unless it was a matter of financial life and death—to accept employment in the same institution. Both had always worked with the kind of physical intensity that kills, and yet they gave the impression this was the only tolerable way in which to function. It meant there was always a sense of peril in what they did, but the peril—according to Everett—made their lives worth living. This, at least, had been his theory twenty years ago when they were young.

8   Now, for whatever unnamed reason, peril had become his enemy and Everett Menlo had begun to look and behave and lose his sleep like a haunted man. But he refused to comment when Mimi asked him what was wrong. Instead, he gave the worst of all possible answers a psychiatrist can hear who seeks an explanation of a patient's silence: he said there was *absolutely nothing wrong.*

9   "You're sure you're not coming down with something?"

10   "Yes."

11   "And you wouldn't like a massage?"

12   "I've already told you: no."

13   "Can I get you anything?"

14   "No."

15   "And you don't want to talk?"

16   "That's right."

17   "Okay, Everett ..."

18   "Okay, what?"

19   "Okay, nothing. I only hope you get some sleep tonight."

20   Everett stood up. "Have you been spying on me, Mimi?"

21   "What do you mean by *spying*?"

22   "Watching me all night long."

23   "Well, Everett, I don't see how I can fail to be aware you aren't asleep when we share this bedroom. I mean—I can hear you grinding your teeth. I can see you lying there wide awake."

24   "When?"

25   "All the time. You're staring at the ceiling."

26   "I've never stared at the ceiling in my whole life. I sleep on my stomach."

27   "You sleep on your stomach *if* you sleep. But you have not been sleeping. Period. No argument."

28   Everett Menlo went to his dresser and got out a pair of clean pyjamas. Turning his back on Mimi, he put them on.

29   Somewhat amused at the coyness of this gesture, Mimi asked what he was hiding.

30   "Nothing!" he shouted at her.

31   Mimi's mouth fell open. Everett never yelled. His anger wasn't like that; it manifested itself in other ways, in silence and withdrawal, never shouts.

32   Everett was staring at her defiantly. He had slammed the bottom drawer of his dresser. Now he was fumbling with the wrapper of a pack of cigarettes.

33   Mimi's stomach tied a knot.

34   Everett hadn't touched a cigarette for weeks.

35   "Please don't smoke those," she said. "You'll only be sorry if you do."

36   "And you," he said, "will be sorry if I don't."

37   "But, dear … ," said Mimi.

38   "Leave me for Christ's sake alone!" Everett yelled.

39   Mimi gave up and sighed and then she said: "all right. Thurber and I will go and sleep in the living-room. Goodnight."

40   Everett sat on the edge of his bed. His hands were shaking.

41   "Please," he said—apparently addressing the floor. "Don't leave me here alone. I couldn't bear that."

42   This was perhaps the most chilling thing he could have said to her. Mimi was alarmed; her husband was genuinely terrified of something and he would not say what it was. If she had not been who she was— if she had not known what she knew—if her years of training had not prepared her to watch for signs like this, she might have been better off. As it was, she had to face the possibility the strongest, most sensible man on earth was having a nervous breakdown of major proportions. Lots of people have breakdowns, of course, but not, she had thought, the gods of reason.

43   "All right," she said—her voice maintaining the kind of calm she knew a child afraid of the dark would appreciate. "In a minute I'll get us something to drink. But first I'll go and change...."

44   Mimi went into the sanctum of the bathroom, where her nightgown waited for her—a portable hiding-place hanging on the back of the door. "You stay here," she said to Thurber, who had padded after her. "Mama will be out in just a moment."

45   Even in the dark, she could gauge Everett's tension. His shadow—all she could see of him—twitched from time to time and the twitching took on a kind of lurching rhythm, something like the broken clock in their living-room.

46   Mimi lay on her side and tried to close her eyes. But her eyes were tied to a will of their own and would not obey her. Now she, too, was caught in the same irreversible tide of sleeplessness that bore her husband backward through the night. Four or five times she watched him lighting cigarettes—blowing out the matches, courting disaster in the bedclothes—conjuring the worst of deaths for the three of them: a flaming pyre on the twentieth floor.

47   All this behaviour was utterly unlike him; foreign to his code of disciplines and ethics; alien to everything he said and believed. *Openness, directness, sharing of ideas, encouraging imaginative response to every problem. Never hide troubles. Never allow despair ...* These were his directives in everything he did. Now, he had thrown them over.

48   One thing was certain. She was not the cause of his sleeplessness. She didn't have affairs and neither did he. He might be ill—but whenever he'd been ill before, there had been no trauma; never a trauma like this one, at any rate. Perhaps it was something about a patient—one of his tougher cases; a wall in the patient's condition they could not break through; some circumstance of someone's lack of progress—a sudden veering towards a catatonic state, for instance—something that Everett had not foreseen that had stymied him and was slowly ... what? Destroying his sense of professional control? His self-esteem? His scientific certainty? If only he would speak.

49   Mimi thought about her own worst case: a child whose obstinant refusal to communicate was currently breaking her heart and, thus, her ability to help. If ever she had needed Everett to talk to, it was now. All her fellow doctors were locked in a battle over this child; they wanted to take him away from her. Mimi refused to give him up; he might as well have been her own flesh and blood. Everything had been done—from gentle holding sessions to violent bouts of manufactured anger—in her attempt to make the child react. She was staying with him every day from the moment he was roused to the moment he was induced to sleep with drugs.

50   His name was Brian Bassett and he was eight years old. He sat on the floor in the furthest corner he could achieve in one of the observation-isolation rooms where all the autistic children were placed when

nothing else in their treatment—nothing of love or expertise—had managed to break their silence. Mostly, this was a signal they were coming to the end of life.

51   There in his four-square, glass-box room, surrounded by all that can tempt a child if a child can be tempted—toys and food and story-book companions—Brian Bassett was in the process, now, of fading away. His eyes were never closed and his arms were restrained. He was attached to three machines that nurtured him with all that science can offer. But of course, the spirit and the will to live cannot be fed by force to those who do not want to feed.

52   Now, in the light of Brian Bassett's utter lack of willing contact with the world around him—his utter refusal to communicate—Mimi watched her husband through the night. Everett stared at the ceiling, lit by the Manulife building's distant lamps, borne on his back further and further out to sea. She had lost him, she was certain.

53   When, at last, he saw that Mimi had drifted into her own and welcome sleep, Everett rose from the bed and went out into the hall, past the simulated jungle of the solarium, until he reached the dining-room. There, all the way till dawn, he amused himself with two decks of cards and endless games of Dead Man's Solitaire.

54   Thurber rose and shuffled after him. The dining-room was one of Thurber's favourite places in all his confined but privileged world, for it was here—as in the kitchen—that from time to time a hand descended filled with the miracle of food. But whatever it was that his master was doing up there above him on the table-top, it wasn't anything to do with feeding or with being fed. The playing cards had an old and dusty dryness to their scent and they held no appeal for the dog. So he once again lay down and he took up his dreams, which at least gave his paws some exercise. This way, he failed to hear the advent of a new dimension to his master's problems. This occurred precisely at 5:45 A.M. when the telephone rang and Everett Menlo, having rushed to answer it, waited breathless for a minute while he listened and then said: "yes" in a curious, strangulated fashion. Thurber—had he been awake—would have recognized in his master's voice the signal for disaster.

55   For weeks now, Everett had been working with a patient who was severely and uniquely schizophrenic. This patient's name was Kenneth Albright, and while he was deeply suspicious, he was also oddly caring. Kenneth Albright loved the detritus of life, such as bits of woolly dust and wads of discarded paper. He loved all dried-up leaves that had drifted from their parent trees and he loved the dead bees that had curled up to die along the window-sill of his ward. He also loved the spiderwebs seen high up in the corners of the rooms where he sat on plastic chairs and ate with plastic spoons.

56   Kenneth Albright talked a lot about his dreams. But his dreams had become, of late, a major stumbling block in the process of his

recovery. Back in the days when Kenneth had first become Doctor Menlo's patient, the dreams had been overburdened with detail: "overcast," as he would say, "with characters" and over-produced, again in Kenneth's phrase, "as if I were dreaming the dreams of Cecil B. de Mille."

57   Then he had said: "but a person can't really dream someone else's dreams. Or can they, Doctor Menlo?"

58   "No" had been Everett's answer—definite and certain.

59   Everett Menlo had been delighted, at first, with Kenneth Albright's dreams. They had been immensely entertaining—complex and filled with intriguing detail. Kenneth himself was at a loss to explain the meaning of these dreams, but as Everett had said, it wasn't Kenneth's job to explain. That was Everett's job. His job and his pleasure. For quite a long while, during these early sessions, Everett had written out the dreams, taken them home and recounted them to Mimi.

60   Kenneth Albright was a paranoid schizophrenic. Four times now, he had attempted suicide. He was a fiercely angry man at times—and at other times as gentle and as pleasant as a docile child. He had suffered so greatly, in the very worst moments of his disease, that he could no longer work. His job—it was almost an incidental detail in his life and had no importance for him, so it seemed—was returning reference books, in the Metro Library, to their places in the stacks. Sometimes—mostly late of an afternoon—he might begin a psychotic episode of such profound dimensions that he would attempt his suicide right behind the counter and even once, in the full view of everyone, while riding in the glass-walled elevator. It was after this last occasion that he was brought, in restraints, to be a resident patient at the Queen Street Mental Health Centre. He had slashed his wrists with a razor—but not before he had also slashed and destroyed an antique copy of *Don Quixote*, the pages of which he pasted to the walls with blood.

61   For a week thereafter, Kenneth Albright—just like Brian Bassett—had refused to speak or to move. Everett had him kept in an isolation cell, force-fed and drugged. Slowly, by dint of patience, encouragement and caring even Kenneth could recognize as genuine, Everett Menlo had broken through the barrier. Kenneth was removed from isolation, pampered with food and cigarettes, and he began relating his dreams.

62   At first there seemed to be only the dreams and nothing else in Kenneth's memory. Broken pencils, discarded toys and the telephone directory all had roles to play in these dreams but there were never any people. All the weather was bleak and all the landscapes were empty. Houses, motor cars and office buildings never made an appearance. Sounds and smells had some importance, the wind would blow, the scent of unseen fires was often described. Stairwells were plentiful, leading nowhere, all of them rising from a subterranean world that Kenneth either did not dare to visit or would not describe.

63   The dreams had little variation, one from another. The themes had mostly to do with loss and with being lost. The broken pencils were all

given names and the discarded toys were given to one another as companions. The telephone books were the sources of recitations—hours and hours of repeated names and numbers, some of which—Everett had noted with surprise—were absolutely accurate.

64   All of this held fast until an incident occurred one morning that changed the face of Kenneth Albright's schizophrenia forever; an incident that stemmed—so it seemed—from something he had dreamed the night before.

65   Bearing in mind his previous attempts at suicide, it will be obvious that Kenneth Albright was never far from sight at the Queen Street Mental Health Centre. He was, in fact, under constant observation; constant, that is, as human beings and modern technology can manage. In the ward to which he was ultimately consigned, for instance, the toilet cabinets had no doors and the shower-rooms had no locks. Therefore, a person could not ever be alone with water, glass or shaving utensils. (All the razors were cordless automatics.) Scissors and knives were banned, as were pieces of string and rubber bands. A person could not even kill his feet and hands by binding up his wrists and ankles. Nothing poisonous was anywhere available. All the windows were barred. All the double doors between this ward and the corridors beyond were doors with triple locks and a guard was always near at hand.

66   Still, if people want to die, they will find a way. Mimi Menlo would discover this to her everlasting sorrow with Brian Bassett. Everett Menlo would discover this to his everlasting horror with Kenneth Albright.

67   On the morning of April 19th, a Tuesday, Everett Menlo, in the best of health, had welcomed a brand-new patient into his office. This was Anne Marie Wilson, a young and brilliant pianist whose promising career had been halted mid-flight by a schizophrenic incident involving her ambition. She was, it seemed, no longer able to play and all her dreams were shattered. The cause was simple, to all appearances: Anne Marie had a sense of how, precisely, the music should be and she had not been able to master it accordingly. "Everything I attempt is terrible," she had said—in spite of all her critical accolades and all her professional success. Other doctors had tried and failed to break the barriers in Anne Marie, whose hands had taken on a life of their own, refusing altogether to work for her. Now it was Menlo's turn and hope was high.

68   Everett had been looking forward to his session with this prodigy. He loved all music and he thought to find some means within its discipline to reach her. She seemed so fragile, sitting there in the sunlight, and he had just begun to take his first notes when the door flew open and Louise, his secretary, had said: "I'm sorry, Doctor Menlo. There's a problem. Can you come with me at once?"

69   Everett excused himself.

70 Anne Marie was left in the sunlight to bide her time. Her fingers were moving around in her lap and she put them in her mouth to make them quiet.

71 Even as he'd heard his secretary speak, Everett had known the problem would be Kenneth Albright. Something in Kenneth's eyes had warned him there was trouble on the way: a certain wariness that indicated all was not as placid as it should have been, given his regimen of drugs. He had stayed long hours in one position, moving his fingers over his thighs as if to dry them on his trousers; watching his fellow patients come and go with abnormal interest—never, however, rising from his chair. An incident was on the horizon and Everett had been waiting for it, hoping it would come.

72 Louise had said that Doctor Menlo was to go at once to Kenneth Albright's ward. Everett had run the whole way. Only after the attendant had let him past the double doors, did he slow his pace to a hurried walk and wipe his brow. He didn't want Kenneth to know how alarmed he had been.

73 Coming to the appointed place, he paused before he entered, closing his eyes, preparing himself for whatever he might have to see. *Other people have killed themselves: I've seen it often enough*, he was thinking. *I simply won't let it affect me.* Then he went in.

74 The room was small and white—a dining-room—and Kenneth was sitting down in a corner, his back pressed out against the walls on either side of him. His head was bowed and his legs drawn up and he was obviously trying to hide without much success. An intern was standing above him and a nurse was kneeling down beside him. Several pieces of bandaging with blood on them were scattered near Kenneth's feet and there was a white enamel basin filled with pinkish water on the floor beside the nurse.

75 "Morowetz," Everett said to the intern. "Tell me what happened here." He said this just the way he posed such questions when he took the interns through the wards at examination time, quizzing them on symptoms and prognoses.

76 But Morowetz the intern had no answer. He was puzzled. What had happened had no sane explanation.

77 Everett turned to Charterhouse, the nurse.

78 "On the morning of April 19th, at roughly ten-fifteen, I found Kenneth Albright covered with blood," Ms Charterhouse was to write in her report. "His hands, his arms, his face and his neck were stained. I would say the blood was fresh and the patient's clothing—mostly his shirt—was wet with it. Some—a very small amount of it—had dried on his forehead. The rest was uniformly the kind of blood you expect to find free-flowing from a wound. I called for assistance and meanwhile attempted to ascertain where Mister Albright might have been injured. I performed this examination without success. I could find no source of bleeding anywhere on Mister Albright's body."

79   Morowetz concurred.

80   The blood was someone else's.

81   "Was there a weapon of any kind?" Doctor Menlo had wanted to know.

82   "No, sir. Nothing," said Charterhouse.

83   "And was he alone when you found him?"

84   "Yes, sir. Just like this in the corner."

85   "And the others?"

86   "All the patients in the ward were examined," Morowetz told him.

87   "And?"

88   "Not one of them was bleeding."

89   Everett said: "I see."

90   He looked down at Kenneth.

91   "This is Doctor Menlo, Kenneth. Have you anything to tell me?"

92   Kenneth did not reply.

93   Everett said: "When you've got him back in his room and tranquil-lized, will you call me, please?"

94   Morowetz nodded.

95   The call never came. Kenneth had fallen asleep. Either the drugs he was given had knocked him out cold, or he had opted for silence. Either way, he was incommunicado.

96   No one was discovered bleeding. Nothing was found to indicate an accident, a violent attack, an epileptic seizure. A weapon was not located. Kenneth Albright had not a single scratch on his flesh from stem, as Everett put it, to gudgeon. The blood, it seemed, had fallen like the rain from heaven: unexplained and inexplicable.

97   Later, as the day was ending, Everett Menlo left the Queen Street Mental Health Centre. He made his way home on the Queen streetcar and the Bay bus. When he reached the apartment, Thurber was waiting for him. Mimi was at a goddamned meeting.

98   That was the night Everett Menlo suffered the first of his failures to sleep. It was occasioned by the fact that, when he awakened sometime after three, he had just been dreaming. This, of course, was not unusual—but the dream itself was perturbing. There was someone lying there, in the bright white landscape of a hospital dining-room. Whether it was a man or a woman could not be told, it was just a human body, lying down in a pool of blood.

99   Kenneth Albright was kneeling beside this body; pulling it open the way a child will pull a Christmas present open—yanking at its strings and ribbons, wanting only to see the contents. Everett saw this scene from several angles, never speaking, never being spoken to. In all the time he watched—the usual dream eternity—the silence was broken only by the sound of water dripping from an unseen tap. Then, Kenneth Albright rose and was covered with blood, the way he had been that morning. He stared at Doctor Menlo, looked right through him and departed. Nothing remained in the dining-room but plastic tables and plastic chairs and the bright red thing on the floor that once

had been a person. Everett Menlo did not know and could not guess who this person might have been. He only knew that Kenneth Albright had left this person's body in Everett Menlo's dream.

100   Three nights running, the corpse remained in its place and every time that Everett entered the dining-room in the nightmare he was certain he would find out who it was. On the fourth night, fully expecting to discover he himself was the victim, he beheld the face and saw it was a stranger.

101   *But there are no strangers in dreams*; he knew that now after twenty years of practice. *There are no strangers; there are only people in disguise.*

102   Mimi made one final attempt in Brian Bassett's behalf to turn away the fate to which his other doctors—both medical and psychiatric—had consigned him. Not that, as a group, they had failed to expend the full weight of all they knew and all they could do to save him. One of his medical doctors—a woman whose name was Juliet Bateman—had moved a cot into his isolation room and stayed with him twenty-four hours a day for over a week. But her health had been undermined by this and when she succumbed to the Shanghai flu she removed herself for fear of infecting Brian Bassett.

103   The parents had come and gone on a daily basis for months in a killing routine of visits. But parents, their presence and their loving, are not the answer when a child has fallen into an autistic state. They might as well have been strangers. And so they had been advised to stay away.

104   Brian Bassett was eight years old—*unlucky eight*, as one of his therapists had said—and in every other way, in terms of physical development and mental capability, he had always been a perfectly normal child. Now, in the final moments of his life, he weighed a scant thirty pounds, when he should have weighed twice that much.

105   Brian had not been heard to speak a single word in over a year of constant observation. Earlier—long ago as seven months—a few expressions would visit his face from time to time. Never a smile—but often a kind of sneer, a passing of judgement, terrifying in its intensity. Other times, a pinched expression would appear—a signal of the shyness peculiar to autistic children, who think of light as being unfriendly.

106   Mimi's militant efforts in behalf of Brian had been exemplary. Her fellow doctors thought of her as *Bassett's crazy guardian angel*. They begged her to remove herself in order to preserve her health. Being wise, being practical, they saw that all her efforts would not save him. But Mimi's version of being a guardian angel was more like being a surrogate warrior: a hired gun or a samurai. Her cool determination to thwart the enemies of silence, stillness and starvation gave her strengths that even she had been unaware were hers to command.

107   Brian Bassett, seated in his corner on the floor, maintained a solemn composure that lent his features a kind of unearthly beauty. His back

was straight, his hands were poised, his hair was so fine he looked the very picture of a spirit waiting to enter a newborn creature. Sometimes Mimi wondered if this creature Brian Bassett waited to inhabit could be human. She thought of all the animals she had ever seen in all her travels and she fell upon the image of a newborn fawn as being the most tranquil and the most in need of stillness in order to survive. If only all the natural energy and curiosity of a newborn beast could have entered into Brian Bassett, surely, they would have transformed the boy in the corner into a vibrant, joyous human being. But it was not to be.

108   On the 29th of April—one week and three days after Everett had entered into his crisis of insomnia—Mimi sat on the floor in Brian Bassett's isolation room, gently massaging his arms and legs as she held him in her lap.

109   His weight, by now, was shocking—and his skin had become translucent. His eyes had not been closed for days—for weeks—and their expression might have been carved in stone.

110   "Speak to me. Speak," she whispered to him as she cradled his head beneath her chin. "Please at least speak before you die."

111   Nothing happened. Only silence.

112   Juliet Bateman—wrapped in a blanket—was watching through the observation glass as Mimi lifted up Brian Bassett and placed him in his cot. The cot had metal sides—and the sides were raised. Juliet Bateman could see Brian Bassett's eyes and his hands as Mimi stepped away.

113   Mimi looked at Juliet and shook her head. Juliet closed her eyes and pulled her blanket tighter like a skin that might protect her from the next five minutes.

114   Mimi went around the cot to the other side and dragged the IV stand in closer to the head. She fumbled for a moment with the long plastic lifelines—anti-dehydrants, nutrients—and she adjusted the needles and brought them down inside the nest of the cot where Brian Bassett lay and she lifted up his arm in order to insert the tubes and bind them into place with tape.

115   This was when it happened—just as Mimi Menlo was preparing to insert the second tube.

116   Brian Bassett looked at her and spoke.

117   "No," he said. "Don't."

118   *Don't* meant death.

119   Mimi paused—considered—and set the tube aside. Then she withdrew the tube already in place and she hung them both on the IV stand.

120   *All right*, she said to Brian Bassett in her mind, *you win*.

121   She looked down then with her arm along the side of the cot—and one hand trailing down so Brian Bassett could touch it if he wanted to. She smiled at him and said to him: "not to worry. None of us is ever going to trouble you again." He watched her carefully. "Goodbye, Brian," she said. "I love you."

122 Juliet Bateman saw Mimi Menlo say all this and was fairly sure she had read the words on Mimi's lips just as they had been spoken.

123 Mimi started out of the room. She was determined now there was no turning back and that Brian Bassett was free to go his way. But just as she was turning the handle and pressing her weight against the door—she heard Brian Bassett speak again.

124 "Goodbye," he said.

125 And died.

126 Mimi went back and Juliet Bateman, too, and they stayed with him another hour before they turned out his lights. "Someone else can cover his face," said Mimi. "I'm not going to do it." Juliet agreed and they came back out to tell the nurse on duty that their ward had died and their work with him was over.

127 On the 30th of April—a Saturday—Mimi stayed home and made her notes and she wondered if and when she would weep for Brian Bassett. Her hand, as she wrote, was steady and her throat was not constricted and her eyes had no sensation beyond the burning itch of fatigue. She wondered what she looked like in the mirror, but resisted that dis- covery. Some things could wait. Outside it rained. Thurber dreamed in the corner. Bay Street rumbled in the basement.

128 Everett, in the meantime, had reached his own crisis and because of his desperate straits a part of Mimi Menlo's mind was on her husband. Now he had not slept for almost ten days. *We really ought to consign ourselves to hospital beds*, she thought. Somehow, the idea held no per- suasion. It occurred to her that laughter might do a better job, if only they could find it. The brain, when over-extended, gives us the most surprisingly simple propositions, she concluded. *Stop*, it says to us. *Lie down and sleep.*

129 Five minutes later, Mimi found herself still sitting at the desk, with her fountain pen capped and her fingers raised to her lips in an atti- tude of gentle prayer. It required some effort to re-adjust her gaze and re-establish her focus on the surface of the window glass beyond which her mind had wandered. Sitting up, she had been asleep.

130 Thurber muttered something and stretched his legs and yawned, still asleep. Mimi glanced in his direction. *We've both been dreaming,* she thought, *but his dream continues.*

131 Somewhere behind her, the broken clock was attempting to strike the hour of three. Its voice was dull and rusty, needing oil.

132 Looking down, she saw the words BRIAN BASSETT written on the page before her and it occurred to her that, without this person, the words were nothing more than extrapolations from the alphabet— something fanciful we call a "name" in the hope that, one day, it will take on meaning.

133 She thought of Brian Bassett with his building blocks—pushing the letters around on the floor and coming up with more acceptable arrangements: *TINA STERABBS ... IAN BRETT BASS ... BEST STAB the*

RAIN: a sentence. He had known all along, of course, that *BRIAN BAS-SETT* wasn't what he wanted because it wasn't what he was. He had come here against his will, was held here against his better judgement, fought against his captors and finally escaped.

134 But where was here to Brett Bass? Where was here to Tina Sterabbs? Like Brian Bassett, they had all been here in someone else's dreams, and had to wait for someone else to wake before they could make their getaway.

135 Slowly, Mimi uncapped her fountain pen and drew a firm black line through Brian Bassett's name. *We dreamed him*, she wrote, *that's all. And then we let him go.*

136 Seeing Everett standing in the doorway, knowing he had just returned from another Kenneth Albright crisis, she had no sense of apprehension. All this was only as it should be. Given the way that everything was going, it stood to reason Kenneth Albright's crisis had to come in this moment. If he managed, at last, to kill himself then at least her husband might begin to sleep again.

137 Far in the back of her mind a carping, critical voice remarked that any such thoughts were *deeply unfeeling and verging on the barbaric.* But Mimi dismissed this voice and another part of her brain stepped forward in her defence. *I will weep for Kenneth Albright*, she thought, *when I can weep for Brian Bassett. Now, all that matters is that Everett and I survive.*

138 Then she strode forward and put out her hand for Everett's briefcase, set the briefcase down and helped him out of his topcoat. She was playing wife. It seemed to be the thing to do.

139 For the next twenty minutes Everett had nothing to say, and after he had poured himself a drink and after Mimi had done the same, they sat in their chairs and waited for Everett to catch his breath.

140 The first thing he said when he finally spoke was: "finish your notes?"

141 "Just about," Mimi told him. "I've written everything I can for now." She did not elaborate. "You're home early," she said, hoping to goad him into saying something new about Kenneth Albright.

142 "Yes," he said. "I am." But that was all.

143 Then he stood up—threw back the last of his drink and poured another. He lighted a cigarette and Mimi didn't even wince. He had been smoking now three days. The atmosphere between them had been, since then, enlivened with a magnetic kind of tension. But it was a moribund tension, slowly beginning to dissipate.

144 Mimi watched her husband's silent torment now with a kind of clinical detachment. This was the result, she liked to tell herself, of her training and her discipline. The lover in her could regard Everett warmly and with concern, but the psychiatrist in her could also watch him as someone suffering a nervous breakdown, someone who could

not be helped until the symptoms had multiplied and declared themselves more openly.

145   Everett went into the darkest corner of the room and sat down hard in one of Mimi's straight-backed chairs: the ones inherited from her mother. He sat, prim, like a patient in a doctor's office, totally unrelaxed and nervy; expressionless. Either he had come to receive a deadly diagnosis, or he would get a clean bill of health.

146   Mimi glided over to the sofa in the window, plush and red and deeply comfortable; a place to recuperate. The view—if she chose to turn only slightly sideways—was one of the gentle rain that was falling onto Bay Street. Sopping-wet pigeons huddled on the window-sill; people across the street in the Manulife building were turning on their lights.

147   A renegade robin, nesting in their eaves, began to sing.

148   Everett Menlo began to talk.

149   "Please don't interrupt," he said at first.

150   "You know I won't," said Mimi. It was a rule that neither one should interrupt the telling of a case until they had been invited to do so.

151   Mimi put her fingers into her glass so the ice-cubes wouldn't click. She waited.

152   Everett spoke—but he spoke as if in someone else's voice, perhaps the voice of Kenneth Albright. This was not entirely unusual. Often, both Mimi and Everett Menlo spoke in the voices of their patients. What was unusual, this time, was that, speaking in Kenneth's voice, Everett began to sweat profusely—so profusely that Mimi was able to watch his shirt front darkening with perspiration.

153   "As you know," he said, "I have not been sleeping."

154   This was the understatement of the year. Mimi was silent. "I have not been sleeping because—to put it in a nutshell—I have been afraid to dream."

155   Mimi was somewhat startled by this. Not by the fact that Everett was afraid to dream, but only because she had just been thinking of dreams herself.

156   "I have been afraid to dream, because in all my dreams there have been bodies. Corpses. Murder victims."

157   Mimi—not really listening—idly wondered if she had been one of them.

158   "In all my dreams, there have been corpses," Everett repeated. "But I am not the murderer. Kenneth Albright is the murderer, and up to this moment, he has left behind him fifteen bodies: none of them people I recognize."

159   Mimi nodded. The ice-cubes in her drink were beginning to freeze her fingers. Any minute now, she prayed, they would surely melt.

160   "I gave up dreaming almost a week ago," said Everett, "thinking that if I did, the killing pattern might be altered; broken." Then he said tersely; "it was not. The killings have continued...."

161 "How do you know the killings have continued, Everett, if you've given up dreaming? Wouldn't this mean he had no place to hide the bodies?"

162 In spite of the fact she had disobeyed their rule about not speaking, Everett answered her.

163 "I know they are being continued because I have seen the blood."

164 "Ah, yes. I see."

165 "No, Mimi. No. You don't see. The blood is not a figment of my imagination. The blood, in fact, is the only thing not dreamed." He explained the stains on Kenneth Albright's hands and arms and clothes and he said: "It happens every day. We have searched his person for signs of cuts and gashes—even for internal and rectal bleeding. Nothing. We have searched his quarters and all the other quarters in his ward. His ward is locked. His ward is isolated in the extreme. None of his fellow patients was ever found bleeding—never had cause to bleed. There were no injuries—no self-inflicted wounds. We thought of animals. Perhaps a mouse—a rat. But nothing. Nothing. Nothing ... We also went so far as to strip-search all the members of the staff who entered that ward and I, too, offered myself for this experiment. Still nothing. Nothing. No one had bled."

166 Everett was now beginning to perspire so heavily he removed his jacket and threw it on the floor. Thurber woke and stared at it, startled. At first, it appeared to be the beast that had just pursued him through the woods and down the road. But, then, it sighed and settled and was just a coat; a rumpled jacket lying down on the rug.

167 Everett said: "we had taken samples of the blood on the patient's hands—on Kenneth Albright's hands and on his clothing and we had these samples analyzed. No. It was not his own blood. No, it was not the blood of an animal. No, it was not the blood of a fellow patient. No, it was not the blood of any members of the staff...."

168 Everett's voice had risen.

169 "Whose blood was it?" he almost cried. "Whose the hell was it?"

170 Mimi waited.

171 Everett Menlo lighted another cigarette. He took a great gulp of his drink.

172 "Well ..." He was calmer now; calmer of necessity. He had to marshall the evidence. He had to put it all in order—bring it into line with reason. "Did this mean that—somehow—the patient had managed to leave the premises—do some bloody deed and return without our knowledge of it? That is, after all, the only possible explanation. Isn't it?"

173 Mimi waited.

174 "Isn't it?" he repeated.

175 "Yes," she said. "It's the only possible explanation."

176 "Except there is no way out of that place. There is absolutely no way out."

177 Now, there was a pause.

178   "But one," he added—his voice, again, a whisper.

179   Mimi was silent. Fearful—watching his twisted face.

180   "Tell me," Everett Menlo said—the perfect innocent, almost the perfect child in quest of forbidden knowledge.

181   "Answer me this—be honest: is there blood in dreams?"

182   Mimi could not respond. She felt herself go pale. Her husband—after all, the sanest man alive—had just suggested something so completely mad he might as well have handed over his reason in a paper bag and said to her, *burn this*.

183   "The only place that Kenneth Albright goes, I tell you, is into dreams," Everett said. "That is the only place beyond the ward into which the patient can or does escape."

184   Another—briefer—pause.

185   "It is real blood, Mimi. And he gets it all from dreams. *My dreams*."

186   They waited for this to settle.

187   Everett said: "I'm tired. I'm tired. I cannot bear this any more. I'm tired...."

188   Mimi thought, *good. No matter what else happens, he will sleep tonight.*

189   He did. And so, at last, did she.

190   Mimi's dreams were rarely of the kind that engender fear. She dreamt more gentle scenes with open spaces that did not intimidate. She would dream quite often of water and of animals. Always, she was nothing more than an observer; roles were not assigned her; often, this was sad. Somehow, she seemed at times locked out, unable to participate. These were the dreams she endured when Brian Bassett died: field trips to see him in some desert setting; underwater excursions to watch him floating amongst the seaweed. He never spoke, and, indeed, he never appeared to be aware of her presence.

191   That night, when Everett fell into his bed exhausted and she did likewise, Mimi's dream of Brian Bassett was the last she would ever have of him and somehow, in the dream, she knew this. What she saw was what, in magical terms, would be called a disappearing act. Brian Bassett vanished. Gone.

192   Sometime after midnight on May Day morning, Mimi Menlo awoke from her dream of Brian to the sound of Thurber thumping the floor in a dream of his own.

193   Everett was not in his bed and Mimi cursed. She put on her wrapper and her slippers and went beyond the bedroom into the hall.

194   No lights were shining but the street lamps far below and the windows gave no sign of stars.

195   Mimi made her way past the jungle, searching for Everett in the living-room. He was not there. She would dream of this one day; it was a certainty.

196   "Everett?"

197   He did not reply.

198   Mimi turned and went back through the bedroom.

199   "Everett?"

200   She heard him. He was in the bathroom and she went in through the door.

201   "Oh," she said, when she saw him. "Oh, my God."

202   Everett Menlo was standing in the bathtub, removing his pyjamas. They were soaking wet, but not with perspiration. They were soaking wet with blood.

203   For a moment, holding his jacket, letting its arms hang down across his belly and his groin, Everett stared at Mimi, blank-eyed from his nightmare.

204   Mimi raised her hand to her mouth. She felt as one must feel, if helpless, watching someone burn alive.

205   Everett threw the jacket down and started to remove his trousers. His pyjamas, made of cotton, had been green. His eyes were blinded now with blood and his hands reached out to find the shower taps.

206   "Please don't look at me," he said. "I ... Please go away."

207   Mimi said: "no." She sat on the toilet seat. "I'm waiting here," she told him, "until we both wake up."

(1988)

Alice Munro (b. 1931)

Munro spent her youth in southwestern Ontario, the setting for many of
her short stories. Her unaffected but finely subtle style and her focus on the
lives of adolescent and adult women have twice won her the Governor
General's Award.

Boys and Girls

1   My father was a fox farmer. That is, he raised silver foxes, in pens; and
in the fall and early winter, when their fur was prime, he killed them
and skinned them and sold their pelts to the Hudson's Bay Company
or the Montreal Fur Traders. These companies supplied us with heroic
calendars to hang, one on each side of the kitchen door. Against a
background of cold blue sky and black pine forests and treacherous
northern rivers, plumed adventurers planted the flags of England and
France; magnificent savages bent their backs to the portage.

2   For several weeks before Christmas, my father worked after supper
in the cellar of our house. The cellar was whitewashed, and lit by a
hundred-watt bulb over the worktable. My brother Laird and I sat on
the top step and watched. My father removed the pelt inside-out from
the body of the fox, which looked surprisingly small, mean and rat-
like, deprived of its arrogant weight of fur. The naked, slippery bodies
were collected in a sack and buried at the dump. One time the hired
man, Henry Bailey, had taken a swipe at me with the sack, saying,
"Christmas present!" My mother thought that was not funny. In fact
she disliked the whole pelting operation—that was what the killing,
skinning, and preparation of the furs was called—and wished it did
not have to take place in the house. There was the smell. After the pelt
had been stretched inside-out on a long board my father scraped away
delicately, removing the little clotted webs of blood vessels, the bubbles
of fat; the smell of blood and animal fat, with the strong primitive odor
of the fox itself, penetrated all parts of the house. I found it reassur-
ingly seasonal, like the smell of oranges and pine needles.

3   Henry Bailey suffered from bronchial troubles. He would cough and
cough until his narrow face turned scarlet, and his light blue, derisive
eyes filled up with tears; then he took the lid off the stove, and,
standing well back, shot out a great clot of phlegm—hsss—straight
into the heart of the flames. We admired him for this performance and
for his ability to make his stomach growl at will, and for his laughter,
which was full of high whistlings and gurglings and involved the

whole faulty machinery of his chest. It was sometimes hard to tell what he was laughing at, and always possible that it might be us.

4   After we had been sent to bed we could smell fox and still hear Henry's laugh, but these things, reminders of the warm, safe, brightly lit downstairs world, seemed lost and diminished, floating on the stale cold air upstairs. We were afraid at night in the winter. We were not afraid of *outside* though this was the time of year when snowdrifts curled around our house like sleeping whales and the wind harassed us all night, coming up from the buried fields, the frozen swamp, with its old bugbear chorus of threats and misery. We were afraid of *inside*, the room where we slept. At this time the upstairs of our house was not finished. A brick chimney went up one wall. In the middle of the floor was a square hole, with a wooden railing around it; that was where the stairs came up. On the other side of the stairwell were the things that nobody had any use for any more—a soldiery roll of linoleum, standing on end, a wicker baby carriage, a fern basket, china jugs and basins with cracks in them, a picture of the Battle of Balaclava,[1] very sad to look at. I had told Laird, as soon as he was old enough to understand such things, that bats and skeletons lived over there; whenever a man escaped from the county jail, twenty miles away, I imagined that he had somehow let himself in the window and was hiding behind the linoleum. But we had rules to keep us safe. When the light was on, we were safe as long as we did not step off the square of worn carpet which defined our bedroom-space; when the light was off no place was safe but the beds themselves. I had to turn out the light kneeling on the end of my bed, and stretching as far as I could to reach the cord.

5   In the dark we lay on our beds, our narrow life rafts, and fixed our eyes on the faint light coming up the stairwell, and sang songs. Laird sang "Jingle Bells," which he would sing any time, whether it was Christmas or not, and I sang "Danny Boy." I loved the sound of my own voice, frail and supplicating, rising in the dark. We could make out the tall frosted shapes of the windows now, gloomy and white. When I came to the part *When I am dead, as dead I well may be*—a fit of shivering caused not by the cold sheets but by pleasurable emotion almost silenced me. *You'll kneel and say an Ave there above me*—What is an Ave? Every day I forgot to find out.

6   Laird went straight from singing to sleep. I could hear his long, satisfied, bubbly breaths. Now for the time that remained to me, the most perfectly private and perhaps the best time of the whole day, I arranged myself tightly under the covers and went on with one of the stories I was telling myself from night to night. These stories were about myself, when I had grown a little older; they took place in a world that was recognizably mine, yet one that presented opportunities for

---

1. One of the battles in the Crimean War of 1853–56, in which Britain and France allied with Turkey against Tsarist Russia.

courage, boldness and self-sacrifice, as mine never did. I rescued people from a bombarded building (it had discouraged me that the real war had gone on so far away from Jubilee). I shot two rabid wolves who were menacing the schoolyard (the teachers cowered terrified at my back). I rode a fine horse spiritedly down the main street of Jubilee, acknowledging the townspeople's gratitude for some yet-to-be-worked-out piece of heroism (nobody ever rode a horse there, except King Billy in the Orangemen's Day[2] parade). There was always riding and shooting in these stories, though I had only been on a horse twice—bareback because we did not own a saddle—and the second time I had slid right around and dropped under the horse's feet; it had stepped placidly over me. I really was learning to shoot, but I could not hit anything yet, not even tin cans on fence posts.

7   Alive, the foxes inhabited a world my father made for them. It was surrounded by a high guard fence, like a medieval town, with a gate that was padlocked at night. Along the streets of this town were ranged large, sturdy pens. Each of them had a real door that a man could go through, a wooden ramp along the wire, for the foxes to run up and down on, and a kennel—something like a clothes chest with air-holes—where they slept in winter and had their young. There were feeding and watering dishes attached to the wire in such a way that they could be emptied and cleaned from the outside. The dishes were made of old tin cans, and the ramps and kennels of odds and ends of old lumber. Everything was tidy and ingenious; my father was tirelessly inventive and his favorite book in the world was Robinson Crusoe.[3] He had fitted a tin drum on a wheelbarrow, for bringing water down to the pens. This was my job in summer, when the foxes had to have water twice a day. Between nine and ten o'clock in the morning, and again after supper, I filled the drum at the pump and trundled it down through the barnyard to the pens, where I parked it, and filled my watering can and went along the streets. Laird came too, with his little cream and green gardening can, filled too full and knocking against his legs and slopping water on his canvas shoes. I had the real watering can, my father's, though I could only carry it three-quarters full.

8   The foxes all had names, which were printed on a tin plate and hung beside their doors. They were not named when they were born, but when they survived the first year's pelting and were added to the breeding stock. Those my father had named were called names like

---

2. Irish Protestant association named after William of Orange, who later became William III ("King Billy") of England, defeating the Catholic James II. The society holds annual parades on July 12 to commemorate the Battle of the Boyne in 1690, in which James II's army was defeated.

3. Daniel Defoe's novel (1719) about a shipwrecked sailor who survives on a desert island through his ability to improvise and devise ingenious contraptions.

Prince, Bob, Wally and Betty. Those I had named were called Star or Turk, or Maureen or Diana. Laird named one Maud after a hired girl we had when he was little, one Harold after a boy at school, and one Mexico, he did not say why.

9   Naming them did not make pets out of them, or anything like it. Nobody but my father ever went into the pens, and he had twice had blood-poisoning bites. When I was bringing them their water they prowled up and down on the paths they had made inside their pens, barking seldom—they saved that for nighttime, when they might get up a chorus of community frenzy—but always watching me, their eyes burning, clear gold, in their pointed, malevolent faces. They were beautiful for their delicate legs and heavy, aristocratic tails and the bright fur sprinkled on dark down their backs—which gave them their name—but especially for their faces, drawn exquisitely sharp in pure hostility, and their golden eyes.

10   Besides carrying water I helped my father when he cut the long grass, and the lamb's quarter and flowering money-musk that grew between the pens. He cut with the scythe and I raked into piles. Then he took a pitchfork and threw fresh-cut grass all over the top of the pens, to keep the foxes cooler and shade their coats, which were browned by too much sun. My father did not talk to me unless it was about the job we were doing. In this he was quite different from my mother, who, if she was feeling cheerful, would tell me all sorts of things—the name of a dog she had had when she was a little girl, the names of boys she had gone out with later on when she was grown up, and what certain dresses of hers had looked like—she could not imagine now what had become of them. Whatever thoughts and stories my father had were private, and I was shy of him and would never ask him questions. Nevertheless I worked willingly under his eyes, and with a feeling of pride. One time a feed salesman came down into the pens to talk to him and my father said, "Like to have you meet my new hired man." I turned away and raked furiously, red in the face with pleasure.

11   "Could of fooled me," said the salesman. "I thought it was only a girl."

12   After the grass was cut, it seemed suddenly much later in the year. I walked on stubble in the earlier evening, aware of the reddening skies, the entering silences, of fall. When I wheeled the tank out of the gate and put the padlock on, it was almost dark. One night at this time I saw my mother and father standing talking on the little rise of ground we called the gangway, in front of the barn. My father had just come from the meathouse; he had his stiff bloody apron on, and a pail of cut-up meat in his hand.

13   It was an odd thing to see my mother down at the barn. She did not often come out of the house unless it was to do something—hang out the wash or dig potatoes in the garden. She looked out of place, with her bare lumpy legs, not touched by the sun, her apron still on and

damp across the stomach from the supper dishes. Her hair was tied up in a kerchief, wisps of it falling out. She would tie her hair up like this in the morning, saying she did not have time to do it properly, and it would stay tied up all day. It was true, too; she really did not have time. These days our back porch was piled with baskets of peaches and grapes and pears, bought in town, and onions and tomatoes and cucumbers grown at home, all waiting to be made into jelly and jam preserves, pickles and chili sauce. In the kitchen there was a fire in the stove all day, jars clinked in boiling water, sometimes a cheesecloth bag was strung on a pole between two chairs straining blue-black grape pulp for jelly. I was given jobs to do and I would sit at the table peeling peaches that had been soaked in the hot water, or cutting up onions, my eyes smarting and streaming. As soon as I was done I ran out of the house, trying to get out of earshot before my mother thought of what she wanted me to do next. I hated the hot dark kitchen in the summer, the green blinds and the flypapers, the same old oilcloth table and wavy mirror and bumpy linoleum. My mother was too tired and pre-occupied to talk to me, she had no heart to tell about the Normal School Graduation Dance; sweat trickled over her face and she was always counting under her breath, pointing at jars, dumping cups of sugar. It seemed to me that work in the house was endless, dreary and peculiarly depressing; work done out of doors, and in my father's service, was ritualistically important.

14   I wheeled the tank up to the barn, where it was kept, and I heard my mother saying, "Wait till Laird gets a little bigger, then you'll have a real help."

15   What my father said I did not hear. I was pleased by the way he stood listening, politely as he would to a salesman or a stranger, but with an air of wanting to get on with his real work. I felt my mother had no business down here and I wanted him to feel the same way. What did she mean about Laird? He was no help to anybody. Where was he now? Swinging himself sick on the swing, going around in cir-cles, or trying to catch caterpillars. He never once stayed with me till I was finished.

16   "And then I can use her more in the house," I heard my mother say. She had a dead-quiet, regretful way of talking about me that always made me uneasy. "I just get my back turned and she runs off. It's not like I had a girl in the family at all."

17   I went and sat on a feed bag in the corner of the barn, not wanting to appear when this conversation was going on. My mother, I felt, was not to be trusted. She was kinder than my father and more easily fooled, but you could not depend on her, and the real reasons for the things she said and did were not to be known. She loved me, and she sat up late at night making a dress of the difficult style I wanted, for me to wear when school started, but she was also my enemy. She was always plotting. She was plotting now to get me to stay in the house more, although she knew I hated it (*because* she knew I hated it) and

keep me from working for my father. It seemed to me she would do this simply out of perversity, and to try her power. It did not occur to me that she could be lonely, or jealous. No grown-up could be; they were too fortunate. I sat and kicked my heels monotonously against a feed bag, raising dust, and did not come out till she was gone.

18   At any rate, I did not expect my father to pay any attention to what she said. Who could imagine Laird doing my work—Laird remembering the padlock and cleaning out the watering dishes with a leaf on the end of a stick, or even wheeling the tank without tumbling over? It showed how little my mother knew about the way things really were.

19   I have forgotten to say what the foxes were fed. My father's bloody apron reminded me. They were fed horsemeat. At this time most farmers still kept horses, and when a horse got too old to work, or broke a leg or got down and would not get up, as they sometimes did, the owner would call my father, and he and Henry went out to the farm in the truck. Usually they shot and butchered the horse there, paying the farmer from five to twelve dollars. If they had already too much meat on hand, they would bring the horse back alive, and keep it for a few days or weeks in our stable, until the meat was needed. After the war the farmers were buying tractors and gradually getting rid of horses altogether, so it sometimes happened that we got a good healthy horse, that there was just no use for any more. If this happened in the winter we might keep the horse in our stable till spring, for we had plenty of hay and if there was a lot of snow—and the plow did not always get our road cleared—it was convenient to be able to go to town with a horse and cutter.[4]

20   The winter I was eleven years old we had two horses in the stable. We did not know what names they had had before, so we called them Mack and Flora. Mack was an old black workhorse, sooty and indifferent. Flora was a sorrel mare, a driver. We took them both out in the cutter. Mack was slow and easy to handle. Flora was given to fits of violent alarm, veering at cars and even at other horses, but we loved her speed and high-stepping, her general air of gallantry and abandon. On Saturdays we went down to the stable and as soon as we opened the door on its cosy, animal-smelling darkness Flora threw up her head, rolled her eyes, whinnied despairingly and pulled herself through a crisis of nerves on the spot. It was not safe to go into her stall; she would kick.

21   This winter also I began to hear a great deal more on the theme my mother had sounded when she had been talking in front of the barn. I no longer felt safe. It seemed that in the minds of the people around me there was a steady undercurrent of thought, not to be deflected, on this one subject. The word *girl* had formerly seemed to me innocent and unburdened, like the word *child*; now it appeared that it was no such thing. A girl was not, as I had supposed, simply what I was; it was

---

4. Light, horse-drawn sleigh.

what I had to become. It was a definition, always touched with emphasis, with reproach and disappointment. Also it was a joke on me. Once Laird and I were fighting, and for the first time ever I had to use all my strength against him: even so, he caught and pinned my arm for a moment, really hurting me. Henry saw this, and laughed, saying, "Oh, that there Laird's gonna show you, one of these days!" Laird was getting a lot bigger. But I was getting bigger too.

22   My grandmother came to stay with us for a few weeks and I heard other things. "Girls don't slam doors like that." "Girls keep their knees together when they sit down." And worse still, when I asked some questions, "That's none of girls' business." I continued to slam the doors and sit as awkwardly as possible, thinking that by such measures I kept myself free.

23   When spring came, the horses were let out in the barnyard. Mack stood against the barn wall trying to scratch his neck and haunches, but Flora trotted up and down and reared at fences, clattering her hooves against the rails. Snow drifts dwindled quickly, revealing the hard gray and brown earth, the familiar rise and fall of the ground, plain and bare after the fantastic landscape of winter. There was a great feeling of opening-out, of release. We just wore rubbers now, over our shoes; our feet felt ridiculously light. One Saturday we went out to the stable and found all the doors open, letting in the unaccustomed sunlight and fresh air. Henry was there, just idling around looking at his collection of calendars which were tacked up behind the stalls in a part of the stable my mother had probably never seen.

24   "Come to say goodbye to your old friend Mack?" Henry said. "Here, you give him a taste of oats." He poured some oats into Laird's cupped hands and Laird went to feed Mack. Mack's teeth were in bad shape. He ate very slowly, patiently shifting the oats around in his mouth, trying to find a stump of a molar to grind it on. "Poor old Mack," said Henry mournfully. "When a horse's teeth's gone, he's gone. That's about the way."

25   "Are you going to shoot him today?" I said. Mack and Flora had been in the stable so long I had almost forgotten they were going to be shot.

26   Henry didn't answer me. Instead he started to sing in a high, trembly, mocking-sorrowful voice. *Oh, there's no more work, for poor Uncle Ned, he's gone where the good darkies go.*[5] Mack's thick, blackish tongue worked diligently at Laird's hand. I went out before the song was ended and sat down on the gangway.

27   I had never seen them shoot a horse, but I knew where it was done. Last summer Laird and I had come upon a horse's entrails before they were buried. We had thought it was a big black snake, coiled up in the sun. That was around the field that ran up beside the barn. I thought

---

5. Lines from "Old Uncle Ned" by American popular songwriter Stephen Foster (1826–1864).

that if we went inside the barn, and found a side crack or a knothole to look through, we would be able to see them do it. It was not something I wanted to see: just the same, if a thing really happened, it was better to see it, and know.

28 My father came down from the house, carrying the gun.

29 "What are you doing here?" he said.

30 "Nothing."

31 "Go on up and play around the house."

32 He sent Laird out of the stable. I said to Laird, "Do you want to see them shoot Mack?" and without waiting for an answer led him around to the front door of the barn, opened it carefully, and went in. "Be quiet or they'll hear us," I said. We could hear Henry and my father talking in the stable, then the heavy, shuffling steps of Mack being backed out of his stall.

33 In the loft it was cold and dark. Thin, crisscrossed beams of sunlight fell through the cracks. The hay was low. It was a rolling country, hills and hollows, slipping under our feet. About four feet up was a beam going around the walls. We piled hay up in one corner and I boosted Laird up and hoisted myself. The beam was not very wide; we crept along it with our hands flat on the barn walls. There were plenty of knotholes, and I found one that gave me the view I wanted—a corner of the barnyard, the gate, part of the field. Laird did not have a knothole and began to complain.

34 I showed him a widened crack between two boards. "Be quiet and wait. If they hear you you'll get us into trouble."

35 My father came in sight carrying the gun. Henry was leading Mack by the halter. He dropped it and took out his cigarette paper and tobacco; he rolled cigarettes for my father and himself. While this was going on Mack nosed around in the old, dead grass along the fence. Then my father opened the gate and they took Mack through. Henry led Mack away from the path to a patch of ground and they talked together, not loud enough for us to hear. Mack again began searching for a mouthful of fresh grass, which was not to be found. My father walked away in a straight line, and stopped short at a distance which seemed to suit him. Henry was walking away from Mack too, but sideways, still negligently holding on to the halter. My father raised the gun and Mack looked up as if he had noticed something and my father shot him.

36 Mack did not collapse at once but swayed, lurched sideways and fell, first on his side: then he rolled over on his back and, amazingly, kicked his legs for a few seconds in the air. At this Henry laughed, as if Mack had done a trick for him. Laird, who had drawn a long, groaning breath of surprise when the shot was fired, said out loud, "He's not dead." And it seemed to me it might be true. But his legs stopped, he rolled on his side again, his muscles quivered and sank. The two men walked over and looked at him in a businesslike way;

they bent down and examined his forehead where the bullet had gone in, and now I saw his blood on the brown grass.

37 "Now they just skin him and cut him up," I said. "Let's go." My legs were a little shaky and I jumped gratefully down into the hay. "Now you've seen how they shoot a horse," I said in a congratulatory way, as if I had seen it many times before. "Let's see if any barn cat's had kittens in the hay." Laird jumped. He seemed young and obedient again. Suddenly I remembered how, when he was little, I had brought him into the barn and told him to climb the ladder to the top beam. That was in the spring, too, when the hay was low. I had done it out of a need for excitement, a desire for something to happen so that I could tell about it. He was wearing a little bulky brown and white checked coat, made down from one of mine. He went all the way up just as I told him, and sat down on the top beam with all the hay far below him on one side, and the barn floor and some old machinery on the other. Then I ran screaming to my father. "Laird's up on the top beam!" My father came, my mother came, my father went up the ladder talking very quietly and brought Laird down under his arm, at which my mother leaned against the ladder and began to cry. They said to me, "Why weren't you watching him?" but nobody ever knew the truth. Laird did not know enough to tell. But whenever I saw the brown and white checked coat hanging in the closet, or at the bottom of the rag bag, which was where it ended up, I felt a weight in my stomach, the sadness of unexorcised guilt.

38 I looked at Laird, who did not even remember this, and I did not like the look on his thin, winter-pale face. His expression was not frightened or upset, but remote, concentrating. "Listen," I said, in an unusually bright and friendly voice, "you aren't going to tell, are you?"

39 "No," he said absently.

40 "Promise."

41 "Promise," he said. I grabbed the hand behind his back to make sure he was not crossing his fingers. Even so, he might have a nightmare; it might come out that way. I decided I had better work hard to get all thoughts of what he had seen out of his mind—which, it seemed to me, could not hold very many things at a time. I got some money I had saved and that afternoon we went into Jubilee and saw a show, with Judy Canova,[6] at which we both laughed a great deal. After that I thought it would be all right.

42 Two weeks later I knew they were going to shoot Flora. I knew from the night before, when I heard my mother ask if the hay was holding out all right, and my father said, "Well, after tomorrow there'll just be the cow, and we should be able to put her out to grass in another week." So I knew it was Flora's turn in the morning.

43 This time I didn't think of watching it. That was something to see just one time. I had not thought about it very often since, but some-

---

6. American comedian known for her yodelling in "hillbilly" movies of the 1940s.

500 Alice Munro

times when I was busy, working at school, or standing in front of the mirror combing my hair and wondering if I would be pretty when I grew up, the whole scene would flash into my mind: I would see the easy, practised way my father raised the gun, and hear Henry laughing when Mack kicked his legs in the air. I did not have any great feeling of horror and opposition, such as a city child might have had; I was too used to seeing the death of animals as a necessity by which we lived. Yet I felt a little ashamed, and there was a new wariness, a sense of holding-off, in my attitude to my father and his work.

44   It was a fine day, and we were going around the yard picking up tree branches that had been torn off in winter storms. This was something we had been told to do, and also we wanted to use them as a teepee. We heard Flora whinny, and then my father's voice and Henry's shouting and we ran down to the barnyard to see what was going on.

45   The stable door was open. Henry had just brought Flora out, and she had broken away from him. She was running free in the barnyard, from one end to the other. We climbed up on the fence. It was exciting to see her running, whinnying, going up on her hind legs, prancing and threatening like a horse in a Western movie, an unbroken ranch horse, though she was just an old driver, an old sorrel mare. My father and Henry ran after her and tried to grab the dangling halter. They tried to work her into a corner, and they had almost succeeded when she made a run between them, wild-eyed, and disappeared around the corner of the barn. We heard the rails clatter down as she got over the fence, and Henry yelled, "She's into the field now!"

46   That meant she was in the long L-shaped field that ran up by the house. If she got around the center, heading towards the lane, the gate was open; the truck had been driven into the field this morning. My father shouted to me, because I was on the other side of the fence, nearest to the lane, "Go shut the gate!"

47   I could run very fast. I ran across the garden, past the tree where our swing was hung, and jumped across a ditch into the lane. There was the open gate. She had not got out, I could not see her up on the road; she must have run to the other end of the field. The gate was heavy. I lifted it out of the gravel and carried it across the roadway. I had it halfway across when she came in sight, galloping straight towards me. There was just time to get the chain on. Laird came scrambling through the ditch to help me.

48   Instead of shutting the gate, I opened it as wide as I could. I did not make any decision to do this, it was just what I did. Flora never slowed down: she galloped straight past me, and Laird jumped up and down, yelling, "Shut it, shut it!" even after it was too late. My father and Henry appeared in the field a moment too late to see what I had done. They only saw Flora heading for the township road. They would think I had not got there in time.

49   They did not waste any time asking about it. They went back to the barn and got the gun and the knives they used, and put these in

NEL

the truck; then they turned the truck around and came bouncing up the field toward us. Laird called to them, "Let me go too, let me go too!" and Henry stopped the truck and they took him in. I shut the gate after they were all gone.

50 I supposed Laird would tell. I wondered what would happen to me. I had never disobeyed my father before, and I could not understand why I had done it. Flora would not really get away. They would catch up with her in the truck. Or if they did not catch her this morning somebody would see her and telephone us this afternoon or tomorrow. There was no wild country here for her to run to, only farms. What was more, my father had paid for her, we needed the meat to feed the foxes, we needed the foxes to make our living. All I had done was make more work for my father who worked hard enough already. And when my father found out about it he was not going to trust me any more; he would know that I was not entirely on his side. I was on Flora's side, and that made me no use to anybody, not even to her. Just the same, I did not regret it; when she came running at me and I held the gate open, that was the only thing I could do.

51 I went back to the house, and my mother said, "What's all the commotion?" I told her that Flora kicked down the fence and got away. "Your poor father," she said, "now he'll have to go chasing over the countryside. Well, there isn't any use planning dinner before one." She put up the ironing board. I wanted to tell her, but thought better of it and went upstairs and sat on my bed.

52 Lately I had been trying to make my part of the room fancy, spreading the bed with old lace curtains, and fixing myself a dressing table with some leftovers of cretonne for a skirt. I planned to put up some kind of barricade between my bed and Laird's, to keep my section separate from his. In the sunlight, the lace curtains were just dusty rags. We did not sing at night any more. One night when I was singing Laird said, "You sound silly," and I went right on but the next night I did not start. There was not so much need to anyway, we were no longer afraid. We knew it was just old furniture over there, old jumble and confusion. We did not keep to the rules. I still stayed awake after Laird was asleep and told myself stories, but even in these stories something different was happening, mysterious alterations took place. A story might start off in the old way, with a spectacular danger, a fire or wild animals, and for a while I might rescue people; then things would change around, and instead, somebody would be rescuing me. It might be a boy from our class at school, or even Mr. Campbell, our teacher, who tickled girls under the arms. And at this point the story concerned itself at great length with what I looked like—how long my hair was, and what kind of dress I had on; by the time I had these details worked out the real excitement of the story was lost.

53 It was later than one o'clock when the truck came back. The tarpaulin was over the back, which meant there was meat in it. My mother had to heat dinner all over again. Henry and my father had

changed from their bloody overalls into ordinary working overalls in the barn, and they washed their arms and necks and faces at the sink, and splashed water on their hair and combed it. Laird lifted his arm to show off a streak of blood. "We shot Flora," he said, "and cut her up in fifty pieces."

54 "Well I don't want to hear about it," my mother said. "And don't come to my table like that."

55 My father made him go and wash the blood off.

56 We sat down and my father said grace and Henry pasted his chewing gum on the end of his fork, the way he always did; when he took it off he would have us admire the pattern. We began to pass the bowls of steaming, overcooked vegetables. Laird looked across the table at me and said proudly, distinctly, "Anyway it was her fault Flora got away."

57 "What?" my father said.

58 "She could of shut the gate and she didn't. She just open' it up and Flora run out."

59 "Is that right?" my father said.

60 Everybody at the table was looking at me. I nodded, swallowing food with great difficulty. To my shame, tears flooded my eyes.

61 My father made a curt sound of disgust. "What did you do that for?"

62 I did not answer. I put down my fork and waited to be sent from the table, still not looking up.

63 But this did not happen. For some time nobody said anything, then Laird said matter-of-factly, "She's crying."

64 "Never mind," my father said. He spoke with resignation, even good humour, the words which absolved and dismissed me for good. "She's only a girl," he said.

65 I didn't protest that, even in my heart. Maybe it was true.

(1968)

Rudy Wiebe (b. 1934)

*A two-time winner of the Governor General's Award, Rudy Wiebe was born
on the family farm in Fairholme, Saskatchewan, to Mennonite parents from
the Soviet Union. Wiebe was educated at the University of Alberta and at
Tübingen, Germany, and went on to study theology at the Mennonite
Brethren College, Winnipeg, and creative writing at the University of Iowa.
An emeritus professor of the University of Alberta, Wiebe is preoccupied
with rewriting mainstream history, with meaning, justice, cross-cultural
comprehension, belief systems, technical rationalities, and the visionary
possibilities of art.*

Where Is the Voice Coming From?

1   The problem is to make the story.

2   One difficulty of this making may have been excellently stated by
Teilhard de Chardin[1]: "We are continually inclined to isolate ourselves
from the things and events which surround us ... as though we were
spectators, not elements, in what goes on." Arnold Toynbee[2] does venture, "For all that we know, Reality is the undifferentiated unity of the
mystical experience," but that need not here be considered. This story
ended long ago; it is one of finite acts, of orders, or elemental feelings
and reactions, of obvious legal restrictions and requirements.

3   Presumably all the parts of the story are themselves available. A difficulty is that they are, as always, available only in bits and pieces.
Though the acts themselves seem quite clear, some written reports of
the acts contradict each other. As if these acts were, at one time, too
well-known; as if the original nodule of each particular fact had from
somewhere received non-factual accretions; or even more, as if, since
the basic facts were so clear perhaps there were a larger number of facts
than any one reporter, or several, or even any reporter had ever
attempted to record. About facts that are simply told by this mouth to
that ear, of course, even less can be expected.

---

1. Pierre Teilhard de Chardin (1881–1955) combined paleontology with a religious
   vocation as a Jesuit priest, aiming to reconstruct science and faith in the process.
   His religious teachings were prohibited by the Vatican.
2. Arnold Toynbee (1889–1975), British historian who considered the past in terms
   of a series of civilizations rather than of political entities.

4   An affair seventy-five years old should acquire some of the shiny transparency of an old man's skin. It should.

5   Sometimes it would seem that it would be enough—perhaps more than enough—to hear the names only. The grandfather One Arrow; the mother Spotted Calf; the father Sounding Sky; the wife (wives rather, but only one of them seems to have a name, though their fathers are Napaise, Kapahoo, Old Dust, The Rump)—the one wife named, of all things, Pale Face; the cousin Going-Up-To-Sky; the brother-in-law (again, of all things) Dublin. The names of the police sound very much alike; they all begin with Constable or Corporal or Sergeant, but here and there an Inspector, then a Superintendent and eventually all the resonance of an Assistant Commissioner echoes down. More, Herself: Victoria, by the Grace of God etc., etc., QUEEN, defender of the Faith, etc., etc.; and witness "Our Right Trusty and Right Well-Beloved Cousin and Councillor the Right Honorable Sir John Campbell Hamilton-Gordon, Earl of Aberdeen; Viscount Formartine, Baron Haddo, Methlic, Tarves and Kellie in the Peerage of Scotland; Viscount Gordon of Aberdeen, County of Aberdeen in the Peerage of the United Kingdom; Baronet of Nova Scotia, Knight Grand Cross of Our Most Distinguished Order of Saint Michael and Saint George, etc., Governor General of Canada." And of course himself: in the award proclamation named "Jean-Baptiste" but otherwise known only as Almighty Voice.[3]

6   But hearing cannot be enough; not even hearing all the thunder of A Proclamation: "Now Hear Ye that a reward of FIVE HUNDRED DOL-LARS will be paid to any person or persons who will give such information as will lead ... (etc. etc.) this Twentieth day of April, in the year of Our Lord one thousand eight hundred and ninety-six, and the Fifty-ninth year of Our Reign ..." etc. and etc.

7   Such hearing cannot be enough. The first item to be seen is the piece of white bone. It is almost triangular, slightly convex—concave actually as it is positioned at this moment with its corners slightly raised—graduating from perhaps a strong eighth to a weak quarter of an inch in thickness, its scattered pore structure varying between larger and smaller on its perhaps polished, certainly shiny surface. Precision is difficult since the glass showcase is at least thirteen inches deep and therefore an eye cannot be brought as close as the minute inspection of such a small, though certainly quite adequate, sample of skull would normally require. Also, because of the position it cannot be determined whether the several hairs, well over a foot long, are still in some manner attached to it or not.

8   The seven-pounder cannon can be seen standing almost shyly between the showcase and the interior wall. Officially it is known as a gun, not a cannon, and clearly its bore is not large enough to admit a

---

3. By many accounts, the story of Almighty Voice (Shu-Kwe-weetam), son of John Sounding Sky (a prominent figure in the 1885 Rebellion), begins with the slaughter of a stray cow for his wedding feast and ends with the deaths of Almighty Voice and two friends, one civilian, and three policemen.

large man's fist. Even if it can be believed that this gun was used in the 1885 Rebellion[4] and that on the evening of Saturday, May 29, 1897 (while the nine-pounder, now unidentified, was in the process of arriving with the police on the special train from Regina), seven shells (all that were available in Prince Albert at that time) from it were sent shrieking into the poplar bluffs as night fell, clearly such shelling could not and would not disembowel the whole earth. Its carriage is now nicely lacquered, the perhaps oak spokes of its petite wheels (little higher than a knee) have been recently scraped, puttied and varnished; the brilliant burnish of its brass breeching testifies with what meticulous care charmen and women have used nationally advertised cleaners and restorers.

9   Though it can also be seen, even a careless glance reveals that the same concern has not been expended on the one (of two) .44 calibre 1866 model Winchesters apparently found at the last in the pit with Almighty Voice. It is also preserved in a glass case; the number 1536735 is still, though barely, distinguishable on the brass cartridge section just below the brass saddle ring. However, perhaps because the case was imperfectly sealed at one time (though sealed enough not to warrant disturbance now), or because of simple neglect, the rifle is obviously spotted here and there with blotches of rust and the brass itself reveals discolorations almost like mildew. The rifle bore, the three long strands of hair themselves, actually bristle with clots of dust. It may be that this museum cannot afford to be as concerned as the other; conversely, the disfiguration may be something inherent in the items themselves.

10   The small building which was the police guardroom at Duck Lake, Saskatchewan Territory, in 1895 may also be seen. It had subsequently been moved from its original place and used to house small animals, chickens perhaps, or pigs—such as a woman might be expected to have under her responsibility. It is, of course, now perfectly empty, and clean so that the public may enter with no more discomfort than a bend under the doorway and a heavy encounter with disinfectant. The door-jamb has obviously been replaced; the bar network at one window is, however, said to be original; smooth still, very smooth. The logs inside have been smeared again and again with whitewash, perhaps paint, to an insistent point of identity-defying characterlessness. Within the small rectangular box of these logs not a sound can be heard from the streets of the, probably dead, town.

> Hey Injun you'll get hung
> for stealing that steer
> Hey Injun for killing that government cow you'll get three weeks on
> the woodpile
> Hey Injun

4. The 1885 Rebellion led by Louis Riel and put down by the North West Mounted Police.

11 The place named Kinistino seems to have disappeared from the map but the Minnechinass Hills have not. Whether they have ever been on a map is doubtful but they will, of course, not disappear from the landscape as long as the grass grows and the rivers run. Contrary to general report and belief, the Canadian prairies are rarely, if ever, flat and the Minnechinass (spelled five different ways and translated sometimes as "The Outside Hill," sometimes as "Beautiful Bare Hills") are dissimilar from any other of the numberless hills that everywhere block out the prairie horizon. They are bare; poplars lie tattered along their tops, almost black against the straw-pale grass and sharp green against the grey soil of the plowing laid in half-mile rectangular blocks upon their western slopes. Poles holding various wires stick out of the fields, back down the bend of the valley; what was once a farmhouse is weathering into the cultivated earth. The poplar bluff where Almighty Voice made his stand has, of course, disappeared.

12 The policemen he shot and killed (not the ones he wounded, of course) are easily located. Six miles east, thirty-nine miles north in Prince Albert, the English Cemetery. Sergeant Colin Campbell Colebrook, North West Mounted Police Registration Number 605, lies presumably under a gravestone there. His name is seventeenth in a very long "list of non-commissioned officers and men who have died in the service since the inception of the force." The date is October 29, 1895, and the cause of death is anonymous: "Shot by escaping Indian prisoner near Prince Albert." At the foot of this grave are two others: Constable John R. Kerr, No. 3040, and Corporal C. H. S. Hockin, No. 3106. Their cause of death on May 28, 1897 is even more anonymous, but the place is relatively precise: "Shot by Indians at Min-etch-inass Hills, Prince Albert District."

13 The gravestone, if he has one, of the fourth man Almighty Voice killed is more difficult to locate. Mr. Ernest Grundy, postmaster at Duck Lake in 1897, apparently shut his window the afternoon of Friday, May 28, armed himself, rode east twenty miles, participated in the second charge into the bluff at about 6:30 p.m., and on the third sweep of that charge was shot dead at the edge of the pit. It would seem that he thereby contributed substantially not only to the Indians' bullet supply, but his clothing warmed them as well.

14 The burial place of Dublin and Going-Up-To-Sky is unknown, as is the grave of Almighty Voice. It is said that a Métis named Henry Smith lifted the latter's body from the pit in the bluff and gave it to Spotted Calf. The place of burial is not, of course, of ultimate significance. A gravestone is always less evidence than a triangular piece of skull, provided it is large enough.

15 Whatever further evidence there is to be gathered may rest on pictures. There are, presumably, almost numberless pictures of the policemen in the case, but the only one with direct bearing is one of Sergeant Colebrook who apparently insisted on advancing to complete an arrest after being warned three times that if he took another step he

would be shot. The picture must have been taken before he joined the force; it reveals him a large-eared young man, hair brush-cut and ascot tie, his eyelids slightly drooping, almost hooded under thick brows. Unfortunately a picture of Constable R. C. Dickson, into whose charge Almighty Voice was apparently committed in that guardroom and who after Colebrook's death was convicted of negligence, sentenced to two months hard labour and discharged, does not seem to be available.

16   There are no pictures to be found of either Dublin (killed early by rifle fire) or Going-Up-To-Sky (killed in the pit), the two teen-age boys who gave their ultimate fealty to Almighty Voice. There is, however, one said to be of Almighty Voice, Junior. He may have been born to Pale Face during the year, two hundred and twenty-one days that his father was a fugitive. In the picture he is kneeling before what could be a tent, he wears striped denim overalls and displays twin babies whose sex cannot be determined from the double-laced dark bonnets they wear. In the supposed picture of Spotted Calf and Sounding Sky, Sounding Sky stands slightly before his wife; he wears a white shirt and a striped blanket folded over his left shoulder in such a manner that the arm in which he cradles a long rifle cannot be seen. His head is thrown back; the rim of his hat appears as a black half-moon above eyes that are pressed shut in, as it were, profound concentration; above a mouth clenched thin in a downward curve. Spotted Calf wears a long dress, a sweater which could also be a man's dress coat, and a large fringed and embroidered shawl which would appear distinctly Dukhobor in origin if the scroll patterns on it were more irregular. Her head is small and turned slightly towards her husband so as to reveal her right ear. There is what can only be called a quizzical expression on her crumpled face; it may be she does not understand what is happening and that she would have asked a question, perhaps of her husband, perhaps of the photographers, perhaps even of anyone, anywhere in the world if such questioning were possible for an Indian woman.

17   There is one final picture. That is one of Almighty Voice himself. At least it is purported to be of Almighty Voice himself. In the Royal Canadian Mounted Police Museum on the Barracks Grounds just off Dewdney Avenue in Regina, Saskatchewan, it lies in the same show-case, as a matter of fact immediately beside that triangular piece of skull. Both are unequivocally labelled, and it must be assumed that a police force with a world-wide reputation would not label *such* evidence incorrectly. But here emerges an ultimate problem in making the story.

18   There are two official descriptions of Almighty Voice. The first reads: "Height about five feet, ten inches, slight build, rather good looking, a sharp hooked nose with a remarkably flat point. Has a bullet scar on the left side of his face about 1-1/2 inches long running from near corner of mouth towards ear. The scar cannot be noticed when his face is painted but otherwise is plain. Skin fair for an Indian." The

second description is on the Award Proclamation: "About twenty-two years old, five feet ten inches in height, weight about eleven stone, slightly erect, neat small feet and hands; complexion inclined to be fair, wavey dark hair to shoulders, large dark eyes, broad forehead, sharp features and parrot nose with flat tip, scar on left cheek running from mouth towards ear, feminine appearance."

19   So run the descriptions that were, presumably, to identify a well-known fugitive in so precise a manner that an informant could collect five hundred dollars—a considerable sum when a police constable earned between one and two dollars a day. The nexus of the problems appears when these supposed official descriptions are compared to the supposed official picture. The man in the picture is standing on a small rug. The fingers on his left hand touch a curved Victorian settee, behind him a photographer's backdrop of scrolled patterns merges to vaguely paradisiacal trees and perhaps a sky. The moccasins he wears make it impossible to deduce whether his feet are "neat small." He may be five feet, ten inches tall, may weigh eleven stone, he certainly is "rather good looking" and, though it is a frontal view, it may be that the point of his long and flaring nose could be "remarkably flat." The photograph is slightly over-illuminated and so the unpainted complexion could be "inclined to be fair"; however, nothing can be seen of a scar, the hair is not wavy and shoulder-length but hangs almost to the waist in two thick straight braids worked through with beads, fur, ribbons and cords. The right hand that holds the corner of the blanket-like coat in position is large and, even in the high illumination, heavily veined. The neck is concealed under coiled beads and the forehead seems more low than "broad."

20   Perhaps, somehow, these picture details could be reconciled with the official description if the face as a whole were not so devastating.

21   On a cloth-backed sheet two feet by two and one-half feet in size, under the Great Seal of the Lion and the Unicorn, dignified by the names of the Deputy of the Minister of Justice, the Secretary of State, the Queen herself and all the heaped detail of her "Right Trusty and Right Well-beloved Cousin," this description concludes: "feminine appearance." But the pictures: any face of history, any believed face that the world acknowledges as *man*—Socrates, Jesus, Attila, Genghis Khan, Mahatma Gandhi, Joseph Stalin—no believed face is more *man* than this face. The mouth, the nose, the clenched brows, the eyes—the eyes are large, yes, and dark, but even in this watered-down reproduction of unending reproductions of that original, a steady look into those eyes cannot be endured. It is a face like an axe.

22   It is now evident that the de Chardin statement quoted at the beginning has relevance only as it proves itself inadequate to explain what has happened. At the same time, the inadequacy of Aristotle's much more famous statement becomes evident: "The true difference [between the historian and the poet] is that one relates what *has* hap-

pened, the other what *may* happen." These statements cannot explain the storymaker's activity since, despite the most rigid application of impersonal investigation, the elements of the story have now run me aground. If ever I could, I can no longer pretend to objective, omnipotent disinterestedness. I am no longer *spectator* of what *has* happened or what *may* happen: I am become *element* in what is happening at this very moment.

23   For it is, of course, I myself who cannot endure the shadows on that paper which are those eyes. It is I who stand beside this broken veranda post where two corner shingles have been torn away, where barbed wire tangles the dead weeds on the edge of this field. The bluff that sheltered Almighty Voice and his two friends has not disappeared from the slope of the Minnechinass, no more than the sound of Constable Dickson's voice in that guardhouse is silent. The sound of his speaking is there even if it has never been recorded in an official report:

> hey injun you'll get
> hung
> for stealing that steer
> hey injun for killing that government
> cow you'll get three
> weeks on the woodpile hey injun

24   The unknown contradictory words about an unprovable act that move a boy to defiance, an implacable Cree warrior long after the three-hundred-and-fifty-year war is ended, a war already lost the day the Cree watch Cartier hoist his guns ashore at Hochelaga and they begin the long retreat west; these words of incomprehension, of threatened incomprehensible law are there to be heard just as the unmoving tableau of the three-day siege is there to be seen on the slopes of the Minnechinass. Sounding Sky is somewhere not there, under arrest, but Spotted Calf stands on a shoulder of the Hills a little to the left, her arms upraised to the setting sun. Her mouth is open. A horse rears, riderless, above the scrub willow at the edge of the bluff, smoke puffs, screams tangle in rifle barrage, there are wounds, somewhere. The bluff is so green this spring, it will not burn and the ragged line of seven police and two civilians is staggering through, faces twisted in rage, terror, and rifles sputter. Nothing moves. There is no sound of frogs in the night; twenty-seven policemen and five civilians stand in cordon at thirty-yard intervals and a body also lies in the shelter of a gully. Only a voice rises from the bluff:

> We have fought well
> You have died like braves
> I have worked hard and am hungry
> Give me food

but nothing moves. The bluff lies, a bright green island on the grassy slope surrounded by men hunched forward rigid over their long rifles, men clumped out of rifle-range, thirty-five men dressed as for fall hunting on a sharp spring day, a small gun positioned on a ridge above. A crow is falling out of the sky into the bluff, its feathers sprayed as by an explosion. The first gun and the second gun are in position, the beginning and end of the bristling surround of thirty-five Prince Albert Volunteers, thirteen civilians and fifty-six policemen in position relative to the bluff and relative to the unnumbered whites astride their horses, standing up in their carts, staring and pointing across the valley, in position relative to the bluff and the unnumbered Indians squatting silent along the higher ridges of the Hills, motionless mounds, faceless against the Sunday morning sunlight edging between and over them down along the tree tips, down into the shadows of the bluff. Nothing moves. Beside the second gun the red-coated officer has flung a handful of grass into the motionless air, almost to the rim of the red sun.

25   And there is a voice. It is an incredible voice that rises from among the young poplars ripped of their spring bark, from among the dead somewhere lying there, out of the arm-deep pit shorter than a man a voice rises over the exploding smoke and thunder of guns that reel back in their positions, worked over, serviced by the grimed motionless men in bright coats and glinting buttons, a voice so high and clear, so unbelievably high and strong in its unending wordless cry.

26   The voice of "Gitchie-Manitou Wayo"—interpreted as "voice of the Great Spirit"—that is, The Almighty Voice. His death chant no less incredible in its beauty than in its incomprehensible happiness.

27   I say "wordless cry" because that is the way it sounds to me. I could be more accurate if I had a reliable interpreter who would make a reliable interpretation. For I do not, of course, understand the Cree myself.

(1971, 1982)

Margaret Atwood (b. 1939)

Equally at home with essays, fiction, and poetry, Atwood has also achieved
some of her considerable stature from her work as a literary critic. Her
interest in fictional form is demonstrated in "Happy Endings," an amusing
survey of the bare-bones possibilities of fiction. See "Through the One-Way
Mirror," p. 58, and Atwood's poems, p. 317.

Happy Endings

1   John and Mary meet.
2   What happens next?
3   If you want a happy ending, try A.

4   A. John and Mary fall in love and get married. They both have
    worthwhile and remunerative jobs which they find stimulating
    and challenging. They buy a charming house. Real estate values
    go up. Eventually, when they can afford live-in help, they have
    two children, to whom they are devoted. The children turn out
    well. John and Mary have a stimulating and challenging sex life
    and worthwhile friends. They go on fun vacations together. They
    retire. They both have hobbies which they find stimulating and
    challenging. Eventually they die. This is the end of the story.

5   B. Mary falls in love with John but John doesn't fall in love with
    Mary. He merely uses her body for selfish pleasure and ego grat-
    ification of a tepid kind. He comes to her apartment twice a week
    and she cooks him dinner, you'll notice that he doesn't even con-
    sider her worth the price of a dinner out, and after he's eaten he
    fucks her and after that he falls asleep, while she does the dishes
    so he won't think she's untidy, having all those dirty dishes lying
    around, and puts on fresh lipstick so she'll look good when he
    wakes up, but when he wakes up he doesn't even notice, he puts
    on his socks and his shorts and his pants and his shirt and his tie
    and his shoes, the reverse order from the one in which he took
    them off. He doesn't take off Mary's clothes, she takes them off
    herself, she acts as if she's dying for it every time, not because she
    likes sex exactly, she doesn't, but she wants John to think she
    does because if they do it often enough surely he'll get used to
    her, he'll come to depend on her and they will get married, but
    John goes out the door with hardly so much as a good-night and

three days later he turns up at six o'clock and they do the whole thing over again.

6   Mary gets run-down. Crying is bad for your face, everyone knows that and so does Mary but she can't stop. People at work notice. Her friends tell her John is a rat, a pig, a dog, he isn't good enough for her, but she can't believe it. Inside John, she thinks, is another John, who is much nicer. This other John will emerge like a butterfly from a cocoon, a jack from a box, a pit from a prune, if the first John is only squeezed enough.

7   One evening John complains about the food. He has never complained about the food before. Mary is hurt.

8   Her friends tell her they've seen him in a restaurant with another woman, whose name is Madge. It's not even Madge that finally gets to Mary: it's the restaurant. John has never taken Mary to a restaurant. Mary collects all the sleeping pills and aspirins she can find, and takes them and a half a bottle of sherry. You can see what kind of a woman she is by the fact that it's not even whiskey. She leaves a note for John. She hopes he'll discover her and get her to the hospital in time and repent and then they can get married, but this fails to happen and so she dies.

9   John marries Madge and everything continues as in A.

10 C. John, who is an older man, falls in love with Mary, and Mary, who is only twenty-two, feels sorry for him because he's worried about his hair falling out. She sleeps with him even though she's not in love with him. She met him at work. She's in love with someone called James, who is twenty-two and not yet ready to settle down.

11   John on the contrary settled down long ago: this is what is bothering him. John has a steady, respectable job and is getting ahead in his field, but Mary isn't impressed by him, she's impressed by James, who has a motorcycle and a fabulous record collection. But James is often away on his motorcycle, being free. Freedom isn't the same for girls, so in the meantime Mary spends Thursday evenings with John. Thursdays are the only days John can get away.

12   John is married to a woman called Madge and they have two children, a charming house which they bought just before the real estate values went up, and hobbies which they find stimulating and challenging, when they have the time. John tells Mary how important she is to him, but of course he can't leave his wife because a commitment is a commitment. He goes on about this more than is necessary and Mary finds it boring, but older men can keep it up longer so on the whole she has a fairly good time.

13   One day James breezes in on his motorcycle with some top-grade California hybrid and James and Mary get higher than you'd believe possible and they climb into bed. Everything becomes very underwater, but along comes John, who has a key

to Mary's apartment. He finds them stoned and entwined. He's hardly in any position to be jealous, considering Madge, but nevertheless he's overcome with despair. Finally he's middle-aged, in two years he'll be bald as an egg and he can't stand it. He purchases a handgun, saying he needs it for target practice—this is the thin part of the plot, but it can be dealt with later—and shoots the two of them and himself.

14   Madge, after a suitable period of mourning, marries an understanding man called Fred and everything continues as in A, but under different names.

15   D. Fred and Madge have no problems. They get along exceptionally well and are good at working out any little difficulties that may arise. But their charming house is by the seashore and one day a giant tidal wave approaches. Real estate values go down. The rest of the story is about what caused the tidal wave and how they escape from it. They do, though thousands drown, but Fred and Madge are virtuous and lucky. Finally on high ground they clasp each other, wet and dripping and grateful, and continue as in A.

16   E. Yes, but Fred has a bad heart. The rest of the story is about how kind and understanding they both are until Fred dies. Then Madge devotes herself to charity work until the end of A. If you like, it can be "Madge," "cancer," "guilty and confused," and "bird watching."

17   F. If you think this is all too bourgeois, make John a revolutionary and Mary a counterespionage agent and see how far that gets you. Remember, this is Canada. You'll still end up with A, though in between you may get a lustful brawling saga of passionate involvement, a chronicle of our times, sort of.

18   You'll have to face it, the endings are the same however you slice it. Don't be deluded by any other endings, they're all fake, either deliberately fake, with malicious intent to deceive, or just motivated by excessive optimism if not downright sentimentality.

19   The only authentic ending is the one provided here:

20   *John and Mary die. John and Mary die. John and Mary die.*

21   So much for endings. Beginnings are always more fun. True connoisseurs, however, are known to favor the stretch in between, since it's the hardest to do anything with.

22   That's about all that can be said for plots, which anyway are just one thing after another, a what and a what and a what.

23   Now try How and Why.

(1983)

Toni Cade Bambara (b. 1939)

Born in New York, Bambara has written short stories, novels, and screen-
plays in which she presents portraits of black urban life in America. In
"The Lesson," she offers an unsentimental, lively, and humorous explanation
of the neighbourhood and wider world of her adolescent protagonists.

The Lesson

1   Back in the days when everyone was old and stupid or young and foolish and me and Sugar were the only ones just right, this lady moved on our block with nappy hair and proper speech and no makeup. And quite naturally we laughed at her, laughed the way we did at the junk man who went about his business like he was some big-time president and his sorry-ass horse his secretary. And we kinda hated her too, hated the way we did the winos who cluttered up our parks and pissed on our handball walls and stank up our hallways so you couldn't halfway play hide-and-seek without a goddamn gas mask. Miss Moore was her name. The only woman on the block with no first name. And she was black as hell, cept for her feet, which were fish-white and spooky. And she was always planning these boring-ass things for us to do, us being my cousin, mostly, who lived on the block cause we all moved North the same time and to the same apartment then spread out gradual to breathe. And our parents would yank our heads into some kinda shape and crisp up our clothes so we'd be presentable for travel with Miss Moore, who always looked like she was going to church, though she never did. Which is just one of the things grown-ups talked about when they talked behind her back like a dog. But when she came calling with some sachet she'd sewed up or some gingerbread she'd made or some book, why then they'd all be too embarrassed to turn her down and we'd get handed over all spruced up. She'd been to college and said it was only right that she should take responsibility for the young ones' education, and she not even related by marriage or blood. So they'd go for it. Specially, Aunt Gretchen. She been screwed into the go-along for so long, it's a blood-deep natural thing with her. Which is how she got saddled with me and Sugar and Junior in the first place while our mothers were in a la-de-da apartment up the block having a good ole time.

2   So this one day Miss Moore rounds us all up at the mailbox and it's puredee hot and she's knockin herself out about arithmetic. And school suppose to let up in summer I heard, but she don't never let up.

And the starch in my pinafore scratching the shit outta me and I'm really hating this nappy-head bitch and her goddamn college degree. I'd much rather go to the pool or to the show where it's cool. So me and Sugar leaning on the mailbox being surly, which is a Miss Moore word. And Flyboy checking out what everybody brought for lunch. And Fat Butt already wasting his peanut-butter-and-jelly sandwich like the pig he is. And Junebug punchin on Q.T.'s arm for potato chips. And Rosie Giraffe shifting from one hip to the other waiting for somebody to step on her foot or ask her if she from Georgia so she can kick ass, preferably Mercedes'. And Miss Moore asking us do we know what money is, like we a bunch of retards. I mean real money, she say, like it's only poker chips or monopoly papers we lay on the grocer. So right away I'm tired of this and say so. And would much rather snatch Sugar and go to the Sunset and terrorize the West Indian kids and take their hair ribbons and their money too. And Miss Moore files that remark away for next week's lesson on brotherhood, I can tell. And finally I say we oughta get to the subway cause it's cooler and besides we might meet some cute boys. Sugar done swiped her mama's lipstick, so we ready.

3   So we heading down the street and she's boring us silly about what things cost and what our parents make and how much goes for rent and how money ain't divided up right in this country. And then she gets to the part about we all poor and live in the slums, which I don't feature. And I'm ready to speak on that, but she steps out in the street and hails two cabs just like that. Then she hustles half the crew in with her and hands me a five-dollar bill and tells me to calculate 10 percent tip for the driver. And we're off. Me and Sugar and Junebug and Flyboy hangin out the window and hollering to everybody, putting lipstick on each other cause Flyboy a faggot anyway, and making farts with our sweaty armpits. But I'm mostly trying to figure how to spend this money. But they all fascinated with the meter ticking and Junebug starts laying bets as to how much it'll read when Flyboy can't hold his breath no more. Then Sugar lays bets as to how much it'll be when we get there. So I'm stuck. Don't nobody want to go for my plan, which is to jump out at the next light and run off to the first bar-b-que we can find. Then the driver tells us to get the hell out cause we there already. And the meter reads eighty-five cents. And I'm stalling to figure out the tip and Sugar say give him a dime. And I decide he don't need it so bad as I do, so later for him. But then he tries to take off with Junebug foot still in the door as we talk about his mama something ferocious. Then we check out that we on Fifth Avenue and everybody dressed up in stockings. One lady in a fur coat, hot as it is. White folks crazy.

4   "This is the place," Miss Moore say, presenting it to us in the voice she uses at the museum. "Let's look in the windows before we go in."

5   "Can we steal?" Sugar asks very serious like she's getting the ground rules squared away before she plays. "I beg your pardon," say Miss Moore, and we fall out. So she leads us around the windows of the toy

store and me and Sugar screaming, "This is mine, that's mine, I gotta have that, that was made for me, I was born for that," till Big Butt drowns us out.

6   "Hey, I'm going to buy that there."

7   "That there? You don't even know what it is, stupid."

8   "I do so," he say punching on Rosie Giraffe. "It's a microscope."

9   "Whatcha gonna do with a microscope, fool?"

10   "Look at things."

11   "Like what, Ronald?" ask Miss Moore. And Big Butt ain't got the first notion. So here go Miss Moore gabbing about the thousands of bacteria in a drop of water and the somethinorother in a speck of blood and the million and one living things in the air around us is invisible to the naked eye. And what she say that for? Junebug go to town on that "naked" and we rolling. Then Miss Moore ask what it cost. So we all jam into the window smudgin it up and the price tag say $300. So then she ask how long'd take for Big Butt and Junebug to save up their allowances. "Too long," I say. "Yeh," adds Sugar, "outgrown it by that time." And Miss Moore say no, you never outgrow learning instruments. "Why, even medical students and interns and," blah, blah, blah. And we ready to choke Big Butt for bringing it up in the first damn place.

12   "This here costs four hundred eighty dollars," says Rosie Giraffe. So we pile up all over her to see what she pointin out. My eyes tell me it's a chunk of glass cracked with something heavy, and different-color inks dipped into the splits, then the whole thing put into a oven or something. But for $480 it don't make sense.

13   "That's a paperweight made of semi-precious stones fused together under tremendous pressure," she explains slowly, with her hands doing the mining and all the factory work.

14   "So what's a paperweight?" asks Rosie Giraffe.

15   "To weigh paper with, dumbbell," say Flyboy, the wise man from the East.

16   "Not exactly," say Miss Moore, which is what she say when you warm or way off too. "It's to weight paper down so it won't scatter and make your desk untidy." So right away me and Sugar curtsy to each other and then to Mercedes who is more the tidy type.

17   "We don't keep paper on top of the desk in my class," say Junebug, figuring Miss Moore crazy or lyin one.

18   "At home, then," she say. "Don't you have a calendar and a pencil case and a blotter and a letter-opener on your desk at home where you do your homework?" And she know damn well what our homes look like cause she nosys around in them every chance she gets.

19   "I don't even have a desk," say Junebug. "Do we?"

20   "No. And I don't get no more homework neither," say Big Butt.

21   "And I don't even have a home," say Flyboy like he do at school to keep white folks off his back and sorry for him. Send this poor kid to camp posters, is his specialty.

22   "I do," says Mercedes. "I have a box of stationery on my desk and a picture of my cat. My godmother bought the stationery and the desk. There's big rose on each sheet and the envelopes smell like roses."

23   "Who wants to know about your smelly-ass stationery," says Rosie Giraffe fore I can get my two cents in.

24   "It's important to have a work area all your own so that ..."

25   "Will you look at this sailboat, please," say Flyboy, cuttin her off and pointin to the thing like it was his. So once again we tumble all over each other to gaze at this magnificent thing in the toy store which is just big enough to maybe sail two kittens across the pond if you strap them to the posts tight. We all start reciting the price tag like we in assembly. "Handcrafted sailboat of fiberglass at one thousand one hundred ninety-five dollars."

26   "Unbelievable," I hear myself say and am really stunned. I read it again for myself just in case the group recitation put me in a trance. Same thing. For some reason this pisses me off. We look at Miss Moore and she lookin at us, waiting for I dunno what.

27   "Who'd pay all that when you can buy a sailboat for a quarter at Pop's, a tube of glue for a dime, and a ball of string for eight cents? It must have a motor and a whole lot else besides," I say. "My sailboat cost me about fifty cents."

28   "But will it take water?" say Mercedes with her smart ass.

29   "Took mine to Alley Pond Park once," say Flyboy. "String broke. Lost it. Pity."

30   "Sailed mine in Central Park and it keeled over and sank. Had to ask my father for another dollar."

31   "And you got the strap," laugh Big Butt. "The jerk didn't even have a string on it. My old man wailed on his behind."

32   Little Q.T. was staring hard at the sailboat and you could see he wanted it bad. But he too little and somebody'd just take it from him. So what the hell. "This boat for kids, Miss Moore?"

33   "Parents silly to buy something like that just to get all broke up," say Rosie Giraffe.

34   "That much money it should last forever," I figure.

35   "My father'd buy it for me if I wanted it."

36   "Your father, my ass," say Rosie Giraffe getting a chance to finally push Mercedes.

37   "Must be rich people shop here," say Q.T.

38   "You are a very bright boy," say Flyboy. "What was your first clue?" And he rap him on the head with the back of his knuckles, since Q.T. the only one he could get away with. Though Q.T. liable to come up behind you years later and get his licks in when you half expect it.

39   "What I want to know is," I says to Miss Moore though I never talk to her, I wouldn't give the bitch that satisfaction, "is how much a real boat costs? I figure a thousand'd get you a yacht any day."

40   "Why don't you check that out," she says, "and report back to the group?" Which really pains my ass. If you gonna mess up a perfectly

good swim day least you could do is have some answers. "Let's go in," she say like she got something up her sleeve. Only she don't lead the way. So me and Sugar turn the corner to where the entrance is, but when we get there I kinda hang back. Not that I'm scared, what's there to be afraid of, just a toy store. But I feel funny, shame. But what I got to be ashamed about? Got as much right to go in as anybody. But somehow I can't seem to get hold of the door, so I step away for Sugar to lead. But she hangs back too. And I look at her and she looks at me and this is ridiculous. I mean, damn, I have never ever been shy about doing nothing or going nowhere. But then Mercedes steps up and then Rosie Giraffe and Big Butt crowd in behind and shove, and next thing we all stuffed into the doorway with only Mercedes squeezing past us, smoothing out her jumper and walking right down the aisle. Then the rest of us tumble in like a glued-together jigsaw done all wrong. And people lookin at us. And it's like the time me and Sugar crashed into the Catholic church on a dare. But once we got in there and everything so hushed and holy and the candles and the bowin and the handker-chiefs on all the drooping heads, I just couldn't go through with the plan. Which was for me to run up to the altar and do a tap dance while Sugar played the nose flute and messed around in the holy water. And Sugar kept giving me the elbow. Then later teased me so bad I tied her up in the shower and turned it on and locked her in. And she'd be there till this day if Aunt Gretchen hadn't finally figured I was lyin about the boarder takin a shower.

41   Same thing in the store. We all walkin on tiptoe and hardly touchin the games and puzzles and things. And I watched Miss Moore who is steady watchin us like she waiting for a sign. Like Mama Drewery watches the sky and sniffs the air and takes note of just how much slant is in the bird formation. Then me and Sugar bump smack into each other, so busy gazing at the toys, 'specially the sailboat. But we don't laugh and go into our fat-day bump-stomach routine. We just stare at that price tag. Then Sugar runs a finger over the whole boat. And I'm jealous and want to hit her. Maybe not her, but I sure want to punch somebody in the mouth.

42   "Watcha bring us here for, Miss Moore?"

43   "You sound angry, Sylvia. Are you mad about something?" Givin me one of them grins like she tellin a grown-up joke that never turns out to be funny. And she's lookin very closely at me like maybe she plannin to do my portrait from memory. I'm mad, but I won't give her that satisfac-tion. So I slouch around the store bein very bored and say, "Let's go."

44   Me and Sugar at the back of the train watchin the tracks whizzin by large then small then gettin gobbled up in the dark. I'm thinking about this tricky toy I saw in the store. A clown that somersaults on a bar then does chin-ups just cause you yank lightly at his leg. Cost $35. I could see me askin my mother for a $35 birthday clown. "You wanna who that costs what?" she'd say, cocking her head to the side to get a better view of the hole in my head. Thirty-five dollars could buy new

bunk beds for Junior and Gretchen's boy. Thirty-five dollars and the whole household could go visit Granddaddy Nelson in the country. Thirty-five dollars would pay for the rent and the piano bill too. Who are these people that spend that much for performing clowns and $1,000 for toy sailboats? What kinda work they do and how they live and how come we ain't in on it? Where we are is who we are, Miss Moore always pointin out. But it don't necessarily have to be that way, she always adds then waits for somebody to say that poor people have to wake up and demand their share of the pie and don't none of us know what kind of pie she talkin about in the first damn place. But she ain't so smart cause I still got her four dollars from the taxi and she sure ain't gettin it. Messin up my day with this shit. Sugar nudges me in my pocket and winks.

45 Miss Moore lines us up in front of the mailbox where we started from, seem like years ago, and I got a headache for thinkin so hard. And we lean all over each other so we can hold up under the draggy-ass lecture she always finishes us off with at the end before we thank her for borin us to tears. But she just looks at us like she readin tea leaves. Finally she say, "Well, what did you think of F.A.O. Schwartz?"

46 Rosie Giraffe mumbles, "White folks crazy."

47 "I'd like to go there again when I get my birthday money," says Mercedes, and we shove her out the pack so she has to lean on the mailbox by herself.

48 "I'd like a shower. Tiring day," say Flyboy.

49 Then Sugar surprises me by sayin, "You know, Miss Moore, I don't think all of us here put together eat in a year what that sailboat costs." And Miss Moore lights up like somebody goosed her. "And?" she say, urging Sugar on. Only I'm standin on her foot so she don't continue.

50 "Imagine for a minute what kind of society it is in which some people can spend on a toy what it would cost to feed a family of six or seven. What do you think?"

51 "I think," say Sugar pushing me off her feet like she never done before, cause I whip her ass in a minute, "that this is not much of a democracy if you ask me. Equal chance to pursue happiness means an equal crack at the dough, don't it?" Miss Moore is beside herself and I am disgusted with Sugar's treachery. So I stand on her foot one more time to see if she'll shove me. She shuts up and Miss Moore looks at me, sorrowfully I'm thinkin. And somethin weird is going on, I can feel it in my chest.

52 "Anybody else learn anything today?" lookin dead at me. I walk away and Sugar has to run to catch up and don't even seem to notice when I shrug her arm off my shoulder.

53 "Well, we got four dollars anyway," she says.

54 "Uh hunh."

55 "We could go to Hascombs and get half a chocolate layer and then go to the Sunset and still have plenty money for potato chips and ice-cream sodas."

56   "Uh hunh."

57   "Race you to Hascombs," she say.

58   We start down the block and she gets ahead which is O.K. by me cause I'm going to the West End and then over the Drive to think this day through. She can run if she want to and even run faster. But ain't nobody gonna beat me at nuthin.

(1972)

Thomas King (b. 1943)

Born in Oklahoma of Greek-German and Cherokee parents, King is a Canadian as well as an American citizen. While teaching Native studies at the University of Lethbridge, he began his creative writing career. He has published poems and short stories in many Canadian periodicals and edited a special issue of Canadian Fiction Magazine *(1987) and* All My Relations: An Anthology of Contemporary Canadian Native Writing *(1990). He is currently a member of the English Department at the University of Guelph.*

The One About Coyote Going West

1   This one is about Coyote. She was going west. Visiting her relations. That's what she said. You got to watch that one. Tricky one. Full of bad business. No, no, no, no, that one says. I'm just visiting.

2   Going to see Raven.

3   Boy, I says. That's another tricky one.

4   Coyote comes by my place. She wag her tail. Make them happy noises. Sit on my porch. Look around. With them teeth. With that smile. Coyote put her nose in my tea. My good tea. Get that nose out of my tea, I says.

5   I'm going to see my friends, she says. Tell those stories. Fix this world. Straighten it up.

6   Oh boy, pretty scary that, Coyote fix the world, again.

7   Sit down, I says. Eat some food. Hard work that fix up the world. Maybe you have a song. Maybe you have a good joke.

8   Sure, says Coyote. That one wink her ears. Lick her whiskers.

9   I tuck my feet under that chair. Got to hide my toes. Sometimes that tricky one leave her skin sit in that chair. Coyote skin. No Coyote. Sneak around. Bite them toes. Make you jump.

10   I been reading those books, she says.

11   You must be one smart Coyote, I says.

12   You bet, she says.

13   Maybe you got a good story for me, I says.

14   I been reading about that history, says Coyote. She tricks that nose back in my tea. All about who found us Indians.

15   Ho, I says. I like those old ones. Them ones are the best. You tell me your story, I says. Maybe some biscuits will visit us. Maybe some moose-meat stew come along, listen to your story.

16   Okay, she says and she sings her story song.

Snow's on the ground the snakes are asleep.
Snow's on the ground my voice is strong.
Snow's on the ground the snakes are asleep.
Snow's on the ground my voice is strong.

17 She sings like that. With that tail, wagging. With that smile. Sitting there.

18 Maybe I tell you the one about Eric the Lucky and the Vikings play hockey for the Old-timers, find us Indians in Newfoundland, she says.

19 Maybe I tell you the one about Christopher Cartier looking for something good to eat. Find us Indians in a restaurant in Montreal.

20 Maybe I tell you the one about Jacques Columbus come along that river, Indians waiting for him. We all wave and say, here we are, here we are.

21 Everyone knows those stories, I says. White man stories. Baby stories you got in your mouth.

22 No, no, no, no, says the Coyote. I read these ones in that old book.

23 Ho, I says. You are trying to bite my toes. Everyone knows who found us Indians. Eric the Lucky and that Christopher Cartier and that Jacques Columbus come along later. Those ones get lost. Float about. Walk around. Get mixed up. Ho, ho, ho, ho, those ones cry, we are lost. So we got to find them. Help them out. Feed them. Show them around.

24 Boy, I says. Bad mistake that one.

25 You are very wise, grandmother, says Coyote, bring her eyes down. Like she is sleepy. Maybe you know who discovered Indians.

26 Sure, I says. Everyone knows that. It was Coyote. She was the one.

27 Oh, grandfather, that Coyote says. Tell me that story. I love those stories about that sneaky one. I don't think I know that story, she says.

28 All right, I says. Pay attention.

29 Coyote was heading west. That's how I always start this story. There was nothing else in this world. Just Coyote. She could see all the way, too. No mountains then. No rivers then. No forests then. Pretty flat then. So she starts to make things. So she starts to fix this world.

30 This is exciting, says Coyote, and she takes her nose out of my tea.

31 Yes, I says. Just the beginning, too. Coyote got a lot of things to make.

32 Tell me, grandmother, says Coyote. What does the clever one make first?

33 Well, I says. Maybe she makes that tree grows by the river. Maybe she makes that buffalo. Maybe she makes that mountain. Maybe she makes them clouds.

34 Maybe she makes that beautiful rainbow, says Coyote.

35 No, I says. She don't make that thing. Mink makes that.

36 Maybe she makes that beautiful moon, says Coyote.

37 No, I says. She don't do that either. Otter finds that moon in a pond later on.

38 Maybe she makes the oceans with that blue water, says Coyote.

39   No, I says. Oceans are already here. She don't do any of that. The first thing Coyote makes, I tell Coyote, is a mistake.

40   Boy, Coyote sit up straight. Them eyes pop open. That tail stop wagging. That one swallow that smile.

41   Big one, too, I says. Coyote is going west thinking of things to make. That one is trying to think of everything to make at once. So she don't see that hole. So she falls in that hole. Then those thoughts bump around. They run into each other. Those ones fall out of Coyote's ears. In that hole. Ho, that Coyote cries. I have fallen into a hole. I must have made a mistake. And she did.

42   So, there is that hole. And there is that Coyote in that hole. And there is that big mistake in that hole with Coyote. Ho, says that mistake. You must be Coyote.

43   That mistake is real big and that hole is small. Not much room. I don't want to tell you what that mistake looks like. First mistake in the world. Pretty scary. Boy, I can't look. I got to close my eyes. You better close your eyes, too, I tell Coyote.

44   Okay, I'll do that, she says, and she puts her hands over her eyes. But she don't fool me. I can see she's peeking.

45   Don't peek, I says.

46   Okay, she says. I won't do that.

47   Well, you know, that Coyote thinks about the hole. And she thinks about how she's going to get out of that hole. She thinks how she's going to get that big mistake back in her head.

48   Say, says that mistake. What is that you're thinking about?

49   I'm thinking of a song, says Coyote. I'm thinking of a song to make this hole bigger.

50   That's a good idea, says that mistake. Let me hear your hole song.

51   But that's not what Coyote sings. She sings a song to make the mistake smaller. But that mistake hears her. And that mistake grabs Coyote's nose. And that one pulls off her mouth so she can't sing. And that one jumps up and down on Coyote until she is flat. Then that one leaps out of that hole, wanders around looking for things to do.

52   Well, Coyote is feeling pretty bad, all flat her nice fur coat full of stomp holes. So she thinks hard, and she thinks about a healing song. And she tries to sing a healing song, but her mouth is in other places. So she thinks harder and tries to sing that song through her nose. But that nose don't make any sound, just drip a lot. She tries to sing that song out her ears, but those ears don't hear anything.

53   So, that silly one thinks real hard and tries to sing out her butt-hole. Pssst! Pssst! That is what that butt-hole says, and right away things don't smell so good in that hole. Pssst.

54   Boy, Coyote thinks. Something smells.

55   That Coyote lies there flat and practise and practise. Pretty soon, maybe two days, maybe one year, she teach that butt-hole to sing. That song. That healing song. So that butt-hole sings that song. And Coyote

begins to feel better. And Coyote don't feel so flat anymore. Pssst! Pssst! Things still smell pretty bad, but Coyote is okay.

56 That one look around in that hole. Find her mouth. Put that mouth back. So, she says to that butt-hole. Okay, you can stop singing now. You can stop making them smells now. But, you know, that butt-hole is liking all that singing, and so that butt-hole keeps on singing.

57 Stop that, says Coyote. You going to stink up the whole world. But it don't. So Coyote jumps out of that hole and runs across the prairies real fast. But that butt-hole follows her. Pssst. Pssst. Coyote jumps into a lake, but that butt-hole don't drown. It just keeps on singing.

58 Hey, who is doing all that singing, someone says.

59 Yes, and who is making that bad smell, says another voice.

60 It must be Coyote, says a third voice.

61 Yes, says a fourth voice. I believe it is Coyote.

62 That Coyote sit in my chair, put her nose in my tea, say, I know who that voice is. It is that big mistake playing a trick. Nothing else is made yet.

63 No, I says. That mistake is doing other things.

64 Then those voices are spirits, says Coyote.

65 No, I say. Them voices belong to them ducks.

66 Coyote stand up on my chair. Hey, she says, where did them ducks come from?

67 Calm down, I says. This story is going to be okay. This story is doing just fine. This story knows where it is going. Sit down. Keep your skin on.

68 So.

69 Coyote look around, and she see them four ducks. In that lake. Ho, she says. Where did you ducks come from? I didn't make you yet.

70 Yes, says them ducks. We were waiting around, but you didn't come. So we got tired of waiting. So we did it ourselves.

71 I was in a hole, says Coyote.

72 Psst. Psst.

73 What's that noise, says them ducks. What's that bad smell?

74 Never mind, says Coyote. Maybe you've seen something go by. Maybe you can help me find something I lost. Maybe you can help me get it back.

75 Those ducks swim around and talk to themselves. Was it something awful to look at? Yes, says Coyote, it certainly was. Was it something with ugly fur? Yes, says Coyote, I think it had that, too. Was it something that made a lot of noise? ask them ducks. Yes, it was pretty noisy, says Coyote. Did it smell bad, them ducks want to know. Yes, says Coyote. I guess you ducks have seen my something.

76 Yes, says them ducks. It is right there behind you.

77 So that Coyote turn around, and there is nothing there.

78 It's still behind you, says those ducks.

79 So Coyote turn around again but she don't see anything.

80 Psst! Psst!

81 Boy, says those ducks. What a noise! What a smell! They say that, too. What an ugly thing with all that fur!

82 Never mind, says that Coyote, again. That is not what I'm looking for. I'm looking for something else.

83 Maybe you're looking for Indians, says those ducks.

84 Well, that Coyote is real surprised because she hasn't created Indians, either. Boy, says that one, mischief is everywhere. This world is getting bent.

85 All right.

86 So Coyote and those ducks are talking, and pretty soon they hear a noise. And pretty soon there is something coming. And those ducks says, oh, oh, oh, oh. They say that like they see trouble, but it is not trouble. What comes along is a river.

87 Hello, says that river. Nice day. Maybe you want to take a swim. But Coyote don't want to swim, and she looks at the river and she looks at that river again. Something's not right here, she says. Where are those rocks? Where are those rapids? What did you do with them waterfalls? How come you're so straight?

88 And Coyote is right. That river is nice and straight and smooth without any bumps or twists. It runs both ways, too, not like a modern river.

89 We got to fix this, says Coyote, and she does. She puts some rocks in that river, and she fixes it so it only runs one way. She puts a couple of waterfalls in and makes a bunch of rapids where things get shallow fast.

90 Coyote is tired with all this work, and those ducks are tired just watching. So that Coyote sits down. So she closes her eyes. So she puts her nose in her tail. So those ducks shout, wake up, wake up! Something big is heading this way! And they are right.

91 Mountain comes sliding along, whistling. Real happy mountain. Nice and round. This mountain is full of grapes and other good things to eat. Apples, peaches, cherries. Howdy-do, says that polite mountain, nice day for whistling.

92 Coyote looks at that mountain, and that one shakes her head. Oh, no, she says, this mountain is all wrong. How come you're so nice and round. Where are those craggy peaks? Where are all them cliffs? What happened to all that snow? Boy, we got to fix this thing, too. So she does.

93 Grandfather, grandfather, says that Coyote, sit in my chair, put her nose in my tea. Why is that Coyote changing all those good things?

94 That is a real sly one, ask me that question. I look at those eyes. Grab them ears. Squeeze that nose. Hey, let go my nose, that Coyote says.

95 Okay, I says. Coyote still in Coyote skin. I bet you know why Coyote change that happy river. Why she change that mountain sliding along whistling.

96   No, says that Coyote, look around my house, lick her lips, make them baby noises.

97   Maybe it's because she is mean, I says.

98   Oh, no, says Coyote. That one is sweet and kind.

99   Maybe it's because that one is not too smart.

100   Oh, no, says Coyote. That Coyote is very wise.

101   Maybe it's because she made a mistake.

102   Oh, no, says Coyote. She made one of those already.

103   All right, I says. Then Coyote must be doing the right thing. She must be fixing up the world so it is perfect.

104   Yes, says Coyote. That must be it. What does that brilliant one do next?

105   Everyone knows what Coyote does next, I says. Little babies know what Coyote does next.

106   Oh no, says Coyote. I have never heard this story. You are a wonderful storyteller. You tell me your good Coyote story.

107   Boy, you got to watch that one all the time. Hide them toes.

108   Well, I says. Coyote thinks about that river. And she thinks about that mountain. And she thinks somebody is fooling around. So she goes looking around. She goes looking for that one who is messing up the world.

109   She goes to the north, and there is nothing. She goes to the south, and there is nothing there, either. She goes to the east, and there is still nothing there. She goes to the west, and there is a pile of snow tires.

110   And there is some televisions. And there is some vacuum cleaners. And there is a bunch of pastel sheets. And there is an air humidifier. And there is a big mistake sitting on a portable gas barbecue reading a book. Big book. Department store catalogue.

111   Hello, says that mistake. Maybe you want a hydraulic jack.

112   No, says that Coyote. I don't want one of them. But she don't tell that mistake what she wants because she don't want to miss her mouth again. But when she thinks about being flat and full of stomp holes, that butt-hole wakes up and begins to sing. Pssst. Pssst.

113   What's that noise? says that big mistake.

114   I'm looking for Indians, says that Coyote, real quick. Have you seen any?

115   What's that bad smell?

116   Never mind, says Coyote. Maybe you have some Indians around here.

117   I got some toaster ovens, says that mistake.

118   We don't need that stuff, says Coyote. You got to stop making all those things. You're going to fill up this world.

119   Maybe you want a computer with a colour monitor. That mistake keeps looking through that book and those things keep landing in piles all around Coyote.

120   Stop, stop, cries Coyote. Golf cart lands on her foot. Golf balls bounce off her head. You got to give me that book before the world gets lopsided.

121   These are good things, says that mistake. We need these things to make up the world. Indians are going to need this stuff.

122   We don't have any Indians, says Coyote.

123   And that mistake can see that that's right. Maybe we better make some Indians, says that mistake. So that one looks in that catalogue, but it don't have any Indians. And Coyote don't know how to do that, either. She has already made four things.

124   I've made four things already, she says. I got to have help.

125   We can help, says some voices and it is those ducks come swimming along. We can help you make Indians, says the white duck. Yes, we can do that, says the green duck. We have been thinking about this, says that blue duck. We have a plan, says the red duck.

126   Well, that Coyote don't know what to do. So she tells them ducks to go ahead because this story is pretty long and it's getting late and everyone wants to go home.

127   You still awake, I says to Coyote. You still here?

128   Oh yes, grandmother, says Coyote. What do those clever ducks do?

129   So I tell Coyote that those ducks lay some eggs. Ducks do that, you know. That white duck lay an egg, and it is blue. That red duck lay an egg, and it is green. That blue duck lay an egg, and it is red. That green duck lay an egg, and it is white.

130   Come on, says those ducks. We got to sing a song. We got to do a dance. So they do. Coyote and that big mistake and those four ducks dance around the eggs. So they dance and sing for a long time, and pretty soon Coyote gets hungry.

131   I know this dance, she says, but you got to close your eyes when you do it or nothing will happen. You got to close your eyes tight. Okay, says those ducks. We can do that. And they do. And that big mistake closes its eyes, too.

132   But Coyote, she don't close her eyes, and all of them start dancing again, and Coyote dances up close to that white duck, and she grabs that white duck by her neck.

133   When Coyote grabs that duck, that duck flaps her wings, and that big mistake hears the noise and opens them eyes. Say, says that big mistake, that's not the way the dance goes.

134   By golly, you're right, says Coyote, and she lets that duck go. I am getting it mixed up with another dance.

135   So they start to dance again. And Coyote is very hungry, and she grabs that blue duck, and she grabs his wings, too. But Coyote's stomach starts to make hungry noises, and that mistake opens them eyes and sees Coyote with the blue duck. Hey, says that mistake, you got yourself mixed up again.

136   That's right, says Coyote, and she drops that duck and straightens out that neck. It sure is good you're around to help me with this dance.

NEL

137   They all start that dance again, and, this time, Coyote grab the green duck real quick and tries to stuff it down that greedy throat, and there is nothing hanging out but them yellow duck feet. But those feet are flapping in Coyote's eyes, and she can't see where she is going, and she bumps into the big mistake and the mistake turns around to see what has happened.

138   Ho, says that big mistake, you can't see where you're going with them yellow duck feet flapping in your eyes, and that mistake pulls that green duck out of Coyote's throat. You could hurt yourself dancing like that.

139   You are one good friend, look after me like that, says Coyote.

140   Those ducks start to dance again, and Coyote dances with them, but that red duck says, we better dance with one eye open, so we can help Coyote with this dance. So they dance some more, and, then, those eggs begin to move around, and those eggs crack open. And if you look hard, you can see something inside those eggs.

141   I know, I know, says that Coyote, jump up and down on my chair, shake up my good tea. Indians come out of those eggs. I remember this story, now. Inside those eggs are the Indians Coyote's been looking for.

142   No, I says. You are one crazy Coyote. What comes out of those duck eggs are baby ducks. You better sit down, I says. You may fall and hurt yourself. You may spill my tea. You may fall on top of this story and make it flat.

143   Where are the Indians? says that Coyote. This story is about how Coyote found the Indians. Maybe the Indians are in the eggs with the baby ducks.

144   No, I says, nothing in those eggs but little ducks. Indians will be along in a while. Don't lose your skin.

145   So.

146   When those ducks see what has come out of the eggs, they says, boy, we didn't get that quite right. We better try that again. So they do. They lay them eggs. They dance that dance. They sing that song. Those eggs crack open and out comes some more baby ducks. They do this seven times and each time, they get more ducks.

147   By golly, says those four ducks. We got more ducks than we need. I guess we got to be the Indians. And so they do that. Before Coyote or that big mistake can mess things up, those four ducks turn into Indians, two women and two men. Good-looking Indians, too. They don't look at all like ducks anymore.

148   But those duck-Indians aren't too happy. They look at each other and they begin to cry. This is pretty disgusting, they says. All this ugly skin. All these bumpy bones. All this awful black hair. Where are our nice soft feathers? Where are our beautiful feet? What happened to our wonderful wings? It's probably all that Coyote's fault because she didn't do the dance right, and those four duck-Indians come over and stomp all over Coyote until she is flat like before. Then they leave. That big

mistake leave, too. And that Coyote, she starts to think about a healing song.

149   Psst. Psst.

150   That's it, I says. It is done.

151   But what happens to Coyote, says Coyote. That wonderful one is still flat.

152   Some of these stories are flat, I says. That's what happens when you try to fix this world. This world is pretty good all by itself. Best to leave it alone. Stop messing around with it.

153   I better get going, says Coyote. I will tell Raven your good story. We going to fix this world for sure. We know how to do it now. We know how to do it right.

154   So, Coyote drinks my tea and that one leave. And I can't talk anymore because I got to watch the sky. Got to watch out for falling things that land in piles. When that Coyote's wandering around looking to fix things, nobody in this world is safe.

(1990)

Donna E. Smyth (b. 1943)

Novelist, playwright, short-story writer, and peace activist, Smyth currently teaches English in Nova Scotia. Her works include Quilt *(1982) and* Subversive Elements *(1986). In "Red Hot," Smyth raises questions not only about the abuse of women but also about the boundaries between fiction and reality.*

Red Hot

1   *(In November, 1982, the Crown charged that Jane Stafford of Bangs Falls, Nova Scotia, willfully and deliberately took the life of her common-law husband William [Billy] Stafford. All direct quotations in the following piece are taken from the Liverpool* Advance's *coverage of this case.)*

***

2   This is written in the Valley of the Shadow where we read death in the horrorscopes of movie stars, musicians and whales. In the cold northern light, people are building bomb shelters.

***

3   This is a ritual. Billy beats Jane like Jane's father beat her mother. Billy beat his first wife and his second wife and he beat Jane like Jane's father beat her mother.

***

4   This is written in hunting season when the wild geese on the river talk to each other all night long. Rising in flight into the frozen dawn, shot-gun scatter plucks them from the sky. The old moon, aghast, rolls on her back. The hunter takes another drink of rye.

***

5   Smelling like a fetid beast, this city heaves itself into the black and blue night. He forces a stick between her teeth so she cannot speak. Video flicker in a rented room. He strokes her throat with a razor. In the room the watchers groan. He grinds his teeth and says: I'm drilling for oil. Nothing can stop me! The watchers sigh and shift in their chairs.

He chains her to the operating table, her feet are in stirrups as if she is giving birth. He approaches with a scalpel, whispering: Tell me you like it! Tell me you like it!

***

6   The forensic firearms expert said: When a shotgun is fired at close range it causes the skull to explode. There was gross destruction of the victim's skull. The truck was full of blood and brain particles. It was like an explosion had taken place.

***

7   The late night talk show host smiles with his perfect teeth. He says to his female guest
—In our modern society, surely censorship is a dangerous weapon. Was it Roland Barthes[1] who said censorship is the bourgeois revenge on the erotic principle?
8   Cut to the beer commercial. Four men on a fishing trip. Not a woman in sight. The fish are jumping. They are happy.
9   Flip back to the female guest who never cracks a smile as she says
—This has nothing to do with sex. We're talking about power.

***

10   February, 1981. Jane said: "... a friend came to visit our home. We were sitting in the kitchen. Bill wasn't drinking and he went to bed. We were just sitting there talking about old times, not bothering anybody, when he came charging out of the bedroom with a 30-30, put it to her (my friend's) head and told her to get out. He then began beating me with the gun. I was knocked out...."

***

11   This is a ritual. To be on the football team, he has to prove he is a man. Stick it in a hot dog bun, slather it with mustard. Mustard? Yes, and ketchup too. The works! As if they're going to eat it BUT! Then they bring the ice and he must put it on ice until it melts 'cause he is hot, red hot! Later, in an interview, the coach chuckles
—Well, things maybe got a little out of hand. You know what guys are like.

***

---

1. Roland Barthes (1915–1980), French literary critic and one of the originators of modern theories of semiotics, which perceive literature, along with gesture and other forms of communication, as an elaborate system of signs.

12   November, 1982. Pauline, Billy's first wife, said: "He was a very cruel man in the six years I was married to him." He hit me, kicked me when I was pregnant. Once "he almost drowned me in a bucket of water." He beat our children too, "quite badly from the time they were six months old." He took one of the kids and stood her outside the house and threw knives at her to see how close he could come. Another time he sat the children down on the steps, threatened them with lit cigarettes and then made them eat the butts.

***

13   Video rerun. Close-up of her hands clutching the table. Glazed faces in a rented room. Black scarf tied over her mouth so she cannot scream. She is chained face-down on the table, a meat-cutting table. The room smells of smoke and booze and pickled herrings. A meat-cutting table where the saw whines with desire. Her hands clutching. The watchers groan. Whine of the saw rises, louder, louder than ambulance screams.
14   Cut.
15   The talk show host smiles disarmingly
    —Think of *Ulysses*. Think of *Lady Chatterley's Lover*.[2] Think of all the great works of art. Would you really want to censor the human imagination?
16   Cut.

***

17   Alan, Jane's teenage son, said that he often found his mother unconscious on the floor after Billy had beaten her. He said that often Billy would fire a gun in the house for no good reason. Once Billy took a shot at Jane while she was putting wood in the stove. Another time he fired when she was in the garden. Even the dog, said Alan. Our St. Bernard was "crazy from the beatings." Billy would "kick the dog in the mouth, bite its nose or even hit it with a piece of wood." We were all scared of Billy. That's what Alan said.

***

18   The female guest on the talk show says
    —These tapes show incredible violence against women and children. We asked this particular chain of stores, called Red Hot, to take the tapes off their shelves. They refused. We asked the Attorney-General to do something about it. He set up a committee to study the issue. Our point is: we don't need to study the issue!
19   Cut.

---

2. Both James Joyce's *Ulysses* (1922) and D.H. Lawrence's *Lady Chatterley's Lover* (1928) were originally censored in Britain and in the United States.

20   To Wayne Gretzky scoring a goal!

21   Cut.

22   Back to the host who now introduces Professor Arnold Armstrong. The Professor has written a scholarly book: *Eros Erectus: Paradigms of Sexuality and Civilization*. Along with his pipe, he brings to the discussion a word of caution
—If you interfere with what people do in the privacy of their own homes, you're violating their civil liberties. To quote our Prime Minister: "The state has no business in the bedrooms of the nation."

***

23   The judge said: Mrs. Stafford, will you please speak up. We can hardly hear you.

24   Jane said: At first Billy was not violent but after I had Darren, our four-year-old, "things started getting different." "Billy wanted a baby girl" and he said "I was no good" because I had the operation so I couldn't have any more children. He started to beat me and make me do things …

25   The lawyer said: What kind of things?

26   Jane said: Things in bed.
       : Sexually?
       : Yes.
       : Bondage?
       : Yes.
       : Bestiality?
       : Yes.
       : Why didn't you tell someone?
       : No one would believe me.
       : How did he treat the children?
       : He never taught Darren anything good. It was always hit, fight, get what you want. Sometimes Billy would pick him up by the hair, right off his feet, and hold a butcher knife to his throat. Darren was never supposed to cry because Billy told him "men don't cry."

***

27   November, 1982. In one night the Vancouver Wimmin's Fire Brigade burned two of the Red Hot shops. On the shelves the ghostly videotape figures writhed and hissed. Red hot. Red hot. The firemen had trouble putting out this purgatorial blaze. The Attorney-General spluttered and said: Taking the law into their own hands is no solution. Our Committee has been studying the issue for six months! The man-in-the-street, interviewed, said: They can't do this to me! In the privacy of my own home I can do what I want. That's what democracy is all about. We're not living in Soviet Russia. At least not yet.

***

28   Jane said: "I stayed in the truck; whenever he passed out in the truck I'd have to stay until he woke up. I just sat there; everything he had said about what he was going to do started sinking in. He said he was going to burn out Margaret Joudrey, my friend who I consider like a mother, and he said he was going to *deal* with Alan. All this started sinking in and I finally said to hell with it. I wasn't going to live like that anymore.... I put the gun in the window (the gun Alan brought me from the house) and pulled the trigger...."

***

29   Cut.

30   Professor Armstrong has forgotten his pipe, he is well-launched into his subject
—Society is always trying to chain up the erotic impulse like they locked up de Sade[3] in a madhouse. To the liberal man of conscience, de Sade is a revolutionary figure. A hero!

31   The female guest tries to interrupt
—But I....

32   And is cut off by the host who says
—I'm sorry. We're running out of time again.

33   Cut.

34   To the streets where the firemen are putting away their gear. The Red Hot shops are charred and smouldering. Into the first delicate light of dawn a car speeds along the Fraser Valley highway. Inside are three women who smell of gasoline and tension and fire. Inside are three women smiling.

***

35   November, 1982. After deliberating for 18 hours, the jury returned the verdict that Jane Stafford was NOT GUILTY. The spectator section of the courtroom burst into applause and people shouted: "Praise the Lord!" Jane's neighbour, Roger, said: "I never thought Jane would have enough gumption to do something like that." The Crown said they would appeal. Jane said: Thank you.

***

36   This is written in the Valley of the Shadow where the wind whips the sea to bitter fury and the old moon holds the new moon in her arms.

(1989)

---

3. The Marquis de Sade (1740–1814), French novelist who celebrated gaining sexual pleasure from physical cruelty to others in his novel *Justine* (1791). The term "sadism" is derived from his name.

Alice Walker (b. 1944)

The daughter of Georgia sharecroppers, Walker established her literary rep-
utation as an editor and writer of poetry and fiction. The Color Purple
(1982), which examines the effects of racism, won the Pulitzer Prize for
Fiction in 1983. Other works include The Third Life of Grange Copeland
(1970), Meridian *(1976), and* The Temple of My Familiar *(1989).*

Nineteen Fifty-Five

1955

1   The car is a brandnew red Thunderbird convertible, and it's passed the
house more than once. It slows down real slow now, and stops at the
curb. An older gentleman dressed like a Baptist deacon gets out on the
side near the house, and a young fellow who looks about sixteen gets
out on the driver's side. They are white, and I wonder what in the
world they doing in this neighborhood.

2   Well, I say to J.T., put your shirt on, anyway, and let me clean these
glasses offa the table.

3   We had been watching the ballgame on TV. I wasn't actually
watching, I was sort of daydreaming, with my foots up in J.T.'s lap.

4   I seen 'em coming on up the walk, brisk, like they coming to sell
something, and then they rung the bell, and J.T. declined to put on a
shirt but instead disappeared into the bedroom where the other television is. I turned down the one in the living room; I figured I'd be
rid of these two double quick and J.T. could come back out again.

5   Are you Gracie Mae Still? asked the old guy, when I opened the
door and put my hand on the lock inside the screen.

6   And I don't need to buy a thing, said I.

7   What makes you think we're sellin'? he asks, in that hearty
Southern way that makes my eyeballs ache.

8   Well, one way or another and they're inside the house and the first
thing the young fellow does is raise the TV a couple of decibels. He's
about five feet nine, sort of womanish looking, with real dark white
skin and a red pouting mouth. His hair is black and curly and he
looks like a Loosianna creole.

9   About one of your songs, says the deacon. He is maybe sixty, with white hair and beard, white silk shirt, black linen suit, black tie and black shoes. His cold gray eyes look like they're sweating.

10   One of my songs?

11   Traynor here just loves your songs. Don't you, Traynor? He nudges Traynor with his elbow. Traynor blinks, says something I can't catch in a pitch I don't register.

12   The boy learned to sing and dance livin' around you people out in the country. Practically cut his teeth on you.

13   Traynor looks up at me and bites his thumbnail.

14   I laugh.

15   Well, one way or another they leave with my agreement that they can record one of my songs. The deacon writes me a check for five hundred dollars, the boy grunts his awareness of the transaction, and I am laughing all over myself by the time I rejoin J.T.

16   Just as I am snuggling down beside him though I hear the front door bell going off again.

17   Forgit his hat? asks J.T.

18   I hope not, I say.

19   The deacon stands there leaning on the door frame and once again I'm thinking of those sweaty-looking eyeballs of his. I wonder if sweat makes your eyeballs pink because his are sure pink. Pink and gray and it strikes me that nobody I'd care to know is behind them.

20   I forgot one little thing, he says pleasantly. I forgot to tell you Traynor and I would like to buy up all of those records you made of the song. I tell you we sure do love it.

21   Well, love it or not, I'm not so stupid as to let them do that without making 'em pay. So I says, Well, that's gonna cost you. Because, really, that song never did sell all that good, so I was glad they was going to buy it up. But on the other hand, them two listening to my song by themselves, and nobody else getting to hear me sing it, give me a pause.

22   Well, one way or another the deacon showed me where I would come out ahead on any deal he had proposed so far. Didn't I give you five hundred dollars? he asked. What white man—and don't even need to mention colored—would give you more? We buy up all your records of that particular song: first, you git royalties. Let me ask you, how much you sell that song for in the first place? Fifty dollars? A hundred, I say. And no royalties from it yet, right? Right. Well, when we buy up all of them records you gonna git royalties. And that's gonna make all them race record shops sit up and take notice of Gracie Mae Still. And they gonna push all them other records of yourn they got. And you no doubt will become one of the big name colored recording artists. And then we can offer you another five hundred dollars for letting us do all this for you. And by God you'll be sittin' pretty! You can go out and buy you the kind of outfit a star should have. Plenty sequins and yards of red satin.

23   I had done unlocked the screen when I saw I could get some more money out of him. Now I held it wide open while he squeezed through the opening between me and the door. He whipped out another piece of paper and I signed it.

24   He sort of trotted out to the car and slid in beside Traynor, whose head was back against the seat. They swung around in a u-turn in front of the house and then they were gone.

25   J.T. was putting his shirt on when I got back to the bedroom. Yankees beat the Orioles 10-6, he said. I believe I'll drive out to Paschal's pond and go fishing. Wanta go?

26   While I was putting on my pants J.T. was holding the two checks.

27   I'm real proud of a woman that can make cash money without leavin' home, he said. And I said *Umph*. Because we met on the road with me singing in first one little low-life jook after another, making ten dollars a night for myself if I was lucky, and sometimes bringin' home nothing but my life. And J.T. just loved them times. The way I was fast and flashy and always on the go from one town to another. He loved the way my singin' made the dirt farmers cry like babies and the womens shout Honey, hush! But that's mens. They loves any style to which you can get 'em accustomed.

1956

28   My little grandbaby called me one night on the phone: Little Mama, Little Mama, there's a white man on the television singing one of your songs! Turn on channel 5.

29   Lord, if it wasn't Traynor. Still looking half asleep from the neck up, but kind of awake in a nasty way from the waist down. He wasn't doing too bad with my song either, but it wasn't just the song the people in the audience was screeching and screaming over, it was that nasty little jerk he was doing from the waist down.

30   Well, Lord have mercy. I said, listening to him. If I'da closed my eyes, it could have been me. He had followed every turning of my voice, side streets, avenues, red lights, train crossings and all. It give me a chill.

31   Everywhere I went I hear Traynor singing my song, and all the little white girls just eating it up. I never had so many ponytails switched across my line of vision in my life. They was so *proud*. He was a *genius*.

32   Well, all that year I was trying to lose weight anyway and that and high blood pressure and sugar kept me pretty well occupied. Traynor had made a smash from a song of mine. I still have seven hundred dollars of the original one thousand dollars in the bank, and I felt if I could just bring my weight down, life would be sweet.

1957

33   I lost ten pounds in 1956. That's what I give myself for Christmas. And J.T. and me and the children and their friends and grandkids of all description had just finished dinner—over which I had put on nine and a half of my lost ten—when who should appear at the front door but Traynor. Little Mama, Little Mama! It's that white man who sings—— —— ——. The children didn't call it my song anymore. Nobody did. It was funny how that happened. Traynor and the deacon had bought up all my records, true, but on his record he had put "written by Gracie Mae Still." But that was just another name on the label, like "produced by Apex Records."

34   On the TV he was inclined to dress like the deacon told him. But now he looked presentable.

35   Merry Christmas, said he.

36   And same to you, Son.

37   I don't know why I called him Son. Well, one way or another they're all our sons. The only requirement is that they be younger than us. But then again Traynor seemed to be aging by the minute.

38   You looks tired, I said. Come on in and have a glass of Christmas cheer.

39   J.T. ain't never in his life been able to act decent to a white man he wasn't working for, but he poured Traynor a glass of bourbon and water, then he took all the children and grandkids and friends and whatnot out to the den. After a while I heard Traynor's voice singing the song, coming from the stereo console. It was just the kind of Christmas present my kids would consider cute.

40   I looked at Traynor, complicit. But he looked like it was the last thing in the world he wanted to hear. His head was pitched forward over his lap, his hands holding his glass and his elbows on his knees.

41   I done sung that song seem like a million times this year, he said. I sung it on the Grand Ole Opry, I sung it on the Ed Sullivan show. I sung it on Mike Douglas, I sung it at the Cotton Bowl, the Orange Bowl. I sung it at Festivals. I sung it at Fairs. I sung it overseas in Rome, Italy, and once in a submarine *underseas*. I've sung it and sung it, and I'm making forty thousand dollars a day offa it, and you know what, I don't have the faintest notion what that song means.

42   Whatchumean, what do it mean? It mean what it says. All I could think was: these suckers is making forty thousand a *day* offa my song and now they gonna come back and try to swindle me out of the original thousand.

43   It's just a song, I said. Cagey. When you fool around with a lot of no count mens you sing a bunch of 'em. I shrugged.

44   Oh, he said. Well. He started brightening up. I just come by to tell you I think you are a great singer.

45   He didn't blush, saying that. Just said it straight out.

46 And I brought you a little Christmas present too. Now you take this little box and you hold it until I drive off. Then you take it out-side under the first streetlight back up the street aways in front of that green house. Then you open the box and see ... Well, just *see*.

47 What had come over this boy, I wondered, holding the box. I looked out the window in time to see another white man come up and get in the car with him and then two more cars full of white mens start out behind him. They was all in long black cars that looked like a funeral procession.

48 Little Mama, Little Mama, what it is? One of my grandkids came running up and started pulling at the box. It was wrapped in gay Christmas paper—the thick, rich kind that it's hard to picture folks making just to throw away.

49 J.T. and the rest of the crowd followed me out the house, up the street to the streetlight and in front of the green house. Nothing was there but somebody's gold-grille white Cadillac. Brandnew and most distracting. We got to looking at it so till I almost forgot the little box in my hand. While the others were busy making 'miration I carefully took off the paper and ribbon and folded them up and put them in my pants pocket. What should I see but a pair of genuine solid gold caddy keys.

50 Dangling the keys in front of everybody's nose, I unlocked the caddy, motioned for J.T. to git in on the other side, and us didn't come back home for two days.

1960

51 Well, the boy was sure nuff famous by now. He was still a mite shy of twenty but already they was calling him the Emperor of Rock and Roll.

52 Then what should happen but the draft.

53 Well, says J.T. There goes all this Emperor of Rock and Roll business.

54 But even in the army the womens was on him like white on rice. We watched it on the News.

> *Dear Gracie Mae [he wrote from Germany],*
>
> *How you? Fine I hope as this leaves me doing real well. Before I come in the army I was gaining a lot of weight and gitting jittery from making all them dumb movies. But now I exercise and eat right and get plenty of rest. I'm more awake than I been in ten years.*
> *I wonder if you are writing any more songs?*
> *Sincerely,*
> *Traynor*

55 I wrote him back:

Dear Son,

We is all fine in the Lord's good grace and hope this finds you the same. J.T. and me be out all times of the day and night in that car you give me—which you know you didn't have to do. Oh, and I do appreciate the mink and the new self-cleaning oven. But if you send anymore stuff to eat from Germany I'm going to have to open up a store in the neighborhood just to get rid of it. Really, we have more than enough of everything. The Lord is good to us and we don't know Want.

Glad to here you is well and gitting your right rest. There ain't nothing like exercising to help that along. J.T. and me work some part of every day that we don't go fishing in the garden.

Well, so long Soldier.
Sincerely,
Gracie Mae

56   He wrote:

Dear Gracie Mae,

I hope you and J.T. like that automatic power tiller I had one of the stores back home send you. I went through a mountain of catalogs looking for it—I wanted something that even a woman could use.

I've been thinking about writing some songs of my own but every time I finish one it don't seem to be about nothing I've actually lived myself. My agent keeps sending me other people's songs but they just sound mooney. I can hardly git through 'em without gagging.

Everybody still loves that song of yours. They ask me all the time what do I think it means, really. I mean, they want to know just what I want to know. Where out of your life did it come from?
Sincerely,
Traynor

1968

57   I didn't see the boy for seven years. No. Eight. Because just about everybody was dead when I saw him again. Malcolm X, King, the president and his brother[1] and even J.T. J.T. died of a head cold. It just settled in his head like a block of ice, he said, and nothing we did moved it until one day he just leaned out the bed and died.

58   His good friend Horace helped me put him away, and then about a year later Horace and me started going together. We was sitting out

---

1. Malcolm X (1925–1965), African-American founder of the Black Muslim movement. Martin Luther King, Jr. (1929–1968), U.S. civil rights leader who successfully led a movement of non-violent resistance against racial segregation in the United States. John F. Kennedy (1917–1963), U.S. president who supported racial integration. Robert F. Kennedy (1925–1968), the president's brother who served as U.S. attorney general. All four were killed by assassins.

on the front porch swing one summer night, dusk-dark, and I saw this great procession of lights winding to a stop.

59   Holy Toledo! said Horace. (He's got a real sexy voice like Ray Charles.[2]) Look *at* it. He meant the long line of flashy cars and the white men in white summer suits jumping out on the drivers' sides and standing at attention. With wings they could pass for angels, with hoods they could be the Klan.

60   Traynor comes waddling up the walk.

61   And suddenly I know what it is he could pass for. An Arab like the ones you see in storybooks. Plump and soft and with never a care about weight. Because with so much money, who cares? Traynor is almost dressed like someone from a storybook too. He has on, I swear, about ten necklaces. Two sets of bracelets on his arms, at least one ring on every finger, and some kind of shining buckles on his shoes, so that when he walks you get quite a few twinkling lights.

62   Gracie Mae, he says, coming up to give me a hug. J.T.

63   I explain that J.T. passed. That this is Horace.

64   Horace, he says, puzzled but polite, sort of rocking back on his heels, Horace.

65   That's it for Horace. He goes in the house and don't come back.

66   Looks like you and me is gained a few, I say.

67   He laughs. The first time I ever heard him laugh. It don't sound much like a laugh and I can't swear that it's better than no laugh at a'tall.

68   He's gitting fat for sure, but he's still slim compared to me. I'll never see three hundred pounds again and I've just about said (excuse me) fuck it. I got to thinking about it one day an' I thought: aside from the fact that they say it's unhealthy, my fat ain't never been no trouble. Men always have loved me. My kids ain't never complained. Plus they's fat. And fat like I is I looks distinguished. You see me coming and know somebody's *there*.

69   Gracie Mae, he says, I've come with a personal invitation to you to my house tomorrow for dinner. He laughed. What did it sound like? I couldn't place it. See them men out there? he asked me. I'm sick and tired of eating with them. But if you come to dinner tomorrow we can talk about the old days. You can tell me about that farm I bought you.

70   I sold it, I said.

71   You did?

72   Yeah, I said. I did. Just cause I said I like to exercise by working in a garden didn't mean I wanted five hundred acres! Anyhow, I'm a city girl now. Raised in the country it's true. Dirt poor—the whole bit—but that's all behind me now.

73   Oh well, he said. I didn't mean to offend you.

74   We sat a few minutes listening to the crickets.

---

2. African-American rhythm and blues singer who became famous during the 1950s.

75   Then he said: You wrote that song while you was still on the farm, didn't you, or was it right after you left?

76   You had somebody spying on me? I asked.

77   You and Bessie Smith[3] got into a fight over it once, he said.

78   You *is* been spying on me!

79   But I don't know what the fight was about, he said. Just like I don't know what happened to your second husband. Your first one died in the Texas electric chair. Did you know that? Your third one beat you up, stole your touring costumes and your car and retired with a chorine[4] to Tuskegee. He laughed. He's still there.

80   I had been mad, but suddenly I calmed down. Traynor was talking very dreamily. It was dark but seems like I could tell his eyes weren't right. It was like *something* was sitting there talking to me but not necessarily with a person behind it.

81   You gave up on marrying and seem happier for it. He laughed again. I married but it never went like it was supposed to. I never could squeeze any of my own life either into it or out of it. It was like singing somebody else's record. I copied the way it was supposed to be *exactly* but I never had a clue what marriage meant.

82   I bought her a diamond ring big as your fist. I bought her clothes. I built her a mansion. But right away she didn't want the boys to stay there. Said they smoked up the bottom floor. Hell, there were *five* floors.

83   No need to grieve, I said. No need to. Plenty more where she comes from.

84   He perked up. That's part of what that song means, ain't it? No need to grieve. Whatever it is, there's plenty more down the line.

85   I never really believed that way back when I wrote the song, I said. It was all bluffing then. The trick is to live long enough to put your young bluffs to use. Now if I was going to sing that song today I'd tear it up. 'Cause I done lived long enough to know it's *true*. Them words could hold me up.

86   I ain't lived that long, he said.

87   Look like you on your way, I said. I don't know why, but the boy seemed to need some encouraging. And I don't know, seem like one way or another you talk to rich white folks and you end up reassuring *them*. But what the hell, by now I feel something for the boy. I wouldn't be in his bed all alone in the middle of the night for nothing. Couldn't be nothing worse than being famous the world over for something you don't even understand. That's what I tried to tell Bessie. She wanted that same song. Overheard me practising it one day, said, with her hands on her hips: Gracie Mae, I'ma sing your song tonight. I *likes* it.

---

3. Bessie Smith (c. 1898–1937), Southern-American singer who became famous during the 1920s as the "Empress of the Blues."
4. Chorus dancer (derogatory).

88　　Your lips be too swole to sing, I said. She was mean and she was strong, but I trounced her.

89　　Ain't you famous enough with your own stuff? I said. Leave mine alone. Later on, she thanked me. By then she was Miss Bessie Smith to the World, and I was still Miss Gracie Mae Nobody from Notasulga.

90　　The next day all these limousines arrived to pick me up. Five cars and twelve bodyguards. Horace picked that morning to start painting the kitchen.

91　　Don't paint the kitchen, fool, I said. The only reason that dumb boy of ours is going to show me his mansion is because he intends to present us with a new house.

92　　What you gonna do with it? he asked me, standing there in his shirt-sleeves stirring the paint.

93　　Sell it. Give it to the children. Live in it on weekends. It don't matter what I do. He sure don't care.

94　　Horace just stood there shaking his head. Mama you sure looks *good*, he says. Wake me up when you git back.

95　　*Fool*, I say, and pat my wig in front of the mirror.

96　　The boy's house is something else. First you come to this mountain, and then you commence to drive up this road that's lined with magnolias. Do magnolias grow on mountains? I was wondering. And you come to lakes and you come to ponds and you come to deer and you come up on some sheep. And I figure these two is sposed to represent England and Wales. Or something out of Europe. And you just keep on coming to stuff. And it's all pretty. Only the man driving my car don't look at nothing but the road. Fool. And then *finally*, after all this time, you begin to go up the driveway. And there's more magnolias— only they're not in such good shape. It's sort of cool up this high and I don't think they're gonna make it. And then I see this building that looks like if it had a name it would be The Tara Hotel.[5] Columns and steps and outdoor chandeliers and rocking chairs. Rocking chairs? Well, and there's the boy on the steps dressed in a dark green satin jacket like you see folks wearing on TV late at night, and he looks sort of like a fat dracula with all that house rising behind him, and standing beside him there's this little white vision of loveliness that he introduces as his wife.

97　　He's nervous when he introduces us and he says to her: This is Gracie Mae Still, I want you to know me. I mean … and she gives him a look that would fry meat.

98　　Won't you come in, Grace May, she says, and that's the last I see of her.

---

5. From Tara, the home of Scarlett O'Hara in Margaret Mitchell's novel, *Gone With the Wind*.

99   He fishes around for something to say or do and decides to escort me to the kitchen. We go through the entry and the parlor and the breakfast room and the dining room and the servants' passage and finally get there. The first thing I notice is that, altogether, there are five stoves. He looks about to introduce me to one.

100   Wait a minute, I say. Kitchens don't do nothing for me. Let's go sit on the front porch.

101   Well, we hike back and we sit in the rocking chairs rocking until dinner.

102 Gracie Mae, he says down the table, taking a piece of fried chicken from the woman standing over him, I got a little surprise for you.

103   It's a house, ain't it? I ask, spearing a chitlin.[6]

104   You're getting *spoiled*, he says. And the way he says *spoiled* sounds funny. He slurs it. It sounds like his tongue is too thick for his mouth. Just that quick he's finished the chicken and is now eating chitlins, *and* a pork chop. *Me* spoiled, I'm thinking.

105   I already got a house. Horace is right this minute painting the kitchen. I bought that house. My kids feel comfortable in that house.

106   But this one I bought you is just like mine. Only a little smaller.

107   I still don't need no house. And anyway who would clean it?

108   He looks surprised.

109   Really, I think, some peoples advance *so* slowly.

110   I hadn't thought of that. But what the hell. I'll get you somebody to live in.

111   I don't want other folks living 'round me. Makes me nervous.

112   You *don't*? It *do*?

113   What I want to wake up and see folks I don't even know for?

114   He just sits there downtable staring at me. Some of that feeling is in the song, ain't it? Not the words, the *feeling*. What I want to wake up and see folks I don't even know for? But I see twenty folks a day I don't even know, including my wife.

115   This food wouldn't be bad to wake up to though, I said. The boy had found the genius of corn bread.

116   He looked at me real hard. He laughed. Short. They want what you got but they don't want you. They want what I got only it ain't mine. That's what makes 'em so hungry for me when I sing. They getting the flavor of something but they ain't getting the thing itself. They like a pack of hound dogs trying to gobble up a scent.

117   You talking 'bout your fans?

118   Right. Right. He says.

119   Don't worry 'bout your fans, I say. They don't know their asses from a hole in the ground. I doubt there's a honest one in the bunch.

---

6. Chitterlings are pigs' intestines, cleaned and fried with spices, a popular Southern dish.

120   That's the point. Dammit, that's the point! He hits the table with his fist. It's so solid it don't even quiver. You need a honest audience! You can't have folks that's just gonna lie right back to you.

121   Yeah, I say, it was small compared to yours, but I had one. It would have been worth my life to try to sing 'em somebody else's stuff that I didn't know nothing about.

122   He must have pressed a buzzer under the table. One of his flunkies zombies up.

123   Git Johnny Carson, he says.

124   On the phone? asks the zombie.

125   On the phone, says Traynor, what you think I mean, git him offa the front porch? Move your ass.

126 So two weeks later we's on the Johnny Carson show.

127 Traynor is all corseted down nice and looks a little bit fat but mostly good. And all the women that grew up on him and my song squeal and squeal. Traynor says: The lady who wrote my first hit record is here with us tonight, and she's agreed to sing it for all of us, just like she sung it forty-five years ago. Ladies and Gentlemen, the great Gracie Mae Still!

128   Well, I had tried to lose a couple of pounds my own self, but failing that I had me a very big dress made. So I sort of rolls over next to Traynor, who is dwarfed by me, so that when he puts his arms around back of me to try to hug me it looks funny to the audience and they laugh.

129   I can see this pisses him off. But I smile out there at 'em. Imagine squealing for twenty years and not knowing why you're squealing? No more sense of endings and beginnings than hogs.

130   It don't matter, Son, I say. Don't fret none over me.

131   I commence to sing. And I sound—wonderful. Being able to sing good ain't all about having a good singing voice a'tall. A good singing voice helps. But when you come up in the Hard Shell Baptist church like I did you understand early that the fellow that sings is the singer. Them that waits for programs and arrangements and letters from home is just good voices occupying body space.

132   So there I am singing my own song, my own way. And I give it all I got and enjoy every minute of it. When I finish Traynor is standing up clapping and clapping and beaming at first me and then the audience like I'm his mama for true. The audience claps politely for about two seconds.

133   Traynor looks disgusted.

134   He comes over and tries to hug me again. The audience laughs.

135   Johnny Carson looks at us like we both weird.

136   Traynor is mad as hell. He's supposed to sing something called a love ballad. But instead he takes the mike, turns to me and says: Now see if my imitation still holds up. He goes into the same song, *our*

song, I think, looking out at his flaky audience. And he sings it just the way he always did. My voice, my tone, my inflection, everything. But he forgets a couple of lines. Even before he's finished the matronly squeals begin.

137   He sits down next to me looking whipped.

138   It don't matter, Son, I say, patting his head. You don't even know those people. Try to make the people you know happy.

139   Is that in the song? he asks.

140   Maybe. I say.

1977

141   For a few years I hear from him, then nothing. But trying to lose weight takes all the attention I got to spare. I finally faced up to the fact that my fat is the hurt I don't admit, not even to myself, and that I been trying to bury it from the day I was born. But also when you git real old, to tell the truth, it ain't as pleasant. It gits lumpy and slack. So one day I said to Horace, I'ma git this shit offa me.

142   And he fell in with the program like he always try to do and Lord such a procession of salads and cottage cheese and fruit juice!

143   One night I dreamed Traynor had split up with his fifteenth wife. He said: *You meet 'em for no reason. You date 'em for no reason. You marry 'em for no reason. I do it all but I swear it's just like somebody else doing it. I feel like I can't remember Life.*

144   The boy's in trouble, I said to Horace.

145   You've always said that, he said.

146   I have?

147   Yeah. You always said he looked asleep. You can't sleep through life if you wants to live it.

148   You not such a fool after all, I said, pushing myself up with my cane and hobbling over to where he was. Let me sit down on your lap, I said, while this salad I ate takes effect.

149   In the morning we heard that Traynor was dead. Some said fat, some said heart, some said alcohol, some said drugs. One of the children called from Detroit. Them dumb fans of his on a crying rampage, she said. You just ought to turn on the TV.

150   But I didn't want to see 'em. They was crying and crying and didn't even know what they was crying for. One day this is going to be a pitiful country, I thought.

(1981)

Lee Maracle (b. 1950)

*Born in Vancouver of Métis and Salish parents, Maracle did not complete
high school, but studied at Simon Fraser University in 1987. Education is a
central concern of her work, which remains true to the principles of Native
oratory. A gifted poet, novelist, short-story writer, and commentator,
Maracle draws her readers into her work to "become the trickster, the architect of great social transformations at whatever level [they] choose."*

Yin Chin

for Sharon Lee, whose real name is Sky, and for Jim Wong-Chu

1   she is tough,
she is verbose,
she has lived a thousand lives

2   she is sweet,
she is not,
she is blossoming
and dying every moment

3   a flower
unsweetened by rain
untarnished by simpering
uncuckolded by men
not coquettish enough
for say the gals
who make a career of shopping
at the Pacific Centre Mall

4   PACIFIC CENTRE, my gawd
do North Americans never tire
of claiming the centre
of the universe, the Pacific and
everywhere else ...

5   I am weary
of North Americans
so I listen to SKY

6   Standing in the crowded college dining hall, coffee in hand, my face is drawn to a noisy group of Chinese youth; I mentally cancel them out. No place to sit—no place meaning there aren't any Indians in the room. It is a reflexive action on my part to assume that any company that isn't Indian company is generally unacceptable, but there it was: the absence of Indians, not chairs, determined the absence of a space for me. Soft of heart, guilt-ridden liberals might argue defensively that such sweeping judgement is not different from any of the generalizations made about us. So be it; after all, it is not their humanity I am calling into question. It is mine. Along with that thought dances another. I have lived in this city in the same neighbourhood as Chinese people for over twenty-two years now and don't know a single Chinese person.

7   It scares me just a little. It wasn't always that way. The memory of a skinny little waif drops into the frame of moving pictures rolling across my mind. Unabashed, she stands next to the door of Mad Sam's market across from the Powell Street[1] grounds, surveying "Chinamen" with accusatory eyes. Once a month on a Saturday the process repeats itself: the little girl of noble heart studies the old men. Not once in all her childhood years did she ever see an old man steal a little kid. She gave up, not because she became convinced that the accusation was unfounded, but because she got too big to worry about it.

8   "Cun-a-muck-ah-you-da-puppy-shaw, that's Chinee for how are you," and the old Pa'pa-y-ah would laugh. "Don't wander around town or the old Chinamen will get you, steal you, ... Chinkee, chinkee Chinamen went down town, turned around the corner and his pants fell down," and other such truck is buried somewhere in the useless information file tucked in the basement of my mind, but the shape of my social life is frighteningly influenced by those absurd sounds. The movie is just starting to lag and the literary theme of the pictures is coming into focus when a small breath of air, a gentle touch of a small woman's hand invites me to sit. How embarrassing. I'd been gaping and gawking at a table-load of Hans long enough for my coffee to cool.

9   It doesn't take long. Invariably, when people of colour get together they discuss white people. They are the butt of our jokes, the fountain of our bitterness and pain and the infinite well-spring of every dilemma life ever presented to us. The humour eases the pain, but always whites figure front and centre of our joint communication. If I had a dollar for every word ever said about them, instead of to them, I'd be the richest welfare bum in the country. No wonder they suffer from inflated egoism.

10   I sit at the table-load of Chinese people and towards the end of the hour I want to tell them about Mad Sam's, Powell Street and the old men. Wisely, I think now, I didn't. Our sense of humour was different then. In the face of a crass white world we had erased so much of our-

---

1. Thoroughfare in Vancouver's Chinatown.

selves, and sketched so many cartoon characters of white people over top of the emptiness inside, that it would have been too much for us to face the fact that we really did feel just like them. I sat at that table more than a dozen times but not once did it occur to any of us that we were friends. Eventually, the march of a relentless clock, my hasty departure from college the following semester and my failure to return for fifteen years took its toll—now even their names escape me.

11 Last Saturday—seems like a hundred years later—was different. This time the table-load of people was Asian and Native. We laughed at ourselves and spoke very seriously about our writing. "We really believe we are writers," someone said, and the room shook with the hysteria of it all. We ran on and on about our growth and development, and not once did the white man ever enter the room. It just seemed too incredible that a dozen Hans and Natives could sit and discuss all things under heaven, including racism, and not talk about white people. It had only taken a half-dozen revolutions in the third world, seventeen riots in America, one hundred demonstrations against racism in Canada and thirty-seven dead Native youth in my life to become. I could have told them about the waif, but it didn't seem relevant. We had crossed a millennium of bridges over rivers swollen with the floodwaters of dark humanity's tenacious struggle to extricate ourselves from oppression, and we knew it. We had been born during the first sword wound that the third world swung at imperialism. We were children of that wound, invincible, conscious and movin' on up. We could laugh because we were no longer a joke. But somewhere along the line we forgot to tell the others, the thousands of our folks who still tell their kids about old Chinamen.

* * *

12 It's Tuesday and I'm circling the block at Gore and Powell trying to find a parking space, windows open, driving like I belong here. A sharp, "Don't come near me, why you bother me?" jars me loose. An old Chinese woman swings a ratty old umbrella at a Native man who is pushing her, cursing her and otherwise giving her a hard time. I lean toward the passenger side and shout at him from the safety of my car: "Leave her alone, asshole."

13 "Shuddup you f.ck.ng rag-head." I jump out of the car without bothering to park it. No one honks; they just stare at me. The man sees my face and my cowichan,[2] bends deeply and says sarcastically that he didn't know I was a squaw. Well, I'm no pacifist, I admit: I belt him, give him a what for, and the coward leaves. I help the old woman across the street, then return to park my car. She stays there, where I left her, still shaking, so I stop to try to quell her fear.

---

2. Usually the word is capitalized. It refers to the heavy, handknit sweaters made and sometimes worn by the Cowichan band.

14   She isn't afraid. She is ashamed of her own people—men who passed her by, walking around her or crossing the street to avoid trying to rescue her from the taunts of one of my people. The world rages around inside me while she copiously describes every Chinese man who saw her and kept walking. I listen to her in silence and think of me and old Sam again.

15   Mad Sam was a pioneer of discount foods. Slightly overripe bananas (great for peanut-butter-and-banana bannock sandwiches), bruised apples and day-old bread were always available at half the price of Safeway's, and we shopped there regularly for years. I am not sure if he sold meat. In any case, we never bought meat; we were fish-eaters then. I doubt very much that Sam knew we called him "Mad" but I know now that "mad" was intended for the low prices and the crowds in his little store, not for him. In the fifties, there were still storeowners who concerned themselves with their customers, established relationships with them, exchanged gossip and shared a few laughs. Sam was good to us.

16   If you press your nose up against the window to the left of the door you can still see me standing there, ghost-like, skinny brown body with huge eyes riveted on the street and the Powell Street grounds. Sometimes my eyes take a slow shift from left to right, then right to left. I'm watchin' ol' Chinamen, makin' sure they don't grab little kids. Once a month for several years I assume my post and keep my private vigil. No one on the street seems to know what I'm doing or why, but it doesn't matter. The object of my vigil is not appreciation but catchin' the old Chinamen in the act.

17   My nose is pressed up against the window pane; the cold circles the end of my flattened nose; it feels good. Outside, the window pane is freckled with crystal water drops; inside, it is smooth and dry, but for a little wisp of fog from my breath. Round o's of water splotch onto the clear glass. Not perfectly round, but just the right amount of roundness that allows you to call them o's. Each o is kind of wobbly and different, like on the page at school when you first print o's for teacher.

18   I can see the rain-distorted street scene at the park through the round o's of water. There are no flowers or grass in this park, no elaborate floral themes or landscape designs, just a dozen or so benches around a wasteland of gravel, sand and comfrey root (weeds), and a softball backstop at one end. (What a bloody long time ago that was, mama.)

19   Blat. A raindrop hits the window, scrunching up the park bench I am looking at. The round o of rain makes the park bench wiggle towards my corner of the store. I giggle.

20   "Mad Sam's ... Mad Sam's ... Mad Sam's?" What begins as a senseless repetition of a household phrase ends as a question. I know that Mad Sam is a Chinaman ... Chinee, the old people call them—but then, the old people can't speak goot Inklish. But what in the world makes him mad? I breathe at the window. It fogs up. The only kind of

mad I know is when everyone runs aroun' hollering and kicking up dust.

21   I rock back and forth while my finger traces out a large circle which my hand had cleared. Two old men on the bench across the street break my thoughts of Sam's madness. One of them rises. He is wearing one of those grey tweed wool hats that people think of as English and associate with sports cars. He has a cane, a light beige cane. He half bends at the waist before he leaves the bench, turns, and with his arms stretched out from his shoulders flails them back and forth a few times, accentuating his words to the other old man seated there.

22   It would have looked funny if Pa'pa-y-ah had done it, or ol' Mike, but I am acutely aware that this is a Chinaman. Ol' Chinamen are not funny. They are serious, and the words of the world echo violently in my ears: "Don't wander off or the ol' Chinamen will get you and eat you." I wonder about the fact that mama has never warned me about them.

23   A woman with a black car coat and a white pill box hat disturbs the scene. Screech, the door of her Buick opens. Squeak, slam, it bangs shut. There she be, blonde as all get out, slightly hippy, heaving her bare leg, partially constrained by her skirt, onto the bumper of her car and cranking at whatever has to be cranked to make the damn thing go. There is something humorously inelegant about a white lady with spiked heels, tight skirt and a pill box hat cranking up a '39 Buick. (Thanks, mama, for having me soon enough to have seen it.) All of this wonderfulness comes squiggling to me through a little puddle of clear rain on the window. The Buick finally takes off and from the tail end of its departure I can see the little old man still shuffling his way across the street. Funny, all the cars stop for him. Odd, the little Chinee boy talks to him, unafraid.

24   Shuffle, shuffle, plunk of his cane, shuffle, shuffle, plunk; on he trudges. The breath from the corner near my window comes out in shorter and louder gasps. It punctuates the window with an on-again, off-again choo-choo rhythm of clarity. Breath and fog, shuffle, shuffle, plunk, breath and fog. BOOM! And the old man's face is right on mine. My scream is indelicate. Mad Sam and mama come running.

25   "Whatsa matter?" ... "Wah iss it?" from Sam and mama respectively.

26   Half hesitating, I point out the window. "The Chinaman was looking at me." I can see that this is not the right answer. Mama's eyes yell *for pete's sake* and her cheeks shine red with shame—not embarrassment, shame. Sam's face is clearly, definably hurt. Not the kind of hurt that shows when adults burn themselves or something, but the kind of hurt you can sometimes see in the eyes of people who have been cheated. The total picture spells something I cannot define.

27   Grandmothers, you said if I was ever caught doing nothing you would take me away for all eternity. The silence is thick, cloying and paralyzing. It stops my brain and stills my emotions. It deafens my ears

to the rain. I cannot look out to see if the old man is still there. No grannies come to spare me.

28   My eyes fall unseeing on a parsnip just exactly in front of my face. They rest there until everyone stops looking at my treacherous little body and resumes talking about whatever they were talking about before I brought the world to a momentary halt with my astounding stupidity. What surprises me now, years later, is that they did eventually carry on as though nothing were wrong.

29   The floor sways beneath me, while I try hard to make it swallow me. A hand holding a pear in front of my face jars my eyes loose from the parsnip.

30   "Here," the small, pained smile on Sam's face stills the floor, but the memory remains a moving moment in my life.

* * *

31   The old woman is holding my hands, saying she feels better now. All that time I wasn't thinking about what she said, or speaking. I just nodded my head back and forth and relived my memory of Mad Sam's.

32   "How unkind of the world to school us in ignorance" is all I say, and I make my way back to the car.

(1990)

Guy Vanderhaeghe (b. 1951)

Born in Saskatchewan, Vanderhaeghe worked as a teacher, researcher, and
archivist before turning to writing. He won the Governor General's Award
for fiction for his first book, Man Descending *(1982), and for* The
Englishman's Boy *(1996). He regards himself "as a writer who celebrates*
... the endurance of the ordinary person whose life is a series of small
victories fashioned from small resources."

Drummer

1   You'd think my old man was the Pope's nephew or something if you'd
seen how wild he went when he learned I'd been sneaking off Sundays
to Faith Baptist Church. Instead of going to eleven o'clock Mass like he
figured I was.

2   Which is kind of funny. Because although Mom is solid R.C.—eight
o'clock Mass and saying a rosary at the drop of a hat—nobody ever
accused Pop of being a religious fanatic by no means. He goes to confession regular like an oil change, every five thousand miles, or Easter,
whichever comes first.

3   Take the Knights of Columbus. He wouldn't join those guys for no
money. Whenever Mom starts in on him about enlisting he just
answers back that he can't afford the outlay on armour and where'd he
keep a horse? Which is his idea of a joke. So it isn't exactly as if he was
St. Joan of Arc himself to go criticizing me.

4   And Pop wouldn't have been none the wiser if it wasn't for my older
brother Gene, the prick. Don't think I don't know who told. But I can't
expect nothing different from that horse's ass.

5   So, as I was saying, my old man didn't exactly take it all in stride.
"Baptists! *Baptists!* I'm having your head examined. Do you hear me?
I'm having it *examined!* Just keep it up and see if I don't, you crazy little
pecker. They roll in the aisles, Baptists, for chrissakes!"

6   "I been three times already and nobody rolled in an aisle once."

7   "Three times? *Three times?* Now it all comes out. Three, eh?"
He actually hits himself in the forehead with the heel of his palm.
Twice. "Jesus Christ Almighty, I'm blessed with a son like this?
What's the matter with you? Why can't you ever do something I can
understand?"

8   "Like wrecking cars?" This is a swift kick in the old fun sack. Pop's just getting over Gene's totalling off the first new car he's bought in eight years. A 1966 Chevy Impala.

9   "Shut your smart mouth. Don't go dragging your brother into this. Anyway what he done to the car was *accidental*. But not you. Oh no, you marched into that collection of religious screwballs, holy belly-floppers, and linoleum-beaters under your own steam. On purpose. For God's sake, Billy, that's no religion that—it's exercise. Stay away from them Baptists."

10   "Can't," I says to him.

11   "Can't? *Can't?* Why the hell not?"

12   "Matter of principle."

13   They teach us that in school, matters of principle. I swear it's a plot to get us all slaughtered the day they graduate us out the door. It's their revenge, see? Here we are reading books in literature class about some banana who's only got one oar in the water to start with, and then he pops it out worrying about principles. Like that Hamlet, or what's his name in *A Tale of Two Cities*.[1] Ever notice how many of those guys are alive at the end of those books they teach us from?

14   "I'll principle you," says the old man.

15   The only teacher who maybe believes all that crock of stale horse-shit about principles is Miss Clark, who's fresh out of wherever they bake Social Studies teachers. She's got principles on the brain. For one thing, old Clarkie has pretty nearly wallpapered her room with pic-tures of that Negro, Martin Luther King, and some character who's modelling the latest in Wabasso sheets and looks like maybe he'd kill for a hamburger—Gandhi is his name—and that hairy old fart Tolstoy, who wrote the books you need a front-end loader to lift. From what Clarkie tells us, I gather they're what you call non-violent shit-dis-turbers.

16   Me too. Being a smart-ass runs in the Simpson family. It's what you call hereditary, like a disease. That's why all of a sudden, before I even *think* for chrissakes, I hear myself lecturing the old man in this fruity voice that's a halfway decent imitation of old Clarkie, and I am using the exact words which I've heard her say myself.

17   "Come, come, surely by this day and age everybody has progressed to the point where we can all agree on the necessity of freedom of wor-ship. If we can't agree on anything else, at least we can agree on that."

18   I got news for her. My old man don't agree to no such thing. He up and bangs me one to the side of the head. A backhander special. You see, nobody in our house is allowed an opinion until they're twenty-one.

19   Of course, I could holler Religious Persecution. Not that it would do any good. But it's something I happen to know quite a bit about, seeing

---

1. Novel by Charles Dickens about the French Revolution.

as Religious Persecution was my assignment in Social Studies that time we studied Man's Inhumanity to Man. The idea was to write a two-thousand-word report proving how everybody has been a shit to everybody else through the ages, and where did it ever get them? This is supposed to improve us somehow, I guess.

20 Anyway, as usual anything good went fast. Powbrowski got A. Hitler, Keller put dibs on Ivan the Terrible, Langly asked for Genghis Khan. By the time old Clarkie got around to me there was just a bunch of crap left like No Votes For Women. So I asked, please, could I do a project on Mr. Keeler? Keeler is the dim-witted bat's fart who's principal of our school.

21 For being rude, Miss Clark took away my "privilege" of picking and said I had to do Religious Persecution. Everybody was avoiding that one like the plague.

22 Actually, I found Religious Persecution quite interesting. It's got principles too, number one being that whatever you're doing to some poor son of a bitch—roasting his chestnuts over an open fire, or stretching his pant-leg from a 29-incher to a 36-incher on the rack—why, you're doing it for his own good. So he'll start thinking right. Which is more or less what my old man was saying when he told me I can't go out of the house on Sundays any more. He says to me, "You aren't setting a foot outside that door [he actually points to it] of a Sunday until you come to your senses and quit with all the Baptist bullshit."

23 Not that that's any heavy-duty torture. What he don't know is that these Baptists have something called Prayer, Praise and Healing on Wednesday nights. My old man hasn't locked me up Wednesday nights yet by no means.

24 I figure if my old man wants somebody to blame for me becoming a Baptist he ought to take a peek in my older brother Gene's direction. He started it.

25 Which sounds awful funny if you know anything about Gene. Because if Gene was smart enough to have ever thought about it, he'd come out pretty strong against religion, since it's generally opposed to most things he's in favour of.

26 Still, nobody thinks the worse of my brother for doing what he likes to do. They make a lot of excuses for you in a dinky mining town that's the arsehole of the world if you bat .456 and score ninety-eight goals in a thirty-five-game season. Shit, last year they passed the hat around to all the big shots on the recreation board and collected the dough for one of Gene's liquor fines and give it to him on the q.t.

27 But I'm trying to explain my brother. If I had to sum him up I'd probably just say he's the kind of guy doesn't have to dance. What I mean is, you take your average, normal female: they slobber to dance. The guys that stand around leaning against walls are as popular to

them as syphilis. You don't dance, you're a pathetic dope—even the ugly ones despise you.

28   But not Gene. He don't dance and they all cream. You explain it. Do they figure he's too superior to be bothered? Because it's not true. I'm his brother and I know. The dink just can't dance. That simple. But if I mention this little fact to anybody, they look at me like I been playing out in the sun too long. Everybody around here figures Mr. Wonderful could split the fucking atom with a hammer and a chisel if he put his mind to it.

29   Well, almost everybody. There's a born doubter in every crowd. Ernie Powers is one of these. He's the kind of stupid fuck who's sure they rig the Stanley Cup and the Oscars and nobody ever went up in space. Everything is a hoax to him. Yet he believes professional wrestling is on the up and up. You wonder—was he dropped on his head, or what? Otherwise you got to have a plan to grow up that ignorant.

30   So it was just like Einstein to bet Gene ten dollars he couldn't take out Nancy Williams. He did that while we were eating a plate of chips and gravy together in the Rite Spot and listening to Gene going on about who's been getting the benefit of his poking lately. Powers, who is a very jealous person because he's going steady with his right hand, says, oh yeah sure, maybe her, but he'd bet ten bucks somebody like Nancy Williams in 11B wouldn't even go out with Gene.

31   "Get serious," says my brother when he hears that. He considers himself irresistible to the opposite sex.

32   "Ten bucks. She's strictly off-limits even to you, Mr. Dreamboat. It's all going to waste. That great little gunga-poochy-snuggy-bum, that great matched set. Us guys in 11B, you know what we call them? The Untouchables. Like on TV."

33   "What a fucking sad bunch. Untouchables for you guys, maybe. If any of you queers saw a real live piece of pelt you'd throw your hat over it and run."

34   "Talk's cheap," says Ernie, real offended. "You don't know nothing about her. My sister says Miss High-and-Mighty didn't go out for cheerleading because the outfits were *too revealing.* My sister says Nancy Williams belongs to some religion doesn't allow her to dance. Me I saw her pray over a hard-boiled egg for about a half-hour before she ate it in the school lunch-room. Right out where everybody could see, she prayed. No way somebody like that is going to go out with you, Simpson. If she does I'll eat my shorts."

35   "Start looking for the ten bucks, shitface, and skip dinner, because I'm taking Nancy Williams to the Christmas Dance," my brother answers him right back. Was Gene all of a sudden hostile, or was he hostile? I overheard our hockey coach say one time that my brother Gene's the kind of guy rises to a challenge. The man's got a point. I lived with Gene my whole life, which is sixteen years now, and I ought to know. Unless he gets mad he's useless as tits on a boar.

36   You better believe Gene was mad. He called her up right away from the pay phone in the Rite Spot. It was a toss-up as to which of those two jerks was the most entertaining. Powers kept saying, "There's no way she'll go out with him. No way." And every time he thought of parting with a ten-spot, a look came over his face like he just pinched a nut or something. The guy's so christly tight he squeaks when he walks. He was sharing *my* chips and gravy, if you know what I mean?

37   And then there was Gene. I must say, I've always enjoyed watching him operate. I mean, even on the telephone he looks so sincere I could just puke. It's not unconscious by no means. My brother explained to me once what his trick is. To look that way you got to think that way is his motto. "What I do, Billy," he told me once, "is make myself believe, really believe, say ... well, that an H-bomb went off, or that some kind of disease which only attacks women wiped out every female on the face of the earth but the one I'm talking to. That makes her the last piece of tail on the face of the earth, Billy! It's just natural then to be extra nice." Even though he's my brother, I swear to God he had to been left on our doorstep.

38   Of course, you can't argue with success. As soon as Gene hung up and smiled, Powers knew he was diddled. Once. But my brother don't show much mercy. Twice was coming. It turned out that Nancy Williams had a cousin staying with her for Christmas vacation. She wondered if maybe Gene could get this cousin a date? When Powers heard that, he pretty nearly went off in his pants. Nobody'll go out with him. He's fat and he sweats and he never brushes his teeth, there's stuff grows on them looks like that crap that floats on top of a slough. Even the really desperate girls figure no date is less damaging to their reputations than a date with Powers. You got to hold the line somewhere is how they look at it.

39   So Ernie's big yap cost him fifteen dollars. He blew that month's baby bonus (which his old lady gives him because he promises to finish school) and part of his allowance. The other five bucks is what he had to pay when Gene sold him Nancy Williams' cousin. It damn near killed him.

40   All right. Maybe I ought to've said something when Gene marched fat Ernie over to the Bank of Montreal to make a withdrawal on this account Powers has had since he was seven and started saving for a bike. He never got around to getting the bike because he couldn't bring himself to ever see that balance go down. Which is typical.

41   Already then I *knew* Ernie wasn't taking the cousin to no Christmas Dance. I'd heard once too often from that moron how Whipper Billy Watson would hang a licking on Cassius Clay, or how all the baseball owners get together in the spring to decide which team will win the World Series in the fall. He might learn to keep his hole shut for once.

42   The thing is I'd made up my mind to take the cousin. For nothing. It just so happens that, Gene being mad, he'd kind of forgot he's not

allowed to touch the old man's vehicle. Seeing as he tied a chrome granny knot around a telephone pole with the last one.

43   Gene didn't realize it yet but he wasn't going nowhere unless I drove. And I was going to drive because I'd happened to notice Nancy Williams around. She seemed like a very nice person who maybe had what Miss Clark says are principles. I suspected that if that was true, Gene for once was going to strike out, and no way was I going to miss *that*. Fuck, I'd have killed to see that. No exaggeration.

44   On the night of the Christmas Dance it's snowing like a bitch. Not that it's cold for December, mind you, but snowing. Sticky, sloppy stuff that almost qualifies for sleet, coming down like crazy. I had to put the windshield wipers on. In December yet.

45   Nancy Williams lives on the edge of town way hell and gone, in new company housing. The mine manager is the dick who named it Green Meadows. What a joke. Nobody lives there seen a blade of grass yet nor pavement neither. They call it Gumboot Flats because if it's not frozen it's mud. No street-lights neither. It took me a fuck of a long time to find her house in the dark. When I did I shut off the motor and me and Gene just sat.

46   "Well?" I says after a bit. I was waiting for Gene to get out first.

47   "Well what?"

48   "Well, maybe we should go get them?"

49   Gene didn't answer. He leans across me and plays "Shave and a haircut, two bits" on the horn.

50   "You're a geek," I tell him. He don't care.

51   We wait. No girls. Gene gives a couple of long, long blasts on the hooter. I was wishing he wouldn't. This time somebody pulls open the living-room drapes. There stands this character in suspenders, for chrissakes, and a pair of pants stops about two inches shy of his armpits. He looked like somebody's father and what you'd call belligerent.

52   "I think he wants us to come to the door."

53   "He can want all he like. Jesus Murphy, it's snowing out there. I got no rubbers."

54   "Oh, Christ," I says, "I'll go get them, Gene. It's such a big deal."

55   Easier said than done. I practically had to present a medical certificate. By the time Nancy's father got through with me I was starting to sound like that meatball Chip on *My Three Sons*.[2] Yes sir. No sir. He wasn't too impressed with the hornblowing episode, let me tell you. And then Nancy's old lady totes out a Kodak to get some "snaps" for Nancy's scrapbook. I didn't say nothing but I felt maybe they were getting evidence for the trial in case they had to slap a charge on me later. You'd have to see it to believe it. Here I was standing with Nancy and her cousin, grinning like I was in my right mind, flash bulbs going

---

2. Popular television comedy series of the 1960s.

off in my face, nodding away to the old man, who was running a safe-driving clinic for yours truly on the sidelines. Gene, I says to myself, Gene, you're going to pay.

56   At last, after practically swearing a blood oath to get his precious girls home, undamaged, by twelve-thirty, I chase the women out the door. And while they run through the snow, giggling, Stirling Moss[3] delays me on the doorstep, in this blizzard, showing me for about the thousandth time how to pull a car out of a skid on ice. I kid you not.

57   From that point on everything goes rapidly downhill.

58   Don't get me wrong. I got no complaints against the girls. Doreen, the cousin, wasn't going to break no mirrors, and she sure was a lot more lively than I expected. Case in point. When I finally get to the car, fucking near frozen, what do I see? Old Doreen hauling up about a yard of her skirt, which she rolled around her waist like the spare tire on a fat guy. Then she pulled her sweater down to hide it. You bet I was staring.

59   "Uncle Bob wouldn't let me wear my mini," she says. "Got a smoke? I haven't had one for days."

60   It seems she wasn't the only one had a bit of a problem with the dress code that night. In the back seat I could hear Nancy apologizing to Gene for the outfit her mother had made her special for the dance. Of course, I thought Nancy looked quite nice. But with her frame she couldn't help, even though she was got up a bit peculiar. What I mean is, she had on this dress made out of the same kind of shiny material my mother wanted for drapes. But the old man said she couldn't have it because it was too heavy. It'd pull the curtain rods off the wall.

61   I could tell poor old Nancy Williams sure was nervous. She just got finished apologizing for how she looked and then she started in suck-holing to Gene to please excuse her because she wasn't the world's best dancer. As a matter of fact this was her first dance ever. Thank heavens for Doreen, who was such a good sport. She'd been teaching her to dance all week. But it takes lots and lots of practice to get the hang of it. She hoped she didn't break his toes stepping on them. Ha ha ha. Just remember, she was still learning.

62   Gene said he'd be glad to teach her anything he figured she needed to know.

63   Nancy didn't catch on because she doesn't have that kind of mind. "That would be sweet of you, Gene," she says.

64   The band didn't show because of the storm. An act of God they call it. I'll say. So I drove around this dump for about an hour while Gene tried to molest Nancy. She put up a fair-to-middling struggle from what I could hear. The stuff her dress was made of was so stiff it crackled when she moved. Sort of like tin foil. Anyway, the two of them had it

---

3. (b. 1929), British racing car driver, six-time Grand Prix winner.

snapping and crackling like a bonfire there in the back seat while they fought a pitched battle over her body. She wasn't having none of that first time out of the chute.

65   *"Gene!"*

66   "Well for chrissakes, relax!"

67   "Don't take the Lord's name in vain."

68   "What's that supposed to mean?"

69   "Don't swear."

70   "Who's swearing?"

71   "Don't snap my nylons, Gene. Gene, what in the world are you … *Gene!"*

72   "Some people don't know when they're having a good time," says Doreen. I think she was a little pissed I hadn't parked and give her some action. But Lord knows what might've happened to Nancy if I'd done that.

73   Then, all of a sudden, Nancy calls out, sounding what you'd call desperate, "Hey, everybody, who wants a Coke!"

74   "Nobody wants a Coke," mumbles Gene, sort of through his teeth.

75   "Well, maybe we could go some place?" Meaning somewhere well-lit where this octopus will lay off for five seconds.

76   "I'll take you some place," Gene mutters. "You want to go somewhere, we'll go to Zipper's. Hey Billy, let's take them to Zipper's."

77   "I don't know, Gene …"

78   The way I said that perked Doreen up right away. As far as she was concerned, anything was better than driving around with a dope, looking at a snowstorm. "Hey," she hollers, "that sounds like *fun!"* Fun like a mental farm.

79   That clinched it though. "Sure," says Gene, "we'll check out Zipper's."

80   What could I say?

81   Don't get me wrong. Like everybody else I go to Zipper's and do stuff you can't do any place else in town. That's not it. But I wouldn't take anybody nice there on purpose. And I'm not trying to say that Zipper and his mother are bad people neither. It's just that so many shitty things have happened to those two that they've become kind of unpredictable. If you aren't used to that it can seem pretty weird.

82   I mean, look at Zipper. This guy is a not entirely normal human being who tries to tattoo himself with geometry dividers and Indian ink. He has this home poke on his arm which he claims is an American bald eagle but looks like a demented turkey or something. He did it himself, and the worst is he doesn't know how homely that bird is. The dumb prick shows it to people to admire.

83   Also, I should say a year ago he quits school to teach himself to be a drummer. That's all. He doesn't get a job or nothing, just sits at home and drums, and his mother, who's a widow and doesn't know any better, lets him. I guess that that's not any big surprise. She's a pretty

hopeless drunk who's been taking her orders from Zipper since he was six. That's when his old man got electrocuted out at the mine.

84   Still, I'm not saying that the way Zipper is is entirely his fault. Though he can be a real creep all right. Like once when he was about ten years old Momma Zipper gets a jag on and passes out naked in the bedroom, and he lets any of his friends look at his mother with no clothes on for chrissakes, if they pay him a dime. His own mother, mind you.

85   But in his defence I'd say he's seen a lot of "uncles" come and go in his time, some of which figured they'd make like the man of the house and tune him in. For a while there when he was eleven, twelve maybe, half the time he was coming to school with a black eye.

86   Now you take Gene, he figures Zipper's house is heaven on earth. Of course, nothing's entirely free. At Zipper's you got to bring a bottle or a case of beer and give Mrs. Zipper a few snorts, then everything is hunky-dory. Gene had a bottle of Five Star stashed under the back seat for the big Christmas Dance, so we were okay in that department.

87   But that night the lady of the house didn't seem to be around, or mobile anyway. Zipper himself came to the door, sweating like a pig in a filthy T-shirt. He'd been drumming along to the radio.

88   "What do you guys want?" says Zipper.

89   Gene holds up the bottle. "Party time."

90   "I'm practising," says Zipper.

91   "So you're practising. What's that to us?"

92   "My old lady's sleeping on the sofa," says Zipper, opening the door wide. "You want to fuck around here you do it in the basement." Which means his old lady'd passed out. Nobody sleeps through Zipper on the drums.

93   "Gene," Nancy was looking a bit shy, believe me.

94   My brother didn't let on he'd even heard her. "Do I look particular? You know me, Zip."

95   Zipper looked like maybe he had to think about that one. To tell the truth, he didn't seem quite all there. At last he says, "Sure. Sure, I know you. Keep a cool tool." And then, just like that, he wanders off to his drums, and leaves us standing there.

96   Gene laughs and shakes his head. "What a meatball."

97   It makes me feel empty lots of times when I see Zipper. He's so skinny and yellow and his eyes are always weepy-looking. They say there's something gone wrong with his kidneys from all the gas and glue he sniffed when he was in elementary school.

98   Boy, he loves his drums though. Zipper's really what you'd call dedicated. The sad thing is that the poor guy's got no talent. He just makes a big fucking racket and he don't know any better. You see, Zipper really thinks he's going to make himself somebody with those drums, he really does. Who'd tell him any different?

99   Gene found some dirty coffee cups in the kitchen sink and started rinsing them out. While he did that I watched Nancy Williams. She

hadn't taken her coat off, in fact she was hugging it tight to her chest like she figured somebody was going to tear it off of her. I hadn't noticed before she had on a little bit of lipstick. But now her face had gone so pale it made her mouth look bright and red and pinched like somebody had just slapped it, hard.

100   Zipper commenced slamming away just as the four of us got into the basement. Down there it sounded as if we were right inside a great big drum and Zipper was beating the skin directly over our heads.

101   And boy, did it *stink* in that place. Like the sewer had maybe backed up. But then there were piles of dirty laundry humped up on the floor all around an old wringer washing machine, so that could've been the smell too.

102   It was cold and sour down there and we had nothing to sit on but a couple of lawn chairs and a chesterfield that was all split and stained with what I think was you know what. Nancy looked like she wished she had a newspaper to spread out over it before she sat down. As I said before, you shouldn't never take anybody nice to Zipper's.

103   Gene poured rye into the coffee mugs he'd washed out and passed them around. Nancy didn't want hers. "No thank you," she told him.

104   "You're embarrassing me, Nancy," says Doreen. The way my date was sitting in the lawn chair beside me in her make-do mini I knew why Gene was all scrunched down on that wrecked chesterfield.

105   "You know I don't drink, Doreen." Let me explain that when Nancy said that it didn't sound snotty. Just quiet and well-mannered like when a polite person passes up the parsnips. Nobody in their right mind holds it against them.

106   "You don't do much, do you?" That was Gene's two bits' worth.

107   "I'll say," chips in Doreen.

108   Nancy doesn't answer. I could hear old Zipper crashing and banging away like a madman upstairs.

109   "You don't do much, do you?" Gene's much louder this time.

110   "I suppose not." I can barely hear her answer because her head's down. She's checking out the backs of her hands.

111   "Somebody in your position ought to try harder," Doreen pipes up. "You don't make yourself too popular when you go spoiling parties."

112   Gene shoves the coffee mug at Nancy again. "Have a drink."

113   She won't take it. Principles.

114   "Have a drink!"

115   "Whyn't you lay off her?"

116   Gene's pissed off because he can't make Nancy Williams do what he says, so he jumps off the chesterfield and starts yelling at me. "Who's going to make me?" he hollers. "You? You going to make me?"

117   I can't do nothing but get up too. I never won a fight with my brother yet, but that don't mean I got to lay down and die for him. "You better take that sweater off," I says, pointing, "it's mine and I don't want blood on it." He always wears my clothes.

118   That's when the cousin Doreen slides in between us. She's the kind of girl loves fights. They put her centre stage. That is, if she can wriggle herself in and get involved in breaking them up. Fights give her a chance to act all emotional and hysterical like she can't stand all the violence. Because she's so sensitive. Blessed are the peace-makers.

119   "Don't fight! Please, don't fight! Come on, Gene," she cries, latching on to his arm, "don't fight over her. Come away and cool down. I got to go to the bathroom. You show me where the bathroom is, Gene. Okay?"

120   "Don't give me that. You can find the bathroom yourself." Old Gene has still got his eyes fixed on me. He's acting the role. Both of them are nuts.

121   "Come on, Gene, I'm scared to go upstairs with that Zipper person there! He's so strange, I don't know what he might get it in his head to do. Come on, take me upstairs." Meanwhile this Doreen, who is as strong as your average sensitive ox, is sort of dragging my brother in the direction of the stairs. Him pretending he don't really want to go and have a fuss made over him, because he's got this strong urge to murder me or cripple me or something.

122   "You wait" is all he says to me.

123   "Ah, quit it or I'll die of shock," I tell him.

124   "Please, Gene. That Zipper person is *weird.*"

125   At last he goes with her. I hear Gene on the stairs. "Zipper ain't much," he says, "I know lots of guys crazier than him."

126   I look over to Nancy sitting quietly on that grungy chesterfield, feet together, hands turned palms up on her lap. Her dress kind of sticks out from under the hem of her coat all stiff and shiny and funny-looking.

127   "I shouldn't have let her make me this dress," she says, angry. "We ought to have gone downtown and bought a proper one. But she had this *material.*" She stops, pulls at the buttons of her coat and opens it. "Look at this thing. No wonder Gene doesn't like it, I bet."

128   At first I don't know what to say when she looks at me like that, her face all white except for two hot spots on her cheekbones. Zipper is going nuts upstairs. He's hot tonight. It almost sounds like something recognizable. "Don't pay Gene any attention," I say, "he's a goof."

129   "It's awful, this dress."

130   She isn't that dumb. But a person needs a reason for why things go wrong. I'm not telling her she's just a way to win ten dollars and prove a point.

131   "Maybe it's because I wouldn't drink that whiskey? Is that it?"

132   "Well, kind of. That's part of it. He's just a jerk. Take it from me, I know. Forget it."

133   "I never even thought he knew I was alive. Never guessed. And here I was, crazy about him. Just crazy. I'd watch him in the hallway, you

know? I traded lockers with Susan Braithwaite just to get closer to his. I went to all the hockey games to see him play. I worshipped him."

134 The way she says that, well, it was too personal. Somebody oughtn't say that kind of a thing to a practical stranger. It was worse than if she'd climbed out of her clothes. It made me embarrassed.

135 "And funny thing is, all that time he really did think I was cute. He told me on the phone. But he never once thought to ask me out because I'm a Baptist. He was sure I couldn't go. Because I'm a Baptist he thought I couldn't go. But he thought I was cute all along."

136 "Well, yeah."

137 "And now," she says, "look at this. I begged and begged Dad to let me come. I practically got down on my hands and knees. And all those dancing lessons and everything and the band doesn't show. Imagine."

138 "Gene wouldn't have danced with you anyway. He doesn't dance."

139 Nancy smiled at me. As if I was mental. She didn't half believe me.

140 "Hey," I says, just like that, you never know what's going to get into you, "Nancy, you want to dance?"

141 "Now?"

142 "Now. Sure. Come on. We got the one-man band, Zipper, upstairs. Why not?"

143 "What'll Gene say?"

144 "To hell with Gene. Make him jealous."

145 She was human at least. She liked the idea of Gene jealous.

146 "Okay."

147 And here I got a confession to make. I go on all the time about Gene not being able to dance. Well, me neither. But I figured what the fuck. You just hop around and hope to hell you don't look too much like you're having a convulsion.

148 Neither of us knew how to get started. We just stood gawking at one another. Upstairs Zipper was going out of his tree. It sounded like there was four of him. As musical as a bag of hammers he is.

149 "The natives are restless tonight, Giles," I says. I was not uncomfortable. Let me tell you another one.

150 "Pardon?"

151 "Nothing. It was just dumb."

152 Nancy starts to sway from side to side, shuffling her feet. I figure that's the signal. I hop or whatever. So does she. We're out of the gates, off and running.

153 To be perfectly honest, Nancy Williams can't dance for shit. She gets this intense look on her face like she's counting off in her head, and starts to jerk. Which gets some pretty interesting action out of the notorious matched set but otherwise is pretty shoddy. And me? Well, I'm none too co-ordinated myself, so don't go getting no mental picture of Fred Astaire or whoever.

154 In the end what you had was two people who can't dance, dancing to the beat of a guy who can't drum. Still, Zipper didn't know no better

and at the time neither did we. We were just what you'd call mad dancing fools. We danced and danced and Zipper drummed and drummed and we were all together and didn't know it. Son of a bitch, the harder we danced the hotter and happier Nancy Williams' face got. It just smoothed the unhappiness right out of it. Mine too, I guess.

155   That is, until all of a sudden it hit her. She stops dead in her tracks and asks, "Where's Doreen and Gene?"

156   Good question. They'd buggered off in my old man's car. Zipper didn't know where.

157   The rest of the evening was kind of a horror story. It took me a fair while to convince Nancy they hadn't gone for Cokes or something and would be right back. In the end she took it like a trooper. The only thing she'd say was, "That Doreen. *That Doreen,*" and shake her head. Of course she said it about a thousand times. I was wishing she'd shut up, or maybe give us a little variety like, "*That Gene.*" No way.

158   I had a problem. How to get Cinderella home before twelve-thirty, seeing as Gene had the family chariot. I tried Harvey's Taxi but no luck. Harvey's Taxi is one car and Harvey, and both were out driving lunches to a crew doing overtime at the mine.

159   Finally, at exactly twelve-thirty, we struck out on foot in this blizzard. Jesus, was it snowing. There was slush and ice water and every kind of shit and corruption all over the road. Every time some hunyak roared by us we got splattered by a sheet of cold slop. The snow melted in our hair and run down our necks and faces. By the time we went six blocks we were soaked. Nancy was the worst off because she wasn't dressed too good with nylons and the famous dress and such. I seen I had to be a gentleman so I stopped and give her my gloves, and my scarf to tie around her head. The two of us looked like those German soldiers I seen on TV making the death march out of Russia, on that series *Canada at War.* That was a very educational series. It made you think of man's inhumanity to man quite often.

160   "I could just die," she kept saying. "Dad is going to kill me. This is my last dance ever. I could just die. I could just die. *That Doreen.* Honestly!"

161   When we stumbled up her street, all black because of the lack of street-lights, I could see that her house was all lit up. Bad news. I stopped on the corner. Just then it quits snowing. That's typical.

162   She stares at the house. "Dad's waiting."

163   "I guess I better go no further."

164   Nancy Williams bends down and feels her dress where it sticks out from under her coat. "It's soaked. I don't know how much it cost a yard. I could just die."

165   "Well," I says, repeating myself like an idiot, "I guess I better go no further." Then I try and kiss her. She sort of straight-arms me. I get the palm of my own glove in the face.

166   "What're you doing?" She sounds mad.

167 "Well, you know—"

168 "I'm not *your* date," she says, real offended. "I'm your brother's date."

169 "Maybe we could go out some time?"

170 "I won't be going anywhere for a long time. Look at me. He's going to kill me."

171 "Well, when you do? I'm in no hurry."

172 "Don't you understand? Don't you understand? Daddy will never let me go out with anybody named Simpson again. Ever. Not after tonight."

173 "Ever?"

174 "I can't imagine what you'd have to do to redeem yourself after this mess. That's how Daddy puts it—you've got to redeem yourself. I don't even know how I'm going to do it. And none of it's my fault."

175 "Yeah," I says, "he'll remember me. I'm the one he took the picture of."

176 She didn't seem too upset at not having me calling. "Everything is ruined," she says. "If you only knew."

177 Nancy Williams turns away from me then and goes up that dark, dark street where there's nobody awake except at her house. Wearing my hat and gloves.

178 Nancy Williams sits third pew from the front, left-hand side. I sit behind her, on the other side so's I can watch her real close. Second Sunday I was there she wore her Christmas Dance dress.

179 Funny thing, everything changes. At first I thought I'd start going and maybe that would redeem myself with her old man. Didn't work. He just looks straight through me.

180 You ought to see her face when she sings those Baptist hymns. It gets all hot and happy-looking, exactly like it did when we were dancing together and Zipper was pounding away there up above us, where we never even saw him. When her face gets like that there's no trouble in it, by no means.

181 It's like she's dancing then, I swear. But to what I don't know. I try to hear it. I try and try. I listen and listen to catch it. Christ, somebody tell me. What's she dancing to? Who's the drummer?

(1982)

Rohinton Mistry (b. 1952)

Born into the Parsi community in Bombay and educated at the University of Bombay, Mistry immigrated to Canada in 1975. He worked for a bank and completed a B.A. in English and philosophy at the University of Toronto. When he won two Hart House Prizes for his first short stories, he committed to writing full time. His first collection, Tales from Firozsha Baag *(1987), was shortlisted for a Governor General's Award;* Such a Long Journey *(1991) received the Governor General's Award, among others;* A Fine Balance *(1995) won the Giller Prize.*

Swimming Lessons

1   The old man's wheelchair is audible today as he creaks by in the hallway: on some days it's just a smooth whirr. Maybe the way he slumps in it, or the way his weight rests has something to do with it. Down to the lobby he goes, and sits there most of the time, talking to people on their way out or in. That's where he first spoke to me a few days ago. I was waiting for the elevator, back from Eaton's with my new pair of swimming-trunks.

2   "Hullo," he said. I nodded, smiled.

3   "Beautiful summer day we've got."

4   "Yes," I said, "it's lovely outside."

5   He shifted the wheelchair to face me squarely. "How old do you think I am?"

6   I looked at him blankly, and he said, "Go on, take a guess."

7   I understood the game; he seemed about seventy-five although the hair was still black, so I said, "Sixty-five?" He made a sound between a chuckle and a wheeze: "I'll be seventy-seven next month." Close enough.

8   I've heard him ask that question several times since, and everybody plays by the rules. Their faked guesses range from sixty to seventy. They pick a lower number when he's more depressed than usual. He reminds me of Grandpa as he sits on the sofa in the lobby, staring out vacantly at the parking lot. Only difference is, he sits with the stillness of stroke victims, while Grandpa's Parkinson's disease would bounce his thighs and legs and arms all over the place. When he could no longer hold the *Bombay Samachar* steady enough to read, Grandpa took to sitting on the veranda and staring emptily at the

traffic passing outside Firozsha Baag. Or waving to anyone who went by in the compound: Rustomji, Nariman Hansotia in his 1932 Mercedes-Benz, the fat ayah Jaakaylee with her shopping-bag, the *kuchrawalli* with her basket and long bamboo broom.

9   The Portuguese woman across the hall has told me a little about the old man. She is the communicator for the apartment building. To gather and disseminate information, she takes the liberty of un-abashedly throwing open her door when newsworthy events tran-spire. Not for Portuguese Woman the furtive peerings from thin cracks or spyholes. She reminds me of a character in a movie, *Barefoot In The Park* I think it was, who left empty beer cans by the landing for anyone passing to stumble and give her the signal. But PW does not need beer cans. The gutang-khutang of the elevator opening and closing is enough.

10   The old man's daughter looks after him. He was living alone till his stroke, which coincided with his youngest daughter's divorce in Vancouver. She returned to him and they moved into this low-rise in Don Mills. PW says the daughter talks to no one in the building but takes good care of her father.

11   Mummy used to take good care of Grandpa, too, till things became complicated and he was moved to the Parsi General Hospital. Parkin-sonism and osteoporosis laid him low. The doctor explained that Grandpa's hip did not break because he fell, but he fell because the hip, gradually growing brittle, snapped on that fatal day. That's what osteoporosis does, hollows out the bones and turns effect into cause. It has an unusually high incidence in the Parsi community, he said, but did not say why. Just one of those mysterious things. We are the chosen people where osteoporosis is concerned. And divorce. The Parsi community has the highest divorce rate in India. It also claims to be the most westernized community in India. Which is the result of the other? Confusion again, of cause and effect.

12   The hip was put in traction. Single-handed, Mummy struggled valiantly with bedpans and dressings for bedsores which soon appeared like grim spectres on his back. *Mamaiji*, bent double with her weak back, could give no assistance. My help would be enlisted to roll him over on his side while Mummy changed the dressing. But after three months, the doctor pronounced a patch upon Grandpa's lungs, and the male ward of Parsi General swallowed him up. There was no money for a private nursing home. I went to see him once, at Mummy's insistence. She used to say that the blessings of an old person were the most valuable and potent of all, they would last my whole life long. The ward had rows and rows of beds; the din was enormous, the smells nauseating, and it was just as well that Grandpa passed most of his time in a less than conscious state.

13   But I should have gone to see him more often. Whenever Grandpa went out, while he still could in the days before parkinsonism, he would bring back pink and white sugar-coated almonds for Percy and

me. Every time I remember Grandpa, I remember that; and then I think: I should have gone to see him more often. That's what I also thought when our telephone-owning neighbour, esteemed by all for that reason, sent his son to tell us the hospital had phoned that Grandpa died an hour ago.

14 *The postman rang the doorbell the way he always did, long and continuous; Mother went to open it, wanting to give him a piece of her mind but thought better of it, she did not want to risk the vengeance of postmen, it was so easy for them to destroy letters; workers nowadays thought no end of themselves, strutting around like peacocks, ever since all this Shiv Sena agitation about Maharashtra or Maharashtrians, threatening strikes and Bombay bundh all the time, with no respect for the public; bus drivers and conductors were the worst, behaving as if they owned the buses and were doing favours to commuters, pulling the bell before you were in the bus, the driver purposely braking and moving with big jerks to make the standees lose their balance, the conductor so rude if you did not have the right change.*

15 *But when she saw the airmail envelope with a Canadian stamp her face lit up, she said wait to the postman, and went in for a fifty paisa piece, a little baksheesh[1] for you, she told him, then shut the door and kissed the envelope, went in running, saying my son has written, my son has sent a letter, and Father looked up from the newspaper and said, don't get too excited, first read it, you know what kind of letters he writes, a few lines of empty words, I'm fine, hope you are all right, your loving son—that kind of writing I don't call letter-writing.*

16 *Then Mother opened the envelope and took out one small page and began to read silently, and the joy brought to her face by the letter's arrival began to ebb; Father saw it happening and knew he was right, he said read aloud, let me also hear what our son is writing this time, so Mother read: My dear Mummy and Daddy, Last winter was terrible, we had record-breaking low temperatures all through February and March, and the first official day of spring was colder than the first official day of winter had been, but it's getting warmer now. Looks like it will be a nice warm summer. You asked me about my new apartment. It's small, but not bad at all. This is just a quick note to let you know I'm fine, so you won't worry about me. Hope everything is okay at home.*

17 *After Mother put it back in the envelope, Father said everything about his life is locked in silence and secrecy. I still don't understand why he bothered to visit us last year if he had nothing to say; every letter of his has been a quick note so we won't worry—what does he think we worry about, his health, in that country everyone eats well whether they work or not, he should be worrying about us with all the black market and rationing, has he forgotten already how he used to go to the ration-shop and wait in line every week; and what kind of apartment description is*

---

1. Baksheesh: gratuity or tip.

that, not bad at all; and if it is a Canadian weather report I need from him, I can go with Nariman Hansotia from A Block to the Cawasji Framji Memorial Library and read all about it, there they get newspapers from all over the world.

18   The sun is hot today. Two women are sunbathing on the stretch of patchy lawn at the periphery of the parking lot. I can see them clearly from my kitchen. They're wearing bikinis and I'd love to take a closer look. But I have no binoculars. Nor do I have a car to saunter out to and pretend to look under the hood. They're both luscious and gleaming. From time to time they smear lotion over their skin, on the bellies, on the inside of the thighs, on the shoulders. Then one of them gets the other to undo the string of her top and spread some there. She lies on her stomach with the straps undone. I wait. I pray that the heat and haze make her forget, when it's time to turn over, that the straps are undone.

19   But the sun is not hot enough to work this magic for me. When it's time to come in, she flips over, deftly holding up the cups, and reties the top. They arise, pick up towels, lotions and magazines, and return to the building.

20   This is my chance to see them closer. I race down the stairs to the lobby. The old man says hullo. "Down again?"

21   "My mailbox," I mumble.

22   "It's Saturday," he chortles. For some reason he finds it extremely funny. My eye is on the door leading in from the parking lot.

23   Through the glass panel I see them approaching. I hurry to the elevator and wait. In the dimly lit lobby I can see their eyes are having trouble adjusting after the bright sun. They don't seem as attractive as they did from the kitchen window. The elevator arrives and I hold it open, inviting them in with what I think is a gallant flourish. Under the fluorescent glare in the elevator I see their wrinkled skin, aging hands, sagging bottoms, varicose veins. The lustrous trick of sun and lotion and distance has ended.

24   I step out and they continue to the third floor. I have Monday night to look forward to, my first swimming lesson. The high school behind the apartment building is offering, among its usual assortment of macramé and ceramics and pottery classes, a class for non-swimming adults.

25   The woman at the registration desk is quite friendly. She even gives me the opening to satisfy the compulsion I have about explaining my non-swimming status.

26   "Are you from India?" she asks. I nod. "I hope you don't mind my asking, but I was curious because an Indian couple, husband and wife, also registered a few minutes ago. Is swimming not encouraged in India?"

27   "On the contrary," I say. "Most Indians swim like fish. I'm an exception to the rule. My house was five minutes walking distance

from Chaupatty beach in Bombay. It's one of the most beautiful beaches in Bombay, or was, before the filth took over. Anyway, even though we lived so close to it, I never learned to swim. It's just one of those things."

28 "Well," says the woman, "that happens sometimes. Take me, for instance. I never learned to ride a bicycle. It was the mounting that used to scare me, I was afraid of falling." People have lined up behind me. "It's been very nice talking to you," she says, "hope you enjoy the course."

29 The art of swimming had been trapped between the devil and the deep blue sea. The devil was money, always scarce, and kept the private swimming clubs out of reach; the deep blue sea of Chaupatty beach was grey and murky with garbage, too filthy to swim in. Every so often we would muster our courage and Mummy would take me there to try and teach me. But a few minutes of paddling was all we could endure. Sooner or later something would float up against our legs or thighs or waists, depending on how deep we'd gone in, and we'd be revulsed and stride out to the sand.

30 Water imagery in my life is recurring. Chaupatty beach, now the high-school swimming pool. The universal symbol of life and regeneration did nothing but frustrate me. Perhaps the swimming pool will overturn that failure.

31 When images and symbols abound in this manner, sprawling or rolling across the page without guile or artifice, one is prone to say, how obvious, how skilless; symbols, after all, should be still and gentle with dewdrops, tiny, yet shining with a world of meaning. But what happens when, on the page of life itself, one encounters the ever-moving, all-engirdling sprawl of the filthy sea? Dewdrops and oceans both have their rightful places; Nariman Hansotia certainly knew that when he told his stories to the boys of Firozsha Baag.

32 The sea of Chaupatty was fated to endure the finales of life's everyday functions. It seemed that the dirtier it became, the more crowds it attracted: street urchins and beggars and beachcombers, looking through the junk that washed up. (Or was it the crowds that made it dirtier?—another instance of cause and effect blurring and evading identification.)

33 Too many religious festivals also used the sea as repository for their finales. Its use should have been rationed, like rice and kerosene. On Ganesh Chaturthi, clay idols of the god Ganesh, adorned with garlands and all manner of finery, were carried in processions to the accompaniment of drums and a variety of wind instruments. The music got more frenzied the closer the procession got to Chaupatty and to the moment of immersion.

34 Then there was Coconut Day, which was never as popular as Ganesh Chaturthi. From a bystander's viewpoint, coconuts chucked into the sea do not provide as much of a spectacle. We used the sea, too, to deposit the leftovers from Parsi religious ceremonies, things

such as flowers, or the ashes of the sacred sandalwood fire, which just could not be dumped with the regular garbage but had to be entrusted to the care of Avan Yazad, the guardian of the sea. And things which were of no use but which no one had the heart to destroy were also given to Avan Yazad. Such as old photographs.

35   After Grandpa died, some of his things were flung out to sea. It was high tide; we always checked the newspaper when going to perform these disposals; an ebb would mean a long walk in squelchy sand before finding water. Most of the things were probably washed up on shore. But we tried to throw them as far out as possible, then waited a few minutes; if they did not float back right away we would pretend they were in the permanent safekeeping of Avan Yazad, which was a comforting thought. I can't remember everything we sent out to sea, but his brush and comb were in the parcel, his *kusti*,[2] and some Kemadrin pills, which he used to take to keep the parkinsonism under control.

36   Our paddling session stopped for lack of enthusiasm on my part. Mummy wasn't too keen either, because of the filth. But my main concern was the little guttersnipes, like naked fish with little buoyant penises, taunting me with their skills, swimming underwater and emerging unexpectedly all around me, or pretending to masturbate— I think they were too young to achieve ejaculation. It was embarrassing. When I look back, I'm surprised that Mummy and I kept going as long as we did.

37   I examine the swimming-trunks I bought last week. Surf King, says the label, Made in Canada-Fabriqué Au Canada. I've been learning bits and pieces of French from bilingual labels at the supermarket too. These trunks are extremely sleek and stream-lined hipsters, the distance from waistband to pouch tip the barest minimum. I wonder how everything will stay in place, not that I'm boastful about my endowments. I try them on, and feel that the tip of my member lingers perilously close to the exit. Too close, in fact, to conceal the exigencies of my swimming lesson fantasy: a gorgeous woman in the class for non-swimmers, at whose sight I will be instantly aroused, and she, spying the shape of my desire, will look me straight in the eye with her intentions; she will come home with me, to taste the pleasures of my delectable Asian brown body whose strangeness has intrigued her and unleashed uncontrollable surges of passion inside her throughout the duration of the swimming lesson.

38   I drop the Eaton's bag and wrapper in the garbage can. The swimming-trunks cost fifteen dollars, same as the fee for the ten weekly lessons. The garbage bag is almost full. I tie it up and take it outside. There is a medicinal smell in the hallway; the old man must have just returned to his apartment.

---

2. Kusti: woollen cord worn round the waist by Parsis.

39   PW opens her door and says, "Two ladies from the third floor were lying in the sun this morning. In bikinis."

40   "That's nice," I say, and walk to the incinerator chute. She reminds me of Najamai in Firozsha Baag, except that Najamai employed a bit more subtlety while going about her life's chosen work.

41   PW withdraws and shuts her door.

42   *Mother had to reply because Father said he did not want to write to his son till his son had something sensible to write to him, his questions had been ignored long enough, and if he wanted to keep his life a secret, he would get no letters from his father.*

43   *But after Mother started the letter he went and looked over her shoulder, telling her what to ask him, because if they kept on writing the same questions, maybe he would understand how interested they were in knowing about things over there; Father said go on, ask him what his work is at the insurance company, tell him to take some courses at night school, that's how everyone moves ahead over there, tell him not to be discouraged if his job is just clerical right now, hard work will get him ahead, remind him he is a Zoroastrian: manashni, gavashni, kunashni, better write the translation also: good thoughts, good words, good deeds—he must have forgotten what it means, and tell him to say prayers and do kusti at least twice a day.*

44   *Writing it all down sadly, Mother did not believe he wore his sudra and kusti any more, she would be very surprised if he remembered any of the prayers; when she had asked him if he needed new sudras he said not to take any trouble because the Zoroastrian Society of Ontario imported them from Bombay for their members, and this sounded like a story he was making up, but she was leaving it in the hands of God, ten thousand miles away there was nothing she could do but write a letter and hope for the best.*

45   *Then she sealed it, and Father wrote the address on it as usual because his writing was much neater than hers, handwriting was important in the address and she did not want the postman in Canada to make any mistake; she took it to the post office herself, it was impossible to trust anyone to mail it ever since the postage rates went up because people just tore off the stamps for their own use and threw away the letter, the only safe way was to hand it over the counter and make the clerk cancel the stamps before your own eyes.*

46   Berthe, the building superintendent, is yelling at her son in the parking lot. He tinkers away with his van. This happens every fine-weathered Sunday. It must be the van that Berthe dislikes because I've seen mother and son together in other quite amicable situations.

47   Berthe is a big Yugoslavian with high cheekbones. Her nationality was disclosed to me by PW. Berthe speaks a very rough-hewn English, I've overheard her in the lobby scolding tenants for late rents and leaving dirty lint screens in the dryers. It's exciting to listen to

her, her words fall like rocks and boulders, and one can never tell where or how the next few will drop. But her Slavic yells at her son are a different matter, the words fly swift and true, well-aimed missiles that never miss. Finally, the son slams down the hood in disgust, wipes his hands on a rag, accompanies mother Berthe inside.

48   Berthe's husband has a job in a factory. But he loses several days of work every month when he succumbs to booze, a word Berthe uses often in her Slavic tirades on those days, the only one I can understand, as it clunks down heavily out of the tight-flying formation of Yugoslavian sentences. He lolls around in the lobby, submitting passively to his wife's tongue-lashings. The bags under his bloodshot eyes, his stringy moustache, stubbled chin, dirty hair are so vulnerable to the poison-laden barbs (poison works the same way in any language) emanating from deep within the powerful watermelon bosom. No one's presence can embarrass or dignify her into silence.

49   No one except the old man who arrives now. "Good morning," he says, and Berthe turns, stops yelling, and smiles. Her husband rises, positions the wheelchair at the favourite angle. The lobby will be peaceful as long as the old man is there.

*

50   It was hopeless. My first swimming lesson. The water terrified me. When did that happen, I wonder, I used to love splashing at Chaupatty, carried about by the waves. And this was only a swimming pool. Where did all that terror come from? I'm trying to remember.

51   Armed with my Surf King I enter the high school and go to the pool area. A sheet with instructions for the new class is pinned to the bulletin board. All students must shower and then assemble at eight by the shallow end. As I enter the showers three young boys, probably from a previous class, emerge. One of them holds his nose. The second begins to hum, under his breath: Paki Paki, smell like curry. The third says to the first two: pretty soon all the water's going to taste of curry. They leave.

52   It's a mixed class, but the gorgeous woman of my fantasy is missing. I have to settle for another, in a pink one-piece suit, with brown hair and a bit of a stomach. She must be about thirty-five. Plain-looking.

53   The instructor is called Ron. He gives us a pep talk, sensing some nervousness in the group. We're finally all in the water, in the shallow end. He demonstrates floating on the back, then asks for a volunteer. The pink one-piece suit wades forward. He supports her, tells her to lean back and let her head drop in the water.

54   She does very well. And as we all regard her floating body, I see what was not visible outside the pool: her bush, curly bits of it, straying out of the pink Spandex V. Tongues of water lapping against her delta, as if caressing it teasingly, make the brown hair come alive

in the most tantalizing manner. The crests and troughs of little waves, set off by the movement of our bodies in a circle around her, dutifully irrigate her; the curls alternately wave free inside the crest, then adhere to her wet thighs, beached by the inevitable trough. I could watch this forever, and I wish the floating demonstration would never end.

55   Next we are shown how to grasp the rail and paddle, face down in the water. Between practising floating and paddling, the hour is almost gone. I have been trying to observe the pink one-piece suit, getting glimpses of her straying pubic hair from various angles. Finally, Ron wants a volunteer for the last demonstration, and I go forward. To my horror he leads the class to the deep end. Fifteen feet of water. It is so blue, and I can see the bottom. He picks up a metal hoop attached to a long wooden stick. He wants me to grasp the hoop, jump in the water, and paddle, while he guides me by the stick. Perfectly safe, he tells me. A demonstration of how paddling propels the body.

56   It's too late to back out; besides, I'm so terrified I couldn't find the words to do so even if I wanted to. Everything he says I do as if in a trance. I don't remember the moment of jumping. The next thing I know is, I'm swallowing water and floundering, hanging on to the hoop for dear life. Ron draws me to the rails and helps me out. The class applauds.

57   We disperse and one thought is on my mind: what if I'd lost my grip? Fifteen feet of water under me. I shudder and take deep breaths. This is it. I'm not coming next week. This instructor is an irresponsible person. Or he does not value the lives of non-white immigrants. I remember the three teenagers. Maybe the swimming pool is the hangout of some racist group, bent on eliminating all non-white swimmers, to keep their waters pure and their white sisters unogled.

58   The elevator takes me upstairs. Then gutang-khutang. PW opens her door as I turn the corridor of medicinal smells. "Berthe was screaming loudly at her husband tonight," she tells me.

59   "Good for her," I say, and she frowns indignantly at me.

60   The old man is in the lobby. He's wearing thick wool gloves. He wants to know how the swimming was, must have seen me leaving with my towel yesterday. Not bad, I say.

61   "I used to swim a lot. Very good for the circulation." He wheezes. "My feet are cold all the time. Cold as ice. Hands too."

62   Summer is winding down, so I say stupidly, "Yes, it's not so warm any more."

63   The thought of the next swimming lesson sickens me. But as I comb through the memories of that terrifying Monday, I come upon the straying curls of brown pubic hair. Inexorably drawn by them, I decide to go.

64   It's a mistake, of course. This time I'm scared even to venture in the shallow end. When everyone has entered the water and I'm the only one outside, I feel a little foolish and slide in.

65   Instructor Ron says we should start by reviewing the floating technique. I'm in no hurry. I watch the pink one-piece pull the swim-suit down around her cheeks and flip back to achieve perfect flotation. And then reap disappointment. The pink Spandex triangle is perfectly streamlined today, nothing strays, not a trace of fuzz, not one filament, not even a sign of post-depilation irritation. Like the air-brushed parts of glamour magazine models. The barrenness of her impeccably packaged apex is a betrayal. Now she is shorn like the other women in the class. Why did she have to do it?

66   The weight of this disappointment makes the water less manageable, more lung-penetrating. With trepidation, I float and paddle my way through the remainder of the hour, jerking my head out every two seconds and breathing deeply, to continually shore up a supply of precious, precious air without, at the same time, seeming too anxious and losing my dignity.

67   I don't attend the remaining classes. After I've missed three, Ron the instructor telephones. I tell him I've had the flu and am still feeling poorly, but I'll try to be there the following week.

68   He does not call again. My Surf King is relegated to an unused drawer. Total losses: one fantasy plus thirty dollars. And no watery rebirth. The swimming pool, like Chaupatty beach, has produced a stillbirth. But there is a difference. Water means regeneration only if it is pure and cleansing. Chaupatty beach was filthy, the pool was not. Failure to swim through filth must mean something other than failure of rebirth—failure of symbolic death? Does that equal success of symbolic life? death of a symbolic failure? death of a symbol? What is the equation?

69   *The postman did not bring a letter but a parcel, he was smiling because he knew that every time something came from Canada his baksheesh was guaranteed, and this time because it was a parcel Mother gave him a whole rupee, she was quite excited, there were so many stickers on it besides the stamps, one for Small Parcel, another Printed Papers, a red sticker saying Insured; she showed it to Father, and opened it, then put both hands on her cheeks, not able to speak because the surprise and happiness was so great, tears came to her eyes and she could not stop smiling, till Father became impatient to know and finally got up and came to the table.*

70   *When he saw it he was surprised and happy too, he began to grin, then hugged Mother saying our son is a writer, and we didn't even know it, he never told us a thing, here we are thinking he is still clerking away at the insurance company, and he has written a book of stories, all these years in school and college he kept his talent hidden, making us think he was just like one of the boys in the Baag, shouting and playing the fool in the*

compound, and now what a surprise; then Father opened the book and begin reading it, heading back to the easy chair, and Mother so excited, still holding his arm, walked with him, saying it was not fair him reading it first, she wanted to read it too, and they agreed that he would read the first story, then give it to her so she could also read it, and they would take turns in that manner.

71   *Mother removed the staples from the padded envelope in which he had mailed the book, and threw them away, then straightened the folded edges of the envelope and put it away safely with the other envelopes and letters she had collected since he left.*

72   The leaves are beginning to fall. The only ones I can identify are maple. The days are dwindling like the leaves. I've started a habit of taking long walks every evening. The old man is in the lobby when I leave, he waves as I go by. By the time I'm back, the lobby is usually empty.

73   Today I was woken up by a grating sound outside that made my flesh crawl. I went to the window and saw Berthe raking the leaves in the parking lot. Not in the expanse of patchy lawn on the periphery, but in the parking lot proper. She was raking the black tarred surface. I went back to bed and dragged a pillow over my head, not releasing it till noon.

74   When I return from my walk in the evening, PW, summoned by the elevator's gutang-khutang, says, "Berthe filled six black garbage bags with leaves today."

75   "Six bags!" I say. "Wow!"

76   Since the weather turned cold, Berthe's son does not tinker with his van on Sundays under my window. I'm able to sleep late.

77   Around eleven, there's a commotion outside. I reach out and switch on the clock radio. It's a sunny day, the window curtains are bright. I get up, curious, and see a black Olds Ninety-Eight in the parking lot, by the entrance to the building. The old man is in his wheelchair, bundled up, with a scarf wound several times round his neck as though to immobilize it, like a surgical collar. His daughter and another man, the car-owner, are helping him from the wheelchair into the front seat, encouraging him with words like: that's it, easy does it, attaboy. From the open door of the lobby, Berthe is shouting encouragement too, but hers is confined to one word: yah, repeated at different levels of pitch and volume, with variations on vowel-length. The stranger could be the old man's son, he has the same jet black hair and piercing eyes.

78   Maybe the old man is not well, it's an emergency. But I quickly scrap that thought—this isn't Bombay, an ambulance would have arrived. They're probably taking him out for a ride. If he is his son, where has he been all this time, I wonder.

79   The old man finally settles in the front seat, the wheelchair goes in the trunk, and they're off. The one I think is the son looks up and

catches me at the window before I can move away, so I wave, and he waves back.

80   In the afternoon I take down a load of clothes to the laundry room. Both machines have completed their cycles, the clothes inside are waiting to be transferred to dryers. Should I remove them and place them on top of a dryer, or wait? I decide to wait. After a few minutes, two women arrive, they are in bathrobes, and smoking. It takes me a while to realize that these are the two disappointments who were sunbathing in bikinis last summer.

81   "You didn't have to wait, you could have removed the clothes and carried on, dear," says one. She has a Scottish accent. It's one of the few I've learned to identify. Like maple leaves.

82   "Well," I say, "some people might not like strangers touching their clothes."

83   "You're not a stranger, dear," she says, "you live in this building, we've seen you before."

84   "Besides, your hands are clean," the other one pipes in. "You can touch my things any time you like."

85   Horny old cow. I wonder what they've got on under their bathrobes. Not much, I find, as they bend over to place their clothes in the dryers.

86   "See you soon," they say, and exit, leaving me behind in an erotic wake of smoke and perfume and deep images of cleavages. I start the washers and depart, and when I come back later, the dryers are empty.

87   PW tells me, "The old man's son took him out for a drive today. He has a big beautiful black car."

88   I see my chance, and shoot back: "Olds Ninety-Eight."

89   "What?"

90   "The car," I explain, "it's an Oldsmobile Ninety-Eight."

91   She does not like this at all, my giving her information. She is visibly nettled, and retreats with a sour face.

92   *Mother and Father read the first five stories, and she was very sad after reading some of them, she said he must be so unhappy there, all his stories are about Bombay, he remembers every little thing about his childhood, he is thinking about it all the time even though he is ten thousand miles away, my poor son, I think he misses his home and us and everything he left behind, because if he likes it over there why would he not write stories about that, there must be so many new ideas that his new life could give him.*

93   *But Father did not agree with this, he said it did not mean that he was unhappy, all writers worked in the same way, they used their memories and experiences and made stories out of them, changing some things, adding some, imagining some, all writers were very good at remembering details of their lives.*

94   *Mother said, how can you be sure that he is remembering because he is a writer, or whether he started to write because he is unhappy and thinks of his past, and wants to save it all by making stories of it; and Father said that is not a sensible question, anyway, it is now my turn to read the next story.*

95   The first snow has fallen, and the air is crisp. It's not very deep, about two inches, just right to go for a walk in. I've been told that immigrants from hot countries always enjoy the snow the first year, maybe for a couple of years more, then inevitably the dread sets in, and the approach of winter gets them fretting and moping. On the other hand, if it hadn't been for my conversation with the woman at the swimming registration desk, they might now be saying that India is a nation of non-swimmers.

96   Berthe is outside, shovelling the snow off the walkway in the parking lot. She has a heavy, wide pusher which she wields expertly.

97   The old radiators in the apartment alarm me incessantly. They continue to broadcast a series of variations on death throes, and go from hot to cold and cold to hot at will, there's no controlling their temperature. I speak to Berthe about it in the lobby. The old man is there too, his chin seems to have sunk deeper into his chest, and his face is yellowish grey.

98   "Nothing, not to worry about anything," says Berthe, dropping rough-hewn chunks of language around me. "Radiator no work, you tell me. You feel cold, you come to me, I keep you warm," and she opens her arms wide, laughing. I step back, and she advances, her breasts preceding her like the gallant prows of two ice-breakers. She looks at the old man to see if he is appreciating the act: "You no feel scared, I keep you safe and warm."

99   But the old man is staring outside, at the flakes of falling snow. What thoughts is he thinking as he watches them? Of childhood days, perhaps, and snowmen with hats and pipes, and snowball fights, and white Christmases, and Christmas trees? What will I think of, old in this country, when I sit and watch the snow come down? For me, it is already too late for snowmen and snowball fights, and all I will have is thoughts about childhood thoughts and dreams, built around snowscapes and winter-wonderlands on the Christmas cards so popular in Bombay; my snowmen and snowball fights and Christmas trees are in the pages of Enid Blyton's[3] books, dispersed amidst the adventures of the Famous Five, and the Five Find-Outers, and the Secret Seven. My snowflakes are even less forgettable than the old man's, for they never melt.

---

3. British author (1887–1968) of over 600 books for children.

100   It finally happened. The heat went. Not the usual intermittent coming
and going, but out completely. Stone cold. The radiators are like ice.
And so is everything else. There's no hot water. Naturally. It's the hot
water that goes through the rads and heats them. Or is it the other way
around? Is there no hot water because the rads have stopped circulating it? I don't care, I'm too cold to sort out the cause and effect relationship. Maybe there is no connection at all.

101   I dress quickly, put on my winter jacket, and go down to the lobby.
The elevator is not working because the power is out, so I take the
stairs. Several people are gathered, and Berthe has announced that
she has telephoned the office, they are sending a man. I go back
upstairs. It's only one floor, the elevator is just a bad habit. Back in
Firozsha Baag, they were broken most of the time. The stairway
enters the corridor outside the old man's apartment, and I think of
his cold feet and hands. Poor man, it must be horrible for him
without heat.

102   As I walk down the long hallway, I feel there's something different
but I can't pin it down. I look at the carpet, the ceiling, the wallpaper:
it all seems the same. Maybe it's the freezing cold that imparts a
feeling of difference.

103   PW opens her door: "The old man had another stroke yesterday.
They took him to the hospital."

104   The medicinal smell. That's it. It's not in the hallway any more.

105   *In the stories that he'd read so far Father said that all the Parsi families
were poor or middle-class, but that was okay; nor did he mind that the
seeds for the stories were picked from the sufferings of their own lives;
but there should also have been something positive about Parsis, there
was so much to be proud of: the great Tatas and their contribution to the
steel industry, or Sir Dinshaw Petit in the textile industry who made
Bombay the Manchester of the East, or Dadabhai Naoroji in the freedom
movement, where he was the first to use the word* swaraj, *and the first to
be elected to the British Parliament where he carried on his campaign; he
should have found some way to bring some of these wonderful facts into
his stories, what would people reading these stories think, those who did
not know about Parsis—that the whole community was full of cranky,
bigoted people; and in reality it was the richest, most advanced and phil-
anthropic community in India, and he did not need to tell his own son
that Parsis had a reputation for being generous and family-oriented. And
he could have written something also about the historic background,
how Parsis came to India from Persia because of Islamic persecution in
the seventh century, and were the descendants of Cyrus the Great and
the magnificent Persian Empire. He could have made a story of all this,
couldn't he?*

106   *Mother said what she liked best was his remembering everything so
well, how beautifully he wrote about it all, even the sad things, and*

though he changed some of it, and used his imagination, there was truth in it.

107   *My hope is, Father said, that there will be some story based on his Canadian experience, that way we will know something about our son's life there, if not through his letters then in his stories; so far they are all about Parsis in Bombay, and the one with a little about Toronto, where a man perches on top of the toilet, is shameful and disgusting, although it is funny at times and did make me laugh, I have to admit, but where does he get such an imagination from, what is the point of such a fantasy; and Mother said that she would also enjoy some stories about Toronto and the people there; it puzzles me, she said, why he writes nothing about it, especially since you say that writers use their own experience to make stories out of.*

108   *Then Father said this is true, but he is probably not using his Toronto experience because it is too early; what do you mean, too early, asked Mother and Father explained it takes a writer about ten years time after an experience before he is able to use it in his writing, it takes that long to be absorbed internally and understood, thought out and thought about, over and over again, he haunts it and it haunts him if it is valuable enough, till the writer is comfortable with it to be able to use it as he wants; but this is only one theory I read somewhere, it may or may not be true.*

109   *That means, said Mother that his childhood in Bombay and our home here is the most valuable thing in his life just now, because he is able to remember it all to write about it, and you were so bitterly saying he is forgetting where he came from; and that may be true, said Father, but that is not what the theory means, according to the theory he is writing of these things because they are far enough in the past for him to deal with objectively, he is able to achieve what critics call artistic distance, without emotions interfering; and what do you mean emotions, said Mother, you are saying he does not feel anything for his characters, how can he write so beautifully about so many sad things without any feelings in his heart?*

110   *But before Father could explain more, about beauty and emotion and inspiration and imagination, Mother took the book and said it was her turn now and too much theory she did not want to listen to, it was confusing and did not make as much sense as reading the stories, she would read them her way and Father could read them his.*

111   My books on the windowsill have been damaged. Ice has been forming on the inside ledge, which I did not notice, and melting when the sun shines in. I spread them in a corner of the living room to dry out.

112   The winter drags on. Berthe wields her snow pusher as expertly as ever, but there are signs of weariness in her performance. Neither husband nor son is ever outside with a shovel. Or anywhere else, for that matter. It occurs to me that the son's van is missing, too.

113   The medicinal smell is in the hall again, I sniff happily and look forward to seeing the old man in the lobby. I go downstairs and peer into the mailbox, see the blue and magenta of an Indian aerogramme with Don Mills, Ontario, Canada in Father's flawless hand through the slot.

114   I pocket the letter and enter the main lobby. The old man is there, but not in his usual place. He is not looking out through the glass door. His wheelchair is facing a bare wall where the wallpaper is torn in places. As though he is not interested in the outside world any more, having finished with all that, and now it's time to see inside. What does he see inside, I wonder? I go up to him and say hullo. He says hullo without raising his sunken chin. After a few seconds his grey countenance faces me. "How old do you think I am?" His eyes are dull and glazed; he is looking even further inside than I first presumed.

115   "Well, let's see, you're probably close to sixty-four."

116   "I'll be seventy-eight next August." But he does not chuckle or wheeze. Instead, he continues softly, "I wish my feet did not feel so cold all the time. And my hands." He lets his chin fall again.

117   In the elevator I start opening the aerogramme, a tricky business because a crooked tear means lost words. Absorbed in this while emerging, I don't notice PW occupying the centre of the hallway, arms folded across her chest: "They had a big fight. Both of them have left."

118   I don't immediately understand her agitation. "What … who?"

119   "Berthe. Husband and son both left her. Now she is all alone."

120   Her tone and stance suggest we should not be standing here talking but do something to bring Berthe's family back. "That's very sad," I say, and go in. I picture father and son in the van, driving away, driving across the snow-covered country, in the dead of winter, away from wife and mother; away to where? how far will they go? Not son's van nor father's booze can take them far enough. And the further they go, the more they'll remember, they can take it from me.

121   *All the stories were read by Father and Mother, and they were sorry when the book was finished, they felt they had come to know their son better now, yet there was much more to know, they wished there were many more stories; and this is what they mean, said Father, when they say that the whole story can never be told, the whole truth can never be known; what do you mean, they say, asked Mother, who they, and Father said writers, poets, philosophers. I don't care what they say, said Mother, my son will write as much or as little as he wants to, and if I can read it I will be happy.*

122   *The last story they liked the best of all because it had the most about Canada, and now they felt they knew at least a little bit, even if it was a very little bit, about his day-to-day life in his apartment; and Father said if he continues to write about such things he will become popular because*

I am sure they are interested there in reading about life through the eyes of an immigrant, it provides a different viewpoint; the only danger is if he changes and becomes so much like them that he will write like one of them and lose the important difference.

123   The bathroom needs cleaning. I open a new can of Ajax and scour the tub. Sloshing with mug from bucket was standard bathing procedure in the bathrooms of Firozsha Baag, so my preference now is always for a shower. I've never used the tub as yet; besides, it would be too much like Chaupatty or the swimming pool, wallowing in my own dirt. Still, it must be cleaned.

124   When I've finished, I prepare for a shower. But the clean gleaming tub and the nearness of the vernal equinox give me the urge to do something different today. I find the drain plug in the bathroom cabinet, and run the bath.

125   I've spoken so often to the old man, but I don't know his name. I should have asked him the last time I saw him, when his wheelchair was facing the bare wall because he had seen all there was to see outside and it was time to see what was inside. Well, tomorrow. Or better yet, I can look it up in the directory in the lobby. Why didn't I think of that before? It will only have an initial and a last name, but then I can surprise him with: hullo Mr. Wilson, or whatever it is.

126   The bath is full. Water imagery is recurring in my life: Chaupatty beach, swimming pool, bathtub. I step in and immerse myself up to the neck. It feels good. The hot water loses its opacity when the chlorine, or whatever it is, has cleared. My hair is still dry. I close my eyes, hold my breath, and dunk my head. Fighting the panic, I stay under and count to thirty. I come out, clear my lungs and breathe deeply.

127   I do it again. This time I open my eyes under water, and stare blindly without seeing, it takes all my will to keep the lids from closing. Then I am slowly able to discern the underwater objects. The drain plug looks different, slightly distorted; there is a hair trapped between the hole and the plug, it waves and dances with the movement of the water. I come up, refresh my lungs, examine quickly the overwater world of the washroom, and go in again. I do it several times, over and over. The world outside the water I have seen a lot of, it is now time to see what is inside.

128   The spring session for adult non-swimmers will begin in a few days at the high school. I must not forget the registration date.

129   The dwindled days of winter are now all but forgotten; they have grown and attained a respectable span. I resume my evening walks, it's spring, and a vigorous thaw is on. The snowbanks are melting, the sound of water on its gushing, gurgling journey to the drains is beautiful. I plan to buy a book of trees, so I can identify more than the maple as they begin to bloom.

130   When I return to the building, I wipe my feet energetically on the mat because some people are entering behind me, and I want to set a good example. Then I go to the board with its little plastic letters and numbers. The old man's apartment is the one on the corner by the stairway, that makes in number 201. I run down the list, come to 201, but there are no little white plastic letters beside it. Just the empty black rectangle with holes where the letters would be squeezed in. That's strange. Well, I can introduce myself to him, then ask his name.

131   However, the lobby is empty. I take the elevator, exit at the second floor, wait for the gutang-khutang. It does not come: the door closes noiselessly, smoothly. Berthe has been at work, or has made sure someone else has. PW's cue has been lubricated out of existence.

132   But she must have the ears of a cockroach. She is waiting for me. I whistle my way down the corridor. She fixes me with an accusing look. She waits till I stop whistling, then says: "You know the old man died last night."

133   I cease groping for my key. She turns to go and I take a step towards her, my hand still in my trouser pocket. "Did you know his last name?" I ask, but she leaves without answering.

(1987)

Lynda Barry (b. 1956)

Lynda Barry is a Wisconsin-born author, illustrator, playwright, and con-tributor to various periodicals. "Automatic Timer," a story that plays with the idea of photographic representation, captures the voice of youthful ado-lescence. Barry herself has said that childhood is "the only place to go if you're looking for answers."

Automatic Timer

1 My father. For a long time I thought about him and then I didn't think about him and then yesterday I started thinking about him again. I was in the basement, and for no reason I went around under the steps and suddenly saw his camera case on this high shelf, and it was like that thing of where you're drowning and your whole life flashes in front of your eyes. Except it wasn't my whole life. It was just one day from a million years ago when he lived with us still and this room was glowing glowing red from the darkroom light. I was standing on a chair, watching his hand pull a piece of paper back and forth under the water, him saying, "Watch honey, now watch." And then I saw the reverse disappearing ghost of my face showing itself slow onto that paper, and him saying what he always said when he did something like that. "Okay, honey. Who's the best dad?"

2 Some nights he would tilt out the lamp shade in the front room and set his stacks of pictures on a TV tray under it. I'd watch him smoking and coloring me and my sister and my mom with Q-Tips and oils and special midget paint tubes and then, for his last finishing touch, he would draw on our eyelashes with a tiny red pencil with Life Magazine printed on the side. He would ask me to hold it up for him to look at and I'd watch him lean back and say "Ahhhhhhh. Another Perfect Masterpiece by Raymond Robert Arkins!" And then my mother would see it and yell at him for making us look like a bunch of Mexican whores.

3 Mom found a picture of another lady colored the same way. It was in the street in front of our house. I guess it fell out of his car. It was Pat, the checker at his store. Pat with the small teeth who did a wink to my mom and rang our meat up really cheap. Pat colored in and smiling under a tire mark, with her hands up behind her head and no top on. My mom put it on our front door with so many rows of Scotch tape that it looked like Pat was sinking in a deep aquarium.

4   I can remember the sound of my dad's feet coming up the steps and then stopping. Then him coming in and saying it didn't mean anything.

5   A long time later, when my dad left, my mother took everything that ever belonged to him and put it out on the front porch for Goodwill. Afterwards, I remember coming into the kitchen and seeing her holding her curved fingernail scissors, flipping through all our photo books and cutting his head out of every picture there was of him. I remember the pile of my dad's heads in the ashtray, her cigarette burning on top, and her singing along with the radio. I remember hearing the bathroom door close, me sneaking into the kitchen and taking three pictures to save. One of him and her holding me, one of him squatting on a beach in an Air Force uniform, and one of him laughing with his eyes shut, holding a dog I didn't know and a glass of beer. The last picture he had colored. He colored the dog in blue.

6   I reached my hand up and pulled down the camera. It was the kind with the flip-open top viewer and I remembered once how I watched him and Pat drunk through it, them singing upside down at the company picnic. My mom was at work and Dad took me and my sister. He kept singing "Welcome to my world" and she kept laughing. I won the footrace and I ran to show him my silver dollar, then me seeing them kissing, and then her trying to act nice to me, and later in the car him telling me how lucky he was to have a kid like me. A kid who understood his saying Don't Make Waves.

7   I saw a yellow number eight through the square glass window. There was still film. My hand started to kind of freak out. It was like a backwards version of that Alfred Hitchcock Hour where the camera comes from something like the thirteenth dimension and can take pictures of the future. The moral of it was something like, Don't Mess with Your Regular Life. I put the camera back on the shelf, and then I took it back down. I put it under my shirt and walked up the stairs past my mom in the kitchen.

8   My friend Vicky Talluso's brother Victor has a darkroom in their rec room bathroom and said for two joints he would develop the film for me. I had one roach. He said okay. Me and Vicky stood in the pitch dark and I could hear Victor dropping things and saying "Fuck." Then he handed me a container and he said keep shaking it and he lit the roach and Vicky lit a Kool and Mrs. Talluso pounded on the door yelling "What in the hell is going on in there?" She made us come out and each blow on her nose and busted Victor and Vicky for smoking and made me go home.

9   This morning at school Vicky came running across the parking lot saying she had a present for me. She opened her folder and handed me some pictures. "Only three came out," she said. The first one was of Pat in front of a car. Then two kids at a birthday with Pat smiling and

talking on the phone. Then my dad and Pat with their arms around each other, kissing.

10   I remembered the sound of the automatic timer. How my dad would set it and run fast across the room to get into the picture.

11   "Who's it of?" Vicky says.

(1990)

Evelyn Lau (b. 1971)

The diaries recording Evelyn Lau's street life after running away from her Vancouver home at the age of fourteen were published as Runaway: Diary of a Street Kid *(1989) and brought to life in the film* The Diary of Evelyn Lau *(1994). Reluctant to become a spokesperson for street people or to be characterized as a Chinese-Canadian writer, Lau identifies less with her family or ethnic community than with the older men who populate her writing. Winner of the Milton Acorn People's Poetry Prize and the Canadian Authors' Association Air Canada Prize, Lau is the author of several poetry collections,* Fresh Girls and Other Stories *(1993), the novel* Other Women *(1995), and* Inside Out: Reflections on a Life So Far *(2001).*

Marriage

1 His gold wedding band catches the light between the two walls of flesh that are our bodies in bed. It is a wide band with a perforated design, and it fits loosely on his finger. When he draws his hand up between us to touch me, the hand seems to take on a separate entity—as though it is a stranger's hand encountered in a crowded bus or an empty alley, the ring as hard as a weapon. I feel the coldness of it branding my skin. Yet I am drawn to it compulsively, this symbol of his commitment to another, as though it is a private part of him that will derive pleasure from my touch: rubbing it, twisting it, pulling it up to his knuckle and back down again.

2 In the morning we go for a walk in Queen Elizabeth Park, where a wedding is taking place. There are photographers bent on one knee in the grass, children with flowers looped through their hair, a bride in her layers of misty white. We watch from a bridge over a creek nearby, and then from the top of a waterfall. From that height the members of the wedding appear toy-like, diminished by the vast green slopes, the overflowing flower beds. When I glance sideways, I see him serenely observing the activity below, his hands draped over the low rail. I want then to step behind him, put my hands between his shoulders, and push him over, if only to recognize something in his face, some anxiety or pain to correspond with what I am feeling.

3 The people we pass in the park see a middle-aged man in a suit with his arm around a nineteen-year-old girl. They invariably pause, look

twice with curiosity. At first I look back boldly, meeting their eyes in the harsh sunlight, but as the walk wears on my gaze falters. I keep my eyes trained on the ground, my pointy white high heels keeping step with his freshly polished black leather shoes. I don't know what people are thinking; I know they don't think I am his daughter. Their stares make me feel unclean, as if there is something illicit about me. Suddenly I wonder if my skirt is too short, my lipstick too red, my hair too teased. I concentrate hard on pretending that there is something natural about my odd pairing with this man.

4   He is oblivious to their looks; if anything, he is pleased by them, as though people are looking because the girl his arm holds captive is particularly striking. He does not see that the looks are more often edged with pity than any degree of approval or jealousy.

5   He tells me afterwards that he is proud to be seen with me.

6   Sometimes when he visits me he is carrying his beeper. He has just completed the crawl to the foot of my bed, drawn up the comforter tent-like over his head and shoulders, and is preparing in the fuzzy dark to attack my body with his tongue. And then from deep in the grey huddle of his pants on the floor rises the berating call of the beeper, causing the anonymous bulk under the covers to jump and hit his head against the soft ceiling of the comforter. I resist the urge to reach out and rub that dome under my comforter, like it is a teddy bear or my own bunched-up knees.

7   Naked, he digs into the mass of material on the floor, extracts the beeper, and seats himself on the edge of the bed. I tuck my hair behind my ear and examine his back as he dials a series of numbers to access his answering service, the hospital, other doctors.

8   "Good afternoon," he says. "Is this Dr. Martin? Yes … yes … how is she? All right, one milligram lorazepam to be administered at bedtime …" while he remains half-erect between his long white thighs, one hand groping behind him 'til it finds and begins to squeeze my breast and then its nipple. Even though he has tucked the phone between his ear and shoulder so that the hand that flaps the air is not the one that wears the ring, I still feel it belongs to someone other than him as it rounds the blank canvas of his back and pats air and pillow before touching skin. I am reminded of the card in my desk drawer: on Valentine's Day four months ago he gave me a card that read, in a floral script, "I Love You." He said, almost immediately, "I hope you don't get vindictive and send that card to my wife. It's got my handwriting on it."

9   It never would have occurred to me to do so if he hadn't told me. What he said inspired me to keep the card in a special drawer, where I will not lose it. I put it away feeling reassured that at last I had some power over him. I had something I could hurt him with. I now know I saved the card because it was my only proof of his love for me, it is the only part of him that belongs to me.

10 The night before his wife's return from the conference she's attending in Los Angeles, we drive to our usual restaurant where the Japanese waiter smiles at us in a way he interprets as friendly, while I recognize amusement dancing at the corners of his mouth. I lift my purse into my lap and politely ask permission to smoke.

11 "I'd rather you didn't. My wife has a good nose for tobacco."

12 How much I want his wife to come home to the smell of smoke in the family car. After she has walked off the plane and through the terminal to where her luggage revolves on the carousel, after she has picked out his face among the faces of other husbands waiting to greet their wives and take them home, I can see her leaning back in the passenger seat, rubbing her neck, tired after her flight and eager for sleep—then the trace of smoke acrid in her nostrils, mingled perhaps with my perfume. In my fantasy she turns to him, wild-eyed and tearful, she demands that he stop the car, she wrenches the perforated wedding band from her finger and throws it at him before she opens the door and leaves. *Give it to that slut*, she will say.

13 "Maybe I'm subconsciously trying to ruin your marriage," I smile as I light a cigarette and watch the smoke momentarily fill up the front of the car.

14 "Please don't," he says calmly. I think a man whose marriage is in my hands should sound a little more desperate, but in the dark I can only see his profile against the stores and buildings blurring outside the window, and it is unreadable. I wish afterwards that I had looked at his hands, to see if they tightened on the wheel.

15 He tells me that we will have lots of time together over the years but I have no concept of time. I ask him to leave the city with me.

16 "Would you really do that?" he asks. "Run off with me?"

17 "Yes."

18 "I'm very flattered."

19 "Don't be. It wasn't meant to be flattering." I pause. I want to say, *It meant more than that.* "Why can't we just take off?"

20 "I can't do it right now," he says. "I have people depending on me— my patients. I'd love to. I can't."

21 "I have just as much to lose as you do, you know," I say, but he doesn't believe me. He has been feeding me whisky all evening, and I am swaying in a chair in front of him. He places my hands together between his own and pulls me out of the chair, collapsing me to my knees. Kneeling, I sway back and forth and squint up at him, my hands stranded in his lap.

22 "You should go," I say.

23 "Yes, I have to work tomorrow morning."

24 "And you have to pick your wife up from the airport," I say, struggling to my feet to press the colour of my lips against his white cheek.

25 I do not realize I am clutching the sleeve of his suit jacket until we have reached the door, where he chuckles and pries my fingers loose.

He adjusts his beeper inside his pocket and walks out into the rain-misted night.

26   Back inside the apartment I am intent on finishing the bottle of Chivas he left behind on the kitchen counter, but when I go to it I find an envelope next to the bottle, weighted by an ashtray. I tear it open, my heart beating painfully—it could be a letter, he could be saying that he can no longer live without me, that tonight he will finally tell his wife about us. Instead I pull out a greeting card with a picture on the front of a girl standing by a seashore. She is bare-legged, with dimpled knees, wearing a loose frock the colour of daffodils. She looks about twelve years old.

27   Inside are no words, just two new hundred-dollar bills.

28   He tries to alleviate his guilt by giving me money: cheques left folded on the kitchen table, crisp bills tucked inside cards. He takes me shopping for groceries and clothes, he never visits my apartment without bringing me some small gift, as though all this entitles him to leave afterwards and return home to his wife. But I have no similar method of striking such bargains with my conscience. The dregs of our affair stick to my body like semen. Because I do think of his wife—of the way she must sink into bed beside him in the dark, putting her face against his chest and breathing him in, his scent carried with her into her dreams. I do think of the pain she would feel if she knew, and I am frightened sometimes by the force of my desire to inflict that pain upon her—this wife who is to be pitied in her faithless marriage, this wife whom I envy.

29   And tonight I want more than anything to take those smooth brown bills between my fingers and tear them up. Does he think I'm like one of those teen hookers in thigh-high boots and bustiers he says he used to pick up downtown before he met me? My hands are shaking, I want so badly to get rid of his money. Instead I go over to the chest of drawers beside my bed and add this latest contribution to the growing stack of cards and cash I have hidden there.

30   He often says to me, "If you were my daughter ..." My lips twist and he has to add each time, "You know what I mean." If things were different, he means. If we weren't sleeping together. We cultivate fantasies for each other of what a loving, doting father he would have made me; of what a pretty, accomplished daughter I would have made him. "I adore you," he says to me. "I wish I could marry you." And then, "I wish you were my daughter," as he kisses my neck, my shoulders, my breasts, his fingers slipping between my thighs. As things are, I see we don't have anything that comes close to the illusion.

31   His cologne has found places to lodge in my blankets, clothing, cushions. No matter how many loads of laundry I carry down the back stairs, the smell of him has taken up residence in the corners of my apartment, as though to stay.

32   He tells me little about his activities, but the spare portraits he paints grow vivid in my mind. This weekend he will visit Vancouver Island with his family. I picture them on the ferry, with the possibility of grey skies and rain, the mountains concealed by veils of fog, the treed islands rising like the backs of beasts out of the ocean. I wonder if his family will venture onto the deck and look down at the water, I imagine them falling overboard and being ground to pieces by the propellers, staining those foamy waves crimson.

33   He tells me about his three sons and I know they are all teenagers. I know that the oldest is stronger than his father, handsome with a thick head of red hair, and that this son's feisty girlfriend reminds him of me. I know they tease him with the eyeball-rolling exasperation and embarrassment that I've felt towards my own parents.

34   "Oh, Dad," they'd groan in restaurants where he'd be teasing the waitress. "Don't *do* that. She's in our class at school!"

35   I imagine him clambering up the grey steel ladder leading to the top deck of the ferry. He reaches down towards his wife. When she grips his hand his ring bites into her palm, a sensation she has grown used to, as though the ring is now a part of his body.

36   They walk together behind their children, past rows of orange plastic chairs in the non-smoking section, past the cafeteria selling sticky danishes and styrofoam cups of hot coffee, past the gift shop with the little Canadian flags and sweatshirts in the window. They wrestle open the heavy door leading onto the deck and the blast of air sucking them out separates his hair into pieces plastering forward, backward, tight against his cheek.

37   His family races in their sneakers and jeans towards the edges of the ferry, clinging to the railings, and he fights his way through the wind towards them, laughing and shouting. I know for certain that, for once, he is not thinking of me.

(1993)

APPENDIX: WRITING ABOUT LITERATURE

The art of writing has for backbone some fierce attachment to an idea.

—Virginia Woolf

"To write is to make choices," argues Margot Northey. Different occasions, audiences, and purposes require different choices, and we'll focus here on the process of writing essays on literary topics for academic audiences. We'll focus on planning, prewriting, researching, organizing, drafting, and revising, on the tact and tactics needed to know what to include and what to exclude, what to assume and when to elaborate, and how to be responsive, respectful, and rigorous in producing the best products. Writing about literature is a matter of evaluation and enjoyment, evidence and interpretation, quotation and summary, description and explanation, analysis and integration of evidence, accurate documentation of sources, effective introductions, transitions, and conclusions—and, importantly, of finding your own voice. And when we write about our reading, we engage with different viewpoints—those of writers and of other readers (whether peers or professionals)—in ways that can transform our own understandings, build confidence, enhance authority, and expand our horizons.

Literature is itself an intellectual discipline—a way of knowing and communicating insights into history, experience, identities, and issues—and we can learn much from creative writers about writing and about arresting reader attention and making writing memorable. From Virginia Woolf we learn about the importance of writing from a position that we do believe, not one that we feel we ought to uphold. Writing, from this point of view, is about presenting public reasons for private reflections or beliefs. But how do we clarify what we believe about a topic, poem, essay, or short story? We get some direction from W.H. Auden's question, "How do I know what I think until I see what I write?" In other words, the process of writing is itself an important part of discovering knowledge, of defining viewpoints and developing ideas. Be prepared to test your assumptions about a text, to rethink first impressions, and to change your mind. In fact, for Robert Frost, writing is about having ideas—"To learn to write is to learn to have ideas"—so that learning necessarily involves a significant amount of writing.

GETTING STARTED

Sometimes [writing] comes easily and perfectly. Sometimes it is like drilling rock and then blasting it out with charges.

—Ernest Hemingway

If you sometimes find it hard to get started, you are in very good company. Writing *is* hard work. Investing time and effort in the activity is easier if we understand its value, its power to shape people's thinking and lives, their sense of selves and of others. It is also easier if we understand writing about literature not as a subjective but as an evidence-based and rigorous process; if we understand writing not as a solitary activity but as collaborative work building on the writing and thinking of others—whether in reading, writing, speaking, researching, journal writing, or brainstorming (a planning technique to develop an unedited list of words, phrases, and ideas).

But writing is easier if you have a plan; that is, if you establish your objectives (your essay's task) and audience needs (in this case, your instructor's need to be persuaded of your understanding, rigorous reading, correct and coherent writing); identify the resources you require; and develop a course of action to accomplish the plan. Planning and prewriting (and writing) overlap and intersect. If you have an assigned topic, can the terms of the question help you brainstorm? Are you being asked to discuss (to develop points in an orderly way, taking account of contrary ideas and evidence), or to explain (show how and why), or to illustrate (explain by examples), or to compare and contrast (identify similarities and differences between two texts, for example)? Are there words that you might check in the dictionary? The dictionary can generate ideas by reminding you of the history of a word's uses or range of its current meanings. If you are to generate your own topic, focus on manageable topics that interest and challenge you. Be careful neither to pose too large a question (the history of poetic form in Western literature) nor to resort to cliché ("love conquers all"). Although some come to titles after completing their essays, you may find defining your title a useful means of brainstorming, of playing with ideas and words, the sounds of sense, and creating suggestive combinations and clarifying your focus and thesis (the conclusion that your entire essay will aim to support).

You may also find writing about literature hard because literature seems mysterious or intimidating or you think your job is to recover and respect a writer's intention or to uncover a meaning that the writer has "hidden" between the lines. But we bring different experiences—educational, cultural, social, political, and personal—to the act of reading and writing about literature and in the process activate diverse meanings that can enrich us all. Your age, gender, class, and ethnic background will significantly shape how you respond. Consider your own experience of reading a poem or a Shakespeare play in high school and in university and finding new meaning and value in material that was at first alien or unfamiliar. No text, then, has a single or stable meaning, but the text is a place where meanings are made and remade by different readers (or even the same reader) in changing circumstances. So do not be unduly troubled if your own reading differs in substantial ways from that of your instructor or peers, but take account of those different views as you refine your own argument and find the evidence (in the text and in your research and experience) to support your claims.

If words have multiple meanings and writers say more or less than they intend, there are limits to the readings we may generate for any one text. To begin gathering resources to support your essay writing, try re-reading the text and reviewing your class notes about the author, the genre, and the historical context of the text. Re-read actively, underlining key terms and quotations, annotating, and asking (journalists') questions of the text (who, what, when, why, where, how). Although writers may revise many times before publication, works typically appear under one title that begins to orient readers to some of the text's meaningfulness. What expectations does the title raise? Are they realized? What is the opening or closing line, and what is the relationship between them? Is the poem divided into stanzas, and how are they related? Are they complex or simple? Conventional for the time period? What is the setting, speaker, and mood? Accurate description is a necessary prelude to, but no substitute for, effective analysis and interpretation. Answering these questions helps capture the text's distinctiveness (and your response to it) and identify what you need to learn in order to substantiate arguments that take account of features of the text and different readings of it.

RESEARCHING

Research is formalized curiosity. It is poking and prying with a purpose.

—Zora Neale Hurston

To help support or refine your tentative thesis and developing argument, you may turn to secondary reading on the text, biographical information, historical context, or subject matter. Such reading—whether in journal articles, monographs, textbooks, Web sites, or encyclopedias—will challenge you to assess its validity and relevance and also to test and, if necessary, revise your own ideas. Are you persuaded the article or book is accurate, reliable, and current? Are you persuaded the evidence is sufficient and pertinent and the argument addresses important literature (and contrary views) on the topic? Evaluating on-line sources can be especially challenging. For some useful advice, access this resource:

- "Evaluating Information Found on the Internet" by Elizabeth E. Kirk, Head, Entrepreneurial Library Program, Sheridan Libraries, Johns Hopkins University at: http://www.library.jhu.edu/elp/useit/evaluate

DOCUMENTING SOURCES

Writing means responsibility to represent other views fairly and accurately and to acknowledge your dependence on secondary sources—a sign not of laziness but of conscientious contextualizing of issues and ideas. Documenting sources shows the work you have done and obligations you have inevitably incurred, supports your line of argument by adding authorities, and gives readers access to further sources on a particular topic. To document accurately, keep records of names, titles, dates, places, pages, and, in the case of on-line material, the on-line service, the uniform resource locator (URL), and date of access; take careful notes; and distinguish summary, paraphrase, and quotation (whichever serves your purpose and audience).

Quotation

When the source's expression is especially effective or vivid, when the source depends on technical or specialized vocabulary, or when you want to dispute the terms of the source's argument, you will want to quote. Be sure to integrate quotations into your own sentence structure and developing argument; vary introductory words (Jennifer Barton agrees, argues, claims; from Jennifer Barton's point of view;

according to Jennifer Barton). Quote only those words necessary for your purposes, using three spaced periods (. . .) to indicate omitted words within a sentence or four periods when the omission comes at the end of a sentence. Use square brackets ([]) to indicate any changes you may have made to integrate the quotation into your grammar. For example, if you are quoting a first-person account ("I"), in your own discussion, you will want to change the pronouns to fit. For example: When John Barsky argues, "[he prefers] face-to-face communication for sensitive personnel issues," he is . . .

Short Quotations (of four or fewer lines)

These should be run in; that is, incorporated in the regular double-spaced lines of your essay. For example: The male speaker of John Donne's "The Sun Rising" taunts the sun with its irrelevance to the lovers' world that "no season knows, nor clime, / Nor hours, days, months, which are the rags of time." (Note the slash indicates the line division in the poem.)

Long Quotations (longer than four lines)

This type of quotation should be set off from the regular text by indenting the left-hand margin 10 spaces. Use quotation marks only for quotation within an indented quotation. When a complete sentence introduces your indented quotation, the sentence is followed by a colon. For example: The jealous pride of the Duke of Ferrara becomes apparent early in his exchanges with the Count's emissary:

> Sir, 'twas not
> Her husband's presence only, called that spot
> Of joy into the Duchess' cheek: perhaps
> Frà Pandolf chanced to say "Her mantle laps
> Over my lady's wrist too much," or "Paint
> Must never hope to reproduce the faint
> Half-flush that dies along her throat." (13–19)

Summary and Paraphrase

When quotation is not essential, put the source ideas in your own words. Summary involves condensing in your own words the source argument/information. You will summarize when you want to give the gist of the source without supplying details of the developing argument. Paraphrase involves rephrasing in your own words and generally following the source's line of reasoning without any concern to reduce the number of words in the source. Be very careful not to repeat words from your source or to substitute synonyms while retaining the source's sentence structure. If words from the source are helpful or important in your paraphrase, be sure to put quotation marks around those particular words.

Modern Language Association of America (MLA)

Whether you quote, summarize, or paraphrase, you will typically document a literary essay by means of the MLA two-part reference system. MLA uses in-text parenthetical references at the appropriate point in the document and a Works Cited at the end listing all works used in your essay. MLA identifies WHO said (last name), WHERE (page number), and HOW (distinguishing quotation from summary or paraphrase). The parenthetical reference identifies exactly where you have used the source and gives just enough information to identify the relevant entry in the Works Cited. If a work is listed by author in the Works Cited, then your parenthetical reference begins with the author's name (Knockwood 16, for instance); if a work is unsigned and therefore listed by title, use the first significant word (no articles or prepositions) in the title ("Symbols" 16, for instance). For more information, see the *MLA Handbook for Writers of Research Papers*, 6th edition, 2003, or access the MLA Web site at: http://www.mla.org/

ORGANIZING IDEAS

If the writer doesn't start with the bottom line, we—as readers—do. We make the bottom line the top line by skipping ahead. We take charge of the organization because the writer didn't.

—Edward P. Bailey

When you organize the results of brainstorming and research, you find patterns and connections and clarify your assumptions, focus, and overall structure of your draft essay. The typical literary essay has an *introduction* that outlines any necessary background or contextual information and establishes the topic and thesis and a *main body* of paragraphs that support the thesis, including adequate and varied illustration of evidence and quotations, summary, or paraphrase effectively integrated, analyzed, and documented. The *conclusion* gives closure by summarizing key points (David Suzuki's "A Planet for the Taking," for example); incorporating quotations, a vivid image, or compelling stylistic feature (Isabelle Knockwood's "Origins"); returning to and revising opening terms (Margaret Laurence's "Where the World Began"); or elaborating a larger context or set of questions requiring further research.

Whether or not you use a formal outline, you will also need to consider how to organize within and across paragraphs. Organizing controls access and response, creating relationships with readers, ideas, and outcomes, determining what is included or highlighted and what is not. Not all essays need to begin with biographical information about the author; include such information only to the extent it is relevant to your argument. Do ensure that you include information that is *necessary* to sustain your claims and ensure coherence without relying on your reader to supply information (information you know is familiar to your instructor, for example). Be sure too that the topic (or opening) sentence of each paragraph clarifies the focus or main idea of the paragraph. The topic sentence, that is, should not simply repeat plot summary but should connect events to the stage in your argument. For example, instead of merely identifying that Hadrian in D.H. Lawrence's "You Touched Me" returns to England after the Armistice, your topic sentence might take this form: When Hadrian returns to England after the Armistice, the prodigal son again proves to be "one little fly" in the ointment, unsettling relations and precipitating a power struggle in the Rockley household.

When writing on literature, you may use the structure of the literary text to order your own argument. Of course, you can effectively organize otherwise, but you will face extra burdens on your style (to keep clear the order of events or the logic of a character's changing understanding, for example) as well as the dangers of misrepresentation. If your thesis is highly original or controversial, you should follow *climactic* order; that is, begin with your strongest argument to unsettle entrenched views. If you are dealing with a number of texts, you may want to deal with them chronologically to underline changes or continuities over time.

"Comparison and contrast" is a useful organizational strategy to underline the distinctiveness of different but related texts. The easiest way to organize (without undue repetition) comparison and contrast of two texts (images, scenes, etc.) is to discuss the one and then the other, using the introduction, transition, and conclusion to underline key points of identity and difference. You may also discuss the texts together, indicating points of comparison and then points of difference. But you will find that this organization can mean significant repetition to avoid confusing the texts as you move back and forth between them and can also entail some unnecessary comment in efforts to balance discussion. Whatever organization (or modification thereof) you use, always keep your purpose and audience in mind.

POLISHING IT OFF

Writing without revision is like getting dressed without looking in the mirror.

—*Joanne Buckley*

However carefully you consider audience and purpose in drafting, no essay is fit to be read until it has been through revision (literally re-seeing; inserting, replacing, reordering parts); editing (correcting errors and ensuring consistency in grammar, spelling, and punctuation); and proofreading (checking for typographical errors and inconsistencies). This paragraph may usefully get a draft started, but it is insufficiently concise, concrete, and complete at this stage:

> The short stories by Nathaniel Hawthorne and Edgar Allan Poe can be usefully compared and contrasted. "The Cask of Amontillado" and "The Birthmark" both probe sanity but do so from different yet valid perspectives.

The following revised version gives a context for the topic, defines terms, establishes focus, and elaborates the logic of the student's thesis:

> Because humans have a natural propensity to conform, they are often motivated by fear of isolation, by fear of being considered eccentric or even insane because they deviate too radically from social norms. As a result, humans are fascinated with the subject of sanity, especially when it is represented in the engaging and edifying form of a short story. In "The Birthmark" and "The Cask of Amontillado" respectively, Nathaniel Hawthorne and Edgar Allan Poe strategically and ironically explore understandings of sanity by analyzing examples of insanity in the obsessions of New England scientist Aylmer and Italian aristocrat Montresor who share a disproportionate belief in their own sanity and reasoning powers— and with fatal consequences for those close to them.

In revising, you might use the following checklist:

- clear introduction, body, and conclusion
- key terms and contexts defined (who, what, when, why, where, how)
- research review fair and accurate
- evidence relevant, sufficient, varied, integrated, analyzed, documented
- transitions effective (read topic sentences)

- redundancies or missing elements addressed
- over-generalizations modified
- language, tone, level of formality appropriate to audience and purpose

At the editing stage, attend to the following:

- sentences and paragraphs complete and varied
- punctuation and spelling correct and consistent
- subject-verb and pronoun-antecedent agreements
- misplaced and dangling modifiers
- parallelism in lists
- vague references (this, that, which)
- shifts in person, number, tense, and voice
- names and numbers checked

When proofreading, read double-spaced hard copy (not the computer screen), do not *rely on* spell or grammar checkers, and focus on accuracy and fluency. You will need to overcome the tendency to read in what is missing (words or punctuation) and to read out what should not be there (repeated words) and can do so by rewarding yourself (in whatever way suits you) for finding errors. Having conscientiously negotiated each stage of the process of writing an essay on a literary topic, you can now wait confidently for your grade and instructor feedback.

FURTHER READING

Buckley, Joanne. *Fit to Print: The Canadian Guide to Essay Writing*. 6th edition. Toronto: Nelson, 2004.

Northey, Margot. *Making Sense: A Student's Guide to Research and Writing*. 4th edition. Toronto: Oxford UP, 2002.

Rooke, Constance. *The Clear Path: A Guide to Writing English Essays*. 3rd edition. Toronto: Nelson, 2004.

GLOSSARY

Accent Accent, or stress, is emphasis on one syllable in relation to another or others when a word is spoken. It is a prominent feature of speech in English and has, since the fourteenth century, been the basis of rhythmic pattern in the language. *See* SCANSION.

Accentual verse and **accentual-syllabic verse** The most common formal verse measure or METRE is either accentual (where each line of verse has a uniform number of stressed syllables but not of unstressed ones) or accentual-syllabic (where each line has a uniform number of stressed and unstressed syllables). Accentual verse was the metre of Anglo-Saxon poetry; Chaucer popularized accentual-syllabic. For an example of accentual-syllabic verse, *see* the quotation from Alexander Pope under SCANSION. Syllabic verse (where the unit of measurement is the number of syllables exclusively) is much less common. Rarer still (but common in classical Greek and Latin) is quantitative verse, which is based on vowel length. *See also* METRE.

Action In any literary work, not only what the CHARACTERS do or say, but also what happens to them. In some works, the action also includes what the characters feel and how they respond psychologically. *See also* PLOT.

Allegory (a) A NARRATIVE where the sequence of events develops a symbolic pattern of ideas making a moral or philosophical statement. (b) A form of symbolism where CHARACTERS and incidents are presented not for what they signify in themselves but for philosophical, historical, or other references that lie outside the text.

Alliteration The close recurrence of consonants for poetic effect, especially at the beginning of words and in stressed syllables. *See* Gerard Manley Hopkins's "The Windhover" ("*d*apple-*d*awn-*d*rawn Falcon," etc.).

Allusion A reference in a literary work to something (a person, place, work of art, statement, or object of any kind) that is external to the text. *See* the patterns of allusion to literary and biblical sources in John Milton's *Paradise Lost*.

Antagonist *See* CHARACTER.

Anti-hero In twentieth-century literary works, a major CHARACTER who is presented as having qualities antithetical either to those of the traditional HERO or to those of the romantic hero of popular FICTION. Anti-heroes are typically ineffectual and passive, but they may also be obnoxious and obtuse. Prufrock in T.S. Eliot's poem is an anti-hero. *See* HERO/HEROINE.

Antithesis A device of expression that balances opposing concepts to make a contrast. In VERSE, antithesis may occur between lines (Andrew Marvell's "The grave's a fine and private place, / But none, I think, do there embrace") or between parts of single lines, as in the following passage from Alexander Pope's "An Essay on Criticism": "So vast is art, so narrow human wit."

Archetype In literary criticism, a term borrowed from psychology employed to discuss the significance of an IMAGE, CHARACTER, situation, etc. Archetypes are recurring configurations that appear in myth, religion, folklore, fantasy, and dreams, as well as in art and literature. In addition to operating essentially at the subconscious level, archetypes recur universally in human experience: psychologist Carl Jung saw them as manifestations of what he called the "collective unconscious." Archetypal criticism is one of several methods of reading a text. For example, one may trace the archetypes of death and rebirth, the search for the parent, the Promethean rebel, or the scapegoat in poems and short fiction. *See* MOTIF.

Assonance The close repetition of the same or similar vowel sounds in stressed syllables. Alfred, Lord Tennyson's Ulysses complains of those "That h*oa*rd, and sl*ee*p, and f*ee*d, and kn*ow* not m*e*."

Ballad A song that tells a story. Usually anonymous in origin, popular or folk ballads were transmitted from generation to generation for centuries by oral tradition. Instead of a fixed text, they employed composition formulas such as REFRAINS, stock phrases, iambic METRE, a preferred STANZA FORM, and swift ACTION. Literary ballads are those written in the STYLE of the traditional ballad and were first introduced in the Romantic period.

Blank verse Unrhymed IAMBIC PENTAMETER (*see also* METRE). William Wordsworth's "Tintern Abbey" is in blank verse.

Cacophony The use of harsh sounds for poetic effect. The opposite of EUPHONY. *See also* DISSONANCE and ONOMATOPOEIA.

Cadence In VERSE, a rhythmic unit based not on a standard line length or on METRE, but on the spontaneous character of informal speech. *See* FREE VERSE.

Caesura A pause in a line of VERSE. Because its placement may vary from line to line, it is a useful device for altering rhythmic emphasis or flow without breaking away from a metrical pattern. *See* example under SCANSION. Also note the spacing technique used by Earle Birney.

Canon Originally a body of sacred texts accepted by the Christian churches, the term was later applied to secular works accepted by experts as genuine works of particular authors. In contemporary literary terms, the canon consists of works regarded as classics and normally treated in university courses on literature.

Caricature Ludicrously exaggerated CHARACTERIZATION.

Carpe diem (Latin, "seize the day.") A THEME or viewpoint expressed frequently in love LYRICS, but occurring as well in other literature, that since youth is fleeting and death certain, there should be no restraint in enjoying life's pleasures. *See* Andrew Marvell's "To His Coy Mistress."

Character A fictional person in a literary work who may be either purely imaginary or based upon someone real. Many works employ a central character or protagonist, whose ACTIONS are the main focus of attention and represent a struggle against opposing forces that are often summed up in the person of an antagonist. Characters have been variously classified as flat (two-dimensional) or rounded (three-dimensional), types or individuals, and dynamic or static. Dynamic characters undergo change as a result of their experiences. They are frequently attractive because they are unpredictable. Static characters do not necessarily lack depth and complexity. They can be equally full of dramatic interest when a work is organized to allow for progressive revelation of their inner qualities that are not clear at the outset.

Characterization The means an author employs in presenting and developing CHARACTERS. Writers may either describe the qualities of characters directly or present them through ACTION and DIALOGUE. The former TECHNIQUE provides a quick impression; the latter method is a slow, cumulative one, but allows for depth and complexity. Characterization also varies according to the writer's NARRATIVE PERSPECTIVE.

Closure A term borrowed from parliamentary procedure that refers to the call for conclusion to a debate. In literature, it refers to the principle that works should not end arbitrarily, that they ought to conclude with the ACTION, feeling, or exposition being in some sense complete.

Comedy While comedy employs WIT and HUMOUR to make amusing comment on human folly and social values, it frequently strives to instruct as well as delight. Whether it is written as poetry, FICTION, or drama, comedy is usually associated with happy endings, CHAR-ACTERS that are more survivors of trials than victims of fate, and NARRATIVES that sustain a light-hearted TONE. Farce is less subtle than comedy; its characters are frequently more improbable or exaggerated and their situations more ludicrous. Slapstick is even more far-fetched as a representation of life: the characters are more boisterous, the ACTION more physical and violent, and the verbal HUMOUR more at the level of gags, jokes, and insults. *See also* SATIRE.

Comic relief A comic or humorous passage included in works that are basically non-comic in order to relieve tension or dispel excessive gloom. In TRAGEDY, it is also used to heighten the tragic effect.

Conceit A striking or, frequently, outlandish comparison, as in the first SIMILE in T.S. Eliot's "The Love Song of J. Alfred Prufrock." For a more elaborate use of the conceit, *see* the use of twin compasses in John Donne's "A Valediction Forbidding Mourning."

Conflict In literary NARRATIVE, the struggle between opposing forces embodied either in the interaction between CHARACTERS or in the mind of the central figure.

Connotation An association or suggestion attached to a word in addition to its literal meaning. In times of war, for example, propagandists have exploited pleasant associations in words like "pacification" in an attempt to justify unusually severe methods of social control such as bombing civilian targets.

Consonance The close recurrence of consonants with differing vowel sounds in the middle and at the end of words. *See* ALLITER-ATION. The abundance of near-RHYMES (or slant rhymes) in W.B. Yeats's "Easter 1916" is based on consonance.

Convention Writers' customary practice, such as paragraph indentation or chapters in novels. Conventions are rules agreed on between author and reader but seldom made explicit.

Couplet A pair of rhyming VERSE lines. The two most popular forms in English are the four-stress, or octosyllabic, couplet (*see* Andrew Marvell's "To His Coy Mistress") and the five-stress, or heroic, couplet (*see* Alexander Pope's "An Essay on Criticism").

Dénouement French for unknotting or unravelling, the resolution of PLOT CONFLICT in a literary work.

Dialect A non-standard variety of language specific to a region or social group.

Dialogue The conversational language spoken by the CHARACTERS in a literary work. Dialogue may appear to resemble actual speech but at best is always a stylized version of what a character might actually say in a situation. Good dialogue attempts to record the idiom of characters as psychologically and socially observed.

Diction The author's choice of words. Diction may be either formal or informal, obscure or familiar, ornate or plain, depending on the context or the writer's purpose. *See* OBSCURITY.

Discourse A term current in the humanities and social sciences, especially since the 1960s, which insists on language as social practice sustainable within particular social and cultural contexts. Discourse analysis in literary and other studies is concerned with the uses of discourse in written or spoken conversation. A discourse community or culture is one that shares assumptions, beliefs, and modes of exchange.

Dissonance Deliberate placement of words for inharmonious effect. It contrasts with CACOPHONY, which also aims at discordance but employs words that are themselves harsh. In Philip Larkin's "Church Going," dissonance can be seen in "What this accoutred frowsty barn is worth" and cacophony in "suburb-scrub."

Dramatic monologue A poem in which the lines are spoken by, and ironically reveal the personality of, a CHARACTER who addresses either a listener who is present or an imagined audience. Robert Browning's Duke of Ferrara and Eliot's Prufrock are SPEAKERS in dramatic monologues.

Elegy A LYRIC poem expressing a lament for the death of a person or for the passing of an era.

Enjambment A run-on line of VERSE. It occurs when the grammatical sense of a poem forces the reader to finish one line and start the next without a pause. *See* Robert Browning's "My Last Duchess": "I call / That piece a wonder, now." *See also* STANZA.

Epic A long narrative poem on a heroic or quasi-divine subject in an elevated style and elaborating a nation's sense of itself. The Anglo-Saxon *Beowulf* is a traditional or folk epic; John Milton's *Paradise Lost* is a literary epic.

Epigram A concise but weighty statement, often phrased with WIT and elegance. PARADOX is a favourite epigrammatic device.

Euphony The use of pleasant, harmonious, or musical sounds for poetic effect. The opposite of CACOPHONY.

Fable A brief allegorical TALE told to illustrate a moral. Beast fables are folk tales that use animals to illustrate human shortcomings.

Fiction While the word generally refers to any imagined story, in literary works it means prose fiction in the form of a novel, SHORT STORY, TALE, etc. Even when prose fiction is based on facts or a true story, the process of NARRATION requires much elaboration, and this has to be based on invented detail.

 If the novel has been typically oriented toward REALISM, freedom of invention has always characterized the popular romance. Romances originated in medieval court tales of love and adventure. From the eighteenth century onward, as the novel with a bias toward CHARACTER development emerged, a distinction arose between the novel and romance. Although the two overlap in works of mixed GENRE, the freedom of romance to go beyond the novel's limits of probability appeals not only to writers of escapist stories but also to those who see it as a more useful vehicle than realism for serious exploration of particular THEMES and subjects. Nathaniel Hawthorne's "The Birthmark" is an example of a short story in the romance vein. While "novel" (usually a work of more than 50 000 words) is the most familiar term for extended works of prose fiction, "novelette" (15 000 to 50 000 words) is a less well-known term for a short novel. The novella (10 000 to 15 000 words) is more of a long story than a short novel. *See* SHORT STORY.

Figures of speech and **figurative language** Figures of speech are devices of expression, basically metaphorical in nature, that enable writers to make suggestions and statements beyond the literal meanings of words, phrases, comparisons, and sentences. Figurative language is effective in literature when it defines or describes something by making striking comparisons either to dissimilar objects or to objects having a partial resemblance. *See* CONCEIT, HYPERBOLE, IRONY, METAPHOR, METONYMY, OXYMORON, PARADOX, PERSONIFICATION, SIMILE, SYMBOL, and SYNECDOCHE.

First-person narrator A term for a storyteller who is a CHARACTER in the work being narrated and who writes in the first person ("I"). Also called character narrator. *See* NARRATIVE PERSPECTIVE and NARRATOR.

Flashback Episode that returns to the past to narrate events that precede the present of the narrative.

Free verse Verse that is free of regular METRE and other CONVENTIONS of formal poetry. It relies on the CADENCED phrase, on TONE, on its flexibility and adaptability in relation to its subject, and on its ability to approximate where necessary traditional or formal verse rhythms. The works of Walt Whitman and William Carlos Williams illustrate the use of free verse. *See* CADENCE.

Genre Literary works may be classified into major genres or types such as the novel, the SHORT STORY, the play, the poem, and the essay, and into sub-genres such as the problem play or the elegiac poem. Since descriptions of genre and sub-genre characteristics are based on our conventional understanding and past experiences of literature, and since there are both hybrid types and many unclassifiable works, definitions of genre cannot be used prescriptively—especially in the assessment of new writing.

Haiku A Japanese poetic form representing in seventeen syllables over three lines of five, seven, and five syllables a poetic response to an object or scene. Ezra Pound's "In a Station of the Metro" is an example.

Hero/Heroine The central figure around whom the PLOT of a literary work revolves. Originally, before the rise of REALISM, heroes and heroines had noble qualities. In modern literature, the term is often a synonym for PROTAGONIST. Many modern writers employ very ordinary, unheroic central figures. Such protagonists can be timid, awkward, obnoxious, or whatever is required for the author's purpose. *See* ANTI-HERO.

Heroic couplet *See* COUPLET and IAMBIC PENTAMETER.

Humour A way of seeing that observes the ludicrous, the comic, and the amusing. While humour shares this tendency with WIT, it is gentler, more tolerant, and warmer in its approach to life. Thus, in SATIRE, where criticism is central to the writer's purpose, humour is as much a leavener of the NARRATIVE as it is a vehicle for commentary. In satire, humour is most effective when combined with art.

Hyperbole Exaggeration or overstatement frequently employed for humorous purposes. *See* Andrew Marvell: "I would / Love you ten years before the Flood."

Iambic pentameter The most common ACCENTUAL-SYLLABIC VERSE line in English. Its great expressive range makes it the basis for a variety of traditional forms such as BLANK VERSE, the heroic COUPLET, the heroic QUATRAIN, and several STANZA patterns. William Shakespeare's SONNETS are written in five-foot iambics. *See also* METRE and VERSIFICATION.

Image and **Imagery** In literature, an image is a verbal representation of a sense impression. While images are most obviously recognized as visual, they may also be auditory, olfactory, tactile, and even taste-oriented. Depending on the work or context, images may be either literal or figurative, and they may be either frequently or sparsely employed. Imagery is the term used for images in their aggregate form. Because imagery is patterned throughout a work and related images often concentrated in image clusters, analysis of imagistic detail, and of all language with a FIGURATIVE function, is an essential part of defining the quality, the emotional content, and the meaning of a literary work.

In medias res Literally in the middle of things, a PLOT beginning in the middle of the ACTION.

Irony (a) Verbal irony occurs when a statement contradicts its literal meaning. An example of extended verbal irony occurs when events are interpreted through a naïve or unreliable NARRATOR who fails to recognize or admit the significance of what is described. *See* Sir John Betjeman's "In Westminster Abbey." (b) Situational irony occurs when events develop in a pattern opposite to what is expected. *See* Margaret Atwood's "Happy Endings." (c) Dramatic irony occurs when CHARACTERS in a literary work are proceeding without being aware of factors affecting their fate that are known to the audience. Traynor in Alice Walker's "Nineteen Fifty-Five" is such a character.

Litotes Ironic understatement, especially the expression of a positive by a negative ("no mean feat"). Common in Anglo-Saxon poetry.

Lyric A short poem expressing strong personal feeling. As an arrested moment of intense emotion, lyric expression may occur as a tendency in (or in a passage of) a longer work like a play or a novel.

Metafiction A story or novel, the major THEME of which is the nature of FICTION. Margaret Atwood's story "Happy Endings" is an example.

Metaphor An implied comparison of dissimilar objects. As such, it contrasts with SIMILE, which is an explicit comparison. Metaphors apply words to objects where there is no normal, literal, or expected association ("Life's but a walking shadow").

Metonymy The use of an attribute or association of an object to stand for the object itself (as John Milton uses "light" for vision; as we might use "Ottawa" to refer to the federal government).

Metre The pattern of stressed and unstressed syllables that STRUCTURES the RHYTHM of formal VERSE in English. (For informal or non-metrical verse, *see* FREE VERSE.) Formal verse is based on a metrical unit of two or three syllables called a foot. The most familiar in English is the iambic, a two-syllable foot where an unstressed is followed by a stressed syllable (William Shakespeare: To bé, or nót to bé). Other feet are the trochaic, where the stressed precedes the unstressed syllable (Sir John Betjeman: Thínk of whát our Nátion stánds for), and two three-syllable feet, the anapestic (˘˘´) and the dactylic (´˘˘). In response to the need for occasional variation from the norm, substitution of one of the other feet can be employed. In addition to any of the four "base" feet, two other variants are employable in substitution: the spondee (two successive stressed syllables) and the pyrrhic (two successive unstressed syllables). *See also* ACCENTUAL VERSE and ACCENTUAL-SYLLABIC VERSE, IAMBIC PENTAMETER, SCANSION, and VERSIFICATION.

Mimesis (Greek, "imitation.") The theory that literary works are a representation of human ACTION. Mimetic theory and criticism focus on the relevance of a work to human experience rather than on its structural features.

Motif   One of the unifying elements in a work or a frequently recurring element in a number of works by the same author. It may be a phrase, IMAGE, SYMBOL, citation, or some other narrative detail that recurs and helps to elaborate a THEME.

Myth   A traditional narrative usually involving supernatural or imaginary figures and embodying popular ideas on natural, social, or cultural realities. A myth is but part of a larger system of stories—mythology—explaining rules, rituals, and regulations of peoples (Judeo-Christian, Aboriginal, Norse, etc.). *See* the poetry of W.B. Yeats, for example, on the powers of myth and mythology.

Narrative perspective   The point of view or angle from which the ACTION of a literary work is depicted. Character or first-person narration has the perspective of a direct or indirect participant in the action. THIRD-PERSON NARRATION may be omniscient (that is, one that is not limited by time or space and can freely observe and represent thoughts and actions of characters), or it may be limited. In the case of limited third-person narratives, the perspective is restricted to the perceptual level of the CHARACTERS (*see* the Introduction to Short Fiction). In the case of character narration, narrative perspective varies a great deal according to the reliability of the narrator(s) employed. Some of the variables affecting character narration include the degree to which the narrator is being presented ironically, the degree of the narrator's personal involvement in or with or bias in relation to events and persons described, and the narrator's honesty, intelligence, and powers of observation. Because reliability affects our knowledge of what actually happens in a work, authors often include elements to make us question narrative reliability and thus deliberately present us with problems of interpretation.

Narrator (narration, narrative)   The narrator is the storyteller in a prose or VERSE narrative. In works of FICTION or poetry in which the narrator is not involved in the ACTION, the narrative VOICE may or may not be authorial (that is, identified with that of the author—*see* SPEAKER). In addition to authorial narrators, CHARACTERS are frequently employed as speakers and storytellers. Narration is the process of telling an audience what happens. While the narrative is the actual account of what happens, it is always a report from a certain perspective (*see* NARRATIVE PERSPECTIVE). Narrative contrasts with DIALOGUE, which, as a record of the speech of the characters, aims to present the action as it happens.

Obscurity   A quality of language or literature where the writer's meaning is difficult to discern. This may be the result of archaism (the use of words no longer in contemporary speech), neologism (the use of newly coined words), FIGURATIVE LANGUAGE, specialized terminology or technical jargon, slang, or some other unfamiliar form of DICTION or DISCOURSE. It may also be the result of difficult syntax, abstruse thought, or poor writing.

Ode   Originally a lengthy poem or praise designed to celebrate a public event, person, achievement, or ideal. Since the Romantic period, when the form became more personal and subjective, the term has been used to describe a dignified formal LYRIC or meditation, usually expressed in a lofty TONE, on a single THEME or specific subject. Aside from its stately manner, it does not require a specific STANZA, METRE, or length.

Omniscient narrator   Omniscient means "all-knowing." This is the type of NARRATOR employed by Nathaniel Hawthorne in "The Birthmark." This narrator stands outside the ACTION and comments in the third person from a perspective that can freely observe and record thoughts and action of the CHARACTERS. *See* NARRATIVE PERSPECTIVE and THIRD-PERSON NARRATOR.

Onomatopoeia   The use of words that sound like the objects or ACTIONS referred to. *See* Robert Frost's "Out, Out—": "The buzz saw snarled and rattled in the yard."

Oxymoron   A statement with two apparently contradictory components (W.B. Yeats's "terrible beauty"), which is effective as a result of its incongruity.

Parable   A TALE illustrating a moral or religious lesson. Often it includes an enigmatic element to arrest the listener's attention. *See* ALLEGORY.

Paradox   An apparently contradictory statement, as in William Wordsworth's line "The Child is father of the Man."

Parody   A deliberate and clever imitation of an artistic work or STYLE, often for the purpose of ridicule or mockery. Sir John Betjeman's "In Westminster Abbey" parodies a prayer.

Pastoral   Originally, a form of poetry set in a classical rustic Arcadia with shepherds, flowers, flutes, and bucolic emotions. In modern literature, any work that presents rural SETTINGS, THEMES, and CHARACTERS.

Persona   *See* SPEAKER.

Personification   The attribution of human qualities to non-human objects.

Plot   The arrangement of the ACTION and the selection of incidents that best achieve the author's purpose in telling a story.

Point of view   *See* NARRATIVE PERSPECTIVE.

Postcolonial   Writing concerned with the culture, history, and politics of former colonies of European empires. Instead of being the objects of European "expert" scrutiny, postcolonial writers become subjects or active agents who offer accounts of their experience that counter traditional imperial NARRATIVES depicting colonized peoples as quaint, inferior, or uncivilized.

Prose poem   A poem that has abandoned the device of line definition so that as a mode of composition it must be described as prose. However, it retains most of the rhythmic and all of the figurative devices of both formal and FREE VERSE and is fully a poetic form of literary expression. *See* Robert Bly's "Visiting Emily Dickinson's Grave with Robert Francis."

Prosody   The study of the theory, history, and principles of METRE and VERSIFICATION.

Protagonist   *See* CHARACTER.

Pun   A play on words involving distinct meanings for a single word or two similar-sounding words. *See,* for example, puns on "mark(s)," "charter'd," "ban," "forg'd," "black'ning," and "appalls" in William Blake's "London."

Quatrain   A four-line form with a variety of RHYME SCHEMES, the quatrain is the most familiar STANZA in English. An IAMBIC PENTAMETER version rhyming *abab* is sometimes termed an elegiac and sometimes a heroic quatrain (*see* Samuel Johnson's "On the Death of Dr. Robert Levet").

Realism   In terms of subject matter, realism has come to mean literature that deals with the ordinary commonplace world in preference to the world of exceptional circumstances. CHARACTERS are neither rich nor heroic, SETTINGS are prosaic rather than exotic, and yet there is a serious grappling with moral, social, and psychological dilemmas and a normal range of other THEMES and moods. The surface of life is usually carefully and faithfully observed, a plain STYLE of description is employed, and an unintrusive NARRATIVE PERSPECTIVE is preferred, especially in the handling of character motivation and the presentation of interior consciousness.

Refrain A repeated VERSE line, usually at the end of a STANZA, with a function (whether LYRIC, comic, ironic, etc.) that may change throughout a poem. *See* W.B. Yeats's "terrible beauty" refrain in "Easter 1916."

Rhyme The repetition of final vowels, or of a combination of final vowels and consonants, in words at the end of, or within, lines of VERSE. *See also* CONSONANCE.

Rhyme scheme The pattern of rhyme within a fixed VERSE form or STANZA. An elegiac QUATRAIN, for instance, follows an *abab* scheme.

Rhythm The flow of language in either free or measured form. Rhythm in VERSE is arranged in either formal or informal patterns. For informal VERSIFICATION, *see* FREE VERSE.

Satire A treatment of subject matter that can appear in any literary GENRE, satire usually employs devices of ridicule and appeals to amusement, scorn, or contempt to comment on or correct some human vice, social evil, or general tendency to folly.

Scansion The analysis of the metrical structure of VERSE. To scan a line of verse is to mark out the ACCENTS or stresses in relation to metrical feet, pauses, and the number of syllables. The following lines from Alexander Pope are scanned as follows:

True wít / is ná / ture tó / ad ván / tăge dréssed. /
Whăt óft / wăs thóught, // but n'ér / sŏ wéll / ex préssed. /

/ marks the end of each foot, // marks the CAESURA, ´ marks the ACCENT or stress, and ˘ marks the unaccented syllables.

Sensibility That part of a writer's or a CHARACTER's personality that has a capacity for emotional responsiveness and sensitivity. The value of sensibility was heightened in the late eighteenth century when sentimentalism came into fashion in literature and HEROES and HEROINES (and writers) came to be admired for their fine sensitivity to delicate nuances of feeling.

Setting In a NARRATIVE or dramatic work, setting involves the place, historical period, and social circumstances of the ACTION. The setting has significant implications for atmosphere, CHARACTER, PLOT, and THEME.

Shakespearean sonnet   Also known as the English sonnet. *See* SONNET.

Short story   A relatively brief type of prose FICTION. In the early nineteenth century, a number of writers, including Nathaniel Hawthorne (*see* "The Birthmark"), developed the GENRE out of the sketch and literary essay. While the sketch was a relaxed NARRATIVE, usually written for a newspaper or periodical, with limited development of PLOT, CHARACTER, and THEME, the short story became more compact, complex, and ambitious. The short story is often characterized by its highly crafted STRUCTURE and its use of subtle detail within a compressed spatial format. The short story ranges from 500 to 20 000 words, but normal length is from 2000 to 15 000 words.

Simile   A comparison usually expressed with "like," "as," or "as if." An explicit form of METAPHOR.

Sonnet   A poem written in IAMBIC PENTAMETER, consisting of fourteen lines. There are two main patterns: the Italian sonnet, consisting of an octave (rhyming eight lines *abba abba*) and a sestet (six lines rhyming *cde cde*), and the English or SHAKESPEAREAN SONNET, with three QUATRAINS and a final COUPLET (*abab cdcd efef gg*). A variant of the English sonnet is the SPENSERIAN SONNET, notable for its tighter RHYME SCHEME (*abab bcbc cdcd ee*).

Speaker   Just as we refer to a NARRATOR of a story, we call the person who gives VOICE to a poem the speaker. It is crucial for understanding ironic, satiric, humorous, descriptive, and other intentions in an essay or poem to recognize the kind of speaker employed. Where, as in Andrew Marvell's "To His Coy Mistress," the speaker is a CHARACTER involved in the ACTION, it is obvious that the sentiments directly expressed are not the poet's—*see* DRAMATIC MONOLOGUE. But, where the speaker is not involved in the action, the persona or voice expressed may or may not be akin to the writer's own. As an example of the latter, Jonathan Swift's "A Modest Proposal" has a persona who plays the role of the devil's advocate. In many short poems, the speaker may reveal only one small aspect of the poet's personality, or, as in William Carlos Williams's "The Red Wheelbarrow," the voice is merely one adapted to the evocation of a particular mood or response.

Spenserian sonnet   A variant of the English sonnet. *See* SONNET.

Sprung rhythm A distinctive and forceful poetic line developed by Gerard Manley Hopkins. As with trochaic and dactylic feet (*see* METRE), sprung rhythm places the ACCENT on the initial syllable of each foot, but the number of unaccented syllables is irregular.

Stanza Lines of VERSE may be composed in verse paragraphs, or they may be organized into formal units called stanzas. Each stanza provides the poet with a division mark, but frequently (as in Philip Larkin's "Church Going," where there is ENJAMBMENT at the end of three of the poem's seven stanzas) the division is blurred for a purpose discernible in the poem. While enjambment may occur as frequently between stanzas as between lines, it does not in any way diminish the impact of the stanza as a forceful unit in a poem.

Stanza forms Some traditional STANZAS are both fixed and elaborate in format (ottava rima, for instance, an eight-line IAMBIC PENTAMETER stanza, rhyming *abababcc*). Such stanzas are based on a predetermined METRE, RHYME SCHEME, and number of lines and feet per line. Certain basic stanzas like the tercet have fixed variant forms—*see also* COUPLET and QUATRAIN for their variants. While a tercet is a three-line stanza employing a single rhyme, terza rima is a series of tercets with *aba bcb cdc*, interlinking rhymes (*see* Percy Bysshe Shelley's "Ode to the West Wind"). BALLADS often alternate tetrameter and trimeter lines in *abcb* quatrains (*see* "Sir Patrick Spens"). Rhyme royal is a seven-line iambic pentameter stanza rhyming *ababbcc* (*see* Sir Thomas Wyatt's "They Flee from Me"). Modern poets frequently design stanzas for specific poems, and although their stanzas may not vary radically from traditional fixed forms, they do not expect readers to link their chosen pattern to a familiar stanza form.

Stress *See* ACCENT.

Structure The organizing principles of a literary work revealed in such obvious elements of a literary framework as chapter, scene, or STANZA divisions as well as more subtle compositional devices such as the arrangement of IMAGES and ideas. Structure affects THEME and meaning and defines the elements that give unity and coherence to a work.

Style A writer's characteristic way of writing, which may or may not be highly distinctive.

Symbol In a literary work, any CHARACTER, ACTION, situation, SETTING, or object can be a symbol if, in addition to having a clear literal function, it represents something beyond itself. Flora, the horse in Alice Munro's "Boys and Girls," is used symbolically to make a statement about the end of an early phase of the NARRATOR'S life.

Synecdoche The use of the part to stand for the whole ("rhyme" for poem) or the whole to stand for the part ("Canada" for Canadians).

Synesthesia A deliberate confusion of sense impressions; experience of two or more sensations when only one sense is stimulated. *See* John Keats, "Ode to a Nightingale": "Tasting of Flora and the country green, / Dance, and Provençal song, and sunburnt mirth!"

Tale An informal or spontaneous literary NARRATIVE. Originally oral in nature, it is now a loosely constructed story that is told with some of the relish of its folk origins. It contrasts with the typically more tightly structured narrative we call the SHORT STORY.

Technique A device or method of expression in literature and art.

Texture The formal qualities of literary language, as opposed to the content of a work of literature. DICTION, RHYTHM, IMAGERY, FIGURATIVE LANGUAGE, stylistic and prosodic devices, and so on, are aspects of texture, but structural devices such as PLOT and CHARACTER are not.

Theme An idea, moral, social observation, or other generalization that can be recognized as underlying or unifying a literary work. For example, John Milton announces his theme in Book 1 of *Paradise Lost*: to "assert Eternal Providence, / And justify the ways of God to men."

Third-person narrator A NARRATOR who stands outside the ACTION when telling the story. Third-person narrators may be OMNISCIENT, but more commonly they limit their commentary to the perspective level of the CHARACTERS. *See* NARRATIVE PERSPECTIVE.

Tone The cast of VOICE that reveals the SPEAKER'S or writer's attitude to the audience.

Tragedy A literary work (most familiar as a classical form of drama) that involves a PROTAGONIST in a series of events leading to a fatal catastrophe. The DÉNOUEMENT, which results in the violent death of the central figure, must seem the inevitable outcome of the struggle of a valiant but tragically flawed HERO/HEROINE against the odds of a fateful situation. Contrast with COMEDY.

Verse (a) A single line of poetry. "Verse" is sometimes used to refer to a STANZA. (b) A composition either in METRE or CADENCES that uses the line as a rhythmical unit.

Versification The art of making VERSE. Versification is either formal or informal. For informal versification, *see* FREE VERSE. Formal versification employs METRE and a regular line length. Each formal line is named according to its length, with the four-, five-, and six-foot lines being the most familiar (tetrameter, pentameter, hexameter). *See* IAMBIC PENTAMETER. Less well known are monometer, dimeter, trimeter, and heptameter (the one-, two-, three-, and seven-foot lines). Sometimes line length is measured by syllable (*see* COUPLET for a reference to the octosyllabic line).

Villanelle A poem with five tercets and a final QUATRAIN. The opening and closing lines of the initial tercet provide REFRAINS that are placed in a strict pattern as illustrated by Dylan Thomas's "Do Not Go Gentle into That Good Night."

Voice Every literary work, whether a brief LYRIC or a long prose NARRATION, has a SPEAKER or PERSONA. The sense of personal presence behind the speaker's words constitutes voice. The term "voice" reminds us that the significance of what is said is qualified by who is speaking, and the speaker's TONE and feeling. *See* SPEAKER.

Wit Originally, wit was associated specifically with quickness of intellect; an instinct for IRONY, variety, and incongruity; and agility of ideas and language. It now tends to mean, at worst, a proclivity to make quips and, at best, the ability to communicate clever, amusing, or surprising observations that have at least a modicum of intellectual substance. Because wit can be incisive, intolerant, and intellectual, it is a useful element in SATIRE.

CREDITS

Because some selections are now in the public domain in Canada, not all sources are listed below.

ESSAYS

Atwood, Margaret. "Through the One-Way Mirror" originally published in *The Nation,* March 22, 1984. Reprinted by permission of the author.

Bissoondath, Neil. "I'm Not Racist But ..." copyright © 1989 by Neil Bissoondath.

Klein, Naomi. "Buying a Gladiatorial Myth" copyright © Naomi Klein. Reprinted by permission of the author.

Knockwood, Isabelle. "Origins" from *Out of the Depths: The Experiences of Mi'knaw Children at the Indian Residential School at Shubenacadie, Nova Scotia* by Isabelle Knockwood with Gillian Thomas (Lockeport, NS: Roseway Publishing Co., 1993). Reprinted by permission of the author.

Laurence, Margaret. "Where the World Began" from *Heart of a Stranger* by Margaret Laurence. Used by permission, McClelland & Stewart Ltd., *The Canadian Publishers.*

Mallick, Heather. "Women Clamouring at the Gates, But the Boys Still Won't Open Up" by Heather Mallick from *The Globe and Mail* (May 18, 2002). Reprinted with permission of the author.

Mumford, Lewis. "Mechanization of Modern Culture" from *Interpretations and Forecasts: 1922–1972.* Copyright © 1973 by Lewis Mumford, reprinted by permission of Harcourt, Inc.

Ndebele, Njabulo S. "Guilt and Atonement: Unmasking History for the Future." Copyright © Njabulo S. Ndebele 1994. Reprinted by permission of the author.

Nelson, Joyce. "The Temple of Fashion" from *Sign Crimes/Road Kill: From Mediascape to Landscape* (Toronto: Between the Lines, 1992). Copyright © Joyce Nelson. Reprinted by permission of the publisher.

Robertson, Peter. "More Than Meets the Eye" from *Archivaria*, Volume 1, No. 2 (1976): 33–43. Copyright © 1976 Peter Robertson. Reprinted by permission of Peter Robertson.

Saul, John Ralston. "The Grail of Balance" from *The Doubter's Companion* by John Ralston Saul. Copyright © 1994 by John Ralston Saul. Reprinted by permission of Penguin Books Canada Limited.

Suzuki, David T. "A Planet for the Taking" from *The Canadian Forum*, Volume 64, No. 746, February 1985, pp. 6–8. Copyright © 1985 David T. Suzuki. Reprinted with permission of the author.

Taylor, Drew Hayden. "Pretty Like a White Boy: The Adventures of a Blue Eyed Ojibway." © Drew Hayden Taylor. Reprinted by permission of the author.

Tregebov, Rhea. "Some Notes on the Story of Esther" from *Language in Her Eye: Views on Writing and Gender by Canadian Women Writing in English*, edited by Libby Scheier, Sarah Sheard, and Eleanor Wachtel (Toronto: Coach House Press, 1990). Copyright © 1990 Rhea Tregebov. Reprinted by permission of the author.

POETRY

Acorn, Milton. "I've Tasted My Blood" from *Dig Up My Heart* by Milton Acorn. Used by permission, McClelland & Stewart Ltd., *The Canadian Publishers*.

Ammons, A.R. "Needs" copyright © 1968 by A.R. Ammons, from *Collected Poems 1951–1971* by A.R. Ammons. Used by permission of W.W. Norton & Company, Inc.

Armstrong, Jeannette. "History Lesson" from *Breath Tracks* published by Theytus Books, 1991. Reprinted by permission.

Atwood, Margaret. "This Is a Photograph of Me" from *The Circle Game* by Margaret Atwood. © copyright by Margaret Atwood. Reprinted by permission of House of Anansi Press. "The animals in that country" from *Selected Poems 1966–1984*. Copyright © 1990 by Margaret Atwood. Reprinted by permission of Oxford University Press Canada.

Auden, W.H. "Musée des Beaux Arts" and "One Evening" from *Collected Poems of W.H. Auden*, edited by Edward Mendelson (London: Faber & Faber, 1976). Reprinted by permission of Faber & Faber Ltd.

Avison, Margaret. "In a Season of Unemployment" from *The Dumbfounding: Poems of Margaret Avison*. Copyright © 1966 by Margaret Avison. Reprinted by permission of W.W. Norton & Company, Inc.

"Beowulf" translated by Seamus Heaney from *Beowulf*, translated by Seamus Heaney. Copyright © 2000 by Seamus Heaney. Used by permission of W.W. Norton & Company, Inc.

Betjeman, Sir John. "In Westminster Abbey" from *John Betjeman's Collected Poems*, compiled and with an introduction by The Earl of Birkenhead (London: John Murray, 1970). Reprinted by permission of John Murray (Publishers) Ltd.

Birney, Earle. "The Road to Nijmégen," "The Bear on the Delhi Road," and "Anglosaxon Street" from *Collected Poems of Earle Birney*. Used by permission, McClelland & Stewart Ltd., *The Canadian Publishers*.

Bishop, Elizabeth. "Sestina" from *The Complete Poems 1927–1979* by Elizabeth Bishop. Copyright © 1979, 1983 by Alice Helen Methfessel. Reprinted by permission of Farrar, Straus and Giroux, LLC.

Bly, Robert. "Visiting Emily Dickinson's Grave with Robert Francis" from *The Man in the Black Coat Turns* by Robert Bly. Copyright © 1981 by Robert Bly. Used by permission of Doubleday, a division of Random House, Inc.

Bowering, George. "Grandfather" from *Selected Poems: Particular Accidents*, edited with an introduction by Robin Blaser (Vancouver: Talon Books, 1980). Reprinted with permission of Talon Books.

Brand, Dionne. "Amelia still" and "Blues Spiritual for Mammy Prater" from *No Language Is Neutral* by Dionne Brand. Used by permission, McClelland & Stewart Ltd., *The Canadian Publishers*.

Brooks, Gwendolyn. "We Real Cool" from *Blacks* (Chicago: Third World Press, 1991). Copyright Gwendolyn Brooks.

Carillo, Jo. "And When You Leave, Take Your Pictures With You" from *This Bridge Called My Back: Writings by Radical Women of Color* (Third Woman Press: 2002), 3rd ed., Cherrie Moraga and Gloria Anzaldea, eds. ISBN: 0-943219-22-1. Reprinted with permission of the author.

Clarke, George Elliott. "Hammonds Plains African Baptist Church," "Crying the Beloved Country," and "Salvation Army Blues" from *Lush Dreams, Blue Exile: Fugitive Poems 1978–1993*, copyright © 1993 by George Elliott Clarke. Published in Canada by Pottersfields Press.

Cohen, Leonard. "For E.J.P." from *Stranger Music* by Leonard Cohen. Used by permission, McClelland & Stewart Ltd., *The Canadian Publishers*.

Crozier, Lorna. "Marriage: Getting Used To" from *The Garden Going On Within Us* by Lorna Crozier. Used by permission, McClelland & Stewart Ltd., *The Canadian Publishers*.

Cummings, E.E. "since feeling is first" copyright 1926, 1954, © 1991 by the Trustees for the E.E. Cummings Trust. Copyright © 1985 by George James Firmage, "somewhere I have never traveled, gladly beyond" copyright 1931, © 1959, 1991 by the Trustees for the E.E. Cummings Trust. Copyright © 1979 by George James Firmage, "O sweet spontaneous" copyright © 1923, 1951, © 1991 by the Trustees for the E.E. Cummings Trust. Copyright © 1976 by George James Firmage, from *Complete Poems: 1904–1962* by E.E. Cummings, edited by George J. Firmage. Reprinted by permission of Liveright Publishing Corporation.

Day Lewis, C. Extract from "Two Songs" by C. Day Lewis from *The Complete Poems* by C. Day Lewis, published by Sinclair-Stevenson (1992), copyright © 1992 in this edition, and the Estate of C. Day Lewis.

(Doolittle, Hilda) H.D. "Heat" from *Collected Poems 1912–1944*. Copyright © 1982 by The Estate of Hilda Doolittle. Reprinted by permission of New Directions Publishing Corp.

Dumont, Marilyn. "Letter to Sir John A. Macdonald" reprinted by permission of Brick Books.

Eliot, T.S. "The Love Song of J. Alfred Prufrock" and "Journey of the Magi" from *Collected Poems 1909–1962* (London: Faber & Faber, 1964). Reprinted by permission of Faber & Faber Ltd.

Frost, Robert. "Home Burial," and "Out, Out —," from *The Poetry of Robert Frost*, edited by Edward Connery Lathern. Copyright 1916, © 1969 by Henry Holt and Company, copyright 1944, 1958 by Robert

McGraw-Hill Ryerson, 1972). Reprinted by permission of the Estate of Dorothy Livesay.

Lorde, Audre. "Hanging Fire" from *The Black Unicorn* by Audre Lorde. Copyright © 1978 by Audre Lorde. Used by permission of W.W. Norton & Company, Inc.

MacEwen, Gwendolyn. "A Breakfast for Barbarians" from *Magic Animals: Selected Poetry of Gwendolyn MacEwen* (Toronto: Macmillan, 1969). "Dark Pines under Water" from *The Shadow Maker* (Toronto: Macmillan, 1969). Reprinted by permission of the author's family.

MacNeice, Louis. "Snow" from *The Collected Poems of Louis MacNeice*, edited by E.R. Dodds (London: Faber & Faber, 1979). Reprinted by permission of David Higham Associates.

Marlatt, Daphne. "New Moon" and "coming home" from *Net Work: Selected Writing* (Vancouver: Talon Books, 1980). Copyright by Daphne Marlatt. Reprinted by permission of Talon Books.

Marshall, Chief Lindsay. "Clay Pots and Bones" by Chief Lindsay Marshall from *Clay Pots and Bones* (Solus Publishing). Reprinted by permission of the author.

McGuckian, Medbh. "Slips" and "The War Ending" by Medbh McGuckian from *Medbh McGuckian: Selected Poems*. Reprinted by permission of Wake Forest Press.

Moore, Marianne. "Poetry" and "Fish" reprinted with permission of Scribner, an imprint of Simon & Schuster Adult Publishing Group, from *The Collected Poems of Marianne Moore* by Marianne Moore. Copyright © 1935 by Marianne Moore, renewed © 1963 by Marianne Moore and T.S. Eliot.

Muir, Edward. "The Wayside Station" from *Collected Poems* (London: Faber & Faber, 1963). Reprinted by permission of Faber & Faber Ltd.

Nowlan, Alden. "Warren Pryor" from *Selected Poems* (Toronto: House of Anansi Press). Copyright © Claudine Nowlan. Reprinted by the permission of the Estate of Alden Nowlan.

Olds, Sharon. "Leningrad Cemetery, Winter of 1941." First published in *The New Yorker*. Copyright © 1979 Sharon Olds. Reprinted with permission of the author.

Ondaatje, Michael. "Bearhug" and "The Cinnamon Peeler." Copyright © 1979 by Michael Ondaatje. Reprinted by permission of Ellen Levine Literary Agency/Trident Media Group.

Page, P.K. "Stories of Snow" from *The Hidden Room,* Volume One of a two-volume set (Erin: The Porcupine's Quill, 1997). Reprinted with permission of The Porcupine's Quill.

Philip, Marlene Nourbese. "Discourse on the Logic of Language" from *Making a Difference: Canadian Multicultural Literature,* edited by Smaro Kamboureli (Toronto: Oxford University Press, 1996). Reprinted by permission.

Piercy, Marge. "To Be of Use" and "Barbie Doll" from *Circles on the Water.* Copyright © 1982 by Marge Piercy. Used by permission of Alfred A. Knopf, a division of Random House.

Plath, Sylvia. "Morning Song" and "Mirror" from *The Collected Poems by Sylvia Plath,* edited by Ted Hughes. Copyright © Ted Hughes. "Lady Lazarus" from *Ariel* (London: Faber & Faber, 1966). Copyright © 1963 by Ted Hughes. Reprinted by permission of Faber & Faber Ltd.

Pound, Ezra. "In a Station of the Metro" and "The River Merchant's Wife: A Letter" from *Personae.* Copyright © 1926 by Ezra Pound. Reprinted by permission of New Directions Publishing Corp.

Pratt, E.J. "The Shark" and "Silences" from *Collected Poems,* edited by Zailig Pollack, University of Toronto Press. Reprinted by permission of the University of Toronto Press, Inc.

Purdy, Al. "Wilderness Gothic" from *Beyond Remembering: The Collected Poems of Al Purdy* (Harbour Publishing, Madeira Park, BC). Reprinted by permission of Harbour Publishing.

Reed, Henry. "Naming of Parts" from *Collected Poems,* edited by Jon Stallworthy, 1991. Copyright The Executor of Henry Reed's Estate. Reprinted by permission of Oxford University Press.

Rich, Adrienne. "Aunt Jennifer's Tigers." Copyright © 2002, 1951 by Adrienne Rich. "What Kind of Times Are These." Copyright © 2002, 1995 by Adrienne Rich, from *The Fact of a Doorframe: Selected Poems 1950–2001* by Adrienne Rich. Used by permission of W.W. Norton & Company, Inc.

Roethke, Theodore. "My Papa's Waltz" copyright 1942 by Hearst Magazines, Inc. From *The Collected Poems of Theodore Roethke* by

Theodore Roethke. Used by permission of Doubleday, a division of Random House, Inc.

Ruffo, Armand Garnet. "Why I Write" and "Archie Belaney, 1935" from *Grey Owl: The Mystery of Archie Belaney* (Regina: Coteau Books, 1997). Reprinted by permission of Armand Garnet Ruffo.

Sassoon, Siegfried. "Counter-Attack." Copyright Siegfried Sassoon, by permission of George Sassoon.

Scott, F.R. "Spain, 1937" and "Calamity" from *The Collected Poems of F.R. Scott*, edited by John Newlove. Reprinted with the permission of William Toye, literary executor for the Estate of F.R. Scott.

Sexton, Anne. "Cinderella" from *Transformations* by Anne Sexton. Copyright © 1971 by Anne Sexton. Reprinted by permission of Houghton Mifflin Co. All rights reserved.

Shapiro, Karl. "Auto Wreck" from *Collected Poems, 1940–1978* by Karl Shapiro. Random House, Inc. Copyright © Karl Shapiro 1942, 1970. Reprinted by permission of Wieser and Wieser, Inc., New York.

Smith, A.J.M. "The Lonely Land" from *The Classic Shade* by A.J.M. Smith. Reproduced with the permission of William Toye, literary executor for the Estate of A.J.M. Smith.

Smith, Stevie. "Thoughts about the Person from Porlock" from *Collected Poems of Stevie Smith*. Copyright © 1972 by Stevie Smith. Reprinted by permission of New Directions Publishing Corp.

Soyinka, Wole. "Telephone Conversation" copyright © 1962, 1990 by Wole Soyinka. Reprinted by permission of Melanie Jackson Agency, LLC.

Stevens, Wallace. "Anecdote of the Jar" and "The Snow Man" from *The Collected Poems of Wallace Stevens*, copyright 1954 by Wallace Stevens and renewed 1982 by Holly Stevens. Used by permission of Alfred A. Knopf, a division of Random House, Inc.

Tregebov, Rhea. "What Makes You Sure" from *Remembering History* (Toronto: Guernica Editions, 1982). Copyright © 1982 Rhea Tregebov. Reprinted by permission of the author.

Walcott, Derek. "A Far Cry from Africa" from *Collected Poems 1948–1984* by Derek Walcott. Copyright © 1986 by Derek Walcott. Reprinted by permission of Farrar, Straus & Giroux, LLC.

Wallace, Bronwen. "Stunts" from *Common Magic*. Reprinted by permission of Oberon Press.

Wayman, Tom. "Factory Time" from *Did I Miss Anything? Selected Poems of Tom Wayman* (Harbour Publishing: Madeira Park, 1993). Reprinted by permission of Harbour Publishing.

Webb, Phyllis. "Treblinka Gas Chamber" from *Wilson's Bowl* (Toronto: Coach House Press, 1980). Copyright © Phyllis Webb. "Composed Like Them" copyright © Phyllis Webb. Reprinted with permission of Talon Books.

Williams, William Carlos. "The Red Wheelbarrow" from *Collected Poems of William Carlos Williams: 1909–1939*, Volume 1. Copyright © 1938 New Directions Publishing Corp. Reprinted by permission of New Directions Publishing Corp.

SHORT FICTION

Atwood, Margaret. "Happy Endings" from *Murder in the Dark* by Margaret Atwood. Used by permission, McClelland & Stewart Ltd., *The Canadian Publishers*.

Bambara, Toni Cade. "The Lesson" from *Gorilla, My Love* by Toni Cade Bambara. Copyright © 1972 by Toni Cade Bambara. Reprinted by permission of Random House, Inc.

Barry, Lynda. "Automatic Timer" © 1990 Lynda Barry. Reprinted by permission of Darhansoff, Verrill, Feldman Literary Agency.

Faulkner, William. "A Rose for Emily" from *Collected Stories of William Faulkner* by William Faulkner. Copyright © 1930 and renewed 1958 by William Faulkner. Reprinted by permission of Random House, Inc.

Findley, Timothy. "Dreams" from *Stones* by Timothy Findley. Copyright © Pebble Productions Inc., 1988. Reprinted by permission of Penguin Books Canada Ltd.

Gallant, Mavis. "From the Fifteenth District" from *From the Fifteenth District* by Mavis Gallant. Copyright © 1979 by Mavis Gallant. Reprinted by permission of Georges Borchardt, Inc., for the author.

INDEX OF AUTHORS

INDEX OF TITLES AND FIRST LINES OF POEMS